WORLDS OF
childhood

WORLDS OF
childhood

Robert H. Wozniak
Bryn Mawr College

Associate Editors
Mary T. Rourke
Berit I. Haahr
Bryn Mawr College

HarperCollinsCollegePublishers

WORLDS OF CHILDHOOD is a project of DLGHS, Inc., and Contemporary Learning Systems of East Lansing, Inc., in association with GPN, a service agency of the University of Nebraska, Lincoln, with primary funding by HarperCollins College Publishers. The CHILDHOOD television series, which inspired this national educational undertaking, was produced by Thirteen/WNET and The Childhood Project, Inc., in association with Great Britain's Channel 4 Television and Antelope Films, Ltd.

PROJECT DIRECTOR

George A. Colburn, Ph.D.

SUPERVISORY EDITOR

John Ball, Ph.D.

CONTENT ADVISORS

Helen Bee, Ph.D.
Geoff Haines-Stiles
Robert Hinde, Ph.D.
Jerome Kagan, Ph.D.
Julius Segal, Ph.D.

Sponsoring Editor: Anne Harvey
Permissions Editor: Elsa Peterson
Production: Bob Cooper
Development Editor: M. K. Moore
Art Director: Jeffrey Apgar

Reader to accompany Bee WORLDS OF CHILDHOOD

ISBN: 0-06-501332-8

93 94 95 96 9 8 7 6 5 4 3 2 1

CONTENTS

Preface

Although *Worlds of Childhood* traveled the route from initial conception to publication in less than a year, it is the end product of a much longer process that has had many contributors. The inspiration for this reader came from the PBS prime-time television series, *Childhood*, which premiered in the fall of 1991. The idea for the *Chidhood* series was originated in 1985 by long-time public television producers Geoffrey Haines-Stiles (Carl Sagan's *Cosmos*; *Nova*; and the *Creation of the Universe*) and David Loxton (*The Lathe of Heaven*; the *Non-Fiction Television* series, and many dramatic and documentary specials).

Between 1989, when *Childhood* received production clearance, and its appearance in Fall, 1991, the unique intellectual vision which shaped both the television series and this volume was forged in the interaction among producer-director-writers Erna Akuginow, Eugene Marner, and Geoff Haines-Stiles, and several key content advisors. Foremost among these were Jerome Kagan, Urie Bronfenbrenner, Sandra Scarr, Robert Hinde, Marian Wright Edelman, and Melvin Konner, all of whom appeared in *Childhood* as on-camera Observers. Important contributions were also made by an interdisciplinary group of scholars representing psychology, anthropology, sociology, history, and literature, who served on the *Childhood* National Advisory Board, and by *Childhood* researchers Victor Balaban and Meg Kruizenga, who provided a rich archive of published material through which many of the articles in this compilation were initially identified.

Building on the strong foundation provided by the *Childhood* staff, the *Worlds of Childhood* development team came together in late 1991 to begin work on this volume. In addition to Geoff Haines-Stiles, *Worlds of Childhood* Project Director George Colburn was the prime motivational and organizational force keeping the project on time and on target. He and Supervisory Editor John Ball made numerous and invaluable suggestions regarding both the form and content of this volume. Bryn Mawr College student Jennifer Hurley and Haverford College student Rachel Gold searched the appropriate cross-cultural and historical literature on children and turned up a number of the more important articles eventually included in this volume. My Associate Editors, Mary Rourke and Berit Haahr, provided the collegial support, long hours of diligent effort, intellectual challenge, and superb editorial commentary without which the project would never have come to fruition. Joan Copel, Secretary in the Bryn Mawr College Department of Human Development, and Jennifer Lambert, Departmental Assistant, were, as always, there when we needed them—as we frequently did.

Robert Miller, Project Director, and Licia Hurst, Supervising Editor of the Thirteen/WNET CHILDHOOD Viewer's Guide and Claire Elliott, author of the Channel 4 (London) Viewer's Guide helped lay the groundwork for *Worlds of Childhood* by creating some of the small vignettes that are sprinkled throughout the volume. Colleagues in several fields and in many institutions willingly gave of their time to help us in a variety of other ways. Helen Bee, Dorota Biela, Julius Segal, Rebecca Eder, Leslie Rescorla, Anne Fowler, Elissa Newport, Robert Hinde, Jerome Kagan, Carolyn Rovee-Collier, Sharon Lamb, Patricia Draper, and Linda A. Hughes assisted us in locating additional articles for inclusion in the volume and/or provided commentary on drafts of interstitial material.

The efforts of Susan Driscoll, Anne Harvey, and M.K. Moore, at HarperCollins, and Elsa Peterson, our Permissions Editor, are gratefully acknowledged. It is to all of the foregoing individuals as well as to those authors, photographers, and publishers (see publication credits) who have graciously granted us permission to reprint their material that we owe the existence of this volume.

WORLDS OF
childhood

UNIT 1: Introduction

• Worlds of Childhood •

In 1979, when psychologist Urie Bronfenbrenner referred to developmental psychology as "the science of the strange behavior of children, in strange situations with strange adults for the briefest possible periods of time." In the years since, much has changed. Developmental psychologists have become more interested in naturally occurring activities studied in the everyday contexts in which they take place. We now know that children actively construct the world around them, and that much of that construction is fundamentally social in nature. This has led beyond the study of behavior itself to a much broader concern with beliefs, attitudes, and values. The family and the peer group are now more frequent contexts of research, and investigators have become much more comfortable in focusing on processes that take place over periods of time ranging from days to years.

At the heart of this shift has been a growing recognition that development occurs in the interaction between individuals and their environments, that the developing human mind is fundamentally social, and that the environment is a very complex place. Neither characteristics of the individual child nor characteristics of the many contexts within which children live will, by themselves, explain how children come to perceive and talk about the world, act on objects and interact with people. These developments must be understood in terms of the interaction between the physical and social situations in which children find themselves and in terms of the personal characteristics that children bring with them to these situations.

In addition, both children and situations are constantly changing. Children learn to walk, talk, interact with peers, read, work, and explore the broader world. As they grow, the families and neighborhoods in which they live change as well. Baby brothers and sisters may be added to the family; fathers and mothers may enter the work force, change jobs, or become unemployed. Parents may divorce. In their neighborhoods, children will develop particular friendships and learn how to interact in groups. The information that they obtain from friends and peer groups,

2

as well as that from teachers and family members, will help children to develop a sense of self. While all this development is occurring, the subcultures and broader societies that envelop families and neighborhoods will also be changing. Values, economic conditions, political reforms, social policies—all of which affect children—will come and go.

Worlds of Childhood has been specifically designed to bring the work of developmental psychologists together with that of historians of childhood, psychological anthropologists, sociologists, psycholinguists, and experts in other fields, to examine the diversity of children's development in the complex, changing social contexts in which it occurs. In the chapters that follow, we will be studying children as they change within these developing contexts. Through this study we will be led to a deeper understanding of the many forces that bring about change—change in individuals, in families, in societies, and in humankind. Change and children are the human future. In studying children through Worlds of Childhood, we will be preparing ourselves not only to understand and to adjust to change, but to influence the course of change—to influence the course of our own future.

1

Development and Diversity

During the first seven days various reflex actions, namely sneezing, hiccoughing, yawning, stretching, and of course sucking and screaming, were well performed by my infant. On the seventh day, I touched the naked sole of his foot with a bit of paper, and he jerked it away, curling at the same time his toes, like a much older child when tickled. The perfection of these reflex movements show that the extreme imperfection of the voluntary ones is not due to the state of the muscles or the co-ordinating centres. At this time, though so early, it seemed clear to me that a warm, soft hand applied to his face [evoked] a wish to suck. This must be considered as a reflex or an instinctive action, for it is impossible to believe that experience and association with the touch of his mother's breast could so soon have come into play.

–Charles Darwin, *A Biographical Sketch of an Infant*

• INTRODUCTION •

There are many childhoods. There is the childhood of the newborn, the toddler, the first grader, and the adolescent. There is 20th century American childhood; and there is its colonial counterpart. There is childhood as it varies with culture among industrial nations of the world such as Japan, Russia, and the United States; and there is childhood as it is lived in traditional societies such as the Baka of Cameroon. **Worlds of Childhood** provides an introduction to the many lives that children lead. It focuses on developmental phenomena and processes from infancy to adolescence and on the historical and cultural contexts within which development takes place. The three readings in this module have been chosen to provide an overview of the value of the developmental, historical, and cultural perspectives for enhancing our understanding of children. Notice how all three authors, despite variations in perspective, touch on some of the same issues: a) the relationship between original endowment and experience; b) the importance of beliefs about children and childhood in guiding the actions of caregivers; and c) the importance of the social environment.

• • •

The Power and Limitations of Parents
Jerome Kagan

In the following excerpt, Jerome Kagan provides a short, provocative tour of development from infancy to adolescence. He introduces us to four important developmental phenomena and six factors contributing to development that we will soon study in greater depth; and he raises two related issues that will frequently reappear in later readings. The first of these issues involves the contrast between universality and individual difference. Are there psychological characteristics that are universally shared by all human beings everywhere? What are these characteristics, and how do they relate to psychological phenomena that vary between individuals and among cultures? The second issue involves a contrast between biological endowment and experience. Are there psychological

6

characteristics that are largely or wholly determined by the individual's genetic endowment and emerge in development without need for specific experience? Are there psychological phenomena that emerge wholly or largely as a function of experience, little affected, if at all, by the individual's original endowment?

Note that while the foregoing issues are related, they are not identical. Human beings all live in the same physical world. Certain fundamental characteristics of the environment are universally shared. The mere fact of universality, therefore, does not necessarily imply biological origin. Conversely, individual differences are by no means solely a function of experience. Human beings inherit both species general and highly particular characteristics from their ancestors. More importantly, as we shall see, in the view of most psychologists, no matter how important the contribution of original endowment, we should never lose sight of the fact that children are always completely immersed in the world around them. Development from conception onward is, as Kagan suggests, a joint and complex function of a multitude of factors in the individual's biological endowment and environmental, especially social, context. Human development is the product of human nature and human nurture operating in concert.

. . . TWO DEVELOPMENTAL STORIES

Human development has two different stories to tell. One describes the growth of the universal characteristics that are present in all human beings because humans possess a particular set of genes. Humans have a generative language, apes do not; humans experience guilt, shame, and pride; apes do not; humans create laws and mathematics, and apes do not. As long as a child is not locked in a closet or confined to a basement, he or she will resemble other children around the world. The reasons for this universality comprise an interesting story, especially to psychologists, psychiatrists and pediatricians. The moral of the story is that regardless of the family in which a child grows, he or she will demonstrate some of these universal qualities.

The second plot, which is of greater interest to citizens, seeks to explain the psychological differences among us. One hundred people, of any age, are different. In textbooks this idea is called personality. And therefore it is interesting to ask what factors create different personalities.

Kagan, Jerome. (1986). *The Power and Limitations of Parents.* Austin, TX: Hogg Foundation for Mental Health, University of Texas. pp. 3-17.

I shall deal first with the universals and then turn to what we know about the causes of personality.

Biological Preparedness

As the brain grows in accord with its genetic script, the infant becomes able to behave and think in new ways. A six-month-old can neither understand nor speak language no matter what parents do because the brain is not sufficiently mature. However, when the child is twelve to fifteen months old it has reached a level of maturity that enables it to use the experiences of hearing speech to begin to utter words. We say that children are biologically prepared to learn, as long as they hear some language. The key phrase is "biologically prepared." "Zoologists say that birds are biologically prepared to sing the song of their species if they hear that song. So if a canary, hatched and raised in a laboratory and isolated from all birds, hears on tape the song of a canary at the right time in its development, it will later sing its proper song. All the bird needs is a brief exposure. Let us now examine four examples of biological preparedness in the psychological growth of children.

The Growth of Memory

At around eight to ten months of age the human brain reaches an important milestone when the number of synapses in most parts of the brain has reached a peak. As a result the infant can now retrieve memories of the past, as you can remember what you ate for breakfast or what you did last evening. Before infants are eight months old they cannot retrieve the past because their brains are not sufficiently mature to permit them to reach back and recall what happened a minute earlier. After eight months they can. As a result, infants become vulnerable to a special form of anxiety.

One basic occasion for anxiety is remembering the past and comparing it with the present and noting that the two memories do not correspond. Now the person has a problem and if he or she cannot solve that cognitive problem, anxiety results. If the engine on a jet sounds odd, you only become anxious if you can remember what the engine ordinarily sounds like. If you could not retrieve that sound you would not become anxious. You may have noticed that older people who begin to lose their recall memory become less anxious.

At about eight months babies begin to show fear of strangers and fear of separation from their caretakers. You may remember that at about eight to nine months your own child cried when you left the house. A four-month-old rarely cries to that event. The eight-month-old cries because, as the mother leaves, he or she is able to compare the memory of her presence moments ago with the current perception that she is absent. The infant cannot understand that inconsistency and so has a problem. The mother was present moments ago but is not present now. As a result the infant becomes anxious.

8

The anxieties of infancy are a nice illustration of the principle of preparedness. All infants are prepared to become anxious about unfamiliar people and separation from their mothers at a certain age because of the maturation of the brain.

Moral Sense and Empathy

A second example of preparedness that is equally important to our species concerns our moral sense. The tree of knowledge allegory in the Bible may be the wisest statement ever written about humans. You will remember that when Adam and Eve ate from the tree of knowledge God warned them that from then on humans would be different from animals because they would know the difference between right and wrong. Every moral philosopher has acknowledged, in one way or another, that deep truth about our species.

But, after the First World War, American psychology was caught up in a rampant and dogmatic environmentalism that implied that if you didn't teach a child right from wrong he might never know the difference. Psychologists taught their students in the thirties and forties that if a parent did not punish a child and inform him what was right and what was wrong, that child might grow up to be a criminal. But Genesis and Kant were closer to the truth. All children with an intact brain will, between seventeen and twenty-four months, become concerned with broken and flawed objects. This is a time when a child may point to a frayed thread on its shirt and say to the mother, "Mommy, look." The child understands there is something wrong with the shirt. This concern with right and wrong is a prepared characteristic, no different from speech or the improvement in memory at one year.

Another quality that appears at this time is empathy for the emotional state of another. Two-year-olds who live with human beings are able to infer that a person or an animal might be suffering or feeling distress. Hume, the Scottish philosopher, called that feeling sympathy and regarded it as the most fundamental human emotion. Psychologists call it empathy. Empathy for the state of another is a fundamental human emotion that does not have to be taught. It will emerge in all children in the second year. The two-year-old who is capable of empathy has also matured enough to know that if he or she caused the distress of another guilt will also appear. Like empathy, guilt does not have to be taught. Thus humans are biologically prepared to possess a minimal conscience.

Modern psychiatry made a mistake when it invented the word psychopath to apply to criminals. Applying that word to someone who murders with no emotion implies that the killer never had a conscience at any point in his development. I doubt that. As long as the killer was not brain damaged, he once knew right from wrong, and at age two had empathy. What may have happened was that life experiences during childhood and adolescence impaired his adult capacity for empathy. One can lose temporarily a basic human emotion—love is a good example. If a woman is rejected in love twelve times it will become harder for her to fall in love the next time the occasion arises. The experiences of life can reduce the adult capacity for empathy, but every child has that capacity.

Preparedness for Responsibility

Jean Piaget, one of the great psychologists of the twentieth century, said that children passed through stages of intellectual development and that one important stage occurred at about six to seven years of age, although children living in isolated, illiterate villages without schools pass through this stage two or three years later. I believe that at this time the brain has matured in new ways permitting a new set of mental abilities to be actualized.

You will remember that the Catholic church does not require confession of a child before age seven; English Common Law did not view a child as responsible for a crime prior to seven years of age. These facts mean that our ancestors, long before there was child psychology, understood that something profound happens to a child at about seven years of age. In my work in rural Guatemala I found that parents with eight or nine children who did not know their ages would assign a boy the cutting of a new field for corn or assign to a daughter the responsibility of caring for an infant at about seven to eight years of age. Thus it must be that children are giving off some sign informing their parents that they are ready for responsibility.

A second characteristic that occurs at this age is the talent to compare oneself to others. Now the child understands that he or she is prettier, less brave, or a better reader than a friend. A four-year-old cannot compare him or herself with another. This competence or ability to understand how one's qualities compare with those of a larger group has a major effect on the sense of self or self-concept. One of the components of the self-concept is the result of a psychological comparison of self with others. A child cannot know how intelligent he or she is unless he evaluates the other children in his classroom or neighborhood. Without comparative information there is no way to know how attractive, strong, brave, or intelligent one is.

Recognition of Inconsistency

The last preparedness I shall discuss is more abstract but is critical for human functioning. As puberty begins another important maturational change occurs. By twelve or thirteen years of age adolescents begin to examine their beliefs on a particular theme, and if they detect inconsistency among these beliefs they become troubled. Consider the following illustration. An eight-year-old boy can hold these two beliefs and yet not feel uneasy—"My father is a wonderful man;" "My father yells at my mother." Although these ideas are inconsistent, an eight-year-old does not sense their lack of concordance. By contrast, a thirteen-year-old cannot help but sense the inconsistency and is driven to resolve it.

10

Adolescents experience the dissonance that is inherent in their sets of beliefs about God, sex, family, and their future. The tension and stress we attribute to adolescence has less to do with an increase in sex hormones than with a new ability to recognize that one's beliefs are discordant.

This special psychological tension is stronger in the West than in isolated village communities around the world where almost everybody in the community holds the same set of beliefs. As a result, there is little inconsistency and adolescence is a less troubling period than in Western communities where there is so much pluralism in ideology.

Each of these phenomena, the anxiety of infancy as well as the cognitive dissonance of adolescence, will appear whether one's parents are kind or cruel, permissive or restrictive.

Personality

I now turn to the second developmental story which asks how one can account for the differences among children and adults. In order to begin this discussion we have to decide what specific differences we will consider as important. Should we concentrate on swimming ability, how long a person sleeps, or whether a person laughs with gusto at jokes? Each culture values a small number of human qualities, awarding them more seriousness than others.

I believe that four such qualities valued in contemporary American society are: the acquisition of technical abilities, especially academic ones; differences in wealth and status; differences in the ability to enter into close and satisfying social relationships with others; and, finally, differences in happiness. Americans want to know why people differ on these four psychological qualities. Depending upon which of the four you pick, the profile of causative forces will be different.

Influencing Factors

I now want to suggest six conditions which I believe contribute to the differences in technical ability, status, social relationships, and happiness that we see among adults. Depending upon which criterion you pick, the balance of the six conditions will vary. Although the six conditions do not exhaust the domain of causative factors, they are important. You will also note at the end of the discussion that only one of the six is completely within the power of the parent. The remaining five are harder for parents to influence, although they are not beyond their will.

1. *Biological temperament.* The biological temperament of the infant is one of the most basic factors. The biological and psychological differences among infants that we call temperamental can be genetic or prenatal. Babies differ in activity level, irritability, and in how easily they establish a schedule when they return home from the hospital.

11

The temperamental quality I wish to dwell on is one that our research group has been studying for almost eight years.

During the second year of life one sees infants who are extremely timid, fearful, cautious, and shy. They rush to their mother if a stranger comes into the house, and they cry when taken to the doctor. They don't let their mother leave them the first month or two of nursery school and cling whenever they're in an unfamiliar situation, at least until they have become more relaxed. We believe about 10 to 15 percent of children who behave this way were born with a biological predisposition to develop this style. Obviously, it is possible to make a child shy and timid through family experiences.

Another 15 percent of children are born with a predisposition to develop a more sociable, outgoing, and fearless behavioral style. It is hard to frighten such children. We have been following two groups of children who were noted in the second or third year of life to be either timid and shy or sociable and outgoing. We had to observe over 400 volunteer children in our laboratory in order to find these 100 children—50 who are consistently shy and timid and 50 who are sociable, fearless and outgoing. The children in the middle are less consistent. We have followed these children for six years and find remarkable consistency in their styles of behavior. We believe this consistency is due, in part, to differences in the biochemistry of their brains.

Deep in our brains there is an area called the limbic lobe which is the origin of the stress circuits that discharge when we are frightened. The activity of these stress circuits leads us to secrete cortisol, a hormone of the adrenal gland which increases the tension in our muscles, and makes our hearts beat faster. The timid, shy children are reactive in all three of the stress circuits—namely, the pituitary-adrenal axis, the motor system, and the sympathetic chain. This fact suggests that the limbic lobe in the shy, timid children is at a lower threshold of excitability to events that are unfamiliar or challenging.

However, some of these children have changed. We have seen parents of timid two-year-olds gently urge their children to be less shy, and over the years these children have changed. Specifically, about half of our timid, shy children at seven-and-a-half years of age are not extremely shy or timid. However, many families are fatalistic about their children and do not make gentle efforts to alter the child's temperamental qualities. When timid children enter school, many become isolated and loners. If such children come from middle-class families who promote high academic standards they are likely to choose an academic vocation such as history, poetry, or science. I believe that T. S. Eliot was one of these children. If, on the other hand, the parents put excessive pressure on the child to succeed in some domain and the child does not have successes, that child may become extremely anxious and may show pathology later in life.

2. *Birth order.* A second condition contributing to personality differences is the child's birth order; that is, whether the child is first, second, or third born. If we compared a thousand first borns with a thousand later borns we would find that, among middle-class Americans, first borns are generally more responsible and seek to control their environment. First borns get better grades, end up going to better colleges, and,

as adults, commit fewer crimes. When a stress or challenge occurs first borns are less likely to develop symptoms.

By contrast, when later borns are faced with stress they are more likely to develop problems. Later borns are more pragmatic, less idealistic, and a little more likely to be rebellious. Historical studies show that more of the rebels and terrorists of the world are later borns, and more of the idealists and abstract thinkers are first borns. For example, Trotsky the activist was a later born, Marx the scholar a first born.

Let me try to explain these differences. To a first born growing up in a traditional middle-class home, the world looks orderly. Parents are nurturant, predictable, kind people who set high standards. The child is closely attached to and identified with them and the child looks at the world as a just place where, if you do what you are told, all will be well. As first borns enter the period of childhood they ask their parents, "What is it that you want me to do? I will do it."

But the world looks different to a later born. Imagine a later born lying in his crib when suddenly a first born unpredictably shows up and intrudes into the sphere of the younger child. When a later born talks to his older sibling the latter doesn't necessarily reply, but he may seize a toy or pinch the child. Additionally, the first born can stay up until ten o'clock, while the later born has to go to bed at sunset. Imagine these experiences happening week after week, year after year.

What might you predict to be the consequences of this regimen? One reasonable prediction is that later borns should see the world as a little less fair and just, while first borns should be more concerned with the approval of authority and less prone to disagree with or rebel against authority. First borns should want to keep harmonious relationships with authority and have less hostile feelings toward authority. If, as an adult, the person picks science as a vocation, one might predict that if a new scientific theory opposed what authority believed to be correct, and, therefore, threatened the society, the first born would be more likely to question the new idea. The more defiant later born would be more likely to favor it.

We are talking here about theories for which citizens have strong opinions. Educated citizens cared when Copernicus and Darwin said that the Bible's interpretation of the heavens or of man's place in nature was wrong. By contrast, the laser, although a brilliant discovery, did not threaten the average person's beliefs about man and nature. We are concerned here not with brilliant discoveries but with brilliant, new ideas about which most people have fixed beliefs.

Frank Sulloway, a young historian, has done research on this issue. He studied a large number of revolutions in science where the themes were of concern to the society. Some of these revolutions included the ideas of Copernicus, Francis Bacon, Freud, and, of course, Darwin. He then sought to determine what the eminent scientists of the time said about each revolutionary idea in a ten-year period after its original discovery. Was the scientist for or against the new idea and was he a first or later born? In studies of a dozen different scientific revolutions and many hundreds of scientists, he found that those who agreed with a new idea were likely to be later borns, while those who opposed it were likely to be first borns.[1] Thus one's attitude about a new scientific idea is

13

influenced by one's ordinal position and seems to have little to do with that child's specific relationship to its parents.

3. *Parental influence.* Parents assume importance in our third condition, which deals with parental behavior toward the child. Parental behavior tends to assume its greatest importance during the first six or seven years of life.

There are three experiences that parents can provide that have a profound influence on their children. One of the least impeachable facts in child development is that the child's mental development will be stimulated if a parent provides a great deal of variety for the infant. Hence, parents who play with and talk to their children and present them with tameable variety will promote their children's mental development. Parents who do not behave this way will slow their child's intellectual development. Obviously, this variety can be supplied by a babysitter or a daycare center.

Some of the intellectual differences between a working- and a middle-class child are apparent by two to three years of age. Although working-class mothers love their children, they generally provide less variety during the period of infancy. It is not clear why they behave this way. Perhaps they don't believe in the effectiveness of presenting variety to the child.

A second way parents influence their children is through praise and punishment. The child does learn values in accord with what is rewarded and punished. Thus if parents discipline a child for dirtying his shirt or not cleaning his hands and do so consistently, they will get a five-year-old who is a little worried about keeping his shirt and hands clean. If a parent praises schoolwork, the child will become more concerned with doing well in school, at least during the early years of school.

A final source of parental influence involves communicating to the child that the parents value him or her. This experience is more important in our society in this century than it was in the past. You will recall that human beings have a natural tendency to evaluate themselves as good or bad. We all want our consciences to be gentle with us. When the day is done and we ask ourselves in the quiet of the evening, "How are you doing?" we want to be able to answer, "I am a good person." We are essentially moral creatures; in our daily lives we are engaged in a moral mission. A child growing up in a Third World village has to gather wood for the family, prepare supper, or wash clothes in the river. As a result it is obvious to such children that they are good. These seven-year-olds know that they are making a contribution to the family's vitality. Hence no adult has to say to them—and they usually don't—"I love you very much, Maria." Maria has less of a need for this communication because she knows she is of value.

In a society like ours, however, where children make no economic contribution to the family they have to be reassured about their goodness. That is one reason why love, the communication of value, has become so important. Historical changes made loving children, and the communication of love to children, important.

14

Loving a child does not necessarily mean giving that child a great deal of physical affection. John Stuart Mill recalled that his father was a wonderful person but not an emotionally close one. I have been reading an autobiography by a colleague, George Homans, who is now an emeritus professor. He writes of his father, "I could not have been blessed with a better father. I always enjoyed being with him, I respected him. Yet, I must say, I never felt emotionally close to him." A child can feel loved and can love a parent, even though there is not a great deal of physical affection between them. Some young Americans have a hard time understanding that idea because our culture has come to equate parental love with kissing and embracing.

4. *Identification with role models.* The fourth set of conditions is, in my opinion, the most important, and almost every philosopher has made this point, but we continue to forget it. In modern dynamic psychology the phenomenon I am referring to is called identification. Let me explain this idea. The child believes that some of the qualities of his or her parents also belong to the child. The child, as well as the adult, go beyond the objective facts and conclude, "I have the same last name as my family, I have the same color hair as my father, and my aunt noticed that my father and I both have dimples in our chins." The child goes beyond those facts and concludes that "because my father is popular, I must be popular too; because my father is talented, I must also be talented." Or the child can conclude, "No one respects my father; therefore no one will respect me." An identification with the parent can be positive or negative.

I believe that a parent's most important influence on a child originates in his or her status as a role model with whom that child can identify. One problem is that most parents find it difficult to hide their deep qualities, especially if these are undesirable. If a child perceives that the mother is competent, kind, nurturing and attractive, then, fair or unfair, that seven-year-old girl will feel better about herself than she would otherwise. But if the mother is incompetent, not liked, and perceived to be unjust, then the child, even though she possesses none of those qualities, will feel bad, perhaps guilty. Many schizophrenics have identified with a rejecting mother they labeled as bad. As a result, they have these anxious feelings about themselves. A typical statement from a young schizophrenic woman to her psychiatrist is, "I'll tell you my problem, deep inside of me there is a great deal of evil." That feeling is a result of identification with a parent whom one perceives as bad.

Even though parents have limited control over how they present themselves to their children, it is their strongest power for it will influence the child's conception of self for many years. The child can also identify with his or her class or ethnic group. A child who is a member of a disadvantaged minority group is likely to perceive his or her group to be rejected by the larger society. As a result, the child will feel anxiety. In contemporary American society, disadvantaged Hispanic and Black children live with this burden if they identified with their ethnic group when they were young. Even though some grow up to be successful, they can carry the vulnerability for many years. A book that will bring a tear to your cheek, written by John Henry Wideman, is about a pair of

15

black brothers growing up in a ghetto in Pittsburgh. The older brother, a professor of English at the University of Wyoming, has written three novels and is respected in his community. His younger brother is serving a life sentence in a Pennsylvania prison for murder. The older brother, in an attempt to understand his younger brother, wrote a book called *Brothers and Keepers*.[2] In this book he confesses that although he is a professor of English who has written many books, every morning when he wakes up he is afraid he will be discovered. That feeling of vulnerability is a product of an earlier identification. Mr. Wideman may go to his grave anxious and suspecting that one day the larger society will discover this mysterious lack of goodness.

5. *Success and failure.* A fifth condition that influences the child resides in actual environmental successes and failures. Success in school depends in part on the size of the school. Many studies show that if the talent of a child is held constant, the probability of that child being successful is higher if he or she goes to a small school than to a very large one. Similarly, whether the peer group accepts or rejects the child is important. My colleague George Homans was not very popular with his peers and he writes that his classmates bullied and teased him. As a result he decided that he would become talented in schoolwork. The rejection by his peers and the subsequent decision set his life career.[3] It had less to do with his parents than with his experiences in school.

6. *Chance and history.* Finally we consider chance as a factor. Unlike the Chinese and the Malaysians, we in the West are less willing to acknowledge the role of chance in our lives. The Greeks acknowledged the power of the gods' moods. You will remember that in *The Odyssey,* Athena decides what will happen to Odysseus; maybe she will cause a storm or arrange conditions to beach his boat on the rocks. But Americans want to believe that each is a master of his or her fate. If an adult is successful, he wants to believe that he did it through talent and motivation. If one fails, he or she did something wrong. And in our theories of human development we give chance events very little power.

Let me cite a few factors that are outside the control of children or families and, therefore, from that perspective are chance events. What was the size of the town in which the child grew up ? If one leafs through *Who's Who in America* and notes the places where each person grew up, you will find that over 60 percent came from towns under 50,000 although the vast majority of Americans grow up in urban areas. How can we explain that anomaly?

Consider a nine-year-old girl with an I.Q. of 120 who is skilled and has kind parents. On the one hand, let us have her grow up in Salado, Texas; on the other in Chicago. In Salado there will be very few girls as talented as she, and if she stays there through high school she will graduate as a seventeen-year-old who feels very good about herself because she has compared herself with the other girls in the town and realized that she was in the top five percent. In Chicago she will know over two hundred girls who are more talented and pretty than she and, as a result, she will learn humility.

That's why those listed in *Who's Who* spent their childhoods in small towns. Among the first group of astronaut candidates, three-quarters grew up in small towns—towns without great museums, large aquariums, or six-story libraries.

If one is going to succeed in an extraordinary way it is necessary to have an illusion about the self. The adolescent must believe that he or she is much better than others are. Illusion is harder to establish if there are several hundred children one's own age who are more talented, attractive or courageous.

Historical events that influence the entire society comprise another chance factor. The depression of the 1930s is one example. Sociologists have found that if a child was between seven and fifteen years of age during the depression his adult behavior was influenced profoundly. Many who were adolescents in Europe after World War I, the spiritual war that was to solve all of the world's problems, became skeptics for the rest of their lives. . . .

Conclusion

I have listed six factors that can have important effects on the growth of children. Two involve parents. They pertain to what parents do and what they are—their actual practices with their children and how they are viewed as role models for identification. But parents have far less control over the other four factors. That is why I said earlier that parents have power but that power is constrained. The limitation does not mean that parents should not invest effort and care in rearing children. They should be loving and conscientious as parents and should reflect on their actions. Indeed, they cannot do otherwise, for humans are prepared to believe that they can have an effect on the world. But they also must realize that the growing child is a product of the coming together of many, many coherent events, including the child's temperament, historical era, and birth order. An individual life is a complex story with many collaborators.

Notes

1. Sulloway, F., *Family constellations, sibling rivalry and scientific revolutions.* Unpublished manuscript, 1972.

2. Wideman, John Edgar. *Brothers and Keepers.* New York: Holt, Reinhart and Winston, 1984.

3. Homans, G.C., *Coming to My Senses.* New Brunswick, NJ: Transaction Books, 1984.

Our Disconnected Child
William Kessen

Like children and the social conditions in which children grow, our images of childhood change with time. In this brief article, William Kessen introduces the importance of studying children and childhood within the context of history. As he points out, childhood as we think of it—in which young children rarely contribute to the economic well-being of their families and spend large portions of their growing years in age-segregated classrooms interacting with non-familial peers or with adults who may not fully share their values—is a 20th century phenomenon. Our forebears, embedded in communities whose beliefs and values were widely shared, working side-by-side with family members to produce food, clothing, candles, and other necessities of life, and educated in the home and through the church, experienced a very different childhood, guided by different images of children. In the contrast between Locke and Rousseau, we see that the dominant images of children as sustained by nurture or by nature have had a long history. By studying the child in history we learn what childhood has been like and how it has changed with time; and we develop a perspective from which we may look ahead to anticipate what childhood may someday become.

Damnation lay fore and aft the American child two hundred years ago. Primers began with the words "In Adam's Fall, We Sinned All," and the danger of a sin-filled death was proclaimed from every pulpit. Everyone lived under the twin threats of imminent mortality and a fall from grace. The alliance of children and grown-ups in the fear of Satan and the hope of salvation was mirrored in the social organization of the time. No one doubted the unity and strength of Church and State, and the family was seen as "a little Church, a little Commonwealth." Children dressed much like adults and played many of the games that adults played (more frequently, of course, in Europe and the colonial South than in rigorous New England); they lived in the workaday world of adults as smaller colleagues, and they shared in the major and minor rituals of the larger group—weddings, burials, punishments, and gossip. In remarkable measure, the continuity of the community was matched by a continuity of generations.

A short history of children in the United States can be sketched on the theme of their steady separation from both continuities, the story of the child severed from his past and

Kessen, William. (1978). A historical view: Our disconnected child. *Harper's Magazine*, April, Vol. 256. pp. 44-45.

increasingly a traveler from one specialized setting to another. In Europe, where children had been full participants in adult life from a very young age, the segregation of parent and child was under way before 1700. Philippe Ariès, the French historian, has shown that children's games and children's clothes began to differ from those of adults precisely in synchrony with the establishment of schools. (By 1800, children of the middle class were being dressed in the costumes of the lower social orders—little boys wore sailor suits with long, soft trousers, instead of the breeches worn by their fathers—just as their nineteenth century counterparts wore peasant tunics and children today wear overalls and blue jeans.)

The first specialization of the child, in America and Europe, was Child as Student. The school remains the strongest agent of the child's separation from the world of adults. In school, we learn adult values: clock time is truer than body time; order is more to be valued than fooling around; hierarchy is essential for a proper democratic society. With the growth of schools, American children were also gradually drawn away from the world of adult work. At first chores went on, especially in rural areas; but for many children—and in urban areas, for most—the move to school was a move away from the everyday lives of their fathers.

The redefinition of childhood had its philosophers and polemicists in Europe, and their influence was soon felt in America. In 1699 John Locke published *Some Thoughts Concerning Education*, with advice to parents about their children's early training. Locke was as dubious as any colonial preacher about children's ability to grow up well without strict restraint, . . . but he severed them from their demonic origins and held out the possibility of *changing* their behavior. Locke would have had fundamental disagreements with modern behaviorists like B. F. Skinner, but he started us on our way toward behavior modification when he wrote:

> Rewards . . . *and* Punishments *must be proposed to Children, if we intend to work upon them. The Mistake . . . is that those that are generally made use of are* ill chosen . . . Esteem *and Disgrace are, of all others, the most powerful Incentives to the Mind. . . .*

Rousseau's *Emile*, published in 1762, opened another door through which American cultural ideology would run. For Rousseau, the child was not only free of original sin, he was also a being of *Nature*, pregnant with unsuspected possibility.

Childhood was not a time set aside for adults to finish God's work by bringing the child into closer match with adult behavior; it was a time important in itself. "Leave childhood to ripen in your children," Rousseau wrote; ". . . the child's individual bent . . . must be thoroughly known before we can choose the fittest moral training." The child, no longer a passive recipient of instruction, had become a busy, and alert, explorer.

More than a century later, Darwin published *A Biographical Sketch of an Infant*. With chatty scholarship, Darwin offered up the child (his own) as a fit subject for scientific study, a representative of the species' capacity to perfect itself by selective transformation. Before Locke, the child had stood for the stability of family and church. After Darwin, the child became the emblem and the agent of radical change in cultural—even radical change in the nature of man. In 1876, the Reverend W. F. Crafts published *The Coming Man in the Present Child; or Childhood, the Textbook of the Age*. By 1900, the new era was welcomed as the century of the child, the century of limitless growth, renewal, and transformation, the century *led* by children.

Between 1830 and 1880, technical and scientific advances—factory industry, the locomotive, germ theory—had prepared the way for Darwin's vision of man as infinitely perfectible. These developments required the recasting of the American family. Women, who had been partners in labor and in caring for most colonial and early federalist families, were assigned new roles and new chains. The process of change began in the earliest years of the century. Work, particularly commerce and high industry, became man's province—ugly, aggressive, morally diminishing; home, hearth, and heaven became woman's—pure, incorruptible, and pallid. Of course, women kept their children with them in the cloister: somehow, these hopes of the age, these transforming young folk, had to be guarded and enfolded by maternal purity. Children were sweet untroubled innocence, precious and fragile. According to the popular literature of the time, it was better for a child to die than to join the foul world of adult males. The cultural isolation of women and children approached psychological imprisonment.

For nearly one hundred years, Americans have taken hesitant steps toward restoring children to a richer humanity. Wordsworth's romantic belief that "heaven lies about us in our infancy" received rough treatment from Freud, who showed us the dark side of human nature. A general intellectualization of the culture in the mid-twentieth century prepared us for Jean Piaget, with his view of the child as *cognitive*, as cool thinker. Both philosophies make the child into a creature more complex than ever before: both define him primarily in terms of internal processes that shape his development. It is one of the significant ironies of our time that Freud, who stressed the role of instinct, and Piaget, who has focused on pure mind, have come together in their separation of the child from the influences of history and community.

Our formal institutions preserve the child's isolation. School not only serves to teach order, rank, and merit; it is the agency of rigid age-segregation, with children marching through their lives in phalanxes one year wide. The State and the professions have taken on more and more of the work of the familial community, so that decisions about food and clothing and jobs are made far from both the child and his parents. Television can even separate the child from his own experience: what American child sees, in his personal world, the excitement and gore and simplicity of life on TV?

Today, as in colonial times, there is a profound congruence between the definition of childhood and the social order. Our disconnected child—a mosaic of roles, a wardrobe of quick-change social skills—is, unfortunately, fit for our age. He is healthy, independent, preeminently *adaptable*, generally secure from the cruelties of disease and enslavement. Yet somehow, the apotheosis of freedom has become separation from one's own history. We should take a tough look at the modern form of damnation that confronts our children, and ask ourselves not only "Have you hugged your child today?" or "What has your child learned today?" but also "Have you thought what your child will be like when he's forty years old?"

A New Understanding of Childhood
Margaret Mead and Rhoda Metraux

Margaret Mead was a pioneer in cultural studies of children and adolescents. Born in 1901, she first traveled to the South Seas as a twenty-three-year-old, fresh from Barnard College and Columbia University. Describing adolescent sexuality and guilt-free love in the first of her thirty-four books, Coming of Age in Samoa, *she became an almost overnight sensation; and her opinions on sex, education, child-rearing, and culture influenced several generations. In the article reprinted below, Mead and her colleague Rhoda Metraux articulate one of the principal justifications for looking at childhood cross-culturally: we are forced to confront the fact that "there is no one right way to proceed in rearing a child." Like historical periods, cultures each have their own guiding images of childhood, images that in turn shape conceptions of the respective influences of nature and nurture and the role of parents in the child's development. By temporarily stepping outside our own culture to study the many childhoods that exist around the world, we can begin to transcend the constraints of our belief system and come, as Mead suggests, to a deeper understanding of the effects on children of the varied practices found in our own and other cultures.*

We Americans continually try to envision the future as one way of telling ourselves by comparison where we stand now. One question I am often asked is what our descendants, looking back at the twentieth century, will think of as the greatest accomplishment of our time.

There are, of course, many possible answers. No one can really foretell what future generations will select out of the complex past as most relevant to what they have become. But as an anthropologist concerned primarily with our understanding of ourselves as human beings I believe that, looking back, our descendants will regard as one of the great accomplishments of our age the discovery of the nature of childhood and our attempt to put this new knowledge to work in the upbringing of our children.

In my lifetime there has been an extraordinary readiness to accept a kind of understanding about children that was only beginning to shape the thinking of a very few people in my own childhood. Yet we have growing up around us—here and in many parts of the world—a whole generation whose lives have been deeply affected by our

Mead, Margaret & Metraux, Rhoda. (1980). *Aspects of the Present.* New York: Morrow. "A new understanding of childhood." pp. 149-155.

initial efforts to put into practice (as well as, for far too many children, our failure to put into practice) this new knowledge. We cannot know how it will all turn out, for nothing on so large a scale and with so many variations has been tried before. But others in the future may see these first attempts as a turning point.

A great many people, I feel sure, will disagree. After all, they will say, children have existed always and everywhere—seen and heard or seen and not heard, they have been there and have grown up to become adults. We all have been children, reared by parents and teachers and other adults who knew very well the difference between children and adults. Others, mostly young parents in mid-course of bringing up their children, will think about their hesitation and doubts—what choices to make, how to help their children make their way. Is this a change?

I think it is. What has changed is the old, absolute certainty people had that they knew about children and childhood—knew the one right way to proceed in rearing a child, a girl or a boy, from babyhood to become a functioning adult. But one thing we have discovered in this century, by looking at different cultures, is that there are—and were in the past—a great many "right" ways, each different from the others.

The theory that childhood should be regarded as a period of carefree play seemed entirely wrong to those who believed that childhood was a hard apprenticeship to adulthood. That children learned best by making their own mistakes seemed an incredible attitude to people who believe firmly that children must learn what to do and how to do it before they could safely be allowed to take the initiative. When I went to Samoa in the mid-1920s I could ask the question whether adolescence is, the world over, a period of storm and stress, as it undoubtedly was at that time in Western societies. Yet in Samoa it most certainly was not.

What we were learning then by careful observation was that each culture shapes the processes of growth, at whatever stages are recognized as significant, in its own image of a human life. But we were just beginning to ask questions about the processes of development—about what is involved in the conception of the child's "becoming" a person.

Every people has a quite definite image of what a child is at birth. Russians, for example, see the newborn as so strong that they swaddle it firmly to protect it from harming itself. The French, in contrast, see the baby as fragile and vulnerable to anything harmful in the environment—and they softly swaddle the infant to keep it quietly safe.

In Bali a baby is not given a human name at birth. Until it seems clear it will live, the Balinese refer to it as a caterpillar or a mouse. At three months, when it is given a name, it becomes a participating human being whose mother, speaking for it, says the words of polite social response. But if the baby dies before this, people reproach it, saying, "You didn't stay long enough. Next time stay and eat rice with us." For the Balinese believe in reincarnation. They believe the "soul," without any specific personality, is reborn every fourth generation within the same family.

Such beliefs as these—that the newborn child is intrinsically strong or delicate, assertive or compliant, naturally good or bad, a traveler from a different and better

23

world, a soul given one chance for eternal salvation or a soul moving in an endless round of reincarnation—give people assurance that they know what to expect and how to rear a child. And long before the child learns what a child should be, it begins to know whether it fits or doesn't fit the expectations of its parents.

But it is not only conceptions of human nature that are expressed in such images. The basic relationship of parent and child and the procedures of education also are described by analogy. In many Western European cultures the child has been pictured as a plant and the parents as gardeners tending the plant. And there is, in fact, a kind of parallel between the way a people treats plants and children both as living things.

In the English image the gardener, it is believed, must provide the best environment for the plant's own natural growth. In the French image the child is often likened to a young tree that must be given space, with some idea of what it should become, and must be trained, shaped and pruned unremittingly for its best eventual flowering or fruiting by an experienced gardener who knows what the aims of cultivation are. But in the German image the child is more like a flowerpot in which seeds are sprouting, some of them flowers and others weeds, and it is the gardener's duty not only to tend the flowers but to uproot the weeds—weaknesses, errors and faults—so that in time he will produce a sturdy plant that can survive on its own.

In complex societies, of course, analogies like these provided only some of the simpler models for what children and childhood are. But as long as a people considered themselves as somehow representative of what is human and right, they could hold on to traditional beliefs or, from their ideas of what children should be, judge the children they saw around them.

In our time, however, two things in particular changed all this drastically and brought into focus many attempts to think about childhood in another way—not as a stage or state but as a process based in human biology and shaped by the child's relationships to the world of people and things.

One was our growing recognition that although there are extraordinarily different routes from childhood to adulthood, there are also regularities in children's growing—regularities of timing, for example, within wide individual limits, of when children begin to walk or begin to talk. In the face of this our older dependence on absolutes—our insistence on one right way—broke down as students asked how children's capabilities come into play in response to different forms of teaching and learning.

The other discovery grew out of the explorations carried out by the psychoanalyst Sigmund Freud with his patients in which they traced the paths of experience back to childhood—to long-"forgotten" memories, fantasies and conflicts. Freud's belief was that if troubled individuals could recover what was lost and understand what went amiss, they could free themselves to become happier and more productive. But what was also gained was a sense of the wholeness of a human life and of the continuing interplay of past and present in man's relationship to himself and the world around him.

The sequel has been a flowering of work with children themselves—children in many cultures. So for the first time we are beginning to see and understand the relationship between the child's developing capacities and what he experiences from day to day and from month to month, responding to and initiating responses from the people around him.

We are discovering too that many of our most fixed beliefs were simply myths. There was the belief, for example, that for the baby the world at first is, in the phrase of William James, a "buzzing confusion." Far from this, we are finding out that the youngest infants have a working sense of space, that they respond with preference for certain kinds of visual patterns and, especially, are alert to movement and change in what they see and hear.

Equally important, we are finding out that little babies very soon begin to enjoy new variations, and by the time they are a year old are delighted with their own attempts to make quite complex variations on what they have come to know. These are things for which we have so far devised explorations in which babies themselves become partners in the enterprise.

Mothers—observant, loving mothers who enjoy their babies—may have an intuitive sense of what their own babies are reaching out for as they grow. But intuition does not fill the gaps. In our culture, in which babies often are left to lie alone in their own room staring at the blank ceiling, it is a matter of chance whether a mother notices how her baby responds to patterns of light and shadow accidentally cast on the ceiling and whether she finds a way of making these light-birds appear on another day. For her it is this baby—her baby—who responds with delight to the moving play of light and shadow.

What we are finding out now is how babies' developing capabilities come into play at two weeks, four weeks, four months, a year, two years—and also what happens to the child from whom no one, except accidentally, elicits responses of interest and renewed recognition. We need to build this new knowledge into the kind of relationships of babies with those around them that almost any adult, given a lead, can establish—as traditionally mothers and grandmothers and fond aunts played nursery games just for the fun of it.

As our knowledge grows we can also look to the traditional ways of rearing children in different cultures as a way of understanding better the effects on children of special kinds of emphasis. For example, the Chinese give babies a great variety of experiences of looking without touching. The French emphasize sound and believe that to be alert a baby needs to be almost continuously in contact with human voices. In our own country we encourage babies to be physically active—to move and explore, wriggle and reach out, testing the world and their own ability to get what they want. As we examine these varying traditions in child rearing, what we learn from the world's children can be given back to them in new forms to enrich their lives and ours. . . .

25

2

The Ecology of Development

When I was young enough to still spend a long time buttoning my shoes in the morning, I'd listen toward the hall: Daddy upstairs was shaving in the bathroom and Mother was frying the bacon. They would begin whistling back and forth to each other up and down the stairwell. My father would whistle his phrase, my mother would try to whistle, then hum hers. It was their duet. I drew my buttonhook in and out and listened to it—I knew it was "The Merry Widow." The difference was, their song almost floated with laughter: how different from the record, which growled from the beginning, as if the Victrola were only slowly being wound up. They kept it running between them, up and down the stairs where I was now just about ready to run clattering down and show them my shoes.

—Eudora Welty, *One Writer's Beginnings*

• INTRODUCTION •

As we have already observed, the path that children take from birth to adolescence reflects a complex interaction of factors such as biological inheritance, temperament, caregiving, family and peer relationships, schooling, culture, and historical period. Development, in other words, is a joint function of characteristics of the individual person and characteristics of the many contexts in which the person resides. This is an old idea, one that can be traced back at least as far as the pioneer theoretical writings of James Mark Baldwin, John Dewey, and Kurt Lewin; and it is a notion that can be found in the work of developmental psychology's most respected theorists, Jean Piaget and L.S Vygotsky.

Despite the longevity and obvious importance of the concept of Person X Context interaction, however, it has only recently been taken seriously as a potential guide to research. One reason for this is that for a long time psychologists have labored without real theories of the environment, without ways of systematically describing and analyzing the many contexts within which development occurs. Over the past twenty years, this situation has slowly begun to change. Urie Bronfenbrenner has been one of the most influential among a number of psychologists active in promoting this change.

In the first reading in this module, taken from the introduction to *The Ecology of Human Development*, Bronfenbrenner shows us that the child's psychological environment is a very complex affair. In Bronfenbrenner's view, home, neighborhood, school, parental work place, even the halls of government where public policy is made, together with the many connections among these various contexts and the cultural and historical frameworks within which they exist, constitute the ecology of development.

This complex ecology is the subject of our second reading. With specific reference to modern Japan, Joy Hendry offers us a detailed description of three of the most important contexts for the development of young children: home, neighborhood, and nursery school. Through her work, we not only learn about the nature of these varied settings, we also see quite clearly how they relate to one another and how each reflects the overarching culture of Japan.

● ● ●

The Ecology of Human Development
Urie Bronfenbrenner

In this excerpt, Urie Bronfenbrenner introduces us to a few of the fundamental constructs of his ecological perspective on development. For Bronfenbrenner, the environment is a set of nested structures consisting of: a) multiple immediate settings (e.g., home, school) containing the developing child, other people, and a complex set of interrelations among them (microsystems); *b) relations among these settings* (mesosystems); *c) relations among these settings and settings in which the child does not directly participate such as the parent's workplace* (exosystems); *and d) "overarching patterns of ideology and organization of the social institutions common to a particular culture or sub-culture"* (macrosystems). *He argues that "what matters for behavior and development is the environment as it is* perceived *rather than as it may exist in 'objective' reality." He stresses the need for a systems analysis of the reciprocal interactions that take place at each of the various levels of the environment; and suggests that students of development may profit from focusing on the significance of "ecological transitions—shifts in role or setting which occur throughout the lifespan" such as those that accompany the birth of a sibling, school entrance, graduation, first employment, marriage, parenthood, etc.*

In this volume, I offer a new theoretical perspective for research in human development. The perspective is new in its conception of the developing person, of the environment, and especially of the evolving interaction between the two. Thus development is defined in this work as a lasting change in the way in which a person perceives and deals with his environment. For this reason, it is necessary at the outset to give an

Bronfenbrenner, Urie. (1979). *The Ecology of Human Development.* Cambridge, MA: Harvard University Press. Chapter 1 (Purpose and Perspective). pp 3-15.

indication of the somewhat unorthodox concept of the environment presented in this volume. Rather than begin with a formal exposition, I shall first introduce this concept by some concrete examples.

The ecological environment is conceived as a set of nested structures, each inside the next, like a set of Russian dolls. At the innermost level is the immediate setting containing the developing person. This can be the home, the classroom, or as often happens for research purposes—the laboratory or the testing room. So far we appear to be on familiar ground (although there is more to see than has thus far met the investigator's eye). The next step, however, already leads us off the beaten track for it requires looking beyond single settings to the relations between them. I shall argue that such interconnections can be as decisive for development as events taking place within a given setting. A child's ability to learn to read in the primary grades may depend no less on how he is taught than on the existence and nature of ties between the school and the home.

The third level of the ecological environment takes us yet farther afield and evokes a hypothesis that the person's development is profoundly affected by events occurring in settings in which the person is not even present. . . . Among the most powerful influences affecting the development of young children in modern industrialized societies are the conditions of parental employment.

Finally, there is a striking phenomenon pertaining to settings at all three levels of the ecological environment outlined above: within any culture or subculture, settings of a given kind—such as homes, streets, or offices—tend to be very much alike, whereas between cultures they are distinctly different. It is as if within each society or subculture there existed a blueprint for the organization of every type of setting. Furthermore, the blueprint can be changed, with the result that the structure of the settings in a society can become markedly altered and produce corresponding changes in behavior and development. For example, research results suggest that a change in maternity ward practices affecting the relation between mother and newborn can produce effects still detectable five years later. In another case, a severe economic crisis occurring in a society is seen to have positive or negative impact on the subsequent development of children throughout the life span, depending on the age of the child at the time that the family suffered financial duress. . . .

The environment as conceived in the proposed schema differs from earlier formulations not only in scope but also in content and structure. On the first count, the ecological orientation takes seriously and translates into operational terms a theoretical position often lauded in the literature of social science but seldom put into practice in research. This is the thesis, expounded by psychologists and sociologists alike, that what matters for behavior and development is the environment as it is *perceived* rather than as it may exist in "objective" reality. . . .

Different kinds of settings are also analyzed in terms of their structure. Here the approach departs in yet another respect from that of conventional research models: environments are not distinguished by reference to linear variables but are analyzed in systems terms. Beginning at the innermost level of the ecological schema, one of the basic units of analysis is the *dyad*, or two-person system. Although the literature of developmental psychology makes frequent reference to dyads as structures characterized by reciprocal relations, . . . in practice, this principle is often disregarded. In keeping with the traditional focus of the laboratory procedure on a single experimental subject, data are typically collected about only one person at a time, for instance, about either the mother or the child but rarely for both simultaneously. In the few instances in which the latter does occur, the emerging picture reveals new and more dynamic possibilities for both parties. For instance, from dyadic data it appears that if one member of the pair undergoes a process of development, the other does also. Recognition of this relationship provides a key to understanding developmental changes not only in children but also in adults who serve as primary caregivers—mothers, fathers, grandparents, teachers, and so on. The same consideration applies to dyads involving husband and wife, brother and sister, boss and employee, friends, or fellow workers.

In addition, a systems model of the immediate situation extends beyond the dyad and accords equal developmental importance to what are called *N + 2 systems*—triads, tetrads, and larger interpersonal structures. Several findings indicate that the capacity of a dyad to serve as an effective context for human development is crucially dependent on the presence and participation of third parties, such as spouses, relatives, friends, and neighbors. If such third parties are absent, or if they play a disruptive rather than a supportive role, the developmental process, considered as a system, breaks down; like a three-legged stool, it is more easily upset if one leg is broken, or shorter than the others.

The same triadic principle applies to relations between settings. Thus the capacity of a setting—such as the home, school, or workplace—to function effectively as a context for development is seen to depend on the existence and nature of social interconnections between settings, including joint participation, communication, and the existence of information in each setting about the other. This principle accords importance to questions like the following: does a young person enter a new situation such as school, camp, or college alone, or in the company of familiar peers or adults? Are the person and her family provided with any information about or experience in the new setting before actual entry is made? How does such prior knowledge affect the subsequent course of behavior and development in the new setting?

Questions like these highlight the developmental significance and untapped research potential of what are called *ecological transitions*—shifts in role or setting, which occur throughout the life span. Examples of ecological transitions include the arrival of a younger sibling, entry into preschool or school, being promoted, graduating, finding a job, marrying, having a child, changing jobs, moving, and retiring.

The developmental importance of ecological transitions derives from the fact that they almost invariably involve a change in *role*, that is, in the expectations for behavior associated with particular positions in society. Roles have a magiclike power to alter how a person is treated, how she acts, what she does, and thereby even what she thinks and feels. The principle applies not only to the developing person but to the others in her world.

The environmental events that are the most immediate and potent in affecting a person's development are activities that are engaged in by others with that person or in her presence. Active engagement in, or even mere exposure to, what others are doing often inspires the person to undertake similar activities on her own. A three-year-old is more likely to learn to talk if others around her are talking and especially if they speak to her directly. Once the child herself begins to talk, it constitutes evidence that development has actually taken place in the form of a newly acquired *molar activity* (as opposed to molecular behavior, which is momentary and typically devoid of meaning or intent). Finally, the molar activities engaged in by a person constitute both the internal mechanisms and the external manifestations of psychological growth.

The sequence of nested ecological structures and their developmental significance can be illustrated with reference to the same example. We can hypothesize that a child is more likely to learn to talk in a setting containing roles that obligate adults to talk to children or that encourage or enable other persons to do so (such as when one parent does the chores so that the other can read the child a story).

But whether parents can perform effectively in their child-rearing roles within the family depends on role demands, stresses, and supports emanating from other settings. As we shall see, parents' evaluations of their own capacity to function, as well as their view of their child, are related to such external factors as flexibility of job schedules, adequacy of child care arrangements, the presence of friends and neighbors who can help out in large and small emergencies, the quality of health and social services, and neighborhood safety. The availability of supportive settings is, in turn, a function of their existence and frequency in a given culture or subculture. This frequency can be enhanced by the adoption of public policies and practices that create additional settings and societal roles conducive to family life. . . .

The structure of the ecological environment may also be defined in more abstract terms. As we have seen, the ecological environment is conceived as extending far beyond the immediate situation directly affecting the developing person—the objects to which he responds or the people with whom he interacts on a face-to-face basis. Regarded as of equal importance are connections between other persons present in the setting, the nature of these links, and their indirect influence on the developing person through their effect on those who deal with him at first hand. This complex of interrelations within the immediate setting is referred to as the *microsystem*.

The principle of interconnectedness is seen as applying not only within settings but with equal force and consequence to linkages between settings, both those in which the developing person actually participates and those that he may never enter but in which events occur that affect what happens in the person's immediate environment. The former constitute what I shall call *mesosystems*, and the latter *exosystems*.

Finally, the complex of nested, interconnected systems is viewed as a manifestation of overarching patterns of ideology and organization of the social institutions common to a particular culture or subculture. Such generalized patterns are referred to as *macrosystems*. Thus within a given society or social group, the structure and substance of micro-, meso-, and exosystems tend to be similar, as if they were constructed from the same master model, and the systems function in similar ways. Conversely, between different social groups, the constituent systems may vary markedly. Hence by analyzing and comparing the micro-, meso-, and exosystems characterizing different social classes, ethnic and religious groups, or entire societies, it becomes possible to describe systematically and to distinguish the ecological properties of these larger social contexts as environments for human development. . . .

Becoming Japanese: The Arenas and Agents of Socialization
Joy Hendry

For most young children in industrialized societies, home, neighborhood, and preschool constitute significant contexts for development. In reading Joy Hendry's careful description of the way in which these contexts are organized and function in Japan, pay particular attention to the characteristics of each of the three settings as microsystems. In the continuing families that constitute many of Japan's households, for example, notice how relationships between the spouses and the generations may influence the mother's relationship with her child. Observe the mesosytemic links between the home, the neighborhood, and the school. In Japan, contexts of development frequently function in concert to reinforce a remarkably consistent set of values. Exosystem effects are also observable. Japanese fathers, for example, are expected to work long hours. Leaving home in the morning before the children arise and returning after they are asleep, fathers tend to play only a minor role in childcare. Finally, it is evident that the processes that unfold in this complex ecology are also, in many ways, distinctively Japanese. Among the most obvious manifestations of the cultural macrosystem are an extremely protective and indulgent attitude toward infants; benevolent hierarchy in parent-child, sibling, and even neighbor-child relations reflecting traditional Japanese respect for age and seniority; strong concern with cooperative activity; and insistent pressure for achievement leading to the popularity of private after-school lessons even for young children.

Socialization of preschool children in Japan is carried out in three main arenas, whose relative importance ideally changes as a child passes through three generally perceived stages of development. The three arenas are the home, the neighborhood and the kindergarten or day nursery, each of which will be considered in a separate section of this chapter. The three stages are distinguished mainly by vocabulary and attitudes. The first is separated linguistically from the other two as the 'suckling period' (*nyūjiki*), approximately the first year of a child's life, after which the preschool years are taken together as *yōjiki*. The division of the second stage is based on collective ideas that a

Hendry, Joy. (1986). *Becoming Japanese*. Honolulu: University of Hawaii Press. Chapter 2 (The arenas and agents of socialization). pp. 47-69.

34

child of three begins to respond to reason and will therefore 'listen' to its caretakers, so that the approach to rearing may develop from the first 'creation' of the soul, implied in the saying 'the soul of the three-year-old lasts till 100'.

The home is of course important throughout a child's life, but the view is often expressed that a baby or 'suckling' should be moved as little as possible from the immediate environment of its family and their abode. A forcible illustration of this idea arose when my assistant's baby ran a temperature during a couple of nights away from home. On her return, she became adamant that the baby should not be moved again. Her own mother chastised her for taking the baby away, arguing that taking it out amongst people lowers its resistance to germs, excites it, breaks up its routines and rhythms, and could well cause the baby to wake up and cry during the night. Other informants reinforced this view in reference to self-imposed limitations on their usual activities during the first year of a baby's life. Even a mother with employment outside the home tries to entrust a baby to the care of a relative or close neighbor during this early stage, and it is reported that only 1.7 percent of all babies under one year are taken to day nurseries or other such facilities. Seventy-one percent of working women's children under one year are cared for in their own homes, probably usually by a grandparent, and fourteen percent in other homes, so that most are in the charge of individuals.[1] The general disapproval of 'baby hotels' is indicative of the collective idea that home is the more appropriate environment.

As the infant learns to walk, it begins to venture out into the neighborhood, at first accompanied by a caretaker, but as it approaches the age of three it may be allowed to play with other children if the area close to the home is considered sufficiently safe. In Kurotsuchi toddlers are often to be seen playing in the shrine compound, their caretakers nearby but not necessarily interfering with the activities of the children on the swings and slides supplied there, as long as they are in no danger. The view is often expressed that this is the stage when children should start to make friends with other infants of their own age, and in a booklet published by the Chiba prefectural department of education to help mothers of children in the yōji stage, it is said to be necessary (hitsuyō) from the age of two for children to start playing with other children in the neighborhood.[2] At this time, the agents of socialization increase in number as the caretakers of other toddlers enter the scene, and the child begins to learn about its relations with peers. Older children also become important, but inter-relationships are still informal and the child can usually retreat to its home territory if it becomes overwhelmed.

During its fourth or fifth year usually, although this may be earlier, a child will enter a local kindergarten or day nursery, where it comes into contact with institutionalized socialization under the guidance of professional caretakers, although, again, other children may be as much involved in the process as adults are. This is the period also when a child may be enrolled in private classes for particular accomplishments. Now the child is fully entered into the third stage in preschool development and all three arenas have come into play. In the following pages some detail of each stage will be provided, together with a discussion of recent changes.

The Home

The composition of the household in which a child spends its early years varies depending on the family circumstances. Nuclear families, which have become increasingly common in modern Japan, are similar to those found in the West. The archetypal parents-and-two children unit is in fact by far the most common,[3] the two children frequently being born within the space of two or three years, so that large numbers of siblings, common within living memory as important influences in growing up, are now relatively rare. The continuing family, which is the other still common type of domestic arrangement, almost always involves only one conjugal pair in each generation. Thus, the child growing up in such a family is in close contact with one set of grandparents and possibly one or two great-grandparents, as well as its parents, but cousins and married uncles and aunts usually live elsewhere. Unmarried siblings of the parent whose natal home it is may be present for a period, and have a right to stay in the house if they never marry.

In the areas where research was carried out there were both types of family. In Kurotsuchi, a rural community with a large number of farmers, most of the houses were old family lines, so the vast majority were continuing families. Even those who had set up new homes, since only one son in a continuing family remains in the ancestral home, had proceeded in the next generation to bring in a spouse and continue in the traditional way. In Tateyama there was more variety. Details were available in some of the kindergartens where family information was kept, although if a child came from a two-generation household it was impossible to tell from the records whether it was a new nuclear family or a continuing one where the grandparents had died. One of the areas in which I worked was quite rural with a situation similar to Kurotsuchi. Of the 113 children in the local kindergarten, 99 lived in continuing families and 14 in nuclear ones. At Shirayuri Kindergarten, the only private one and therefore representing the better-off of Tateyama, 82 of the pupils lived in continuing families and 98 in nuclear ones. At Tateyama Kindergarten, one of the central public ones in the city, 121 children lived in continuing ones and 252 in nuclear ones. In all these examples, some of the 'nuclear' figures are probably continuing families with only two generations alive. Of the 49 families I interviewed for this investigation, 28 lived with senior parents and 21 in nuclear families, but in this case I know that all the nuclear families are also new families. The Kyushu families in the sample had 18 to four in favor of the continuing line, whereas the Tateyama and Tokyo ones included only 10 continuing families and 17 nuclear ones.

In either type of family, where geographically possible, other close relatives are likely to be frequent visitors and since these seem to be regarded as appropriate people to admonish and teach a child, they may well play quite an important part in their early rearing. Grandparents, in particular, are usually involved, ritually if not practically, and if they live too far for frequent contact, children often spend a week or longer periods in their home during the kindergarten holidays.

36

Thus the categories of human being that a child first learns to distinguish are the parents, grandparents, uncles, aunts and cousins, much as may be the case in Western society. The terminology, too, does not differ greatly. Even where the continuing family is the residential unit, the terms for grandfather and grandmother are the same for both sets of couples, that for the non-resident pair being qualified with a place-name or some other distinguishing feature. No distinction is made between maternal and paternal uncles, aunts and cousins, and second cousins are not usually distinguished terminologically from first cousins. The chief difference between this system and the Western one is that older and younger siblings are distinguished so that there are separate words for elder brother and younger brother, elder sister and younger sister, which introduces an element of hierarchy into the sibling relationship.

All terms of relationship are expressed from the point of view of the youngest member. Thus the terms for grandmother and grandfather are applied by everyone to the oldest generation, even by their own children once they have become parents. As new babies are born, their elder siblings are addressed more and more as 'elder brother' and 'elder sister', rather than by their first names. In principle, seniors address juniors by their first names and juniors use a relationship term for their superiors but the relationship terms are used to children to encourage them to behave in a grown-up manner.

Within this group of close family, then, how are the child-rearing responsibilities distributed? It seems to be the common view nowadays that the ultimate responsibility for a child rests with the mother, whether the domestic arrangements involve three generations or not.[4] From a Western point of view, this may seem to be quite natural, but in a traditional household (*ie*) the children were regarded as belonging to the house, whether the mother was present or not. Thus, if a girl had a baby out of wedlock and subsequently married, the child would often stay in the mother's natal home; or if a woman left a house on divorce or separation, it was usual for the children to remain behind, to be brought up by the new wife or their grandmother. For example, one of my informants in Kurotsuchi lived with his wife and his father's second wife, his own mother having been divorced from his father when he was a baby and now she was living in Hawaii. His young brother, the uterine son of the second wife, had left the house on marriage, since he was not the eldest son, who is preferred to inherit in the system of primogeniture usually practiced. In the past, a common reason for divorce was said to be when the wife failed to get on with her mother-in-law, even if relations with her husband were quite reasonable, but nowadays it seems to be more likely in such circumstances for the young couple to leave the family home, taking their children with them. The legal registration system, which now records each nuclear family as a separate unit, also supports this practice. In case of divorce, it is getting more and more likely that children will remain with their mother.[5]

Evidence for the attitude that the mother bears the ultimate responsibility for her children was provided during research in several ways. For example, where grandmothers taking charge of small children while their mothers were out at work were

37

interviewed about their child-rearing practices, they usually commented that it should really be the mother who answered the questions as they were just standing in. In some cases, grandmothers received pocket money from their daughters or daughters-in-law who were out at work as specific remuneration for child care. When one grandmother was invited to go on a trip with her age-mates, her daughter-in-law was expected to take time off work so that she could go.

Nevertheless, within specific families, mothers often reported that in a difference between mother and grandmother over a matter of child-rearing, the grandmother would still usually be deferred to. When I reported to a PTA group that in England our mothers advise us, but that in the end we English mothers tend to go our own way, the audience responded with gasps of surprise. It has been reported from survey material that many parents prefer to rely on the advice of their own mothers, or their own experience from childhood, than to follow the advice of modern magazines and 'scientific' recommendations.[6] The figures are higher for rural areas than urban ones, but in studies carried out in Nagoya and Okayama cities, these were still around 50 percent of respondents.[7] However, mothers frequently complain that grandmothers do too much for a child so that it fails to learn to do things for itself. They also say that grandparents are too lenient with children, giving them anything they ask for and cancelling punishments meted out by parents. Grandparents are also said to emphasize too often the dangers surrounding the child, thus making it too cautious and unadventurous, though the caretakers defend themselves by pointing out that they must be especially careful with children who are not their own. Grandfathers are often not distinguished from grandmothers in these comments, each apparently as likely to indulge a child as the other. Indeed, in Kurotsuchi, it seemed more often the grandfather who was the culprit in such accusations. It was certainly often the grandfather who spent a large part of the day with the child. . . .

In neither the nuclear nor the continuing family does the father usually play a very active part in the early child-rearing process. Recently there has been some publicity given to the way fathers have begun to become more involved with their babies in Western societies, particularly from a feminist element of Japanese society,[8] and it is said to be good for a father to have as much contact as possible with his children. Indeed, in some families these principles are put into practice and fathers are even helping with feeding and changing of their babies.[9] In general, however, fathers express great interest in child-rearing at a theoretical level, some claiming to have as much contact as possible with their children, but the majority of my female informants report that the father is in practice little involved. In many cases the pressure of work prevents the father from being present much in the family home, many men returning home each evening after their children are asleep, and leaving in the morning before they get up. It is sometimes emphasized that the father's work comes first, even in family businesses where he is actually on the premises all day. Two such wives in the interview sample complained that their husbands spend very little time with the children. Other wives seemed quite resigned to the fact that their husbands spend most of their evenings drinking with their colleagues.

In response to a question put to the families in the interview sample about the role of the father in child-rearing, many families reported that it was he who bathed the child(ren) if he was home in time. It should perhaps be pointed out that the Japanese bath is something of an institution, a relaxing, pleasurable activity, rather than merely being a means to become clean. In most families the children bathe with their parents and grandparents of both sexes until they are quite grown up, and the bath is seen as a good place to be together and discuss the events of the day. The sting in the tail for the mother, where very small children are concerned, is that she must wait outside the bathroom where all the fun is taking place, so that she can dry and dress the children when they come out. But at least it is easier for her to do this than it is for her to dry herself and the babies at the same time if there is no other adult to help. The bath is too deep and too hot to sit babies in by themselves. In continuing families it is often a grandparent who will help out by bathing the children. According to the Norbecks, the baby was often bathed by the father because they shared the privilege of being allowed first in the clean, hot water.[10]

Several families also reported that the father sometimes found time on Sundays to take out his child(ren) or play with them, but this kind of activity tends to increase as the child gets older. In families with a new baby it seems to be regarded as a father's role to help more with the older child. In public places, such as parks and other amusements visited by young families, it is possible to observe this principle in practice, although it is not unusual these days to see a father carrying a baby or pushing round a push-chair. Most fathers seem to draw the line at strapping babies to their backs, however, and when I reported at a PTA meeting at Shirayuri Kindergarten that back-carriers for babies are often carried by men in England, the response was gales of laughter. . . .

An older sibling is usually encouraged to participate in the socialization of the younger one and great emphasis is laid on the status of 'elder brother' or 'elder sister'. This seems to be a successful ploy in many families to avoid jealousy when a new baby is born. The older child is usually encouraged to help and give way to the younger one, and much play is made of the fact that being older one is therefore more experienced and able 'to understand'. A definite superior role is being outlined for the older child, who seems to take great pride in playing it. This places an interesting early emphasis on the concept of hierarchy, since it is the benevolence and responsibility of the superior role which is being encouraged.

The distinction between younger and older brother and sister is also emphasized in a use of language encouraged. Older children 'do things for' a younger child (*naninani o shite ageru*), whereas this phrase is discouraged if used by a younger child to an older one. For example, in the case of the verb to play, the older child does the younger child the favor of playing with it (*asonde ageru*), but in the reverse situation, where it wanted to play with a still older child, it would have to make the suggestion in the form of a request which implies a degree of deference (*asonde kureru*). This introduces the other, inferior side of hierarchial relations and corresponds to speech forms used in polite conversation when one humbles oneself in order to show respect to another. Children

39

are not expected to master these general niceties very early, but the presence of the grandparents is sometimes cited as an opportunity for mothers to encourage them to begin to use simple forms of respect language.

Nowadays no discussion of the agents of socialization in the home would be complete without mention of the television set. Few families are without one, there are numerous channels to choose from, and morning television abounds with programs for pre-school children and their mothers. Many of these shows present quite explicit child-training material, reinforcing the teachings of mothers throughout Japan. . . . The form resembles that of *Sesame Street*, with large, speaking animal-like characters who blunder about behaving in the wrong way so that they can be corrected by a gentle, friendly (sometimes male) mother-figure who explains to them the proper way to proceed. The important points are reinforced in songs and ditties, often sung by children, and a plethora of other devices designed to appeal to and remain in the minds of tiny viewers. Characters of Japanese writing are also featured in an early program, supporting the mothers' claim that their children learn to read through television.

This adds a public dimension to socialization, even in the home, which is of course evident too in the books and pamphlets distributed to mothers of babies and young children. Television programs supplement this literature so that mothers, too, may be socialized in the appropriate way to socialize their children. Since many of these broadcasts and publications are initiated on a national level, even if they are actually put out by the prefectural or municipal authorities, they are probably a strong force for homogeneity in approach throughout the country. Regional variations in child-rearing practices undoubtedly still exist, but it seems likely that they are diminishing in force and number. Although many mothers in the survey mentioned above reported that they followed their own mothers rather than the new 'scientific' methods advised in books and magazines, a number of grandmothers discussed the ways in which they had modified their own rearing methods in the tight of modern advice. . . .

The Neighborhood

In many parts of Japan, there is an institutional aspect to neighborhood relations. Communities may be divided up into fixed groups which share various responsibilities for public property, and, within the groups, members of the houses involved have fixed roles at certain important times for each of the other houses.[11] Typically, neighbors will participate in each other's weddings, births and deaths, as well as perhaps attending the ceremonies associated with the growing up of each other's children. Even where such groups are not formally created, informal aid is usually given between houses popularly delineated as 'the three opposite and one on either side' (*mukōsangen ryōdonari*), although the actual participation in such co-operative activity may not of course be distributed exactly in this way. In cities, where the population of neighborhoods may be more fluid than in the country, it is the custom for a family moving in to take a small gift to the near neighbors as a convenient way of introducing themselves and expressing a willingness to co-operate in local activities. Even in a housing estate near Chiba, where one of the interviewees had recently built a house and all the neighbors were in houses constructed in the last few years, the families had already organized several local co-operative groups.

Thus, it is common in Japan for a family to be acquainted with other families living nearby, and for its members to know and co-operate with their counterparts in neighboring houses. In particular, in this context, mothers of young children meet at the local swings, discuss their problems with each other, and occasionally look after each other's children when the need arises. For the children themselves, these neighbors are probably the first representatives of the world outside the family circle with whom they have repeated contact, and their children may well be their first friends.

Close neighbors may in fact be classified in familial terms, so that other mothers become 'aunts', fathers become 'uncles', and their children become 'big brothers' and 'big sisters', according to their ages. Older children refer to younger ones by their given names, with a diminutive suffix '*chan*', just as is the case within the family. For clarity, the given names or surnames of the individuals concerned may be appended, as may a place or occupational name such as 'the aunt from the corner shop' or 'next door's big brother' and so on. Again, a hierarchical element is present, now perhaps better recognized, as children are explicitly encouraged to be polite to the adults, show a degree of respect for the older children, and help and care for the younger ones. There is again a role for the older ones to teach the younger ones and be benevolent to them when disputes arise: indeed, one of my informants commented that a neighbor's daughter was more efficient than she at socializing her daughter. As we met neighbors in the areas where we stayed, the relative ages of our children was always one of the first matters to be sorted out so that the appropriate terms could be used, and the appropriate behavior encouraged.

Perhaps as important as the hierarchical element, however, it is thought to be necessary at this stage for children to learn to play happily with any other children who happen to be there. This is the beginning of social life, the creation of the social being, and a child who is unsuccessful playing with the children in the neighborhood is thought likely to have trouble in its future social relations. On the household information sheet filled out on entry at kindergartens there is often a space to enter the child's good points in the view of the parents. A point quite frequently mentioned was the child's ability to play with anyone, and if the child had difficulty in this respect, it might be entered in the section for bad points, or points to be rectified. Since any one neighborhood usually has a number of children of different ages, the existence of some accepted ideas about hierarchy seems to aid the likelihood of harmony amongst the children.

Less emphasis is placed at this stage on sex, and indeed, lists of friends of children entering Shirayuri Kindergarten included several examples of children of different sexes as particularly good friends at that time. Later, single-sex groups become common, but in the early stages boys and girls seem to get on well. One family in the interview sample teased a daughter now in a university about the fact that her closest playmate before school had been a little boy. Although they still lived near to the boy's family, she had had little to do with him after starting school and was surprised to find out that he had been so close.

Thus little gangs of children of both sexes may be seen roaming about in many parts of Japan from quite an early age. In the country they will play in the fields, or on the footpaths which crisscross the villages; in cities they will play in quiet back-streets or parks; even apartment buildings often have an open space at one side, or a courtyard in the middle, where children may play. At first mothers may supervise their toddlers as they venture out into this social world, but gradually they will leave them to trail after the bigger children, learning the rules as they go. When sibling groups were larger, five-year-olds were entrusted with the care of babies, but this is rarely observed these days.

Such activities are rather informal for preschool children, serving mainly to introduce them to a social world outside their own home and circle of relatives. Some older children may act as important agents of socialization, reinforcing the teaching of mothers and other caretakers if they take seriously their role of older brother or sister. For others, it may just be a convenient way to learn ball games, and how to catch and keep the insects which abound in the summer. In the past, however, this neighborhood play was seen as an important part of a child's education, and some adults lament the fact that kindergarten and other classes have severely reduced the number of hours children have available for such play. As long ago as the early part of this century, Yanagita Kunio, an influential Japanese folklorist, questioned the value of the middle-class preference to keep their children in, and the separation in kindergarten of children of different ages into groups supervised by adults. He pointed out that as children of different ages played together outside they gradually learned the ideas of equality and justice—important steps on the way to an independent life.[12] Smaller sibling groups and the extension of the kindergartens and day nurseries to include all social classes are factors which have further reduced such experience. Outside play continues, but apparently on a greatly reduced scale to that of the past,[13] when the local community was more involved generally in the rearing of its children.

A still flourishing element of many neighborhoods begins on a more organized basis when children enter school and qualify to join a children's group (*kodomogumi*). These are based on local residential units and the children thus express a formal allegiance with the neighborhood by joining them. Traditionally these groups were active in villages, especially for festivals and other religious activities, but many fell into decline as industrialization proceeded.[14] Recently they have been revived in many areas, organizing sporting activities, outings and school disciplinary groups as well as participating in festivals and other ceremonies in the old way. In neighborhoods in Tokyo, as well as in country villages such as Kurotsuchi, children of a neighborhood gather at a meeting point every morning in order to walk to school together. Thus, the relations established informally at an early age are likely to continue, and even for children whose families move, there are similar groups for them to join in other areas.

Kindergartens, Day Nurseries and Other Classes

Most children in Japan today experience the third arena of institutionalized socialization before they enter compulsory education in their seventh year. In 1981, 65.7 percent of all children of the appropriate age had enrolled in a kindergarten,[15] and most of the rest attend day nurseries, either because the longer hours are convenient for their working mothers, or because day nurseries are more readily available in areas where most mothers do in fact work. . . .

Once children enter a kindergarten or day nursery, they find themselves in a highly structured situation. Usually they are divided by age so that most of their contact with other children will be with peers, great emphasis being placed on the ideal that all the children should be friends (*tomodachi*) and get on well with one another. Best friends are not particularly encouraged, indeed there is not really such a concept at this stage, and a Japanese girl in England recently reeled off to me a whole list of 'best friends' she had made at her English school. Conflict and competition is discouraged, and each child is expected to participate equally in the many and varied communal activities. Duties are allocated to each member of the class each day, but every child has a turn eventually to serve and to discipline the others.

Much is made of the equality and sameness of the 'friends' surrounding one in an establishment such as this. Some have complete uniforms, little distinguishing one child from another, most have at least overalls and caps which are identical for boys and girls, except perhaps that their caps are different colors to indicate the classroom to which they belong. They have identical sets of equipment kept in identical drawers and shelves, although each child does at least have its own personal set, which is more than can be said of English kindergartens and nurseries where crayons, scissors and so forth are usually common property. In Tateyama, each child also has an emergency earthquake hood, again identical, and these are kept on hooks where the children also hang their bags, distinguished from each other only by their names and possibly little stickers, which give the children a chance to express their own identity. Thus, the child who has been much fussed over, and attended to night and day, now finds itself among perhaps thirty-nine other children,[16] each equally important in the eyes of the teacher, and each equally entitled to her attention.

This is not aimed to turn the children into little robots or automatons, as some Western observers like to see it, but to impress upon the child that the world is full of people just like itself whose needs and desires are equally important. Their names are known—the register is read out each day when each child must answer clearly—and their quirks and character differences become common knowledge as the children move through the classes and often into school together. Fun and enjoyment are perfectly possible in a kindergarten—indeed, they are among the aspects most stressed by teachers and parents alike, but they require co-operation and consideration, and the other members of the peer group become forceful agents of socialization into this stage of development.

In most kindergartens and nurseries there is also some opportunity for older and younger children to interact, so that the 'elder brothers' and 'elder sisters' may still be encouraged to set an example to the younger ones, and perhaps take care of them in certain circumstances. At Shirayuri, for example, a new child will be assigned an older one to sit beside on the kindergarten bus, and the older one makes sure that the younger one learns the routine at going-home time. Almost every kindergarten and day nursery seems to have birthday parties from time to time, typically monthly to celebrate all the birthdays of that period at once, and on such an occasion all the children assemble together. Thus it is a good opportunity to point out the activities of the older ones as an example to the younger ones, which provides a responsibility for the former to consider in their singing or whatever activity happens to be the order of the day. If one of the top class should misbehave, it is suggested to them that one of the smaller children might see them and pick up bad behavior, which would be quite inappropriate for big brothers and sisters. In some kindergartens, where numbers are limited, the children of two years' intake may be put together, which gives the teacher plenty of opportunity to use her older children to demonstrate to the younger ones the proper way to do things, again providing the older children with a responsible role and the younger ones with an example.

Of course, the teacher, too, now becomes an important person in the lives of the children. The head of Shirayuri Kindergarten encouraged her teachers to be crisp and efficient and to dress gaily but smartly to carry out the role which she saw as more important than that of a university teacher, since they have the children at such an impressionable age. They were kind with the children, but very firm, and crying was behavior to be ignored rather than indulged. The benevolence of the teacher is for the children who put their energies into co-operating and participating enthusiastically in the many and varied activities she arranges for them. If she is a good teacher, she will show no favoritism, and most of her attention is directed to supervising the class as a body. . . .

Finally, some preschool children begin to be influenced strongly by the teachers of private classes in particular skills. These are more commonly associated with older children preparing for entrance to academic secondary schools, but many classes are also available for primary school and kindergarten pupils. A typical selection open to preschool children in a fairly densely populated area includes art, drawing, calligraphy, piano, violin, electric organ, ballet, rhythmics, Japanese dance, gymnastics, martial arts such as *kendō* and *aikidō*, swimming, football and more academic subjects such as English and Kumon-style mathematics. The nature of the classes is of course quite variable. Some are highly structured and especially sought by parents to provide an element of old fashioned discipline in their children's lives. Among these are *kendō*, where they may also learn the old samurai rules and ideology as a kind of sound philosophy for life; calligraphy, which emphasizes the beauty of the Japanese script and the importance of writing it correctly; and Japanese dance, which is again concerned with very formalized and structured movement. An art or drawing class, on the other hand, may aim to develop some freedom of expression and a feeling for shape and color in the young child. A chain of art schools throughout Japan base their teaching on a famous American school whose ideas are currently popular. The music classes may concentrate on Western classics, but some are very rigid in their teaching methods and discipline is again an important part of their training. The Suzuki violin schools have of course had a great impact in the West in the way they teach very young children to become accomplished musicians. Also popular are piano and electric organ classes. Sports of one sort or another seem to be becoming popular too for youngsters, and skating was a less common option open to preschool children in Tateyama. . . .

Hara has pointed out that these classes, which may well operate at different times for different children in a neighborhood, have removed the possibility of long continuous periods of time for play, particularly when children reach school age and more and more are enrolled for extra tuition of one sort or another. She goes on to add that nowadays children are less involved than they used to be in household chores, partly because of smaller families and the increased use of electric gadgets, but also in the interests of their studies, so there is still time for play, but it is fragmented. Thus, solitary pursuits, such as reading and watching television have come to replace activities with children in the neighborhood. Instead, she goes on, more children are seeking peer group identity among friends who are attending the same tutoring classes, and those who don't attend are being deprived of the opportunity to form peer groups.[17]

This argument was supported by an informant who gave private English classes after school. He claimed that so many friendships are now formed in this way that children who don't attend such classes find themselves without friends, which adds an interesting group element to a phenomenon which must at first have started out to encourage individual achievement. However, another writer on the subject, who also comments on the element of friendship involved, points out that it provides a close interpersonal relationship between pupil and teacher which used to characterize Japanese learning, but which has been lost in recent mass education. Thus, she claims, special classes contain the seeds of 'a positive, progressive educational movement'.[18] Opal Dunn has suggested that for young children the teacher is often more like an 'elder sister' than a formal teacher. At Shirayuri Kindergarten, whose graduates are often dispersed to schools in their own residential areas when they leave, after-school classes in English and music provide excellent opportunities for kindergarten classmates to maintain their friendships throughout their school lives. A similar situation was described by the head of a kindergarten in Kyushu which also specialized in musical training, and continued classes for school children.

It seems to be the case, then, that these after-school classes have a socializing role apart from the obvious one connected with their content. This is likely to be more important for school children than for most younger children, except perhaps for those in some areas of Tokyo and other large cities. Thus, the pre-school period becomes a particularly important time to develop neighborhood contacts, which may, if they are well-established endure sporadically as other areas take on a more and more time-consuming role. The revival of neighborhood children's groups should help to encourage this. With television, the home has perhaps become more important than it

45

used to be, however, since short periods between school, study and outside classes can more profitably be spent there than outside seeking friends.

Notes

1. Economic Welfare Bureau (Japan). 1980. *Current State and Future Problems of the Japanese Household—Outline.* Economic Planning Agency Publication (February), *23.*

2. *Mama Wakatte Ne (You Understand, Don't You, Mummy)* 1981. Chibaken Kyoikuiinkai (Chiba Prefecture Education Department), *3.*

3. Ministry of Foreign Affairs (Japan) Information Bulletin. 1976. Report from the Japanese Side of the World: Fertility Survey, *13.*

4. Maretzki, Thomas W. & Hatsumi Maretzki. 1963. Taira, an Okinawan Village. In Beatrice Whiting, *Six Cultures.* New York and London: John Wiley & Sons, *367.*

5. Ministry of Health and Welfare (Japan) 1979. White paper (in Japanese); ——1979. A Brief Report of Child Welfare Services in Japan. Children and Families Bureau, *28.*

6. Aoi, Kazuo *et al. c* 1970. Comparative Study of Home Discipline. In Hill, R. & R. König, eds. *Families in East West: Socialization Process and Kinship Ties.* The Hague and Paris: Mouton, 58; Koyano, Shogo. 1964. 'Changing family behaviour in four Japanese communities'. *Journal of Marriage and the Family* 26: 149-59.

7. Koyano, *ibid.*

8. See, for example, the magazine *Mothering,* edited by Ikegami Chizuko.

9. Hara, Hiroko. 1980. The childhood in Japanese society during the past 100 years. Paper presented at Kolloquium 'Kindheit, Familie und Poesie im Kulturvergleich'. Goethe-Institut, Kyoto, *10.*

10. Norbeck, Edward. & Margaret Norbeck. 1956. Child Training in a Japanese Fishing Community. In D.G. Haring, ed., *Personal Character and Cultural Milieu.* Syracuse, New York: Syracuse University Press, *657.*

11. See, for example, Fukutake, Tadashi. 1972. *Japanese Rural Society*, trans. R.P. Dore. London: Cornell University Press; Hendry, Joy. 1981. *Marriage in Changing Japan*. London: Croom Helm: chapter 2; Nakane, Chie. 1967. *Kinship and Economic Organization in Rural Japan*. L.S.E. Monographs on Social Anthropology No. 32. London: Athlone; and Beardsley, Richard K. *et al.* 1969. *Village Japan*. Chicago University Press, Phoenix Edition.

12. Hara, Hiroko & Wagatsuma Hiroshi. 1974. *Shitsuke (Child-rearing)*. Tokyo: Kōbundo.

13. Hara, Hiroko. 1980. The childhood in Japanese society during the past 100 years. Paper presented at Kolloquium 'Kindheit, Familie und Poesie im Kulturvergleich'. Goethe-Institut, Kyoto, 9; see, for example, Johnson, Thomas W. 1975. *Shonendan: Adolescent Peer Group Socialization in Rural Japan.* Asian Folklore & Social Life Mongraph No. 68. The Chinese Association for Folklore, 52.

14. Hara, Hiroko & Wagatsuma Hiroshi. 1974. *Shitsuke (Child-Rearing)*. Tokyo: Kōbundo, 62-3; Takeuchi, Toshimi. 1957. *'Kodomogumi ni tsuite'* ('The Children's Group'). *Minzokugaku Kenkyū (Japanese Jounal of Ethnology)* 21,4: 61-7; Sakurai, Tokutaro. 1962. *Kōshudan Seiritsu Katei no Kenkyū (A Study on the Development of Kō Organization)*. Tokyo: Yoshikawa Kōbunkan, 314-325; Seki, Keigo. 1962. *Nenrei Shudan* (Age Groups). In Omachi Tokuzo *et al.* eds. 1962. *Nihon Minzakugaku Taikei (An Outline of Japanese Folklore)*. Vol. 4. Tokyo: Heibonsha, 128-43; variations in such groups are discussed in Johnson, Thomas W. 1975. *Shonemdan: Adolescent Peer Group Socialization in Rural Japan*. Asian Folklore & Social Life Monograph No. 68, 52-60.

15. *Pre-School Education in Japan*. 1981. Ministry of Education, Science and Culture, Tokyo, Japan, 20.

16. *Early Childhood Education* 31 reports 1978 average of 33.5 children per class.

17. Hara, 1980: 20-1; cf. Kondo, Sumio. 1974. 'Off we go to our lessons'. *Japan Interpreter* 9: 15-24.

18. Riggs, Lynne E. 1977. *Ranjuku Jidai.* In 'The idioms of contemporary Japan'. *Japan Interpreter* 11: 549.

UNIT 2: Heredity and Enviroment

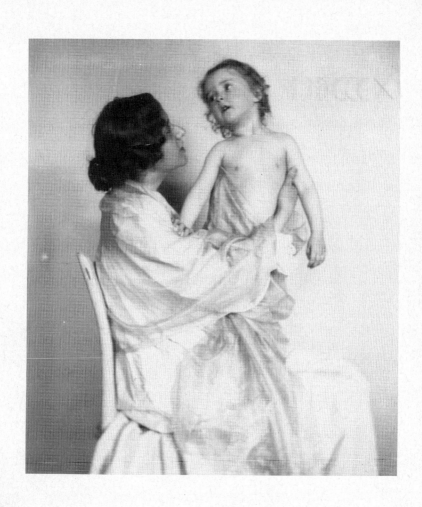

3

Prenatal Development and the Birth Process

In Rajastan, in India, women may communicate the news of their pregnancy to their husbands by making or asking for a *pido*. This is a numeric coloured veil with a red dot at its centre traditionally worn by women who have recently borne a son. For a husband, conception means that his life and name will continue. For the wife, pregnancy means her standing in her husband's home is increased, and her position established.

Fathers prepare for childbirth too. In India, when the wife of a Brahmin becomes pregnant, the husband stops chewing betel—often harder than giving up tobacco and fasts until the child is born. In the Philippines, the father must stop eating sour fruit a week before delivery; otherwise it is believed that the child will have a stomach ache. In China, the man must guard against violent movement or the embryo will suffer in the mother's body. Malayans touch no sharp implements, kill no animals, and avoid any action that injures anything.

It is much easier to study the infant than the fetus. It is easier to observe a child on the first day of school than an infant being born. Perhaps for this reason, the vast majority of research and theory in child development focuses on the postnatal period. Psychological development, however, does not begin in infancy.

As we see in the reading in this chapter, the prenatal period has significant consequences for development. In their description of the growing sophistication of fetal sensitivity and behavior, Marshall and Phyllis Klaus suggest that it is in the prenatal period that we will find the developmental origins of mother/infant reciprocity.

● ● ●

Before Birth: the Dawn of Awareness
Marshall H. Klaus and Phyllis H. Klaus

Compared to most areas of research in child development, the systematic investigation of fetal behavior is still in its infancy. Only within the past twenty years, as ultrasound imaging techniques have become more widely available, as miniaturized electronics have provided researchers with increased opportunity for intrauterine measurement, and as medicine has developed techniques for sustaining life in extreme cases of premature birth have we begun to appreciate the complexity of behavior and sensory sensitivity in the fetus.

In this excerpt from their book, The Amazing Newborn, *Marshall and Phyllis Klaus describe some of what is known about the movement and sensory response capacities of the fetus. Using the newest techniques, researchers have discovered that long before they will be needed postnatally the fetus develops and exercises a wide range of critical sensorimotor patterns (yawning, swallowing, breathing, rooting, smiling, grimacing, sucking, grasping, stretching and curling). This exercise is essential to the neural development that underlies the increasing coordination of these actions.*

As the fetus is learning to coordinate movement, sensitivity to a surprisingly varied array of sensory input is also developing. Sounds from the exterior environment, the internal rumblings of the mother's body, and the complex acoustic patterns of the mother's voice provide the fetus with constant aural stimulation. Recent research has even indicated that fetal apprehension of the sounds of the mother's voice is sufficiently well developed that babies, whose mothers had read the sing-song stories of Dr. Seuss' (e.g., The Cat and the Hat*) aloud during the last trimester of pregnancy, showed a marked preference after birth not only for the mother's voice but for the mother's reading Dr. Seuss.*

Sensitivity to light, touch, and taste also develop prenatally as do the fetus' biological rhythms and sensitivity to maternal emotional states. As the authors point out, long before birth the mother and her baby have begun to accommodate to one another, to engage in dialogue. Although we do not yet know to what extent the parameters of this dialogue will relate to the synchrony of later mother/infant interaction, it seems reasonable to suppose that the developmental roots of the interactional dance that characterizes adaptive interactions between mothers and infants lie in the mutual adjustments of mother and fetus that take place during the period of prenatal development. Just as biological development does not cease with birth, neither does the development of children's relationship to their mothers await the moment of birth.

Years ago the growing fetus was thought to live in an isolated world, an impenetrable castle, impervious to the environment outside its mother's womb. Our notion of what life is like for the human fetus has changed. Ultrasound images and other innovative technologies, as well as careful observations of very premature infants who survived early delivery, have given us a glimpse into the life of the fetus and its capacities to react, to perceive light and sound, to register sensations or sensory messages. We know much more about how intrauterine experience and activities rehearse and prepare the fetus for life outside the uterus.

Ultrasound was first developed during World War II and used extensively to detect enemy submarines. Sound waves are transmitted through water, and as they bounce off an object are reflected back and projected by a computerized technique onto a screen. The ultrasound devices presently used to study the fetus can reveal exquisite details of its body. A small, lightweight instrument placed on the mother's abdomen sends and

Klaus, Marshall H. and Klaus, Phyllis H. (1985). *The Amazing Newborn*. Reading, MA: Addison-Wesley Publishing Co. Chapter 7 (Before birth: the dawn of awareness). pp. 128-138.

receives the sound waves. After these waves bounce off the fetus, they are projected onto a screen that can show both still and moving pictures. . . .

Though ultrasound is probably safe, not everything about its effect is yet known. Most doctors recommend that it be used only when necessary. In practice ultrasound is used mainly to estimate the age of the fetus by measuring the dimensions of its head. This is most accurate when done between fifteen and thirty weeks of pregnancy. It is also used to check for certain problems in development.

Through this window into the womb we can follow the growth of the fetus from its beginning weeks of life. By means of an ultrasound image, one can see that a five-week-old fetus is capable of spontaneous movement.

Mothers first begin to feel the fetus move at about four to five months of pregnancy, and fathers when they rest their hands on the mother's abdomen shortly after that. However, undetected motion already has been occurring for sometime. By seven to eight weeks, the fetus can accomplish very simple movements of a single arm or leg joint, the wrist, elbow, or knee. At twelve weeks, the fetus can move all the joints of an arm or leg together. By thirteen to fourteen weeks, the arms may move with the legs, and sometimes the fetus can even be seen to hold its hands up. By nineteen weeks, the fetus can step, hold itself erect, and scoot itself forward by bracing against a hand. Such abilities have been seen both in ultrasound images and in tiny premature babies.

This astonishing repertoire of motions has many purposes. Motion itself is essential for the growth and development of the muscles and bones as well as for the stimulation of nerve-cell growth in the brain. An extension of the nerve cells in the brain actually grows into an arm or a leg. Motion helps this growth and, at the same time, creates new pathways for future nerves. This process, for example, permits children as they grow to develop very fine hand control. The movements of arms and legs can be compared to the work of a shuttle in a loom that weaves through the warp of the fabric, adding a new row of thread to the cloth with each motion. If movement is prevented in any limb, the joint freezes, muscles and nerves wither, and the bone atrophies. . . .

The fetus lives in the amniotic sac, a fluid-filled container that cushions and protects it. In this floating and weightless environment, the limbs and body have a wide range of freedom to move, keeping the joints flexible. The rocking motions that the baby experiences in utero may explain why, after birth, the newborn derives so much pleasure from being held and rocked.

As researchers have observed the fetus using ultrasound, they have noticed a variety of unexpected behavior. Yawning, swallowing, breathing, rooting, smiling, grimacing, sucking, grasping, stretching, curling, and unfolding appear to be practiced for long periods before they are necessary. This rehearsal, like the training of an athlete, helps make each motion more smooth and coordinated over time.

The fetus develops its own rhythms and patterns. The activities and life of the fetus are governed by a series of internal clocks, each running on a different schedule. The heart beats 140 times a minute, while the timer controlling sleep and awake periods in the uterus is paced very slowly, changing once every thirty minutes. The timing of these sleep and awake states changes with the age of the fetus. Most of the clocks are located in the brain; however, the pacemaker for the fetal heart is part of the heart itself. These many clocks work simultaneously and produce overlapping rhythms in the fetus. A Swiss watchmaker would never get any sleep if he had to keep all these differently timed clocks in good running order! Babies have their own characteristic time tables and rhythms when born, and a perceptive mother will notice clues about these during pregnancy.

The fetus is also bathed in sound. From the earliest period of pregnancy, the environment of the womb is a symphony of sounds and vibrations. Minute microphones placed alongside the fetus at six to seven months have revealed that the maternal sounds have a volume slightly less than that of a busy city street! Swishing of the blood in the mother's large blood vessels, her heartbeat, and her intestinal rumblings make up many of the sounds.

In varying degrees, the fetus is sensitive to external noises as well. Japanese researchers have made a fascinating observation while studying newborns living in the vicinity of Osaka airport, one of the world's busiest. If a pregnant woman moves into the housing near the runway before six and a half months' gestation, her three-day-old newborn will wake up only five percent of the time when a jet takes off. But if a woman moves into the same area after seven months of gestation, her three-day-old newborn will wake up and cry 55 percent of the time at the same occurrence. Similar experiments with buzzers have shown this same ability to "tune out," or "habituate," as researchers call it. Such an ability shows a highly sophisticated level of development in the fetus.

Further evidence of fetal hearing comes from observing the fetus through ultrasound while it is responding to clicking sounds from outside the mother's abdomen. At twenty-eight weeks, an external clicking sound produces an immediate response of the eye. Eye blinks begin in some fetuses as early as twenty-six weeks, and all healthy babies blink by twenty-eight weeks. Researchers cannot yet tell how much of this blinking comes from the actual hearing of the click and how much is related to picking up the vibrations of the click with other sense organs. However, brain waves of very young prematures do show a definite response to pure sound as early as twenty-seven weeks. . . .

Other senses are also well developed long before delivery. Some of the taste receptors are in use between twenty-eight and thirty weeks. Young premature infants will suck with extra vigor when given something sweet and make a face or grimace when given anything tart.

The sense of touch appears very early. When the soles of the feet are touched, the fetus will straighten its legs; and when its fingers come to its lips, it will suck on them. As early as six to eight weeks, if a fetus's hand or foot accidentally touches something in utero, the fingers or toes will curl; and by six months, the hand grasp is strong enough to actually support the fetus's own weight.

The fetus is also sensitive to light while in the womb and develops the capability of sight several months before the pregnancy is complete. When a bright light is flashed on and off on the mother's abdomen, a blink can be seen on ultrasound, but it occurs with a definite delay of one second compared to the immediate blink in response to

55

sound. Very young prematures are sometimes born with their eyelids still fused. However, they do make a blinking motion at the flash of a bright light. Light can be transmitted through the thin wall of the uterus and abdominal wall of the mother, and so the fetus probably experiences night and day. Some premature babies who have spent only thirty to thirty-one weeks in the uterus have visual preferences. When premature infants are shown thick and thin stripes, they demonstrate that they prefer to look mainly at thick stripes. These preferences keep changing, and by thirty-five to thirty-six weeks, they like to look at different kinds of shapes.

The observations of pregnant women add continually to those of researchers. The fetus, by using its newly developing senses, picks up many internal and external signals. In addition, pregnant women report that the fetus responds by a change of activity to their emotions. Obstetricians have also observed that women with chronic stress will have fetuses who have fast heart rates and are very active. By some complicated process, the fetus can be affected by its mother's emotional experiences. Consequently, the mother and her baby are engaged in a dialogue long before the baby's birth. Her activity level and emotional state interlock with the unborn baby's characteristic cycles. As she adjusts to the rhythms of this new life within her, the fetus is already experiencing the tempo of her life as well as that of its father and other members of its family.

4

Evolution, Environment, and Growth

Young people in Western Europe, Japan and North America are growing taller and heavier than their ancestors and even their parents. The caskets of Egyptian pharaohs and the armour of medieval knights seem designed for today's ten year olds. By one estimate 15 year olds were 14 cm taller and 15 kilos heavier in 1955 than they were in 1870. Seats in la Scala opera house in Milan, built in 1778, were 32.5 cm wide. Today comfortable seats need to be 60 cm wide! This change is in part due to improved nutrition and sanitation. Where diet has not altered much over the centuries, or there is insufficient food, there has been little size change—for instance in India, or amongst the Baka hunter-gatherers.

• INTRODUCTION •

Biology and culture interact, as we have already seen, in myriad and complex ways. This interaction is even evident in an arena of development that one would expect to be primarily biological, that of human physical growth and sexual maturation. In the first of two articles reprinted for this module, we are shown how an evolutionarily derived pattern of growth unique to humans—one in which infancy is greatly extended and an additional stage of childhood is inserted between the end of infancy and the transition to sexual maturity—provides conditions that facilitate the emergence and maintenance of culture. In the second article, we are shown how age of menarche, a critical point in the sexual maturation of young women, has decreased markedly with historical changes in cultural and economic conditions.

• • •

The Evolution of Human Childhood
Barry Bogin

In comparison to other mammals, even primates, the human growth pattern is unique. In this article, Barry Bogin reviews data indicating that for most mammals sexual maturity begins where infancy ends, with no noticeable change in growth rate. While sub-human primates and some social carnivores add an intermediate stage of juvenile development between infancy and puberty, this period is essentially only an extension of infancy in that growth velocity continues steadily to decrease. For humans, on the other hand, growth occurs in three clearly defined stages: a rapid decrease in rate during infancy, a gentle decrease during childhood, and a rapid increase with the onset of the adolescent growth spurt. In Bogin's view the intermediate stage of childhood, during which the brain has reached most of its adult size while heads, faces, and bodies retain features eliciting caretaking behavior from adults, provides children

Bogin, Barry. (1990). The evolution of human childhood. *Bioscience*, *40* (1). pp. 16-25.

with the time required for learning while it continues to foster proximity to those capable of teaching. The evolution of childhood, in other words, provides conditions that facilitate the emergence and maintenance of human culture.

The pattern of human growth from birth to adulthood is characterized by a prolonged period of infant dependency, an extended period of childhood and juvenile growth, and a rapid and large acceleration in growth velocity at adolescence that leads to physical and sexual maturation. This pattern is unusual for mammals in that most mammalian species progress from the infant nursing period to adulthood without any intervening stages. Compared with other mammals, nonhuman primates extend the infancy period. Many species of monkeys and apes have a phase of juvenile growth, defined as the time of independence from parental care after weaning and before sexual maturation. Only the human species has childhood as a step in the life cycle, and it is a step which is well defined from both a physiological and behavioral perspective. The purpose of this article is to take an evolutionary approach toward human development and show how childhood may be considered a unique characteristic of *Homo sapiens*. . . .

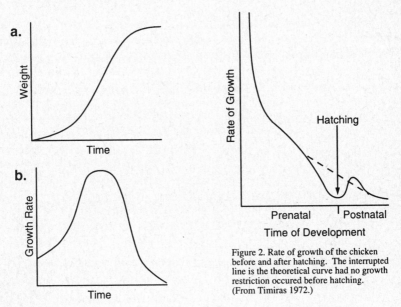

Figure 2. Rate of growth of the chicken before and after hatching. The interrupted line is the theoretical curve had no growth restriction occured before hatching. (From Timiras 1972.)

Figure 1. General growth curves. a. Weight versus time. b. Rate of growth (velocity versus time).

Typical Growth Curves

To better understand the stages of the life cycle, developmental biologists often use mathematics as a tool to describe the pattern of amount and rate of growth for a species. The shape of the mathematical curve of growth of all organisms, parts of organisms, and colonies of cells is virtually identical. It is an S-shaped, or sigmoid, curve characterized by an initial acceleration and then a period of deceleration in growth rate (Figure 1a). The growth of bacteria, chickens, rats, cattle, and even tumors in animals follows this curve (Brody 1945, Laird 1967, Timiras 1972, von Bertalanffy 1960). . . . In Figure 1b, the velocity, or rate of growth, is given; only a single peak, or maximum rate of growth, occurs. . . .

It is fortunate that the biological pattern of growth can be so clearly described mathematically, . . . that growth is a smooth and continuous process. Regular change in amounts and rates of growth allows us to predict the course of development with precision and make quantative and qualitative comparisons among different species of animals in terms of the mathematical properties of their growth curves.

An example of a general growth pattern is given in Figure 2, for the chicken. Only the physical constraints of the egg around the time of hatching interfere with a smooth growth trajectory. The rigid shell and the depletion of nutrients from the yolk sac of the egg slow growth before hatching. After hatching, the growth rate rebounds, but only to the point where an averaging of the prenatal and postnatal growth rates would yield a smoothly decelerating curve.

Von Bertalanffy (1960) showed that the growth of mice and Brahman cattle may be modeled with the same curve used for the chick. Thus, the pattern of growth of these phylogenetically and ecologically distinct organisms was qualitatively identical. Even human perinatal growth is similar to that of birds and other mammals (Figure 3). During the last part of the third trimester of pregnancy, the fetus is large enough to press against the inner surface of the uterus and the placenta, which probably constricts blood vessels and inhibits the fetomaternal exchange of nutrients, gases, and wastes. Fetal growth slows, but it rebounds after parturition so that the child catches up to the size he or she would have achieved if there had been no prenatal decrease in growth rate (Tanner 1978).

Human Growth

The major exception to the general pattern of organic growth is one followed by humans during postnatal life. The human pattern is illustrated in Figure 4, which is based on data from a Swiss longitudinal study of growth (Prader 1984). The curves are drawn from median values of growth, and thus they represent growth of the typical boy or girl from the Swiss study.

The curves in Figure 4 that represent total height at each measurement (the so-called distance curve of growth) are, at first glance, not markedly different from the general sigmoid curve of Figure 1a. However, the velocity curves illustrated in Figure 4b are different from the velocity curves for other animals (Figures 1b and 2).

For the human, there is a rapid decrease in growth rate from birth to approximately the age of four, followed by a more gentle decrease in the rate of growth to approximately age ten for girls and age twelve for boys. The period of rapid deceleration in growth rate (0-4 years) is the infancy stage. The period of gently decreasing growth rate that follows is the childhood stage.

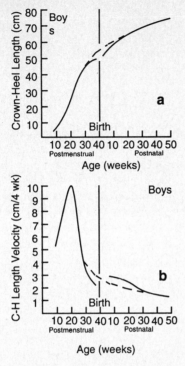

Figure 3. Distance (a) and velocity (b) curves for the growth in body length during human prenatal and early postnatal life. The figure is diagrammatic and based on several sources of data. The interrupted line is the theoretical curve had no growth restriction taken place before birth. (From Tanner 1978.)

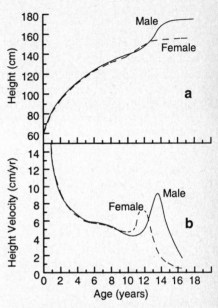

Figure 4. Growth in height of typical European boys and girls. a. Distance curve of growth achieved versus age. b. Velocity curve of growth rate versus age. (From Prader 1984.)

Between the ages of approximately ten and twelve years for girls and twelve and fourteen years for boys, there is a rapid increase in growth rate. The change in growth acceleration from negative to positive marks the onset of the adolescent growth stage. The most obvious feature of growth during this age is the adolescent growth spurt, which peaks at a growth velocity unequaled since early infancy. After the peak growth velocity of the spurt, there is the constant decrease in growth rate that ends with the attainment of adult stature. Thus, qualitative and quantitative differences exist between human growth curves and their nonhuman counterparts.

Unlike the nonhuman curve of growth, the human growth curve cannot be modeled with a single smooth mathematical function. . . . The addition of a childhood stage is one aspect of human growth that makes it unique, even among the primates. A brief review of the growth of primates versus other mammals will clarify the place of childhood in human growth.

61

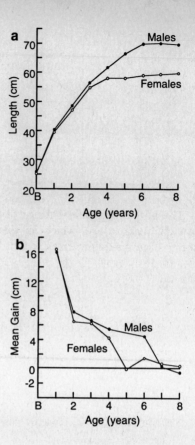

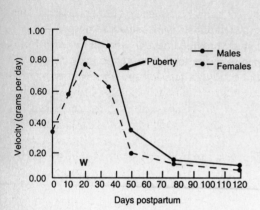

Figure 5. Velocity curves for weight growth in the mouse. In both sexes, puberty (vaginal opening in females or spermatocytes in testes of males) occurs just after the maximal rate of growth. Weaning (W) takes place between days 15 and 20. (After Tanner 1962.)

Figure 6. Distance (a) and velocity (b) curves for crown-rump length in the baboon. Puberty occurs at approximately four years in females and at approximately six years in males. Weaning takes place between the ages of 12 and 18 months. (From Coelho 1985.)

Nonhuman Primate Growth Patterns

Most mammals have evolved a pattern of growth that results in sexual maturation occurring at the point on the growth velocity curve where growth is still taking place but the rate is decelerating rapidly.

It is at this point that infancy ends and adulthood begins, with no noticeable transition in growth rate. Figure 5 displays the mean velocity curves for the male and female mouse, and it illustrates how puberty closely follows weaning. This pattern of growth is typical for nonprimate mammals. Rats, guinea pigs, rabbits, and cattle follow essentially similar patterns of growth and sexual maturation (Tanner 1962, von Bertalanffy 1960). Primates, and some of the social carnivores, postpone puberty by adding to infancy a juvenile stage of development. Juvenile mammals may be defined as "prepubertal individuals that are no longer dependent on their mothers (parents) for survival" (Perieira and Altmann 1985).

The primate pattern of growth is illustrated in Figure 6. The data are based on the work of Coelho (1985), and they show the gains in crown-rump length and weight in a mixed-longitudinal sample of 250 male and 452 female olive baboons (*Papio cynocephalus anubis*). The animals were part of a laboratory colony living under naturalistic conditions in terms of the physical environment and social group composition. All animals were healthy and well nourished, and none showed signs of clinical obesity. The date of birth for all animals was known and the animals were measured once a year.

The mixed-longitudinal design of the study provided data on growth between birth and eight years of age, which for this species is the total span of the growing years. Puberty occurs at approximately four years of age in females and six years of age in males of this species. Note that increments in length velocity generally decrease during the entire growth period.

The maximal rate of growth in the baboon occurs before birth, but for the mouse the maximal rate occurs shortly after birth. This difference between rodent and primate is merely a shift in timing of growth events that are common to both species. The major contrast between the mouse and the monkey is that the time from maximal rate of growth during infancy and the onset of puberty is extended in the primate. The extension of the infant pattern of growth allows for the juvenile stage of development. In terms of growth rate, the juvenile period is essentially an extension of infancy, that is, the velocity of growth continues to decrease steadily. Similar patterns of linear growth before the onset of puberty were found in two other studies of monkey species, the pig-tailed macaque (*Macaca nemestrina*) and the baboon (*Papio cynocephalus*; Orlosky 1982, Sirianni et al. 1982).

The only longitudinal growth data published for apes are for chimpanzees (*Pan troglodytes*). Analyses of these data show a pattern of growth from birth to puberty similar to monkeys; however, the infancy and juvenile periods are further extended (Gavan 1971, Watts and Gavan 1982). For the chimpanzee, weaning takes place at approximately 4.5 years. Females in the wild reach puberty (i.e., first menstruation) at approximately 10 to 11 years (Goodall 1983, Teleki et al. 1976). Watts and Gavan found that a small increase in growth rate occurs at the time of sexual maturation in the long bones of the chimpanzee. Unlike the human adolescent growth spurt, which is easy to detect by simple graphic analysis, the increase in pubertal growth rate of the chimpanzee is revealed only by sophisticated mathematical analysis.

Summarizing the differences in growth between primates and other mammals, Tanner (1962) noted that, "Puberty in other mammals occurs shortly after the maximum velocity of weight growth has been passed, and often when growth is still proceeding fairly vigorously. . . [but in] the primate. . . the essential change is the postponement of the time of puberty" (p.236).

Childhood and Human Growth

. . . Laird (1967) described the uniqueness of human growth as follows:

In the human a further delay has occurred so that adolescent growth with its concomitant development of sexual maturity occupies only the last 1/3 of a prolonged growth period. The delay in the human can be interpreted as being due to the *insertion*, between birth and adolescence, of two growth phases, rather than the single phase identifiable in the monkey and chimpanzee. . . (1967, pp. 351-352, emphasis added).

Humans add childhood as a period of growth between the end of infancy and the start of the juvenile growth period. The addition of a childhood stage to human growth is one evolutionarily novel characteristic of our species. (Some, but not all, researchers also define adolescence as a unique stage in human growth [for a review see Bogin 1988]).

Why did human beings evolve childhood? There are many possible reasons ranging from nutritional factors to reproductive considerations. A review of some of these possible reasons may be found in a recent book (Bogin 1988). In this article, I discuss only two interrelated aspects of the problem: human dependence on learning and culture for survival and the behavior of parents and other adults toward children that permits extensive learning and complex culture.

The Ecology of Learning and Growth

Primates can learn both by imitation and teaching. Jolly (1985) reviewed the data collected by primatologists conducting field studies by monkeys and apes. A common observation was that most imitative learning occurs between females and their offspring. Young baboons and chimpanzees watch their mothers select foods, peel fruits, and interact with conspecifics, and then the young copy their mothers' actions. Chimpanzees learn to use tools, for instance, for termite fishing, in the same imitative way. People also learn by imitation, but purposeful teaching is equally important and, probably, a uniquely human behavior.

The Arunta, a hunting and gathering people of central Australia, illustrate the value of human learning and teaching. In 1943, a severe drought occurred in central Australia. Birdsell (1979) relates that during this time an old Arunta man, Paralji, led a band of people on a 600-kilometer trek in search of water. After passing twenty-five dry waterholes, he led them to a fallback well that the old man had not visited for more than fifty years. That well was also dry, forcing Paralji and his band to trek 350 kilometers on ancient trails, locating water holes by place names learned from initiation rites and ceremonial songs he memorized as a child.

Even the way human hunters and gatherers, such as the Arunta, forage for food requires extensive learning during the childhood and juvenile growth periods. The widely dispersed nature of food resources in their habitat compels the Arunta to live in self-sufficient nuclear families (Service 1978). As soon as they are able, the children follow their mothers and fathers on the daily rounds of food collection and preparation. Elkin (1964) observed boys and girls as young as five years being taken by their fathers on hunting trips and being shown how to collect raw materials and prepare them for spears, points, and other tools. Because it takes more than a decade to become proficient in the manufacture and use of these tools, early learning and slow growth and maturation are mutually beneficial.

Learning is also needed to use foods once they are collected. Many of the foods humans consume are hidden from view (e.g., roots and tubers) or are encased in protective coatings (e.g., fruits and seeds); tools are usually needed to extract and process these foods. The costs of tool manufacture, including the time and energy needed to find and process raw materials, are outweighed by the benefits. Tool-using human gatherers extract twice as many calories from savanna-woodland environments as primates that do not use tools (Lee and Devore 1976).

Some foods are poisonous before processing by washing, leaching, drying, or cooking. Acorns and horse chestnuts, eaten by many North American Indians, and manioc, a staple food of many peoples in the tropics, are toxic if eaten raw. These foods must be leached by boiling in water and dried before consumption.

People survive by having available detailed knowledge of a habitat for the location of food, raw materials, and avoidance of predators or disease. Survival also requires knowledge of intricate procedures such as detoxifying poisonous raw foods, flaking rocks into stone tools, or using the machines and technologies of modern industrial societies. Finally, a myriad of social facts, including knowledge of kinship organization and ritual behavior, are required.

All living humans depend for survival on these complex technologies, social systems, and ideological belief systems or, more simply, culture. The same was likely the case for many of our fossil ancestors of the genus *Homo*. From a purely biological perspective, culture is an adaptive strategy with significant reproductive benefits. This benefit may be seen most clearly by comparing reproductive outcomes among various species. For this comparison, reproductive success is measured by the percentage of live-born offspring that survive to sexual maturity.

At one end of the range of variation of reproductive success for vertebrates are fish, amphibians, and reptiles that deposit dozens or hundreds of eggs, but they do not provide parental care for the eggs or the hatchlings. These species have birth-to-adulthood survival rates that may be lower than 1 percent. For instance, a female codfish produces approximately 30 million eggs, of which 50,000 might hatch, but only two (0.004 percent) reach maturity.

At the other end of the range are social mammals, which have fewer offspring but lavish much care on them. Social mammals usually provide much parental investment to their offspring, such as food provisioning after lactation ends. These animals also extend the infancy growth stage into a juvenile stage, which provides their young a greater opportunity for learning by observation and imitation. Lions are one such species, and they successfully rear 14-16 percent of their offspring to adulthood (Lancaster and Lancaster 1983). Monkeys and apes, with more parental investment and a longer juvenile period than lions, successfully rear 12-38 percent of their offspring to sexual maturity (Altmann 1980, Lancaster and Lancaster 1983). Among nonhuman primates, chimpanzees provide the most investment in offspring. The average period between successful births in the wild in 5.6 years, and young chimpanzees are dependent on their mothers for approximately 4.5 years (Goodall 1983, Teleki et al. 1976). Chimpanzee females in the wild reach menarche (first menstruation) at 10-11 years of age (Goodall 1983). Just to reproduce herself and one mate a female must live to be approximately twenty-five years old.

This period is long for the chimpanzee to struggle for its own existence, find food, avoid predators, and compete with conspecifics. However, Teleki and colleagues and Goodall estimate that in one African game reserve approximately 35 percent of all live-born chimpanzees survive to their mid-twenties. That survival percentage is significantly greater than for most other species of animals. Thus, the reduced number of offspring born, the extended infancy and juvenile growth periods of the young, and the female chimpanzee's parental investment of time and energy are ultimately efficient.

The childhood growth stage delays human reproductive age even more than in chimpanzees. But people often do not wait as long between successive births. The best documented examples of the reproductive histories of people living in traditional hunting and gathering societies are the !Kung of southern Africa. A !Kung woman's age at birth of her first offspring averages 19 years, and subsequent births follow approximately every 3.6 years (Howell 1976, 1979, Short 1976). The reproductive success rate of the !Kung and other traditional peoples is higher than that of nonhuman primates. Among the !Kung, approximately 50 percent of all live births reach adulthood (Lancaster and Lancaster 1983). This high success rate is maintained without the benefits of modern medical care and other western technology.

!Kung parents help ensure this high rate of success by provisioning with food all their children, not just their current infant, for a decade or longer. Lancaster and Lancaster (1983) call this type of parental investment "the hominid adaptation." The !Kung and other people do more, because added to the food provisioning is the intensive investment in cultural teaching and learning that occurs during the childhood dependency period.

The Evolutionary Biology and Psychology of Childhood

Reproductive success is a major force behind the biological evolution of all species. In the course of human evolution, during at least the past two million years since the appearance of *Homo*, natural selection would have favored biological traits that facilitated parental care, teaching, and the learning of cultural behavior. Prolonged growth during childhood and delayed maturation fit the bill, not only because there is so much to learn

66

before adulthood, but also because maturational differences between teachers and students are maximized. Most cultural information is passed from an older, experienced individual to a younger individual. The greater the maturational status difference between teacher and pupil the more likely that the transmission of this type of detailed knowledge will be one way, older to younger (Jolly 1985).

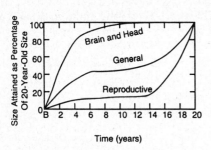

Figure 7. Growth curves for different human body tissues. The general curve represents growth in stature or total body weight. The curve for the brain and head represents the growth of the central nervous system. The reproductive curve represents the growth of the gonads and the primary reproductive organs. Unlike many other mammals, which show an advancement of reproductive tissue growth and function over that of the general body growth curve, human beings delay reproductive development and advance central nervous system growth in comparison with general body growth. (From Scammon 1930.)

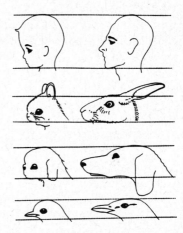

Figure 8. The releasing schema for human prenatal care responses. **Left:** head proportions, perceived as "lovable" (child jerboa, Pekinese dog, and robin). **Right:** related head profiles that do not elicit the parental drive (man, hare, hound, and golden oriole). Note that in all cases, except for the child, the head profiles are drawn from adult animals. (From Lorenz 1971.)

In some cases, however, children and juveniles provide learning benefits to adults. For instance, the young may introduce new behaviors to the elders of a social group. The classic field studies of Japanese macaques conducted by Itani (1958), Kawamura (1959), and Kawai (1965) clearly showed that juvenile primates are more likely than adults to investigate novel items in their environment, including new foods. A juvenile monkey introduced potato washing in one group, and another juvenile introduced swimming in another group. In a similar way, human children, juveniles, and adolescents may provide a service to adults by testing new foods and behaviors for their safety and utility.

67

We are so accustomed to this positivist view of learning and teaching that most of the foregoing may appear obvious. Our prehistoric ancestors, however, may not have seen the immediate or long-term value of parental investment in dependent children, including feeding and teaching. Assuming that life for our ancestors was relatively short (Washburn 1981), then many parents would not have lived to see the fruits of their labor, that is, the successful birthing of their grandchildren. It is possible, therefore, that some biological selection took place for traits that would promote the provisioning of children, their instruction in survival skills, and other forms of parental investment without conscious knowledge of the reasons for this behavior. These traits might, ideally, be closely linked with the pattern of growth during infancy and childhood, the time when parental investment in children and their provisioning and instruction play a crucial role in immediate and long-term survival.

The growth of the brain and head versus the rest of the body provides for much of a child's capacity to learn and the adults's ability to teach, provide food, and care generally for the child. The evolution of human childhood prolonged the total growth period. Most systems in the body (e.g., skeletal, muscular, and reproductive) follow the general course of growth for the body as a whole. The major exception is the central nervous system.

The central nervous system, especially the brain, follows a growth curve that is advanced as compared to the curve for the body as a whole (Figure 7). The brain achieves virtually adult size when body growth is only 40 percent complete and reproductive maturation is only 10 percent complete. Slow somatic growth and delayed sexual maturation result in a relatively small body and greater dependence of the human child during the early learning years than is the case for nonhuman primates. These growth patterns help establish teacher-student roles that remain stable for a decade or more, allowing a great deal of learning, practice, and modification of survival skills to occur.

The advancement of central nervous system development over body growth in general provides the physical basis for the efficient learning and memory of these skills. It also allows for the integration of separately learned behaviors that may be creatively recombined by the individual and result in novel behaviors, suitable for situations that have never been encountered before or for changes in the physical and social environment not foreseen by teachers.

Lorenz (1971) stated that the physical characteristics of mammalian infants, including small body size, a relatively large head with little mandibular or nasal prognathism, relatively large round eyes in proportion to skull size, short thick extremities, and clumsy movements inhibit aggressive behavior by adults and encourage caretaking and nurturing behaviors. Lorenz believed that these neotenous features trigger "innate releasing mechanisms" in adult mammals, including humans, for the protection and care of dependent young.

As evidence for the genetic cause of human parental behavior toward neotenous children, Lorenz cited the fact that people extend nurturing behavior towards other animals with appropriate features (e.g., puppies, kittens, and even adult animals with neotenous features; Figure 8). Lorenz noted the penchant of some pet owners to treat the miniature varieties of dog breeds as if they were infants, even when the animals are mature. Miniaturization in domesticated animals results from a growth process that retains neotenous features (e.g., large, round head and short extremities relative to body size) into adulthood. Lorenz further noted that inanimate objects, such as clouds and rock formations, that resemble neotenous animals can release emotions of tenderness from humans.

Gould (1979) questioned the innateness of the human response to infantile features. Such behavior may be "learned from our immediate experience with babies and grafted upon an evolutionary predisposition for attaching ties of affection to certain learned signals." Whether innate or learned, the resultant behavior is the same. The depth of our reaction to neotenous features is exemplified by Gould's description of the "evolution of Mickey Mouse." From the cartoon creature's first appearance in 1928 to later appearances in the 1950's Mickey's body shape changed. His head and eyes enlarged and arms and legs shortened relative to body size. During this physical evolution, Mickey was transformed socially from an ill-behaved, mischievous rodent to the delightful host of the Magic Kingdom. The physical and behavioral changes are not simply coincidental; rather they are necessary concomitants of human perception based on our reaction to body shape and growth status.

CARDIOIDAL STRAIN

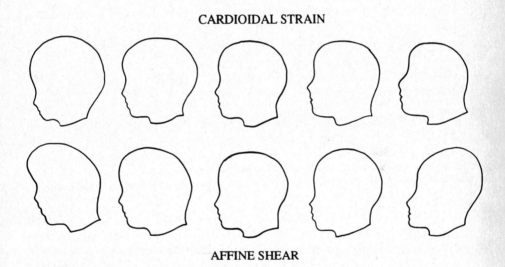

AFFINE SHEAR

Figure 9. Two of the mathematical transformations of human head shape used in the experiments of Todd et al. (1980). The middle profile in each row was drawn from the photograph of a ten-year-old boy. The transformations were applied to the profile of a real child. The cardioidal strain transformation is perceived by most adults as growth. The affine shear transformation is not perceived as growth. (From Bogin 1988.)

An elegant series of psychological experiments performed by Todd et al. (1980) confirm that human perceptions of body shape and growth status are consistent among individuals. When approximately forty adults from the University of Minnesota community were shown a series of profiles of human skull proportions, they could easily arrange them correctly into a hierarchy spanning infancy to adulthood. The adults could also ascribe maturity ratings to skull profiles that were geometrically transformed to imitate the actual changes that occur during growth. This perception was selective because a variety of other types of geometrical transformations elicited no reports of growth or maturation (Figure 9).

When the growth-like mathematical transformations were applied to profile drawings of the heads of birds and dogs, human subjects reported identical perceptions of growth and maturation, even though in reality the development of these animals does not follow the human pattern of skull shape change.

Even more surprising is that subjects reported the perception of growth when the growth-like mathematical transformations were applied to front and side view profiles of Volkswagen "beetles," even though automobiles do not grow.

In another series of experiments, Alley (1983) studied the association between human body shape or size and the tendency of adults to protect and "cuddle" other individuals. The subjects of the experiments (forty-five men and seventy-five women) were shown two sets of drawings. One set were called "shape-variant" drawings (Figure 10a). Alley used the middlemost of the profiles in Figure 10a that varied in height and width but not in shape. These were called "size-variant" drawings. Figure 10b is an example of one of Alley's size-variant drawings. Note that Alley's figures have no facial features, navels, or genitals. Perceptual differences among figures would be due to body shape or size alone, not sex, nasal prognathism, eye size and shape, or stage of sexual maturation.

In the first experiment, the subjects were shown pairs of the shape-variant drawings (i.e., profiles of a newborn and a six-year-old, a two-year-old, a twelve-year-old, and an adult) or pairs of the size-variant drawings and were asked to state which one of the pair they "would feel most compelled to defend should you see them being beaten." The average response was to defend the "younger" of the shape-variant drawings or the smaller of the size-variant drawings. In the second and third experiments, subjects were shown the five shape-variant drawings, one at a time, and asked to rate the drawings on a scale from one (low) to nine (high) "according to how compelled you would feel to intervene if you saw someone striking the human depicted" and according to their feelings to "hug or cuddle" the person depicted. The trends found in both experiments are statistically significant. There was a fairly strong reported willingness to defend "newborns" and "two-year-olds," and a moderate willingness to defend "six- and twelve-year-olds," and the least willingness to defend "adults." The reported willingness to cuddle also decreased with the "age" of the drawings. Alley mentions that American cultural values (e.g., defend the underdog or the weak) may have influenced the results of these experiments.

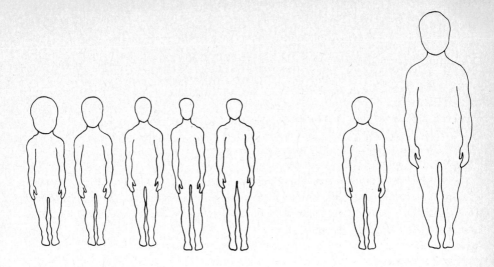

Figure 10. A The series of five shape-variant drawings used in the experiments of Alley (1983). These drawings represent the typical body proportions of a male at (from left) birth, 2, 6, 12, and 25 years of age. **B** An example of the size-variant pairs of drawings used by Alley (1983).

However, placed in the context of the ethological study of parental caretaking in mammals and birds, Alley believes that his results demonstrate a more general tendency to protect or cuddle others based on the perception of maturational status.

The psychological experiments of Todd and colleagues and Alley provide support for the arguments developed in this article for the evolution of human childhood. Human children, and probably the children of ancestral hominid species, retain neotenous characteristics longer than any other mammalian species. This difference is due in part to the slow growth of most parts of the body, especially postcranial regions, and also parts of the head, such as the nose and the jaw. The perception of neoteny is also aided by the relatively faster growth of the brain compared with the face and body, which maintains the round, bulbous cranium of infant mammals throughout human childhood.

These growth patterns of body, face, and brain facilitate parental investment by maintaining the potential for nurturing behavior of adults toward infants and older, but still physically dependent, children. Due to their physical dependence on older individuals, children maintain intimate contact with successful practitioners of their culture for many years. Thus, childhood facilitates a unique style of human cultural learning, both by observation and purposeful teaching. Together, the prolongation of investment by adults in children and the learning by children from adults have been two of the major reasons for the evolutionary success of the human species.

References

Alley, R. R. 1983. Growth-produced changes in body shape and size as determinants of perceived age and adult caregiving. *Child Dev.* 54: 241-248.

Altmann, J. 1980. *Baboon Mothers and Infants*. Harvard University Press, Cambridge, MA.

Birdsell, J. B. 1979. Ecological influences on Australian aboriginal social organization. Pages 117-151 in I. S. Bernstein and R. O. Smith, eds. *Primate Ecology and Human Origins*. Garland, New York.

Bogin, B. 1988. *Patterns of Human Growth*. Cambridge University Press, New York.

Bonner, J. T. 1965. *Size and Cycle*. Princeton University Press, Princeton, NJ.

Brody, S. 1945. *Bioenergetics and Growth*. Reinhold, New York.

Coelho, A. M. Jr. 1985. Baboon dimorphism: growth in weight, length, and adiposity from birth to 8 years of age. Pages 125-159 in E. S. Watts, ed. *Nonhuman Primate Models for Human Growth*. Alan R. Liss, New York.

Elkin, A. P. 1964. *The Australian Aborigines*. Doubleday, New York.

Gavan, J. A. 1971. Longitudinal postnatal growth in the chimpanzee. Pages 46-102 in G. Bourne, ed. *The Chimpanzee*. vol. 4. Karger, Basel, Switzerland.

Goodall, J. 1983. Population dynamics during a 15- year period in one community of tree living chimpanzees in the Gombe National Park, Tanzania. *Z. Tierpsychol.* 61: 1-60.

Gould, S. J. 1979. Mickey Mouse meets Konrad Lorenz. *Nat. Hist.* 88: 30-36.

Howell, N. 1976. The population of the Dobe area !Kung. Pages 137-157 in R. B. Lee and I. DeVore, eds. *Kalahari Hunter-Gatherers*. Harvard University Press, Cambridge, MA.

——— 1979. *Demography of the Dobe !Kung*. Academic Press, San Diego, CA.

Huxley, J. S. 1932. *Problems of Relative Growth*. Methuen, New York. 2nd ed., 1972. Dover, New York.

Itani, J. 1958. On the acquisition and propagation of a new food habit in the troop of Japanese monkeys at Takasakiyama. *Primates* 1: 131-148.

Jolly, A. 1985. *The Evolution of Primate Behavior.* Macmillan, New York.

Kawai, M. 1965. Newly acquired precultural behavior of the natural troop of Japanese monkeys on Koshima Island. *Primates* 6: 1-30.

Kawamura, S. 1959. The process of subcultural propagation among Japanese macaques. *Primates* 2: 43-55

Laird, A. K. 1967. Evolution of the human growth curve. *Growth* 31: 345-355.

Lancaster, J. B., and C. S. Lancaster. 1983. Parental investment: the hominid adaptation. Pages 33-65 in D. J. Ortner, ed. *How Humans Adapt.* Smithsonian Institution Press, Washington, D.C.

Lee, R. B., and I. DeVore 1976. *Kalahari Hunter-Gatherers.* Harvard University Press, Cambridge, MA.

Lorenz, K. 1971. Part and parcel in animal and human societies: a methodological discussion. Pages 115-195 in *Studies in Animal and Human Behavior.* vol. 2. Translated by R. Martin. Harvard University Press, Cambridge, MA.

Medwar, P. B. 1945. Size, shape and age. Pages 157-187 in W.E. LeGros Clark and P.B. Medwar, eds. *Essays on Growth and Form.* Clarendon Press, Oxford, UK.

Orlosky, F. J. 1982. Adolescent midfacial growth in *Macaca nemestrina* and *Papio cynocephalus. Hum. Biol.* 54: 23-29.

Periera, M. E., and J. Altmann. 1985. Development of social behavior in free-living nonhuman primates. Pages 217-309 in E.S. Watts, ed. *Nonhuman Primate Models for Human Growth and Development.* Alan R. Liss, New York.

Prader, A. 1984. Biomedical and endocrinological aspects of normal growth and development. Pages 1-22 in J. Borms, R. Hauspic, A. Sand, C. Susanne, and M. Hebbelink, eds. *Human Growth and Development.* Plenum, New York.

Scammon, R. E. 1930. The measurement of the body in childhood. Pages 173-215 in J.A. Harris, C.M. Jackson, D.G. Paterson, and R.E. Scammon, eds. *The Measurement of Man.* University of Minnesota Press, Minneapolis.

Service, E. R. 1978. The Arunta of Australia. Pages 13-34 in E.R. Service, ed. *Profiles in Ethnology.* Harper & Row, New York.

Short, R. V. 1976. The evolution of human reproduction. *Proc. R. Soc. Lond. Series B* 195: 3-24.

Siriani, J. E., A. L. VanNess, and D. R. Swindler. 1982. Growth of the mandible in adolescent pig-tailed macaques *(Macaca nemestrina). Hum. Biol.* 54: 31-44.

Tanner, J. M. 1962. *Growth at Adolescence.* Blackwell Scientific Publ., Boston.

———1978. *Fetus into Man.* Harvard University Press, Cambridge, MA.

Teleki, G. E., E. Hunt, and J. H. Pfifferling. 1976. Demographic observations (1963-1973) on the chimpanzees of Gombe National Park, Tanzania. *J. Hum. Evol.* 5: 559-598.

Timiras, P. S. 1972. *Developmental Physiology and Aging.* Macmillan, New York.

Todd, J. T., L. S. Mark, R. E. Shaw, and J. B. Pittenger. 1980. The perception of human growth. *Sci. Am.* 242: 132-144.

Von Bertalanffy, L. 1960. Principles and theory of growth. Pages 137-259 in W. N. Nowinski, ed. *Fundamental Aspects of Normal and Malignant Growth.* Elsevier, Amsterdam.

Washburn, S. L. 1981. Longevity in primates. Pages 11-29 in J. L. McGaugh and S. B. Kiesler, eds. *Aging: Biology and Behavior.* Academic Press, San Diego.

Watts, E. S., and J. A. Gavan. 1982. Postnatal growth of nonhuman primates: the problem of the adolescent spurt. *Hum. Biol.* 54: 53-70.

Secular Trend in the Age of Menarche
James M. Tanner

Over the past century and a half, the average age at which young women living in industrialized societies attain menarche has plummeted by anywhere from one and one half to four years. In this short article, written for the Encyclopedia of Adolescence, *James Tanner, one of the world's leading experts on human growth, reviews historical data gathered from Europe, North America, and Japan in support of this trend. Concluding that decrease in age of menarche has reflected improved levels of nutrition, better quality of medical care, wider opportunity for exercise, and increased psychological well-being, Tanner suggests that the trend in age at menarche in developing countries may even be useful as a "guide to whether conditions of life are being ameliorated."*

During at least the last 150 years the average age of menarche, the first menstrual period, has decreased in the populations of the industrialized or "developed" countries. Modern data on menarche is collected by what is called the "status quo" method. An accurate sampling is made of all girls aged nine to sixteen in a given city, country, or geographical area and each individual is simply asked her date of birth and whether she has yet experienced a menstrual period (usually defined as bleeding for at least three days). The percentage of girls responding in the affirmative for successive six-month age periods is plotted, and yields a sigmoid curve. The age at which 50 percent of the girls were postmenarcheal is then estimated, using the statistical technique of probits. (Longitudinal studies giving exact date of menarche have shown that the distribution of age at menarche, at least under good environmental conditions, is Gaussian.) This method is so easy to apply that we now have an enormous list of ages of menarche, including practically all populations in the world (Eveleth & Tanner, 1990). The method yields a standard error of the mean and a test also for homogeneity of the populations examined.

But the status quo method has only been in use since the middle 1950s. Before then most studies relied on questioning adult women—often those admitted to hospital for childbirth—as to their recollection of their age when menstruation occurred for the first time. Some studies are available on the accuracy of this recollection. In a Swedish longitudinal study, 339 girls whose dates were accurately known were questioned some four years after the event. Despite the fact that these girls had participated in a prolonged study that paid particular attention to all aspects of development, the correlation between recollected and true age was only 0.81; less than two-thirds recalled the date to within

Tanner, James M. (1991). Menarche, secular trend in age of. In R.M Lerner; A.C. Peterson; & J. Brooks-Gunn. (Eds.) *The Encyclopedia of Adolescence*. New York: Garland Publishing, Inc. pp. 637-641.

TABLE 1
AVERAGE AGES OF MENARCHE IN UNITED KINGDOM, SCANDINAVIA, GERMANY,
AND RUSSIA IN THE NINETEENTH CENTURY

	YEAR OF MENARCHE (APPROX.)	MEAN AGE AT MENARCHE	PLACE	AUTHOR
Working women				
UK	1815	15.2	Manchester	Roberton (1830)
	1835	15.6	Manchester	Whitehead (1847)
	1830	15.1	London	Guy (1845)
	1830	14.9	London mostly	Murphy (1844-45)
	1855	15.0	London	Rigden (1869)
	1910	15.0	Edinburgh	Kennedy (1933)
Scandinavia,	1785	16.6	Göttingen	Osiander (1795)
Germany, and Russia	1835	16.4	Copenhagen	Ravn (1850)
	1850	16.8	Copenhagen	Hannover (1869)
	1850	16.4	Berlin	Krieger (1869)
	1850	16.8	Munich	Hecker (1864)
	1865	16.6	Bavaria	Schlichting (1880)
	1870	15.6	Oslo	Brudevoll et al. (1979)
	1875	15.7	Russia	Grüsdeff (1894)
	1875	16.5	Helsinki	Malmio (1919)
	1890	15.7	Stockholm	Essen-Möller; in Lenner (1944)
	1895	16.2	Berlin	Schaeffer (1908)
	1900	16.2	Schleswig	Heyn (1920)
	1900	16.0	Helsinki	Malmio (1919)
	1900	14.6	Oslo	Brudevoll et al. (1979)
Middle class				
UK	1835	14.3	Manchester	Whitehead (1847)
	1890	14.4	London	Giles (1901a)
Scandinavia,				
Germany, and Russia	1820	15.0	Norway	Brundtland and Walløc (1976)
	1835	14.4	Copenhagen	Ravn (1850)
	1875	14.4	Russia	Grüsdeff (1894)
	1895	14.4	Berlin	Schaeffer (1908)

Note: The average date of year of menarche has been calculated from the probable mean age of the women studied: it has an error of up to five years.

three months of the true one. In a similar study, at the Harvard University School of Public Health, a correlation of 0.78 was found between the true date and the date recollected nineteen years later. Thus recollected ages have to be dealt with cautiously.

Using historical data may also produce sampling problems. Young women attending a certain hospital in the 1870s, for example, may be exclusively from the lower class (since most middle-class women in Europe had their labors at home at that time), while all social classes might be represented in the same hospital during the 1920s.

In spite of these cautions, the data gives rather clear-cut results. Table 1, taken from my *A History of the Study of Human Growth*, lists most of the data available for Europe in the nineteenth century. Working women had a later menarche than middle- class women, by something approaching two years. The figures for Danish women have recently been carefully reassessed by Helm and Helm *(Annals of Human Biology*, 1987, p. 371). In 1840-50 the average age of menarche for working women was as high as 17.2 years. From 1860 on there was a fairly rapid reduction, amounting to about 0.3 years per decade, so that by 1920 age 15.0 was the average figure. By 1950 the value had fallen to about 13.5. Thereafter the change slowed down; the figure for 1983 was 13.0. Figure 1 summarizes some of the main data.

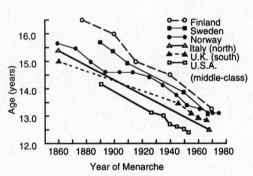

Figure 1. Secular changes in age at menarche, 1860-1980 (from Marshall and Tanner, 1986).

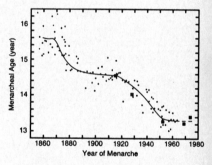

Figure 2. Mean menarcheal age for working-class women (up to 1945; thereafter middle-class also) in Oslo from 1860 to 1975. Recollection data; each point represents the average of about 50 maternity clinic patients. The squares represent status-quo probit-fitted data on Oslo schoolgirls. The curve is a 21-term moving average until 1960. Redrawn from Brudevoll, Liestol, and Walløc (1979).

More detail is available for the city of Oslo, Norway. This data shows that the trend has not always been as linear as it appears in Figure 1. Brudevoll (1973), randomly selected the records of fifty women for each year from the archives of the Oslo City Maternity Hospital and plotted the average recollected age of menarche of these patients year by year. Figure 2 shows the data, with a twenty-one- point moving average line put in. There was a sharp drop between girls born about 1860 and those born about 1880, followed by a period of little change. Then a second sharp drop occurred between those born in 1900 and those born in 1940. There has been little change in the last thirty years.

Brudevoll reports the data in terms of date of birth, and this may well paint a truer historical pic-ture than reporting in terms of date of menarche. The secular trend to earliness is a response to ameliora-tion of the conditions of life, particularly increase of food and decrease of infection. Age at menarche, the end-point of the growth process, is influenced by all the conditions in the preceding years of fetal life and childhood. There is some evidence, however, that it is especially the conditions of the early years, around birth to two, which play the major role (as they do in the secular increase in body size also).

North American data is more limited. About 1890 patients in a Boston and a St. Louis practitioners' dispensary had a recollected age of 14.2 years (see Tanner, 1981); college women had a mean of 13.5 years. Wyshak (1983) studied a large number of mostly middle-class Americans all over the U.S.A. in the course of an epidemiological survey and found a secular trend of 3.2 months per decade between women born around 1920 and those born around 1940. The value for those born in 1940 and later was 12.5, but no further decline has occurred—12.5 is still the expected value for middle-class white Americans.

The greatest of all secular trends in menarche occurred in Japan. From 1900 to 1935 the trend was slight, and from 1935 to 1950 the trend actually reversed, with age at menarche increasing. Then, in improving postwar conditions, there was a decline of some eleven months per decade until 1975, when the trend leveled out to practically zero. The secular change in age at peak height velocity was similar (Marshall & Tanner, 1986).

In a population growing up under optimal circumstances from the points of view of nutrition, infection, exercise, and psychological well-being, age at menarche is a genetically determined characteristic (being simply an element of the more general characteristic called growth tempo). In some developed countries something like these conditions have obtained for several decades, and it seems that menarche has reached or very nearly reached its lower threshold; the secular trend has stopped. (There are differences between populations in the value of this threshold: it is about 13.0 for North-West European populations, for example, but nearer 12.3 for Mediterranean European populations). Similarly, in socially advanced countries, such as Norway and Sweden, there are no differences in age at menarche between children growing up in manual workers' families and those in nonmanual workers' households. But in most other countries, lower-class age of menarche lags behind middle- and upper-class age of menarche.

In the developing countries the trend in age at menarche, which may be zero, is a good guide to whether conditions of life are being ameliorated. Thus economic historians have been interested to interpret data such as those shown in Figure 2, in terms of the history of industrialization. Statistics on age at menarche are one of the most easily obtained indicators of economic well-being.

References

Brudevoll. (1973). *Annals of Human Biology.*

Eveleth, P. B., & Tanner, J. M. (1990). *Worldwide variation in human growth.* (2d Ed.) Cambridge: Cambridge University Press.

Marshall, W. A. & Tanner, J. M. (1986). Puberty. In F. Falkner & J. M. Tanner (Eds.), *Human Growth* (2d Ed., Vol. 2, pp. 171-209). New York: Plenum Press.

Tanner, J. M. (1981). *A history of the study of human growth.* Cambridge: Cambridge University Press.

Wyshak. (1983). *Annals of Human Biology.*

5

Nature and Nurture Interwoven

The Romantic movement in Britain took Rousseau's child of innocence, and idealised it, regarding a child as near to God.

> *Our birth is but a sleep and forgetting:*
> *The Soul that rises with us, our life's Star,*
> *Hath had elsewhere its setting,*
> *And cometh from afar:*
> *Not in entire forgetfulness,*
> *And not in utter nakedness,*
> *But trailing clouds of glory do we come*
> *From God, who is our home:*
> *Heaven lies about us in our infancy!*

—**Wordsworth,** *Intimations of Immortality*

• INTRODUCTION •

Is development a product of biological nature, a function of the environments of nurture, or a joint product of nature expressed in the context of nurture? This question has long been at the center of a continuing debate among those concerned with the human condition. Proponents of each side of the nature/nurture argument have staked out territory in many areas, but of all these areas, none have been so consistently and bitterly contested for such a length of time as those of intelligence and educational achievement.

On the one hand, hereditarians have conceived of intelligence as a fixed capacity predetermined by the genes. In societies characterized by mating patterns that fall heavily along social class and racial lines, it has been easy for those convinced of this view to conclude that differences in IQ test and academic performance between racial and ethnic groups are genetically determined and unalterable.

On the other hand, environmentalists have long pointed out that when a child sits at a desk across from an examiner for the administration of an IQ test or walks into a classroom on the first day of school, that child is entering a setting in which certain skills, attitudes, and beliefs—those reflecting the value system of mainstream culture—are essential for success. For many minority children, whose cultural roots lie in traditions quite different from those of Western Europe and whose cultural experience reflects both those traditions and a long history of economic and racial discrimination, the acquisition of mainstream cultural skills represents a considerable achievement in itself. Therefore it should come as no surprise that, on average, minority children do not perform as well on IQ tests and in school as children who have been raised from birth within the culture that created the tests and designed the schools.

The two readings excerpted in this chapter were chosen to shed light on this issue. The first except is from a book, *Intelligence and Experience*, published in 1961 at the height of what has sometimes been called psychology's "cognitive revolution." In this work, J. McV. Hunt offered a searching analysis of the claim that intelligence is a fixed capacity predetermined by the genes. Reinterpreting research previously thought to support this view and reviewing evidence indicating the cognitive

82

benefits in animals and humans to be gained through infant stimulation, Hunt argued for a new conception of intelligence as a joint product of the interaction of heredity and environment. In the course of elaborating this argument, he also articulated a rationale for environmental enrichment that gave impetus to the then newly emerging compensatory education movement. Under the assumption that the lower IQ and achievement scores of minority children reflected environmental and cultural factors, compensatory education programs were designed to speed the acculturation of minority children into the educational mainstream in the expectation that this would enhance overall IQ and boost educational performance.

In 1969, however, Arthur Jensen published a widely read *Harvard Educational Review* article that challenged this assumption. By pointing to the failure of compensatory educational programs to produce lasting effects on minority children's IQ and achievement, reviewing evidence indicating high heritability of intelligence, and arguing that IQ differences primarily reflect genetic and racial rather than environmental and cultural factors, Jensen re-ignited the long-simmering nature/nurture controversy in American education. Amidst a storm of protest, claims and counter-claims, two issues–the relative roles of genes and environments in the development of behavior and the possibility of genetic differences in intelligence between the races–were once again pushed to the forefront.

In the midst of this superheated atmosphere, Sandra Scarr and Richard Weinberg designed the Minnesota Adoption Studies described in the second excerpt below. What, they wondered, would happen to IQ test performance and school success if black children were raised in homes that were culturally "white"? How would the IQ test and academic performance of black children adopted by white parents compare with that of white children adopted by white parents? How would performance of adoptees, be they white or black, compare with that of adoptive parents' biological children; and how would the IQ scores of adoptees relate to those of their own biological parents? The results of their research, as we shall see, provided strong evidence against any hypothesis of genetic differences in intelligence between races. These results also demonstrated, however, that both genes and environments are important. When children are raised under similar rearing conditions, the contribution to individual differences in their performance on IQ tests and in school is substantially genetic. Under varied environmental conditions, however, development is clearly malleable.

● ● ●

Intelligence and Experience
J. McV. Hunt

Of all the concepts with which psychology is concerned, the concept of "intelligence" is still probably the one most misunderstood. In this classic exposition, J. McV. Hunt analyzes two of the most widespread misconceptions about intelligence—that intelligence is a fixed capacity and that its development is predetermined by the genes. Arguing for the notion that behavior is controlled by central, intellectual processes constructed in early encounters with the environment, Hunt articulates an interactionist view of the relationship between heredity and environment and a rationale for environmental enrichment. Notice that in his concern for potential dangers inherent in overemphasis on intellectual develop-ment, he is careful to point out that children's environments should not only foster an "optimally rapid rate of intellectual development" but a "satisfying life."

Intelligence has been a topic of central concern for those seeking to understand human nature. Even though tests of intelligence and of the aptitudes derived therefrom have been of more practical help than tests of any other kind in selecting people for quality of performance in various situations, discussions of intelligence have typically been marked by polemics. These polemics have usually concerned two of the beliefs or assumptions about intelligence that have dominated thought on the topic from the turn of the twentieth century through World War II. According to these two dominant assumptions intelligence is fixed and immutable, and the development of the individual's basic repertoire of responses and capacities is predetermined by his heredity.

The implications of these two assumptions spilled over in various directions. Intelligence came to be defined as "inherited capacity," and it was looked upon as a basic dimension of an individual person. The hope of improving man's lot was shifted from the euthenic strategy of improving his upbringing and education to the eugenic strategy

Hunt, J. McV. (1961). *Intelligence and Experience*. New York: Ronald Press Co. Chapter 9 (Recapitulation and conclusion). pp. 347-363.

of finding some way to select only the more intelligent for the propagation of the race. . . .

Investigations of the effects of various kinds of experience at various ages on the development of intellectual capacity were discouraged. Practical educational efforts to cultivate intellectual capacity, particularly in the very young, were discouraged. With behavioral development conceived to be a process in which anatomic maturation automatically brought with it the response repertoire, experts warned parents not to overstimulate their infants but rather to leave them alone to grow. . . .

Fixed Intelligence

. . . Evidence consonant with the notion of fixed intelligence came with the finding, artifactual though it was, that the mean IQ obtained from groups of differing ages is constant. Moreover, the scores for individual children showed considerate constancy for the years of later childhood and adolescence; and scores from various tests showed considerable correlation both with each other and with measures of such criterion performances as those in school and those on various types of jobs. Finally, direct evidence of hereditary influence came from the fact that the correlations among the test-scores of people closely related are higher than are those among the test- scores of people not closely related.

Evidence dissonant with the assumption of fixed intelligence came from the fact that the correlation between the IQ's of identical twins reared apart is lower than that for the IQ's of identical twins reared together. More of such evidence came from the fact that the IQ's of infants, obtained at successive ages, show considerable variation, and also from the fact that the IQ's of infants show little correlation with their IQ's as adults. But the import of such facts was largely explained away by assuming that the infant tests lacked validity. . . . Still more such evidence came from the fact that orphanage-reared children score lower on tests than do children reared in foster homes, but this fact was explained away by assuming that the children who got into orphanages are so selected as to be innately inferior to the children who got placed in foster homes. Finally, the finding of improvement in IQ with nursery-school experience was explained away in terms of defects in the designs of the investigations in which they appeared. . . .

Predetermined Development

. . . From this standpoint, development consisted of two essentially distinct processes, maturation and learning. The basic response units were conceived to come automatically with the maturation of the anatomical structures upon which they were presumed to depend. . . .

Evidence apparently consonant with the notion of predetermined development came from several sources. Coghill found the head-to-tail and center-outward orders of anatomical maturation to hold for the development of the swimming reaction in the tadpoles of salamanders (*Amblystoma*). Carmichael found that the tadpoles of frogs and salamanders that had developed without any opportunity for behavior while anesthetized with chloretone swam as well as others that had developed normally in unadulterated water, and he took this to be a demonstration of the existence of "unlearned behavior." When Mary Shirley found not only the head-tailward order of behavioral development in human children but also a marked degree of consistency in the order in which various responses appear in children, her findings were conceived to indicate that principles induced from observing the behavioral development of the lowly salamander generalize to man, and she herself argued that the consistency in order favored the notion of predetermined maturation. The early experiments in which various kinds of experience were either subtracted or added seemed to have little permanent effect on behavior. Chicks reared in darkness for a few days actually learned to peck accurately with a greater rate of improvement than did chicks that had had every opportunity to practice pecking. Children who were given special practice in such skills as tower-building, stair-climbing, cutting with scissors, etc., showed improvement, but children who were not given such special practice appeared to achieve the same degree of mastery of these skills with much less practice at a later age. Dennis found that the Hopi Indian children who were reared on cradle-boards, which prevented their using their legs, learned to walk at the same average age as Hopi children who were reared with full use of their legs.

Bits of evidence clearly dissonant with the conception that development is entirely predetermined also appeared. Altering developmental experience was found to interfere with the development of instinctive patterns. For instance, Birch found that the maternal behavior of female rats reared with collars to prevent them licking their own genitalia ate their young at parturition instead of retrieving them and licking them. Moreover, Riess found that rats reared in cages devoid of nesting materials failed to build nests at parturition even though proper materials were available. It was also observed that when people deprived of visual experiences from birth by congenital cataracts were operated on to restore their vision, they might immediately distinguish between figure and ground and be able to say whether two impressions were the same or different, but they could not recognize objects without months of visual experience. Moreover, various investigators found that insightful responses tended to appear only in those monkeys and chimpanzees who had been observed to play with the tools to be used insightfully.

A New Emphasis on Central Processes

. . . Recently . . . emphasis on central processes has been greatly increased by developments in several areas with important implications for the theory of intelligence. In neuropsychology, Hebb, prompted by noting that behavior is to a considerable degree independent of receptor inputs and failing to find intellectual deficits on standard tests of intelligence following removal of upwards of 20 percent of the mass of the cerebrum in adults while noting that cerebral lesions in infancy produce feeble-mindedness, led off

86

with his attempts to conceptualize the semi-autonomous central processes that intervene between receptor inputs and motor outputs. . . .

Intelligence as Central Processes and as Strategies for the Processing of Information

Hebb's conceptions led to a substantial revision in the conception of intelligence. His notion of the important role of autonomous central processes in behavior suggested . . . that adult intelligence should vary with opportunities for perceptual and perhaps even motor experience in which a variety of inputs with appropriate degrees of redundancy are available. It also stimulated a number of studies of the effects of infantile experience on later learning and problem-solving. These studies have shown that rats reared with ample opportunities for a variety of perceptual experience do learn mazes more readily than rats reared with minimal opportunities for a variety of such experiences. Pet-reared rats with a background of highly varied experience have been found to perform with more facility on the Hebb-Williams test of intelligence than do cage-reared rats with a background of little variation in experience. Similarly, Thompson & Heron have shown that in a wide variety of situations pet-reared dogs behave in a fashion much more intelligent than their litter-mates who were cage-reared for the first eight months of their lives. . . .

In yet another example of the effects of infantile experience, this time on perception, Riesen has found that chimpanzees kept in darkness for the first months of their lives lack object-recognition and the various responses which depend upon such recognition. Moreover, even the anatomic development of the visual apparatus appears to be hampered by lack of visual stimulation.

Combined with Hebb's theorizing and the work stimulated by it in this new emphasis on central processes and their dependence upon experience are other developments. The people who program electronic computers for the solving of problems have begun to systematize the conception of the requirements of problem-solving in terms of strategies for the processing of information. . . . From studies of animal problem-solving, Harlow has shown that by repeatedly learning the solution to any given type of problem, monkeys develop learning sets which give them the capacity to solve that type of problem almost immediately with the information derived from perception of the situation. These "learning sets" look fairly analogous to the strategies for the processing of information that programmers wire into their electronic computers. The thought that the computer and the brain have similarities of operation has prompted a re-examination of the theory of brain function. . . .

Piaget's Observations of the Development of Intelligence

The conception of intelligence deriving from Piaget's observations of the development of adaptive ability in children resembles so much that which derives from considering the computer and the brain and from the work of Hebb and Harlow that his observations may be considered to lend further empirical support to this new conception of intelligence. A basis for the hierarchical arrangement of the central processes that

87

mediate intelligence appears in Piaget's description of behavioral development wherein the sensorimotor organizations of each stage become incorporated, in the course of the child's . . . psychological interactions with the environment, into the more complex sensorimotor organizations of the next stage. Things heard become things to look at; things seen become things to grasp; things grasped become things to suck, etc. In the course of such coordinations, inputs from the distance receptors, and especially the eyes, acquire control over motor activities. Intentions emerge, means are distinguished from ends, interest in activities and in objects develops, and behavior becomes more and more variable and adaptive. All this happens presumably as central processes become both coordinated and redifferentiated. . . .

Some Reinterpretations

In the light of this newer conception of intelligence, which puts its neural basis in autonomous central neural processes located largely in the intrinsic regions of the brain and which explicitly gives its roots in the child's encounters with his environment, the old evidence once considered disturbing is what would be expected. Moreover, the old evidence once conceived to support the assumptions of fixed intelligence and predetermined development can readily be reinterpreted to be consonant with the newer conception. . . .

The fact that the scores from repeated testing in infancy, when the rate of change in the intellectual structures is greatest, fluctuate radically and the fact that such scores show poor predictive validity are precisely what would be expected if intellectual capacity depends to a considerable degree upon the child's encounters with his environment, but such fluctuations are highly embarrassing to the assumptions of fixed intelligence and predetermined development. . . .

The apparent evanescence of the effects of either subtracting or adding experience in the development of various organisms was apparently to some degree a function of the short duration of the subtraction or the addition. When frogs were kept in chloretoned water longer than Carmichael kept them there, they failed to learn to swim properly. When chicks were kept in the dark longer than Cruze kept them there, they lost the pecking response. Although the advantage got from a few weeks of special early practice in tower-building, stair-climbing, buttoning, and scissoring quickly disappeared when the controls, who started later, got to practicing these same skills, when Myrtle McGraw gave her trained twin, Johnny, nearly a year's experience at roller-skating, the untrained twin, Jimmy, was not able to catch up quickly. In fact, where Johnny had had little trouble learning to roller-skate at eleven months of age, Jimmy could not learn the skill at all at twenty-two months of age. . . .

It is hardly surprising that the special practice on such activities as tower-building, stair-climbing, buttoning, scissoring, etc., produced but evanescent superiority in these skills because, presumably, the incidental activities of the control children in these experiments might have been expected to have produced as much development in the central processes mediating these activities as would the direct practice on them, and perhaps even more.

Although the fact that change in the intellectual structures is most rapid during the early months and years suggests that the effects of environmental encounters during the early period should perhaps be most potent, it remains to be determined in crucial fashion how great and how permanent such effects can be.

Probably the question concerning the relative proportion of the variance in intelligence attributable to heredity and to environment, which is the one most frequently asked, has been unfortunate. No general answer to this question is possible. This impossibility has long been recognized by geneticists, for only the phenotype can be measured, and how much any genotype can be altered by experience can be ascertained only by submitting that genotype to all possible life programs of encounters with the environment. Much more pertinent are specific questions relevant to either problems of educational and welfare practice or to the theory of human intelligence and its development. Inasmuch as Dennis has very recently found that in orphanage environments where the variety of stimulation is minimal, only 42 percent of the children sit alone at two years of age, and only 15 percent walk alone at four years of age, it appears to be quite clear that the rate of development is not predetermined by the genes. On the other hand, although it is unlikely that any person has ever achieved his full potential for intellectual development, it is not known how much various procedures for improving the match between circumstances and level of behavioral development to foster the accommodative modification of central structures might increase the rate and the final level of intellectual capacity over the rate and level common under existing circumstances. No general answer can be made to questions of this sort, but a variety of such investigations might be expected to lead to generalizations about the nature of environments rich or poor in their capacity to promote intellectual development. . . .

Conclusion and the Challenge

In view of the conceptual developments and the evidence coming from animals learning to learn, from neuropsychology, from the programming of electronic computers to solve problems, and from the development of intelligence in children, it would appear that intelligence should be conceived as intellectual capacities based on central processes hierarchically arranged within the intrinsic portions of the cerebrum. These central processes are approximately analogous to the strategies for information processing and action with which electronic computers are programmed. With such a conception of intelligence, the assumptions that intelligence is fixed and that its development is predetermined by the genes are no longer tenable.

In the light of these considerations, it appears that the counsel from experts on child-rearing during the third and much of the fourth decades of the twentieth century to let children be while they grow and to avoid excessive stimulation was highly unfortunate. . . .

The problem for the management of child development is to find out how to govern the encounters that children have with their environments to foster both an optimally rapid rate of intellectual development and a satisfying life. . . .

References

BIRCH, H. G. 1956. Sources of order in maternal behavior of animals. *Amer. J. Orthopsychiat.*, **26**, 279-284.

CARMICHAEL, L. 1926. The development of behavior in vertebrates experimentally removed from influence of external stimulation. *Psychol. Rev.*, **33**, 51-58.

CARMICHAEL, L. 1927. A further study of the development of behavior in vertebrates experimentally removed from the influence of external stimulation. *Psychol. Rev.*, **34**, 34-47.

CARMICHAEL, L. 1928. A further study of the development of behavior. *Psychol. Rev.*, **35**, 253-260.

COGHILL, G. E. 1929. *Anatomy and the problem of behavior.* Cambridge: Cambridge Univer. Press; New York: Macmillan.

CRUZE, W. W. 1935. Maturation and learning in chicks. *J. Comp. Psychol.*, **19**, 371-409.

DENNIS, W., & DENNIS, MARSENA G. 1940. The effect of cradling practice upon the onset of walking in Hopi children. *J. genet. Psychol.*, **56** 77-86.

DENNIS, W., & NAJARIAN, PERGROUH I. 1957. Infant development under environmental handicap. *Psychol. Monogr.*, **71**, No. 7 (Whole No. 436).

HARLOW, H. F. 1949. The formation of learning sets. *Psychol. Rev.*, **56**, 51-65.

HEBB, D.O. 1949. *The organization of behavior.* New York: Wiley.

HEBB, D.O., & WILLIAMS, K. 1946. A method of rating animal intelligence. *J. genet. Psychol.*, **34**, 59-65.

LOEB, J. 1890. *Der Heliotropismus der Thiere und seine Überstimmung mit dem Heliotropismus der Pflanzen.* Würzburg: Hertz.

LOEB, J. 1918. *Tropisms, forced movements, and animal conduct*. Philadelphia: Lippincott.

McGRAW, MYRTLE B. 1935. *Growth: a study of Johnny and Jimmy*. New York: Appleton-Century-Crofts.

MORGAN, C. L. 1894. *An introduction to comparative psychology*. (2nd ed.) London: Scott, 1909.

PIAGET, J. 1936. *The origins of intelligence in children*. Trans. by Margaret Cook. New York: Int. Univer. Press, 1952.

RIESEN, A. H., CHOW, K. L., SEMMES, J., & NISSEN, H. W. 1951. Chimpanzee vision after four conditions of light deprivation. *Amer. Psychologist*, **6**, 282 (Abstract).

RIESS, B. F. 1954. The effect of altered environment and of age on mother-young relationships among animals. *Ann. N.Y. Acad. Sci.*, **57**, 606-610.

SHIRLEY, MARY M. 1933. *The first two years*. Minneapolis: Univer. Minnesota Press. 2 vols. **51**.

THOMPSON, W. R., & HERON, W. 1954. The effects of restricting early experience on the problem-solving capacity of dogs. *Canad. J. Psychol.*

WOLFF, C. F. 1759. *Theoria Generationis*. Halle.

WOLFF, C. F. 1768. *Deformatione intestinorum praecipue, tum et de aminio spurio, allisque partibus embryonis gallinacei nodum visis*. *Novi Comment. Acad. Sci. Imp. Petropol.*, **12**. Also 1769, **13**.

The Nature-Nurture Problem Revisited:
The Minnesota Adoption Studies
Sandra Scarr and Richard A. Weinberg

In the following excerpt, Sandra Scarr and Richard Weinberg describe the respective personal journeys by which they came to collaborate on the Minnesota Adoption project and convey a sense of the courage required to undertake this project in the post-Jensen era. Reporting on two large-scale studies of white adoptive families, one involving white, the other Black, White, and interracial adoptees, they conclude that there is no evidence for genetic differences between races in either IQ test performance or school achievement. Both white and black children adopted into White families score above average and similarly on these measures. Within racial groups and between adoptees and birth children, on the other hand, when rearing conditions are similar, there is considerable evidence that differences in performance are more closely related to the IQs of birth parents than to the adoptive environment. Development, in other words, occurring as it does through the expression of a particular genotype in a specific environment, is a joint function of nature and nurture operating in concert.

The role, indeed the very existence, of genetic differences in human behavior has long been a matter of heated debate in the social sciences. Each generation of scientists rediscovers the nature-nurture problem. Throughout intellectual history, although the social, political, and religious contexts have varied, the question has remained about the same: "To what extent are genes *and* environments important variables in accounting for the development of human behavior?" The question seems to remain unanswered despite an expanded knowledge base in the fields of behavioral genetics and psychology, an increased repertoire of methodologies in research design and statistical analyses, and the availability of populations appropriate for studying the problem. Counterbalancing these advances is a plethora of value and moral issues rooted in the rich soil of the social-political and judicial arenas (Weinberg, 1983).

In the past two decades, the writings of Jensen (1973), Lewontin (1970), Herrnstein (1973), and Kamin (1974) have generated an overheated emotional climate. Strong public opinion has been sparked, accompanied by uncontrolled polemics. The

Scarr, Sandra & Weinberg, Richard A. (1990). The nature-nurture problem revisited: The Minnesota adoption studies. In I. Sigel & G. Brody. (Eds.) *Methods of Family Research: Biographies of Research Projects. Volume 1: Normal Families.* Hillsdale, NJ: Lawrence Erlbaum Associates, Inc. pp. 121-151.

has been stoked by questioning the authenticity of Sir Cyril Burt's data, long considered a cornerstone of hereditarian arguments, and by increasingly vigorous interest in sociobiology and its emphasis on the evolutionary roots and adaptive nature of complex social behavior. Charges of racism, genocide, and antifeminism have been made against psychologists, ethologists, anthropologists, and others who have embraced sociobiological perspectives. In their extremes, hereditarian arguments have been used both to defend notions of racial inferiority and supremacy in various domains of human behavior (e.g., intellectual ability) and to attack compensatory education programs such as Head Start and other intervention programs as naive, untenable exploitations of federal funds. "Pure" environmentalists have offered a rationale for developing specific intervention programs and general social policies that guarantee major changes in an individual's behavior presumed to be genetically determined by hereditarians. Environmentalism, run amok, has provided the basis for Pygmalion schemes that promise geniuses in every home and scholars in every classroom.

Like master chess players, advocates from the hereditarian and environmentalist camps have played a rigorous game—accepting theoretical and mathematical assumptions as reasonable when they support an argument, rejecting methodological strategies and research designs as inappropriate when they challenge a position, and shaping data to fit their own particular views. Clad in ideological armor, the combatants have hurled scientific rhetoric and ad hominem insults; while the battlefield remains cluttered, no clear victory has been won by either side. Indeed, undiluted polar positions have characterized discussions of the sources of individual differences in behavior. This "either-or" philosophy must create confusion for many members of the psychological community, whose primary interest is fostering an individual's development by creating optimal environments. If intellectual ability, cognitive skills, school achievement, personality characteristics, and other parameters of behavior are predetermined by genetic blueprints, then what role can environments play in the development of the individual? More specifically, can an environment contribute to the development of a child's behavior? Can the level of an individual's performance be altered as the result of child-rearing, instruction, and interventions? Are there limits to the impact of such interventions?

It is in the context of these issues that our program of research evolved. Coming from different academic and professional backgrounds, we joined forces in 1971 to embark on a fifteen-year collaboration, two major studies and their follow-ups, and over thirty joint publications.

In this chapter we share that odyssey—the kinds of questions we individually posed which led us to this research program, the conceptual model that has guided our research design, the plan for our research, what we have found, and what we think it all means. It is hoped that this insider's view of a research enterprise will help the reader see the personal, subjective side of even the most basic, objective, efforts in science.

Sandra Scarr: What's a Nice Girl Like You Doing In a Place Like This?

"My interest in the possibility of genetic behavioral differences began, when as an undergraduate, I was told there were none. The social science view of the time was that genetics might set limits on species but that each individual within the species was endowed with everything that was important to develop into a beggar, king, attorney, or con artist.

My own observation of human behavior made me curious about their certainty in this matter, especially since I could find no evidence for this view. It seemed to me important to understand human differences rather than to stifle research for fear of unpopular results. I joined the American Civil Liberties Union in my senior year in college, to assure myself and others that an interest in genetic differences did not necessarily go with antidemocratic politics.

In graduate school, I decided to have a closer look at human individuality by doing a doctoral dissertation with Irving Gottesman on genetic variability in motivation. Even then, I was struck by the behavioral individuality of my own first child (compared to my friends' children) and by the resistance among professors of psychology to such ideas.

After moving to the University of Pennsylvania in 1966, a quick glance at the local scene told me that the most interesting question of practical import was, "Why do Black children do so poorly in school and on intellectual tests?" This question had been addressed in hundreds of studies that merely charted the intellectual differences between Blacks and Whites at many age levels and in many locales. There must be, I thought, more analytically powerful ways to get at the causes of these differences in performance.

Two logically possible hypotheses had been offered to explain why Black children do poorly in school and badly on tests: sociocultural disadvantage and racial genetic differences. The advocates of both views asserted their positions with vehemence, but there were no critical tests of either hypothesis.

Thus, in 1967, I began a program of research that continues today, employing five previously unused strategies to study the sources of racial differences in intellectual performance:

1. studies of individual differences within the U.S. Black population by the twin method;

2. the study of genetic markers of degrees of African ancestry and their relation to intellectual differences with the U.S. Black population;

3. the study of transracial adoption by which socially classified Black children are reared in the cultural environment sampled by the tests and the school;

4. cross-cultural studies in which Black children are or are not socially disadvantaged, and

5. educational intervention programs with young children to test ideas about reaction range and malleability.

Evidence against a racial genetic hypothesis and for the importance of genetic individual variability has come from all five sources.

The implications I have drawn from these five lines of research on racial and social class differences are that Black and White children do not differ much, if they have reasonable opportunities to learn the culture of the tests and the schools, but that social class differences among Whites are largely due to genetic differences. Among Blacks, the correlation of social class indicators with IQ test scores are about half of those for Whites, a suggestion that mobility by individual attributes has been historically limited, thereby limiting the contemporary association between genetic differences and social stratification among Blacks.

Individual differences, I find, are predominantly genetic within any group that is reasonably nurtured. Deliberate interventions to improve children's intellectual and academic performance are most effective for those who have little contact with the knowledge and skills to be tested or used in schools. Educational interventions to improve the performance of children who are not considerably disadvantaged have little effect. Framed in the reaction range concept, malleability is a property of organisms within the range of species-normal environments, and development is not so plastic as to be shoved around by any but the most severe environments."

Richard A. Weinberg: Does What We Do Really Make a Difference?

"I received my doctorate in 1968, trained in school psychology with a strong focus on child development. Like most school psychologists, influenced by the writings of the 1960s—Jerome Bruner, B. F. Skinner, J. McVicker Hunt, and Benjamin Bloom, I was a strong advocate of educational interventions and programs that would "make a difference." In fact, my doctoral thesis was a study aimed at modifying children's conceptual tempos using behavioral techniques. As a clinician, I wanted to believe that interventions in the form of alternative curricula, therapeutic programs, and remedial efforts were time well spent. At Teachers College, Columbia University, my first teaching position, I expanded my interests in the early education enterprise and watched the unfolding of the Head Start program, a major early childhood intervention effort and national social experiment (Weinberg, 1979). Then, in 1969, Arthur Jensen published his controversial critique of compensatory education programs and rekindled the nature-nurture controversy in a contemporary context of racial unrest and the quest for civil rights. Jensen's paper (Jensen, 1969) and the responses that followed had a profound impact on me. I had been working with some groups of Black parents and children in Harlem and the Morningside Heights areas of New York. Certainly, I saw individual differences among the children in terms of ability, personality, and attitudes, but these differences appeared also among the advantaged White parents and children who were applicants to a prestigious girls' school for which I consulted. Two different

95

cultures and socioeconomic climates were represented in my experiences, but personally I could not see how *racial* differences and Jensen's account could explain the variance within and between these populations.

Sandra Scarr and I joined the faculty at the University of Minnesota in 1970 and quickly came to share views that represented an appreciation of individual differences and a thirst to know more about why Black children and White children had such disparate school records, why children within the same families could appear so different, and what limits were set by genetic endowment for altering human behavior."

A Conceptual Framework

We joined forces—a developmental behavior geneticist and a developmental school psychologist—to address the nature-nurture problem, taking advantage of the time and place to pursue behavior genetics research.

In developing a conceptual framework for studying the nature-nurture problem, we agreed on some basic assumptions and beliefs. Initially, we acknowledged that the social sciences have been plagued by the controversy over nature *and* nurture, because of a misconception that the conjunction was "or." At the core of the controversy is the idea that genetic variation *fixes* individual and group differences in human behavior. Opponents of the idea believe that genetic differences are antithetical to malleability or change in behavior. A common error underlying this belief is a failure to distinguish environmental and genetic sources of individual differences in behavior from the necessary roles of both genes and environments in behavioral development. One cannot assess the relative impact of heredity or environment in behavioral domains because everyone must have both a viable gene complement and an environment in which the genes can be expressed over development.

Behavioral differences among individuals, on the other hand, can arise in any population from genetic differences, from variations among their environments, or both. Imagine a population of genetically identical clones who are reared in family environments that vary from working to upper-middle class. Any behavioral differences among the clones would necessarily arise from developing within those different environments. Next, imagine a genetically diverse human population reared in laboratory cages. All members experience exactly the same environments. Naturally, all differences among those individuals are accounted for by their genetic variability. Notice, however, that in the two fantasies the organisms all have *both* genes *and* environments for development (Scarr & Weinberg, 1980). Because nearly all families share both genes and environments, it is usually impossible to know why individuals are similar or different from one another. . . .

Our Program of Research: 1973-1976

In our two large-scale studies of adoption in Minnesota, one of White adolescents, the other of Black and interracial children adopted into White homes, we interviewed hundreds of children and their parents; we gave comparable tests for intelligence, interests, and attitudes to both generations; our interviews and tests covered a great deal of information other than IQ. Most important, we were able to assess the relative effects of heredity and environment because we could compare birth and adopted children within the same family, compare adopted children with their birth and their adoptive parents, and explore the origins of differences between children who grow up in similar environments. . . .

The Results of the Studies

Some of our findings were expected. Others surprised us. In general, we found no evidence of genetic differences in IQ between Blacks and Whites; [and] strong evidence of genetic origins of intellectual differences among individuals within each race. . . .

Let us consider the studies in greater detail.

The Adolescent Adoption Study

. . . The adolescents in this study had spent an average of eighteen years in their families—194 adopted children in 115 adoptive families and a comparison group of 237 biological children in 120 other families. All of the adoptees were placed in their families in the first year of life, the median being two-months-of-age. From 1975 to 1977 both groups of children were sixteen-twenty-two years old. Both samples of parents were of similar SES, from working to upper-middle class, and of similar IQ levels on the WAIS. The IQ scores of parents in both adoptive and biological families averaged 115, approximately 1 SD above the population mean. The biological children scored, on the average, an IQ of 113, and the adopted children 7 points lower at 106. The parent-child IQ correlations in the biological families were what we were led to expect from other studies—about .40 when corrected for the restricted range of the parents' scores. The biological midparent-child correlation was .52. The adoptive parent-child correlations were about .13; the adoptive midparent-child correlation was only .14.

The adopted children's IQ scores were more closely correlated with the educational levels of their birth mothers (.28) and fathers (.43) than with those of their adoptive mothers (.09) and fathers (.11). In fact, adopted children's IQ scores were as highly correlated with their natural parents' education as were those of the adolescents in the biological sample (.17 with mothers and .26 with fathers) (Scarr & Weinberg, 1980).

The IQ correlation of the biologically related siblings was .35. However, the IQ correlation of adopted children reared together for eighteen years was zero! These White adolescents reared together from infancy did not resemble their genetically unrelated siblings. . . .

97

The Transracial Adoption Study

The unique and controversial nature of our second study, the transracial adoption project, warrants an especially detailed discussion of its rationale and goals.

Rationale

It is well known that Black children reared by their own families achieve IQ scores that average about a standard deviation (15 points) below Whites (Jensen, 1973; Loehlin, Lindzey, & Spuhler, 1975). This finding is at the heart of a continuing controversy in the educational arena. Studies (e.g., Cleary, Humphreys, Kendrick, & Wesman, 1975) confirm the hypothesis that low IQ scores predict poor school performance, regardless of race. Thus, more Black children than White children fail to achieve academically and to earn the credentials required by higher occupational status, with its concomitant social prestige and economic security (Husen, 1974; Jencks, 1972).

In an attempt to remedy the alarming rate of school failure, compensatory educational programs, which were directed particularly at Black children, were introduced in the 1960s. At the same time, but for different reasons, a more intensive intervention began: the adoption of Black children by White families. Whereas compensatory educational programs involve the child for a few hours per day, we believed that transracial adoption alters the entire social ecology of the child. Transracial adoption is the human analog of the cross-fostering design, commonly used in animal behavior genetics research (e.g., Manosevitz, Lindzey, & Thiessen, 1969). The study of transracial adoption can yield estimates of biological and sociocultural effects on the IQ test performance of cross-fostered children.

We realized that the results of a transracial or cross-fostering study would require careful interpretation. Black children reared in White homes are socially labeled as Black and therefore may suffer racial discrimination. Because of the unmeasured effects of racism, poor IQ test performance by Black children in White homes cannot be uncritically interpreted as a result of genetic limitations. In addition, equal performance by Black and other adoptees cannot be interpreted as an indication of the *same* range of reaction for all groups. Again, the unknown effects of racism may inhibit the intellectual development of the Black adoptees. However, equally high IQs for Black and other adoptees would imply that IQ performance is considerably malleable. . . .

Upper-middle-class White families have an excellent reputation for rearing children who perform well on IQ tests and in school. When such families adopt White children, the adoptees have been found to score above average on IQ tests, but not as highly as the birth offspring of the same and similar families (Burks, 1928; Freeman, Holzinger, & Mitchell, 1928; Leahy, 1935; Munsinger, 1975; Skodak & Skeels, 1949).

If Black children have genetically limited intellectual potential, as some have claimed (Jensen, 1973; Shockley, 1971, 1972), their IQ performance would fall below that of other children reared in White upper-middle-class homes. On the other hand, if Black children have a range of reaction similar to other adoptees, their IQ scores would have a similar distribution. The concept, range of reaction, refers to the fact that genotypes do not usually specify a single phenotype. Rather, genotypes specify a range of phenotypic responses that the organism can make to a variety of environmental conditions.

Minnesota was especially in the forefront of *transracial adoption*. Although the Black population of the state is small (.9 percent in 1970), there were too many Black and interracial children (with one Black and one White or other racial group parent) available for adoption and too few Black families to absorb them. Minority group children—Black, American Indian, Korean, and Vietnamese—have consequently been adopted by White families in large numbers. Furthermore, in recent years, many non-White children have been adopted from other states.

The support for interracial adoption changed dramatically in the late 1950s and early 1960s because of the efforts of public and private agencies and the pioneering White adoptive parents. Several agency and parent organizations were formed to promote the adoption of Black and interracial Black children. The most influential organization was the Open Door Society of Minnesota, formed in 1966 by adoptive parents of socially classified[1] Black children. The founding president of the Open Door Society was a leading columnist on one of the Minneapolis daily newspapers who frequently wrote about his multiracial family. The intellectual and social climate of Minnesota is to this day generally conducive to liberal and humanitarian movements such as interracial adoption.

Goals of the Study and the Sample

We posed four major questions in the study regarding the development of intellectual skills:

1. What is the estimated reaction range for IQ scores of Black/interracial children reared in Black environments or in White adoptive homes?

2. Do interracial children perform at higher levels on IQ tests than do children with two Black parents; that is, does the degree of White ancestry affect IQ scores ?

3. How do the IQ scores of socially classified Black children reared in White homes compare to those of other adopted children and birth White children within the same families; that is, do different racial groups, when exposed to similar environments, have similar distributions of IQ scores?

4. How well do socially classified Black children reared in White families perform in school?

For the Black adoption study, we recruited 101 families (from 136 families eligible to participate) consisting of 176 adopted children (130 who had one or two Black parents; 25 White; 21 others including Asian, North American Indian, and Latin American Indian children) and 145 birth White children. Like our other sample of adoptive parents, these families were above average in income and education, stability and mental health, and interest in children. The birth parents of these adoptees were about average intellectually and educationally, as we determined from the adoption records.

The sample of families lived within a 150-mile radius of the Twin Cities metropolitan area. Although nearly all of the children were adopted in Minnesota, sixty-eight were born outside of the state. Through interstate cooperation, the child placement agencies arranged for the adoption of many non-White children from other states.

The birth children in our studies had the benefits of both genes and environment; the adopted children were born to intellectually average parents but raised in intellectually enriched homes. To make environmental conditions as similar as possible, we most often limited our analyses to the children who had been adopted in the first year of life—most during the first three months.

Answering the Questions

The first question considered whether socially classified Black children reared in economically advantaged White homes would score above those reared in Black environments.

The average IQ score of Black and interracial children, adopted by advantaged White families, was found to be 106. Early-adopted Black and interracial children performed at an even higher level. This mean represents an increase of 1 standard deviation above the average IQ of 90 usually achieved by Black children reared in their own homes in the North Central region. Furthermore, in the Minneapolis public school district, the average performance of fourth-grade children on the *Gates-MacGinities* vocabulary test at a school with 87 percent Black and interracial enrollment in 1973 was about the twenty-first national percentile, which translates to an IQ equivalent of about 90.

Since 68 of the 130 Black children were known to have one White parent and only 29 were known to have had two Black parents (the remainder were of other mixed or unknown parentage), it may seem misleading to compare the adoptees to Black children in the general population. Even if all of the Black children were interracial offspring, we thought a strong genetic hypothesis should not predict that they would score well above the White population average. Nor should they score as highly as White adoptees. In fact, the Black and interracial children of this sample scored as highly on IQ tests as did White adoptees in previous studies with large samples (Burks, 1928; Horn, Loehlin, & Willerman, 1979; Leahy, 1935).

In other words, the range of reaction of socially classified Black children's IQ scores from average (Black) to advantaged (White) environments was at least 1 standard deviation. Conservatively, if we consider only the adopted children with two Black parents (and late and less favorable adoptive experiences), the IQ reaction range was at least 10 points between these environments. If we consider the early-adopted group, the IQ range was as large as 20 points. The level of school achievements among the Black and interracial adoptees was further evidence of their above-average performance on standard intellectual measures.

The dramatic increase in the IQ mean and an additional finding that placement and adoptive family characteristics accounted for a major portion of the IQ differences among the socially classified Black children strongly suggested that the IQ scores of these children are environmentally malleable.

We reasoned that the substantial increase in test performance of the Black and interracial adoptees is because their rearing environments are culturally relevant to the tests and to the school. Amid the IQ controversy, some have argued that standardized measures are inappropriate for children whose cultural background is different from that of the tests. While the rejection of IQ tests as predictors of academic success, on the basis of their cultural bias, is untenable (Jensen, 1974), we strongly believe that the tests and the schools share a common culture to which Black children are not as fully acculturated as are White children. However, the socially classified Black children in this study were fully exposed to the culture of the tests and the school, although they were still socially defined as Black .

The second question concerned a comparison of the IQ scores of children whose parents were both Black with Black children of interracial parentage. The interracial children scored about 12 points higher than those with two Black parents, but this difference was associated with large differences in maternal education and preplacement history. The part correlations suggested that variation in the race of mothers accounted for 3 percent of the children's IQ variance, but even this percentage of variance probably includes some additional and unmeasured environmental differences between the groups.

For example, Black mothers are known to be at greater risk than White mothers for nutritional deficiencies, maternal death, infant mortality, and other reproductive casualties (Scarr-Salapatek & Williams, 1973). The prematurity rate among Black mothers is more than double that of Whites. These risks are often found to be associated with poverty and long-term developmental problems among the children. The interracial children, all but two of whom have White mothers, were less likely to have suffered any of these problems.

The third question asked for comparisons among the scores of Black/interracial, Asian/Indian adoptees, and the birth children of the adoptive families. There were significant differences in IQ scores among the groups. The socially classified Black children scored on the average between the White and Asian/Indian adoptees, but these results were confounded with placement variables. Among the early adoptees, there were too few White and Asian/Indian children to make meaningful comparisons. The Black/interracial early adoptees, however, performed at IQ 110, on the average.

Compared to adopted children in previous studies, the average IQ of 110 for the 99 early adopted Black/interracial children compares well with the 112.6 reported by Leahy

(1935, p. 285) for White adoptees in professional families, with the IQ 108 of the Texas White adoptees from a private adoption home, and with the 106 of the adopted adolescents reported in our other study.

The above-average IQ level of adopted children, reported in all adoption studies, reflects both their better-than-average environments and the elimination of severely retarded children from the pool of potential adoptees. Although Munsinger's (1975) review concluded that adoptive family environments have little or no impact on the intellectual development of adoptees, past studies have not adequately tested this hypothesis. Because children who are selected for adoption are not grossly defective, their predicted IQ level is slightly above that of the general population. In this study, however, the adopted *Black/interracial* children could not have been predicted to have average IQ scores above the mean of the *White* population unless adoptive family environments have considerable impact.

The birth children of the adoptive families scored above the average of the Black/interracial early adoptees. Not only have the birth children been in their families since birth, but their natural parents are considerably brighter than those of the adopted children, regardless of race.

A fourth question focused on the school achievement of the Black/interracial adoptees and the birth children in the adoptive families. Black/interracial adoptees were found to score slightly above average on school-administered achievement and aptitude tests, as predicted by their IQ scores. The natural children of the adoptive families scored higher than the socially classified Black adoptees on school achievement measures, a finding which is congruent with their higher IQ scores. The school achievement data provided validation for our IQ assessment.

Implications of the Findings

What are the implications of these results for developmental plasticity? First, it is clear from the IQ scores of the transracially adopted children that they, like other adoptees, were responsive to the rearing environments in adoptive families, which as a group provided intellectual stimulation and exposure to the skills and knowledge sampled on IQ tests. The mean IQ scores of both samples of adoptees were above the average of agemates, primarily because they benefited from their rearing environments.

Second, individual adoptees differed in their responses to the environmental advantages of adoptive families. Those with natural parents of higher educational levels, and by implication higher intellectual abilities, were more responsive to the rearing environments of adoptive families than were those with natural parents of more limited intellectual skills. Children adopted into families of adoptive parents at and above the average educational and IQ levels of adoptive parents scored higher on the *WAIS* than children of comparable natural mothers adopted into families with less bright adoptive parents. The adolescents whose natural mothers and adoptive parents were both below average scored 10.4 IQ points below those whose natural mothers and adoptive parents

102

were both above average.

Individual differences among the adopted children at both younger and older ages were related to intellectual variation among adoptive parents and their biological parents, even though the average IQ of adoptees most likely exceeded that of their natural parents. Human beings are not infinitely plastic; malleability does not mean that given the same environment, all individuals will end up alike.

At present we are conducting a ten-year follow-up study of the transracially adopted children, who are now ages fourteen to twenty-two. Their intellectual and academic achievements, their personality and social adjustments, and their personal stories are all of interest to our understanding of what families can (and cannot) do for children. . . .

So What?

We have found evidence of genetic sources of variability for all of the psychological characteristics we have studied, from early childhood to the end of the childrearing period. The same studies also provide evidence for the malleability of development—the responsiveness of genotypes to differences in their environments. We think that developmentalists ought to be concerned with individual differences in development under similar rearing conditions, as well as the average level of development expressed under varying environmental conditions. An evolutionary view incorporates both perspectives, because individuals vary genetically in their responses to diverse rearing conditions.

Thus, the view we have embraced is a middle-of-the-road, interactionist perspective that highlights the roles that genes *and* environments play in determining human development and behavior. As a personal observation we can affirm that by staking ground between two well-armed, ideological forces, one becomes an easy target in the crossfire of bitter accusations, conceptual challenges, and verbal assaults that are hurled in defense of respective positions in the field.

The conclusion that our genetic heritage contributes to the complex accounting of variation in our performance is not pessimistic and does not bode evil for social and educational policy. The position we have taken has been summarized as follows:

> *Social policy should be determined by political and ethical values. . . . Once social policy has been determined, however, research can be useful. Governments can do a better job of designing effective intervention programs if people know which variations in the environment make a difference and which do not. The average level of a culture's environment determines the average level of achievement: by providing good schools, nutrition, health care, and psychological services, a society can raise the overall level of health and attainment for the whole population. Resources spent in these areas should eliminate conditions that have definite deleterious effects on individual development.*

But governments will never turn their entire populations into geniuses, or altruists, or entrepreneurs, or whatever their philosophy is. Biological diversity is a fact of life, and respect for individual differences derives from the genetic perspective. (Scarr & Weinberg, 1978, p. 36)

Those of us who devote our professional efforts to the mental health enterprise can appreciate individual differences and accept the challenge to create those environments that effectively "match" a child's abilities and talents. We can attempt to provide the necessary full range of environments that will facilitate optimal psychological outcomes for every child. We can invest our resources in changing those circumstances that clearly leave deleterious effects on development.

Note

1. In the United States, individuals with visible signs of African ancestry are socially labeled or classified as Black.

References

Burks, B. S. (1928). The relative influence of nature and nurture upon mental development: A comparative study of foster parent-foster child and true parent-true child resemblance. *Twenty-Seventh Yearbook of the National Society for the Study of Education*, 219-316.

Cleary, T. A., Humphreys, L. G., Kendrick, S. A., & Wesman, A. (1975). Educational uses of tests with disadvantaged students. *American Psychologist*, *30*, 15-41.

Herrnstein, R. (1973). *IQ in the meritocracy*. Boston: Atlantic, Little, Brown.

Horn, J. M., Loehlin, J C., & Willerman, L. (1979). Intellectual resemblance among adoptive and biological relatives: The Texas adoption project. *Behavior Genetics*, 177-207.

Jensen, A. R. (1969). How much can we boost IQ and scholastic achievement? *Harvard Educational Review*, *39*, 1-123.

Jensen, A. R. (1973). *Educability and group differences*. New York: Basic Books.

Jensen, A. R. (1974). How biased are culture-loaded tests? *Genetic Psychology Monographs*, *90*, 185-244.

Kamin, L. J. (1974). *The science and politics of IQ*. Hillsdale, NJ: Lawrence Erlbaum Associates.

Leahy, A. M. (1935). Nature-nurture and intelligence. *Genetic Psychology Monographs, 17*, 235-307.

Lewontin R. C. (1970). Race and intelligence. *Bulletin of the Atomic Scientists, 26*, 2-8.

Loehlin, J., Lindzey, G., & Spuhler, J. N. (1975). *Race differences in intelligence*. San Francisco, CA: Freeman

Manosevitz, M., Lindzey, G., & Thiessen, D. (Eds.). (1969). *Behavioral genetics*. New York: Appleton-Century-Crofts.

Munsinger, H. (1975). The adopted child's IQ: A critical review. *Psychological Bulletin, 82*, 623-659.

Scarr, S., & Weinberg, R. A. (1978). The influence of "family background" on intellectual attainment. *American Sociological Review, 43*, 674-692.

Scarr, S., & Weinberg, R. A. (1980). Calling all camps! The war is over—A reply to "The non-influence of 'family background' on intellectual attainment: A critique of Scarr and Weinberg." *American Sociological Review, 45*, 859-864.

Scarr-Salapatek, S., & Williams, M. L. (1973). The effects of early stimulation on low-birthweight infants. *Child Development, 44*, 94-101.

Weinberg, R. A. (1979). Early childhood education and intervention: Establishing an American tradition. *American Psychologist, 34*, 912-916.

Weinberg, R. A. (1983). A case of a misplaced conjunction: Nature or nurture? *Journal of School Psychology, 21*, 9-12.

UNIT 3: Culture and Context

6

Culture, Time, and Place

Some rituals are found in many different countries, for instance, the coincidence of two people accidentally saying the same thing at once. In Italy, if this happens, children link little fingers and shake their hands up and down three times, saying, 'uno, due, tre'; they then break their grasp and say either 'flic' or 'floc.' If both choose the same expression they each get a wish. Viennese children have an identical ceremony, but use the poets 'Goethe' or 'Schiller' instead of 'flic' or 'floc.' In France, girls predict weddings—each girls tries to pinch the other, and whoever pinches first will be married first. In Spain, and Bolivia, where the ritual is marked by adults as well as children, women cross their fingers and say, 'may you be the first to have a child'. In Egypt, children say, 'your life is longer than mine,' to wish each other longer life.

• INTRODUCTION •

Within every society, acculturation processes communicate beliefs, values, attitudes, and expectations to children. They define the actions and styles of interaction acceptable or unacceptable in given settings and they foster a sense of belonging to family and to community. In the readings chosen for this module, we are presented with a classic third-person ethnographic description of childhood in pre-World War II Bali and with two highly contrasting first-person accounts of female childhood in America. In these exceptional portraits we see how the intimate interactions and collective rites of everyday life reflect the communal belief system and serve as specific vehicles of acculturation. We observe the way in which tradition, myth, and ritual connect children to the past and to the future and help them to perceive themselves in a broader framework of time and meaning; and we are given striking evidence of the historical and cultural diversity of children's lives.

• • •

Children and Ritual in Bali
Margaret Mead

Writing on the basis of field work done in Bali before the sweeping cultural changes of the post-World War II period, Margaret Mead provides a beautifully-tailored account of the place of children in the rich tapestry of traditional Balinese cultural life. Notice the seamless pattern created by the system of Balinese beliefs regarding the meaning and course of human existence, ideas concerning the nature and place of childhood in the cycle of life and death, forms of caregiving, styles of adult-child interaction, and communal participation in ritual dance and theater. In a context in which aggression and the display of hostility or fear were strongly discouraged, Balinese children had to endure constant and merciless teasing from adults. The tension inherent in this conflict and the opportunity to resolve this tension through participation in the ritualized expression of conflict, destruction, and healing portrayed in

Balinese dance and theater were, in Mead's view, at the core of the Balinese process of acculturation.

In Bali, children are called "small human beings," and the conception of the nature and place of the child is different from that of the West. The whole of life is seen as a circular stage on which human beings, born small, as they grow taller, heavier, and more skilled, play predetermined roles, unchanging in their main outlines, endlessly various and subject to improvisation in detail.

The world of the dead is one part of the circle, from which human souls return, born again into the same family every fourth generation, to stay too briefly—dying before they have shared rice—or for a long time, or even for too long, for it is inappropriate for great-grandparents to be alive at the same time as their great-grandchildren. Such lingerers have to pay a penny to their great-grandchildren, chance-met on the street. The newborn child and the aged great-grandparent are both too close to the other world for easy entrance into the temple. The baby cannot enter until after a special feast at three and a half or seven months, and the very aged enter through a special side gate.

The newborn are treated as celestial creatures entering a more humdrum existence and, at the moment of birth, are addressed with high-sounding honorific phrases reserved for gods, the souls of ancestors, princes, and people of a higher caste. Human beings do not increase in stature and importance, as is so often the case in societies where men have only one life to live; rather, they round a half-circle in which middle age, being farthest from the other world, is the most secular. There is little acceptance of any task being difficult or inappropriate for a child, except that an infant at birth is, of course, expected to do nothing for itself. Words are put into the mouth of the infant, spoken on its behalf by an adult; the hands of the seven-month-old baby are cupped to receive holy water, folded in prayer, opened to waft the incense offered to it as a god, and when the ceremony is over the child sits, dreamily repeating the gestures which its hands have momentarily experienced.

The Balinese may comment with amusement but without surprise if the leading metallophone player in a noted orchestra is so small that he has to have a stool in order to reach the keys; the same mild amusement may be expressed if someone takes up a different art after his hands have a tremor of age to confuse their precision. But in a continuum within which the distinction between the most gifted and the least gifted is muted by the fact that everyone participates, the distinction between child and adult—as performer, as actor, as musician—is lost except in those cases where the distinction is ritual, as where a special dance form requires a little girl who has not reached puberty.

This treatment of human history as an unending series of rebirths is matched in the treatment of the calendar. The Balinese have a whole series of weeks, of three, four,

Mead, Margaret. (1955). Children and ritual in Bali. In M. Mead & M. Wolfenstein. (Eds.). *Childhood in Contemporary Cultures*. Chicago: University of Chicago Press. pp. 40-51.

five, six, up to ten days, which turn on each other, like wheels of different sizes, and there are important occasions when two or three weeks recurrently coincide. These have special names and may be an occasion for festival—like Galoengan, a New Year's feast associated with the souls of the dead, and a postfestival season of special theatricals. But, although there is a way of noting the year in a continuous irreversible sequence, it is seldom used. A man who has labored long to recopy a sacred text on pages of lontar palm will simply note, when his task of intricate elaboration of a beautiful archaic script is over, that this was finished on the such-and-such, a recurrent combination of days—as we might say, on Friday the thirteenth of September. The principal calendrical unit, the ceremonial year, is two hundred and ten days long. The lunar calendar simply marks the pattern of planting and harvest.

Children, then, are smaller and more fragile than adults, as well as closer to the other world. Their essential personality characteristics—gaiety or seriousness, gentleness or harshness—are recognized early, and those around each child combine to set its formal character in an expected mold. The baby of six months with silver bracelets welded on its tiny wrists, waves and bangs its arms; if someone is hurt in the process, there comes the exclamation, "Isama is harsh." It takes only a few such acts to stereotype the judgment which will be echoed and re-echoed through its life, setting and defining its ways, but quite forgotten after death as other events—day of birth, experience in other incarnations—combine to give new personality. So, while the people take ritual pains over a corpse—that the individual may be born again fleeter of foot or more beautiful of face—they cannot describe the character or the looks of someone who died two years ago. Personality characteristics are accidents, held gently constant through any given incarnation, that dissolve at death. But the baby who is identified as "gay and mischievous" has a way of life plotted out for it, which again is independent of age. Old men who have been "gay" all their lives still know who sleeps with whom in the fields at night in the brief, wordless first encounters which for the Balinese represent the height of passion; and men and women, labeled "serious," may bear many children, but people will comment instead on their industriousness in the rice fields or their faithfulness at the temple.

The child is made conscious of its sex very early. People pat the little girl's vulva, repeating an adjective for feminine beauty, and applaud the little boy's phallus with the word for "handsome male." The child is fitted into words appropriate to its caste, gestures appropriate to each ceremony, and before the child can walk, it is taught to dance with its hands. Before he can stand, the little boy, who has sat on his father's knees while his father played the *gamelan*, begins to play himself. Peeking over a house wall, one may see diminutive girls of three, sitting all alone, practicing hand gestures. The child learns to walk around a single walking rail, learning that it is safe as long as it holds to this central support, in danger of falling when it loosens its hold and strays out into the unknown. When it learns to walk, its ventures away from support and parents are controlled by the mother or child nurse mimicking terror and calling it back with threats that are random in content—"Tiger!" "Policeman!" "Snake!" "Feces!"—but constant in theatrical affect, until the child learns that undefined outer space may at any moment be filled with unknown terrors.

In the village, in familiar territory, the child learns the directions—*kadja*, the center of the island, where the high mountain of the gods stands; *kelod*, toward the sea, the point of least sanctity; and *kangin*, to the right, *kaoeh*, to the left, when one faces *kadja*. Every act is likely to be expressed in these terms as babies are bidden to come a little *kadja* or to brush a speck off the *kelod* side of their face, and little boys of different caste play together happily but learn that the boy of higher caste must get into bed first or sit on the *kadja* side of the food tray.

Children learn the vertical hierarchies of life—that the head, even of a casteless peasant child, is something sacred, that a flower which has fallen to the ground from an offering carried on the head may not be replaced in the offering, that those of highest caste or sanctity must be given the highest seats. As they learn to speak, they learn that the words addressed to them by their elders and superiors are never the words in which they may answer, although sometimes the lesson is imperfectly learned, and a low-caste boy will marvel at the fact that "they say Brahman parents are very polite to their children, that they say *tiang* to them," not knowing that the children must reply with an exaggeratedly more polite term, *titiang*, in which the pronoun "I" is made more self-deprecating by a stylized stutter.

From birth until long after they can walk, children live most of their waking hours in human arms, carried in a sling or on the hip, even sleeping suspended about the neck of an adult or a child nurse. They learn a plastic adaptation, to take cognizance of the other's movement in limp relaxation, neither resisting nor wholly following the pounding of the rice or the game the child nurse is playing. When there is teaching to be done, the teacher uses this flaccid adaptivity and, holding the hands and body of the learner with vigorous, precise intent, twists and turns them into place or pattern. Verbal directions are meager; children learn from the feel of other people's bodies and from watching, although this watching itself has a kinesthetic quality. An artist who attempts to draw a group of men will draw himself over and over again, feeling the image. The children are everywhere. Very little babies cannot enter the temple, but the toddler is present in the midst of the most solemn ceremonial, attached to parent or grandparent, watching the blessing of the trance dancer, the throw of coins of the diviner, the killing of the fowl as exorcism. Women attending a theatrical performance carry their babies in their arms, and the front row of every performance is given over to the very small children, who watch and doze and are hastily rescued when the play threatens to break the bounds of the audience square and to involve the crowd in the plot. At the shadow play the children sit in front, and the puppet master increases the number of battles in the plot in proportion to the number of children. As the women kneel in the temple, placing the petals of a flower between their praying fingers, a flower is placed in the hands of the child who is with them. For the temple feast, small children, who at other times may run about stark naked, will appear elaborately dressed, boys in headdress and kris.

113

They look like dolls, and they are treated like playthings, playthings which are more exciting than fighting cocks—over which the men spend many fascinated hours—or the kites and crickets which amuse little boys. Everyone joins in the mild titillating teasing of little babies, flipping their fingers, their toes, their genitals, threatening them, playfully disregarding the sanctity of their heads, and, when the children respond by heightened excitement and mounting tension, the teaser turns away, breaks the thread of interplay, allows no climax. Children learn not to respond, to resist provocation, to skirt the group of elders who would touch or snatch, to refuse the gambit when their mothers borrow babies to make them jealous. They develop an unresponsiveness to the provocative intent of others at the same time that they remain plastic to music and pattern. It is a childhood training which, if followed here, would seem dangerously certain to bring out schizoid trends in the growing child's character.

But there is one great difference between Bali and the changing Western world as we know it. In the Western world children are traumatized in childhood in ways which are new and strange, for which no ritual healing, no artistic form, exists in the culture. Those who are very gifted may become prophets, or artists, or revolutionaries, using their hurt, their made deviancy, or their innate deviancy exaggerated by adult treatment as the basis for a new religion or a new art form. Those who are not so gifted or who are less fortunate in finding a medium for their gifts go mad or dwindle away, using little even of what they have. We are beginning to recognize how damaging a trauma can be—administered by a parent who is ignorant of the world the child lives in and lived out by the child in a still different world later. The present emphasis in America is on the application of psychiatric techniques—in childhood itself—to undo the damage, take out the false stitches, relearn the abandoned stance. Our conception of life is a sequential, changing, and climactic one. So a trauma in childhood is seen as producing mental damage or intolerable yearning, which must then be solved in later life—and solved alone by the traumatized individuals.

Old Bali is a striking example of a quite different solution, in which the child each day meets rituals accurately matched to the intensities and the insatiabilities which are being developed by the interplay between itself and others. Little children are not permitted to quarrel, they are not allowed to struggle over toys, or to pull and claw at each other—there are always elders there to separate them, gently, impersonally, and inexorably, and so completely that, in over two years of living in Balinese villages, I never saw two children or adolescents fight. When conflict arises, the elder child is continually told to give in to the younger; the younger, responding to the invitation of the older, is jealous of every favor and demanding of anything the elder has.

But day after day, as the child is prevented from fighting, he sees magnificent battles on the stage, and the children are part of the crowd that streams down to the river bank to duck some character in the play. He sees the elder brother—who must always be deferred to in real life—insulted, tricked, defeated, in the theater. When his mother teases him in the eerie, disassociated manner of a witch, the child can also watch the witch in the play—the masked witch wearing the accentuated symbols of both sexes, with long protruding tongue, pendulous breasts, covered with repulsive hair—watch her recurrent battle with the dragon, who in his warmer and puppy-like behavior resembles his father. He can see the followers of the dragon attack the witch and fall down in a trance, as if killed, only to be brought back to life again by the magic healing power of the dragon. These followers of the dragon, like the younger brother, go further than he will ever dare to go in showing hostility to his mother, in open resentment of her laughter. He sees his possible destructive wish lived out before his eyes, but in the end no one is slain, no one is destroyed, no one is hurt. The trancers, who have fallen into convulsions when they attack the witch, are revived by holy water and prayers, the play ends, the masks are taken off, the actors lay aside their golden garments for stained workday clothes; the young men who lay twitching in convulsions half an hour ago go off singing gaily for a bath. Over and over again, as babies in their mothers' arms, as toddlers being lifted out of the path of a pair of dancing warriors, as members of the solemn row of children who line the audience square, they see it happen—the play begins, mounts to intensity, ends in ritual safety. And in the villages, when theatrical troupes under the protection of the dragon mask, patron of the theater and enemy of death, parade about a village in which they have just arrived, people buy a little of the dragon's hair as bracelets for their children to protect them from evil dreams.

In this absence of change, the experience of the parent is repeated in that of the child, and the child, a full participant in ritual and art, is presented with the last elaborations almost with its first breath. The people themselves treat time as a circular process rather than a progressive one, with the future ever behind one, unrolling beneath one's feet, an already exposed but undeveloped film. Here we find a perfect expression of the historical nature of culture, in which any separation between cause and effect, any attempt to turn either childhood experience or adult ritual into the cause, one of the other, is seen to be a hopeless endeavor. The two recur together, at every stage; the teased baby of the witchlike human mother watches the witch on the stage, and the teasing mother, even as she teases her baby, also sees the witch, attacked, apparently destroying, but in the end doing no harm. The effect on child and mother must both be reckoned in a round of simultaneous events, repeating and repeating until the child in arms again becomes a parent.

And yet, in spite of their conception of life as a circle, we may, if we wish, break the circle—as they are unwilling to do—and, for purposes of a type of scientific analysis born of our Western conceptions of time, space, and causality, ask the question: What happens as babies born to Balinese parents, equipped at birth with the same potentialities as other human babies, learn to be Balinese? How do they make the ritual of Balinese life part of themselves and so become as able to dance the intricate dances, carve or play or weave or go into trance, as did their parents or their grandparents? How do they learn to be Balinese and so perpetuate Balinese culture? This is no question which treats Balinese culture as a mere projection from childhood experience. The themes enacted in the Balinese theater have a long history. On the shadow-play screen there appear the heroes and heroines of the *Ramayana*, the great Indian epic. The witch Rangda is also the Javanese Tjalonarang, and she is also Derga, the destroyer. The dragon is found around the world—in Japan, in the streets of New York for Chinese New Year, where he blesses the local merchants whose restaurants may contain a juke box or a cigarette-vending machine. It is only in the particular details of the plots that one can find the distinctive mark of Balinese culture—in the refusal to let the witch die, in the permission to show a violence on the stage which is not permitted in real life, and in the way in which artist, actor, and priest participate in everyday life.

But children in Bali, like human children everywhere, are born helpless, dependent, and cultureless and must be bathed and fed and protected, taught to balance and to walk, to touch and to refrain from touching, to relate themselves to other people, to talk, to work, to become sure members of their own sex, and finally to marry and produce and rear children. We cannot find that which is distinctively Balinese in the mere presence of the witch and the dragon, who recur in many forms throughout the world. It is necessary to look at fine details of difference. For example, the Balinese witch has got hold of a dragon's fiery tongue—and the Balinese dragon has no tongue at all. This can be seen as a part of the way in which the witch combines all the gross, overaccentuated aspects of secondary sex characters. In the Balinese ideal physical type, both men and women are slender; male breasts are more pronounced than among us; women's breasts are high and small; hips of both sexes are closer in dimensions. Men are almost beardless, and the muscles of their arms are not developed. The witch's hairy legs and long pendulous breasts accentuate the frightening aspects of highly developed sex differences, and we find, counterpointing her, protecting the people from the illness and death she brings, and presiding with her over the theater, the dragon, a mythical creature, wearing lovely fluffy, feather-like "hair" or crow feathers sent especially by the gods. Only as the Balinese witch is contrasted with her historical predecessors and as the Balinese dragon is seen in a world perspective of other dragons, is it possible to say what is distinctively Balinese. In the same way, by placing Balinese childhood experience in a context of our knowledge of child development, we can see in what particular ways Balinese children, while repeating universal human experiences, also have special ones.

The Balinese infant has preserved a kind of neonatal flexibility, which in the children who have been studied in Western culture tends to disappear very early, so that both the way a baby relaxes in its mother's arms and the way the mother holds it are sharply contrasting to our patterns. The disallowance of infancy, as adults speak in behalf of the child or press its compliant learning hands into ritual gestures, is again distinctive; and the way in which the child is constantly discouraged from walking, taught to use its right hand rather than the left, which is exposed by the carrying posture, left free to drink from its mother's breast when it chooses, as it is carried high above her high breast, but fed in a helpless prone position as a mound of prechewed food is piled on its mouth—all these details go to build the kind of Balinese personality which will be receptive to rituals danced and acted by others who have been treated in the same way. The constant provocative teasing and threatening which never reaches any but a theatrical climax, the denial of all violence and expressed hostility toward siblings, the serial experience of being the pampered baby, the displaced knee baby, and the child nurse, who, as guardian of the baby, stays to see the usurper dethroned in turn, all these form a background for

116

the plots of ritual and theater to which the child is exposed.

But there is something more here than the correspondence between childhood experience and dramatic plot, something different from the sort of cultural situation discussed by Róheim when a terrifying infantile experience—of a male child sleeping beneath the mother—is abreacted by initiation rites in adolescence. In Bali the absence of sequence even in the life-span of the individual and the absence of discontinuity between ritual role and everyday role seem crucial. The artist, the dancer, the priest, is also a husbandman who tills his rice fields. Occasionally an artist becomes so famous that he lets his fingernails grow as he does no other work, and, say the Balinese, he begins to grow fat and careless and lazy, and his artistic skills decrease. The priest may stand robed in White during a ceremony, officiating at the long ritual of inviting the gods down to earth, dressing them, feeding them, bathing them, presenting them with dance and theater, and then sending them back again for another two hundred and ten days in heaven. But the day after the ceremony he is a simple citizen of the village, only owing the land which he cultivates to his work on feast days as guardian of the temple.

Nor is there any gap between professional and amateur. There are virtually no amateurs in Bali, no folk dancing in which people do traditional things without responsibility to an artistic canon. There are enormous differences in skill and grace and beauty of performance, but prince and peasant, very gifted and slightly gifted, all do what they do seriously and become, in turn, critical spectators, laughing with untender laughter at the technical failures of others. Between the audience that gathers to watch the play and the players there is always the bond of professional interest, as the audience criticizes the way the actor or actress who plays the princess postures or sings, rather than identifying with her fate—however lost she may be in some dense theatrical forest.

Nor is there any gap between rehearsal and performance. From the moment an orchestra begins to practice an old piece of music, there is a ring of spectators, aspiring players, substitute players, small boys, and old men, all equally engrossed in the ever fresh creation of a new way of playing an old piece of music. Where in Java the shadow-play screen divided men from women, the women seeing only the faint shadow on the screen, the men the brightly painted figures, in Bali people can sit on either side, in front to watch the finished play, behind—and this is where little boys prefer to sit—to watch the individual designs on the figures and the deft hands of the puppet master. When a village club decides to learn a new play—a play in which the main serious parts are traditional and the parts of clowns, servants, and incidental characters are all improvised, never set, even in consecutive performances—half the village attends the rehearsals, enjoys the discussions of costume, the sharp words of the visiting virtuoso come to teach a dance step, the discovery of some new talent among the actors. In the rectangular piece of ground which becomes a four-sided stage as the audience gathers around it, isolated pairs of curtains borrowed from a theater with a quite different style of handling surprise may be set up near each end. The actors, their crowns a little askew, sit in almost full view dozing behind these curtains or among the audience, and then, as they make their appearance, part the curtain for a prolonged stylized "entrance," from which they later return to their full visibility offstage. People advance from the audience to pin up a dancer's fallen scarf, and dramatic scenes of chase and conquest will be pursued into the midst of the audience.

Thus in Bali the ritual world of art and theater and temple is not a world of fantasy, an endless recurrent daydream, or a new set of daydreams woven from the desperations of the gifted of each generation. It is rather a real world of skill and application—a world in which members of a dance club scheme to get money for the gold of a new headdress or to buy new instruments for the orchestra; where long hours are spent in the basic work of learning to dance; where disciplined hands and wrists and eyes that click to one side in perfect time to the music, are all the result of continuous, although relaxed, rather dreamy, work. And the temple feasts, where many of these activities combine to make a great spectacle, are called appropriately "the work of the Gods."

Children have not only the precocious postural participation in prayer and offering, dance and music, but also a whole series of parallel participations. A little boy will be given bamboo clappers with which to imitate the clapping of the dragon's tongueless jaws and, covered by his mother's cloth shawl—the same shawl with which the witch will dance in the play and which she will carry in her arms as if it were a baby—goes about clapping in imitation of the dragon. In the nonceremonial seasons, when life is a little less crowded, secular dance clubs go about with a tinkly orchestra, which has a hurdy-gurdy quality, and a little girl dancer, who dances with the young men of the village and, in between, dances as the witch, combining the beautiful ballet of the witch's disciples with being the witch herself and placing her foot firmly on the neck of a doll, enacting her role of bringing death.

Children stay in a deep resistant sleep during a childbirth in their houses, a sleep from which it is necessary to shake them awake, lest they see the witches which may come to kill the child. But the same children participate with delight in the play in which the witch child, after stealing a doll, born of a man and dressed as a woman, is chased up a tree or into a nearby stream. Children make puppets of banana leaf and parody the puppet master, especially the puppet master who performs with puppets in the daytime, whose screen has shrunk to a single line of thread. They draw in the sand with twigs while master artists work at little shallow wooden tables. And children may form clubs of their own, make their own dragon and witch, and progress about the village, collecting pennies for further finery for the masks.

If one follows these activities carefully, notes the expressions on the children's faces at different kinds of ceremonies, follows the same child on different occasions, and watches the play in which the children think they are reproducing the full theatricals, one begins to get clues to the dynamic mechanisms by which the children, born human like all other human children, become such very different people from other people—as Balinese. The mother who teases her child—who borrows a baby to provoke its jealousy, although preventing any expression of jealousy of a real sibling; who borrows a baby to set on its head, although at the same time protecting its head from real insult—has learned that all this is a safe game. When she watches the witch dance and watches the men and women who have gone into trance and are slow in coming out, she watches with the same relaxed enjoyment or ready criticism for some ritual or technical defect with which she watches the trance dance in which children dance as goddesses. But the child, teased into a violent temper, screaming and clawing to get the borrowed baby away from his mother's breast, has not yet learned that all this is safe. In his intensity and grief, in his fervent acceptance of his mother's theatrical amends for a real hurt, he still shows a capacity for hurt which will not be manifest later. Even as he withdraws from the recurrently disappointing sequences which have no climax, he learns to trust the arts, and he learns to avoid hurting responsiveness to human stimulation.

The faces of the children who watch the trance dance in which little girls replace dancing wooden puppets—and as child dancers are indulged by their parents and willful in their demands—are as relaxed as their parents' faces. But during the witch dance the children's faces are strained and anxious. When the witch dances or when some woman worshiper in the temple is possessed by the witch, the fingers are flexed backward in a gesture of fear, spoken of as *kapar*—the gesture made by a baby falling or a man falling from a tree—for the witch is both frightening and afraid, the picture of Fear itself. But when children play the witch, especially when they play her without benefit of costume or music or any of the elements which accompany the finished ritual, their hands are bent like claws, and they threaten an attack in witchlike gestures which can be found in many parts of the world. When the young men, who, as followers of the dragon, fall down before the witch's magic, thrust their daggers against their breasts, they thrust them in response to an intolerable itching feeling in their breasts—a possible reciprocal to the mother's breast during the period when they were so teased, provoked, and given only theatrical climaxes.

When Balinese children are frightened of strangers or strange situations, their elders shout at them, "Don't show fear!" and they learn not to run but to stand stock still, often with their hands pressed over their eyes. In situations of danger or uncertainty—during childbirth in a tiny one-room house, after an accident for which one may be blamed—children and older people also fall into a deep sleep from which it is hard to rouse them.

The Balinese move easily in a group. A whole village may make a pilgrimage of two or three days to make offerings at the seaside or in the high mountains. A troupe of Balinese went to the Paris Exposition in 1931, and a troupe visited New York in 1952. But one Balinese, isolated from those he knows and taken to a strange place, wilts and sickens; people say it is because he is *paling*—disoriented—the word used for trance, insanity, for being drunk, confused, or lost. . . .

Following the children as they grow up reveals that, even within the simultaneity of ritual satisfaction and individual fear, the capacity to enjoy such rituals, to dance the lovely dances and fill the air with music, has been—in the case of the Balinese—developed at certain costs. The culture contains—or did contain until the recent upheavals about which we know little—ritual solutions for the instabilities it created, and the people, on their little island, were safe. But it was the safety of a tightrope dancer, beautiful and precarious.

Eighty Years and More
Elizabeth Cady Stanton

Elizabeth Cady Stanton was born in 1815 and died in 1902. Daughter of a well-known lawyer, congressman, and judge, she grew up in Johnstown, New York, in the midst of relative wealth and privilege. As a child she visited her father's law office. There she encountered married women who were being legally deprived of their property or the custody of their children. Impressed with their plight, she became a tireless advocate of woman's rights. In this short and poignant excerpt from her autobiography, we catch a glimpse of female childhood as it was lived in families of the educated Eastern establishment in the early 19th century. Servants, a house large enough to contain a garret and a cellar filled with food for nibbling and nooks for playing hide and seek, and above all time to devote to activities such as studying Greek or learning to manage a horse were luxuries that only a few could afford. Rarer still perhaps, even in this environment, was the opportunity for young women to transcend the cultural message that girls were "an inferior order of beings" and to become, as Elizabeth Cady Stanton became, a national leader in the fight to change that view.

With several generations of vigorous, enterprising ancestors behind me, I commenced the struggle of life under favorable circumstances on the 12th day of November, 1815, the same year that my father, Daniel Cady, a distinguished lawyer and judge in the State of New York, was elected to Congress. Perhaps the excitement of a political campaign, in which my mother took the deepest interest, may have had an influence on my prenatal life and given me the strong desire that I have always felt to participate in the rights and duties of government.

My father was a man of firm character and unimpeachable integrity, and yet sensitive and modest to a painful degree. There were but two places in which he felt at ease—in the courthouse and at his own fireside. Though gentle and tender, he had such a dignified repose and reserve of manner that, as children, we regarded him with fear rather than affection.

My mother, Margaret Livingston, a tall, queenly looking woman, was courageous, self-reliant, and at her ease under all circumstances and in all places. She was the

Stanton, Elizabeth Cady. (1898). *Eighty Years and More: Reminiscences, 1815-1897.* NY: European Publishing Company. pp. 3-8, 20-23.

daughter of Colonel James Livingston, who took an active part in the War of the Revolution. . . .

The first event engraved on my memory was the birth of a sister when I was four years old. It was a cold morning in January when the brawny Scotch nurse carried me to see the little stranger, whose advent was a matter of intense interest to me for many weeks after. The large, pleasant room with the white curtains and bright wood fire on the hearth, where panada, catnip, and all kinds of little messes which we were allowed to taste were kept warm, was the center of attraction for the older children. I heard so many friends remark, "What a pity it is she's a girl!" that I felt a kind of compassion for the little baby. True, our family consisted of five girls and only one boy, but I did not understand at that time that girls were considered an inferior order of beings.

To form some idea of my surroundings at this time, imagine a two-story White frame house with a hall through the middle, rooms on either side, and a large back building with grounds on the side and rear. . . .

Our favorite resorts in the house were the garret and cellar. In the former were barrels of hickory nuts, and, on a long shelf, large cakes of maple sugar and all kinds of dried herbs and sweet flag; spinning wheels, a number of small White cotton bags filled with bundles, marked in ink, "silk," "cotton," "flannel," "calico," etc., as well as ancient masculine and feminine costumes. Here we would crack the nuts, nibble the sharp edges of the maple sugar, chew some favorite herb, play ball with the bags, whirl the old spinning wheels, dress up in our ancestors' clothes, and take a bird's-eye view of the surrounding country from an enticing scuttle hole. This was forbidden ground; but, nevertheless, we often went there on the sly, which only made the little escapades more enjoyable.

The cellar of our house was filled, in winter, with barrels of apples, vegetables, salt meats, cider, butter, pounding barrels, washtubs, etc., offering admirable nooks for playing hide and seek. Two tallow candles threw a faint light over the scene on certain occasions. This cellar was on a level with a large kitchen where we played blind man's bluff and other games when the day's work was done. These two rooms are the center of many of the merriest memories of my childhood days.

I can recall three colored men, Abraham, Peter, and Jacob, who acted as menservants in our youth. In turn they would sometimes play on the banjo for us to dance, taking real enjoyment in our games. . . .

Johnstown was to me a gloomy-looking town. The middle of the streets was paved with large cobblestones, over which the farmer's wagons rattled from morning till night, while the sidewalks were paved with very small cobblestones, over which we carefully picked our way, so that free and graceful walking was out of the question. The streets were lined with solemn poplar trees, from which small yellow worms were continually dangling down. Next to the Prince of Darkness, I feared these worms. They were harmless, but the sight of one made me tremble. So many people shared in this feeling that the poplars were all cut down and elms planted in their stead. The Johnstown academy and churches were large square buildings, painted White, surrounded by these same somber poplars, each edifice having a doleful bell which seemed to be ever tolling for school, funerals, church, or prayer meetings. Next to the worms, those clanging bells filled me with the utmost dread; they seemed like so many warnings of an eternal future. Visions of the Inferno were strongly impressed on my childish imagination. It was thought, in those days, that firm faith in hell and the devil was the greatest help to virtue. It certainly made me very unhappy whenever my mind dwelt on such teachings, and I have always had my doubts of the virtue that is based on the fear of punishment.

Perhaps I may be pardoned a word devoted to my appearance in those days. I have been told that I was a plump little girl, with very fair skin, rosy cheeks, good features, dark-brown hair, and laughing blue eyes. A student in my father's office . . . told me one day, after conning my features carefully, that I had one defect which he could remedy. "Your eyebrows should be darker and heavier," said he, "and if you will let me shave them once or twice, you will be much improved." I consented, and, slight as my eyebrows were, they seemed to have had some expression, for the loss of them had a most singular effect on my appearance. Everybody, including even the operator, laughed at my odd-looking face, and I was in the depths of humiliation during the period while my eyebrows were growing out again. It is scarcely necessary for me to add that I never allowed the young man to repeat the experiment, although strongly urged to do so. . .

When I was eleven years old, two events occurred which changed considerably the current of my life. My only brother, who had just graduated from Union College, came home to die. A young man of great talent and promise, he was the pride of my father's heart. We early felt that this son filled a larger place in our father's affections and future plans than the five daughters together. Well do I remember how tenderly he watched my brother in his last illness, the sighs and tears he gave vent to as he slowly walked up and down the hall, and, when the last sad moment came, and we were all assembled to say farewell in the silent chamber of death, how broken were his utterances as he knelt and prayed for comfort and support. I still recall, too, going into the large darkened parlor to see my brother, and finding the casket, mirrors, and pictures all draped in White, and my father seated by his side, pale and immovable. As he took no notice of me, after standing a long while, I climbed upon his knee, when he mechanically put his arm about me and, with my head resting against his beating heart, we both sat in silence, he thinking of the wreck of all his hopes in the loss of a dear son, and I wondering what could be said or done to fill the void in his breast. At length he heaved a deep sigh and said: "Oh, my daughter, I wish you were a boy!" Throwing my arms about his neck, I replied: "I will try to be all my brother was."

Then and there I resolved that I would not give so much time as heretofore to play, but would study and strive to be at the head of all my classes and thus delight my father's heart. All that day and far into the night I pondered the problem of boyhood. I thought that the chief thing to be done in order to equal boys was to be learned and courageous. So I decided to study Greek and learn to manage a horse. . . .

Soon after this I began to study Latin, Greek, and mathematics with a class of boys in the Academy, many of whom were much older than I. For three years one boy kept his place at the head of the class, and I always stood next. Two prizes were offered in Greek. I strove for one and took the second. How well I remember my joy in receiving that prize. There was no sentiment of ambition, rivalry, or triumph over my companions, nor feeling of satisfaction in receiving this honor in the presence of those assembled on the day of the exhibition. One thought alone filled my mind. "Now," said I, "my father will be satisfied with me." So, as soon as we were dismissed, I ran down the hill, rushed breathless into his office, laid the new Greek Testament, which was my prize, on his table and exclaimed: "There, I got it!" He took up the book, asked me some questions about the class, the teachers, the spectators, and, evidently pleased, handed it back to me. Then, while I stood looking and waiting for him to say something which would show that he recognized the equality of the daughter with the son, he kissed me on the forehead and exclaimed, with a sigh, "Ah, you should have been a boy!"

Mountain Wolf Woman, Sister of Crashing Thunder: The Autobiography of a Winnebago Indian
Mountain Wolf Woman, as told to N. O. Lurie

Mountain Wolf Woman was born among the Winnebago people in 1884 and died in 1960. Growing up in Wisconsin, the youngest of eight children and sister of Crashing Thunder, whose autobiography had been published in 1920 by anthropologist Paul Radin, she was raised in one of the last generations to experience childhood defined by the "old ways." Historically much of the life of the community revolved around activities necessary to the group's survival. Winnebago men were hunters and trappers, while women gathered wild food and tilled the soil. As soon as children were old enough to help, they too were expected to contribute to tribal subsistence. It is from this perspective that Mountain Wolf Woman writes. In this excerpt from her reminiscences, transcribed by anthropologist Nancy Lurie, we are given a glimpse into a world of female childhood in which the gathering and preparation of food, story-telling, ritual, and taboo loomed large: a childhood later in time but far more traditional than that of Elizabeth Cady Stanton.

In March we usually travelled to the Mississippi River close to La Crosse, sometimes even across the river, and then we returned again in the last part of May. We used to live at a place on the edge of the Mississippi called Caved In Breast's Grave. My father, brother-in-law and brothers used to trap there for muskrats. When they killed the muskrats my mother used to save the bodies and hang them up there in great numbers. When there were a lot of muskrats then they used to roast them on a rack. They prepared a lot of wood and built a big fire. They stuck four crotched posts into the ground around the fire and placed poles across the crotches. Then they removed the burning wood and left the embers. They put a lot of fine wood crisscross and very dense on the frame. On this the muskrats were roasted, placed all above the fireplace. As the muskrats began roasting, the grease dripped off nice and brown and then the women used long pointed sticks to turn them over and over. The muskrat meat made a lot of noise as it cooked. When these were cooked, the women put them aside and placed some more on the rack. They cooked a great amount of muskrats—when they were cooled, the women packed them together and stored them for summer use.

In the spring when my father went trapping on the Mississippi and the weather

Lurie, N.O. (1961). *Mountain Wolf Woman, Sister of Crashing Thunder: The Autobiography of a Winnebago Indian*. Ann Arbor, MI: University of Michigan Press. pp. 8-9, 20-23.

became very pleasant once my sister said, "It is here that they dig yellow water lily roots." So, we all went out, my mother and sisters and everybody. When we got to a slough where the water lilies were very dense, they took off their shoes, put on old dresses and went wading into the water. They used their feet to hunt for the roots. They dug them out with their feet and then the roots floated up to the surface. Eventually, my second oldest sister happened upon one. My sister took one of the floating roots, wrapped it about with the edge of her blouse and tucked it into her belt. I thought she did this because it was the usual thing to do. I saw her doing this and when I happened upon a root I took it and did the same thing. I put it in my belt too. And then everybody laughed at me! "Oh, little Siga is doing something! She has a water lily root in her belt!" Everybody laughed at me and yelled at me. My sister had done that because she was pregnant. I suppose she did that to ward off something because she was pregnant. Thus she would not affect the baby and would have good luck finding the roots. Because I saw her do that, I did the same thing, and so they teased me.

When they dug up a lot of roots in this fashion they put them in a gunny sack, filling it half full and even more. Then we carried them back to camp and my mother and all my sisters scraped them. The roots have an outside covering and they scraped that off and sliced them—they look something like a banana. The women then strung the slices and hung them up to dry in order to store them. They dried a great amount, flour sacks full. During the summer they sometimes cooked them with meat and they were really delicious. . . .

We used to blacken our cheeks with charcoal at the time father left in the morning to go hunting. We used coals from the fire to blacken our cheeks and we did not eat all day. I used to play outside but my older sister used to sit indoors and weave yarn belts. When father returned from hunting in the evening he used to say to us, "Go cry to the Thunders." When father was ready to eat he would give us tobacco and say to us, "Here, go cry to the Thunders." Just as it was getting dark my sister and I used to go off a certain distance and she would say to me, "Go stand by a tree and I am going to go farther on." We used to stand there and look at the stars and cry to the Thunders. This is what we used to sing:

Oh Good Spirits
Will they pity me? Here am I, pleading.

We used to sing and scatter tobacco, standing there and watching the stars and the moon. We used to cry because, after all, we were hungry. We used to think we were pitied. We really wanted to mean what we were saying.

When we finished with our song we scattered tobacco at the foot of the tree and returned home. When we got back home father ate and we ate too. We did not eat all day, only at night, and when we had finished eating we put the dishes away. Then father used to say, "All right, prepare your bedding and go to bed and I will tell you some stories." I really enjoyed listening to my father tell stories. Everybody, the entire household, was very quiet and in this atmosphere my father used to tell stories. He

125

used to tell myths, the sacred stories, and that is why I also know some myths. I do not know all of them any more, I just remember parts of stories. . . .

[Another time] the family went on a short hunting trip. After that they went off to find cranberries and on our return we stopped at the home of grandfather Nâqi-Johnga. There it was that mother told me how it is with little girls when they become women. "Some time," she said, "that is going to happen to you. From about the age of thirteen years this happens to girls. When that happens to you, run to the woods and hide some place. You should not look at any one, not even a glance. If you look at a man you will contaminate his blood. Even a glance will cause you to be an evil person. When women are in that condition they are unclean." Once, after our return to grandfather's house, I was in that condition when I awoke in the morning.

Because mother had told me to do so, I ran quite far into the woods where there were some bushes. The snow was still on the ground and the trees were just beginning to bud. In the woods there was a broken tree and I sat down under this fallen tree. I bowed my head with my blanket wrapped over me and there I was, crying and crying. Since they had forbidden me to look around, I sat there with my blanket over my head. I cried. Then, suddenly I heard the sound of voices. My sister Hinakega and my sister-in-law found me. Because I had not come back in the house, they had looked for me. They saw my tracks in the snow, and by my tracks they saw that I ran. They trailed me and found me. "Stay here," they said. "We will go and make a shelter for you," and they went home again. Near the water's edge of a big creek, at the rapids of East Fork River, they built a little wigwam. They covered it with canvas. They built a fire and put straw there for me, and then they came to get me. There I sat in the little wigwam. I was crying. It was far, about a quarter of a mile from home. I was crying and I was frightened. Four times they made me sleep there. I never ate. There they made me fast. That is what they made me do. . . .

7

Changing Families
and Systems of Support

In 1910 Jewish settlers founded the first kibbutz in Israel. The kibbutzim were voluntary communities organized around a collective form of economic and social life. Most adopted a nontraditional, communal approach to childrearing.

Rather than being housed with their parents, children lived together, first in infant and then in toddler houses, and later in mixed-sex groups in a communal children's house. During the day, care was provided by a surrogate parent, a woman called a *metaplete*. Except during the neonatal period, when mothers visited regularly to nurse their newborns, contacts between parents and children tool place only on Saturdays and in the hours after work.

At the time it was feared that if mothers were not readily available, their children might suffer a "partial maternal deprivation." Research indicated, however, that by adolescence, children in the kibbutzim had developed into generally well-balanced individuals. Relative to others of their age, they even exhibited a reduced tendency to sibling rivalry and a greater concern for the social good.

Communal childrearing appeared to work, and some within the kibbutz movement hoped that conventional ideas about the role of the family would gradually wither away. Paradoxically, however, just the reverse occurred. As the kibbutzim became better established, communities were no longer composed of isolated immigrants who felt the need to band together for survival. Family-style housing, which had not even been an option in the early years, became available. Factors such as these led those living in the kibbutzim to demand a return to family-style living. Given the opportunity, even those adults who had been raised communally as children seemed to see the family as the preferred child-rearing unit.

• INTRODUCTION •

Since the late 1950s, American family life has undergone rapid change. Alterations in the career patterns of women; a general aging of the population; higher rates of divorce, remarriage, and the blending of families; and an increase in the number of unmarried mothers who choose to raise their own children have led to fundamental shifts in the nature of the American family. Chief among these changes has been a sharp rise in the number of households headed by a single mother.

In the three readings presented here, we examine contemporary family change in the context of history, culture, and social policy. Although many of the characteristics of the modern American family have historical precedent, the existence of households headed by single women with children, relatively isolated from the community and forced to rely on their own economic and psychological resources, is largely a 20th century phenomenon. Among African Americans, historical, marital, and socioeconomic factors have encouraged single mothers to live within extended families, frequently with the child's maternal grandmother and one or more additional kin. Extended families provide single mothers with communal, psychological, and sometimes economic support; and when the support of an extended family is available, mothers and their children tend to fare better.

Governments also provide support. Indeed, family and child support policies have a major impact on single mothers and their children. From a comparative analysis of family policy in Europe and the United States, it is apparent that American lawmakers, influenced in part by traditional antipathy to forms of family life that depart from our "ideal," have yet to face the full implications of recent family change. Ultimately we may be required to choose between protecting children at the expense of supporting alternatives to the traditional family or adopting policies aimed at preserving the "ideal" form of the family at children's expense.

• • •

Domestic Revolutions: A Social History of American Family Life

Steven Mintz and Susan Kellogg

In a short and powerfully written introduction to the history of American family life, Steven Mintz and Susan Kellogg describe ways in which American families no longer correspond to the post-World War II ideal to which many Americans subscribed. Briefly contrasting the nature of family life in the colonial period with that in the early nineteenth and twentieth centuries, the authors make it clear that recent rapid change in family patterns has had several historical precedents. They suggest that the roots of this change can be found in economic, demographic, and social forces, including transition from domestic industry to factory production, reduction in fertility within marriage, gradual aging of the population, and radical transformations in women's roles. They conclude with an eloquent summary of factors that both contribute to and conflict with the maintenance of strong, stable bonds in the contemporary family.

Until quite recently, most Americans subscribed to a common conception of a "proper" family life—a set of beliefs so widespread that it was largely taken for fact. These were some of the givens of that conception:

A family comprises a married couple and their minor children living together in a common residence

The father, as head of household, should single-handedly earn the family's income and determine the family's residence, and his surname will become that of his wife and children

The mother's primary responsibilities should be to serve as her husband's companion and helper and as facilitator of her children's education and development, staying home and devoting herself full-time to the tasks of child-rearing and homemaking

Marriage is a lifelong commitment and sex should be confined to marriage

Mintz, Steven & Kellogg, Susan. (1988). Domestic Revolutions: A Social History of American Family Life. New York: The Free Press. Introduction. pp. xiii-xx.

129

Parents have exclusive responsibilities for their children's care until the children enter kindergarten and, that even after that time, parents are free to discipline and care for their children as they see fit, without outside interference

Families that fail to conform to one or more of these givens may be regarded as "troubled" or "problem" families.

Over the past two decades, these givens have been subjected to profound inquiry and attack in light of contemporary mores. Today the term "family" is no longer attached exclusively to conjugal or nuclear families comprising a husband, wife, and their dependent children. It is applied to almost any grouping of two or more people domiciled together. These family groupings include single-parent households, blended families made up of stepparents and stepchildren or adoptive parents and their children, and couples cohabiting outside wedlock, including gay couples.

American family life today is markedly different from what it was even two decades ago. Over the past fifteen years, the divorce rate has doubled, as has the number of female-headed families. Today more than half of all mothers with school-age children work outside the home, more than a quarter of all families with children have just one parent, and more than half of all three-to-five year olds are enrolled in nursery schools or day-care centers. Over the course of a generation, the number of children per family has declined by half.

These dramatic changes constitute a fundamental reorientation in American family patterns. But as sudden and far-reaching as they are, they have precedents. Over the past 300 years, American families have undergone a series of far-reaching "domestic revolutions" that profoundly altered their familial life, repeatedly transforming their demographic characteristics, organizational structure, functions, conceptions, and emotional dynamics.

Although the family is seen as the social institution most resistant to change, it is, in fact, as deeply embedded in the historical process as any other institution. The claim that it is essentially a conservative institution—an island of stability in a sea of social, political, and economic change—is largely an illusion. If the family is a conservative institution in the sense that it transmits the moral and cultural values of one generation to the next, it is not conservative in the sense of being static. In structure, role, and conception, the American family has changed dramatically over time.

Three centuries ago the American family was the fundamental economic, educational, political, and religious unit of society. The family, and not the isolated individual, was the unit of which church and state were made. The household was not only the locus of production, it was also the institution primarily responsible for the education of children, the transfer of craft skills, and the care of the elderly and the infirm.

During the early colonial era, the family performed many functions that have since been relegated to nonfamilial institutions. The family was an integral part of the larger society. It was a "little commonwealth," governed by the same principles of hierarchy and deference as the larger society. During the seventeenth century, a sharp division between economics, religion, law, and politics and family life was unimaginable. All these aspects of life were part of a single, unitary, mutually reinforcing matrix.

Compared to seventeenth-century families, today's families are much more isolated from public life and specialized in functions. The family has not only ceased to be a productive unit, but its roles in caring for the aged, providing relief for the poor, and educating the young have increasingly been assumed by public institutions, ranging from government social agencies to insurance companies, banks, public charities, hospitals, and schools. As many of its traditional economic, educational, and welfare functions were transferred outside the home, the family ceased to be a largely autonomous, independent, self-contained, and self-sufficient unit. Instead the family has tended to concentrate on a small number of remaining functions—the socialization of children and the provision of emotional support and affection. . . .

By the time Alexis de Tocqueville visited the United States in 1831 and 1832, he found family patterns vastly different from those of the settlers who had left England in the seventeenth century. The older conception of the family as a "little commonwealth," a microcosm of the larger society, had receded and been replaced by a new image of the family as a "haven in a heartless world," a bastion of morality and tender feeling and a refuge from the aggressive and selfish world of commerce. The family had become a private place, a shelter for higher redeeming values and a shelter from the temptations and corruptions of the outside world. Relations within this new "democratic" family were less formal and hierarchical than they had been in the seventeenth- or eighteenth-century household. Marriages were more and more based on romantic love, relations between husbands and wives had grown increasingly affectionate and egalitarian, children stayed at home longer than before, and parents devoted increased attention to the care and nurture of their offspring. In this family, relations were organized around the principle of "separate spheres," according to which each family member had a special role, or sphere, appropriate to his or her age and gender.

During the early years of the twentieth century, a host of educators, legal scholars, social workers, and academic social scientists created a new ideal of family life that they termed the "companionate family." Responding to an alarming rise in the divorce rate, the falling birthrate, the revolution in morals and manners, and the changing position of women, these experts extolled a new ideal of family life in which spouses would be friends and lovers and parents and children would be pals. According to the new companionate ideal, relations within the family would not be based on patriarchal authority but on affection and mutual interest. The traditional conception of marriage as a sacred duty or obligation gave way to a new ideal of sexual satisfaction, companionship, and emotional support. To achieve this ideal, influential groups recommended liberalized divorce laws; programs of marriage counseling, domestic science, and sex education; and permissive child-rearing practices stressing freedom and self-expression over impulse-control.

Although the intellectual roots of the companionate family lay in the 1920s, the impact of this new ideal of family life was delayed by the depression and World War II, only to resurface dramatically after the war. By the mid-1950s, the ideal of the companionate family seemed well on the way to fulfillment. Family "togetherness" became a cultural watchword. Couples married earlier than their parents had, and women bore more children, had them at younger ages, and spaced them closer together. The increase in the divorce rate was lower than in preceding years. And rising real income permitted a growing majority of the nation's families to buy their own homes. At the same time, outside institutions continued to take on traditional family functions. As the proportion of the population over the age of sixty-five grew, the economic burden of supporting the elderly was increasingly assumed by public and private pensions. Similarly, more responsibility for the training of young people fell to separate age-segregated institutions.

Since the late 1950s, confidence that the American family is growing progressively stronger has eroded. The family, once viewed as the deepest source of affection and emotional support, increasingly came to be seen as an impediment to individual self-fulfillment. In those years the relationship between family values and the values of individualism and personal autonomy has grown ever more problematic. One source of strain lies in a continuing escalation in the expectations of what marriage can and ought to fulfill. Rising expectations have proved difficult to meet, and the result has been mounting divorce rates. A further source of strain has been individuals' increased desire for personal fulfillment, especially the middle-class belief that happiness can only be achieved through a successful, independent career. Career expectations frequently come into conflict with a more traditional view of marriage as an institution in which the spouses, particularly the wife, must sacrifice for the good of the family unit. Increasingly, this desire for greater personal freedom and fulfillment has been met by a proliferation of nonmarital relationships—most notably, a sharp rise in the number of couples cohabiting outside of marriage.

The distinguishing characteristic of American family life since 1960 has been increasing diversity in family arrangements. Today, as a growing number of young adults defer marriage and more and more elderly live by themselves, nearly a quarter of all American households consist of just a single member. As the divorce rate climbed, the number of stepfamilies increased, and now more than a tenth of the nation's children live with one stepparent and one natural parent. Higher divorce rates coupled with a sharp increase in the number of children born to single women have led to a marked upturn in the number of female-headed families. Female-headed families now account for 13 percent of White families and 44 percent of Black families.

Today the United States is a society without a clear unitary set of family ideals and values. Many Americans are groping for a new paradigm of American family life, but in the meantime a profound sense of confusion and ambivalence reigns. One consequence of this confusion has been deep social division over which responsibilities the individual family should shoulder and which should be assumed by other, nonfamilial institutions. As a society we vigorously debate the pros and cons of institutionalized child care, the emotional and psychological costs of divorce, and the advantages and disadvantages of placing seriously ill older persons in nursing homes or the severely mentally ill in custodial institutions, but the nation has found it increasingly difficult to agree on a plan of action.

Since the 1960s America has become a permissive society, not merely in the superficial sense of becoming more open and tolerant, but in the more profound sense of becoming reluctant to accept responsibility for the economic and social consenquences of social change—most notably for such phenomena as increasing numbers of divorces, working mothers, and teenage pregnancies. Individuals, families, and society as a whole have been hesitant to accept full responsibility for the care of young children, the elderly, the poor, the handicapped, or the mentally ill or for sex education or questions of birth control. Responsibility has been splintered, and as a result many family-related problems are dealt with in a piecemeal or makeshift manner. Unable to decide whether further to encourage the transfer of traditional family functions to public institutions or to help families to become more capable of handling these problems on their own, Americans have responded with a pervasive sense of uncertainty.

How are we to explain the extraordinary evolution of the American family over the past four centuries? The causes of familial change cannot be reduced to any simple formula. The critical transformations that have occurred in the family are aspects of broader demographic, economic, social, and philosophic transformations that have reshaped all aspects of American life. Three fundamental factors, however, stand out.

Changes in the economy have been a principal force for change in all other areas. Three centuries ago most American families were largely self-sufficient agricultural units. Few families sought to maximize their income by producing specialized goods destined for distant markets; their goal was to build up family farms or family enterprises in order to maintain familial independence, to protect family property and status and produce dowries or an inheritance for their children. Although specialized craftsmen made shoes, saddles, hats, iron implements, and men's clothing, most families produced most of the goods they needed, including food, furniture, cloth, soap, candles, and leather. Parental authority was reinforced by control of property (land) or a craft skill that could be transmitted to the children. The family was not merely an emotional unit; it was also an interdependent unit of labor in which all family members contributed to a collective "family economy."

By the late eighteenth century, a marked loosening of the economic relationships among family members had taken place—a transition marked by parents' diminishing control over their children's choice of marriage partners. Household self-sufficiency declined as a growing number of farm households began to specialize in the production of cash crops and to use the proceeds to purchase household goods produced outside the home. Domestic industries that had employed large numbers of women and older children gradually disappeared as an increasing proportion of goods were produced in factories or other businesses. For the middle class, older children ceased to be economic assets, no longer employed in household industries or fostered out as servants or apprentices. Instead they became economic dependents requiring significant investments in the form of education. The effect of these changes was to transform the family from a public unit serving as workplace, a school, and a welfare agency into a more private, specialized unit.

Another potent force for change in American family life has been demography. Such fundamental characteristics of a population as age distribution and the proportion of the sexes exert strong influences on the size and composition of families, the marriage rate, the death rate, the birthrate, and other attributes of family life. Two key demographic changes have had especially far-reaching consequences for family life. The first is a gradual reduction of fertility within marriage. Beginning in the last quarter of the eighteenth century, American women began bearing fewer children, spacing children closer together, and ceasing childbearing at earlier ages. Smaller families meant that parents could invest more emotion and financial resources in each child, while closer spacing of children meant that mothers could expect to devote fewer years to bearing and rearing young children.

A second fundamental demographic change has been a gradual aging of the population. Some 150 years ago the average age in the United States was just seventeen, a figure comparable to the youngest populations in the world today. Now the median age has climbed to nearly thirty, giving the United States one of the oldest populations in the world. This shift means that a growing proportion of the American population now experiences aspects of family life less well known in the past, such as a period of marriage when children are no longer responsibilities, grandparenthood, and prolonged widowhood.

A third basic force for familial change lies in a series of profound transformations in women's roles. During the early nineteenth century, as production was increasingly transferred outside the home, married women lost many traditional "productive" economic roles. Many middle-class women concentrated on motherhood and household management. According to a new conception of sex roles, women's task was to shape the character of the children, make the home a haven of peace and order, and exert a moral and uplifting influence on men.

Especially since World War II, this process of privatizing the role of women has been reversed as the number of married women participating in the labor force has dramatically increased. A massive influx of wives and mothers into the work force has, in turn, made wives less financially dependent on their husbands and called into question traditional assumptions about the sexual division of roles in housekeeping and child rearing.

For over three centuries, Americans have worried about the future of the family. Within decades of the Puritans' arrival in Massachusetts Bay Colony, Puritan jeremiads were already decrying the increasing fragility of marriage, the growing selfishness and irresponsibility of parents, and the increasing rebelliousness of children. Despite nearly four centuries of fears that the family is decaying, the institution has, of course, survived. But it has—for better and worse— changed in important ways.

Clearly, on the positive side of the ledger, families today are far less likely than those in the past to lose children as a result of high rates of infant mortality, and children are far less likely to be orphaned while growing up. Unlike parents in the past, parents now can anticipate seeing all of their children reach adulthood. Since mothers no longer bear children every two years after marriage until menopause or death, they can expect to spend a far smaller proportion of their adult lives rearing young children and can more easily combine family life with a career. And, finally, longer life expectancies and closer spacing of children mean that married couples can anticipate a period together after their children have ceased to be responsibilities.

At the same time, however, today's families are more isolated than their predecessors from the worlds of work, kinship, and community life, and there can be no doubt that the structural isolation of the contemporary family has made it in certain respects a more fragile institution. Shorn of traditional educational and productive functions, the stability of today's families rests on the tenuous basis of affection, compatibility, and mutual interest. Family members today are no longer tied together by their mutual participation in a collective family economy. As a result of smaller families and closer spacing of children, parents devote less time to the rearing of young children and have more time to ponder the quality of their interpersonal relations. Parental authority is no longer reinforced by control of property or craft skills or by the supervision of the surrounding community. Nor is authority buttressed by common sets of values held by large groups of people. Given the erosion of these earlier kinds of supports, it is not surprising to find that while families today are less likely to be disrupted by premature death, they are more vulnerable to divorce. The paradox of the modern American family is that while we attach far greater psychological and ideological significance to a happy family life than did our ancestors, our work lives, our emphasis on personal fulfillment, and our political behavior all conflict with strong, stable family bonds.

Child Development in the Context of the Black Extended Family
Melvin N. Wilson

As the previous article pointed out, the "ideal" nuclear American family—an original marriage, father the primary bread winner, and two or three children (sometimes called the "Dick and Jane" family)—is becoming progressively rarer on the American scene. One important and increasingly common alternative to this "ideal" is the extended family. Among African-Americans, extended families frequently involve a single mother and child living with the child's maternal grandmother and one or more additional kin. In this reading, Melvin Wilson describes historical, marital and interpersonal, and socioeconomic factors that have influenced the formation of the extended family in the African-American community. Pointing out that the impact of the extended family on the child appears to be more indirect than direct, he reviews evidence suggesting that extended family members are more likely to relieve the single mother of household tasks than to perform primary child care, that they increase the opportunity of interaction between adults but not between nonmaternal adults and children, and that they serve to provide the mother with emotional support.

. . . Extended families represent a significant proportion of families in the Black community. The Black child is surrounded by a kin organization of significant family associations and family influences that go beyond mother, father, and children to include parental, sibling, avuncular and cousin links of spouses and offspring. This article addresses two aspects of Black child development in the context of the extended family: factors that influence the formation of the extended family, and the direct and indirect influences of the extended family on the behavior of and relationship between extended family members.

The Formation of the Extended Family

The family is an ever-evolving system that responds to normal and nonnormal changes and events through adaptation of available family resources. The most typical instances of normal changes and events are marriage, the birth of the first child, the

Wilson, Melvin N. (1989). Child development in the context of the Black extended family. *American Psychologist, 44* (2). pp 180-185. [See the original article for a much more extensive set of citations.]

entrance of the first child into school, and the young adult child leaving home. Likewise, the nonnormal changes and events include divorce, hospitalization, and unemployment. Family resources depend on the ability of family members to contribute tangible help such as material support, income, child care, and assistance in performing household tasks, and nontangible help such as expressive interaction, emotional support, counseling, instruction, and social regulation. Families mitigate stress for their members by defining and addressing stressful situations as familial rather than individual concerns (Barbarin, 1983).

The extended family's central feature, the familial support network, is manifested by utilitarian procedures of propinquity, communication, and cooperation. A strong sense of familial obligation serves as the motivational rule that facilitates this system. Wilson (1986) asserted that nonnormal changes and events are a primary reason for the formation of extended-family support networks. A common stressful situation in the Black community is the lack of adequate adult resources in single-parent family units. The formation occurs when one family unit absorbs another one. Once formed, the extended family occupies most of the family life span. The formation of the extended family is facilitated by a constant interplay of complex historical, socioeconomic, and marital factors. In order to understand the Black extended family's impact on child development and family life, the factors that influence its formation must be considered.

Historical Factors

Historical accounts indicate the existence of strong familial affiliations among slaves even when the rules of slavery did not sanction such relationships (Flanagan, 1978; Genovese, 1976; Gutman, 1976). Because of the devastation of African families and kinship patterns caused by the slave trade, slaves invested non-kin with symbolic kin status; that is, they established fictive kin. As a result, African-American slave families and related kin groups emerged from the initial disruptions associated with enslavement and the early creation of symbolic kin networks. The development of multigenerational linkages among slave families was accompanied by a conception of family and kin obligations of mutual support and assistance. Reliably replicated historical studies suggest that 70 percent of the children born into slavery were born into long-standing conjugal relationships (Agresti, 1978; Gutman, 1976; Otto & Burns, 1983); family units were eventually reconstituted or blended into step-family situations when families were separated when a member was sold to another plantation (Dykstra & Manfra, 1985; Meacham, 1983); and plantations usually contained large extended families by 1825 (Cohen, 1984; Genovese, 1976; Herskovits, 1966). Patterns of familial organization evolved over successive generations and led to the emergence from slavery of families that were multigenerational, collateral, and extranuclear.

Marital and Interpersonal Factors

Demographic and census research indicate that the composition of Black families changes frequently. For example, according to several studies, 62 percent of Black parents were divorced, separated, widowed, or never married; 55 percent of Black births were to unmarried mothers; and 28 percent of Black births were to adolescents (Glick, 1976; 1981; "Black Population," 1984; Reid, 1982; Sweet, 1977). The rates of Black family status changes suggest that Black children are exposed to a significant level of fluidity in the formation of families. Black low-income, extended, and one-parent families are more likely to make frequent changes in their living arrangements than are their respective counterparts (Furstenberg, 1980; Slesinger, 1980; Smith, 1980; Stack, 1974). Adolescent and single, adult mothers often change their living situations. Such situations include independent living, cohabitation, marital arrangements, and living with their families of origin.

Many young single mothers ultimately return to reside with their family of origin, resulting in the formation of extended families. Generally, the single mother's increased participation in extended family activities appears to be related to her feelings of aloneness, powerlessness, and alienation (McLanahan, Wedemeyer, & Adelbery, 1981; Smith, 1980).

Socioeconomic Factors

The persistent and concentrated poverty of high proportions of Black families, especially single-parent Black families, is probably the most important factor correlated with extended family formation. Although most Black families are not poor, 31 percent of them in recent decades lived in poverty. Among one-parent families, poverty is particularly evident—52.9 percent of Black one-parent families were classified as poor (Duncan, 1968; Reid, 1982; U.S. Bureau of the Census, 1986). Poverty is often considered by people to be the cause of chronic stress. Belle, Longfellow, and Makosky (1982), for example, found that Black single mothers who experienced a high frequency of nonnormal changes and events more often blamed their depressive conditions on low income and chronic money problems than on any other stressful nonnormal events. It is the chronic effects of low income that present the most difficulties for Black families. . . .

The Impact of Black Extended Families on Children and Their Caregivers

The direct and indirect influences of the extended family on its family members reflect the successive adjustments to and interactions with a changing American environment. Overall, the literature suggests that the impact of extended family may have more indirect than direct effects on the child. The involvement of extended-family members in one-parent families facilitates the mothers' participation in self-improvement activities, increases the quality of child care, and reduces negative effects of single parenting. Clearly, more research is needed on the relation between family structures and child outcomes. The limited amount of research on the direct effects of the extended family on child development has typically been focused on the effect of a grandmother's presence on the children of adolescent mothers.

Studies of parenting by adolescent mothers who live in three-generation households indicate that child care is provided by both mothers and grandmothers (Badger, 1981; Field, Widmayer, Stringer, & Ignatoff, 1980; Hardy, King, Shipp, & Welcher, 1981). When the grandmother is primarily a homemaker, she is typically the child's primary caregiver. Adolescent mothers spend less time performing child-care tasks, because they are involved in some form of self-improvement. In a home observation study, adolescent mothers were slightly less active in playing with, talking to, and teaching their twelve- to twenty-four- month-old children in the grandmother's presence (Field & Ignotoff, 1981). In the mother's presence, grandmothers spent more time watching the mother-infant interaction than interacting either with mother and infant or with the infant alone. The total amount of child care the infant received was not lessened, however, because of the combined interaction time of mothers and infants and grandmothers and infants.

Grandmothers may represent a model for effective caregiving in that they reported more responsive and less punitive interactions with their infant grandchildren than did their teenaged daughters (Stevens, 1984). Stevens has suggested that the presence of a young infant seems to provide the context in which the grandmother helps the young mother acquire accurate information about her baby's normative development. The young mothers reported feeling that their mothers supported them in their role as parents. Living in the extended-family household offset some of the negative outcomes of adolescent extramarital pregnancy. Consistent with this suggestion, infants' attachment classification, in general, was more likely to change from anxiously attached at twelve months to securely attached at eighteen months if the infants were living in three-generation households composed of their mothers, their maternal grandmothers, and their mothers' siblings (Egeland & Sroufe, 1981). Furthermore, Crockenberg (1981) found that the presence of a responsive, sensitive grandmother seemed to buffer the infant against the deleterious influence of an insensitive mother.

Extended family structure may support children's long-term achievement and social adjustments. Like children from two-parent families, children from families consisting of mothers and grandmothers, mothers and aunts, and mothers and others achieved and adjusted adequately (Kellam, Ensminger, & Turner, 1977; Kellam, Adams, Brown, & Ensminger, 1982). In contrast, children from families with mothers only or mothers and stepfathers were functioning below the rates of the other children. When one-parent families shared residence with their extended family, mothers exerted more parental control and children exerted less autonomy in family decision making than in one-adult family situations (Dornbush et al., 1985). Furthermore, adolescent children of one-parent families who lived with extended families participated in fewer deviant activities than did

139

adolescent children who lived in one-parent situations.

Several studies indicate that an extended family's involvement with child care indirectly benefited the child of an adolescent mother because it allows mothers the opportunity to improve their situations. Adolescent mothers who remained in their mother's household were more likely to complete school and were less likely to continue to receive public assistance when compared to adolescent mothers who set up separate households (Furstenberg & Crawford, 1978). Adolescent mothers who continued to live at home were less involved in child-care tasks, and thus were able to spend more time on self-improvement and were more connected to their peer social networks than were adolescent mothers who set up independent households. Variations in the amount, source, and impact of social support available to adolescent mothers depend on the mother's needs (Colletta 1981; Colletta & Lee, 1983). Studies have shown that adolescent mothers who attended school or worked outside the home received more assistance with child care, living arrangements, and housework, and they reported more peer group and individual support than did adolescents who neither worked outside the home nor attended school; they also more often reported feeling control over their lives.

The extended family also provides support to mother's whose children have special needs. For example, mothers of children experiencing chronic pain from sickle cell anemia depended most often on the child's father for emotional aid and encouragement, independent of whether the father was present or absent in the home (Slaughter & Dilworth-Anderson, 1985). But studies show that extended-family members offered more assistance when the father was absent than when he was present in the home. Mothers reported that the family members' assistance usually took the form of relieving the mother from other chores, such as cleaning, meal preparation, and transportation rather than direct assistance with the care of the sick child. Maternal kin assisted more often than paternal kin, and usually the mother's mother provided instrumental services, whereas the mother's sisters offered emotional support to the mother.

Research on the role of the extended family in normal, functional family situations has focused on the impact of family structure on perceived and actual child-rearing experiences. Grandmothers perceived themselves and were perceived as being actively involved in child-rearing activities (Wilson, 1984) and affecting the attitudes of their daughters (Staples & Smith, 1954) when the daughters lived with the family as opposed to when they lived in the community. Observational research indicates, however, that grandmothers act more as relievers than as primary caregivers (Wilson & Tolson, 1986).

Consistent with the research focusing on the support of grandmothers to mothers, recent studies on the involvement of elderly Blacks in extended-family activities have found that the elderly Black population had a high level of interaction and exchange in extended-family support systems, usually as the donors of services (Allen, 1979; Cantor, 1979; Hofferth, 1984; Mindel, 1980, 1983; Mutran, 1985; Rubenstein, 1971). These studies largely involved elderly Black women who generally reported being active in large familial networks. Grandmothers support their daughters and grandchildren in an extended-family system that mitigates the stresses of living in a one-parent family situation.

Conclusion

The extended-family organization is a coping mechanism with a long history. The extended family structure persists in Black communities because of a high incidence of poverty, unemployment, extramarital births, and marital dissolutions. Single mothers, elderly family members, and children of single-parent families are more involved in extended family activities than are their counterparts. Interestingly, the influence of the extended family is probably more indirect than direct. Usually, extended-family members relieve the single mother of household tasks rather than primary child care; they increase the opportunity of interaction between adults but not between nonmaternal adults and children, and they provide emotional support to the mother. . . .

References

Agresti, B. F. (1978). The first decades of freedom: Black families in a southern county, 1870-1885. *Journal of Marriage and the Family, 46,* 697-706.

Allen, W. R. (1979). Class, culture, and family organization: The effects of class and race on family structure in Urban America. *Journal of Comparative Family Studies, 10,* 301-313.

Badger, E. (1981). Effects of parent education program on teenage mothers and their offspring. In K. G. Scott, T. Field, & E. G. Robertson (Eds.), *Teenage parents and their offspring* (pp. 201-227). New York: Grune & Stratton.

Barbarin, O. A. (1983). Coping with ecological transitions by Black families: A psychosocial model. *Journal of Community Psychology, 11,* 308-322.

Belle, D., Longfellow, C., & Makosky, V. P. (1982). Stress, depression and the mother-child relationship: A report of a field study. *International Journal of Sociology of the Family, 12,* 251-263.

The Black population: A statistical view, 1970-82. (1984). *Monthly Labor Review, 107*(4), 44-51.

Cantor, M. A. (1979). Neighbors and friends: An overlooked resource in the informal support system. *Research on Aging, 1,* 434-463.

Cohen, M. (1984). The ethnomedicine of Garfina (Black Caribs) of Rio Tinto Honduras. *Anthropological Quarterly, 57,* 16-27.

Colletta. N. D. (1981). Social support and risk of maternal rejection by adolescent mothers. *Journal of Psychology, 109*(2), 191-197.

Colletta, N. D., & Lee, D. (1983) The impact of support for Black adolescent mothers. *Journal of Family Issues, 4,* 127-143.

Crockenberg, S. B. (1981). Infant irritability, mother responsiveness and social support influences in the security of infant-mother attachment. *Child Development, 52,* 857-865.

Dornbush, S. M., Carlsmith, J. M., Bushwall, S. J., Ritter, P. L., Leiderman, H., Hastorf, A. H., & Gross, R. T. (1985). Single parents, extended households, and the control of adolescence. *Child Development, 56,* 326-341.

Duncan, O. D. (1968). Inheritance of poverty or inheritance of race? In D. P. Moynihan (Ed.), *On understanding poverty* (pp.116-149). New York: Basic Books.

Dykstra, R. R., & Manfra, J. A. (1985). Serial marriage and the origin of the Black stepfamily: The Rowonty evidence. *The Journal of American History, 72*(1), 18-44.

Egeland, B., & Sroufe, L. A. (1981). Attachment and early maltreatment. *Child Development, 52,* 44-52.

Field, T. M., & Ignatoff, E. (1981). Videotaping effects on play and interaction behaviors of low-income mothers and their infants. *Journal of Applied Developmental Psychology, 2,* 227-236.

Field, T. M., Widmayer, S. M., Stringer, S., & Ignatoff. E. (1980). Teenage, lower class, Black mothers and their preterm infants: An intervention and developmental follow-up. *Child Development, 51,* 426-436.

Flanagan, W. G. (1978, August). *The extended family as an agent of social change.* Paper presented at 9th World Congress of the International Sociological Association, Uppsala University, Uppsala, Sweden.

Furstenberg. F. (1980). Burdens and benefits: The impact of early childbearing on the family. *Journal of Social Issues, 36,* 64-87.

Furstenberg, F., & Crawford, D. B. (1978). Family support: Helping teenagers to cope. *Family Planning Perspectives, 10,* 322-333.

Genovese, E. D. (1976). *Roll, Jordan, roll.* New York: Random House.

Glick, P. (1976). Living arrangements of children and young adults. *Journal of Com parative Family Studies, 7,* 321-333.

Glick, P. (1981). A demographic picture of Black families. In H. P. McAdoo (Ed.) *Black families* (pp. 106-126). Beverly Hills, CA: Sage.

Gutman, H. G.(1976). *The Black family in slavery and freedom,* 1750-1925. New York: Vintage Press.

Hardy, J. B., King, T. M., Shipp, D. A., & Welcher, D. W. (1981). A comprehensive approach to adolescent pregnancy. In K. G. Scott, T. Field, & E. G. Robertson (Eds.), *Teenage parents and their offspring.* New York: Grune & Stratton.

Herskovits, M. J. (1966). *The myth of the Negro past.* Boston: Beach Press.

Hofferth, S. L. (1984). Kin network, race, and family structure. *Journal of Marriage and the Family, 46,* 791-806.

Kellam, S. G., Ensminger, M. A., & Turner, J. T. (1977). Family structure and the mental health of children. *Archives of General Psychiatry, 34,* 1012-1022.

Kellam, S. G., Adams, R. G., Brown, C. H., & Ensminger, M. E. (1982). The long-term evolution of the family structure of teenage and older mothers. *Journal of Marriage and the Family, 46,* 539-554.

McLanahan, S. S., Wedemeyer, N. V., & Adelbery, J. (1981). Network structure, social support and psychological well-being in the single-parent family. *Journal of Marriage and the Family, 43,* 601-611.

Meacham, M. (1983). The myth of the Black matriarchy under slavery. *Mid-American Review of Sociology-8,* 13-41.

Mindel, C. H. (1980). Extended familism among urban Mexican American Anglos and Blacks. *Hispanic Journal of Behavior Science, 2,* 21-34.

Mindel, C. H. (1983). The elderly in the minority family. In T. H. Brubaker (Ed.), *Family relationships in late life* (pp. 193-209). Beverly Hills, CA: Sage.

Mutran, E. (1985). Intergenerational family support among Blacks and Whites: Responses to culture or to socioeconomic differences. *Journal of Gerontology, 40,* 382-389.

Otto, J. J., & Burns, A. M., III. (1983). Black folks and poor buckras: Archeological evidence of slave and overseer living conditions on an antebellum plantation. *Journal of Black Studies*, *14*, 185-200.

Reid, J. (1982). Black America in the 1980's. *Population Bulletin*, *37*(4), 1-37.

Rubenstein, D. (1971). An examination of social participation of Black and White elderly. *Aging and Human Development*, *2*, 172-188.

Slaughter, D. T., & Dilworth-Anderson, P. (1985, April). *Childcare of Black sickle cell anemic children: Impact of father's presence and absence from households.* Paper presented at the Biennial Meeting of the Society for Research in Child Development, Toronto, Canada.

Slesinger, D. P. (1980). Rapid changes in household composition among low income mothers. *Family Relations*, *29*, 221-228.

Smith, M. J. (1980). The social consequences of single parenthood: A longitudinal perspective. *Family Relations*, *29*, 75-81.

Stack, C. (1974). *All our kin: Strategies for survival in the Black community.* New York: Harper & Row.

Staples, R., & Smith, J. W. (1954). Attitudes of grandmothers and mothers toward child rearing practices. *Child Development*, *25*, 91-97.

Stevens, J. H. (1984). Black grandmothers' and Black adolescent mothers' knowledge about parenting. *Developmental Psychology*, *20*(6), 1017-1025.

Sweet, J. A. (1977, October). *Further indicators of family structure and process for racial and ethnic minorities.* Paper presented at the Conference on the Demography of Racial and Ethnic Groups, Austin, TX.

U.S. Bureau of the Census. (1986). *Household and family characteristics: March, 1985* (Current Population Report Series P-20, No. 411). Washington, DC: U.S. Government Printing Office.

Wilson, M. N. (1984). Mothers' and grandmothers' perception of parental behavior in three-generational Black families. *Child Development*, *55*(4), 1333-1339.

Wilson, M. N. (1986). The Black extended family: An analytical review. *Developmental Psychology*, *22*(2), 246-258.

Wilson, M. N., & Tolson, T. F. J. (1986). A social interaction analysis of two- and three-generational Black families. In P. Dail & R. Jewson (Eds.), *In praise of fifty years: Groves Conference on the Conservation of Marriage and the Family* (pp. 43-53). Lake Mills, IA: Graphic Publishing.

What Europe Does for Single-Parent Families
Sheila Kamerman and Alfred Kahn

Most single-parent families, with only one wage-earner and child-care responsibilities, find it difficult to manage without help. As Melvin Wilson pointed out in the previous article, time and emotional support are important forms of assistance provided single mothers by members of the extended family. Responsibility for financial support, however, often rests with the government. While the United States has been extremely slow to react to the economic needs of single parents, many European countries have moved rapidly to adjust to increasing rates of divorce and single parenting. In this article, Sheila Kamerman and Alfred Kahn review four different approaches taken by various European countries to address the economic problems faced by single mothers. While it is evident that there is no perfect family policy, some countries have adopted measures that appear to be much more effective than others in achieving the objective of helping mother-headed households remain financially viable while enhancing family well-being.

Female-headed single-parent families have more than doubled in numbers and as a proportion of all families with children in the United States since 1970. They are a major component of the "feminization of poverty" and of child poverty, and they are at the heart of the welfare conundrum. These demographic trends are shared with Western Europe, but the societal responses have been, for the most part, strikingly different.

There are few countries in Europe in which one-parent or mother-only families are high on the public-policy agenda or the subject of major attention. Nor is there a uniform European policy response. Some countries have addressed the single-parent question directly, while others have considered it only as part of a larger poverty problem. Nevertheless, a continuum of European policy strategies can be described under the rubric of four alternative models.

Four Strategies of Concern

1. An *antipoverty strategy* attempts to meet the general needs of the poor and thus help the family headed by a single mother as well. Britain is the best illustration of this model. A single mother in Britain today may remain at home and receive a means-tested

Kamerman, Sheila B. and Kahn, Alfred J. (1989). What Europe does for single-parent families. *Transatlantic Perspectives, No. 19*. pp. 9-11.

assistance grant until her child or children are sixteen years of age. Although half of all single parents are assisted by Income Support, the program is unlike America's Aid to Families with Dependent Children (AFDC) because most recipients are two-parent families, the long-term unemployed, or the elderly.

There is no pressure on single mothers to take on training or a job. The tax and welfare systems operate so as to create a disincentive for part-time work; but full-time jobs are hard to come by, and mothers of very young children require child care that is largely unavailable or unaffordable. Single mothers who work at least twenty-four hours a week at low wages are ineligible for a wage supplement. Nevertheless, most single mothers stay at home with their children. Their families are also helped by child allowances, the national health service, and priority access to public housing.

Despite this assistance, the situation of these families has become worse in recent years. In 1979 the average gross income of a one-parent family was about 51 percent of that of a couple with two children. By 1984 the figure was down to 39.5 percent. The value of the child allowance has not kept up with inflation, while the income of two-parent families has increased. The proportion of single mothers who are supported by public aid has increased substantially, from about 38 percent in 1979 to more than half in 1985.

2. *A categorical strategy for single mothers* is geared to providing special financial aid to single mothers, supporting them so that they can remain at home with their children. (This was once the mission of AFDC in the United States.)

Norway is a country that pays special attention to mother-only families. It is the most generous country in supporting these families, and it clearly expects most single mothers to stay home until their children are ten years old.

The Transitional Benefit, a special income-tested cash benefit, is available to a woman in a cohabiting relationship as well, as long as the couple does not have a child together. The benefit has a tapered phase-out: 60 percent of earnings may be kept until wages equal three times the grant. It supplements the child allowance (provided for all children), the guaranteed minimum child-support benefit (provided if the noncustodial spouse does not pay), a housing allowance, medical care, and various tax considerations. The special financial assistance provided to single-mother families is sufficient to eliminate poverty for these families but not enough to maintain them at the level of husband/wife families. One result is that single mothers have far lower labor-force participation rates than married mothers: they find it hard to enter the labor force when their children reach age ten and the Transitional Benefit ends.

3. *A universal, young-child strategy* aims to provide cash benefits for all families with children, in particular those with children under age three, so that a parent may choose to remain home during the child's first years. Single mothers may have special add-ons, but they are mostly aided by the overall active family policy.

French family policy is designed to benefit all families with children. Its main instruments are an elaborate system of both universal and income-tested (but nonstigmatized) family allowances, including a basic allowance, family-allowance supplements, housing allowances, maternity and paternity leaves, and special allowances for mothers of very young children. The formal objectives—as enunciated in the ninth national plan (1985)—are to equalize the economic burdens of those with children and those without, to assure a minimum standard of living to families with children, to aid in the care and rearing of very young children, to make child-rearing compatible with employment for parents, and to encourage families to have a third child. Helping the parents of children under age three is a central component of French family policy, since these are the years when it is particularly difficult for mothers to work, and the additional financial aid allows the parents either to pay for child care or to exercise the option of remaining home for some time after childbirth. Obviously, this can be especially helpful to the single mother—but it is regarded as transitional help.

French policy offers all mothers of children under age three a choice of whether to work or remain at home; it provides a transitional benefit conferring modest support for one year to poor single mothers with children over that age. Once children reach age three, parents, including single mothers, are expected to work if they are in financial need. While family and housing allowances provide a continuing and valued foundation, the special allowances for the very young do end, and earnings become critical for mothers with older children. At 78 percent, the labor-force participation rate of single mothers is very high in France, far higher than that of married mothers.

4. *Combining labor market and family policy to permit a successful union of parenting and work.* Here the policy is to provide a variety of cash benefits and policy supports for families with children. Young mothers are encouraged to enter and remain in the work force, earning income to support their families, instead of being supported at a low standard at home by public income-transfer payments. These family-policy measures buttress labor-market measures in Sweden to create a supportive nexus.

In contrast to Britain and France, Sweden has implemented social policies that stress the importance of full employment and the role of labor-market programs; and unlike Britain or the United States, its policies seek to reduce inequality more than poverty. Like Norway, Sweden provides a special benefit for single parents; however, this benefit is designed only to help maintain the children, and not to support the mother and full family at home. Finally, like France, Sweden provides assistance to all families with children, in particular those with very young children; but much of what is done is designed to support parents in their efforts to balance work and family life. What Sweden seems to have done is to create a generous family policy, and to support it with parallel labor-market efforts.

Wages are viewed as the fundamental source of family income in Sweden. Women, like men, are expected to work, even if they are parents. There is an active labor-market policy: government invests heavily in job creation, if necessary, and in training, retraining, education, and relocation. Transfer payments—social benefits—are at best either

148

transitional (and very short-term) or supplementary if and when earnings are low. Work—the prevailing pattern for both married and single mothers—and parenting are supported by a generous social infrastructure that includes health care, child care services, and a variety of benefits designed to ease the tension between work and family life. Single parents participate in a basic family-benefit system for all, which includes child allowances and housing allowances. All working parents are guaranteed a one-year paid parental leave following childbirth. There are generous provisions for a parent to stay home with a sick child, to visit school, and to reduce daily work hours when a child is young. In addition, single parents collect either child support from the noncustodial parent or a minimum, but generous, government support benefit.

Policies Designed to Enhance Family Well-being

One big difference between the United States and Europe is that the European countries have moved rapidly over the last decade (if not earlier) to develop new social policies in response to the increase in divorce. All the Nordic countries (Norway, Sweden, Denmark, Finland, and Iceland) have established some form of guaranteed child-support payment, paid for by the government when noncustodial parents fail to pay or pay inadequately. A government agency assumes responsibility for collection from the noncustodial parent.

These benefits are available to all custodial parents, regardless of income. Where they exist, they add significantly to income from earnings. More importantly, receipt of adequate child support, provided by the guaranteed minimum, protects women and children from needing to claim a stigmatized social-assistance benefit, while also providing incentives to work.

Other countries are also moving in this direction. In effect, divorce is being redefined in Europe as a social rather than an individual risk, which has negative economic consequences for women and warrants protection through the public-income maintenance system. This has not occurred in the United States, but is being discussed; one experiment in Wisconsin guarantees child support, if not from the absent parent, then from the state.

In most countries, single mothers are already expected to work; it is an emerging expectation even in those countries in which single mothers are still supported at home. However, if mothers are to work, an adequate social infrastructure must exist. It is here that European countries are far ahead of the United States, in providing basic social services like health insurance, child-care services, maternity and parenting benefits and leaves, and housing subsidies.

Scandinavian and British women are likely to work part-time, but in most countries single mothers are more likely to work full-time. Part-time work is not remunerative enough when income-tested social benefits are lost as a consequence. But for many, especially when their children are young, full-time work is not feasible because of time and child-care problems. No country has yet resolved the problem posed by the need for a full-time wage coupled with the inability to cope with the time pressures of a full-time job. Currently the extent to which work is expected of single mothers is in part a function of unemployment rates. In general, Britain is still supporting single mothers at home, while Sweden, Finland, Denmark, Germany, and France expect them to work.

One major new development suggests convergence among policies designed to enhance family well-being, to make it possible for mothers to work, and to help low-income mothers. This is the policy of giving special support to parents with children under age three. This support is designed to promote numerous policy goals: to improve the labor market (by lessening the pressure on it when unemployment rates are high) to increase the population (by making it easier for women to have more children), to reduce public expenditures (by providing less government-financed child care), and to further equality between the sexes (by making it easier for women to work while still being able to rear children).

These policies involve extending paid and job-protected maternity/parenting leaves with supplementary leaves and cash benefits, the latter usually at a lower level than the immediate post-childbirth benefit. In some countries (Sweden, Finland, Austria), these benefits are contingent on prior work, and therefore create both strong incentives for early labor-market participation and strong disincentives to adolescent parenting. By assuring job protection, the policies facilitate a return to work for women who might otherwise find it difficult to get jobs. In some countries, such as Germany, prior work is not a criterion for eligibility. Where this is the case, it could be difficult for women to find employment when they enter the labor market.

Will Punitive Policies Be the Choice?

Americans rightly worry about the unanticipated consequences of policies. But European data, reports and analyses consistently arrive at this reassuring conclusion: women do not have babies in order to qualify for social benefits, and couples do not break up to get benefits. Social policies do not cause these developments. But once an unwed mother has a baby, and once a couple divorces, the existence of social benefits makes the single-parent family possible in various ways, depending on the policy.

In both the United States and Europe, single-parent families with children face economic difficulties, because families cannot manage financially with only one wage earner. The difference between the United States and Europe, however, is that the European countries have understood this and have addressed the problem—the United States has not. In addition, the Europeans have gone much further in making work viable for parents (by providing maternity and parental leaves, flexible work time, leave to take care of a sick child, etc.). The result is that most single-parent families are better off economically in Europe than in the United States.

In effect, the European countries that expect single mothers to work, and their families to do well, have invested in and implemented policies designed to achieve this goal. The United States, despite its professed concern about work for "welfare mothers," has not yet adopted the measures necessary to show full concern for family well-being.

Ultimately, the major question for America may be deciding whether to protect the economic and social situation of children (even if it means facilitating alternatives to the traditional family that are the objects of disapproval), or to impose punitive policies so as to constrain or shape the behavior of adults (even if it means harming children).

UNIT 4: Children and Families

8

Individual Differences and Developmental Milestones

By letting an infant's personality and actions speak louder than words, ongoing research is revealing surprising capabilities among infants. In Dr. Carolyn Rovee-Collier's studies, for example, an infant is placed on her back in a crib so that she can look up at a mobile. When a baby is excited, she kicks; and Dr. Rovee-Collier and her colleagues first establish the baby's basic rate of kicking. Then a ribbon tied to the baby's foot is connected to the mobile. When the baby's kicking shakes the mobile, the infant begins to kick more often and more purposefully. An infant even appears to remember the relationship between her own movements and the effects on the mobile after an interval of three days. Memory, will, and intention, in other words, seem to be present even in these very young infants. As Dr. Rovee-Collier herself concludes: "Most people who work with human adults think that babies are like rats until they're eight or nine months of age. . . . What we've shown is that babies are very human from the moment they're born."

● INTRODUCTION ●

The great American psychologist William James (1892) once described the consciousness of the human infant as "one big blooming, buzzing Confusion." For many years this was the commonly held view. Modern research on infants, however, has forced psychologists to modify this conclusion. Very young infants have been found to be surprisingly sophisticated in their ability to cognize aspects of the complex world into which they have been born. Available evidence even suggests that many of these skills develop with little or no specific experience. Babies, in other words, come evolutionarily prepared to make sense of fundamental properties of the physical and social world. The excerpts in this chapter have been taken from some of the classic studies that have forced us to revise our views of infants. Note the ingenious methods employed in this research. Many psychologists think that we have only begun to appreciate infant cognitive abilities. Our understanding of how much babies know seems to be limited only by our capacity to devise techniques to assess infant skills.

● ● ●

The Visual Cliff
Eleanor J. Gibson and Richard D. Walk

In one of developmental psychology's most famous studies, Eleanor Gibson and Richard Walk focused on young children's ability to perceive and react to depth. In this context, they posed a question that has motivated much of the infancy research of the past twenty-five years: "Is experience really the teacher? Or is . . . ability . . . part of the child's original endowment?" In the excerpt presented here, we read about an extremely simple piece of apparatus, the "visual cliff," that the authors devised to assess infants' ability to discriminate depth. Results of research with the visual cliff make it clear that this ability is present as soon as babies can crawl.

Gibson, E.J. & Walk, R.D. (1960). The visual cliff. *Scientific American, 202.* pp. 64-71

Human infants at the creeping and toddling stage are notoriously prone to falls from more or less high places. They must be kept from going over the brink by side panels on their cribs, gates on stairways and the vigilance of adults. As their muscular coordination matures they begin to avoid such accidents on their own. Common sense might suggest that the child learns to recognize falling-off places by experience—that is, by falling and hurting himself. But is experience really the teacher? Or is the ability to perceive and avoid a brink part of the child's original endowment? . . .

At Cornell University we have been investigating these problems by means of a simple experiment setup that we call a visual cliff. The cliff is a simulated one and hence makes it possible not only to control the optical and other stimuli (auditory and tactual, for instance) but also to protect the experimental subjects. It consists of a board laid across a large sheet of heavy glass which is supported a foot or more above the floor. On one side of the board a sheet of patterned material is placed flush against the under surface of the glass, giving the glass the appearance as well as the substance of solidity. On the other side a sheet of the same material is laid upon the floor; this side of the board thus becomes the visual cliff. We tested thirty-six infants ranging in age from six months to fourteen months on the visual cliff. Each child was placed upon the center board, and his mother called him to her from the cliff side and the shallow side successively. All of the twenty-seven infants who moved off the board crawled out on the shallow side at least once; only three of them crept off the brink onto the glass suspended above the pattern on the floor. Many of the infants crawled away from the mother when she called to them from the cliff side; others cried when she stood there, because they could not come to her without crossing an apparent chasm. The experiment thus demonstrated that most human infants can discriminate depth as soon as they can crawl.

The behavior of the children in this situation gave clear evidence of their dependence on vision. Often they would peer down through the glass on the deep side and then back away. Others would pat the glass with their hands, yet despite this tactual assurance of solidity would refuse to cross. It was equally clear that their perception of depth had matured more rapidly than had their locomotor abilities. Many supported themselves on the glass over the deep side as they maneuvered awkwardly on the board; some even backed out onto the glass as they started toward the mother on the shallow side. Were it not for the glass some of the children would have fallen off the board. Evidently infants should not be left close to a brink, no matter how well they may discriminate depth. . .

Intermodal Matching by Human Neonates
Andrew N. Meltzoff and Richard W. Borton

Another well-known test of the hypothesis that certain basic, human cognitive-perceptual capacities develop "without the need for learned correlations" is described by Andrew Meltzoff and Richard Borton. In this research, the authors focus on the infant's ability to detect similarity of shapes presented in two different sensory modalities—touch and vision. Once again, results indicate surprisingly sophisticated abilities even in babies under one month of age. In reading this excerpt, pay particular attention to the care with which the infant was tested. Even the youngest of infants is extremely sensitive to cues provided by adults. If the experimenters who test and observe the infant know where the baby is expected to look, their expectations may influence their own behavior in subtle ways that in turn affect the direction of the baby's gaze. By using multiple experimenters, Meltzoff and Borton ruled out possible effects of unconscious experimenter bias that would have invalidated their interpretation.

Normal human adults judge two identical objects to have the same shape even when they are perceived through different modalities, such as touch and vision. The ontogenesis of man's capacity to recognize such intermodal matches has long been debated. One hypothesis is that humans begin life with independent sense modalities and that simultaneous tactual and visual exploration of shapes is needed to learn to correlate the separate tactual and visual sense impressions of them.[1,2,3] A second hypothesis is that the detection of shape invariants across different modalities is a fundamental characteristic of man's perceptual-cognitive system, available without the need for learned correlations.[4,5,6,7] Recent research has shown that six- to twelve-month-old infants can recognize certain tactual-visual matches.[8,9,10,11] However, such data cannot help resolve the classic theoretical debate. Infants of this age repeatedly reach out and touch objects they see, and such simultaneous bimodal exploration presumably offers ample opportunity for learning to correlate tactual and visual sense impressions. The experiments reported here show that humans can recognize intermodal matches without the benefit of months of experience in simultaneous tactual-visual exploration. We demonstrate that twenty-nine-day-old infants can recognize which of two visually perceived shapes matches one they previously explored tactually, thus supporting the second hypothesis listed above.

Meltzoff, A.N. & Borton, R.W. (1979). Intermodal matching by human neonates. *Nature, 282*. pp. 403-404.

For our assessment of intermodal matching, we adapted a paradigm used to test infant memory. We began with a brief familiarization period during which the infant tactually explored an object. Next, the infant was shown a pair of visual shapes, only one of which matched the tactual stimulus. Visual fixation to the matching versus non-matching shape .was then recorded. Three experimenters were used to ensure objectivity of the results. One experimenter selected the tactual shape and the left-right positioning of the visual shapes. This experimenter was not involved with testing the infant. A second experimenter administered the tactual stimulus. He was not informed about the left-right positioning of the visual shapes. A third experimenter observed the infant's visual fixations through a 0.64-cm peephole in the center of the rear wall of the testing chamber. He was unaware of both the tactual shape used and the left-right positioning of the visual shapes. Corneal reflections of the test objects were visible to this scorer, but the shapes of the objects were not resolvable. He scored the infant as fixating the left object when the left reflection was visible in either of the infant's pupils, and as fixating the right object when the right reflection was visible. . . .

Thirty-two full-term infants ranging from twenty-six to thirty-three days old (mean 29.4 d) served as subjects. . . . As infants of this age will not explore objects manually, the tactual stimuli were constructed by modifying pacifiers so that small, hard-rubber shapes could be mounted on them (Figure 1). The matching shapes used for the visual test were constructed from dense Styrofoam and painted bright orange (diameter 6.4 cm). The experiment started with a 90-s tactual familiarization period during which infants orally explored one of the tactual stimuli. This stimulus was then removed and the infant presented with both visual shapes for a 20-s visual test. Care was taken to ensure that the

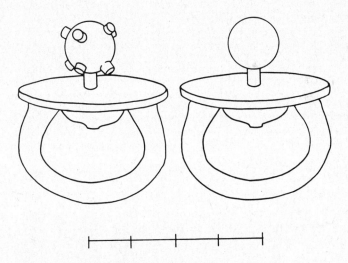

Figure 1   The tactual objects.

tactual stimulus was administered and removed without the infant seeing it. The shape used for tactual familiarization, the left-right positioning of the visual objects, and the sex of the infants were counterbalanced. Thus, half the infants were tactually familiarized with the sphere and half with the sphere-with-nubs; half the infants in each of these groups were shown the familiar shape on the left and half on the right; half the infants within each of these subgroups were male and half female.

The results clearly demonstrate that infants under one month of age are capable of intermodal matching. . . . Of the thirty-two infants, twenty-four fixated the shape matching the tactual stimulus longer than the non-matching shape. These results were significantly different from chance ($P < 0.01$; binomial test). The mean percent of total fixation time directed to the matching shape was 71.8 percent as compared with the chance level of 50 percent ($t = 3.07$; $P < 0.01$). There were no significant differences due to sex of the infant, familiarization object or method of feeding (breast or bottle), nor were there significant preferences for fixating the right versus left side or for fixating the sphere versus sphere-with-nubs. . . .

Positive results from such a task indicate that neonates can (1) tactually discriminate between the shapes presented, (2) visually discriminate between them, (3) store some representation of the tactually perceived shape, and (4) relate a subsequent visual perception to the stored representation of the tactually perceived shape. . . .

1. Locke, J. *An Essay Concerning Human Understanding* (Basset, London, 1690).

2. Berkeley, G. *An Essay Toward a New Theory of Vision* (Pepyat, Dublin, 1709).

3. Piaget, J. *The Origins of Intelligence* (Norton, New York, 1952); *The Construction of Reality* (Basic, New York, 1954); *Play, Dreams and Imitation in Childhood* (Norton, New York, 1962).

4. Gibson, J.J. *The Senses Considered as Perceptual Systems* (Houghton Mifflin, New York, 1966).

5. Gibson, E.J. *Principles of Perceptual Learning and Development* (Appleton-Century-Crofts, New York, 1969).

6. Bower, T.G.R. *Development in Infancy* (Freeman, San Francisco, 1974).

7. Meltzoff, A.N. & Moore, M.K. *Science* **195**, 75-78 (1977).

8. Bryant, P.E., Jones, P., Claxton, V. & Perkins, G.M. *Nature* **240**, 303-304 (1972).

9. Bryant, P.E. *Perception and Understanding in Children* (Methuen, London, 1974).

10. Gottfried, A.W., Rose, S.A. & Bridger, W.H. *Child Dev.* **48**, 118-123 (1977).

11. Ruff, H.A. & Kohler, C.J. *Infant Behav. Dev.* **1**, 259-264 (1978).

Object Permanence in Five-Month-Old Infants
Renee Baillargeon, Elizabeth S. Spelke, and Stanley Wasserman

In his influential study of the sensorimotor development of the human infant, Jean Piaget observed babies' reactions to the disappearance of objects. Based on these observations, he argued that before the fourth substage of the sensorimotor period, at about nine months of age, infants fail to treat hidden objects as permanent entities that continue to exist. In support of this claim, he showed that prior to substage 4, infants given the opportunity to search for an attractive toy that has been hidden under a cloth in full sight of the child will fail to do so. The child appears to act as though the toy has been annihilated. More recently, however, it has been suggested that the young infant's failure to search for the hidden toy may be less a reflection of lack of object permanence than of lack of ability to coordinate actions. In the study described here, the authors report results from an ingenious test of object permanence that did not require the infant to engage in search for a hidden object. When the requirement for coordinated action was removed, five month old infants, far younger than those in Piaget's fourth sensorimotor substage, reacted as though an object should have continued to exist even though it was no longer visible. In more recent research, Baillargeon has replicated this finding with three and one-half month-olds and extended it to show that young infants give evidence of cognizing not only continued existence but even such properties of hidden objects as height, location, and trajectory.

We sought a new means of testing object permanence in young infants. . . . The method we devised . . . focused on infants' understanding of the principle that a solid object cannot move through the space occupied by another solid object ("solidity principle"). Infants' understanding of this principle was tested in a situation involving a visible object and an occluded object. If infants were surprised when the visible object appeared to move through the space occupied by the occluded object, it would suggest that they took account of the existence and the location of the occluded object. In other words, evidence that infants applied the solidity principle would also provide evidence that they possessed object permanence.

Baillargeon, Renee; Spelke, Elizabeth S. & Wasserman Stanley. (1985). Object permanence in five-month-old infants. *Cognition. 20*, pp. 191-208.

In the experiment, a box was placed on a surface behind a wooden screen. The screen initially lay flat, so that the box was clearly visible. The screen was then raised, in the manner of a drawbridge, thus hiding the box from view. Infants were shown two test events: a possible event and an impossible event. In the possible event, the screen moved until it reached the occluded box, stopped, and then returned to its initial position (see Figure 1A). In the impossible event, the screen moved until it reached the occluded box—and then kept on going as though the box were no longer there! The screen completed a full 180-degree arc before it reversed direction and returned to its initial position, revealing the box standing intact in the same location as before (see Figure 1B). To adults, the possible event is consistent with the solidity principle: the screen stops when it encounters the box. The impossible event, in contrast, violates the principle: the screen appears to move freely through the space occupied by the box. Note that adults would not perceive the event as impossible if they did not believe that the box continued to exist, in its same location, after it was occluded by the screen.

Figure 1. Schematic representation of the possible and impossible test events used in the principal experiment.

A. Possible Event

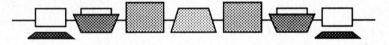

B. Impossible Event

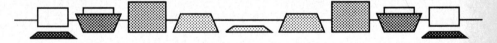

To test infants' perception of these events, we used a habituation paradigm. Infants were habituated to the screen moving back and forth through a 180-degree arc, with no box present. After infants reached habituation, the box was placed behind the screen, and infants were shown the possible and impossible events. Our reasoning was as follows. If infants understood that (1) the box continued to exist, in its same location, after it was occluded by the screen, and (2) the screen could not move through the space occupied by the box, then they should perceive the impossible event to be novel, surprising, or both. On the basis of the commonly-held assumption that infants react to novel or surprising events with prolonged attention, we predicted that infants would look longer at the impossible than at the possible event. On the other hand, if infants did not understand that the box continued to exist after it was occluded by the screen, then they should attend to the movement of the screen without concerning themselves with the presence of the box in its path. Since the screen movement was the same in the impossible and the habituation events (in both events the screen moved through a 180-degree arc), we predicted that infants would look longer at the possible event, which depicted a novel, shorter screen movement.

There was one foreseeable difficulty with the design of our experiment. Infants might look longer at the impossible than at the possible event, not because they understood the underlying structure of the events, but because they found the 180-degree movement intrinsically more interesting than the 120-degree movement. To check this possibility, we ran a control experiment that was similar to the first experiment except that the box was placed behind and to the side of the screen, out of its path of motion. Therefore, neither the 180- nor the 120-degree screen movement violated the solidity principle. We reasoned that if infants in the first experiment looked longer at the impossible event because they found the 180-degree movement intrinsically more interesting than the 120-degree movement, then infants in the control experiment should look longer at the 180-degree event. On the other hand, if infants in the first experiment looked longer at the impossible event because they viewed it as impossible, then infants in the control experiment should look equally at the 180- and the 120-degree events, since neither was impossible, or they should look longer at the 120-degree event, since it involved a novel screen movement. . . .

Results

The results of the principal experiment were clear-cut: infants showed a strong, consistent preference for the impossible over the possible test event.

Figure 2A presents the mean looking times during the habituation and test phases of the experiment. . . .

The results of the control experiment were quite different: infants showed no overall preference between the 180- and the 120-degree test events.

Figure 2B presents the mean looking times to the habituation and test events.

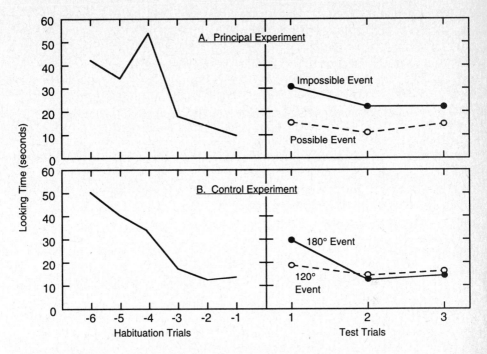

Figure 2. Looking times of subjects in the principal and control experiments to the habituation and test trials.*

* The habituation trials are numbered backwards from the trial in which criterion was reached.

Discussion

The results of the principal experiment are easily summarized: infants showed a marked preference for the impossible over the possible event. Further, infants showed this preference on all three pairs of test trials, regardless of the order in which they saw the two events. The results of the control experiment were very different: only infants who saw the 180-degree event first showed a preference for that event, and that only on the first test pair; infants who saw the 120-degree event first looked equally at the two events on all three test pairs. These results provide evidence that infants in the principal experiment looked longer at the impossible event not because they preferred the 180-degree screen movement, but because they expected the screen to stop against the occluded box and were surprised, or puzzled, when it failed to do so.

The results of these experiments indicate that five-month-old infants understand that an object continues to exist when occluded. . . .

Becoming a Native Listener
Janet F. Werker

Most of us would perhaps be shocked to learn that there is a sophisticated perceptual task on which infants perform at a much higher level than adults. Yet this is just what researchers studying speech perception have reported. As Werker explains, young infants have consistently been shown to discriminate virtually all of the phonemic contrasts relevant to all of the world's languages. Older children and adults, however, have considerable difficulty with discriminations that are not relevant to their own native language. Here the question of the effects of original endowment versus the role of experience is given an unusual twist. In speech perception, experience seems to lead to the loss of an ability with which infants are apparently originally endowed. In reading this excerpt, notice how carefully Werker pursues her question from experiment to experiment, generalizing her findings across languages and validating cross-sectional developmental trends with longitudinal data.

The syllables, words, and sentences used in all human languages are formed from a set of speech sounds called phones. Only a subset of the phones is used in any particular language. Adults can easily perceive the differences among the phones used to contrast meaning in their own language, but young infants go much farther: they are able to discriminate nearly every phonetic contrast on which they have been tested, including those they have never before heard. Our research has shown that this broad-based sensitivity declines by the time a baby is one year old. This phenomenon provides a way to describe basic abilities in the young infant and explore the effects of experience on human speech perception.

To put infants' abilities in perspective, adult speech perception must be understood. The phones that distinguish meaning in a particular language are called phonemes. There is considerable acoustic variability in the way each individual phoneme is realized in speech. For example, the phoneme /b/ is very different before the vowel /ee/ in "beet" from the way it is before the vowel /oo/ in "boot." How do adults handle this variability? As first demonstrated in a classic study by Liberman and his colleagues (1967), they treat these acoustically distinct instances of a single phoneme as equivalent. This equivalency is demonstrated in the laboratory by presenting listeners with a series of pairs of computer-synthe-sized speech stimuli that differ by only one acoustic step along a physical continuum and asking them first to label and then to try to discriminate between

Werker, Janet F. (1989). Becoming a native listener. *American Scientist*, 77. pp. 54-59.

the stimuli. Adult listeners are able to discriminate reliably only stimuli that they have labeled as different—that is, they cannot easily discriminate between two acoustically different stimuli that they labeled /pa/, but they can discriminate between two similar stimuli if one is from their /ba/ category and one from their /pa/ category.

The phenomenon by which labeling limits discrimination is referred to as categorical perception. This has obvious advantages for language processing. It allows a listener to segment the words he hears immediately according to the phonemic categories of his language and to ignore unessential variations within a category.

Given that adults perceive speech categorically, when do such perceptual capabilities appear? To find out, Eimas and his colleagues (1971) adapted the so-called high-amplitude sucking procedure for use in a speech discrimination task. This procedure involves teaching infants to suck on a pacifier attached to a pressure transducer in order to receive a visual or auditory stimulus. After repeated presentations of the same sight or sound, the sucking rate declines, indicating that the infants are becoming bored. The infants are then presented with a new stimulus. Presumably, if they can discriminate the new sight or sound from the old, they will increase their sucking rate.

In Eimas's experiment, infants one and four months old heard speech sounds that varied in equal steps from /ba/ to /pa/. Like adults, they discriminated between differences in the vicinity of the /ba/-/pa/ boundary but were unable to discriminate equal acoustic changes from within the /ba/ category. Rather than having to learn about phonemic categories, then, infants seem capable of grouping speech stimuli soon after birth.

Experiments in the seventeen years since Eimas's original study have shown that infants can discriminate nearly every phonetic contrast on which they are tested but are generally unable to discriminate differences within a single phonemic category (for a review, see Kuhl 1987). That is, like adults, infants perceive acoustically distinct instances of a single phoneme as equivalent but easily discriminate speech sounds from two different categories that are not more acoustically distinct.

Of special interest are demonstrations that young infants are even able to discriminate phonetic contrasts not used in their native language. In an early study, Streeter (1976) used the high-amplitude sucking procedure to test Kikuyu infants on their ability to discriminate the English /ba/-/pa/ distinction, which is not used in Kikuyu. She found that the infants could discriminate these two syllable types. Similar results have been obtained from a variety of laboratories using other nonnative phonetic contrasts (Lasky et al. 1975; Trehub 1976; Aslin et al. 1981; Eilers et al. 1982). This pattern of results indicates that the ability to discriminate phones from the universal phonetic inventory may be present at birth.

Developmental Changes

Given these broad-based infant abilities, one might expect that adults would also be able to discriminate nearly all phonetic contrasts. However, research suggests that adults often have difficulty discriminating phones that do not contrast meaning in their own language. An English-speaking adult, for example, has difficulty perceiving the difference between the two /p/ phones that are used in Thai (Lisker and Abramson 1970). So too, a Japanese speaking adult initially cannot distinguish between the English /ra/ and /la/, because Japanese uses a single phoneme intermediate between the two English phonemes (Miyawaki et al. 1975; MacKain et al. 1981). This pattern of extensive infant capabilities and more limited capabilities in the adult led to the suggestion that infants may have a biological predisposition to perceive all possible phonetic contrasts and that there is a decline in this universal phonetic sensitivity by adulthood as a function of acquiring a particular language (Eimas 1975; Trehub 1976).

My work has been designed to explore this intriguing possibility. In particular, I wanted to trace how speech perception changes during development. Are infants actually able to discriminate some pairs of speech sounds better than adults, or have they simply been tested with more sensitive procedures? If infants do have greater discriminative capacities than adults, when does the decline occur and why?

The first problem that my colleagues and I faced was to find a testing procedure which could be used with infants, children of all ages, and adults. We could then begin a program of studies comparing their relative abilities to perceive the differences between phonetic contrasts of both native and nonnative languages.

The testing routine we chose is a variation of the so-called infant head turn procedure (for a complete description, see Kuhl 1987). Subjects are presented with several slightly different versions of the same phoneme (e.g., /ba/) repeated continuously at 2-sec intervals. On a random basis every four to twenty repetitions, a new phoneme is introduced. For example, a subject will hear "ba," "ba," "ba," "ba," "ba," "da," "da." Babies are conditioned to turn their heads toward the source of the sound when they detect the change from one phoneme to another (e.g., from "ba" to "da"). Correct head turns are reinforced with the activation of a little toy animal and with clapping and praise from the experimental assistant. . . . Adults and children are tested the same way, except that they press a button instead of turning their heads when they detect a change in the phoneme, and the reinforcement is age-appropriate.

In the first series of experiments, we compared English-speaking adults, infants from English-speaking families, and Hindi-speaking adults on their ability to discriminate the /ba/-/da/ distinction, which is used in both Hindi and English, as well as two pairs of syllables that are used in Hindi but not in English (Werker et al. 1981). The two pairs of Hindi syllables were chosen on the basis of their relative difficulty. The first pair contrasts two "t" sounds that are not used in English. In English, we articulate "t" sounds by placing the tongue a bit behind the teeth at the alveolar ridge. In Hindi, there are two different "t" phonemes. One is produced by placing the tongue on the teeth (a dental t—written /t/). The other is produced by curling the tip of the tongue back and placing it against the roof of the mouth (a retroflex t— written /T/). This contrast is not used in English, and is in fact very rare among the world's languages.

The second pair of Hindi syllables involves different categories of voicing—the timing of the release of a consonant and the amount of air released with the consonant. Although these phonemes, called /t^h/ and /d^h/, are not used in English, we had reason to believe

168

that they might be easier for English-speaking adults to discriminate than the /t/-/T/ distinction. The timing difference between /tʰ/ and /dʰ/ spans the English /t/-/d/ boundary. Moreover, this contrast is more common among the world's languages.

The results of this study, which are presented in Figure 1A, were consistent with the hypothesis of universal phonetic sensitivity in the young infant and a decline by adulthood. As expected, all subjects could discriminate /ba/ from /da/. Of more interest, the infants aged six to eight months performed like the Hindi adults and were able to discriminate both pairs of Hindi speech contrasts. The English-speaking adults, on the other hand, were considerably less able to make the Hindi distinctions, especially the difficult dental-retroflex one.

Timing of Developmental Changes

The next series of experiments was aimed at determining when the decline in nonnative sensitivity occurs. It was originally believed that this decline would coincide with puberty, when, as Lenneberg (1967) claims, language flexibility decreases. However, our work showed that twelve-year-old English-speaking children were no more able to discriminate non-English syllables than were English-speaking adults (Werker and Tees 1983). We then tested eight- and four-year-old English-speaking children, and, to our surprise, even the four-year-olds could not discriminate the Hindi contrasts. Hindi-speaking four-year-olds, of course, showed no trouble with this discrimination.

Before testing children even younger than age four, we felt it was necessary to determine that the phenomenon of developmental loss extended to other languages. To this end, we chose a phonemic contrast from a North American Indian language of the Interior Salish family, called Nthlakapmx by native speakers in British Columbia but also referred to as Thompson.

North American Indian languages include many consonants produced in the back of the vocal tract behind our English /k/ and /g/. The pair of sounds we chose contrasts a "k" sound produced at the velum with another "k" sound (written /q/) produced by raising the back of the tongue against the uvula. Both are glottalized—that is, there is an ejective portion (similar to a click) at the beginning of the release of the consonants.

Again, we compared English-speaking adults, infants from English-speaking families, and Nthlakapmx-speaking adults in their abilities to discriminate this pair of sounds (Werker and Tees 1984a). As was the case with the Hindi syllables, both the Nthlakapmx-speaking adults and the infants could discriminate the non-English phonemes, but the English-speaking adults could not.

We were now satisfied that there is at least some generality to the notion that young infants can discriminate across the whole phonetic inventory but that there is a developmental decline in this universal sensitivity. Our next series of experiments involved testing children between eight months and four years of age to try to determine just when the decline in sensitivity might start. It quickly became apparent that something important was happening within the first year of life. We accordingly compared three groups of infants aged six to eight, eight to ten, and ten to twelve months. Half of each group were tested with the Hindi (/ta/-/Ta/) and half with the Nthlakapmx (/ki/-/gi/) contrast.

As shown in Figure 1B, the majority of the six-to-eight-month-old infants from English-speaking families could discriminate the two non-English contrasts, whereas only about one-half of the eight-to-ten-month-olds could do so. Only two out of ten ten-to-twelve-month-olds could discriminate the Hindi contrast, and only one out of ten of the Nthlakapmx. This provided strong evidence that the decline in universal phonetic sensitivity was occurring between six and twelve months of age. As a further test to see if this developmental change would be apparent within the same individuals, six infants from English-speaking families were tested at two-month intervals beginning when they were about six to eight months old. All six infants could discriminate both the Hindi and Nthlakapmx contrasts at the first testing, but by the third testing session, when they were ten to twelve months old, they were not able to discriminate either contrast. . . .

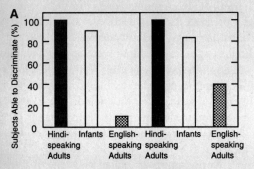

A

Figure 1-A. When tested on their ability to discriminate two Hindi syllables that are not used in English, six-to-eight-month-old infants from English-speaking families do nearly as well as Hindi-speaking adults. English-speaking adults, however, have great difficulty with this discrimination task, depending on the degree of difference from English sounds. The graph on the left shows a contrast involving two "t" sounds, one dental (i.e., made with the tip of the tongue touching the upper front teeth) and the other retroflex (made with the tongue curled back under the palate). This contrast is rare in the world's languages. The contrast in the graph on the right involves two kinds of voicing, a phenomenon that is less unusual and thus some- what more recognizable to English-speaking adults. (After Werker et al. 1981.)

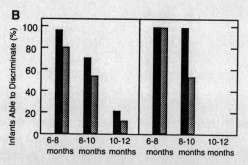

B

Figure 1-B. Infants show a decline in the universal phonetic sensitivity demonstrated in Figure A during the second half of their first year, as shown heare in the results of experiments performed with babies from English-speaking families and involving non-English syllables from Hindi (*black bars*) and Nthlakapmx, a language spoken by some native Indians in British Columbia (*gray bars*). The graph on the left gives results from experiments with three groups of infants aged six to eight months, eight to ten months, and ten to twelve months. The graph on the right gives results from testing one group of infants three times at the appropriate ages. None of the latter group were able to discriminate either of the non-English contrasts when they were ten to twelve months old. (After Werker and Tees 1984a.)

References

Aslin, R. N., D. B. Pisoni, B. L. Hennessy, and A. J. Perey. 1981. Discrimination of voice onset time by human infants: New findings and implications for the effect of early experience. *Child Devel.* 52:1135-45.

Eilers, R. E., W. J. Gavin, and D. K. Oller. 1982. Cross-linguistic perception in infancy: Early effects of linguistic experience. *J. Child Lang.* 9:289-302.

Eimas, P. D. 1975. Developmental studies in speech perception. In *Infant Perception: From Sensation to Cognition*, ed. L. B. Cohen and P. Salapatek, vol. 2, pp. 193-231. Academic Press.

Eimas, P. D., E. R. Siqueland, P. W. Jusczyk, and J. Vigorito. 1971. Speech perception in infants. *Science* 171:303-06.

Kuhl, P. K. 1987. Perception of speech and sound in early infancy. In *Handbook of Infant Perception*, ed. P. Salapatek and L. Cohen, vol. 2, pp. 275-382. Academic Press.

Lasky, R. E., A. Syrdal-Lasky, and R.E. Klein 1975. VOT discrimination by four to six and a half month old infants from Spanish environments. J. *Exper. Child Psychol.* 20:215-25.

Lenneberg, E. H. 1967. *Biological Foundations of Language*. Wiley.

Liberman, A. M., F. S. Cooper, D. P. Shankweiler, and M. Studdert-Kennedy. 1967. Perception of the speech code. *Psychol. Rev.* 74: 431-61.

Lisker, L., and A. S. Abramson. 1970. The voicing dimension: Some experiments in comparative phonetics. In *Proceedings of the 6th International Congress of Phonetic Sciences*, pp. 563-67. Prague: Academia.

MacKain, K. S., C. T. Best, and W. Strange. 1981. Categorical perception of English /r/ and /l/ by Japanese bilinguals. *Appl. Psycholing.* 2:269-90

Miyawaki, K., et al. 1975. An effect of linguistic experience: The discrimination of [r] and [l] by native speakers of Japanese and English. *Percept. Psychophys.* 18:331-40.

Streeter, L. A. 1976. Language perception of two-month old infants shows effects of both innate mechanisms and experience. *Nature* 259: 39-41.

Trehub, S. 1976. The discrimination of foreign speech contrasts by infants and adults. *Child Devel.* 47:466-72.

Werker, J. F., J. H. V. Gilbert, K. Humphrey, and R. C. Tees. 1981. Developmental aspects of cross-language speech perception. *Child Devel.* 52:349-53.

Werker, J. F., and R. C. Tees. 1983. Developmental changes across childhood in the perception of non-active speech sounds. *Can. J. Psychol.* 37:278-86.

————1984. Cross-language speech perception: Evidence for perceptual reorganization during the first year of life. *Infant Behav. Devel.* 7: 49-63.

Temperamental Influences on the Preservation of Styles of Social Behavior
Jerome Kagan

In the research excerpts presented earlier, the authors were primarily concerned with general developmental trends, summarized across the performances of individual infants. If you look back at the results reported, you will notice that infants typically do not show general effects to the same degree. Indeed, it is not uncommon for certain infants even to behave in ways that run counter to the general trend. Thus, for example, of the twenty-seven children who moved off the center board on Gibson and Walk's visual cliff, three actually crawled off on the deep side, and of the thirty-two infants observed by Meltzoff and Borton, eight failed to make an intermodal match. Although researchers investigating infant perception have not, for the most part, studied individual differences of this sort, one area of research that has focused on variation among infants is that concerned with temperament. "Temperament" has been generally defined to consist of biologically based individual differences in behavioral dispositions that appear early in life and remain relatively stable across situations and over time. Although psychologists do not always agree on basic categories of temperament, specific temperament concepts usually refer in some way to infants' emotionality, frequency and intensity of motor activity, or sociability. In the article excerpted below, Kagan describes a program of research that has addressed a characteristic of temperament, extreme behavioral inhibition in the face of novelty, that appears to be related to all three of these characteristics.

. . . The term temperament in contemporary theory is used by most to refer to those psychological characteristics that display variation among young children and have a relatively, but not indefinitely, stable biological basis in the person's genotype. . . .

The temperamental qualities that are most obvious to contemporary parents and studied most often by psychologists and psychiatrists are excessive irritability, activity level, regularity, ease of adaptation to new situations, smiling, vocalization, and laughter. These particular variables are popular because they have implications for the ease with which parents can socialize their infants. . . .

Kagan, Jerome. (1989). Temperamental influences on the preservation of styles of social behavior. *McLean Hospital Journal*, XIV. pp. 23-24.

Categories of Inhibited and Uninhibited Children

Steven Reznick, Nancy Snidman, and I, together with Cynthia Garcia-Coll, Wendy Coster, Michelle Gersten, and many others in our laboratory, have been studying two temperamental categories. We began this work by focusing on one and one-half to three-year old children who were observed in a variety of unfamiliar situations.[1,2] Some children consistently become quiet, restrained and retreat to the parent while they assess the situation and act only after they have assimilated the unfamiliarity. Another small group of children consistently act with spontaneity as though the unfamiliarity of the setting or objects were relatively unimportant. The contexts that reveal these two qualities most often in children between one and one-half and three years of age are unfamiliar children or adults. I suspect this is because other people are a frequent basis for categorizing a setting as unfamiliar.

It is rare to find a large number of children who are consistently shy and restrained, on the one hand, or outgoing and spontaneous, on the other, regardless of the social context. There is, however, a small group of children, we estimate at 15 percent, who usually bring one or the other of these behavioral styles to new situations. We have called the shy, fearful, children "inhibited" and the sociable, spontaneous, children "uninhibited." . . .

Our current investigation of these categories goes back to an early collaboration with Howard Moss, the results of which were published in *Birth to Maturity* in 1962[3]. Moss and I studied a large group of families who were participating in the Fels Institute's longitudinal project which was initiated in the early 1930s. The Caucasian children from these intact families were observed from birth to adolescence in many settings. Moss rated each child on a set of variables for consecutive, chronological epochs from a large corpus of information while I interviewed these same subjects who were then in their twenties. We also administered a relevant battery of tests. One of the most important discoveries emanating from this project was that the only two psychological characteristics that were preserved from the first three years of life through adulthood were the characteristics that we now call inhibited and uninhibited. A small group of children who were very shy and fearful during the early years—about 15 percent of the total sample—retained that characteristic through adulthood. The contrasting group of sociable, fearless infants became extroverts when they were adults. Even though Moss and I suggested tentatively that these predispositions might be a partial function of genetics, the dominant belief during the early 1960s was that temperamental factors were of minimal significance. Our own faith in a temperamental interpretation was not sufficiently strong and neither of us pursued these phenomena.

Fortunately, a later collaboration with Richard Kearsley and Philip Zelazo led to a return of the repressed[4]. The three of us were investigating the effect of daycare on children in the first three years of life and observed Chinese-American and Caucasian infants from similar social class backgrounds in a longitudinal investigation. Although the effect of regular daycare on cognitive and affective characteristics was minimal, the

Chinese infants, whether they were attending our daycare center regularly or were raised only at home, were, compared with the Caucasian infants, more shy and fearful when they encountered unfamiliar adults or children in laboratory settings. The Chinese infants also cried more intensely when their mother left them for a brief separation. We also found that the Chinese children had less variable heart rates across the numerous laboratory assessments from three through twenty-nine months of age. This provocative and unexpected association provided one of the incentives for our current work.

During the last ten years we have been studying three cohorts of children. The first two were selected to be extreme on inhibited or uninhibited behavior. Cohort 1 was selected at twenty-one months; Cohort 2 at thirty-one months. We had to screen over 400 children in order to find 54 inhibited and 53 uninhibited children, about 15 percent of all the children screened. We also decided to have equal numbers of boys and girls in each of the groups. These children have been seen on three additional occasions. At the last assessment, when they were seven and one-half years old, there were 41 children in each of the two cohorts, which is a loss of about 20 percent of the original sample.[5]

The third cohort was an unselected volunteer sample typical of the groups studied by child psychologists. The original sample began with 100 children at 14 months and ended with 77 children at four years of age. From this group we selected the extremely inhibited and uninhibited children and saw the smaller samples when they were five and one-half years of age.

Details of the assessments at each of the ages can be found in our published papers.[1,2,5,6] The children in Cohort 1, selected at twenty-one months of age, were observed on two occasions when they encountered unfamiliar women and objects in unfamiliar laboratory rooms. The signs of inhibition were prolonged clinging to or remaining proximal to the mother, cessation of vocalization, and reluctance to approach the unfamiliar events. The selection of children for Cohort 2 at thirty-one months of age was based on behavior with an unfamiliar child of the same sex and age in a laboratory playroom and a subsequent episode in which the child encountered an unfamiliar woman dressed in an unusual costume. The indexes of inhibition, similar to those used with Cohort 1, were long latencies to play, to speak, and to interact with the unfamiliar child and woman, as well as long periods of time spent proximal to the mother. The indexes of inhibition on the later assessments were based on behavior in laboratory play sessions with an unfamiliar child, or children, of the same sex and age and behavior with an unfamiliar female examiner administering a cognitive battery. At five and one-half years of age, the children were observed in their classrooms and coded for degree of interaction with other children.

About three-fourths of the children in each of the first two cohorts retained their expected behavioral classification, based on whether their score on an aggregate index of inhibition at seven and one-half years was positive or negative. Further, the children who were most extreme in their early behavior were most likely to retain their temperamental style. A small number of uninhibited children—about 10 percent—became timid and shy at seven and one-half years of age.

In addition, the majority of the inhibited seven and one-half year olds compared with

175

only twenty-five percent of the uninhibited group had several unusual fears. Typical fears characteristic of the inhibited children included speaking voluntarily in the classroom, attending summer camp, being alone in the home, taking out the rubbish at night, or going to their bedroom alone in the evening. Follow-up studies of clinical samples reveal that about one-third of young children diagnosed as having severe phobias remain anxious as adults and often seek vocations with minimal risk.

In addition, inhibited children may be at some risk for social phobia in adulthood and perhaps panic and agoraphobia because panic patients report being shy and timid as children. In addition, in a collaborative study with Gerald Rosenbaum and Joseph Biederman of the Massachusetts General Hospital, we have found that four to seven year-old children living with parents who were or had been panic patients were significantly more likely to be inhibited than were control children.

These results were found for children who had been selected originally to be either extremely inhibited or uninhibited. However, some scientists believe that shyness and sociability lie in a continuum; hence, it is important to determine whether inhibited and uninhibited children represent two qualitative categories. . . .

Support for this suggestion comes from our study of the third cohort mentioned earlier. The 100 children in this third unselected cohort were observed initially at fourteen months and again at twenty, thirty-two, and forty-eight months of age; 77 children were seen at forty-eight months. The indexes of inhibited and uninhibited behavior were similar to those used in our other studies. The indexes of inhibition at fourteen and twenty months did not predict variation in behavior at four years of age for the entire sample. We only found preservation of the two styles when we restricted the analysis to those children who fell to the top and bottom 20 percent of the distribution of behavioral inhibition at both fourteen and twenty months.

We recently evaluated these two extreme groups when they were five and one-half years of age in test situations used with our other two cohorts. The behavioral differences have been preserved. About two-thirds of the original inhibited children were still very inhibited; not one had become extremely sociable. Three-fourths of the uninhibited children remained uninhibited and not one child had become unusually shy. The total corpus of results implies that the constructs, inhibited and uninhibited, refer to qualitative categories and not to a behavioral continuum that ranges from shyness to sociability, even though such a continuum can be constructed. . . .

1. Garcia-Coll C, Kagan J, Reznick JS: Behavioral inhibition in young children. Child Devel 55:1005-1019, 1984.

2. Snidman N: Behavioral restraint and the central nervous system. Unpublished doctoral dissertation. UCLA, 1984.

3. Kagan J, Moss HA: Birth to Maturity. New York, New Haven, Yale Univ Press, 1983.

4. Kagan J, Kearsley R, Zelazo P: Infancy: Its Place in Human Development. Cambridge MA, Harvard Univ Press, 1978.

5. Kagan J, Reznick JS, Snidman N, Gibbons J, et al: Childhood derivatives of inhibition and lack of inhibition to the unfamiliar. Child Dev 59: 1580-1589, 1988.

6. Kagan J, Reznick JS, Snidman N: Biological basis of childhood shyness. Science 240: 167-171, 1988.

9

Symbol Formation and the Acquisition of Language

Usually we are so young when we begin to speak that we are unable years later to recall the experience of those first words. But in rare cases a child may not acquire language until a later age. Helen Keller was such a child. Deaf and blind after a childhood illness, she was eight years old when she understood her first word. Perhaps all children experience the same sense of joy when they first realized the power of language:

One day . . . we walked down the path to the wellhouse. . . Someone was drawing water, and my teacher placed my hand under the spout. As the cool stream gushed over one hand, she spelled into the other the word 'water,' first slowly then rapidly. I stood still, my whole attention fixed on the motions of her fingers. Suddenly, I felt a misty consciousness as of something forgotten—A thrill of returning thought; and somehow the mystery of language was revealed to me. I knew then that w-a-t-e-r meant the wonderful, cool something that was flowing over my hand. That living word awakened my soul, gave it light, hope, joy, set it free!

— **Helen Keller,** *The Story of My Life*

• INTRODUCTION •

Language is one of our most complicated skills and most powerful tools. There are few, if any, events within the realm of human experience, no matter how complex, that we cannot think about or discuss with others using language. Language is an extraordinary ability: in its range, flexibility, and generativity, it sets human beings apart from all of the other creatures of nature. Yet language, for all its complexity and sophistication, is among the earliest skills that children acquire. Long before they can ride bicycles, cut with scissors, draw human figures, find their way around department stores, or drive automobiles, children speak or sign in forms barely distinguishable from those used by adults. Incredibly, the process starts even before the first birthday, and much of the hard work of sorting out problems of word order and word form is over before children leave preschool.

Although there is much about language development that we still do not understand, research over the past 25 years has greatly enriched our conception of the language acquisition process. The three readings chosen for this module describe outstanding examples of this research. In the first article, John de Cuevas introduces us to the early history of modern child language study as it developed in the Harvard laboratory of Roger Brown. Brown originated techniques of study, formulated and provided data on the classic questions, and helped train an entire generation of scholars in the area of child language. Among the most important generalizations to emerge from this work was the recognition that in the early stages of speech the order of emergence of certain basic grammatical structures is similar among children, even though they may be acquiring language at different rates and under varied social conditions. This discovery has been widely interpreted as supporting the notion that elements of the process of language acquisition are universal, common to all children acquiring all languages everywhere.

In the second reading, Dan Slobin reviews cross-linguistic evidence consonant with this view. Languages, as everyone knows, differ markedly from one another. Spoken languages each have their own particular constellation from the total corpus of human speech sounds. Rules for word order and word form vary widely. Despite this variability, certain features of the acquisition process are consistent across languages. These universal principles of language acquisition seem to imply the existence, as Slobin puts it, of "developmental universals of human mind."

Deaf children may not acquire spoken language at all. Instead they may be raised to be fluent in one or another form of sign language. Sign languages, we now know, are fully developed languages with their own complex systems of rules for word formation and word order. Yet manual communication is visual-gestural rather than auditory-phonemic. The case for universality would be considerably strengthened if languages using a modality other than speech were shown to exhibit the same basic principles of acquisition that characterize spoken languages. In our third reading, Richard Meier reviews evidence that supports just such a notion.

● ● ●

"No, she holded them loosely"
John de Cuevas

Roger Brown is a pioneer in the study of child language. In this article, John de Cuevas describes several generally accepted regularities in language acquisition originally clarified by the work of Brown and his students. These include the nature of the two-word, "telegraphic" utterances that emerge around eighteen months; children's ability to formulate rules about language (such as how to form plurals or make the past tense) and apply them in novel contexts; the invariant order of emergence of certain basic early grammatical structures; and the fact that acquisition order is independent of the frequency with which these structures appear in adult speech. In his discussion, de Cuevas also raises an issue with which we are now quite familiar, the issue of nature/nurture. The existence of principles of language acquisition common across children and seemingly independent of the specifics of language input is interpreted by many to support the view that children are not only biologically predisposed to learn language, but innately constrained to learn in certain ways and not in others.

de Cuevas, John. (1990). "No, she holded them loosely." *Harvard Magazine,* September-October. pp. 60-70.

Language is a natural endowment. We all learned to speak as naturally as we learned to walk or run, and by the time we were five years old we had mastered most of the subtleties and complexities of our native language. We didn't have to be taught it or go to school to learn. We picked it up automatically, without thinking about it or making a special effort. Of course, in the beginning when we were very small, our parents spoke to us more slowly than they spoke to adults. They used simpler phrases and sentences, and exaggerated their tone of voice to emphasize how words and ideas went together. That is to say, they spoke baby talk to us (what some call *motherese*). But that doesn't explain how we learned. Anyone who has tried to learn a foreign language in adult years will immediately recognize how hard it is to acquire vocabulary and to master rules of grammar, syntax, and the subtleties of usage to the point of being able to respond appropriately and fluently in any given context. Yet preschool children learn to do just that without formal training of any kind. It is an astonishing feat. How they do it, how they learn language, is a question that people have been trying to answer for a very long time.

In 1962 Roger Brown—now the Lindsley professor of psychology in memory of William James at Harvard—undertook to study the question systematically. Brown is a tall, handsome man ("the Cary Grant of psychology" according to a former student), whose soft-spoken manner, quiet sense of humor, and gentle patience would put any child at ease. He and some of his graduate students tape-recorded the speech of three children—Brown called them Adam, Eve, and Sarah—at regular intervals over a period of several years. They chose those three children, according to Brown, "primarily because they were all just beginning to speak multiword utterances, had highly intelligible speech, and were highly voluble, which meant we would not have to sit around forever to get usefully large transcriptions." Or as Ursula Bellugi—one of Brown's students at the time, now director of the Laboratory for Language and Cognitive Studies at the Salk Institute for Biological Studies in California—put it, "because they talked a lot."

Adam and Eve were recorded for two hours every other week, Sarah for about an hour every week. Eve was only a year and a half old when the studies began, and unfortunately the recordings of her speech had to end after about eleven months, when her family unexpectedly left Cambridge for Nova Scotia. But Adam and Sarah, who were both twenty-seven months old when studies of their speech began, were recorded over a period of several years. From the beginning of the project, Brown and his students met at a weekly seminar to discuss the material they were collecting and to analyze what was happening in the speech of the children. The seminar was not limited to those who did the recordings but was open to anyone interested in language development. In fact, the seminar ran for several years and became a training ground for those who attended, many going on to become leading scholars in the field of psycho-linguistics. Dan Slobin, one of the students who attended, now professor of psychology at Berkeley, called it "The Garden of Eden."

It may be said without much exaggeration that Brown and his seminar gave rise to an entire generation of scholars of language development. His influence in that respect has been enormous; a list of the names of his former students reads like a *Who's Who* of the field. When he began the project with Adam and Eve, only a handful of people were investigating the speech of children. Today child language is a basic part of most courses in psychology, and last October the Conference on Language Development, held annually at Boston University, attracted more than five hundred participants from around the world. Based on the studies, Brown wrote an analysis of children's speech in a book called *A First Language*, one of the most influential works on the subject of language development in children ever written, in which he concluded that the way children learn language is "approximately invariant across children learning the same language and, at a higher level of abstraction, across children learning any language."

Brown's pioneering work became the model for countless studies of child language that followed and gave rise to the flourishing field known as developmental psycholinguistics. By now so much has been written on language learning in children that no one could ever read it all, but in spite of all the work, no one has yet been able to explain fully how children learn their first language, although the pattern of development is well established for children learning English and a number of other languages as well.

All children cry at birth. Within hours of being born, they can distinguish sounds and are especially attentive to the human voice. They begin cooing at six weeks and babbling at six months, by which time they are also capable of distinguishing speech sounds and hearing the difference between consonants like *p* and *b* or *t* and *d*. At eight months they vary their intonations in mimicry of adult speech. In fact, mothers hearing infants from English, Russian, or Chinese backgrounds can pick out the infants from their own language group but cannot distinguish between the other two. English speakers, for instance, can tell which infants have English-speaking mothers but not which ones have Chinese- or Russian-speaking mothers.

Most children say their first words when they are about a year old, but children vary enormously in their rates of development. Some begin speaking earlier, while others may not begin until their third year. (Being early or late, by the way, says nothing about intelligence or mental capacities in general.) At about eighteen months, most children progress to the two-word stage, which means only that the average length of their utterances is about two words: they may utter four or five in a row. Brown coined the term *telegraphic speech* to characterize children's early utterances ("more milk," "allgone cookie," "What dóing, Mommy?") because pronouns, prepositions, inflectional word endings, and other niceties are omitted. As every mother knows, however, the one- and two-word stages are far richer in meaning than the bare words might indicate. The child hearing a car pulling up at the front door might say, "Daddy come," clearly understanding though unable to express that daddy himself will appear in a few moments.

Children progress quickly and by two and a half can produce complex sentences that are indistinguishable from those an adult might utter. Which is not to say that at two and a half they are capable of adult speech, only that they often come up with what sounds like the real thing. At twenty-seven months, Eve could say, "I go get a pencil 'n' write," and "I put them in the refrigerator to freeze." She had acquired a number of function words—those pronouns, prepositions, auxiliary verbs, and the like that are indispensable parts of the structure of the English language. Children at that age often know how words should sound but can't manage the right pronunciation. Brown tells of a child who spoke of "a fis." Brown queried, "Fis?" The child forcefully said "fis" as if to correct him. Then Brown said "fish," and the child nodded, "Yeah, fis." Children also understand more than they can say; they understand utterances more complex than any they can produce themselves. In the language of psychologists, comprehension exceeds production.

It is by now quite clear that children don't learn to speak by imitating adults. Moreover, parents rarely correct children's mistakes or reward them for good grammar; they are more often concerned with the content of what children say. Children seem to learn independently of what their parents or other adults say, as if they followed a program of their own, looking for regularities in language as they went along and forming notions of how to do things with words. Take, for example, the child who had understood that possessive pronouns (*its, his, ours, yours.* etc.) all ended in *s*, including *mines*. "Dis is mines," she said to an older playmate one day, "dat's yours." "That's mine," he agreed, whereupon, aware of a difficulty, she said, "Dis is mine," and a few moments later, "I keep stealing all your." It had suddenly occurred to her that something was wrong with her old rule.

One of the commonest mistakes children make in English is to overgeneralize the regular ending for the past tense. Here is an often quoted exchange:

Child: My teacher holded the baby rabbits and we petted them.
Mother: Did you say your teacher held the baby rabbits?
Child: Yes.
Mother: What did you say she did?
Child: She holded the baby rabbits and we petted them.
Mother: Did you say she held them tightly?
Child: No, she holded them loosely.

Children often stick to their notions of language, disregarding those who try to correct them, persisting in their peculiar usages until they are ready to adopt new ones. Another often cited example is that of the child who said, "Nobody don't like me." His mother tried to correct him by saying, "Nobody likes me." They repeated this exchange no fewer than eight times until it dawned on the boy that he had been making a mistake. "Oh!" he said at last, "nobody don't *likes* me."

At two and a half most children ask questions and make negative statements, although it is usually another year or two before they master the intricacies of combining *no* or *not* with forms of *to be* in sentences such as "Isn't Daddy here?" They first learn to ask questions with a rising intonation ("You like this?") and only later that the words *what, when, where, who, why,* and *how* can be used to introduce questions. Children are also late to learn the subject verb inversion that questions in English require, as in "Where can we go?" and the even more complicated use of auxiliary verbs, as in "Why are you doing that?" The tag questions, as in "You'd like to play with my toys, wouldn't you?" come later still.

By the time they are five, children have mastered most of the complex constructions that characterize everyday social speech and are able to understand and generate passive constructions ("We were driven to school"), indirect requests ("Would you mind passing the salt?"), and many other sophisticated forms of adult language, although some subtleties continue to elude them. Take this exchange between a researcher and a child of five:

> Researcher (showing the child a blindfolded doll): Is the doll easy or hard to see?
> Child: Hard to see.
> Researcher: Will you make her easy to see?
> Child: If I can get this untied.
> Researcher: Why was she hard to see?
> Child: Because she had a blindfold.

At eight years of age some children still have trouble with expressions like "hard to see," but not at ten, for by then they have matured fully in their understanding of speech, and their progress past that age consists almost entirely of enlarging their vocabulary.

How *do* children learn language? Steven Pinker, a former student of Brown's, now professor of brain and cognitive sciences and a director of the Center for Cognitive Science at M.I.T., has called language "the jewel in the crown of cognition—it is what everyone wants to explain." Are we born with empty minds and is everything we know, including language, the result of learning and experience? Or are we born with predispositions that not only endow us with the capacity for language but also determine what we can learn and how we perceive the world around us? Nowadays, the more fashionable view is that we are predisposed, not just for language, but also for music or math or culture. Some believe that specific structures in the brain mediate specific functions, such as language. That may not be the universal view, but most psychologists today would agree that we are constrained to some extent in what we know and the way we learn by innate knowledge.

It was not always so. Forty years ago, most psychologists in the United States believed children learned language through imitation and conditioning. Psychology was then dominated by behaviorism, which focused exclusively on external behavior and shunned questions about the nature of consciousness, memory, and the like as unscientific and not amenable to experimental investigation. Mental states, mind itself, were not fit subjects of inquiry because they were neither observable nor measurable. Taking a cue from the Russian physiologist Ivan Pavlov, who made the conditioned reflex almost a household phrase, the behaviorists sought to explain all behavior in terms of conditioning—that is, of stimulus and response. Living organisms, they argued, whether animals

185

or people, respond passively to stimuli, and the responses are either discouraged by punishment or reinforced by reward. Harvard's B. F. Skinner, the best-known representative of the behaviorist school, at one time dazzled the world with demonstrations of the kinds of seemingly complex behavior he could induce by conditioning. He trained pigeons with precise timed rewards of food to press buttons on command, to dance like dervishes, even to play Ping-Pong. In a book called *Verbal Behavior*, he argued that language, too, could be understood as the result of conditioning.

The behaviorists were successful in explaining many forms of behavior as the result of conditioning, but as Noam Chomsky showed in a famous critique of Skinner's book, they could not explain language, or for that matter, creativity in general. Speakers of a language can produce and understand an infinite number of novel utterances, a capacity that cannot be accounted for by operant conditioning. "The child who learns a language," wrote Chomsky, "has in some sense constructed the grammar for himself on the basis of his observation of sentences and nonsentences . . . and . . . has succeeded in carrying out what from the formal point of view, at least, seems to be a remarkable type of theory construction. Furthermore, this task is accomplished in an astonishingly short time, to a large extent independently of intelligence, and in a comparable way by all children."

Enter Brown. He came to Harvard as an instructor in 1952, having earned his doctorate in psychology at Michigan the year before. Oddly enough he never took a course in linguistics, and his interest in the subject did not really develop until after he had taken his degree. As a postdoc, he attended a seminar at Michigan where he heard a talk on traditional descriptive linguistics and became fascinated by the subject. He taught a course in the psychology of language while still at Michigan, and when he came to Harvard, he quite naturally taught a similar course. In 1958 he published his first book, *Words and Things*, an engaging and highly readable reflection on some "very old" problems of language—Brown called them "a set of real chestnuts"—such as the nature of meaning and the relation between language and thought. The book is still in print today.

Brown was aware at the time—it was a well known phenomenon in psychology, he says—that children made systematic errors in speech. Those errors suggested that they were formulating rules about language as they went along. If, for example, a child said, "they goed away," or "I digged a hole," a kind of mistake all children learning English make at some point, the child had probably formulated a rule about the past tense: add *-ed* to the ends of all verbs. Oddly enough, children learn certain irregular forms of the past tense before they learn the regular ones, forms like *went* and *saw*, which are among the oldest verbs in the English language and among the most frequently used. Children learn them as words, however, rather than as forms of the past tense.

Children, of course, don't think of the past tense as the subject of a rule (if they think of it at all). Rather, they know that different sounds must be added at the ends of certain verbs to form the past— after verbs like *walk,* for example, they must add a *t* sound; after verbs like *play* they must add a *d* sound; and after verbs like *wade* they must add an *ed* sound, which includes an unstressed vowel sound linguists call *schwa*. Similarly, children know that certain words take the sound of *s* to form the plural (as in *cats*), others take the sound of *z* (as in *dogs*), and yet others take the sound of *ez*, which also includes a schwa, (as in *horses*).

Children seem to formulate many such rules about language and to be able to apply them in novel contexts. Among the earliest rules that children learning English seem to master are how to form the plurals of words and how to form the past tense. A classic study of the phenomenon was done under Brown's guidance by one of his first graduate students at Harvard, Jean Berko, now Jean Berko Gleason and professor of psychology at Boston University. For her doctoral research, she devised an ingenious set of experiments to test how well children understood certain forms. She invented nonsense words for imaginary objects and actions, and illustrated them with cartoon drawings. She showed the drawings to children of various ages and asked them questions to see how they responded. For example, she would present a child with a cartoon drawing depicting odd, birdlike creatures and explain, "This is a wug. Now there is another one. There are two of them. There are two _____." She would pause, and the child might say, "wugs," correctly pronouncing the *s* like a *z*. Or she would show a drawing of a man with a strange instrument in his hands and explain, "This is a man who knows how to rick. He is ricking. He did the same thing yesterday. Yesterday he _____," and the child might say, "He ricked," supplying the correct *t* sound for the past tense.

Berko Gleason's approach represented a method that could be used in a variety of ways to test children's understanding of language. For example, children might be shown a drawing of a container with a spaghetti-like substance that someone appeared to be kneading. They might then be told, "In this picture you can see a niss," or "you can see some niss." or "you can see someone nissing," and if they understood the distinctions among the three statements, their attention would be drawn respectively to the container, the substance, or the action. Then they might be shown three separate pictures—the container alone, the spaghetti-like substance alone, or the action of kneading something—and be told "show me *a* niss," "show me *some* niss," or "show me *nissing*," which would require them to point to one of the three pictures. Most children, even at two years of age, respond correctly. They already know how a specific object, a mass noun, and an action are marked in English and can distinguish accordingly between object, substance, and action.

Experiments of this kind strongly supported the idea that children weren't learning language by rote or by imitation but by formulating rules. Moreover, as soon as they formulated a rule, they were apt to apply it universally and, often enough, incorrectly. Hence they would say "digged" instead of "dug," or "foots" instead of "feet," and might not learn the correct forms for irregular words until much later. Indeed, children's errors appeared to be systematic, and it was this systematicness that prompted Brown to undertake the studies of Adam, Eve, and Sarah; if such errors were characteristic of all children learning English, they might throw some light on the psychological processes at work below the surface.

In 1962 Brown, with the help of Ursula Bellugi and Colin Fraser (Fraser is now lecturer in psychology at Cambridge University in England), began a study of the speech of about thirty children in Cambridge (Massachusetts), visiting them in their homes and recording samples of their conversation. At first Brown concentrated on the development of specific forms—plurals, past tenses, and the like. He and his students wrote a number of papers on their methods of research and the findings that resulted from them. But Brown soon realized that the approach was only piecemeal. He really wanted to investigate more fundamental psychological processes in children's acquisition of speech. That would require a study extending over time, so he decided to follow a few children throughout their preschool years of language learning. That is how the studies of Adam, Eve, and Sarah began.

Adam and Eve came first, Bellugi recording Adam, and Fraser Eve. About a year later, Courtney Cazden, now professor of education at the Harvard Graduate School of Education, joined the group and undertook to record Sarah. The project required more than merely taping the children's words. Notes had to be taken of the context in which all speech was uttered, both that of the children and of any adults who might be present. Brown made it a rule that the tapes be transcribed within two or three days of the time they were made while memories of the recording sessions were still fresh in the minds of the investigators. And great care had to be taken in transcribing the children's speech to mark the presence or absence of words and inflections. It was essential, for instance, to know whether a child said "Mommy shoe" or "Mommy's shoe," whether "that mine" or "that's mine." (On one occasion, Adam was asked, "which is right, 'two shoes' or 'two shoe'?" His answer, as Brown describes it, "produced with explosive enthusiasm, was 'Pop goes the weasel!' The two-year-old child," he added, "does not make a perfectly docile experimental subject.")

The studies of Adam and Eve and Sarah were unexpectedly successful. The three children, whose families were not known to each other and who came from different social and economic backgrounds, exhibited a similarity in the way they acquired language that Brown says still amazes him. Although they differed in their rates of development, all three acquired certain forms of language in the same order. For instance, all three learned the present progressive (the -ing ending of verbs) before they learned to combine it with a form of to be. They would all say things like "baby talking" long before they said "baby is talking." All three used on and in before they used any other prepositions. All three acquired, in the same order, first the use of the articles a and the, then the possessive 's, then the regular past, and then the various contractions, as in "Mommy's going" or "no, don't." It was as if a basic plan of development were unfolding in the children, one that Brown has likened in its intricacy to the biological development of an embryo. . . .

Brown tried to account for the phenomenon of why children learning English acquired certain forms of speech in one particular order rather than another, and why the order should be the same in all children. He examined the possibility that the forms children hear most often in the speech of their parents and other adults were the ones they acquired earliest, but he concluded from the evidence in the transcripts that the frequency with which forms appeared in adult speech had little effect on what children

188

learned first. For instance, the articles *a* and *the* are among the words most frequently used by all adults, yet they ranked only seventh in order of acquisition in the list of fourteen morphemes.

Perhaps not surprisingly, what seemed mainly to determine the order of acquisition was what Brown called "cumulative complexity," which included both a semantic component (how many meanings a word carries) and a grammatical component (how many rules determine a word's formation). Cumulative complexity can be illustrated by the combination of the plural, which signifies number, and the past tense, which signifies what Brown termed "earlierness." Before children can acquire the plural they must understand number, and before they can acquire the past tense they must understand earlierness. (Number appears to be an easier concept for them to grasp than earlierness because they acquire it sooner.) To acquire and use *were* correctly, for instance, children must understand both number and earlierness. *Were* is more complex than either the plural or the past tense alone because it combines the two notions, and children must have grasped them in combination before they can use the word correctly. As Brown observed, "There is evidently, and this is simply an empirical discovery, some additional knowledge involved in putting the component items of knowledge together to make the more complex construction."

A First Language dealt only with the early stages of children's speech. Brown did not go beyond them because he could no longer find the same regularities in the later stages that characterized the early ones, nor could he reduce the data he and his students had collected to manageable proportions. "What impels the child to 'improve' his speech at all," he wrote, "remains something of a mystery". . . .

Children and Language: They Learn the Same Way All Around the World
Dan I. Slobin

Whether they are learning Russian, Serbo-Croatian, Finnish, Turkish, Tzeltal (Mayan), Samoan, Mandarin Chinese, English, or any of a number of other languages that have been studied, children learn to speak in surprisingly similar ways. In this article, Dan Slobin reviews a basic set of linguistic universals that appear to span the diversity of human tongues. The child's first word typically names an object, animal, or person in the immediate environment. At about eighteen months, children begin to combine words into two-word phrases designed to convey a basic set of fundamental meanings (e.g., identification, location, repetition, etc.). No matter how flexible the word order requirements of a language in adult form, children seem to rely heavily on word order in early acquisition. Although developmental limitations early in the two- and three-word stages are severe, children can use context to communicate ideas that exceed the limits of their language productivity. In acquiring more complex grammatical structures, children first attach new elements to old sentences and only then learn to use the correct word order. Finally, in all studied languages, the child's grammar bias is so powerful that errors reflecting over-generalization of rules may persist for years. Principles of language acquisition, in other words, are not only common across children, they are common across languages as well. Such evidence strengthens the case for biological constraints on language learning.

According to the account of linguistic history set forth in the book of Genesis, all men spoke the same language until they dared to unite to build the Tower of Babel. So that men could not cooperate to build a tower that would reach into heaven, God acted to "confound the language of all the earth" to insure that groups of men "may not understand one another's speech."

What was the original universal language of mankind? This is the question that Psammetichus, ruler of Egypt in the seventh century B.C., asked in the first controlled psychological experiment in recorded history—an experiment in developmental psycholinguistics reported by Herodotus:

Slobin, Dan I. (1972). Children and language: They learn the same way all around the world. *Psychology Today*, July. pp. 71-74, 82.

"Psammetichus . . . took at random, from an ordinary family, two newly born infants and gave them to a shepherd to be brought up amongst his flocks, under strict orders that no one should utter a word in their presence. They were to be kept by themselves in a lonely cottage. . . ."

Psammetichus wanted to know whether isolated children would speak Egyptian words spontaneously— thus proving, on the premise that ontogeny recapitulates phylogeny, that Egyptians were the original race of mankind.

In two years, the children spoke their first word: *becos*, which turned out to be the Phrygian word for bread. The Egyptians withdrew their claim that they were the world's most ancient people and admitted the greater antiquity of the Phrygians.

Same. We no longer believe, of course, that Phrygian was the original language of all the earth (nor that it was Hebrew, as King James VII of Scotland thought). No one knows which of the thousands of languages is the oldest—perhaps we will never know. But recent work in developmental psycholinguistics indicates that the languages of the earth are not as confounded as we once believed. Children in all nations seem to learn their native languages in much the same way. Despite the diversity of tongues, there are linguistic universals that seem to rest upon the developmental universals of the human mind. Every language is learnable by children of preschool-age, and it is becoming apparent that little children have some definite ideas about how a language is structured and what it can be used for:

Mmm, I want to eat maize.
What?
Where is the maize?
There is no more maize.
Mmm.
Mmm.
[Child seizes an ear of corn]:
What's this?
It's not our maize.
Whose is it?
It belongs to grandmother.
Who harvested it?
They harvested it.
Where did they harvest it?
They harvested it down over there.
Way down over there?
Mmm. [yes]
Let's look for some too.
You look for some.
Fine.
Mmm.
[Child begins to hum]

The dialogue is between a mother and a two and one-half year-old girl. Anthropologist Brian Stross of the University of Texas recorded it in a thatched hut in an isolated Mayan village in Chiapas, Mexico. Except for the fact that the topic was maize and the language was Tzeltal, the conversation could have taken place anywhere, as any parent will recognize. The child uses short, simple sentences, and her mother answers in kind. The girl expresses her needs and seeks information about such things as location, possession, past action, and so on. She does not ask about time, remote possibilities, contingencies, and the like—such things don't readily occur to the two-year-old in any culture, or in any language.

Our research team at the University of California at Berkeley has been studying the way children learn languages in several countries and cultures. We have been aided by similar research at Harvard and at several other American universities, and by the work of foreign colleagues. We have gathered reasonably firm data on the acquisition of 18 languages, and have suggestive findings on twelve others. Although the data are still scanty for many of these languages, a common picture of human-language development is beginning to emerge.

In all cultures the child's first word generally is a noun or proper name, identifying some object, animal, or person he sees every day. At about two years—give or take a few months—a child begins to put two words together to form rudimentary sentences. The two-word stage seems to be universal.

To get his meaning across, a child at the two-word stage relies heavily on gesture, tone and context. Lois Bloom, . . . Teachers College, Columbia University, reported a little American girl who said *Mommy sock* on two distinct occasions: on finding her mother's sock and on being dressed by her mother. Thus the same phrase expressed posession in one context (*Mommy's sock*) and an agent-object relationship in another (*Mommy is putting on the sock*).

But even with a two-word horizon, children can get a wealth of meanings across:

IDENTIFICATION: *See doggie.*
LOCATION: *Book there.*
REPETITION: *More milk.*
NONEXISTENCE: *Allgone thing.*
NEGATION: *Not wolf.*
POSSESSION: *My candy.*
ATTRIBUTION: *Big car.*
AGENT-ACTION: *Mama walk.*
AGENT-OBJECT: *Mama book* (meaning, "Mama read book").
ACTION-LOCATION: *Sit chair.*
ACTION-DIRECT OBJECT: *Hit you.*
ACTION-INDIRECT OBJECT: *Give papa.*
ACTION-INSTRUMENT: *Cut knife.*
QUESTION: *Where ball?*

The striking thing about this list is its universality. The examples are drawn from child talk in English, German, Russian, Finnish, Turkish, Samoan and Luo, but the entire list could probably be made up of examples from two-year-old speech in any language.

Word. A child easily figures out that the speech he hears around him contains discrete, meaningful elements, and that these elements can be combined. And children make the combinations themselves— many of their meaningful phrases would never be heard in adult speech. For example, Martin Braine studied a child who said things like *allgone outside* when he returned home and shut the door, *more page* when he didn't want a story to end, *other fix* when he wanted something repaired, and so on. These clearly are expressions created by the child, not mimicry of his parents. The matter is especially clear in the Russian language, in which noun endings vary with the role the noun plays in a sentence. As a rule, Russian children first use only the nominative ending in all combinations, even when it is grammatically incorrect. What is important to children is the *word*, not the ending; the *meaning*, not the grammar.

At first, the two-word limit is quite severe. A child may be able to say *daddy throw, throw ball,* and *daddy ball*—indicating that he understands the full proposition, *daddy throw ball*—yet be unable to produce all three words in one stretch. Again, though the data are limited, this seems to be a universal fact about children's speech.

Tools. Later a child develops a rudimentary grammar within the two-word format. These first grammatical devices are the most basic formal tools of human language: intonation, word order, and inflection.

A child uses intonation to distinguish meanings even at the one-word stage, as when he indicates a request by a rising tone, or a demand with a loud, insistent tone. But at the two-word stage another device, a contrastive stress, becomes available. An English speaking child might say BABY *chair* to indicate possession, and *baby* CHAIR to indicate location or destination.

English sentences typically follow a subject-verbobject sequence, and children learn the rules early. In the example presented earlier, *daddy throw ball,* children use some two-word combinations (*daddy throw, throw ball, daddy ball*) but not others (*ball daddy, ball throw, throw daddy*). Samoan children follow the standard order of possessed-possessor. A child may be sensitive to word order even if his native language does not stress it. Russian children will sometimes adhere strictly to one word order, even when other orders would be equally acceptable.

Some languages provide different word-endings (inflections) to express various meanings, and children who learn these languages are quick to acquire the word-endings that express direct objects, indirect objects and locations. The direct-object inflection is one of the first endings that children pick up in such languages as Russian, Serbo-Croatian, Latvian, Hungarian, Finnish and Turkish. Children learning English, an Indo-European language, usually take a long time to learn locative prepositions such as *on, in, under,* etc. But in Hungary, Finland, or Turkey, where the languages express location with case-endings on the nouns, children learn how to express locative distinctions quite early.

Place. Children seem to be attuned to the ends of words. German children learn the inflection system relatively late, probably because it is attached to articles (*der, die, das,* etc.) that appear before the nouns. The Slavic, Hungarian, Finnish and Turkish inflectional systems, based on noun suffixes, seem relatively easy to learn. And it is not just a matter of articles being difficult to learn, because Bulgarian articles which are noun suffixes are learned very early. The relevant factor seems to be the position of the grammatical marker relative to a main content word.

By the time he reaches the end of the two-word stage, the child has much of the basic grammatical machinery he needs to acquire any particular native language: words that can be combined in order and modified by intonation and inflection. These rules occur, in varying degrees, in all languages, so that all languages are about equally easy for children to learn.

Gap. When a child first uses three words in one phrase, the third word usually fills in the part that was implicit in his two-word statements. Again, this seems to be a universal pattern of development. It is dramatically explicit when the child expands his own communication as he repeats it: *Want that . . . Andrew want that.*

Just as the two-word structure resulted in idiosyncratic pairings, the three-word stage imposes its own limits. When an English-speaking child wishes to add an adjective to the subject-verb-object form, something must go. He can say *Mama drink coffee* or *Drink hot coffee*, but not *Mama drink hot coffee*. This developmental limitation on sentence span seems to be universal: the child's mental ability to express ideas grows faster than his ability to formulate the ideas in complete sentences. As the child learns to construct longer sentences, he uses more complex grammatical operations. He attaches new elements to old sentences (*Where I can sleep?*) before he learns how to order the elements correctly (*Where can I sleep?*). When the child learns to combine two sentences he first compresses them end-to-end (*the boy fell down that was running*) then finally he embeds one within the other (*the boy that was running fell down*).

Across. These are the basic operations of grammar, and to the extent of our present knowledge, they all are acquired by about age four, regardless of native language or social setting. The underlying principles emerge so regularly and so uniformly across diverse languages that they seem to make up an essential part of the child's basic means of information processing. They seem to be comparable to the principles of object constancy and depth perception. Once the child develops these guidelines he spends most of his years of language acquisition learning the specific details and applications of these principles to his particular native language.

Lapse. Inflection systems are splendid examples of the sort of linguistic detail that children must master. English-speaking children must learn the great irregularities of some of our most frequently used words. Many common verbs have irregular past tenses: *came, fell, broke*. The young child may speak these irregular forms correctly the first time—apparently by memorizing a separate past tense form for each verb—only to lapse into immature talk (*comed, falled, breaked*) once he begins to recognize regularities in the way most verbs are conjugated. These over-regularized forms persist for years,

194

often well into elementary school. Apparently regularity heavily outranks previous practice, reinforcement, and imitation of adult forms in influence on children. The child seeks regularity and is deaf to exceptions. . . .

Talk. When we began our cross-cultural studies at Berkeley, we wrote a manual for our field researchers so that they could record samples of mother-child interaction in other cultures with the same systematic measures we had used to study language development in middle-class American children. But most of our field workers returned to tell us that, by and large, mothers in other cultures do not speak to children very much—children hear speech mainly from other children. The isolated American middle-class home, in which a mother spends long periods alone with her children, may be a relatively rare social situation in the world. The only similar patterns we observed were in some European countries and in a Mayan village.

This raised an important question: Does it matter—for purposes of grammatical development—whether the main interlocutor for a small child is his mother?

The evidence suggests that it does not. First of all, the rate and course of grammatical development seem to be strikingly similar in all of the cultures we have studied. Further, nowhere does a mother devote great effort to correcting a child's grammar. Most of her corrections are directed at speech etiquette and communication, and, as Roger Brown has noted, reinforcement tends to focus on the truth of a child's utterance rather than on the correctness of his grammar. . . .

In this country, Harvard anthropologist Claudia Mitchell-Kernnan has studied language development in black children in an urban ghetto. There, as in foreign countries, children got most of their speech input from older children rather than from their mothers. These children learned English rules as quickly as did the middle class white children that Roger Brown studied, and in the same order. Further, mother-to-child English is simple—very much like child-to-child English. I expect that our cross-cultural studies will find a similar picture in other countries.

How. A child is set to learn a language—any language—as long as it occurs in a direct and active context. In these conditions, every normal child masters his particular native tongue, and learns basic principles in a universal order common to all children, resulting in our adult Babel of linguistic diversity. And he does all this without being able to say how. The Soviet scholar Kornei Ivanovich Chukovsky emphasized this unconscious aspect of linguistic discovery in his famous book on child language, *From Two to Five:*

"It is frightening to think what an enormous number of grammatical forms are poured over the poor head of the young child. And he, as if it were nothing at all, adjusts to all this chaos, constantly sorting out into rubrics the disorderly elements of the words he hears, without noticing as he does this, his gigantic effort. If an adult had to master so many grammatical rules within so short a time, his head would surely burst. . . . In truth, the young child is the hardest mental toiler on our planet. Fortunately, he does not even suspect this."

Language Acquisition by Deaf Children
Richard P. Meier

The linguistic experiences of deaf children may differ from those of hearing children in a number of significant ways. In this article, Richard Meier discusses four such factors: a) impoverishment of the early linguistic environment when deaf babies are born to hearing parents who do not sign; b) immersion in a visual-gestural rather than an auditory-acoustic symbolic environment when parents do sign; c) variation among deaf children in age of first exposure to a sign environment; and d) a relatively less arbitrary (more iconic) relationship between meaning and form for certain signs than for most words.

Arguing for the existence of biological constraints on language acquisition, Meier reviews evidence suggesting that principles of spoken language learning believed to be universal also hold for the acquisition of sign language. Even in the absence of linguistic stimuli, deaf children invent their own gestural systems and spontaneously combine signs in systematic ways. The typical milestones of language acquisition are reached by deaf children who are learning sign in the same order and at approximately the same ages as they are achieved by hearing children; and grammatical rather than iconic properties of signs appear to determine ease of acquisition.

Studies of the deaf, on the other hand, also make it clear that the character of the linguistic environment is critical. Fluency in using the most sophisticated grammatical markers, those having to do with gestural forms rather than word order, varies with the age at which children are first exposed to a rich sign environment. This suggests that environment not only plays the obvious but essential role of determining which language a child will learn, but may provide early input necessary to the eventual attainment of full native fluency. In language, as in other areas, development reflects the interaction of nature and nurture.

Contemporary linguists have argued that the ability to learn language is more than an ordinary human skill; it is biologically based. Language is something we are born knowing how to know. Yet the hypothesis that there are biological underpinnings to

Meier, Richard P. (1991). Language acquisition by deaf children. *American Scientist, 79.* pp. 60-70 human linguistic ability does not explain everything. There may indeed be an innate language capacity, a so-called universal grammar, but despite the proponents of Esperanto, there is no universal language. Depending on the accidents of birth, a child may end up a native speaker of any one of roughly 4,000 languages. Thus the predisposition to acquire language seems to be remarkably flexible as well as strong.

Given that our innate language capacity does not prescribe a particular language but instead sets the boundaries of the class of possible languages, what precisely is the relation between nature and nurture in language acquisition? What do nature (the innate ability) and nurture (the linguistic environment) each contribute when a child is acquiring a language?

This question is easy to ask but very difficult to answer. The obvious experiments would involve manipulating a child's linguistic input. For example, one might expose a child only to an artificial language that violates a hypothesized rule of universal grammar. Could the child acquire such a language? Or one might deprive a child of all linguistic input to see if he or she would develop a language in a linguistic vacuum. Of course, performing such experiments with a human subject is unthinkable.

Similar questions can be answered, however, by studying deaf children, whose linguistic experiences are very different from those of the hearing population. For example, it turns out that a child who has no access to a spoken language will readily acquire a sign language, and that a child deprived of both spoken and signed language sometimes invents his or her own gestural system of communication.

Studies of deaf children make it clear that human linguistic competence is in some sense deeper than the mode of expression. Language can assume either the vocal or the gestural mode as circumstances dictate. In other words, although we are biologically equipped to use language, we are not biologically limited to speech.

Evidence of Innateness

Several lines of evidence support the notion that a child has a biologically based capacity to learn language. At first what is most striking about the world's languages is their diversity, but closer study uncovers many universal elements. All known languages share certain organizational principles. For example, in all languages sentences have a hierarchical structure: words are grouped into phrases, and phrases are combined to form sentences. In no language are the words simply strung together like pearls on a necklace.

Moreover, as Noam Chomsky of the Massachusetts Institute of Technology has observed, it is easy to invent syntactic rules that seem reasonable but that occur in no known language. For example, in no language is an interrogative sentence formed by perfectly inverting the word order of the corresponding declarative sentence. Thus "The linguist from Austin was writing a paper," is never converted into a question having the form, "Paper a writing was Austin from linguist the?" One explanation for these language universals, and for many others that are more subtle, is that they are somehow part of our biological capacity.

A second line of evidence derives from close examination of the linguistic input children receive when they are learning a language. That input appears to be deficient in one key respect. Mature speakers know which sentences are grammatical in their dialect and which are not, but children are not taught the distinction in any straightforward way. As Roger Brown and Camille Hanlon of Harvard University were the first to show, a child typically is given many examples of grammatical sentences but very little information about grammatical errors.

Children obviously make grammatical errors, but it seems parents seldom correct them. When a child says, "Me want cookie," the parent seldom explains that only the Cookie Monster on "Sesame Street" says it that way. In any case, whether the child obtains the coveted cookie will probably have more to do with the time remaining until dinner than with the grammatical correctness of his or her request. Furthermore, there are many interesting classes of errors that children never make. It may be that children need little explicit instruction in grammar because they are biologically provided with a universal grammar, and that they never make some types of errors because those errors would violate principles of the universal grammar.

A third line of evidence comes from the study of pidgins and creoles, forms of language that arise when groups of people with no common language find themselves in prolonged contact. Such situations arose on the sugar-cane plantations of Hawaii in the 1890s, for example. Pidgins are simplified, limited-purpose languages. Creole languages, in contrast, are complete and fully serviceable languages. Derek Bickerton of the University of Hawaii argues that the creole languages were the creation of the first generation of children born into the polyglot plantation societies. He considers their linguistic input to have been the local pidgin, which provided them with a sizable vocabulary, but with a limited and highly variable syntactic model. The creole they created and continued to speak as adults shows grammatical regularities not present in the pidgin or, for that matter, in any of the other languages spoken in Hawaii. This finding and the remarkable similarity of the syntaxes of the world's creole languages led Bickerton to conclude that the grammars of such languages are the product of what he calls the child's "language bioprogram."

Although each of these areas of research is fascinating, there are many questions they do not answer and that probably cannot be answered by studying hearing children exposed to spoken languages. Research on language acquisition by deaf children can further our understanding of the language capacity we all share.

Linguistic Environments

The linguistic environment of deaf children often differs in important ways from the typical linguistic environment of early childhood.

The most fundamental property of the typical language-learning environment is that it provides linguistic input that is accessible to the child. The deaf children of hearing parents, however, may not have significant exposure to any language in early childhood.

Because of their sensory loss, these children perceive little of their parents' speech. Because in most cases the parents do not sign, the children are also not exposed to a conventional sign language. In the face of this linguistic deprivation, are these children mute?

A second property of the typical language-learning environment is that the input is auditory. Here the best counterexample is provided by the deaf children of deaf parents, who are exposed from birth to a sign language. For these children, linguistic input is visual rather than auditory. Studies of such children can therefore address the question: Does the acquisition of a visual-gestural language proceed in the same way as the acquisition of a spoken language?

A third property of the typical linguistic environment is that the child is exposed to language from birth. The deaf children of hearing parents, however, may not have significant exposure to any language, either signed or spoken, until they are of school age, or even until they are teens or young adults. This circumstance gives access to another question: If exposure to language is delayed, can the learner still achieve the competence of a native speaker or signer?

A fourth property is that linguistic input is arbitrary rather than iconic. Although there are exceptions, most spoken words do not sound like the things or actions or concepts they represent. Some sign languages, however, have many iconic signs, or at least the signs seem iconic to adults. Do the resemblances between the signs and their referents make it easier for the child to learn to sign?

Absence of Linguistic Stimuli

More than 90 percent of prelingually deaf children are born to hearing parents. Because of their sensory loss, these children are largely deprived of exposure to a spoken language. Acquiring speech is for them a long, frustrating and difficult endeavor, but many of them have had no alternative but to try. Until recently, the education of the deaf emphasized speech training to the exclusion of sign language. Hearing parents were discouraged from signing to their children and were told that the use of a sign language would impede their child's progress in learning English. Consequently, the deaf children of hearing parents, who were deprived of exposure to spoken language by biology, were deprived of exposure to sign language by society.

Although children in this situation had little exposure to language, they presumably wished to communicate with their parents and others. How did they accomplish this? The answer is that they invented their own gestural systems of communication. Susan Goldin-Meadow and her colleagues at the University of Chicago followed the development of ten deaf children of hearing parents. The parents had decided to educate their children solely through speech and did not sign to them. When Goldin-Meadow first saw these children, at ages between thirteen months and about four years, they had not yet shown significant progress in English.

At an early age, the children produced isolated gestures. These were either pointing gestures or gestures that in some way resembled the object or event to which the child was referring. For example, a gesture meaning "open jar" was a twisting movement of the hand; a gesture for "eat" took the form of a repeated bobbing movement of the fist at the child's mouth.

More impressively, however, the children soon began to combine gestures to form sentences. In such sentences, two or more gestures were concatenated without intervening pauses. The gestures were not produced at random; all of the children showed statistically reliable gesture-order tendencies. A typical ordering was *patient-act*, where *patient* indicates a gesture referring to an object that is acted upon and *act* indicates a verb-like gesture. (Goldin-Meadow avoids the standard terms for parts of speech to avoid imputing to the children a grammatical sophistication she has not yet demonstrated they have.)

The word ordering the children used could not have been borrowed, because it is characteristic neither of English nor of American Sign Language. For example, one child pointed to food, then made a gesture meaning "eat," then pointed to his addressee. This sentence could be transcribed word-for-word as "That eat you," but its meaning is "You eat that." Moreover, the children's word-order tendencies did not seem to have been shaped by any input from their parents. The parents' gesturing was quite limited, and the comparatively few multi-gesture sequences they did produce had no consistent ordering.

These invented gestural systems suggest that certain linguistic properties, including word order and some aspects of vocabulary, are quite resilient in the face of very limited linguistic input. One way to explain this resiliency is to assume that children are biologically prepared to acquire these properties.

The Native Signer

The linguistic environment of deaf children born into deaf families differs from the typical language-learning environment in one crucial respect: the children are exposed to a gestural language, not a spoken one. In the United States and much of Canada, the gestural language is American Sign Language (ASL). Does the acquisition of a sign language differ from that of a spoken language?

A sign language is not merely a transliterated version of a spoken language. ASL, for example, is a complete and well-formed language whose grammar is quite distinct from that of English. It developed naturally within the American deaf community, and it is not mutually intelligible with the sign languages used elsewhere, including those used in other English-speaking countries. (Oliver Sacks's recent book *Seeing Voices: A Journey into the World of the Deaf* offers a good overview of this subject.)

That ASL is a language in its own right and is organized around the same principles as other languages might lead one to expect that it would be acquired like any other. Yet the ubiquity of spoken languages suggests that the mode of linguistic expression is not a matter of total indifference. Although auxiliary sign languages are relatively common among Native Americans and Australian Aborigines, the primary language of every hearing community is a spoken language. Moreover, there is considerable evidence that *Homo sapiens* and speech have co-evolved. For example, evolutionary changes in the

24-1 Figure 1. Novel system of gestures was invented by a deaf child, David, raised in the home of hearing parents. In the absence of either spoken language or signed language, David developed his own means of communication, which was documented in studies by Susan Goldin-Meadow and her colleagues at the University of Chicago. Here David produces a fluent, rapidly articulated sequence of three gestures: With a toy in his hand he points to a tray of food (left drawing), makes a bobbing gesture in front of his mouth (middle) and finally points to Goldin-Meadow, who was sitting in front of him (right). The meaning of this sentence-like sequence of gestures is "You eat that," but the order of the gestures is "That eat you." Goldin-Meadow observed that David consistently employed this ordering principle, which differs from the usual word order in both English and ASL. In particular, David regularly ordered verb-like gestures after gestures referring to an object that is acted upon. The drawings are based on a videotape made by Goldin-Meadow.

position of the larynx and in the structure of the vocal tract enable us to articulate a wider range of sounds than the great apes. These anatomical changes were not without costs—they put us at greater risk of choking—but the advantage they conferred apparently outweighed the costs. Taken together, considerations such as these suggest that children might be slower to acquire signed languages than spoken languages and that the process by which signed languages are acquired might be atypical.

   In acquiring a spoken language children pass a series of milestones at relatively predictable ages. Hearing children generally produce their first words at twelve months. They acquire a rudimentary syntax between eighteen and twenty-four months; at this stage they combine words to form simple two-word sentences. English inflectional morphology (such as word endings that mark tense and number) generally emerges between the ages of two and a half and three and a half years. The American linguist Eric H. Lenneberg pointed out that children tend to pass these milestones in the same

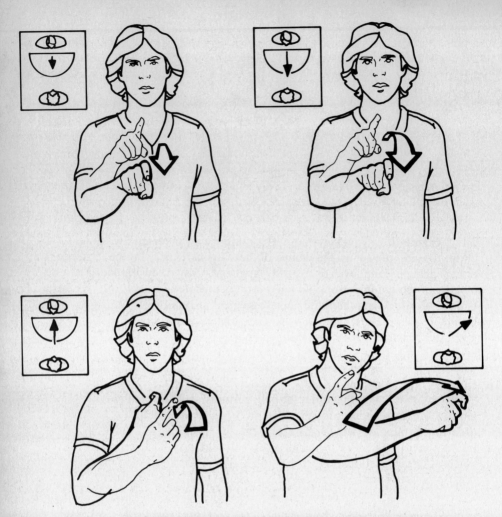

24-2 Figure 2. Sign for ASK in ASL has inflected forms much like those of a verb in a spoken language. Mastery of such morphological complexities is often one of the later milestones of language development. The citation form of ASK_the form that would be listed in a dictionary_is uninflected. The other three forms must agree with both the subject and the object of the sentence. When the sign means "I ask you," the direction of the motion is from the signer toward his conversational partner. When the sign means "You ask me," the direction of motion is reversed. Ask can also agree with subjects or objects whose referents are not present, but which can be assigned to an empty location in the space in front of the signer. For example, the sign for "You ask him (or her)" begins close to the sequence at roughly the same ages no matter what their linguistic environment (although there is evidence that the timing of the acquisition of morphology varies across languages). He argued that this regularity suggests language acquisition is fundamentally controlled by maturation.

Do signing children pass the same milestones at the same ages? From a review of the literature on the acquisition of ASL, Elissa Newport of the University of Rochester and I concluded that they do. Thus by twelve months, signing children, like speaking children, are at the one-word stage. They produce isolated signs drawn from the vocabulary of the adult language. Between eighteen and twenty-four months, signing children enter the two-word stage. They begin to concatenate signs to form simple sentences. Although the considerable differences between ASL and English make further comparison difficult, it can be said that the children continue to pass comparable milestones at comparable ages. For example, the signer's mastery of ASL rules of verb agreement occurs at roughly the same age as the speaker's mastery of complex verb conjugations.

The two-word stage in the acquisition of English has one particularly interesting feature: Even at the outset, children make few errors in word order. Is this also true for the acquisition of ASL? Before I can answer this question, I must introduce a little of ASL's grammar. In adult ASL, as in English, the canonical word order is subject-verb-object (SVO). For example, in the simple declarative sentence "Mathilda kissed Bob," the postverbal position of "Bob" identifies it as the direct object of the verb "kissed." Consequently, we understand that Bob was the person who was kissed, not the one who did the kissing. Although ASL has the same canonical word order, it allows considerably more freedom in word order than English does. One reason is that ASL allows the identity of the subject and the object to be conveyed by the verb, by means of a rule of verb agreement. (My use of the term "object" masks a number of syntactic complexities.) Spoken languages with elaborate systems of verb agreement, such as Spanish and Italian, generally also permit considerable freedom in word order.

As English speakers, we have some acquaintance with verb agreement. If a present-tense verb has the suffix -s, we know that the subject of the sentence is in the third-person singular. Thus we say "I kick the football" but "She kicks the football." ASL exploits linguistic devices of this kind more fully. In particular, the verb may agree with both the subject and the object of the sentence. Figure 2 shows four forms of the ASL verb ASK. The citation form, or dictionary entry form, of this verb is an outward excursion of the hand. When the signer is the subject and his or her addressee is the object, the excursion is longer, and it is directed toward the addressee. When the addressee is the subject and the signer is the object, the direction of motion is reversed. Finally, if the signer wants to refer to an absent person, a third, vacant, position can serve as a kind of pronoun. Verbs can then agree with that position.

Bearing in mind the grammatical differences between ASL and English, do deaf children display the same facility in the use of word order as hearing children? It appears that deaf children begin to use word order to indicate the syntactic relations of a verb and its noun arguments early in the two-word stage, even at age two. According to studies done by Robert J. Hoffmeister of Boston University and by Newport and Ashbrook, signing children reliably use SVO order in the two- and three-word stages of language development. Indeed, they may continue to do so even after they have acquired the ASL rule of verb agreement that allows freer ordering. In their reliance on word order, beginning signers resemble beginning English speakers.

In summary, the same sequence of milestones seems to characterize the acquisition of ASL and of spoken language. Nor is there any evidence that language acquisition is delayed in deaf children. Although human beings may have highly evolved mechanisms for the production and processing of speech, those mechanisms are apparently sufficiently flexible that the acquisition of signed languages is not disadvantaged. Helen J. Neville, Albert Schmidt and Marta Kutas, working at the Salk Institute, have uncovered neuropsychological evidence for such plasticity. Their studies of evoked potentials suggest that temporal-lobe regions implicated in auditory processing in the hearing can be reassigned to visual processing in subjects who have been deaf from birth.

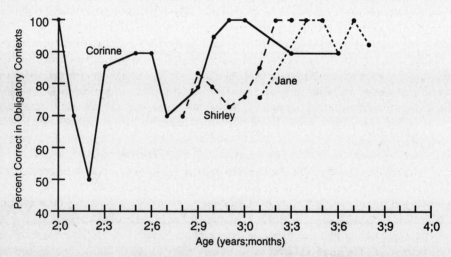

Figure 3. Milestones in language acquisition are the same for speaking and for signing children; furthermore, they pass these milestones in the same sequence and at roughly the same times. The progress of three deaf children toward mastery of ASL verb agreement was studied by the author. All three children achieved consistent command of verb agreement in the first half of their third year. Hearing children master English verb agreement at roughly the same age. One child, Corinne, provides an instance of a common learning pattern: near-perfect initial performance followed by deteriorating accuacy and a slower return to mastery. The child's initial performance is thought to be based on rote learning of a limited number of verbs inflected for agreement.

So far I have been concerned to show that the sign-language learner is not at a disadvantage. But there is even some evidence that signing children pass the very first milestones of language development *before* their speaking counterparts. The most persuasive evidence has to do with the age at which the child produces his or her first word and the age at which he or she has a small vocabulary. For example, John D. Bonvillian and his colleagues at the University of Virginia have reported that thirteen signing children of deaf parents had amassed a ten-sign vocabulary by a mean age of 13.2 months. This is significantly earlier than the eighteen English-speaking children studied by Katherine Nelson of the City University of New York, who did not reach the same milestone until a mean age of 15.1 months.

There are a number of plausible, although yet untested, explanations for the apparent precociousness of signing children. It may have a biological basis: the perceptual and motor systems subserving signed language may mature earlier than those required for speech. It is also possible, however, that the youngchild simply finds manual signs more perspicuous than spoken words, or even that parents (and linguists) are more likely to recognize a child's fumbling attempts at signs than his or her attempts at spoken words. The literature on neurological development provides some support for the first and strongest of these candidate explanations; it turns out that the post-thalamic visual pathways are fully myelinated at an earlier age than the comparable auditory pathways.

It may be that signing children provide a clearer window onto some parts of the language-acquisition process than speaking children do. In particular, the deaf children may begin to sign as soon as they have the linguistic and cognitive maturity to do so. Hearing children, on the other hand, may be delayed by slower development of perceptual or motor abilities needed for the modality of speech.

The Late Learner

In addition to arguing that the process of language acquisition is maturationally determined, Lenneberg hypothesized that children can gain a native speaker's competence only if they are exposed to linguistic stimuli during a critical period. He argued that this period, whose boundaries are presumably set by neurological development, extends roughly from the age of two (when children begin using two-word combinations) to thirteen (the onset of puberty).

In developmental biology the classic example of a critical period is the imprinting of birds. Ducklings, for example, will follow the first moving object, duck or nonduck, to which they are exposed from nine to twenty-one hours after hatching. Maturationally determined critical periods also characterize song learning in some birds, such as the white-crowned sparrow. Given the long philosophical tradition in which language is taken as the distinguishing mark of humanity, we might be reluctant to suppose it shares anything with imprinting in birds. But what does the evidence suggest?

205

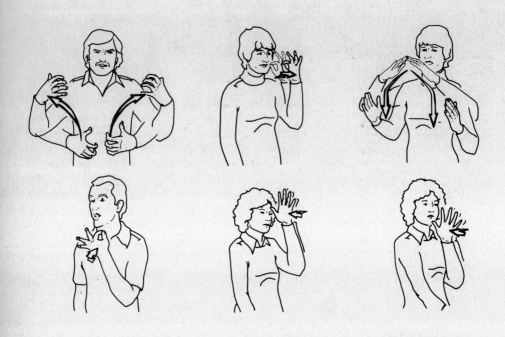

24-4 Figure 4. Iconic signs in ASL—signs that resemble the things they denote—seem conspicuous to English speakers who learn ASL as a second language in adulthood. Three such signs are shown in the upper row of drawings: HOUSE, CAT and ANGRY. It is tempting to suppose the young language learner uses the resemblance between the sign and its referent to guess at the meaning of the sign. There are several problems with this hypothesis, however. ASL is not consistently iconic. It has many arbitrary signs as well, such as those of the lower row: MOTHER, FATHER and CURIOUS. Moreover, the resemblances are much less apparent in a conversation then they are in drawings of signs, and native signers report being unaware of them. (Drawings by Frank A. Paul, from A Basic Course in American Sign Language.)

Of course, it is more difficult to test Lenneberg's hypothesis than those concerning critical periods in animals. Lenneberg himself marshalled evidence having to do with the acquisition of a second language, the probability of recovery from aphasia, and language acquisition by children with Down's syndrome. For example, the age at first exposure to a second language turns out to be a much better predictor of ultimate proficiency than the number of years of exposure.

The most direct test of Lenneberg's hypothesis is delayed exposure to a first language. In the hearing population, such delays occur rarely and even then they are difficult to interpret. There are interesting historical cases of abandoned children who could not speak when they were found, such as Victor, the wild child of Avignon, but accounts of these cases often reveal more about the history of ideas than about linguistic development.

A more recent case was discussed by Susan Curtiss of the University of California at Los Angeles. A girl whom Curtiss calls Genie was isolated in a back bedroom of her Los Angeles home by an abusive father. From the age of two until she was thirteen and a half Genie had virtually no exposure to language. At the time of her discovery, she neither spoke nor understood any English. Genie eventually succeeded in acquiring some hallmarks of fluency, such as a sizable vocabulary and command of word order and subordination, but she failed to acquire others, such as inflectional morphology and a command of auxiliary verbs and of the passive voice. Moreover, her speech was phonologically abnormal.

This outcome is certainly consistent with Lenneberg's hypothesis. What prevents us from reaching any firmer conclusions is that Genie's delayed exposure to language was part of a pattern of abuse. She was deprived not only of speech, but also of social, visual and auditory stimulation in general. Moreover, she was physically abused and malnourished.

A stronger test of Lenneberg's hypothesis is afforded by one segment of the deaf population: deaf children born into hearing families. In years past, these children often had little exposure to any language, either spoken or signed, during early childhood. Most of them eventually encountered ASL, but their age at first exposure varied enormously. For many, the first encounter came at age five or six, when they entered a residential school for the deaf. Even there they learned ASL not in the classroom but in the dormitories—from a few schoolmates who were fluent native signers. Other children, who attended strongly oralist day schools, did not encounter ASL until their early twenties.

Newport and Ted Supalla addressed the question of delayed exposure to language in a study of thirty adults who considered ASL to be their primary language. (Their English skills, in contrast, were quite limited.) The subjects all had 30 or more years of exposure to ASL, but the age at which they were initially exposed varied. All of them had attended the same residential school, but some were native signers who were exposed to ASL from birth, some were early learners who first encountered ASL when they enrolled in the residential school at ages between four and six, and others were late learners, whose first encounter occurred after age twelve.

207

Newport and Supalla gave the subjects a battery of tests examining their ability to produce and comprehend various grammatical constructions in ASL. One result is particularly interesting in the light of the other evidence I have discussed. It turned out that a signer's knowledge of ASL word order was unrelated to his or her age of initial exposure; the performance of all three groups was almost error-free. This is consistent with the reliable use of gesture order by the children Goldin-Meadow studied, with the early mastery of basic word order by both beginning speakers and beginning signers, and with Genie's successful acquisition of basic word order.

Another set of tests yielded a very different pattern of results, however. These tests examined the production and comprehension of morphologically complex signs. In English, morphologically complex words are those that have more than one meaningful part. For example, *walked* consists of two morphemes: the verb stem *walk* and the past-tense inflection *-ed*. Similarly, in ASL the inflected form of the verb ASK meaning "You ask me" is made up of three morphemes: the verb stem ASK and the agreement markers for subject and object. Newport and Supalla found that the earlier a signer had been exposed to ASL, the better he or she scored on these tests. Native signers did better than early learners, who in turn did better than late learners.

Newport and Supalla's study provides strong support for the claim that a child can gain native competence in a language only if he or she is exposed to that language during a critical period. These data are particularly significant because signers are the only large population that undergoes delayed exposure to a primary language.

Iconic Language

Only rarely is it possible to infer the meaning of an English word from its sound. The occasional onomatopoeic word, such as *bow-wow* or *meow*, is the exception rather than the rule. More typical is a word such as *give*: nothing about it in any way resembles the action of transferring an object from one person's possession to another's. In fact an arbitrary relation between the form of a word and the form of its referent is so usual that Ferdinand de Saussure, the Swiss linguist whose *Course in General Linguistics* laid the foundations of structuralism, insisted it is a fundamental property of all human language.

Saussure's conclusion rested entirely on the analysis of spoken languages. ASL, by contrast, has many iconic signs. Unlike the English *give*, or for that matter the Spanish *dar* or the French *donner*, the ASL sign GIVE is "motivated." As Figure 5 shows, GIVE closely resembles the act of handing a small object to another person. Many other ASL verbs with inflections that mark subject and object, such as TAKE and GET, also seem impressively pictorial.

At least they seem so to adults acquiring ASL as a second language. But are children acquiring ASL as a first language equally impressed by the iconic aspects of the language? Do the similarities between form and meaning make it easier for children to acquire an ASL vocabulary? Or are they "expecting" to encounter arbitrary mappings

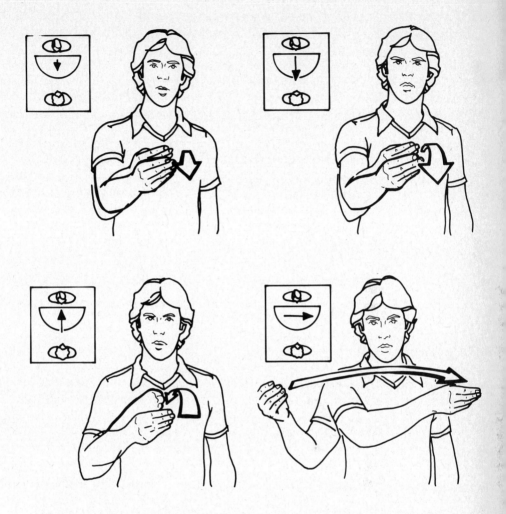

24-5 Figure 5. Inflections of the verb GIVE suggest a means of testing the importance of iconic content in ASL. The various forms exhibit different degrees and different forms of iconicity. The citation form and the form translated as "I give you" are iconic in the sense that the gesture is a mime of the action of giving. The forms "You give me" and "He (She) gives her (him)," in contrast, are not accurate mimes of the action they denote. All three inflected forms (but not the citation form) are iconic in a different way: they map the positions of the giver and the recipient in space. If either kind of iconicity aids language acquisition, children ought to learn the iconic between form and meaning?

This is not a simple question to answer. For one thing, it is difficult to isolate the iconic elements in ASL. ASL has many iconic signs, but it also has many arbitrary ones. Such common signs as MOTHER, FATHER, WHITE, BLACK and AMERICA are essentially unmotivated. In addition, the formation of an ASL sign is never determined solely by resemblance to an object or act; it is also constrained by a complex system of grammatical rules. Finally, even when a sign has an iconic origin, a fluent signer may not experience its iconic content in normal discourse, any more than a native speaker of English is ordinarily aware of a word's etymology—such as the sense of "tongue" in the word "linguistics."

Because iconicity is not a simple phenomenon, it is even conceivable that instead of assisting the language learner, it could place pitfalls in his or her way. For example, a child guided by iconicity might suppose that GIVE could only be used when the verb and the act were very similar. But the sign GIVE can be used to describe the transference of elephants and automobiles as well as of handheld items. Furthermore, the child who attended to iconicity would have to switch strategies when confronted by verbs such as PITY, ASK, HATE and INFORM. These verbs inflect in much the same way as GIVE, but they are not otherwise iconic in form.

I have examined the effect of iconic language in a study of the acquisition of verb agreement by deaf children of deaf parents. I proposed two models of iconic resemblance. One model assumed that children would be attuned to verbs that happen to be enactments, or mimes, of an action. The second model assumed that children would be attuned to verbs that map the spatial relations of the actors. Because these models pin down the somewhat vaporous notion of the iconic, they make precise predictions. For example, according to the model favoring enactments, the child would tend to learn the first two forms of GIVE shown in Figure 5 (the citation form and the form translated as "I give you") before the third and fourth forms ("You give me" and "He gives her"). The first two forms are simple mimes of the action of giving, whereas the last two forms do not have as straight-forward a relation to the action referred to. According to the model emphasizing the spatial relations of actors, the child would learn the last three forms of GIVE before the citation form or before other forms of GIVE that happen not to agree with the agent who gives.

It turned out that the children followed neither model; indeed they seemed quite oblivious to the iconic elements of signs. Three aspects of the study are interesting: the children's progress toward error free performance, the age at which they achieved error-free performance, and the type of errors they made. I was able to follow one child, Corinne, long enough to capture the acquisition process in detail (See Figure 3). Corinne's use of verb agreement seemed nearly perfect at the age of two, but then deteriorated precipitously. She did not again inflect verbs reliably until ten months later. This pattern resembles the U-shaped trajectory followed by hearing children learning the rules for morphologically complex forms of words, such as the past tense. At first the children's performance is surprisingly good, apparently because they learn high-frequency words by rote. Later, as they begin to grapple with general rules rather than specific

210

instances, their performance slips. Much the same seems to be true of Corinne. Her early success was largely confined to the use of one verb in a single inflected form. (Parents of two-year-olds will not be surprised to learn that the verb was SAY-NO and the form was second-person object agreement: "I say no to you.")

At what age did the children acquire verb agreement? According to the criterion I chose for the acquisition of a linguistic rule, the children I studied acquired verb agreement at the ages of three years, three years and three months and three years and six months. Under the same criterion, hearing children acquire English verb agreement at ages between two and a half and three and a half. Thus, the acquisition of ASL verb agreement does not seem to be advanced by the iconic properties of many ASL verb forms. Instead the rules for ASL verb agreement seem to be acquired at much the same time as the rules for English verb agreement.

The children in my study showed no tendency to use iconic verb forms—as defined by either of my models—earlier than arbitrary verb forms. And the errors the children made were inconsistent with the notion that they were attending to the iconic properties of the signs. They often erred by omitting verb agreement altogether, and quite frequently the erroneous verb forms were less iconic than the correct forms. As it happens, hearing children also tend to err by omission when they are learning inflectional morphology. For

	Acquisition of English: hearing children	Acquisition of ASL: deaf children of deaf parents	Minimal linguistic input: deaf children of hearing parents	Delayed exposure to a spoken language: Genie	Delayed exposure to a sign language: deaf, late learners of ASL
Vocabulary	First word at 12 months	First sign at 12 months (or somewhat earlier)	Gestural vocabulary developed	Successful acquisition of a large vocabulary	Large sign vocabulary
Word Order	Reliable English word order early in two-word period	Reliable ASL sign order early in two-sign period	Reliable gesture-ordering tendencies	Reliable English word order acquired	Age of first exposure has no effect on knowledge of sign order
Morphology	English morphology begins to emerge at roughly 30 months	ASL morphology begins to emerge at roughly 30 months	Some spontaneous morphological development (?)	Very poor control over English morphology	Age of exposure has significant effect on knowledge of ASL morphology

Figure 9. Comparison of population of children with different linguistic experiences demonstrates that some aspects of language are extremely robust, whereas others are more fragile. A large vocabulary and consistent word order are acquired even under the most unpromising conditions. But command of morphologically complex words and signs is affected by the child's linguistic upbringing. Hearing and deaf children attain similar proficiency in similar language-learning environments; it appears not to matter whether the child's first language is a spoken or a signed one.

211

example, a child will say "two shoe" instead of "two shoes." In sign language as in spoken language, it seems grammatical complexity determines which errors children make. Typical errors often yield verb forms that are less iconic than the correct form, but that are grammatically simpler. In another study, I asked ten native-signing children to imitate sentences containing agreeing verbs, and the errors they made also support the claim that it is grammatical complexity that matters.

My studies converge with those of other aspects of ASL. Whether the topic is early vocabulary acquisition, the acquisition of pronouns, or the acquisition of the complex morphology of ASL verbs of motion and location, it seems children are remarkably insensitive to the nonarbitrary properties of ASL signs. Although at first blush ASL sometimes strikes adults as pantomime, children respond as though it were a fully arbitrary language.

Conclusion

As we have seen, the linguistic properties of ASL and the demography of the signing community allow us to ask interesting questions about the relation between linguistic input and language development.

The gestural systems invented by the deaf children of hearing parents show that certain linguistic properties emerge even when the child is raised in a virtual language vacuum. This finding suggests that children may come to the task of language acquisition with expectations about how languages are organized, a notion consistent with the assertion that there is an innate, species-specific capacity to acquire language.

On the other hand, we have also seen that children's expectations about language are not so constraining that they find it harder to learn a sign language than to learn a spoken language. The acquisition process itself is relatively independent of modality; acquisition of a language—whether signed or spoken—follows a single maturational schedule.

Finally, we have seen that children are quite insensitive to certain properties of their linguistic input. Adult learners of ASL are charmed by the iconicity of some signs, but children appear to be oblivious to it. It may be that their expectations about language lead them to attend to some aspects of their linguistic input and not to others.

Deaf language learners provide a remarkable opportunity to investigate the child's ability to acquire, and even to create, language. But we must always remember that one reason they do so is that they have so often been denied input from a natural sign language such as ASL.

Bibliography

Bonvillian, J. D., M. D. Orlansky and L. L. Novack. 1983. Developmental milestones: Sign language acquisition and motor development. *Child Development* 54:1435-1445.

Brown, R., and C. Hanlon. 1970. Derivational complexity and order of acquisition in child speech. In *Cognition and the Development of Language.*, ed. J. R. Hayes, John Wiley and Sons.

Chomsky, N. 1988. *Language and Problems of Knowledge.* The MIT Press.

Curtiss, S. 1977. *Genie: A Psycholinguistic Study of a Modern-Day "Wild Child."* Academic Press.

Feldman, H., S. Goldin-Meadow and L. R. Gleitman. 1978. Beyond Herodotus: The creation of language by linguistically deprived deaf children. In *Action, Symbol, and Gesture: The Emergence of Language*, ed. A. Lock, pp. 351-414. Academic Press.

Goldin-Meadow, S., and C. Mylander. 1983. Gestural communication in deaf children: Noneffect of parental input on language development. *Science* 221:372-374.

Goldin-Meadow, S., and C. Mylander. 1990. Beyond the input given: The child's role in the acquisition of language. *Language* 66: 323-355.

Hess, E. H. 1959. Imprinting. *Science* 130:133-141.

Hoffmeister, R. J. 1978. Word order in the acquisition of ASL. Paper presented at the Boston University Conference on Language Development.

Johnson, J. S., and E. L. Newport. 1989. Critical period effects in second language learning: The influence of maturational state on the acquisition of English as a second language. *Cognitive Psychology* 21:60-99.

Klima, E. S., and U. Bellugi. 1979. *The Signs of Language.* Harvard University Press.

Lane, H. 1984. *When the Mind Hears: A History of the Deaf.* Random House.

Lecours, A. R. 1975. Myelogenetic correlates of the development of speech and language. In *Foundations of Language Development*, ed. E. H. Lenneberg, pp. 121-135. Academic Press.

Lenneberg, E. H. 1967. *Biological Foundations of Language.* John Wiley and Sons.

Lieberman, P. 1984. *The Biology and Evolution of Language.* Harvard University Press.

Marler, P., and P. Mundinger. 1971. Vocal learning in birds. In *The Ontogeny of Vertebrate Behavior,* ed. H. Moltz, pp. 389-450. Academic Press.

Meier, R. P. 1981. Icons and morphemes: Models of the acquisition of verb agreement in ASL. *Papers and Reports on Child Language Development* 20:92-99.

Meier, R. P. 1982. *Icons, Analogues, and Morphemes: The Acquisition of Verb Agreement in American Sign Language.* Dissertation, University of California at San Diego.

Meier, R. P. 1987. Elicited imitation of verb agreement in American Sign Language. *Journal of Memory and Language* 26:362-376.

Meier, R. P., and E. L. Newport. 1990. Out of the hands of babes: On a possible sign advantage in language acquisition. *Language* 66:1-23.

Nelson, K. 1973. *Structure and Strategy in Learning to Talk.* Monographs of the Society for Research in Child Development (serial no. 149), Vol. 38, Nos. 1-2.

Neville, H. J., A. Schmidt and M. Kutas. 1983. Altered visual-evoked potentials in congenitally deaf adults. *Brain Research* 266:127-132.

Newport, E. L. 1990. Maturational constraints on language learning. *Cognitive Science* 14:11-28.

Newport, E. L., and E. Ashbrook. 1977. The emergence of semantic relations in ASL. *Papers and Reports on Child Language Development* 13:16-21.

Newport, E. L., and R. P. Meier. 1985. The acquisition of American Sign Language. In *The Crosslinguistic Study of Language Acquisition*, Vol. 1, ed. D. I. Slobin, pp. 881-938. Lawrence Erlbaum Associates.

Orlansky, M. D., and J. D. Bonvillian. 1984. The role of iconicity in early sign language acquisition. *Journal of Speech and Hearing Disorders* 49:287-292.

Oyama, S. 1976. A sensitive period for the acquisition of a nonnative phonological system. *Journal of Psycholinguistic Research* 5:261-285.

Patkowsky, M. S. 1980. The sensitive period for the acquisition of syntax in a second language. *Language Learning* 30:449-72.

Petitto, L. A. 1987. On the autonomy of language and gesture: Evidence from the acquisition of personal pronouns in American Sign Language. *Cognition* 27:1-52.

Sacks, 0. 1989. *Seeing Voices: A Journey into the World of the Deaf*. University of California Press.

Saussure, F. de. 1959. *Course in General Linguistics*. Reprint of third edition (1915). McGraw Hill.

Supalla, T. 1982. Structure and acquisition of verbs of motion and location in American Sign Language. Dissertation, University of California at San Diego.

Umiker-Sebeok, D. J., and T. A. Sebeok (eds). 1978. *Aboriginal Sign Languages of the Americas and Australia*. Plenum Publishers.

10

Concepts and Categories, Meanings and Memories

Before a child can think scientifically, he must understand that things can be grouped systematically, according to common properties. Piaget referred to the mental act of forming such groups as *classification*. For example, thinking of all puppies and kittens as members of a general class of pets or animals is an example of classification.

Like conservation, classification is a concrete operation that emerges during the five to seven transition. During this period, children develop the ability to think simultaneously in terms of more than one class, to relate classes to one another, and to see the relation of a class to the larger class of which it is a part. Now they can not only reason about all dogs but also recognize that both dogs and cats are subordinate to the larger class of animals.

One of Piaget's most famous experiments was designed to study the emergence of this ability. Children, shown a picture of eight roses and four daisies, are asked, "Are there more roses or more flowers?" Preschoolers cannot mentally manipulate the relationship between roses as a class and the larger class of flowers, which includes both roses and daisies. Struck by the appearance of a larger number of roses and unable to reason simultaneously about roses and flowers, they typically assert that there are more roses. After the transition to concrete operations, when children have achieved an understanding of classification, however, they understand immediately that there cannot be more roses than flowers, that roses and daisies belong to the larger, superordinate class of flowers, and that there are therefore more flowers than roses.

● INTRODUCTION ●

As children experience the world in which they live, they retain information about that world for future use. An infant who is given the opportunity to shake a rattle learns that rattles make a certain kind of sound and will expect to hear that sound given the opportunity to shake the rattle again. The infant, in effect, now knows something about rattles. A four-year-old who makes her first trip to the zoo may experience giraffes. Asked about giraffes on a future occasion, she can describe the fact that giraffes have long necks and are very tall. Based on her experience, she has come to know something about giraffes. The knowledge system, evident in both children, is the system of mental representations that contains the information that human beings have extracted from the sum total of their experience over time.

Most psychologists think of the knowledge system as consisting of networks of concepts. Each concept is an abstract, general representation of some set of objects or events that share an overlapping set of common properties. Concepts are tied together in elaborate sets of interconnections. The child's concept of "dog," for example, carries information about what is more or less general among dogs varying from Chihuahuas to Great Danes and is more closely connected to the child's concept of "cat" than it is to the child's concept of "arithmetic."

The common properties of objects and events are themselves represented in the form of attributes of the concept. Attributes of "dog," for example, might include "living," "meat-eating," "four-legged," "domesticated," and so forth. Some concepts are also arranged according to certain hierarchical principles of organization and generality. They have what psychologists refer to as a categorical structure. "Animal," for example, is a superordinate category for "dog;" and "Chihuahua" and "Great Dane" are subordinate categories.

In the three articles presented in this chapter, we are introduced to the way in which children's developing knowledge affects their performance in a variety of critical ways. Carolyn Mervis shows how children's acquisition of word meanings depends on the categorical structure of their knowledge. Lynette Bradley and Peter Bryant demonstrate the importance of children's knowledge of the phonemic categories of speech for the ease with which they learn to read and spell. Michelene Chi shows that memory performance may depend more on the knowledge that the individual brings to the domain to be remembered than it does on general principles of development that vary with age. The developing knowledge system, in other words, both reflects the child's growing experience with the world and underlies the child's developing ability to give that world new and richer meaning.

● ● ●

Child-Basic Object Categories and Early Lexical Development
Carolyn B. Mervis

Spoken words are meaningful patterns of sound that stand for collections of objects, events, relationships, mental states, and other aspects of our experience. The meanings that we give to words are directly related to our knowledge base. A physicist, for example, who hears the phrase "scanning electron microscope" will relate it to a richer, more elaborated system of related concepts than will the average adult. For the physicist, the words will have more and different meaning than they will for another adult; and for a three-year-old, who has few if any of the necessary concepts, the phrase will be essentially meaningless.

Lexical development, the acquisition of word meanings, depends directly on children's gradual elaboration of a knowledge base with increasing exposure to language and to those aspects of experience that are symbolized through language. In this important theoretical article, Carolyn Mervis introduces us to two of the most fundamental characteristics of the child's developing knowledge base, the fact that category knowledge is hierarchical, consisting of basic (e.g., "car"), superordinate (e.g., "vehicle"), and subordinate (e.g., "sedan") levels; and the fact that children's initial categories are basic-level categories.

That children focus at the basic-level in their initial categorization of the world is not surprising. The fundamental nature of basic-level categories has been demonstrated with children and adults in a wide range of studies. As Mervis suggests here, this finding may be due to the fact that basic-level categories "stand out" as the most general categories whose members still share a high level of similarity in important features such as shape, configuration of parts, or function. Thus, for example, the basic-level category, car, *which includes sedans, convertibles, sports cars, limousines, etc. is much more general than the subordinate category,* sedan. *At the same time, however, the various members of the car category have much more in common with one another (e.g., relatively similar shape) than the even more general but highly variable superordinate category,* vehicle.

Although children's initial categories are formed at the basic level, one of the most interesting facts about lexical development is that children's initial use of words to stand for these categories often fails to correspond to adult usage. Thus, for example, relative to adults, very young children first acquiring words will both overextend (e.g., calling a round pin cushion a "ball") and underextend (e.g., refusing to call a football a "ball") word usage. It is the author's view that lexical preferences reflect what young children know or do not yet know about the cultural significance, relevance or importance of various categorical attributes. Thus, the child who calls a pin cushion "ball" knows that roundness and throwability are important attributes of balls but does not yet know that pin cushions serve a cultural function that is largely incompatible with throwing and catching. Similarly, the child who refuses to call a "football" a "ball" is unaware of the fact that despite their peculiar shape, footballs are thrown and caught.

How then do children come to comprehend new adult-basic labels and begin to reorganize their categories in line with adult usage? In concluding this article, Mervis describes a number of circumstances under which adults might use an adult-basic name for an object that the child does not include in the relevant category. In the author's view, those circumstances in which the relevant and important attributes are made explicit, either because the child is already attending to a relevant attribute or because the adult provides a concrete illustration, are likely to become the occasions for developmental change in category structure and word usage or for the acquisition of new vocabulary.

Children's initial categories are basic-level categories. This seems reasonable, because as Rosch and I have argued previously (Rosch, Mervis, Gray, Johnson, & Boyes-Braem 1976), categories at the basic level are more fundamental psychologically than categories at other taxonomic levels. For example, *chair* (a basic-level category) is more fundamental than either *kitchen chair* (a subordinate category) or *furniture* (a superordinate category). Categories at the basic level "stand out" as categories. These categories are based on large clusters of (subjectively) correlated attributes that overlap very little from category to category. In our world, these basic-level categories are the most general categories whose members share similar overall shapes (or similar parts in particular configurations; Tversky & Hemenway 1984) and similar functions or characteristic actions. Recent research has indicated that two-year-olds can form basic-level categories easily, while formation of superordinate and subordinate categories is considerably more difficult (Daehler, Lonardo & Bukatko 1979; Mervis & Crisafi 1982).

But children's initial basic-level categories often will not correspond to the adult-basic category labeled by the same word. Such differences are to be expected. . . . The actual categories formed on the basis of these principles will vary because different groups notice or emphasize different attributes of the same object as a function of different experiences or different degrees of expertise. Very young children often do not share adults' knowledge of culturally appropriate functions of objects and the correlated form attributes, leading children to deemphasize attributes of an object that are important from an adult perspective. At the same time, children may notice a function (and its correlated form attributes) for that object that adults ignore. In such cases, children would emphasize attributes of the object that are unimportant to adults. Therefore, very young children's basic-level categories will oftentimes differ from the corresponding adult-basic categories. Mothers are often aware of these differences, and many mothers indicate this knowledge explicitly by labeling objects with the names corresponding to their child-basic category assignments, even when these names are incorrect by adult standards (Mervis & Mervis 1982). . . . . Mothers tend to accept their young child's use of child-basic names for objects, although labels that mothers perceive as arbitrary are corrected. . . . Mothers also tend to accept their young child's use of an object in accordance with its child-basic function, even when the function is inappropriate from an adult perspective. The child's categories are not derived simply from maternal input, however (see Mervis 1984; Mervis & Mervis 1984; and below).

When differences between child-basic and adult-basic categories occur, several relationships between the two types of categories may result. First, the child-basic category may be broader than the corresponding adult-basic category. These broad categories sometimes correspond to a more general level in the same taxonomy. . . . For example, the child-basic *kitty* category might correspond to the adult *feline* category. In other cases, the child's broad category contains exemplars from several adult taxonomies. For example, the child-basic *ball* category might include round candles, round coin banks, and multisided beads, as well as objects adults would consider balls. Second, the

Mervis, Carolyn B. (1987). Child-basic object categories and early lexical development. In U. Neisser (Ed.) *Concepts and Conceptual Development: Ecological and Intellectual Factors in Categorization.* Cambridge: Cambridge University Press. pp. 201-233.

child's category may be narrower than the corresponding adult category. For example, the child-basic *chair* category might not include beanbag chairs. Third, the child's category may overlap the adult's category; that is, the child's category may include objects that are excluded from the adult category while at the same time excluding objects that are included in the adult category. For example, the child-basic *car* category might include trucks but exclude dune buggies.

Previous theories of early lexical development have accounted for the differences between child and adult categories by postulating that children and adults attend to different numbers of attributes when making categorization decisions. Thus, Clark (1973) has claimed that the child attends to a proper subset of the attributes relevant to an adult. Consequently, the child's categories corresponding to his or her early words are broader than the adult categories labeled by the same words. Nelson (1974) has claimed that the child attends to a superset of the attributes relevant to an adult. Consequently, the child's categories are initially narrower than the corresponding adult categories. Development consists of either adding relevant attributes . . . or subtracting irrelevant attributes . . . until the appropriate adult category is acquired. In contrast, I believe that, although some differences between child and adult categories may be due to variations in the number of attributes attended to, this is not the major source of difference. Instead, one of the most important causes of the differences between child and adult categories is that children are attending to or emphasizing different attributes from adults. . . .

For child-basic categories that are broader than the corresponding adult-basic categories, there are three reasons why a child might attend to a different set of attributes or assign a different weight to an attribute. First, the child may not know about the cultural significance of certain attributes. For example, the child may not realize that a bank is for storing money. Therefore, the slot and the keyhole of a round bank may be ignored, in favor of known attributes such as "round," "rolls," "can be thrown." The round bank accordingly will be assigned to the child's *ball* category. Second, the child may be aware of the attributes that are important to the adult category assignment, but the salience of these attributes may sometimes be less for him or her than the salience of a different set of attributes. Thus, a child may consider a round bank to be both a bank and a ball. Third, the child may include false attributes in his or her decision process. For example, the mistaken belief that a leopard says "meow" (as the child's mother may tell him or her . . .) may contribute to the child's decision to categorize it as a kitty.

For child-basic categories that are narrower than the corresponding adult-basic category, the child often defines the acceptable range of values for a given attribute more narrowly, for attributes that both children and adults include in their decision processes. This situation often occurs because the child is not aware of cultural conventions concerning stylized representations. For example, both children and adults expect bears to have fur. Very young children, however, may require this fur to be plush and relatively plain. Thus, a toy bear made out of a flower-print cotton fabric may be excluded from a child's *bear* category but included in an adult's *bear* category.

In many cases for which the child-basic category overlaps the corresponding adult-basic category, the factors that contribute to overly broad and overly narrow categories operate simultaneously. For example, the child may include round banks and round candles in his or her *ball* category, because he or she is unaware of the cultural significance of the slot or the wick. At the same time, the child may exclude footballs from his or her *ball* category because the shape is too deviant from round. In other cases, the factor that is primarily responsible for overgeneralization may lead to overlap: the child emphasizes attributes that are irrelevant to the adult category, while ignoring an attribute that is crucial for the adult category. For example, Keil (1987) has argued that young children emphasize such attributes as being a friend of one's father and bringing one presents in determining membership in their *uncle* category. Young children ignore the kinship criteria that adults use. Thus, young children would be expected to include not only actual adult uncles but also close male friends of the father in *uncle*, while excluding juveniles who are uncles by the kinship criterion.

Which objects, then, should be included in an initial child-basic category? The principle that basic-level categories are the most general categories whose members share similar overall shapes and similar functions or characteristic actions can be used to make predictions. An initial child-basic category should include those objects that, from a child's perspective, have similar overall shapes (or similar parts in particular configurations) and similar characteristic actions and/or can be used for similar functions.

This prediction is a general one. "Similarity" must be defined separately for each child; as Kogan (1971) has demonstrated, the breadth of any given category may vary from child to child. This variability, however, should occur only with regard to the inclusion or exclusion of borderline members/nonmembers (e.g., for the *chair* category, such items as beanbag chairs, sassy seats, and stools with backs). Thus, if the exemplars used in a study include only objects that either clearly should be included in the category being investigated (good or moderate exemplars) or clearly should not be included, then predictions across children concerning category membership can still be made.

Another factor that limits the predictability of the composition of child-basic categories concerns the initial exemplar or exemplars on which the child bases his or her category. As Pani and I have shown (Mervis & Pani 1980), when the initial exemplar is a good example of its category, a person (either child or adult) is likely to generalize appropriately to include other predicted members in his or her category. When the initial exemplar is a poor example of its category, however, the person is not likely to generalize appropriately at first. In many cases, he or she will form a category that is much narrower than the predicted category. Thus, the predictions made based on the basic-level principle will be correct when children first form a category only if the initial exemplar is a good example of its category. The predictions eventually will hold even if the initial exemplar was a poor example. The child first will have to realize, however, that the good examples are also members of the category.

In summary, very young children form basic-level categories whose composition often differs from that of adult-basic-level categories. Children's categories may be broader than, narrower than, or may overlap, the corresponding adult categories. These differences occur because the child's limited knowledge of culturally appropriate functions of objects and their correlated form attributes leads him or her to emphasize different attributes than adults do, for the same object. . . .

Evolution of Initial Child-Basic Categories

Many initial child-basic categories will not be identical to the corresponding adult-basic categories. When an adult is conversing with a child, there are four circumstances under which the adult can use the adult-basic label for an object the child does not include in its adult-basic category, thus providing the child with an opportunity to learn this label and to change his or her categorization scheme. First, the child might notice important attributes on his or her own, and then call these attributes to an adult's attention. The adult would be likely to respond by acknowledging the attribute that the child had indicated and then labeling the object with its adult-basic name. For example, the child might point out a round candle's wick to the mother, in which case she probably would respond by commenting on the wick and then labeling the object, "candle."

If the child has not noticed these important attributes on his or her own (or if the adult does not realize the child has), the adult may choose to point them out. This may be accomplished in two ways. First, the adult can show the child a critical form attribute(s) and/or demonstrate a critical function attribute(s) of an object, that serve to make it a member of its adult-basic category. Coincident with this highlighting of a critical attribute, the adult may label the object with its adult-basic name. These illustrations are often accompanied by verbal description. For example, the adult might run a finger along the slot of a round bank, drop in a coin, and tell the child that this is a slot into which you put money. The adult would then label the object, "bank." Alternatively, the adult might provide a verbal description, without a concrete illustration. Both of these strategies could be used either spontaneously or in response to the child's use of a child-basic name to label the object in question.

Finally, the adult may label the object with its adult-basic name without either an implied request from the child (the first circumstance described) or some form of explanation (the second and third circumstances). The use of an adult-basic label alone constitutes an implicit statement of the existence of attributes that make the object a member of the named category. This strategy may also be used spontaneously or as a correction of the child's use of a child-basic name to label the object in question.

The four circumstances under which the adult labels an object with its adult-basic name should be differentially associated with success at leading the child to comprehend the new adult-basic label and to begin to form a new category. Success should be most likely to occur if either the child points out a relevant attribute or the adult provides a concrete illustration. In these cases, because the important attributes have been made explicit in a concrete manner, even the very young child often is able to see that they form the basis for a new category, or, in the case of an initially undergeneralized category, the basis for assignment of the object to its appropriate category. Success when the adult provides a verbal explanation without a concrete illustration is less likely. The very young child is unlikely to understand the explanation. The success of this method should increase as the child's vocabulary size increases. Success when the adult uses an adult-basic label without either a request from the child or an explanation is considerably less likely for younger children. If the labeled object already is included in a different child-basic category, success is extremely unlikely. The metacognition required to realize that categories should be altered simply because a different label is used is relatively sophisticated. If the object has not yet been assigned to any category, and the child already has the appropriate category for this object, success is more likely. Indeed, children eventually believe that all objects should belong to some category, and therefore "look" for a category to which the unassigned object could be assigned. In some cases, the child may even ask, "What's that?" in reference to an unassigned object. Success in these cases is very likely.

References

Clark, E. V. (1973). What's in a word? On the child's acquisition of semantics in his first language. In T. E. Moore (Ed.), *Cognitive development and the acquisition of language* (pp. 65-110). New York: Academic Press.

Daehler, M. W., Lonardo, R., & Bukatko, D. (1979). Matching and equivalence judgments in very young children. *Child Development, 50,* 170-179.

Keil, F., (1987). Conceptual development and category structure. In U. Neisser (Ed.), *Concepts and conceptual development: Ecological and intellectual factors in categorization* (pp. 175-200). Cambridge: Cambridge University Press.

Mervis, C.B., (1984). Early lexical development: The contributions of mother and child. In C. Sophian (Ed.), *Origins of cognitive skills* (pp. 339-370). Hillsdale, NJ: Erlbaum.

Mervis, C.B., and Crisafi, M.A. (1982). Order of acquisition of subordinate, basic, and superordinate categories. *Child development, 53,* 258-266.

Mervis, C.B., and Mervis, C.A. (1982). Leopards are kitty-cats: Object labeling by mothers for their 13 month olds. *Child development, 53,* 267-273.

(1984, July). *Reduction of lexical overextensions: The roles of maternal attribute illustrations and corrections.* Paper presented at the Third International Congress for the Study of Child Language, Austin, TX.

Mervis, C.B., & Pani, J.R. (1980). Acquisition of basic object categories. *Cognitive Psychology, 12,* 496-522.

Nelson, K. (1974). Concept, word, and sentence: Interrelations in acquisition and development. *Psychological Review*, *81*, 267-285.

Rosch, E., Mervis, C.B., Gray, W.D., Johnson, D.M., & Boyes-Braem, P. (1976). Basic objects in natural categories. *Cognitive Psychology*, *8*, 382-439.

Tversky, B., & Hemenway, K. (1984). Objects, parts, and categories. *Journal of Experimental Psychology: General*, *113*, 169-193.

Categorizing Sounds and Learning to Read—
A Causal Connection
Lynette Bradley and Peter E. Bryant

Spoken language involves both sounds and meanings. The sound structure of language is referred to as its phonology. *In order to speak correctly, children must acquire knowledge of the phonological structures of their native language. Interestingly, however, children learning to speak are not, for the most part, any more aware of this aspect of language than they are of the complex rules of grammar that they are also acquiring. When children learn to speak, the focus of their attention is on meaning, on the topic about which they wish to communicate. In order to become aware of the sound structure of language, they must learn to use their phonological knowledge to attend to the sound patterns present in spoken speech.*

Over the past few years, evidence has been rapidly accumulating to suggest that phonological awareness makes an important contribution to the process of learning to read. When children are first confronted with written language (orthography), they must learn to detect the spelling patterns in orthography that have a reasonably regular relationship to the sound patterns in spoken language. This, in turn, requires that they have the ability to attend to the sound structure of speech.

In a beautifully designed set of studies, Lynette Bradley and Peter Bryant employed two complementary methods to pin down the relationship between children's capacity to categorize sounds and the facility with which they learn to read and spell. Assessing four- and five-year-olds' ability to pick out the one word in a series of words that did not share a common phoneme with the other words in the series, the authors first related individual differences in this ability to individual differences in children's spelling and reading performance three years later. The findings were striking. Even when differences in intelligence and memory were statistically controlled, ability to categorize sounds was a potent predictor of the child's later skill in reading and spelling.

As the authors point out, however, only through the addition of a training study in which children with poor phonemic awareness were provided with instruction designed to improve sound categorization was it possible to assess the causal relationship between children's ability to categorize speech sounds and their facility in reading and spelling acquisition. Comparing the performance of two trained groups (with and without simultaneous exposure to letters) to that of control groups, the authors found that training (and especially training carried out in connection with the alphabet) significantly facilitated children's reading and spelling performance. Explicit knowledge of speech sounds, in other words, appears to play a significant role in reading and spelling.

Our study combined two different methods. The first was longitudinal. We measured 403 children's skills at sound categorization before they had started to read, and related these to their progress in reading and spelling over the next four years: at the end of this time the size of our group was 368. The second was intensive training in sound categorization or other forms of categorization given to a subsample of our larger group. We used both methods because we reasoned that neither on its own is a sufficient test of a causal hypothesis and that the strengths and weaknesses of the two are complementary. Properly controlled training studies demonstrate cause-effect relationships, but these could be arbitrary; one cannot be sure that such relationships exist in real life. On the other hand longitudinal studies which control for other variables such as intelligence do demonstrate genuine relationships; but it is not certain that these are causal. For example simply to show that children's skills at categorizing sounds predict their success in reading later on would not exclude the possibility that both are determined by some unknown *tertium quid*. Thus the strength of each method makes up for the weakness of the other. Together they can isolate existing relationships and establish whether these are causal.

This combination of methods has not been used in studies of reading or, as far as we can establish, in developmental research in general.

Initially we tested 118 four-year-olds and 285 five-year-old children . . . on categorizing sounds. None of the children could read (that is, were able to read any word in the Schonell reading test). Our method . . . was to say three or four words per trial, all but one of which shared a common phoneme (Table 1): the child had to detect the odd word. There were thirty trials. In such a task the child must remember the words as well as categorize their sounds. To control for this we also gave them thirty memory trials: the child heard the same words and had to recall them straightaway. In addition we tested verbal intelligence (EPVT).

At the end of the project (as well as at other times) we gave the children standardized tests of reading and spelling, and we also tested their IQ (WISC/R) to exclude the effects of intellectual differences. To check that our results were specific to reading and spelling

Bradley, L. & Bryant, P.E. (1983). Categorizing sounds and learning to read—a causal connection. *Nature, 301,* pp. 419-421.

Table 1. Examples of words used in initial sound categorization tests and mean scores on these tests

	4-yr group					5-yr group				
	Words given to children			Mean correct (out of 10)		Words given to children				Mean correct (out of 10)
Sounds in common										
First sound	*hill*	pig	pin			bud	bun	bus	*ng*	
	bus	bun	*ng*	5.69 (1.90)		pip	pin	*hill*	pig	5.36 (2.29)
Middle sound	cot	pot	*hat*			lot	cot	hat	pot	
	pin	bun	gun	7.53 (1.96)		fun	*pin*	bun	gun	6.89 (2.35)
End sound	pin	win	*sit*			pin	win	*sit*	fin	
	doll	hop	top	7.42 (2.09)		*doll*	hop	top	pop	6.67 (2.33)

Standard deviations given in parentheses.

and not to educational achievement in general we also included a standardized mathematical test (MATB-NFER), which we administered to 263 of our total sample of 368.

There were high correlations between the initial sound categorization scores and the children's reading and spelling over three years later (Table 2). . . . These relationships remained strong even when the influence of intellectual level at the time of the initial and the final tests and of differences in memory were removed (Table 3). In every case categorizing sound accounted for a significant proportion of the variance in reading and spelling with these other factors controlled.

So a definite relationship does exist between a child's skill in categorizing sounds and his eventual success in reading and spelling. The design of the project, for the reasons just given, included a training study as a check that any such relationship is a causal one. Sixty-five children were selected from our sample and divided into four groups closely matched for age, verbal intelligence and their original scores on sound categorization. These children were drawn from those with lower scores on sound categorization (at least two standard deviations below the mean); they could not read when the training began. Starting in the second year of the project two of the groups (I and II) received intensive training in categorizing sounds. The training involved forty individual sessions which were spread over two years. With the help of colored pictures of familiar objects the children were taught that the same word shared common beginning (hen, hat), middle (hen, pet) and end (hen, man) sounds with other words and thus could be categorized in different ways. Group I received this training only, but Group II in addition was taught, with the help of plastic letters, how each common sound was represented by a letter of the alphabet (see ref. 1 for further details of this method). The other two groups were controls. Group III was also taught over the same period in as many sessions and with

Table 2. Correlations between initial sound categorization and final reading and spelling levels

Correlations between initial scores and final scores

Initial scores:

		Sound categorization		EPVT		Memory	
Final scores		4	5	4	5	4	5
Reading:	Schonell	0.57	0.44	0.52	0.39	0.40	0.22
Reading:	Neale	0.53	0.48	0.52	0.44	0.40	0.25
Spelling:	Schonell	0.48	0.44	0.33	0.31	0.33	0.20

Multiple regressions testing relationship of initial sound categorization to final reading and spelling levels

	Schonell reading		Neale reading		Schonell spelling	
	4	5	4	5	4	5
% Of total variance accounted for by all variables	47.98	29.88	47.55	34.52	33.59	24.77
% Of total variance accounted for by sound categorization*	9.84†	4.06†	6.24†	4.56†	8.09†	5.59†

* IQ, EPVT, final CA and memory controlled.
† $P<0.001$.

the same pictures how to categorize but here the categories were conceptual ones; the children were taught that the same word could be classified in several different ways (for example, hen, bat (animals); hen, pig (farm animals)). Group IV received no training at all.

Table 3. Training study: details of groups and mean final reading, spelling and mathematics levels

		Mean scores			
		Experimental groups		Control groups	
	Groups	I	II	III	IV
	N	13	13	26	13
Aptitude tests					
Initial EPVT		103.00	103.00	102.34	102.69
Final IQ (WISC/R)		97.15	101.23	102.96	100.15
Final educational tests					
Schonell: reading age (months)		92.23	96.96	88.48	84.46
Neale: reading age (months)		93.47	99.77	89.09	85.70
Schonell: spelling age (months)		85.97	98.81	81.76	75.15
	N	9	8	20	7
Maths MATB (ratio score)		91.27	91.09	87.99	84.13

Reading, spelling and mathematics mean scores are adjusted for two covariates: age and IQ.

The training had a considerable effect which was specific to reading and spelling (Table 3). At the end of the project Group I (trained on sound categorization only) was ahead of Group III (trained on conceptual categorization only) by three to four months in standardized tests of reading and spelling. This suggests a causal relationship between sound categorization and reading and spelling. Group II (trained with alphabetic letters as well as on sound categorization) succeeded even better than Group I (trained on sound categorization only) in reading and particularly in spelling. This suggests that training in sound categorization is more effective when it also involves an explicit connection with the alphabet. That the relationship is specific to these two skills is shown by the mathematics results where the differences were a great deal smaller. . . .

Put together our longitudinal and training results provide strong support for the hypothesis that the awareness of rhyme and alliteration which children acquire before they go to school, possibly as a result of their experiences at home, has a powerful influence on their eventual success in learning to read and to spell. Although others have suggested a link between phonological awareness and reading, [2,3,4] our study is the first adequate empirical evidence that the link is causal. Our results also show how specific experiences which a child has before he goes to school may affect his progress once he gets there.

References

1. Bradley, L. *Assessing Reading Difficulties* 225, (Macmillan, London, 1980).

2. Goldstein, D.M. *J. educ. Psychol.* **68**, 680-688 (1976).

3. Liberman, I. *et al.* in *Toward a Psychology of Reading* (eds Reber, A. & Scarborough, D.) (L. Erlbaum Associates, Hillsdale, New Jersey, 1977).

4. Lundberg, I., Olofsson, A., & Wall, S., *Scand. J. Psychol.* **21**, 159-173 (1980).

Knowledge Structures and Memory Development
Michelene T.H. Chi

*One of the oldest and most consistent findings in the literature on child development is the general improvement in memory performance that accompanies increasing age. As a rule, the older the children, the better their average performance will be on a wide range of memory tasks, including memory for a series of numbers (*digit span*), objects or object pictures, or words. Since most theories conceptualize memory as some sort of storage device (like a filing cabinet, a library, or a computer's hard disc), it would seem reasonable to assume that memory improvement with increased age represents increased storage capacity.*

In the following article, Michelene Chi argues that memory development does not reflect capacity change (at least after age five or so) and introduces us to two alternative explanations. One involves developmental change in strategy use, the other increasing size of the knowledge base. In study after study, older children and adults have been shown to be much better than younger children at using strategies for manipulating information as it is being placed in a memory store and for retrieving that information once it has been stored. Indeed, very young children seem to make little use of strategies. Strategies, which only begin to emerge at the end of the preschool period, are not used with any consistency until the school years.

*As strategy use is increasing, however, so too is the individual's knowledge base. All other things being equal, the longer a human being has been alive, the more they have experienced the world—the greater their experience, the more opportunity they have had for developing and interrelating new concepts. When material to be remembered can be related to an elaborated knowledge base, the subject in a memory task can more easily group that information into meaningful units (*chunks*) that will enhance memory performance. Older children and adults generally know more than do younger children and their better memory performance may simply reflect that greater knowledge.*

In one of the most widely cited studies in the literature on cognitive development, Chi set out to test the hypothesis that memory performance reflects size and elaboration of the knowledge base. How, she asked herself, could she unconfound age (and concomitant improvement in strategy use) and knowledge; and how could she rule out capacity differences? The answer to these questions was simple but clever–find a domain for which there are children whose knowledge is greater than that of most adults and compare children's memory performance to that of adults both within the domain of the children's specialized knowledge and on a traditional memory task such as digit span.   Focusing on chess and chess knowledge, this is just what the author did.   As we will see, her results suggest quite strongly that the degree of elaboration of the knowledge base is a powerful determinant of memory performance.

. . . Three factors influence memory development: strategies, knowledge, and capacity. The influences of each are briefly elaborated.

Strategy

The strategy component is an important factor in memory development because older children are adept at acquiring and using strategies to cope with memory tasks. . . . The strategy component may arise from older children's ability to perceive the useful outcomes of strategic intervention. . . .

What is a strategy? Broadly, a strategy is a set of decision processes that determines what sequences of actions to perform. Some strategies that have been extensively studied are rehearsal, recoding, and grouping. As we will see, there are also many subsidiary strategies that a person can adopt for a given situation.

The findings on strategy development have consistently shown that the use of strategies increases with age. It is clear that part of memory and the improvement of metamemory performance must reflect this factor.

Why do we need to go beyond this? Why not simply adopt the view that strategy changes are responsible for all memory . . . development? There are three reasons: (1) If an adult strategy is taught to children, recall is still generally better in adults (Butterfield, Wambold, & Belmont, 1973); (2) if a strategy is taught to both children and adults, the initial difference in performance is generally maintained (Huttenlocher & Burke, 1976); and (3) if adults are prevented from using certain strategies, their performance remains superior to that of children (Chi, 1977). In general, it is becoming more and more apparent that strategies (at least our traditional notion of strategies) do not account for all the developmental trends or individual differences in memory performance. Hence, it is necessary that we turn to other factors to account for the remaining differences.

Chi, Michelene T.H. (1978).   Knowledge structures and memory development.   In R.S. Siegler (Ed.) *Children's Thinking: What Develops?*   NJ: Erlbaum.   pp. 73-96.

233

Knowledge

Knowledge affects development through the growth of the knowledge base. By growth I mean simply that there are more concepts, more relations among concepts, and so on in the semantic memory of an adult as compared to a child. Associated with the growth of knowledge is a better structure for that knowledge. A better structure may be one that has, in some sense, a more appropriate or valid set of relations among the concepts as well as a greater number of relations.

No one disputes the assumption that adults have a richer knowledge base than children. However, if one looks at the developmental literature on memory, few researchers emphasize this difference or test directly its effect on memory performance. Researchers often regard knowledge as a catchall for any age differences not explained by the experimental variables. No one is certain of the extent to which knowledge influences performance.

This chapter highlights the contribution of amount and structure of knowledge to memory and metamemory performance. The contributions of other components, particularly strategies, have been amply stressed elsewhere. This chapter attempts to place the knowledge factor in a proper perspective.

Capacity

The capacity hypothesis states that the improvement of performance with age can be partially explained by an increase in the capacity of working memory (Baron, in press; Carroll, 1976; Case, 1974). If one examines the developmental data in the area, the hypothesis of capacity increases seems obvious. However, the data may obscure an important issue, namely, that age and knowledge are often confounded.

To define what I mean by *capacity*, one needs to distinguish *performance* capacity from *actual* capacity. Memory capacity can be estimated empirically only by measuring the performance of an individual on a given task. For example, in a memory-span task, the digit span for college students is about 7.98 units (Brener, 1940), whereas for five-year-olds it is about four units (Starr, 1923; see Figure 1). Hence, the performance capacity of an adult is superior to that of a child.

Since the introduction of the concept of the chunk (Miller, 1956), researchers have concluded that the actual capacity of working memory for adults is around seven chunks. For any given domain of stimuli, then, adults' performances can vary, as demonstrated in the memory-span estimates, but the theoretical interpretation is that the underlying chunk capacity of working memory is invariant (Simon, 1974). The solid lines in Figure 1 summarize the literature on performance estimates for various stimulus materials.

For any given domain of stimuli, children consistently exhibit a smaller memory span. The obvious dilemma is whether the results depicted in Figure 1 reflect a smaller actual capacity in children or a smaller chunk size. In other words, it could be argued from Figure 1 that children are simply unfamiliar with these stimulus materials and that

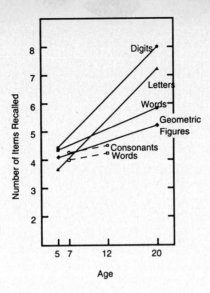

Figure 1. Solid lines summarize results in the literature for memory-span performance for different stimulus materials as a function of age. Dotted lines are Dempster's (1976) results for consonants (open circles) and words (open squares).

the variability in the adults' data is due to different amounts of experience with (or knowledge about) the stimuli.

Both Chi (1976) and Dempster (1976) used the latter notion to argue that memory capacity is constant, at least beyond the age of five years or so. That is, they assumed that children show a smaller memory span in all the materials shown in Figure 1 because these materials are less familiar to them. It follows from this argument that if a class of stimulus materials can be found that is equally familiar (or unfamiliar) to both age groups, then children and adults should exhibit the same memory span. Indeed, Dempster found that with consonants and words, span estimates for first graders (4.3 and 4.07) were not significantly different from those for sixth graders (4.6 and 4.3). These data suggest that knowledge of stimuli may be the critical variable in producing differences in memory-span performance among age groups. However, these data are not sufficient to conclude that capacity is invariant with age. Further data are needed to (1) pinpoint knowledge of the stimuli as the critical variable producing age differences in memory-span performances and (2) show better recall in children than in adults when the stimulus materials are more familiar to children. . . .

Memory For Chess Positions

As mentioned previously, in order to converge on the notion of constant capacity, we need to attribute developmental differences in recall performance to alternative factors. . . . I have argued that in addition to the role played by strategies, recall performance is further influenced by the amount and structure of knowledge children and adults have about the stimuli. The intention of the following study is to assess the extent to which knowledge can affect memory performance independent of age.

235

Because knowledge generally increases with age and because there appears to be a relation between developmental differences in recall and knowledge of the stimuli (Dempster, 1976), it seems at least plausible to assume that recall improves with age primarily because adults know more, rather than because adults have a bigger capacity. We already know, for example, that recall varies directly with knowledge for adults. Chase and Simon (1973) found that chess knowledge influenced performance on both a perception and a memory task, and similar results have been found with games such as "Go" (Eisenstadt & Kareev, 1975; Reitman, 1976) and baseball (Chiesi, Spilich, & Voss, 1977). However, such a direct relation between knowledge and recall cannot be inferred from existing developmental studies, even though we normally assume that adults know more than children. This is because, first, the amount of knowledge an age group has about a set of stimuli has seldom been directly measured, and second, too many other variables exist to permit such a simple deduction. On the other hand, a more direct relation between knowledge and developmental changes in recall can be shown if we demonstrate better recall in children who have greater knowledge in a content area than adults. The purpose of the next study is to provide such a demonstration.

The subjects for this study were six children (third through eighth grade) solicited from a local chess tournament. Their mean age was around 10.5 years. The adult subjects were research assistants and graduate students from an educational research center. All could play chess to some degree.

Two tasks were used to test memory for chess positions: immediate recall and repeated recall. In each condition, a chess position was presented for ten seconds, followed by recall. In the immediate recall task, the subject immediately placed the appropriate chess pieces on a blank board. Pieces, colors, and location all had to be reproduced perfectly for an answer to be counted as correct. On the repeated recall task, if the subject did not reproduce the entire board correctly the first time, the trials continued until perfect performance was achieved. The sequence and timing of each reproduction trial were recorded on audiotape. The stimuli were eight middle-game positions (averaging 22 pieces) selected from a chess quiz book (Reinfeld, 1945). Four positions were used for each memory task. At the end of the repeated recall trials, each subject was asked to draw partitions around those pieces that s/he thought formed a chunk.

Because only one of the twelve subjects had an official chess rating, some way of assessing the chess knowledge of each age group was needed. This was done in two ways: (1) by how well the subject could predict good moves in a position, and (2) by how quickly subjects could perform the knight's tour task. Following the memory trials and the chunk-partitioning task, subjects were asked to predict the next few moves from the same position. The subject made a move and if it was correct, the experimenter replied; the subject then predicted the next move, and so on, for two or three moves, depending on the position. When the subject made a wrong move, the experimenter corrected him/her, and the moves were continued from there. The knight's tour task was a modified version of the one used by Chase and Simon (1973), in which subjects had to move a knight across two rows of the board, with certain constraints, using legal knight moves. The time it takes to complete the moves has been shown to be a gross index of chess knowledge.

As a control, four lists of ten digits were presented for immediate and repeated recall. The procedure was identical to the chess conditions, except that recall consisted of a written response, and no partitionings were requested from the subjects at the end of the repeated recall task.

Results

The mean knight's tour time for children was around 2.5 minutes for the two rows, versus 5.5 minutes for the adults. Hence, the children appeared to have greater knowledge of chess than the adults. On the other indication of chess knowledge, the moves prediction, children's predictions were accurate on about 59 percent of the moves, whereas adults predicted 44 percent of the moves correctly. This prediction task did not seem as sensitive as the knight's tour in assessing chess skill, perhaps because the experimenter corrected the wrong moves, which considerably constrained potential subsequent moves.

The most important result of the experiment, though, was that children's immediate recall for chess positions was far superior to adults' (9.3 versus 5.9 pieces), $F (1,10) = p < 0.05$). In contrast, the children's digit span was lower than that of the adults' (6.1 versus 7.8 digits). Although the digit span difference was not statistically significant, it did replicate the findings in the literature. The same pattern of results was obtained in the repeated recall task. It took children an average of 5.6 trials to learn the entire chess position, whereas adults required 8.4 trials, $F (1 ,10) = 6.2, p < 0.05$. For the digits, on the other hand, the typical developmental trend was again found—children required 3.2 trials to learn a list of 10 digits, whereas adults required only 2.2 trials—although the difference was not significant.

These results are consistent with Chase and Simon's (1973) findings that subjects with high knowledge recognize many more patterns than do subjects with low knowledge. In conjunction with the previous results on naming time, they suggest that memory performance in developmental studies reflects, to a large extent, the influence of knowledge in a specific content area rather than strategies per se. That is, with the exception of knowledge-specific strategies, the availability of general strategies useful for memory performance should have been comparable in both the digit and chess situations. Hence, general strategies such as rehearsal could not have played a major role in determining developmental differences in recall in this study. . . .

References

Baron, J. Intelligence and general strategies. In G. Underwood (Ed.), *Strategies of information processing*. New York: Academic Press, 1978.

Brener, R. An experimental investigation of memory span. *Journal of Experimental Psychology*, 1940, *26*, 467-482.

Butterfield, E. C., Wambold, C., & Belmont, J. On the theory and practice of improving short-term memory. *American Journal of Mental Deficiency*, 1973, *77*, 654-669.

Carroll, J. B. Psychometric tests as cognitive tasks: A new "structure of intellect." In L.B. Resnick (Ed.), *The nature of intelligence*. Hillsdale, N.J.: Lawrence Erlbaum Associates, 1976.

Case, R. Structure and strictures: Some functional limitations on the course of cognitive growth. *Cognitive Psychology*, 1974, *6*, 544-573.

Chase, W. G., & Simon, H. A. The mind's eye in chess. In W. G. Chase (Ed.), *Visual information processing*. New York: Academic Press, 1973.

Chi, M. T. H. Short-term memory limitations in children: Capacity or processing deficits? *Memory and Cognition*, 1976, *4*, 559-572.

Chi, M. T. H. Age differences in memory span. *Journal of Experimental Child Psychology*, 1977, *23*, 266-281.

Chiesi, H. L., Spilich, G., & Voss, J. F. *Cognitive processes and structure in individuals with high and low baseball knowledge: The first inning*. Unpublished manuscript, University of Pittsburgh, 1977.

Dempster, F. N. *Short-term storage capacity and chunking: A developmental study*. Unpublished doctoral disertation, University of California, 1977.

Eisenstadt, M., & Kareev, Y. Aspects of human problem solving: The use of internal representation. In D. A. Norman & D.E. Rumelhardt (Eds.), *Exploration in cognition*. San Francisco, Freeman, 1975.

Huttenlocher, J., & Burke, D., Why does memory span increase with age? *Cognitive Psychology*, 1976, *8*, 1-31.

Miller, G. A. The magical number seven, plus or minus two: Some limits on our capacity for processing information. *Psychological Review*, 1956, *63*, 81-97.

Reitman, J. S. Skilled perception in Go: Deducing memory structures from inter-response times. *Cognitive Psychology*, 1976, *8*, 336-356.

Reinfeld, F. *Win at Chess*. New York: Dover, 1945.

Simon, H. A. How big is a chunk? *Science,* 1974, *183*, 482-488.

Starr, A. S. The diagnostic value of the audio-vocal digit memory span. *Psychological Clinic,* 1923, *15*, 61-84.

11

Responsive Caregiving

Experts have by no means always agreed on the proper procedures by which children can be brought to maturity as successful, happy adults. As Christina Hardyment puts it in her book *Dream Babies*, ". . . while babies and mothers remain constants, advice on the former to the latter veers with the winds of social, philosophical and psychological change. . . ."

Nowhere is this more apparent than in the views of two of the most influential parent advisors of the pre-World War II generation, psychologist John B. Watson and physician Luther Emmett Holt. In his 1928 book, *Psychological Care of Infant and Child*, Watson insisted that "There is a sensible way of treating children. . . . Never hug and kiss them, never let them sit in your lap. If you must, kiss them once on the forehead when they say good night. Shake hands with them in the morning. . . ."

In the *Care and Feeding of Children*, Holt told caregivers in 1929 that "Babies under six months old should never be played with and the less of it at any time the better for the infant." Babies who are played with become "more nervous and irritable, sleep badly, and suffer from indigestion and cease to gain weight."

This is not the advice that one finds in today's child-rearing guides; yet in its day it was taken seriously by many parents. The advice of "experts" has changed over time and continues to change. Because this is so, which "expert" should parents follow? Perhaps the best advice of all in this regard is that provided by Dr. Benjamin Spock, the most famous of modern baby doctors. In his view, "Parents ought to get some idea of how the so-called 'experts' have changed their advice over the decades, so that they won't take them deadly seriously, and so that if the parent has the strong feeling 'I don't like this advice,' that the parent won't feel compelled to follow it."

• INTRODUCTION •

In every society, parents are concerned with safeguarding the health of their children, seeing to it that children acquire skills to become economically self-sustaining as adults, and fostering acculturation to the values of the broader community. The particular constellations of values to which communities subscribe, however, vary from society to society. This variation relates to the social and physical environments within which societies function. Some children live in areas of famine and rampant disease, where mortality among the young is a common occurrence; others are raised in areas of plenty where disease is controlled and children rarely die. For some children, future adult subsistence will be derived from activities that have changed little from those that have supported their parents and generations of forebears. For others, growing up amidst rapid social and technological change, a significant portion of adulthood will be spent training and retraining for shifting demands of changing careers. Cultural values concerning the most desirable outcomes of child-rearing, attitudes about children, and even beliefs about the nature of childhood both reflect and amplify the effect of differential physical and social conditions on children's lives.

In this module, we are presented with two illustrations of the way in which social and economic conditions, cultural values, and specific child-care practices are intertwined. In the first article, Robert LeVine compares child-rearing values and practices of African and American societies characterized by very different childhood mortality and subsistence patterns. In the second article, Nancy Pottishman Weiss contrasts values implicit in child-rearing advice distributed to working and middle-class American mothers early in the century with those inherent in Benjamin Spock's post-war *Baby and Child Care,* a work that has now influenced American middle-class child-rearing practices for several generations.

• • •

A Cross-Cultural Perspective on Parenting
Robert A. LeVine

In the tropical regions of Africa, where infant mortality is high and conditions of subsistence difficult, children are an economic asset: they contribute to the agricultural labor pool, they may bring in "bridewealth" and other payments, and they are expected to care for aging parents. In modern, technologically-oriented societies such as the United States, where infant mortality is low and most families live well above the subsistence level, children are frequently an economic liability. Before adolescence, they are rarely expected to work; they are expensive to raise, and more and more they have turned over the task of caring for elderly parents to agencies outside the family.

In the following article Robert LeVine uses the concept of Parental Investment Strategies *to compare the goals and techniques of child care in tropical African cultures to those in middle-class America. Parental investment strategies are ways in which parents employ economic and psychological resources to achieve their child-rearing goals. In Africa, where children must survive in order to contribute labor to cultivation or provide care to parents in old age, families adopt a strategy tailored to that end. Mothers tend to bear children frequently, as often as every two years, and provide infants with intensive physical care, continual bodily contact, nursing on demand, and attentive response to distress. After weaning, when children's survival is relatively assured, much of their care is turned over to older siblings so that the mother can turn her attention to the succeeding infant. The development of characteristics that are highly valued by the culture–quiescence in infants, obedience and respect for parents in older children–appears to be facilitated by these procedures.*

Among the American middle-class, for whom survival and subsistence are rarely an issue, the benefits of children tend to be construed in affective rather than economic terms. Parents anticipate life-long dialogue with children in whom they can take pride–pride in achievement of status, economic success, and moral autonomy. As LeVine points out, it is characteristic of such parents to value individuality, self-sufficiency, and self-confidence in their children and to assume that the attainment of these

*characteristics will require massive economic and psychological invest-
ment: separate space, personal possessions, a lengthy period of education,
and the focused time, effort, and attention of a parent, usually the mother,
who is devoted to the rearing of each of a small number of children.*

An intelligent consideration of "effective parenting" in our own society requires an understanding of cultural diversity in parental goals, values, and behavior among human societies past and present. Parenthood is at once a universal and highly variable aspect of human behavior. In all human societies, as in infrahuman populations, sexually mature adults protect, nurture, and educate the young, but among humans the patterns of child-rearing are not uniform. In the last forty years, anthropologists have shown, with increasingly convincing evidence, that the environments of infancy and early childhood are shaped by cultural values. These values vary widely among ethnic groups and become firmly established in the personal preferences and inner regulations of individuals who seek to reestablish them in the next generation. Some of the best studies in this area have been conducted by Caudill, comparing middle-class Japanese and Americans (Caudill and Plath, 1966; Caudill and Weinstein, 1969) and by Whiting et al. (1966), comparing Zuni, Texans, and Mormons in New Mexico. It is clear from these studies that parents of different cultural backgrounds define the universal situation of child-rearing differently and attempt to organize the lives of their children accordingly from birth onward.
In this chapter, I try to identify and illustrate both universal and culturally variable aspects of parenting and bring that cross-cultural perspective to bear on issues of parental effectiveness in contemporary American society.

Human parents everywhere can be seen as sharing a common set of goals in their role as parents:

1. The physical survival and health of the child, including (implicitly) the normal development of his reproductive capacity during puberty.

2. The development of the child's behavioral capacity for economic self-maintenance in maturity.

3. The development of the child's behavioral capacities for maximizing other cultural values—for example, morality, prestige, wealth, religious piety, intellectual achievement, personal satisfaction, self-realization—as formulated and symbolically elaborated in culturally distinctive beliefs, norms, and ideologies.

If one asks the question, "What do parents want for their children?" the answers from all human societies would include and be exhausted by these categories. There is a natural hierarchy among these goals because the physical survival of the child is a

LeVine, Robert A. (1980). A cross-cultural perspective on parenting. In M. D. Fantini & R. Cardenas. (Eds.) *Parenting in a Multicultural Society*. NY: Longman. pp. 17-26.

physical survival is threatened, it is likely to become prerequisite of the other two and economic self-maintenance is usually prerequisite to the realization of other cultural values. Thus, if the child's the foremost concern of parents, and if his future economic self-maintenance is considered to be jeopardized, it is likely to assume a high priority among parental goals. There is also a natural developmental sequence in this set of parental goals, in that physical survival and health are normally of greater concern in the first years of life, while the others take precedence after the child's survival seems assured and his capacities for learning are more conspicuous.

Parents do not face the problems of attaining these goals entirely on their own. Each culture contains an adaptive formula for parenthood, a set of customs evolved historically in response to the most prominent hazards in the locally experienced environment of parents that jeopardize attainment of these goals. Thus, in areas where the incidence of disease or danger causes high infant mortality rates, customary patterns of infant care will not only be organized by health and survival goals, but will also embody avoidance of specific local hazards as conceptualized in the folk belief system; in areas of precarious subsistence, the cultural formula for parents will be designed around the priority of enabling the child to make a living in adulthood, particularly after his physical survival is assured. The parents as conforming members of their society can act in accordance with the customary formula without having to make their own encounter with the environmental hazards or devise their own adaptive solutions. It is only in migration or rapid social change, where the environment of child-rearing changes drastically from one generation to the next, that parents are deprived of this comfort, and even then many parents fall back on it, despite the inadequacy of traditional adaptations.

Cultural norms of parenthood are more than hazard-avoidance formulas; they are also designed to maximize positive cultural ideas in the next generation, as indicated in the third set of goals. But for most societies, historical and contemporary, the pressures of disease, physical danger (for example, from cooking fires), and economic uncertainty have contributed more heavily to the design of child-rearing customs than one might conclude from the anthropological literature. (See LeVine, 1974, for some examples of this contribution.) In this context, modern Western societies generally, especially their middle- and upper-class segments, constitute a special case in which parents are uniquely free of the worst hazards of infant mortality and subsistence risk that have been the common human condition for millennia. In comparing our situation and standards with those of Africans, we are in a limited sense examining our own past. This comparison, however, is primarily intended to illustrate how diverse are the human standards of parental behavior and to develop a culturally sophisticated approach to the assessment of parental effectiveness in our own and other societies.

I take the societies of tropical Africa as representing one type of cultural adaptation among non-Western populations because I am best acquainted with them; they share many child-rearing customs with peoples of the Pacific, Latin America, and Asia (as noted below). In making the comparison with the West, I use the concept of parental-investment strategies. This refers to the allocation parents make of their valued resources, including time and attention, in the pursuit of their goals as they perceive

245

them. The goals pursued are usually compromises between what the parents want *for* their children (the three sets of goals outlined above) and what they want *from* their children (sooner or later); the strategies represent culturally acceptable pathways toward the compromise goals. For societies on both sides of the comparison, we shall inquire into the outcomes of their investment strategies, attempting to identify costs as well as benefits.

Among the agricultural populations of tropical Africa, infant mortality has long been high and subsistence precarious, and in many rural places these hard facts have not significantly changed; the child's physical survival and economic future remain in jeopardy and must be salient goals for parental behavior. At the same time, African parents expect their progeny to contribute to the family labor force during childhood and to become filial adults who will support their elderly parents; these goals must also be represented in child-rearing practices. As African parents see it, the investment strategy that best meets these goals is to maximize fertility, giving each one of many children highly attentive physical care in infancy, followed by training in obedience, responsibility, and sharing, much of which is delegated to older siblings. Maximizing fertility increases the probability of having some children who survive infancy to become agricultural workers on the family land and providers of support to parents in their old age. If many survive, more hands and help can always be used, in the extended kin network if not in the immediate family.

In the African context, however, maximizing fertility does not mean giving birth annually, but as often as is consistent with child health, usually every two or three years, permitting the baby to be breast-fed for eighteen to twenty-four months. During that period the lactating mother sleeps with her baby, feeds him on demand, makes sure he is carried most of the time (by herself or a child nurse), and responds rapidly to his cry (usually with feeding, sometimes with shaking). This pattern, which is also found in many non-African tropical areas of high infant mortality, can be seen as folk pediatrics, an attempt to react to the most frequent precipitant of infant death, dehydration from diarrhea, by constant close monitoring for acute discomfort and rapid administration of liquid when the baby cries. It can also be seen as aimed at minimizing the infant's disturbance of the African mother's work in the fields or market, for the baby managed this way is remarkably quiet by Western standards and easily lulled by carrying, shaking, and breast-feeding. Thus, the rural African mother pursuing the goal of the quiescent infant may be serving his health needs as best she can while keeping her primary attention focused on her work.

Once the child is weaned, the mother is ready to give birth again and devote the same attention to the new baby. The weaned child, often as compliant a toddler as he was a quiet infant, learns interdependence by sharing sleeping space, food, and eating bowl with other children, obedience by carrying small items at the command of his elders, and respect by greeting adults appropriately. The customary parental goal for childhood after weaning is formulated by the vernacular term for obedience, a phenomenon found in many agricultural societies in other continents as well as Africa. As Harkness and Super

(1977) found among the Kipsigis of Kenya, mothers shape their small children's behavior toward comprehension of speech without speech production, that is, following maternal orders rather than conversing with mother. Such a child is soon ready to perform useful tasks at home, in the fields, and in the market. Parents see the pursuit of obedience in child-rearing as preparing the child to be a filial son or daughter, a respectful member of the local community, and (potentially) a willing client or apprentice to a powerful patron. This emphasis on obedience, so salient in the child's relationship with his parents, is mitigated by more playful, relaxed, and emotionally nurturing interaction with other children of all ages and with grandparents and other adult kin.

Rural parents of tropical Africa look upon children as an investment; this is by no means an alien perspective to them. They expect themselves to be united with their children in a long-run relationship of "serial reciprocity" in which parents nurture the child physically when he or she is young, providing food and medical care; in return, the children help their parents in cultivation, in bridewealth payments (brought in by the daughter who obediently weds a man of substance), and in material support in old age. They are aware that such expectations are not uniformly met by adult children, and this is a source of much concern, but it serves only to reinforce their conviction that they must have more children to increase their chances of raising some who are as filial, obedient, and grateful as they ought to be. The role of the parent in his or her own investment strategy is as the provider of a nurturing environment; the actual care and training of children is often delegated to others in the family, particularly older children, so that as the child leaves infancy behind, his care may be supervised by parents (closely by mother, remotely by father) but his primary interaction will be with other caretakers and peers. There is much individual variation in this, but the point is that parents are normatively expected to invest most of their time in work and in interaction with other adults; they are not expected to devote much interactive attention to each post-infancy child, and no one will criticize them for not doing so as long as the child is supervised by someone older than himself. By the same token, while parents are expected to feed, house, and clothe each child, they need not provide him or her with separate living space or special possessions until maturity. Thus, parents do not feel unable to afford the cost of having another child; they experience the small cost as outweighed by the potential gain. Once the mother is past the risk of giving birth to a child and the task of carrying him through infancy, the greatest part of the parental investment, in terms of attention and special resources, has been made. (Where schooling and school fees have been introduced, this has begun to change.)

To summarize, rural parents in the agricultural societies of tropical Africa pursue an investment strategy aimed at goals which link the child's welfare to that of the parents and family, in both the long and short run. Since the economic welfare of the family as an agricultural production team and that of the parents as potential dependents in old age are seen as benefitted by raising as many children to maturity as possible, maximizing fertility while minimizing infant mortality is central to this strategy. This is conceived primarily in material terms, beginning with the man's investment through bridewealth in the reproductive capacity of his wife, and continuing in her investment in the physical

247

nurturance of the infant and small child. Once husband and wife are together, the cost of each additional child is seen as minimal, at least in comparison with the anticipated benefits, and this is reflected in the minimal allocation of individual resources to each child and the expectation that the older children will give more attention to their post-infancy juniors than the parents themselves. In infancy the goal of the quiescent child represents the mother's effort to maximize her child's chances of survival while minimizing his disturbance of her work routine. In childhood, the goal of obedience represents the formula for maximizing child labor on the family land, filial support for parents in their later years, and the child's capacity for economic adaptation to an institutional order that demands subordination. The success of this parental investment strategy in terms of benefits and costs will be assessed in comparison with the parental investment strategies of Americans.

It is obvious that Americans have different parental investment strategies. We have a low infant mortality rate, no child labor, and bureaucratically organized sources of care for the elderly; in our largely urban and suburban society, the family is a domestic economic unit sharing income and consumption rather than production. We see children as economic costs with no benefit to the economic welfare of parents and family; benefits tend to be conceptualized in terms of the emotional comfort or moral satisfaction a parent can derive from devoting personal resources to the raising of a new generation and maintaining long-term relationships when he or she would otherwise be lonely. Parents frequently deny any expectation of material return or other calculated reciprocation from their children, and the emotional or moral benefits they hope for are often seen as attainable through having only a few children, sometimes only one, sometimes at least one of each sex. Concerning what parents want *for* their children, the survival problem is not paramount and most parents focus on the child's attainment of a position in life that is equivalent to or an improvement upon that of the parents. The maintenance or improvement of socioeconomic status is perhaps the one widespread parental goal specific enough for rational evaluation of investment strategies directed toward it. Parents tend to experience this goal, however, as part of a cultural ideology requiring the development of character traits such as independence which confer moral as well as practical advantages. In middle-class America, the nurturing of character traits sufficient for socioeconomic success and moral autonomy is assumed to be so costly of human time, effort, and attention as to require a full-time maternal role in which mothers are replaceable only by expensive arrangements simulating the personalized care of the mother herself. This conception of child-rearing virtually guarantees that the preferred parental investment strategy will involve a large investment in each of a small number of children.

A pervasive theme of American child-rearing ideology is independence, which can be considered under three headings: (a) separateness, (b) self-sufficiency, and (c) self-confidence. The emphasis on separateness begins at birth among middle-class Americans, with the allocation of a separate room to the neonate, requiring him to sleep in his own bed removed from others in the family. Compared with Africans, American infants experience a particularly sharp distinction between situations in which they are alone and those in which they are with others—for African infants are never alone and are often present as nonparticipants in situations dominated by adult interaction, while the American infant is often kept in solitary confinement when he is not at the center of adult attention. This creates (for the American) a bifurcation between extremes of isolation and interpersonal excitement that is unknown in Africa and may underlay some of the striking differences in interactive style between peoples of the two continents. The American infant, unlike his African counterpart, has numerous possessions earmarked as belonging to him alone; their number and variety increase as he grows older, permitting him to experience the boundaries of his developing sense of self represented in his physical environment. American parents begin to emphasize sharing only after the child has become habituated to eating, sleeping, and being comforted alone, on his own terms, and with his own properties—which he has become reluctant to give up.

Self-sufficiency is at first closely associated with separateness, for the baby whose separate sleeping arrangements involve crying himself to sleep, even if only occasionally, acquires a primitive capacity for self-comforting not required by infants who always have mother's body available for this purpose. As the American baby gets older, self-sufficiency may be an ideal more than a reality, but it becomes a salient ideal. That is, the American child may not be able to do more for himself than his African counterpart—in practical terms he may be able to do less—but those things he does do receive so much praise and other positive forms of parental attention that he comes to see them as a valued part of himself, a source of pride. The African parents I have worked with generally believe that praise is bad for children because it will make them conceited and potentially disobedient (see LeVine and LeVine, 1966, p. 147), and African children acquire a wide range of skills without receiving (or expecting) praise for their performance. As adults, they take these skills, including the capacity to weave a fine basket or build a strong house, for granted rather than as a badge of honor or a type of invidious distinction the way Americans do. In this perspective, the American child grows up with an excessive but strongly motivating sense of pride in what he can do for himself; it provides a permanent source of striving for an idealized self-sufficiency in which others are not needed and dependence is a mark of failure.

If self-sufficiency represents an ideal for American parents and their children, "self-confidence" is the American folk concept of the psychological process by which the goal is achieved. This concept helps make sense of the lavish praise and enthusiastic attention that American parents give their infants and small children; they believe it gives the child confidence in his own capacity to deal with the world and master unfamiliar situations, a confidence he will need in growing up as an adult. A child who does not receive such attention from his parents is seen as emotionally impoverished, likely to become too fearful and insecure to adapt successfully to the challenges of life, or to adopt an active position (to take initiative) with respect to its opportunities. Americans are continually demonstrating to each other that self-confidence is the key factor in worldly success and even inner contentment, and no parent wants his child to grow up without this powerful kind of positive self-regard.

The American emphasis on the independent individual is so intense one might wonder what standards bear on the small child's social relationships. In contrast with the African parent's concept of serial reciprocity, here we might speak of "concurrent reciprocity" as the American emphasis. From early infancy the child is seen as a separate individual capable of exchange in face-to-face interaction with others, and parents attempt to elicit reactions that can become interactively elaborated in what Brazelton et al. (1975) call "play dialogues." Conversational exchange is the preferred medium for the maintenance of the parent-child relationship. In the long view that African parents take, their children are permanently bound to them, and the physical nurturance they give unilaterally in infancy will be reciprocated in filial support (equally unilateral but reversed) later in the course of the parent-child relationship. In the long view of American parents, their children will be independent and apart from them, and they, therefore, focus on the immediate reciprocity of conversational exchange as the symbol of the positive affect that binds them now and might continue to do so after the period of physical and economic dependence is over. In both the serial reciprocity of material exchange for Africans and the concurrent reciprocity of affective dialogue for Americans, the parent-child relationship can be seen as a normative prototype for other intimate social relationships.

To produce a self-confident, independent adult, love is not considered enough; Americans spend an enormous amount of money on their children, providing the personal space and individual possessions that contribute to their separateness and sense of worth as distinctive individuals. It is estimated that it took an average of $27,578 to raise a child from birth to age eighteen in New York City, starting in 1958, and that it took $84,777 to do so in 1976 (*New York Times*, September 20, 1976). These figures presume a modest standard of living; the allocation per child in the middle and upper classes would be much greater. And they do not include the costs of keeping women out of the labor market to serve as full-time mothers or the costs of day-care arrangements when mothers work. For the present purpose, the figures should be seen as indicating what a large material investment American parents in general, including those of modest means, make in the individual child before maturity. From infancy onwards, the child is encouraged to characterize himself in terms of his favorite toys and foods and those he dislikes; his tastes, aversions, and consumer preferences are viewed as not only legitimate but essential aspects of his growing individuality—a prized quality of the independent person.

The parental investment strategies of Americans, then, involve a large allocation of material and human resources (including maternal attention) to a small number of children, with the goals of producing an independent person who is able to cope with a changing environment, maintain or enhance in his own life the parents' social position, and continue in later child-parent relations the positive affect of early dialogues. There are unconscious meanings involved that make the pursuit and attainment of these goals satisfying for American parents, but they are not the concern of the present discussion, which is centered on whether the parental investment strategies work at a more superficial level. My first answer is that they do work remarkably well in both Africa and America, within limits set by the environment. It is not possible for Africans to solve the infant mortality problem by good mothering nor for Americans to ensure that no child will lose socioeconomic status, but each parental investment strategy that has evolved as a cultural pattern in a changing society represents a compromise formula providing a tested solution for each problem parents face. These solutions are at least effective enough in their milieu to warrant close examination before they are swept away by the advice of experts.

While I cannot provide a complete example of such a close examination in this chapter, I shall illustrate it in the context of the African-American comparison. The first question we might ask concerns the effectiveness of parents as child psychologists: are they able to shape the social behavior of their children in the directions they desire? One bit of comparative data from the Six Cultures Study sheds some light on this question. In that study, Whiting and Whiting (1975, p. 64) distinguish twelve categories of acts and give their frequencies in the naturalistically observed social behaviors of children aged three to ten years old from six culturally diverse communities. For the American children observed, the category "seeks attention" represents 14.6 percent of their (self-initiated) acts; for the African children (from "Nyamsongo" community of the Gusii people of Kenya), the proportion of attention-seeking is only 4.6 percent, less than one-third as much. This can be understood as reflecting outcomes of the divergent parental investment strategies described above. The Gusii do seek the quiescent infant, giving close physical care without a great deal of interpersonal excitement; they omit praise and emphasize obedience as the child gets older. Gusii children do not become exhibitionistic, but tend to avoid "public" attention, particularly that of their elders. This is because in the delegated command system of the family, obedience attracts no attention, but disobedience or other misbehavior does. The child comes to feel safest when not noticed; hence attention-seeking is infrequent. The other non-Western samples in the Six Cultures Study, all drawn from agricultural communities in which obedient children are needed and valued, show proportions of attention-seeking ranging from 3.3 percent to 6.6 percent, much closer to the Gusii than to the Americans.

The relatively high proportion of attention-seeking of the American children can also be seen as shaped by their infant experience—isolated much of the time and lavished with positive attention the rest, with praise and emotionally exciting conversation as basic elements in early social life. The early experience of American children leads them to expect attention to be intrinsically rewarding; hence the peculiar tendency they have to misbehave in order to attract attention, even at the risk of being punished. This tendency in itself, along with the larger pattern of attention-seeking, shows American parents are successful in producing the self-confident children they want, at least in a comparison with a culture of drastically different values, for seeking attention does involve risk, and the American children are less inhibited by it.

The divergent patterns of development indicated here can be analyzed for their costs and benefits as outcomes of parental investment. The data are impressionistic and the analyses speculative, but as illustrations they may prove instructive. On the side of the tropical African agriculturalists, the benefits are clear. The quiescent infants become obedient children who contribute agricultural labor; their support for elderly parents is not as reliable as it used to be, but many children continue to grow up filial. The costs

251

are observable primarily in relation to environmental change. Compliant children used to close supervision are likely to take less initiative and show a less active attitude in coping with the tasks introduced by Western schools; but even this is a judgment of Western observers and not necessarily relevant to the adaptation of the African child. Another cost is experienced in the area of social control. As the community discipline imposed by the mutual supervision of village life decays, it becomes clear that children who are used to close and censorious supervision both need and want to have it continue in adult life. When it is absent, they suffer an anxious anomie and resort to litigation, alcoholism, and crime. In other words, they are not prepared psychologically to fill the void left by social-structural decay.

As for middle-class Americans, the outcomes of their parental investment strategies can also be seen to involve costs as well as benefits. On the benefit side, the evidence as I read it leaves little doubt that the parenting pattern described above produces children with the social competence to perform well in school. Compared with their rural African counterparts and children in many other parts of the world, American middle-class children are relatively uninhibited in the presence of adults and hence freer to act curious, responsive, and competitive in the classroom. They are verbally fluent, accustomed to conversing with adults, and predisposed to seek adult attention and approval through displays of self-sufficient accomplishment. Their strong sense of separateness makes them able to compete with other children without fear of the interpersonal consequences. Having been encouraged earlier to enjoy themselves in artificial problem-solving situations defined by toys and games, many become able to derive pleasure from school work and other utilitarian tasks; for some, this initiates the harnessing of hedonic strivings to work in a pattern that energizes learning and later occupational performance. This type of social competence, so taken for granted in middle-class America that only a comparative perspective brings it into focus, sets the child on an academic pathway toward the higher-ranking occupations and justifies pragmatically the investment parents may be making on moral/emotional/ideological grounds. However the return on this enormous investment might be measured objectively, most middle-class parents regard not only the growing social competence of their children in school and other settings but also their growing capacities for independent judgment and choice, as the unquestionably beneficial results of parental devotion.

Without questioning the benefits, it is possible to begin assessing the costs. The child who receives a great deal of positive and exciting attention at one developmental level brings a high expectation for attention and excitement to the next levels. If it is not forthcoming, he actively seeks it, as in the American sample of the Six Cultures Study mentioned above, and if seeking in a quiet way does not work, he demands it or becomes disruptive enough to co-opt it. In a family with several small children, the demands for parental attention escalate through the simultaneous quest for an exhaustible resource. Parents often report considerable dissatisfaction with this phase in their lives. Aware that they have created in their children the expectation that now burdens them, they are unable or unwilling to deny its fulfillment, and they find themselves allocating more time than anticipated to parenting, while seeking relief in television, peer activities, and anything else that might distract the preschool child. At every stage from birth to puberty, the American middle-class child presents his parents with major demands for attention that are virtually unknown in Africa. From the sleepless weeks for parents before the newborn "sleeps through the night" to the restlessness of rainy weekends and lengthy school holidays, the autonomous centers of activity nurtured by American parents impinge upon adult family life to a degree that rural Africans can not imagine.

The real cost involved here, however, seems to reside in the psychological vulnerability of children with high expectations for attention, stimulation, and exchange. Once their expectations have been elevated in early experience, what happens if their subsequent environment falls short or fails to provide age-appropriate organization for the energy and curiosity that is brought forward? Many of the psychiatric disorders of childhood, from hyperactivity to neurotic symptoms and psychotic conditions, seem to have their origins in a matrix of disrupted or inconsistent patterns of parental attention that presume a child whose expectations for such attention is already high. It is beyond the scope of this paper to do more than speculate briefly about childhood psychopathology and its causes. But I have often wondered if the lower level of interactional excitement to which African infants become habituated does not protect them from a range of emotional disturbances found among middle-class American children, whose exposure to more concentrated attention from fewer persons might entail a higher level of risk. In other words, it might be that the pursuit of American values such as separateness and self-confidence in infant and child care, while resulting in a highly valued social competence in the next generation, also fosters vulnerabilities to emotional problems that mental health practitioners are called upon to treat. This is no more than a hypothesis, but it is one that deserves serious investigation before we advocate the spread of middle-class American styles of child-rearing to other groups in our own and other societies.

Summary and Policy Recommendations

. . . There is no single yardstick for all human parents, but their adaptive responses can be comparably conceptualized as parental investment strategies, in which resources are allocated among immature offspring in such a way as to realize certain culturally formulated goals representing compromises between what parents want *for* their children and what they want *from* them. To illustrate the conditions that belong to future comparative analyses of parental investment strategies, a code comparison of tropical African agriculturalists with middle-class Americans was attempted. Parents of both groups were seen to be pursuing strategies that work (or at least *have* worked) in the sense of realizing values and benefits the parents want, but at costs they might not be aware of.

There is nothing in this trial comparison that gives encouragement to those who would provide "expert" guidance for American parents. The closer one examines the subject calculus of parental behavior in a given culture, the more respect one has for its

253

elements of "folk wisdom," no matter how outdated it has become or how much its failures are disguised. Parents everywhere need (a) information about the environments their children are likely to face, (b) contact and communication with other parents old and young, and (c) confidence in organizing an appropriate environment for their children. Policies that help American parents, who suffer particularly from social isolation, on these terms are timely and should be welcomed. Programs of didactic parent education should be viewed with suspicion if (a) they fail to assess the possible emotional costs in child-rearing practices designed to foster cognitive development and school achievement, (b) they make parents feel excessively responsible for the successes and failures of their children, adding to an already unwieldy burden of guilt, and (c) they tend to be insensitive to the cultural implications of spreading middle-class American child-rearing customs to other groups.

Bibliography

Brazelton, T. B.; Tronick, E.; Adomson, L.; Als, H.; and Wise, S. "Early Mother-Infant Reciprocity." London: *CIBA Symposium* 33: 137, 1975.

Caudill, W., and Plath, D. "Who Sleeps by Whom? Parent-Child Involvement in Urban Japanese Families." *Psychiatry*, Vol. 29, 1966, pp. 344-366.

Caudill, W., and Weinstein, H. "Maternal Care and Infant Behavior in Japan and America." *Psychiatry*, Vol. 32, 1969, 12-43.

Harkness, S., and Super, C. "Why African Children Are So Hard to Test." In L. Adler (Ed.), *Issues in Cross-Cultural Research, Annals of the New York Academy of Sciences*, 1977, Vol. 285, pp. 326-331.

LeVine, R. "Parental Goals: A Cross-Cultural View." *Teachers College Record*, December 1974, Vol. 76, No. 2, pp. 226-239.

LeVine, R., and LeVine, B. *Nyansongo: A Gusii Community in Kenya*. New York: Wiley, 1966.

Whiting, B., and Whiting, J. *Children of Six Cultures*. Cambridge: Harvard University Press, 1975.

Whiting, J. W. M.; Chasdi, E. H., Antonovsky, H. R.; and Ayres, B. C. "The Learning of Values." In E. Z. Voget and E. M. Albert (Eds.), *People of Rimrock*. Cambridge: Harvard University Press, 1966.

Mother, the Invention of Necessity:
Dr. Benjamin Spock's *Baby and Child Care*
Nancy Pottishman Weiss

In traditional societies, where families are in close, continuous contact with one another and generations typically live side by side, caregivers are constantly exposed to the child-rearing values and practices shared by the community. Under such circumstances, there is little need for a systematic guide to child-care. In modern, technologically-oriented societies, on the other hand, parents may find themselves isolated from communal child-rearing support, exposed to divergent values concerning positive outcomes for children's development, and confronted with rapidly changing social conditions for which traditional child-care procedures may not seem to be appropriate. Under these conditions parents sometimes turn to "experts" for advice on what to do. Until very recently, such expert advice was directed exclusively to mothers.

In the following article, Nancy Pottishman Weiss reviews the history of twentieth-century child-care literature. Calling our attention to the way in which child-rearing advice structures mothers' as well as children's lives, she makes it clear that suggestions ostensibly oriented toward the needs of children carry implicit messages regarding the adequacy of mothers. In a superbly crafted analysis, she contrasts two of the century's most influential parenting guides: Infant Care *(1914), published by the Children's Bureau, and* Baby and Child Care *(1945), written by the eminent pediatrician, Dr. Benjamin Spock. Both manuals reflect the American middle-class tendency to focus on the isolated mother/child dyad and to view mothers as professional homemakers; but there the similarity ends. With an emphasis on scheduling the child's day that might seem rigid to many modern parents,* Infant Care *attempted to strike a balance between the child's developmental needs and the mother's need for relief from constant supervision of her children. By recognizing the difficulties inherent in being a parent and a homemaker and by emphasizing the extent to which children contribute to their own development,* Infant Care *appealed to working and middle class mothers, legitimized maternal fears and feelings of inadequacy, and relieved mothers of the burdensome sense that their children's futures were solely dependent on their success as parents.*

When Baby and Child Care first appeared, it offered a very different kind of advice. Friendly and informal in tone, it encouraged mothers to relax and enjoy their children, to allow themselves to follow the child's lead, and above all to feel confident about their ability to create a positive emotional climate within which the child would thrive. As eminently sensible as such advice appears on the surface, it is Weiss's contention that it carries a heavy implicit message of maternal responsibility and a hidden demand for mothers to increase their physical and emotional workload. The permissive message reinforced an unattainable middle-class ideal: perfect mothering in a problem-free family. By failing to recognize just how difficult parenting and family life can sometimes be, it may have added, however unwittingly, to the burden of maternal worry and guilt.

Describing a family at Sunday dinner, a young man told of his father standing at the head of the table carving the chicken. His mother sat next to him and was the first person served; then the father served himself. The storyteller explained, "I was the youngest of five children, and by the time I was served, all the white meat was gone. It looked so delicious, but I never got to taste it. I swore to myself that when I grew up I would eat all the white meat I could. So I'm grown up and a father—and my children get first choice!" This father's lament conveys the swiftness with which child-rearing patterns have changed in the space of three generations. It points as well to a significant facet of child-rearing advice, whatever its particular wisdom—the advice structures the life of the parent as well as the child.

Scholars have assessed rules for rearing the young, but have neglected to ask questions about what these rules meant for adults. Although this article begins with a story about a father, it focuses on the daily existence of a mother. In one serious sense child-rearing manuals might be renamed mother-rearing tracts. Behind every rule concerning desirable child behavior a message to mothers was couched, advising them on how to act and recommending the right, proper, and moral way to conduct their own lives.

Women have left us direct evidence of their reactions to this counsel. They wrote letters to manual authors which unveiled their home life, asked for the clarification of rules, and sometimes scolded them for impractical ideas. This correspondence, paired with the manuals, offers us some important insights into women's lives and provides us a means to understand how mothers interpreted child-rearing lessons. This article will

Weiss, Nancy Pottishman. (1977). Mother, the invention of necessity: Dr. Benjamin Spock's "Baby and Child Care." *American Quarterly*. pp. 519-546.

compare Dr. Spock's *Baby and Child Care* with *Infant Care* of 1914 in light of women's responses to them. Some striking themes in Spock—the increased emotional demands on the mother, the depoliticization of a once political domesticity, the shift from reliance on a network of women to dependence on a patriarchy of doctors, the nagging sense of worry and guilt that underlie self confidence—surface more clearly through comparisons with the earlier manual.

Despite certain similar assumptions about family and home governing child-care literature throughout the century, such as the ideal of the homeostatic, self-sustaining mother-child dyad and the view of the home as a professional enterprise requiring job training, managerial know-how, and scientific expertise, the actual rules of child rearing and their meaning for women have changed dramatically since 1914. Scholars tend to view later manuals as improvements over earlier advice. In this framework, Spock's book represents an advance in salutary counsel for care of the young. However, one can question the idea that child-care dictums were more salubrious later, or that permissive advice is necessarily socially functional, by examining this literature from the perspective of the child rearer. Dysfunction for the caregiver, not social fit, may be associated with the permissive mode which, in turn, may correlate strongly with a high level of maternal anxiety.

Both *Infant Care* and *Baby and Child Care* attracted a large audience, for the books contained information women could obtain nowhere else. Mothers of all backgrounds wanted help and asked for it. Thousands of letters written to the Children's Bureau from 1914 to 1928 point to a need for instructions on care of the young. This correspondence also conveys a nostalgia for a sense of shared enterprise once furnished by female networks. The manuals in this sense serve not only as expert tutors or informed curricula, but also as substitutes for friends and relations. Women used the manuals for purposes other than those intended by the authors: the manuals might have served emotional ends that family or tradition once furnished, and they even filled religious needs, broadly construed as something to believe in. Women frequently referred to *Infant Care* and *Baby and Child Care*, only half jokingly, as their "Bible" or the "Gospel," or the "often-blessed book" that "has been my staff." The historical significance of Dr. Spock's manual can be more richly defined by relating it to the earlier best-seller of the genre, *Infant Care*.

As one of her first official acts, Children's Bureau Chief Julia Lathrop commissioned Mary Mills West, a professional writer, widow, and mother of five children, to write a child care pamphlet. *Infant Care* was the second in a series on child care which Mrs. West's *Prenatal Care* initiated in 1913. Women responded favorably to the literature and the first edition was immediately depleted. Originally free of charge, it was geared to the "average mother of the country" and written in a style "simple enough to be understood by uneducated women and yet not so simple as to seem condescending to the educated," according to Dr. Alice Hamilton, Lathrop's associate. It was, Hamilton claimed, "really an excellent piece of work." Readers concurred, for the demands for *Infant Care* continually exceeded the supply.

257

Any estimate of the circulation of *Infant Care* (or the readership of Dr. Spock's later manual) must necessarily go beyond raw sales figures to take into account the nature of child-rearing advice. Women told other women about techniques that worked, lent copies of manuals to each other, and even learned about child care from their own American-educated children. A mother from Bellingham, Washington, requested a second copy of *Infant Care*. "Unless I learn it by heart," she stated, "it will do me little good, for, as was the case with the first monograph, I am so constantly lending it, that I never have it on hand for quick reference. . . . it could hardly be placed in any more appreciative hands." And in a reversal of traditional mother-daughter patterns, young girls brought the latest child care advice home to their mothers. Learning techniques of baby tending in "Little Mothers' Leagues" at school, they announced, "Don't give the baby herring; Don't give the baby beer to drink; Don't let the baby eat dirty things from the floor that she threw down at first; also pickle." More rules followed. "Don't try to awaken its intelligence and make it laugh"; and the final words for the harried mother, "Don't leave the baby sit on the stove [presumably while heating bath water]. Don't mind your house—mind your children." Here was contemporary child management translated by children to make sense in their own homes.

Letters from mothers reached the bureau in increasing numbers each year, often totaling as many a 125,000. Commonly beginning, "Dear Friend," this correspondence requested advice on rearing children but also revealed lives in livid detail, including unwanted pregnancies, worry over ailing infants, brutal prairie living conditions, poverty, troubled husbands, and a medical profession largely indifferent to their needs. The replies by Julia Lathrop, Mary West, Dr. Grace Meigs, Dr. Anna Rude, or Dr. Dorothy Mendenhall (the latter three from the bureau's Division of Child Hygiene) are the kind that might be anticipated from a friend, but are particularly startling emanating from a Washington bureaucracy. . . .

The bureau letters are interesting documents for several reasons. First, they demonstrate that the pamphlet *Infant Care* circulated among the poor. Secondly, they show that working-class women felt sufficiently interested in the advice to ask for more information. In addition to replying by mail, the Bureau frequently sent emissaries to their letter-writing public. Acting as a cluster of individuals rather than as a federal agency, bureau members provided their correspondents with help in the way of layettes, medical care for lying-in, and donations of money.

Both the quantity and range of mail received by the bureau point to a broad spectrum of women who found advice in *Infant Care* meaningful. Turning to the text of the manual, we see two reasons we might briefly call socioemotional and sociopolitical to explain why the pamphlet appealed to women from differing backgrounds. The socioemotional component relates to the concern for maternal well-being in the context of the mother-child dyad. By more permissive contemporary standards the advice tendered in *Infant Care* of 1914 and the revision of 1921 is typically viewed as strict and harsh to infants. Dr. Spock assesses the earlier wisdom in his own book: "During the first half of this century in this country, babies were usually kept on very strict, regular

258

schedules. . . . Doctors did not know for sure the cause of the serious intestinal infections that afflicted tens of thousands of babies yearly. It was believed that these infections were caused not only by the contamination of milk . . . but also by irregularity in feeding. Doctors and nurses feared irregular feeding so strongly that they came to disapprove of it psychologically, too. . . . In the general enthusiasm for strictness, mothers were usually advised to ignore their baby except at feeding time." And Dr. Spock ends his accounting of earlier practices by stating, "You don't know how lucky you are to be able to be natural and flexible."

Infant Care touted strict scheduling, stopping an infant's crying without cause by ignoring the wails, advocated early toilet training, and advised against rocking, tickling, or playing with infants. However, these rules were more than the dictates of the new pediatrics, for women interpreted the admonitions as protective of mother as well as child. *Infant Care* interpolated the asepsis and scheduling derived from the new pediatrics into a system that benefited the caregiver and emphasized consideration for the mother's role. "The care of a baby is readily reduced to a system," *Infant Care* read, "unless he is sick. Such a system is not only one of the greatest factors in keeping the baby well and in training him in a way which will be of value to him all through life, but it also reduces the work of the mother to the minimum and provides for her certain assured periods of rest and recreation." This "system" was an eminently useful technique for easing a mother's life, a necessity Mrs. West emphatically repeated. Playpen use was not justified in the manual for its educational value or even character-strengthening virtues. Instead, Mrs. West boldly stated, "An older child should be taught to sit on the floor or in his pen or crib during part of his waking hours, or he will be very likely to make too great demands upon his mother's strength." And with the voice of experience, she comments, "No one who has not tried it realizes how much nervous energy can be consumed in 'minding' a baby who can creep or walk about, and who must be continually watched and diverted, and the mother who is taking the baby through this period of his life will need to conserve all her strength, and not waste it in useless activity." Mrs. West developed her perspectives from the large body of information she amassed from women writing to the bureau as well as from her own experience. Letters like the following shaped *Infant Care*'s hints on scheduling the baby. A "*busy* mother of three dear babies—aged three years, twenty months and three months," wrote the bureau that she was on the horns of a dilemma. "I have wanted babies for years," she confides, "and now, when I'm so tired and with unfinished work everywhere I turn, I could scream at their constant prattle." Recognizing that infancy is a fleeting state she continues,

> *I love them until it hurts and know that, when they are out of their babyhood, I can never forgive myself for not making more of these precious years. Is there not some way that I can do all these scientific and hygienic duties for babies, keep our house up in proper fashion and still have time to rock and play with my babies? What of all my housework and baby-care could best be left undone? I do not ask time for myself but it would be nice to have a short period during the evening in which*

to read as I feel that I am growing narrow with no thoughts other than my household.

Thanking you for all the past helps your department has rendered to me. . . .

To the middle-class woman between the Scylla of a comfortable, attractive, sweet-smelling home" and "the 'ten-hour day' in housework," and the Charybdis of eternal vigilance over her children, Mrs. West offered a vast sympathy and some practical short-cuts. For women with a need to improvise ice boxes to chill milk, feed seven or more people routinely, and sew diapers from scratch as well as wash them by hand, Mrs. West also had some helpful hints. The socioemotional element of *Infant Care* shaded into the sociopolitical sphere. . . .

With the advent of behaviorism in the 1920s and its hegemony in child-rearing literature through the 1930's, the care of children began to lose the political effect and concern for maternal well-being that marked Progressive texts. John B. Watson, psychology's *enfant terrible*, wrote popular articles on child rearing for *Collier's* and *Harper's*. His behavioristic psychology, and particularly ideas from *Psychological Care of Infant and Child* (1928), were swiftly incorporated into child-rearing advice of the late twenties and thirties.

"Dedicated to the first mother who brings up a happy child," *Psychological Care of Infant and Child* was as much a diatribe against motherhood as it was currently practiced as a manual forwarding the new applied psychology. The book proves that how things are said is as significant for historical understanding as what is said. The actual advice of Watson's book does not differ radically from *Infant Care*, on a case-by-case comparison; it is the tone in which it is written and the rationale for the procedures that change. In Watson, toilet training is early, habits are critical, crying infants are allowed to cry, scheduling must be maintained at all costs, and indulgence is frowned on, all of which can be found in early *Infant Care*. What changes is the attitude towards the caregiver: the mother in Watson is an impediment to the scientific upbringing of the young and, even worse, a potential threat. Watson made no mention of how useful the advice might be for the mother observing it. Indeed, he is mainly concerned that women restrain their own satisfaction in child care. Reminding the reader of the gravity of her behavior, he enjoins her not to give in to her own self-interest. "When you are tempted to pet your child," he warns, "remember that mother love is a dangerous instrument. An instrument which may inflict a never healing wound, a wound which may make infancy unhappy, adolescence a nightmare, an instrument which may wreck your adult son or daughter's vocational future and their chances for marital happiness." With so much at stake, maternal convenience was hardly a subject worthy of attention. Dr. Spock's manual, although strikingly distant from the techniques or bristling language of Watson, pushes these arguments much further, and through its friendly, informal expression more effectively leads women in their widespread retreat to the private, depoliticized sphere of the new child care.

At first glance, Spock's manual and Watson's tract appear to have little in common. In fact, Spock seems to be reacting directly to the tutelage of the psychologist's book, revamping his directions for feeding, sleeping, toileting, and handling the child. Spock's mentors are Dewey and Freud, not Pavlov. But viewed more closely, the two manuals have more in common than meets the eye. Spock's injunctions also posit a watchful mother, competent to cope with all circumstances that may arise and capable of offering the encouragement, praise, and enrichment the child is presumed to need to gain his or her full potential. The caregiver in Spock is a monitor of her child's development as well as a self-scanner, obliged to have "a natural, easy confidence," "encouraged to be firm" at times, but always readily available for a baby-mother interchange.

Although their child-care techniques differ, Spock and Watson share a central belief: the life of the child can be harmed by improper mother love. In Watson, the mother is a top sergeant who precisely times her interventions in the child's day in order to build good habits. In Spock, the mother is a prime observer who must monitor both the baby and its environment for cues on when to act. In *Infant Care* the life of the child could literally be jeopardized if attentive care were not given to proper feeding and nursing of infant ills. But once accomplished the mother might rest easy, for worry over her child's emotional state was not yet in her lexicon of concerns. This was not entirely an oversight on the part of the bureau, but a deliberate omission of reference to a literature bureau authors thought was still in its infancy. According to Dr. Mendenhall, co-author of the first revision of *Infant Care*, "The literature of child psychology is so muddled and contains so much twaddle, that the average American mother should be warned against it. . . ."

The early manuals of the bureau were concerned with the mother's well-being as well as the child's and advocated a rough equity in the division of labor called for in the child-rearing process. Baby work paralleled mother work, for if the woman was obliged to learn the best techniques of training, cleaning, and provisioning her child, the infant was required to avoid excessive crying, becoming spoiled and fussy, and acting, according to Mrs. West, as "a household tyrant whose continual demands made a slave of the mother." Spoiling the baby for Spock is also a serious matter, but construed as something for which the mother is largely responsible and for which she must use willpower and "a little hardening of the heart" to overcome. Though she must curb herself, it is the baby she must think of.

A division of labor implies a shared enterprise. With Spock, infancy is endowed with a moral neutrality and an emotional tabula rasa even greater than in Watson's environmentalism. This shearing of moral obligations from the child's role accompanies an expansion of maternal moral responsibility in the child-rearing arena and the decline of the only kind of child labor the bureau supported: the child's help in establishing a synchrony of interests in the dyadic relationship. In Spock, an emotional workday is superimposed on the mother's physical workday, in part devoted to monitoring her own behavior so as to provide the proper environment for her offspring's "'self-realization' through 'self-discovery' and 'self-motivated behavior.'" All child work is defined as mother work, for it is she who must preside over the teaching of bathroom protocol, restraint of aggression, and adjustment to peer norms, lessons which lack an explicit correlation with the maternal well-being stressed in the earlier literature. In toileting the child, for example, the energy spared from washing diapers (or sewing them) is reinvested in psychological procedures. Dr. Spock instructs a mother "to watch her child—to see what stage of readiness he is in." Here watching, considering whether or not to intervene, and determining the magnitude of insistence to use in guiding the child's potty behavior replaces and—one can argue—expands other maternal labors. Furthermore, the mother is furnished with a self-scoring achievement test to correlate the result—whether or not the child is trained, and once trained does not lapse back into old habits—with maternal competence, or as Dr. Spock phrases it, "whether the mother has been encouraging or a bit too bossy in her efforts."

Although opposed to the manipulation of the baby's superego, Spock's advice tended to create a modern parental conscience to guarantee proper watchfulness. Mothers had the potential for more lapsed responsibilities, but fathers were not exempt from feeling uneasy either. "Every time I yell at my kids, I have the feeling I'm being reported to some secret psychiatric police force," one father confessed. . . .

Dr. Spock has been disturbed by some of the reactions to advice in *Baby and Child Care* and particularly by the zeal of women heeding his words. His book belongs to a category of genre household terms like kleenex and frigidaire, which young mothers routinely use. Confronting an infant crying without apparent cause, mothers run for their Spocks. Some women make certain they don't have far to run, for they squirrel away copies in bedrooms and bathrooms, as well as in the living room and kitchen, and in the glove compartment of the family car. Dr. Spock himself is chary of his apotheosis as a St. Christopher of motherhood, for he meant to build confidence in natural maternal inclinations, not anxiety nor the elevation of his advice to a creed. Yet, though he has tried to be a "confidence man," in Michael Zuckerman's descriptive phrase, shoring up the fading belief in a young mother's capacities to handle the baffling problems of infants and toddlers, his book has overtones of the second meaning of the term, that of a trickster. The permissive mode, designed to build self-confidence, in fact undercuts it by allusions to the physician's veto power, reminders of the pitfalls of improper child care, and orchestrations of daily events in a mother's life. In the words of one reviewer, "By not identifying these common problems of resentment and loneliness, while being so conscientious about identifying others, the books may contribute to the anxiety of women who read them."

The letters prompted by *Baby and Child Care* indicate a change in audience response. A high degree of literacy marks the letters, indicating more formal schooling among correspondents than analogous mail to *Infant Care*. . . .

Only a few of Spock's correspondents describe serious problems, such as sexual child abuse by a father. But problematic letters receive the uniform suggestion to "get some counseling from a family social agency." Counseling centers are viewed as capable of handling a great variety of difficulties ranging from a four-year-old who fails to speak in sentences, to a five-year-old who wets her pants and whose father is an "overpowering influence" precipitating "violent quarrels while the children are looking on," to a mother who has trouble getting her children to eat nourishing food. It is also to the experts in general but no expert in particular, that Dr. Spock sends the mother suffering a post-partum depression whose husband writes, "I'm asking for your help. I will pay you for your help. Please, please Doctor we need good sound advice and we need it bad."

Even a mother's expertise is insufficient to solve smaller but still troublesome problems. In the final analysis, mothers must rely on outside experts. In letters to Dr. Spock, the ultimate irony is reached, for even women with master's degrees in nutrition have children who refuse to eat fruit and vegetables. One woman confesses: "When I feed my kids the meals I do, I feel—well—apostate. How do I go about getting them to eat new foods without creating an aura of emotion about it? Or had I better not try? I have a very vivid memory of being made to eat food I didn't like. How come my parents got away with it and I can't?" And the woman ventures a guess why. "I know that a lot of my problem is personal, rooted in my own emotionalism and lack of control." Timidly she posits a theory that perhaps things were better in the old days. "Why all the hurry to give them vegetables, cereal, meat? How did babies live before strainers? How do they live in a more primitive state? Honestly, I'm not a reactionary, deploring anything new. Just wondering."

The advice to this woman is meant to be reassuring—that she needs emotional support and guidance and she might turn to a social agency for it. But what Spock fails to acknowledge to his readers is that the social agency is being asked to deflect the magnified emotions engendered by either massive inputs of one adult on a small child in relative isolation or the reverse, massive inputs of a small child on the solitary adult caregiver. For anything that is amiss is amplified to an unbearable decibel level. Still, it is this delicate balance that is considered the norm in the permissive literature and conveyed in casual language meant to assuage worry. . . .

Although Dr. Spock's mail frequently begins by praising him, the letters often end by revealing a substratum of problems experienced by the middle-class, a declension from the ideals depicted in his book. The letters begin briskly, referring to a problem, requesting reference material, and end revealing, unwittingly and indirectly, lives as troubled as those of women who wrote to the Children's Bureau. The difference between the two bodies of mail is that the Spockian generation, trying so intently to lead lives of balance and good cheer, experience difficulty acknowledging aberrations—a husbandless home, a struggle making ends meet, and emotional trouble in pursuing model mothercraft. The woman who wanted reference material on an epileptic son with an explosive personality tells Dr. Spock, "I try to give him a great deal of affection, although I am a working mother—his father left us five years ago. Sometimes it is so difficult to maintain my control that my hands shake." And she ends her letter revealing how unconfident and reliant on experts the Spockian mother has become. "Does he need the help," she writes, "or do I?" A second mother describes her husband who drinks to excess and slams out of the house when her two and one-half-year-old and thirteen month-old children cry or make noise. She requests Dr. Spock's professional opinion about a separation and reveals how well she has learned the lessons of *Baby and Child Care*. "I may have to work full or part-time," she writes. "Do you feel that it would be better for my children to stay with my husband and his poor influence and my upset condition, and the tension, and have me home full time?"

The deviations from the projected norm that often mark letters fulsome with praise for *Baby and Child Care* are related most often as personal failings. "But we continue to find parenthood to C____ an almost unbearable drain. What can we do? What should we do?" one mother asks. And another confesses, "We like to read and listen to music. Maybe we have neglected some aspects of A____'s development in our own selfishness."

This is an extraordinary collection of letters for they tell us among other things, how women have internalized the values *Baby and Child Care* teaches and yet reveal in many cases how difficult it is to live according to this wisdom. When aberrations do occur they are viewed as problems to be tackled by experts and consultants from outside, for the world of *Baby and Child Care* is essentially one of optimism and balance. Curiously, the equanimity that marks the manual has Freudian roots. Accepting Freudian insights on the stages of childhood, the book counsels defusing each of the potentially dangerous phases with maternal behavior like "take it easy and follow his lead" in weaning and toilet training, or "you can distract him with a toy if you want, but don't feel that you've *got* to," on handling the genitals. The manual uniformly stresses the congenial. For the balky two-year-old, the mother is taught, "When it's time for bed, or going outdoors, or coming in, steer him while conversing about pleasant things. Get things done without raising issues." Though *Baby and Child Care* acknowledges Freud, it is not the Freud who wrote *Civilization and its Discontents*. Painting so comforting a world has robbed permissive literature of its true ability to reassure. *Baby and Child Care*'s Freudian world is not only scrubbed of seething ids, constraining and punishing superegos, and fixations in oral, anal, and genital stages in the nursery, it is heavily decathected from the mother's point of view. Insisting on the ultimate ease and benevolence of the world, this regimen leaves behind advisees who are foundering in the breakers of true Freudian waters, the clash of their psychic needs with those of their offspring. Also left out of this scan are the people whose economic struggles preclude the comforts essential to Spock's child-rearing scheme.

The nature of the advice tends to exempt certain mothers. To use permissive techniques requires households with enough bedrooms and belongings for all members. *Baby and Child Care* addresses the problem of whether siblings should share a room, cautioning "out of the parents' room by six months if possible," without considering homes where children must share beds. The advice presumes a catalogue of belongings and a set of relationships: telephones, refrigerators, a pest and rodent free house in adequate repair, accessible physicians, a nuclear family composed of mother, father, and baby, with an occasional recognition of one other sibling. The larder is filled with food, the "feeding problem" being the recalcitrant child, not an inadequate food supply. The modality of child rearing itself involves endless conversations and verbal exchanges. To argue, as sociologists and psychologists recently have, as to whether or not child-rearing practices of the working classes are more or less permissive than those of the middle class pays insufficient heed to the practical dimensions implicit in child-care advice.

The advice in *Infant Care* earlier in the century was also middle-class in orientation. Yet working-class women interpreted this literature to fit their lives. The Children's Bureau encouraged this translation through the celebration of "Baby Weeks," personal visits of bureau personnel, and detailed correspondence with troubled women, as well as with women who wanted to begin informal neighborhood "conferences" on child care. Spockian middle-class rearing rules appear less appealing to the working class and have no provision for the spread of child-rearing lore by an oral mode, or informal network. "Dr. Spock?" one contemporary mother commented, "He's for rich kids. How can he help my children? He doesn't know my child."

Although the ideals set forth in *Infant Care* of 1914 emphasize single family dwellings, sunny nurseries, ample food for mother and child, and adequate maternal rest, there is a recognition of the problematic side of the rearing process for some people: the existence of poverty, rural isolation, and the difficulties of the mother wanting to do her best but proscribed from it by physical or psychological barriers. These dimensions, both emotional and political in a broad sense, are missing from *Baby and Child Care*. Just as *Baby and Child Care* relegates disturbed women to the counseling center, the manual sends poor women to the social worker, for the normal home for Spock has room for neither the personal dilemmas women may face as caregivers nor the social problems of poverty.

References to folk custom or ethnic child-rearing practices, acknowledged in the earlier literature, are absent from *Baby and Child Care*. In trying to guide women to the new scientific child-rearing standards, *Infant Care* alludes to the older ones, thereby including women guided by their lights. Mrs. West speaks of the tradition of "biting the baby's finger nail," believing it "will prevent him from becoming a thief," or feeling "ill luck will follow if the baby looks in the glass." Trying to lead women to the new nurture, *Infant Care* refers to the traditional practices of offering babies table tidbits, wine, cider, beer, or tea and the use of soothing syrups. Although the references are largely negative, mentioning them addresses those women who resorted to them. On traditional practices *Baby and Child Care* is silent, pointing indirectly to a different audience of readers. . . .

The largest body of criticism of *Baby and Child Care* comes not from parent users, disillusioned with its precepts, but from people distrustful of Spock's politics. Dr. Spock has been a controversial political figure, a one-time spokesman for SANE, a defendant in a conspiracy trial for voicing opposition to the war in Vietnam, and a third party vice-presidential candidate in two elections. Dr. Norman Vincent Peale's view of a direct line from self-scheduled babies to indulged, protesting youth sets the tone for negative comments about the book. One furious mother writes, "I have just torn your book apart with my bare hands." Another scrawls "traitor" across the cover and sends the manual to Dr. Spock. . . . The *National Review* publishes a poem entitled "The Spockery of Dr. Quack."

> *I do not love thee, Dr. Spock*
> *The thing is this: I've got a block*
> *Against the sort of seedy hat tricks*
> *You're sneaking into pediatrics.*
> *Let a mother ask you why*
> *Her kid is nervous—you reply*
> *She's stuffed the moppets head with rot*
> *About a Communistic plot*
> *And if she only had a brain*
> *She'd run right out and go in SANE.*
> *Well, Mom, let me say beware*
> *Of all this bogus baby care,*
> *And don't let Benjy muddle you,*
> *You know more than you think you do.*

On a milder note, but still critical of Dr. Spock's political views, the following story was related: "Dr. Spock was giving an anti-war lecture at Western Reserve. There was a poster announcing that Dr. Spock would speak on the war. Some student had written under it 'Next week Gen. Maxwell Taylor will speak on the toilet training of children.'"

It is ironic that Dr. Spock, a political activist in his own life, can be linked with purveying a conservative child-rearing creed. If critics had looked at the ideas conveyed in *Baby and Child Care* more closely, they might have concluded they were antithetical to social and political involvement, rather than conducive to activism. The mother of Dr. Spock's manual is an apolitical person without any social involvements outside of her own home. She exists largely to rear her young and has time off only to pursue a few private activities—"a movie," "the beauty parlor," "a new hat or dress," or a "visit [to] a good friend." The manual's emphasis on getting along, avoiding confrontation, and pursuing a balanced life could, one might imagine, more easily lead to conformity than to political protest.

The variety of stories told about Dr. Spock's activism—some highly critical, some bemused—do point, however, to the schism between the private and social facets of child-centeredness. The split was much less apparent in the Progressive period. Political advocacy on the part of child-care experts like Dr. Josephine Baker, head of the Bureau of Child Hygiene in New York, for example, or of groups like the P.T.A. was not uncommon, nor considered unseemly behavior.

By the 1960s the private and public spheres of child nurture were separate issues, in part encouraged by the success of Spock's own advice. For the very purveyor of this wisdom to take public, political stands on nuclear testing and war outraged his audience. So well had many middle-class Americans absorbed the lesson of the isolated maternal figure along with her offspring mediating their environment to provide optimal experiences, developing cognitive traits, and multiplying sensory input, that the very thought of their patron saint edging them out of the home in a grander cause set them astir. The triumph of the Spockian dictum of a privatized child-rearing world, shorn of political concerns, may, in part, explain the vehemence with which Dr. Spock has been attacked for his own peace activities.

Dr. Spock has stood resolute before critics of his politics, but has yielded to certain faultfinding in *Baby and Child Care*. He has toned down the permissiveness of the first edition in the 1957 and 1968 revisions. A quantitative study of Spock's advice in the area of toilet training, discipline, and children's behavior in articles he wrote for *Redbook* and *Ladies' Home Journal* measures a notable decline from the 1940s to the 1960s in the emphasis on nurturance and a new stress on more structured child-care practices. He indicates why he has changed his mind in the 1968 revision of *Baby and Child Care*: "A lot has been added and changed, especially about discipline, spoiling, and the parents' part. . . . nowadays there seems to be more chance of a conscientious parent's getting into trouble with permissiveness than with strictness. So I have tried to give a more balanced view." Yet the changes are more apparent than real, for the ease and balance of the art of child rearing continue to be underscored, and the privacy surrounding the dyadic relationship of the mother and child is unchallenged.

By 1976, a new revision of *Baby and Child Care* was available. A core assumption of Spock's *oeuvre* appears changed and the mother-child twosome is stretched into a triad to include the father. Affected by feminist critiques of his work and crediting his associations across the country with young people in the anti-war movement in helping him to see the light, Spock assigns a new role to the father in the child-rearing process. In 1976 Spock recanted: "I always assumed that the parent taking the greater share of the care of young children (and of the home) would be the mother, whether or not she wanted an outside career. . . . Now I recognize that the father's responsibility is as great as the mother's." Infants called "he" in earlier versions now become "supposing the baby is a girl"; caregivers become mother, father, child-care center, or sitter (one can "assume for the discussion that it's a woman, though there is no reason why it should not be a man"). In 1945, Dr. Spock had extended the necessity for the continual presence of the maternal figure well beyond the physical requirements of nursing, cautioning that two-year-olds show increased dependence, and "this should be taken into consideration if the mother is thinking for example of taking a job, going on a trip, or having an elective operation." It was not sufficient for the mother to be present most of the time in early Spock, but mandatory that she be present all the time. For home is the school of infancy in this literature, the curriculum is articulated in a child-rearing text, and the teacher-trainer of choice is the mother. By 1976, Dr. Spock saw the plausibility of replacing the maternal figure with a father, baby sitter, or child-care institution. Yet old beliefs, particularly deeply held ones, do not easily change.

The 1976 text continues its emphasis on the primacy of the sequestered home the book has always stressed. "While we're waiting and working for a more humane society

I hope there will always be men and women," Dr. Spock muses, "who feel that the care of children and home is at least as important and soul satisfying as any other activity, and that neither men nor women will feel the need to apologize for deciding to make that their main career." The elevation of the father to an active participant in the household has created the new configuration of the triad, but it is a tableau which on the whole is still a solitary and isolated one. The formulation of the triad continues to stress the private features implicit in the cult of childhood to the exclusion of attention to child rearing's place in the larger social fabric.

Baby and Child Care emphasizes the symbiosis that rests at the heart of permissive advice. Curiously, the interdependence of mother and child has a commercial as well as a moral element. The language in which child rearing is discussed is often that of modern marketing. Children are a product to be turned out by the home. The mother, not only literally the original producer, is more importantly its refiner and packager. The lure is held out before her that with attentiveness, emotional vigilance, and her uninterrupted presence she can provide an environment from which a superior individual will emerge. Spock's correspondents fathom the product orientation and product maintenance implicit in the manual. The first fan letter written to Dr. Spock from a new father stated, "In largely the same manner that I have previously sat down and studied manuals on the operation of the contact camera or the proper upbringing of Irish setters . . . I entered the realm of pediatrics with the good Doctor Spock as guide and mentor." Thirteen years later a mother sent Dr. Spock a revealing parody, equating a child with a product. She remarked, "Today on purchasing even the simplest modern contrivance, a parts check list, and assembling and oiling instruction sheet is included that prominently proclaims, 'STOP—READ THIS FIRST,' for even the simplest minded owner's edification. . . . A glossary of terms, language, schedules, with appendices and footnotes should be required reading for parents while infant is still hospital incarcerated."

Product maintenance advice in the manual has useful consumer features, particularly in medical diagnosis. Through Dr. Spock's words one mother recognized signs of pyloric stenotosis before her physician and a second woman noticed intussusception in her baby. Yet *Baby and Child Care* is more than a medical dictionary, or a first aid manual, or even a Heath kit. It embodies a world view, just as the earlier literature did. This world of rearing the young, in contrast to that of 1914, is free of dissonance or conflict, or the recognition of poverty or cultural difference. Such a world has invented a motherhood that excludes the experience of many mothers.

12

Interactional Styles and Attachment

Anna Freud and Sophie Dann studied six German-Jewish orphans rescued from a concentration camp following the Second World War. Aged between six and twelve months, they had all arrived individually at the Tereszin Camp and lived there for two or three years. They were conscientiously cared for and medically supervised, but their caregivers were also inmates, who were overworked and frequently deported. They had no toys. On their liberation the children were flown to England, where they remained in their group of six. In their new camp, they behaved in a wild, restless and uncontrollably noisy manner. They destroyed toys and furniture. They would ignore adults, except when they had some immediate need, and were frequently hostile to them. Their positive feelings were reserved for each other. They were inseparable, and became upset if away from each other even for a few moments. These children were parentless in the fullest sense of the word. They had no mothers or mother-substitutes but they did have each other.

• INTRODUCTION •

Human infants are well prepared from birth to participate in creating their own social worlds. They perceive and react to faces, cry when they are wet, hungry, or distressed, and respond to touch and movement. Caregivers who are sensitive to the baby's cues will find themselves involved in a series of subtle, shifting, and ever more complex interactions, a kind of dance in which first one partner and then the other takes the lead.

One of the most important outcomes of this process of interaction is that babies begin to form lasting attachments to those around them. When the infant's attachment to primary caregivers is secure, it is a tie of mutual affection and trust. Secure children expect a predictable response to their overtures. From this predictability, they learn that they are valued and that they have the power to influence those around them. Available research suggests that this element of predictability may be critical to the child's later emotional well-being.

The readings in this module have been chosen to introduce the concept of attachment and the theoretical and empirical contributions that have furthered our understanding of the attachment system. In the course of this discussion, Robert Karen presents us with a survey of some of the most important results of attachment research and a description of the origin and format of the "Strange Situation," a widely used but sometimes criticized laboratory technique designed to assess the quality of the caregiver/child bond.

Pay particular attention to the nature of the criticisms that have been leveled at attachment research. Keep in mind that the "Strange Situation," like any measuring device, provides no more than an index of the construct it is designed to measure. Any given child's behavior in the "Strange Situation" on any given day is at best a reasonably faithful reflection of the quality of the attachment relationship. While attachment researchers report data suggesting that the "Strange Situation" does indeed provide a remarkably informative and robust reflection of the attachment bond, others have challenged this view. Critics such as Robert LeVine and Patrice Miller argue that cultural differences in behavior in the "Strange Situation" may be less an index of attachment than of differential socialization experiences that vary with cultural values. Given the psychological importance of the first relationship and the powerful implications of attachment research for parenting and social policy, this is a criticism that must be taken seriously.

● ● ●

Becoming Attached
Robert Karen

For the past fifteen years, work relating infant attachment status (indexed by children's behavior in the "Strange Situation" at twelve months of age) to concurrent or later personality development has been among the most exciting and productive areas of child development research. In this article, Robert Karen describes the intellectual origins of the attachment concept and introduces us to John Bowlby and Mary Ainsworth, whose seminal work initiated the current interest in attachment. Reviewing a body of research literature that some regard as one of psychology's most important achievements, Karen describes procedures by which infants are classified as securely attached, ambivalent, avoidant, or disorganized, and discusses studies in Uganda and Baltimore that led Ainsworth to conclude that attachment status was related to sensitivity and predictability of caregiver reactions to infant signals.

Since that early research, a vast quantity of attachment data has been amassed, much of it relating to the power of attachment classification to predict aspects of the child's later social adjustment. Reviewing some of the criticisms that have been leveled at attachment research by psychologists such as Jerome Kagan, Karen makes it clear that the striking findings and social policy implications of attachment research cannot yet be taken to represent established principle. Until the controversy is resolved, however, the concept of attachment will continue to maintain a powerful hold on the interest of many developmental psychologists.

The struggle to understand the infant-mother bond ranks as one of the great quests of modern psychology—one that touches us deeply, because it holds so many clues to how we became who we are. I have a friend who does not want to be a father, because he fears he will be as emotionally stingy with his child as his mother was with him. This dread, that our character mirrors one of our parents', is very common, and the terrible certainty some of us have that we will re-enact the worst aspects of our upbringing with our own children is not only widespread but seems distressingly well founded. The abused child does indeed often become the child-abuser, and evidence suggests that many other behavioral and emotional tendencies are passed down through the generations.

Theories to explain this unwanted inheritance are plentiful. But scientifically verifiable explanations have been elusive. Indeed, until the past two decades nothing could be said with scientific authority about almost any dimension of the mother-child bond, let alone how aspects of relatedness, good or bad, are transmitted. The multitude of voices confuses not only parents but also the judges and government agencies that make decisions about young lives.

What do children need, at a minimum, in order to feel that the world of people is a positive place and that they themselves have value? What experiences in infancy will enable them to feel confident enough to explore, to develop healthy peer relations, to rebound from adversity? What custody or foster-care arrangements will best serve their emotional needs if the family should dissolve, and at what point do we decide that a neglectful or abusive mother is worse than a kind stranger? Which of us are at risk of being parents who will raise insecure children, and what can be done to minimize that risk? These are all questions of huge theoretical and practical interest.

Today, with mothers spending less time at home, with families falling apart and being reshaped in new combinations, and with debates raging about the emotional needs of schoolchildren and the advantages and disadvantages of day care, understanding all this seems more urgent than ever. One group of researchers and clinicians, known as attachment theorists, claim that they've discovered some answers and are on the road to finding the rest. But although they've dazzled many of their peers, altering some of our most basic attitudes toward early child care, their contributions have frequently met with skepticism, opposition, or rebuke.

In 1958 Harry Harlow reported a study that every student now learns of in Introductory Psych. Inspired by the pioneering work of the psychoanalyst René Spitz, who had shown that infants raised in foundling homes without handling or loving attention withered away and often died, Harlow, an animal-learning theorist, devised an experiment with rhesus monkeys. He took infant monkeys from their mothers shortly after birth and raised them with two surrogate "mothers"—one made of bale-wire mesh, the other covered with terry cloth. Either "mother" could be equipped with a feeding nipple. Even when the bale-wire "mother" was the only one providing food, the infant monkeys became more attached to the terry-cloth "mother," cuddling it, running to it

Karen, Robert. (1990). Becoming attached. *The Atlantic Monthly*, February. pp. 37-70.

when frightened, and using it as a base for explorations. The experiment appeared to disprove the assumption, common among both Freudian and social-learning theorists, that infant attachment to the mother is mainly a function of feeding. To rhesus monkeys, at least, warm contact seemed more important.

As persuasive as Harlow's study was, experiments with monkeys can tell us nothing definitive about human attachment. And given the restrictions on what a researcher can do with human subjects, a more conclusive statement on the infant-mother bond seemed unlikely.

But a decade after Harlow began putting infant monkeys through a variety of extreme deprivations in order to capture the essentials of mothering, Mary Ainsworth, with much the same goal, was conducting experimental observations of human babies in a Baltimore lab. Using a technique called the Strange Situation, Ainsworth embarked upon a longitudinal study of attachment during the infants' first year. In an approach that was extremely unusual at the time, researchers closely observed mothers and children in their homes, paying careful attention to each mother's style of responding to her infant in a number of fundamental areas: feeding, crying, cuddling, eye contact, and smiling. At twelve months the infant and his mother were taken to the lab and the infant was observed as the mother was separated from him. During two intervals a stranger was in the room; during another the baby was alone.

Ainsworth spotted three distinct patterns in the babies' reactions. One group of infants protested or cried on separation, but when the mother returned, they greeted her with pleasure, frequently stretching out their arms to be picked up and molding to her body. They were relatively easy to console. Ainsworth labeled this group "securely attached."

She labeled the other two groups "insecurely" or "anxiously" attached. One group of anxious babies, called "ambivalent," tended to be clingy from the beginning and afraid to explore the room on their own. They became terribly anxious and agitated upon separation, often crying profusely. An ambivalent baby typically sought contact with his mother when she returned, but simultaneously arched away from her angrily, resisting all efforts to be soothed.

The second group, called "avoidant," gave the impression of independence. They explored the new environment without using their mothers as a base, and they didn't turn around to be certain of their mothers' presence, as those labeled securely attached did. When the mother left, the avoidant infant didn't seem affected. And on her return he snubbed or avoided her.

Without the painstaking observation that had come before, Ainsworth's findings would have been relatively insignificant, no more than a demonstration that babies reacted differently when separated from and reunited with their mothers. But because Ainsworth's team had observed each of these mother-child pairs for seventy-two hours over the prior year, they were able to make specific associations between the babies' attachment styles and the mothers' styles of parenting. Mothers of securely attached children were found to be more responsive to the feeding signals and the crying of their infants, and to readily return the infants' smiles. Mothers of anxiously attached children were inconsistent, unresponsive, or rejecting. The three patterns seen in laboratory observation proved directly related to the way the babies were being raised.

The importance of the Strange Situation was not immediately apparent when Ainsworth's article describing her research was published, in 1969. But her findings marked the beginning of a critical shift in perceptions about infancy and child-rearing, set in motion a prolonged debate that divides infancy researchers to this day, and signaled a revolution in the field of developmental psychology. . . . Before Ainsworth, numerous methods had been devised to measure conceptual and cognitive development. Many of them had been introduced by the Swiss psychologist Jean Piaget, who showed the steps by which a child's mind grasps the complexity of his world. But almost no procedures were available for assessing or measuring an infant's social and emotional development—certainly none at this level of complexity. Although real-life experiences were widely assumed to shape personality, no one had been able to demonstrate exactly which experiences mattered. Ainsworth, at a stroke, changed all that, and in subsequent research she and her followers laid siege to much of the received wisdom of the field, offering new explanations of how our inner world is developed and organized and what all this means in terms of security, personality, and future relationships.

In succeeding studies attachment researchers found that without intervention or changes in family circumstances, attachment patterns formed in infancy persist. At age two, insecurely attached children tend to lack self-reliance and show little enthusiasm for problem solving. At three and a half to five years, according to their teachers, they are often problem kids, with poor peer relations and little resilience. At six, they tend to display hopelessness in response to imagined separations. Reliable, statistically verifiable information like this—about what infants need in order to feel secure and how they are likely to feel and behave in later years if they don't get it—had never before been available.

Parents, too, were examined. Mary Main, a former student of Ainsworth's and now a professor at the University of California, Berkeley, found that the way parents remember and organize their own childhood experiences is a powerful predictor of which attachment group their children will fall into. This was the first research both to show intergenerational transmission of secure and insecure attachment and to attempt to distinguish between adults who have retained the negative legacy of their childhood and those who have worked through it.

Questions about child-rearing that had only been speculated about could now be answered with greater authority. For years mothers had been warned against picking up their babies when they cried. It seemed contrary to nature and intuition, but behavioral theory asserted that picking up the child reinforced the crying, and if you did it enough you'd have a monstrous crybaby on your hands. Attachment research seems to have disproved this, at least as a general principle.

Ainsworth's central premise was that the responsive mother provides a secure base. The infant needs to know that his primary caregiver is steady, dependable, there for him. (Throughout this article, for simplicity's sake, I'll refer to the primary caregiver as the mother—though fathers and nonrelated adults can also be primary caregivers—and I'll use the male pronoun for the infant.) Fortified with the knowledge of his mother's availability, the child is able to go forth and explore the world. Lacking it, he is insecure, and his exploratory behavior is stunted. This was an astonishing assertion in the behaviorist-dominated atmosphere of the late 1960s, when most experts warned against spoiling children with too much responsiveness.

Warm, sensitive care, Ainsworth insisted, does not create dependency; it liberates, and enables autonomy. "It's a good thing to give a baby and a young child physical contact," she says, "especially when they want it and seek it. It doesn't spoil them. It doesn't make them clingy. It doesn't make them addicted to being held."

To many mothers, Ainsworth's prescriptions seem as natural as maternity itself. (Of course you pick up your baby when he cries!) But as pleasing as it is to discover that psychology is catching up to intuition—finding that little children do indeed need nurturing and consistency, that the way you are with your baby will profoundly affect his personality development, that what happens to him when he's little will influence what he becomes later—it is equally displeasing to encounter a body of evidence suggesting that you yourself haven't been or aren't or won't be doing it right. Attachment theory, which seems implicitly to advocate a stay-at-home role for the mother, has thus provoked both rage and enchantment.

The day-care issue has been the most explosive (see "Babes in Day Care," by Ellen Ruppel Shell, August, 1988, *Atlantic*). Attachment-theory proponents tend to see full-time day care in the first year as a risk, and Jay Belsky, an attachment researcher at Pennsylvania State University, has voiced the concern that if you put your baby in substitute care for more than twenty hours a week, you are running a serious risk of his becoming anxiously attached—which could skew his subsequent efforts to relate to the outside world. Such assertions, needless to say, have drawn heavy fire, and bristle with political implications.

In twenty years of Strange Situation research, stable middle-class American homes have consistently produced babies of whom about two-thirds are securely attached and one-third are insecurely attached. As these numbers suggest, being securely attached hardly ensures that babies will grow up free of neuroses or even of insecurities. It means only that they have been given confidence that someone will be there for them and that they are thus at least minimally capable of forming satisfying relationships and of passing on that ability to their children. But in unstable homes, where parents, often single, are under great stress, and where neglect or abuse is more common, this minimal bulwark is often missing and the numbers of insecure children swell. Larry Aber, the director of the Barnard Center for Toddler Development, at Columbia University, estimates that of the 100,000 four-year-olds in New York City today, as many as half may be insecurely attached. He believes that we need "dramatic preventive measures" to help these children and expects that attachment research will make its most important clinical contribution in the search for such measures. Other experts would reject both ends of this assertion.

The controversy adds urgency to the question of whether attachment principles can be justly claimed to have scientific validity. Resistance has certainly been vigorous among classical analysts, behaviorists, and those who favor a genetic view. Jerome Kagan, a developmental psychologist at Harvard, believes that the Strange Situation is not a reliable measure, and thus that much of attachment thinking is flawed. "Ainsworth had a very small sample," Kagan says; "it was restricted in variety; it's certainly not enough to build a theory on." Besides, he asks, can we really expect six minutes of reunion behavior in an unfamiliar room to reveal an emotional history between parent and child "comprising over a half-million minutes in the home"?

Friendlier critics are concerned about a reductionist tendency to assume that quality of attachment is all-important. They argue that other aspects of parenting, such as teaching, playing, and having fun, may go well even if attachment goes poorly. Others believe that in focusing so much on the primary caregiver, which usually means the mother, attachment theory has not paid adequate attention to the father's role.

Nevertheless, leading psychoanalytically oriented infancy researchers, such as Daniel Stern and Stanley Greenspan, acknowledge that attachment theory has filled in a piece of the puzzle. "It's too early to say how big a piece," Stern says, "but it's certainly a piece, and it's a nice piece." Psychotherapists are finding that familiarity with attachment concepts is helping them in their work with patients. "My training in the attachment interview," says Arietta Slade, of New York's City University, "has dramatically changed the way I listen to how patients talk." And attachment concepts have increasingly influenced the advice that baby doctors give both parents and lawmakers. T. Berry Brazelton, a famed Boston pediatrician who has popularized his own brand of attachment theory, says, "My whole thinking has been based on it."

Attachment theory was itself born of three unlikely parents: ethology, developmental psychology, and psychoanalysis—disciplines that have not traditionally troubled themselves with one another's findings. But in 1951 the biologist Sir Julian Huxley began talking ethology to John Bowlby, the British psychoanalyst who originated attachment theory. Huxley urged Bowlby to read Konrad Lorenz, considered the father of modern ethology, particularly Lorenz's work on imprinting in newborn goslings, a phenomenon by which the infant birds attach themselves to the first moving object they see. Bowlby did so and became imprinted himself.

Captivated by ethological ideas, Bowlby now had a biological basis for his belief that a child needs a reliable ongoing attachment to a primary caregiver and that he suffers grievously, even irreparably, if that attachment is interrupted or lost. He developed the concept of "internal working models" to describe how the infant's sense of self and other unfolds through interactions with that primary caregiver. A brilliant synthesizer, Bowlby was the first theorist to exhaustively combine cognitive and emotional development, to build a bridge between Piaget and Freud. Having written the three-volume work, *Attachment and Loss*, he is the uncontested father of the movement. But Mary Salter Ainsworth's Strange Situation put attachment theory on the map, by providing empirical evidence for a number of conclusions that until then had only been intuited. She made the bridge from Piaget to Freud sturdy enough for half the field of developmental psychology to traverse. "Our whole developmental approach was cognitive until she came along," Brazelton says, referring to the pre-Ainsworth emphasis on such functions as perception, memory, and abstraction. "She enabled psychology to look at the emotional development of children in a reliable, quantifiable way." Says Bowlby, "Her work has been indispensable. It's difficult to know what might have happened otherwise."

Ainsworth, now seventy-six, lives in semi-retirement in a suburban home near the University of Virginia in Charlottesville, where she taught for many years. "The fact that the Strange Situation was not in the home environment, that it was in the lab, really helped," she says with a laugh. "I only did it as an adjunct to my naturalistic research, but it was the thing that everyone could accept somehow. It was so *demonstrable*."

A bright-eyed woman whose short brown hair is streaked with white and blond, Ainsworth has a face that changes gently from intellectual delight to feisty engagement to shy vulnerability. In discussing her work she reveals both pride and modesty, and an uncommon willingness to credit others. The penetrating gaze she trains on an interviewer is suggestive of her years as a teacher and a clinician.

Although she never had children of her own, Ainsworth is the matriarch of a far-flung but close-knit family of attachment researchers and theorists, many of whom have been intellectually nurtured by her since their graduate-school days and still see her as a guiding force in their work. . . .

The Search for a Theory of Relatedness

By 1950, when Ainsworth and Bowlby first met, many researchers had grown dissatisfied with the lack of attention paid by classical analysis to the influences of relationships, especially in early life. It wasn't that Freud ignored relationships or failed to see that the way one was raised would influence one's emotional well-being. But after discarding his trauma (or "seduction") theory about the origin of neurosis, he came to place more and more emphasis on the unconscious workings of the individual psyche and the instincts or "drives" that motivate it. Classical analysts retained this tight focus—often ignoring Freud's speculative thoughts in other directions—and in their writings the nature of the patient's relationships, past or present, often seemed incidental.

But Freud wasn't even in his grave before new schools of thought were generating new questions about our first relationships and their lasting impact on us. Soon interpersonal and social theorists, family-systems theorists, and object-relations theorists (in psychoanalysis the unfortunate word *object* usually means "person") were all struggling over the relational ground left uncharted by the classical Freudian model.

When, at sixteen, Ainsworth (then Mary Salter) entered the University of Toronto, in 1929, she quickly found that her first mentor, William Blatz, had his own ideas about relatedness. The subject matter of Blatz's abnormal-psychology class consisted almost entirely of his "security theory," and, troubled by insecurity herself, she was drawn to it. "I was impressed with his idea that the child derives security from being near his parents," Ainsworth says. "That security enables him to move out to explore his world, to learn about it, and to acquire the skills to master what he encounters out there. I don't remember if he called that 'using the parent as a secure base from which to explore the world,' but that is how I finally came to phrase it."

Ainsworth recalls Toronto's psychology department as being imbued with a messianic feeling, one that she quickly came to share, and retains to this day: that the science of psychology could be used to improve the quality of human life fundamentally. She became a psychology major, did her doctoral dissertation on Blatz's security theory, and in 1939 became a lecturer at the university, before doing a three-year stint as an army major in charge of personnel selection during the Second World War. In 1946 she returned to the University of Toronto, where she and Blatz co-directed a team studying security in various aspects of adult life. She also began training as a diagnostician during those years, and later co-authored a volume on ink-blot technique with Bruno Klopfer, the leading Rorschach interpreter of the day.

Blessed with a quick mind and a keen eye, the young psychologist was a brilliant and eager researcher. But she had neither the hunger nor the disposition of a scientist on the make. Although intellectually tough, interpersonally she was often softer. In 1950, when she married Len Ainsworth, who was younger than she and had recently completed his masters degree in psychology, she readily dropped her work in favor of his education. "It didn't seem like a good idea for Len to remain at the U of T for his Ph.D., so we went to England. He got admitted to University College, London, and I went along."

If Ainsworth did not have destiny writ large in her features, the man who placed the help-wanted ad that she answered in the London *Times* did. Bowlby had opinions, determination, and presence. Ainsworth's four years with him and his small team would alter the course of her career. She was taken not only with his ideas but also with his formidable and secure personality. "He made no bones about the fact that he was single-handedly fighting the analytic establishment, that it pained him some, but that he was convinced he was on the right track. It was a long time before I felt any sense of getting close to him or being a friend. But I had no difficulty whatsoever making him into a surrogate father figure—even though he's not much older than I."

During that first interview Ainsworth and Bowlby discovered that their interests coincided to a remarkable degree. It was the beginning of a professional marriage that would prove as fruitful and enduring as any in the history of psychology.

Bowlby

Seven years her senior, John Bowlby had already made a name for himself with the publication of *Forty-four Juvenile Thieves*, which noted the high proportion of delinquent boys who had suffered early maternal separations. He was now at work on a report to the World Health Organization on the mental health of homeless children, who were a big problem in the postwar years. Published in 1951, *Maternal Care and Mental Health* warned against separating children from their mothers—even mothers who were untidy and neglectful. It asserted that children suffering maternal deprivation are at increased risk for physical and mental illness, and that even a clean, well-meaning, and well-run

278

institution—unless it somehow provided a true maternal substitute—was unlikely to save a small child from being irreversibly damaged by the age of three.

During the late thirties Bowlby was supervised in child treatment by Melanie Klein, a brilliant and original Vienna-born analyst and the inventor of psychoanalytic play therapy, who had won a large following in England after arriving there in 1926. One of the first avowed object-relations theorists and a giant in the field to this day, Klein is also remembered by some for being eccentric, devious, and nasty.

"I trained with the Kleinians," says Bowlby, eighty-three, a soft-featured man with bushy white eyebrows, thinning white hair, and a proper, somewhat detached upper-class bearing. "But I parted company with them, because I held that real-life events—the way parents treat a child—are of key importance in determining development, and Melanie Klein would have none of it. The object relations that she was talking about were entirely internal relationships"—that is, fantasy. "The notion that internal relationships reflect external relationships was totally missing from her thinking."

The very first case in which Klein supervised Bowlby, in the spring of 1938, set the tone. "I was seeing a small hyperactive boy five days a week. He was anxious, in and out of the room, all over the place. His mother used to bring him, and her job was to sit in the waiting room and take him home again. She was an extremely anxious, distressed woman, who was wringing her hands, in a very tense, unhappy state. But I was forbidden by Melanie Klein to talk to this poor woman."

In Bowlby's earlier work at the London Child Guidance Clinic, he says, "we were seeing parents as much as children and dealing, so far as we could, with parents' emotional problems," an approach that has become widespread today. But Klein was a purist and insisted that he see only the child.

"Well, I found this a rather painful situation, really. After three months the news reached me that the mother had been taken to a mental hospital, which didn't surprise me. And when I came to report this to Melanie Klein, her attitude was What a nuisance—we shall have to find another case. The fact that this poor woman had a breakdown was of no clinical interest to her whatever; it might have been the man in the moon who was bringing this boy. So this horrified me, to be quite frank. And from that point onwards, my mission in life was to demonstrate that real-life experiences have a very important effect on development."

When a goose or a duck is born, it attaches itself to the first moving object it sees. Almost invariably that will be its mother; although if a human scientist elbows his way into view first, the gosling or duckling will become hopelessly attached to him and follow him everywhere. Other instincts can similarly be distorted, or fail to develop at all, depending on what the young animal encounters or fails to encounter in its environment. We know this and many other facts about the bonding behavior of birds and mammals, thanks to the work of ethologists like Konrad Lorenz and Niko Tinbergen. While Ainsworth was in London, Bowlby became, as he puts it, "addicted" to the work of these men. He immediately sensed that human beings, too, must have such bonding behaviors and intergenerational cues, that they, too, must be predisposed toward some sort of relational experience, and that with them, too, nature's intentions could go awry—as they obviously had with that hyperactive boy—if the environment failed them.

"I mean, talk about *eureka*," he says. "They were brilliant, first-class scientists, brilliant observers, and studying family relationships in other species—relationships which were obviously analogous with those of human beings—and doing it so frightfully well. We were fumbling around in the dark; they were already in brilliant sunshine."

In addition to suggesting improved strategies of investigation, ethology gave Bowlby an explanation: separations from the mother are disastrous developmentally because they thwart an instinctual need. Bowlby soon declared that clinging, sucking, and following are all part of the child's instinctual repertoire, and that the goal of these behaviors is precisely to keep the mother close by. He saw the child's smile as a "social releaser" that elicits maternal care. And he abandoned the Freudian notion of drives, arising out of hidden forces like libido and aggression, which accumulate within us and crave discharge. Instead, Bowlby saw an array of innate behavior patterns—relationship-seeking patterns like smiling, babbling, looking, and listening—that are enriched and developed by the responses they call forth from the environment.

Bowlby proceeded to define a series of developmental stages based on the maternal bond. During the first year the child is gradually able to display a complete range of "attachment behaviors," protesting his mother's departure, greeting her return, clinging when frightened, following when able. Such actions are instinctual and rooted in the biological fact that proximity to one's mother is satisfying, because it is essential to survival. The establishment, maintenance, and renewal of that proximity begets feelings of love, security, and joy. A lasting or untimely disruption brings on anxiety, grief, and depression.

Both Melanie Klein and Anna Freud, the rival doyennes of British psychoanalysis, found the analytic-ethological concoction Bowlby was brewing distasteful, and they let their followers know it. Analytic critics charged him with, among other things, gross simplification of psychological theory; assuming that all pathology results from disturbances of the infant-mother bond (when it was well known that early medical and environmental traumas could equally be at fault); and overlooking the infant's ability to develop a negative concept of his mother on wholly irrational grounds—such as a failure to relieve his suffering despite her best efforts, or the arrival of a new sibling, which can bring forth intolerable feelings of abandonment, rage, and guilt. The debate was bitter, even though the participants were largely in the same camp, all of them psychoanalysts who accepted basic analytic principles. Even René Spitz, whose work on institutionalized children Bowlby respectfully cited, joined the public scolding.

Bowlby did find some fellow analysts at least cordial to his views. Most closely kindred was D. W. Winnicott, a pediatrician turned psychoanalyst who had attained great stature as a theorist and was also the British equivalent of Dr. Spock. Winnicott, too, had taken strong positions, some of them pre-dating Bowlby's, on both the centrality of the infant-mother bond and the critical importance of the quality of mothering. His ideological proximity, although expressed in different language, gave Bowlby some comfort during this time.

But regardless of whether Bowlby's radical restructuring of psychoanalytic concepts was correct, he had plainly found a hole in analytic theory. For however closely attuned psychoanalysts had become in their practices to the impact of real-life events and the ways in which parenting styles affect personality, their theories did not reflect it. In their writings psychoanalysts still focused mainly on the individual psyche and the workings of the unconscious in the average expectable environment. That was a big gap, and Bowlby was determined to fill it. He chose to do so by studying separations in and disruptions of the parent-child relationship in the first five years of life, "because I thought that was researchable." Such investigations became the focus of his little unit at the Tavistock Clinic.

Ainsworth's responsibility in Bowlby's unit was to analyze and make sense of an enormous quantity of data that his people had collected, and to determine the direction for future research. One of those whose material she reviewed was James Robertson, a social worker who died recently, at the age of seventy-seven. Robertson had been making detailed observations of young children who were being sent to the hospital, where, in the early 1950s, parents were allowed only very limited visits. Robertson's skillful observations captured the inconsolable agony and despair these separations created. When psychiatric experts insisted that no such trauma could have occurred, Robertson was infuriated. He decided to buy a camera and film the thing. His harrowing documentary, *A Two Year Old Goes to Hospital*, about little Laura's eight-day separation from her parents, was influential in changing hospital practice to allow parents to make routine visits and to stay the night with their hospitalized children

"It was Jimmy's work I most admired," says Ainsworth, who spent many hours wrestling Robertson's raw data into theory. "In studying separation he got acquainted with the families before the child was separated; he did observations of their behavior during the separation, and followed them when they came home. And I made up my mind that whenever I went elsewhere and could start a project, it would be a study of this sort—direct observation in the natural environment—and that is what I did in Uganda."

Ainsworth's Home Studies

In 1954 Ainsworth followed her husband to Uganda, where she launched one of the pioneering studies in modern infant research. With no lab, with meager institutional support, with no help in collecting or analyzing the data, accompanied only by her interpreter, she rounded up twenty-eight unweaned babies from several villages near Kampala and began observing them in their homes, using the careful, naturalistic techniques that Lorenz and Tinbergen had applied to goslings and stickleback fish. It was a happy time for her. She loved doing research, and she loved the contact with babies, which her own marriage had failed to produce.

Ainsworth immediately felt that Bowlby had been right. A baby is not a passive-recipient creature who becomes attached to his mother because she satisfies his needs. "These were very active babies. They went after what they wanted. I began to see certain behaviors that indicated that the baby was becoming attached, and I was able to list them in chronological order of appearance. There was, for instance, the differential stopping of crying. The mother picked up the baby, the baby would stop crying, but if somebody else tried to pick him up at that point, he would continue to cry. Differential smiling. Differential vocalizations. I began to see different situations where attachment to the mother could be spotted; and you could differentiate an attachment figure from some other person, even a familiar person."

Ainsworth classified the twenty-eight Ganda babies she saw as secure, insecure, or nonattached (a category she would later discard), and created some crude scales to rate the degree of sensitivity and responsiveness in the mother. These classifications and ratings would become much more refined in her next project.

For a third time Ainsworth changed countries to follow her husband—this time to Baltimore, where, within a few weeks, a teaching and clinical job was patched together for her at Johns Hopkins University. Seven years passed before she managed to start her next longitudinal study, during which time she divorced her husband and began her own analysis. The connection with Bowlby had grown thin, but when he visited her in 1960, just as her marriage was dissolving, she presented him with the findings that she eventually published as *Infancy in Uganda*. This was the only major study done outside his own unit offering empirical support for his theory. In terms of their relationship, Ainsworth says, "that made all the difference." Once his most capable adherent, she had become an equal colleague. In a few years she would be a partner.

"What I hoped to do in the Baltimore study was to replicate the Uganda research and make it more systematic. But now that I'd done one study, there were specific things I was curious to observe; I wasn't just letting the moving finger write on the blank slate anymore."

Backed by a solid research grant, Ainsworth got together a team of four observers to make eighteen four-hour home visits to each of twenty-six families. Other researchers had observed infant-mother interaction in the lab—even, in one case, a lab that was fitted out to look just like a home. But to Ainsworth, a home in a lab was not the same as a real home.

"Just take feeding. In the home environment I could see how a mother responded to infant signals when she had a lot of other demands on her time, with the telephone and housekeeping and other kids. I saw one mother who was working very hard to put her six-week-old baby on three meals a day—and she was breast-feeding at that! She would say, 'I don't know why the baby's crying. He was fed at seven o'clock this morning'—it now being after twelve. She would pick it up and play with it very nicely for a while and then put it down, and it would cry again. She would dangle a rattle, she would do this, do that, she even gave it a bath one day to fill up the time till one o'clock, with the baby off and on screaming. You would never observe that type of thing in the lab."

Ainsworth and her colleagues acted like friends, not furniture—talking, helping, holding the babies, becoming part of the family—in order to encourage the mother to act naturally. "To have somebody there for an extended period of time just watching and taking notes could be very tension-producing. Besides, I wanted to see whether the baby would smile at us, whether he would cuddle when we picked him up, and how the baby would behave with us in comparison with the mother. She was excited to find that the behaviors she'd identified as attachment behaviors in the Kampala infants were also abundantly evident in Baltimore, suggesting that babies everywhere speak the same attachment language.

If Ainsworth had stopped there, she would have produced another valuable pioneering study. But she had a problem in making a certain critical comparison between Ugandan and middle-class American babies. "I all along had this idea about a secure base. It was so conspicuous with the Ganda babies. If the mother was there, the kid would roam all around the room and explore things, looking back at her and maybe giving her a smile, but focusing most of his attention on the environment. And just as soon as the mother got up to leave the room, the chances were the baby would shriek and absolutely stop any kind of exploratory behavior."

"Now, the Ganda babies are used to having their mother with them all the time. Whereas the Baltimore babies were used to having their mothers come and go, come and go, and they were much less likely to cry when their mother left the room. So when they were happily exploring, it wasn't clear if it was because the mother was there or not."

For Ainsworth, these questions brought to mind a paper she had read in 1943 called "Young Children in an Insecure Situation," by Jean Arsenian, who had put babies into a playroom, some with their mothers and others by themselves. "Arsenian didn't talk about exploratory behavior, but she made it quite clear that the ones brought in with their mothers could take a constructive interest in the environment, while the others spent most of their time crying. I always remembered that.

"So I thought, all right, if you don't see the secure-base phenomenon very clearly at home, that doesn't necessarily mean it doesn't exist. It could very well be different in a strange environment, such as Arsenian used. If I could bring the children into the university with their mothers, maybe I could see how they used the mother to explore." Thus the Strange Situation was born. New research by Harry Harlow, in which rhesus monkeys were able to explore a frightening new environment only when accompanied by their cloth "mothers," further confirmed her thinking:

"I thought, we'll have the mother and baby together in a strange environment with a lot of toys to invite exploration. Then we'll introduce a stranger when the mother's still there, and see how the baby responds. Then we'll have a separation situation where the mother leaves the baby with the stranger. How does the baby respond to the departure? And when the mother returns, how does the baby respond to the reunion? But since the stranger was in the room during the first departure, maybe we'd better have an episode in which the mother leaves the baby entirely alone. Then we could see whether the return of the stranger lessens whatever distress has occurred. Finally, we'll have another reunion with the mother. We devised this thing in half an hour."

Ainsworth divided the twenty-three babies who went through the first Strange Situation into three main groups and eight subgroups, and, to her amazement, these categories have held up for twenty years and through studies of thousands of children.

"The thing that blew my mind was the avoidant response." The avoidant children, who seemed indifferent to their mothers' comings and goings, even to the point of snubbing them on reunion—who looked so extraordinarily independent—had appeared quite insecure in the home. They had cried and showed more separation distress than the secure babies. And they turned out to have mothers whom the observers had rated as interfering, rejecting, or neglectful.

Ainsworth noticed that in the Strange Situation these avoidant one-year-olds behaved like the older child who has had a long depriving separation and comes home and ignores his mother. "Here were these kids who had never had a serious separation behaving just that way." The avoidant response suggested that the infant and the older child were using the same coping defense. Further, it implied that Ainsworth had hit upon the thing that Bowlby had only dreamed of—a procedure to assess the effects not of drastic separations and loss but of the everyday details of parenting.

"I did not intend this as a way of assessing attachment," she says, "but it certainly wound up as that. We began to realize that it fit in with our impressions after seventy-two hours of observation in an amazing way. But instead of seventy-two hours of observation we could do a Strange Situation in twenty minutes."

In the history of psychology a great many procedures had been devised for assessing individuals, and new ways of diagnosing, describing, and categorizing them were repeatedly being developed—but no one before had come up with a method of assessing relatedness. And no one before had found a way to assess how styles of parenting contributed to individual differences. Through this ingenious project, capping years of research, Ainsworth had begun her revolution.

For the next twenty years Ainsworth would be occupied with the fallout from this work. Because she had made such a painstaking description of each infant-mother pair, the statistical analyses took years to work through. Meanwhile, she would be training others to use the Strange Situation technique, supervising new research, writing, teaching, and serving as the leader of a growing attachment community. Of the Baltimore study Ainsworth now says, "It turned out to be everything that I hoped it would be, and it has drawn together all the threads of my professional career. Each piece of data analysis we did, with very few exceptions, had some sort of bang to it. It was always such a pleasure to find things working out, and we had an awful lot of things work out." The constantly appearing evidence, meanwhile, constituted more raw material for Bowlby's grand synthesizing machine. It was fed into the three volumes of his *Attachment and Loss*, which made their way into publication from 1969 to 1982.

Years passed, however, before the importance of what Ainsworth had done became apparent. The Baltimore study had been conducted from 1963 through 1967, but its findings did not begin to appear in published form until 1969, and Ainsworth's book, *Patterns of Attachment*, was not completed until 1978. The Strange Situation procedure could not easily be learned from a manual; developmentalists had to go through training to master it. The longitudinal studies that Ainsworth's students conducted, which supported and extended her work, did not start seeing print until the late seventies. And beyond all that, scientists are cautious, new ideas are slow to catch on, and the attachment ideas turned out to be especially problematic for some, offending reigning theorists and threatening others by calling specific parenting styles into question. Even Bowlby took Ainsworth's work in stride at first. As he himself eventually said, "I hadn't yet seen the payoff."

The Payoff

"I got interested in the field because I went to her lectures," says Inge Bretherton, who was a thirty-four-year-old undergraduate, returning to college after her children started elementary school, when she first heard Ainsworth speak, at Johns Hopkins, in 1969. "I thought, oh, here is somebody who's studying real children in real environments. Almost nobody else was doing that at the time. Back then everybody was a behaviorist. You couldn't talk about the inner life, so to speak, or the internal world. Not in developmental psychology. I had gone to lectures in Cambridge where every time the person talked about consciousness he made quotation marks in the air. That was the sort of climate in which all this developed."

Bretherton, now a leading attachment scholar who teaches psychology at the University of Wisconsin, was just one of many bright students Ainsworth began attracting at that time, people who would carry attachment work with them to other universities throughout the seventies and eighties.

Everett Waters was an undergraduate chemistry major at Johns Hopkins when he met Ainsworth in 1971, and volunteered to help in her research. Waters, who now teaches at the State University of New York at Stonybrook, soon abandoned chemistry and in 1972 entered the psychology doctoral program at the University of Minnesota. There he met Alan Sroufe, a young assistant professor. Sroufe was intrigued by what Waters told him about Ainsworth's work, and before long the university was buzzing with attachment research. . . .

"In the past," Sroufe explains, "developmental psychology thought there were two ways of doing things—you either counted discrete behaviors or you did global ratings. The problem with discrete behaviors is it takes a tremendous amount of observation to get anything that's worthwhile, and it's hard to know what they mean. To know that one mother picks up her kid more than another mother does, or that one child talks to other children more than a second child does—that may tell you something, but it probably doesn't."

Global ratings, on the other hand, allow an observer to use his own judgment: How sensitive is this mother? How sociable is that child? "But," Sroufe says, "global ratings have always had the reputation of being subjective and unreliable." People can't agree. Well, Ainsworth's methodology is neither of those.

"She has one scale called Cooperation and Interference. On the cooperative end the parents fit what they do to the child. They do things in a timely manner, they do things when the child is open to them, they don't do things at cross-purposes to the child. On the other end, interfering, the parent is coming in doing things when the child isn't ready.

Ainsworth showed that mothers of babies who later are avoidant hold their babies as much as mothers of babies who later are secure. So if you just measure frequency of holding you get no difference. But there's one circumstance in which mothers of babies who are later avoidant do not hold them, and that's when the baby signals that it wants to be held. So you could have counted a lot of holding and you would have gotten nothing."

Blessed with sophisticated facilities, a steady flow of cash from funding agencies, their own nursery on campus staffed by teachers trained to do their ratings, fleets of observers when needed, and summer camps equipped with remote cameras, the Minnesota researchers have been able to follow various samples of children from different socioeconomic strata, taking the initial attachment patterns observed by Ainsworth and extending their implications to later and later periods of life.

They have found that two-year-olds assessed as secure at eighteen months were enthusiastic and persistent in solving easy tasks and effective in using maternal assistance when the tasks became more difficult. In contrast, their anxiously attached counterparts tended to be frustrated and whiny. They found that preschoolers who had been judged securely attached as infants were significantly more flexible, curious, socially competent, and self-reliant than their anxiously attached counterparts. The securely attached children were more sympathetic to the distress of their peers, more assertive about what they wanted, and more likely to be leaders. Similar findings persisted through elementary school age.

Some of the most intriguing Minnesota material, much of it since confirmed by other studies, concerned avoidant kids. They have proved far less able to engage in fantasy play than securely attached children, and when they have engaged in such play, it has more often been characterized by irresolvable conflict. Children with histories of secure attachment tend to be neither victims nor exploiters when placed in pairs, but avoidant kids often victimize other insecurely attached children. Critics had claimed that infants labeled "avoidant" were simply more independent, but the fact that they grew up to be four-year-olds who sought contact with their teachers at a greater rate than securely attached children suggested otherwise. That they were frequently sullen or oppositional and not inclined to seek help when injured or disappointed, however, spoke poignantly of their avoidant patterns.

According to Sroufe, many teachers react with tragic consistency when dealing with the three types of children. They tend to treat securely attached children in matter-of-fact, age-appropriate ways; to excuse and infantilize the clingier ambivalent children; and to be controlling and angry with avoidant ones. "Whenever I see a teacher who looks as if she wants to pick a kid up by the shoulders and stuff him in the trash," Sroufe says, "I know that kid had an avoidant attachment history."

In following a sample of 180 children from poor homes, Sroufe and his colleague Byron Egeland have found that nurses' ratings of the mothers' interest in their new babies accurately predicted future quality of attachment. They have also discovered that a child's attachment classification can change, usually as a result of a major alteration in the mother's circumstances: for instance, a single mother's forming a stable partnership with

286

a new man. That the first year's effects, though still assumed to be profound, are not necessarily indelible is a hopeful sign.

The 180 Minnesota children are now heading into adolescence. "You couldn't name a federal priority that we can't access with the data coming up!" Sroufe says. "Drug abuse, delinquency, AIDS, teenage mothers—we'll be able to tell what their histories were and who was in the risk group." Needless to say, he expects security of attachment to be a principal factor in predicting healthy functioning in the teenage years.

They Are Leaning Out for Love

If attachment theory is correct, the insecurely attached child has developed a strategy for dealing with his mother's unavailability or inconsistency. The ambivalent child (ambivalent children represent about 10 percent of children from middle-class U.S. homes) is desperately trying to influence her. He is hooked by the fact that she does indeed come through on occasion. He picks up that she will respond sometimes—perhaps out of guilt—if he pleads and makes a big enough fuss. And so he is constantly trying to hold on to her or to punish her for being unavailable. He is wildly addicted to her and to his efforts to make her change.

The avoidant child (20 to 25 percent) takes the opposite tack. He becomes angry and distant (even though he remains no less attached). His pleas for attention have been painfully rejected, and reaching out seems impossible. The child seems to say, Who needs you—I can do it on my own! Often in conjunction with this attitude grandiose ideas about the self develop: I am great, I don't need anybody. Indeed, some parents unwittingly promote such grandiosity in the child. If the mother can convince herself that her child is vastly superior to other children, she has an excuse for her lack of nurturing attention: This kid is special, he barely needs me, he's been doing his own thing practically since he was born.

In such cases the mother's lack of nurturance likely has its own tragic reasons, often originating in the neglect that she experienced when she herself was young. Needs and longings that she has long repressed make her angry, depressed, or disgusted when she sees them in her child. Meanwhile, if she, too, is somewhat grandiose, the idea of a superior kid, who has no needs, will reinforce her own sense of superiority. This style of nonrelatedness can thus pass down through the generations, along with values that conveniently support it (our family believes in independence; we're not namby-pambies).

Some of these patterns of anxious attachment may be responsible for certain well-known maladaptive syndromes. Bowlby believes that avoidant attachment lies at the heart of narcissistic personality traits, one of the predominant psychiatric concerns of our time. It may also be at work in the legions of people who achieve a rigid independence from their families by becoming emotionally cut off, a pattern first identified by the family theorist Murray Bowen. Other correlations are sure to emerge.

Insecurely attached children are believed to be relatively amenable to change throughout their early years. Avoidant children, for example, will seek attachments with teachers and other adults, and if they are lucky, they will find a special person who will

287

provide them with an alternative model of relatedness. Recent research has shown that if a child is securely attached to his father (or to another secondary caregiver), that will be the greatest help in overcoming an insecure attachment to his mother. Even if it's only an aunt the child sees occasionally, the knowledge that she cares will keep a different quality of relatedness alive in him. Studies of resiliency indicate that a child's having had such a person in his life can make an enormous difference in his ability to believe in himself and overcome adversity.

But the insecurely attached youngster often has difficulty finding such an alternate attachment figure, because the strategies he has adopted for getting along in the world tend to alienate him from the very people who might otherwise be able to help. The behavior of the insecurely attached child—whether aggressive or cloying, all puffed up or easily deflated—often tries the patience of peers and adults alike. It elicits reactions that repeatedly reconfirm the child's distorted view of the world. People will never love me, they treat me like an irritation, they don't trust me, and so on.

Even a mother who has sought therapy, who has found a stable mate, who has overcome distracting financial problems—who is now able to be more nurturant—may have a hard time reaching the child who has adopted such survival strategies. She may find it hard, for example, to persuade him to give up his angry estrangement and be open to receiving love from her again; or to let go of the clinginess, the guilt, and the power struggles, and trust that she has changed, that she will not neglect him this time, that he can let her be a separate person and she will still be there for his needs. Getting such a message across requires the patience and consistency to persist until the child builds up a new set of expectations, or, if you will, a revised internal working model.

Roger Kobak, a psychologist at the University of Delaware, believes that distorted attachment patterns grow out of the way the child learns to deal with negative feelings. A secure child is able to communicate negative feelings like anger, hurt, jealousy, and resentment in a meaningful way. He can cry or shout, fall silent, or say "I hate you," confident of a sensitive response. The insecure child does not have this confidence. His mother, unable to handle her own negative feelings, either becomes dismissive or overreacts. As a result, his negative feelings are either walled off from his consciousness or revved up to the point where they overwhelm him. His ability to communicate his pain is gradually shrunken and distorted until it virtually demands misinterpretation.

Indeed, parents of insecurely attached children consistently misinterpret their behavior. "Parents often think these anxiously attached kids don't love them," Sroufe says. "They think the kid's rejecting them. The mothers of ambivalent kids think, he doesn't like me, he's just ornery, and so forth. Are you kidding? He doesn't like you? You are the center of the universe!". . .

Abused children have typically been found to fall within a fourth attachment category, called "disorganized." A child in this category seeks proximity with his mother in distorted ways. He may approach her backwards, or freeze suddenly in the middle of a movement, or sit for a time and stare off into space. His reactions, unlike the strategies of avoidant and ambivalent babies, seem to suggest the collapse of strategy.

When parents hear about all this, they may wonder, could I get a Strange Situation done on my kid? And yet that by itself would be pointless. The assessment was devised as a research tool, and its power is based on percentages. Some infants who receive sensitive care look anxiously attached, and some who have neglectful parents look secure. Sroufe has been asked by courts to help settle custody cases by putting the child through a Strange Situation with each of his parents, but he has steadfastly refused, because a certain percentage of children will either be mislabeled or reveal patterns that do not result from the predictable parenting styles.

Structures of the Mind

The attention given to the interpersonal strategies and outlooks of young children inevitably raises the question of how these mental constructs show up in adults. In what form do early attachment patterns persist in our lives? If we can't watch adults' reunion behavior, if we can't put adults in a lab and see them crying, crawling to their mothers, or allowing themselves to be comforted, can we in some other way access their internal working models? That is the question that has occupied Mary Main, and she has come up with some ingenious answers.

Main began by examining the parents of securely and anxiously attached children to see what correlations she could find. She used a sample of mothers and fathers of six-year-olds whose attachments had been assessed at twelve or eighteen months. In the course of a cleverly devised and very demanding sixty- to ninety-minute interview, which seems to evoke in adults some of the same feelings that the Strange Situation evokes in infants, she asked the parents to describe their childhoods and their important relationships. She later analyzed the interview transcripts for variations in the ways they responded. Four patterns emerged.

One group, which Main labeled "autonomous," easily remembered early experiences with their parents and clearly saw them as telling. They seemed self-reliant, objective, and able to incorporate painful memories into their discussion. Main was confident that these adults either had had secure attachments as children or had somehow been able to rework insecure early models in order to achieve a more balanced and realistic view of what it means to relate to others. To the extent that their childhood experience was bad, they were able to acknowledge it and had insights about its effects. In some cases they could understand and forgive their parents. Their children were for the most part securely attached.

A second group, which Main described as "dismissive of early attachments," tended to be indifferent to their deepest feelings about relationships. They remembered little of their childhood bonds and offered idealized portraits of their parents. When probed, however, they recalled incidents that contradicted this perfection, with details that suggested parental neglect or rejection. These detached adults typically presented themselves as strong and independent, but they were in many ways reminiscent of avoidant children, still unable to face the reality of their early disappointments and hurt. The majority of their children showed an avoidant attachment pattern.

The third group, which Main labeled "preoccupied with early attachments," came across as somewhat confused and incoherent about their relational past. During the interview they tended to become flooded with intense negative memories, which brought forth feelings of anger and dependency that they could not easily manage. The childhood struggle with their parents, and their ongoing efforts to please them, seemed palpably present. Their children tended to display an ambivalent attachment pattern.

A fourth group of adults corresponds fairly consistently with the fourth—"disorganized"—group of children. Adults in the fourth category are typically found to be suffering from unresolved childhood traumas, such as physical abuse or the loss of a parent.

Main has found that her assessment of adults corresponds to the attachment classification of their children 76 percent of the time. Another study has found a match-up of 85 percent. The work of Main and her students on the transmission of attachment patterns may bring us closer to understanding the process by which our parents become a part of us. It helps explain why we seem to go through life maddeningly constrained to one of four roles—mother, father, self with mother, self with father—in our relationships with others.

Psychoanalysis has a rich body of concepts concerning just this process, and attachment theorists sometimes seem to be reinventing this psychoanalytic wheel. If so, it is a wheel with a difference. For it is one thing to talk about internal structures of the mind—especially the mind of an infant, who has few or no words—and quite another to investigate them empirically. This difference represents a second aspect of the attachment revolution.

The Temperament Debate

To many young developmentalists and to others who have heard about attachment principles through popular authors, one of the attractions of the material has been how commonsensical it is. It seems only right that our earliest relationships become a part of us, and that something like an internal working model accounts for the types of relationships we develop later in life.

"It's intuitively pleasing, that's what's getting in the way," says Jerome Kagan, one of Ainsworth's most consistent antagonists. "Because it makes intuitive sense, people are assuming it's right. But most of the time intuition is wrong. I mean, intuitively the sun goes around the earth, right? Intuitively the earth is flat, right? Why is psychology the least advanced science? Because our intuitions aren't very good."

Kagan, an influential psychologist at Harvard University . . . believes that too much attention is paid to early experience. Children, he argues, even after suffering extreme loss, are far more resilient than we tend to think. He cites studies of teenagers who experienced deprivation when very young and rebounded handsomely in adolescence.

According to Kagan, the commotion about attachment is mainly a sign of contemporary mores. "In the forties and fifties the children now called securely attached were called overprotected, and that was a bad thing. My view is, if you're attached, you are motivated to adopt the values of your parents. If your parent values autonomy, you'll be autonomous; if your parent values dependency, you'll be dependent. Because most American parents in this historical moment value autonomy, their attached children are autonomous."

Kagan argues that some of the children whom Ainsworth has labeled securely attached become upset when left alone in the Strange Situation not because they're securely attached but because they're unable to deal with uncertainty. They've been trained for dependency, and are showing the ill effects of this training.

Similarly, Kagan believes that many children who have been classified as avoidant in the Strange Situation have simply been trained to control their fearful responses. They learn such control not because they've been ill treated but because control is something their parents value. He further charges that attachment theorists have placed too much emphasis on security—that is something *they* value—and are not attentive enough to the advantages that our society confers on those able to handle adversity. Thus a parent rated as insensitive on Ainsworth's scales might actually be giving a child superior training for the modern world.

Needless to say, such interpretations challenge the very core of attachment theory—that consistent availability and warmth yields autonomous children. They also run counter to many of Sroufe's empirical findings.

A researcher who investigates inborn temperament, Kagan . . . cites studies that indicate that children who are assessed as irritable shortly after birth are likely to be classified as anxious a year later. He insists that many children classified as avoidant appear indifferent to their mothers' comings and goings not because they've given up hope of getting anything from their mothers but because they are better able to handle stress. Compared with their counterparts who have been labeled secure or ambivalent (with equal injustice, according to Kagan), the so-called avoidant children are simply constitutionally less fearful. He remains unmoved by Minnesota studies showing that the heart rate of an avoidant child goes way up when the mother leaves the room and way up again when she returns, even as the child's behavior remains calm, data that seem to suggest that the avoidant child is indeed angrily estranged. Kagan argues that heart-rate acceleration in such situations may be a function of temperament and says he has unpublished data suggesting just that.

Other developmentalists similarly favor a genetic approach, and in recent years an eruption of new research—much of it on identical twins who have been raised separately—seems to have convincingly established that a great many of what we think of as personality traits are inherited. There seems to be a genetic predisposition toward shyness or sociability, toward thrill-seeking or placidity, toward easygoingness or irritability. But whether you trust others or not, whether you anticipate love or rejection, whether you feel good about yourself as a person—are these things inherited? No, Ainsworth says. These are not inherited traits, they are learned; and although subject to change, they are initially determined by the sensitivity and reliability of the care you received in your first years. Although Sroufe goes so far as to contest that any baby is inherently difficult, some attachment theorists will now acknowledge that at the extreme fringes of temperament, which are what Kagan tends to study, anxious attachment may indeed have some genetic basis. But generally they believe it is far more likely that temperament alters the *style* of a secure or insecure pattern, not the pattern itself. . . .

One of the charged issues tucked into temperament debate is the blaming and defending of mothers. Attachment theorists are careful to point out that attachment isn't everything—an insensitive caregiver is not the only road to psychopathology. Nevertheless, the emphasis placed on attachment classifications, and the assumption that those classifications reflect maternal sensitivity exclusively, can give the impression that all psychiatric sorrows emanate from bad mothering. At this point in its evolution attachment theory does not seem to account adequately for the poor mother-infant fit; the mother who has a hard time relating to the infant but does come alive to the toddler; or the baby who, because he is extremely irritable or aggressive, because he is not as smiley and responsive as some, or because he is constitutionally unable to take much pleasure in the attachment relationship, may require an unusual degree of sensitivity and patience. A mother who might be fine with the average baby may not have the emotional wherewithal to handle a baby closer to the temperamental fringe. Studies of mothers with children in more than one attachment category seem to support this idea in certain cases. The mother's difficulty with a particular child may also owe much to her life circumstances, such as receiving inadequate emotional support from either her husband or society as a whole. And it may be complicated by unnecessary self-blame. In all such cases, attributing anxious attachment simply to maternal insensitivity would be both unscientific and unfair. . . .

Even at this level the temperament debate may never be completely settled. For it can always be said, no matter how abysmal the mother's parenting style or how dysfunctional the child, that a miserable mother has simply passed on her miserable genes. And as Ainsworth says, "There's no way of winning that argument." At the current stage of research a lot depends on whose statistics and judgment you trust and what makes the most sense. A lot also depends on how much faith you have in Ainsworth's seminal study of a quarter century ago.

Ainsworth's study was not unimpeachable. As her former student Michael Lamb, now the chief of the Section on Social and Emotional Development at the National Institute of Child Health and Human Development, pointed out in a controversial 1984 critique, Ainsworth was not able to get perfect reliability checks on all observers in the home situations (were they definitely measuring the same thing?). No videotapes were available for review. Also, except for research in Germany by Klaus and Karin Grossmann, Ainsworth's study has rarely been replicated, which is quite surprising when one considers the skyscraper of research and theoretical conclusions that is balancing on this small base. In every study that begins by assessing infants in a Strange Situation at twelve or eighteen months and continues to evaluate those children for years afterward, assumptions are being made about the style of the parenting each child has received, and conclusions are being drawn about the effect that style has had on every aspect of the child's life. But the parenting itself is almost never assessed. It is only inferred from the infant's Strange Situation classification. That inference is possible mainly because of Ainsworth's twenty-three Baltimore families. If her study is flawed and the correlations it demonstrated are open to question, the whole attachment edifice begins to wobble.

Ainsworth is not insensitive to this and would like to see more replications. But longitudinal studies of that magnitude take time, money, and immense effort. Young workers prefer breaking new ground to tilling the old. Although Ainsworth believes that much has been established in partial replication, the question lingers.

Attachment and Modern Living

. . . There is something simple and life-affirming in the attachment message—that the only thing your child needs in order to thrive emotionally is your emotional availability and responsiveness. You don't need to be rich or smart or talented or funny; you just have to be there, in both senses of the phrase. To your child, none of the rest matters, except inasmuch as it enables you to give of yourself. What's more, you don't have to be an outstanding mother, just—in Winnicott's famous phrase—a "good enough" mother.

The pressures on people to think otherwise, however, are relentless, especially in an urban environment where whether you get your child into the right nursery school can seem more critical than how he experiences your love. The "superbaby" phenomenon, which encourages parents to believe that what kids really need is to have their IQs juiced up with a rigorous program of infant stimulation, is emblematic of those pressures.

"I don't think it's healthy," Ainsworth says, "to be *at* the child too much, to have him taste this, and smell that, and feel this, trying to enrich all aspects of his life. It's too much, it's intrusive. The normal kind of interaction that takes place in the course of routines, where there is some conversation and smiling back and forth and perhaps a little play, or in periods that are consciously devoted to play—I think that is what the infant needs in the way of stimulation. That doesn't mean the child's interest in other things shouldn't be encouraged, but he'll have that interest if he just has a chance to explore. Stimulation is something you *do* to somebody else. It's experience the child needs."

Where Ainsworth's message has been heard, it has helped to refocus child-rearing debates away from arguments over specific techniques and toward the more comprehensive issue of sensitivity. Questions like whether to breast-feed or bottle-feed or at what age to introduce solid foods, though still important, no longer carry the same urgency. Attachment theory suggests that babies thrive emotionally because of the overall quality of the care they've experienced, not because of specific techniques. A bottle-fed baby whose mother is sensitively attuned will do better than a breast-fed baby whose mother is mechanical and distant.

Ainsworth has been accused by some feminists of being out of touch with what they see as current life-styles, because she is skeptical about the viability of working motherhood. But she contends that it's the children who are out of touch, by perhaps millions of years, for that is when our evolutionary adaptations were forming—including

293

adaptations that may have made proximity to the primary caregiver a cornerstone of secure development. "It's very hard to become a sensitively responsive mother if you're away from your child ten hours a day," she says. "It really is."

But unlike Bowlby, who strongly believes in full-time caregiving, who contends that women are best equipped biologically to play this role, and who would like to see a campaign equivalent to the Attorney General's crusade against smoking to convince parents that day care is bad for their babies, Ainsworth admits the possibility that supplemental mothering could be arranged without harm to the child. "From the point of view of the child's general welfare, the mother should be pretty consistently available. That doesn't mean she has to be there every moment, can never go out, never have anybody else look after the child, or anything like that. But fairly consistently available. Women's-lib people have been finding it comfortable to assume that it doesn't matter what you do and that a woman owes it to herself to work and do what fulfills her. People who focus primarily on the welfare of children tend to ignore what suits the mother. But it's really a matter of how do we adjust these two things. Had I myself had the children I longed for, I like to believe I could have arrived at some satisfactory combination of mothering and a career, but I do not believe that there is any universal, easy, ready-made solution."

As for currently available day care, the research itself is still in its infancy, and Ainsworth prefers not to comment. We don't know how the quality of day care affects attachment outcomes, how many kids are really at risk, how the risk differs at different ages, or whether (to state the case at its most extreme) a mother who stays home bored and resentful is better than one who comes home happy and fulfilled.

Important, too, are the larger societal trends of which day care is only a part. Ainsworth sees the pressures and penchants of modern life pushing us toward anxious attachment, with the unhappy consequences of psychological distress, discordant relationships, and weakening social ties. "People used to have more leisure, more time for fun, for sociability. Now everybody's too busy to be sociable. It's sad."

Economic and social conditions in many Western countries tend to force both parents to work, to penalize those who put their careers on hold for several years, and to give little support to parents, working or not. Traditional societies, as Bowlby stresses, often enjoyed an abundance of secondary attachment figures. Families were stationary, interdependent, and surrounded by relatives, from grandmothers to adolescent aunts, who all pitched in with baby care. While this way of life may be irrevocably lost, compensations could be developed. We could make it easier for mothers and fathers to take time off from work for infant care, train teachers to deal constructively with anxious attachment styles, put additional adults in classrooms to allow for the supplemental connections that seem to benefit kids who are anxiously attached to their mothers, and provide greater support to families. Needless to say, we are ages away from making such commitments. . . .

Cross-Cultural Validity of Attachment Theory
Robert A. LeVine and Patrice M. Miller

One of the most compelling criticisms of the attachment literature involves the assertion that the theory of attachment (oriented as it is to the isolated mother/child dyad), the "Strange Situation" as a technique for the measurement of attachment, and the unquestioned assumption that "autonomy" is a positive developmental outcome, are shot through with American middle-class values. Attachment effects, it is suggested, may not generalize beyond the cultural context within which attachment research has been pursued.

In this article, Robert LeVine and Patrice Miller examine one facet of this criticism. Reminding us that Ainsworth originally developed the "Strange Situation" as a culture-specific procedure designed to elicit from Baltimore babies responses for which elicitation was unnecessary in Uganda, the authors analyze features of the "Strange Situation" that might lead one to expect culture-sensitive performance. The authors suggest that children whose experiences with strange people, strange places, the exploration of strange objects, separation from the mother, and rituals of reunion depart widely from the American norm cannot be meaningfully assessed in the "Strange Situation" without systematic validation of their performance in relation to naturalistic observations of prevailing child-care practices.

The evidence reviewed . . . demonstrates what observers of infants in diverse settings, including Mary D.S. Ainsworth, have long known—that cultural variations in infant environments produce divergent patterns of attachment behavior. This finding casts serious doubt on claims to species universality and optimality of the developmental patterns observed among middle-class Americans through the 'Strange Situation'. It suggests that the 'Strange Situation', though effective in revealing similarities and differences across populations, is attuned to conditions prevailing among middle-class Americans and cannot be used intelligibly in other groups without naturalistic assessments of their prevailing conditions of infant care.

In this commentary we consider how cultural factors influence attachment behavior and suggest that familiarity effects produced by infant care practices may account for cultural differences in response to the 'Strange Situation'. First, however, we return to

LeVine, R.A. & Miller, P.M. (1990). Commentary. *Human Development*, *33*. pp. 73-80.

the origins of the 'Strange Situation' method in Ainsworth's comparison of her Ganda and Baltimore observations.

Cultural Origins of the 'Strange Situation'

In the preface to their volume on the 'Strange Situation', Ainsworth et al. [1978] provide the following history of its invention:

> The strange situation was originally devised in 1964 for use in conjunction with an intensive longitudinal study of the development of infant-mother attachment throughout the first year of life, a naturalistic study in which infants were observed in their familiar home environments. This study of twenty-six mother-infant pairs living in the Baltimore area had been preceded by a comparable but less intensive study of twenty-eight dyads living in country villages in Uganda (Ainsworth, 1967). Despite many similarities between the two samples in regard to attachment behavior, three behavioral patterns that had been highlighted in the Ganda study emerged less strikingly in the American study: the use of the mother as a secure base from which to explore; distress in brief, everyday separations from the mother; and fear when encountering a stranger. Perhaps if stronger instigation were provided, the American babies might be induced to behave in much the same ways as had the Ganda infants. In the belief that these behaviors might be evoked more incisively in an unfamiliar situation than in the familiar home environment, the strange situation was devised [p. viii].

This statement leaves no doubt that the 'Strange Situation' was invented as a *culture-specific* laboratory procedure designed to elicit from the Baltimore babies responses that had already been observed more intensely and frequently ('strikingly') without an elicitation procedure among the Ganda. . . .

Ainsworth's Interpretations of Cross-Cultural Data

In interpreting cross-cultural evidence a decade ago, before the 'Strange Situation' had been applied outside of the USA, Ainsworth [1977] used her naturalistic observations of the Uganda and Baltimore children, as well as Konner's [1972] observations of Kalahari (!Kung or Zhun/Twa) Bushmen. Her analysis is instructive, not only because it is directly relevant to the reason the 'Strange Situation' was invented—that the Baltimore children did not spontaneously show certain attachment behaviors as intensely and frequently as the Ganda had—but also because Ainsworth explained these differences in terms of infant expectations acquired from consistently different experiences, thus illustrating how culture-specific patterns of infant care might influence attachment. Furthermore, Ainsworth did not claim that the American mothers or infants represented an optimal pattern of attachment in comparison with the Ganda.

Ainsworth [1977] reported that intense separation protest (even before weaning) was more frequent among the Ganda babies than in those of Baltimore:

> *(This) is attributable to two major factors. First, the American babies had more experience with frequent maternal comings and goings than had Ganda infants. During our visits, American mothers left the room 3.4 times per hour, on the average, whereas Ganda mothers were unlikely to leave as often as once per hour.*
>
> *The typical mother in the American sample left her baby for fairly long periods in one place, often enough confined, and came in and out frequently in the course of her household activities. In contrast, the Ganda mother, when she left her baby to work in the garden, left him for a period of three or four hours or more. When she was at home she tended either to stay put or to take the baby with her. Thus the securely-attached American infant presumably developed expectations that when his mother left him, say, to go to the kitchen or even upstairs, she would return soon, and perhaps the baby learned also that she would be readily summoned if he needed her. Secure in such expectations, her many brief departures in her familiar environment of the home came to activate protest infrequently. In contrast, even the securely-attached Ganda infant built up expectations that his mother's departure signaled a longer absence during which his mother was inaccessible to his signals, so that even when left in the familiar home environment with familiar caregivers her departure tended to activate protest, unless the baby were able to follow his mother when she left. In short, it seems that separation protest is much influenced by an infant's confidence in his mother's accessibility and the expectations that constitute that confidence are influenced by real-life experiences [p. 141f].*

By the same reasoning, the strong separation protest elicited from Japanese babies left alone in the 'Strange Situation', as described by Takahashi, . . . might be attributed to the fact that their mothers reported leaving the infant with another person an average of only 2.2 times in the past month, so that there had been no opportunity to develop through repeated experience the confidence that mother would return.

Ainsworth reported that the Ganda babies nine twelve months old, like the !Kung observed by Konner [1972], showed much more fear of strangers than their Baltimore counterparts. She concluded:

> *To me, the most reasonable explanation is that the two samples differed in the extent of their general experience with strangers and that infants living in Ganda villages fear strangers because they have little experience with any people except their own families, immediate neighbors and visiting relatives. . . The babies in the American sample, on the other hand, were early taken, and relatively frequently, to supermarkets and other places where they encountered unfamiliar people in great variety, under circumstances of proximity and often interaction and even contact [Ainsworth, 1977, p. 142].*

Here again, an explanation in terms of prior experience is offered for cross-cultural difference in a response (reaction to a stranger) that, like reaction to separation from mother, is part of the 'Strange Situation'.

Ainsworth [1977] also responded, in the same article, to Konner's [1972] report that infant-mother attachment among the !Kung Bushmen involved breast-feeding much more than the Bowlby-Ainsworth model allowed. She showed that this was also true of those Ganda children who had been breastfed on demand and whose weaning was deferred until after attachment to the mother was established: 'Under these circumstances, feeding behavior is so enmeshed in the organization of the attachment relationship that weaning may threaten the whole relationship' [Ainsworth, 1977, p. 128]. Without going into this point in detail, as she did, we want to emphasize that, though the independence of attachment from feeding is central to the Bowlby-Ainsworth model and distinguishes it from orthodox Freudian and S-R secondary drive models, Ainsworth here elaborated the environmental conditions under which breast-feeding could become an important part of the child's 'working model' of attachment to the mother—conditions found widely in African and many other non-Western societies. This shows that in Ainsworth's view as presented in 1977, the meaning of attachment to the child and its behavioral manifestations were culturally variable.

Finally, Ainsworth [1977] found more optimal characteristics among the Ganda mothers: '(My) impression is that more of them than of the Baltimore mothers were sensitive to infant signals and communications, and fewer of them insensitive, rejecting, inaccessible or interfering' [p. 126]. This might lead one to expect that the Ganda infants would more frequently be securely attached, but without comparable assessment through the 'Strange Situation', a direct comparison was not possible. [In the original Uganda report, Ainsworth, 1967, p. 388, classified 57 percent of the Ganda sample as secure-attached, 25 percent as insecure-attached and 18 percent as 'non-attached'.] On the whole she treated the two samples as equivalent in security of attachment while recognizing a greater frequency of separation protest and intensity of fear response to strangers among the Ganda babies.

In this cross-cultural comparison of 1977, then, Ainsworth invoked culture-specific patterns of child care that condition the infant's expectancies to account for group differences in fear of strangers and separation protest, while claiming that the group in which infants were more fearful and less tolerant of maternal separation contained the more sensitive mothers. The implication is that security of attachment is independent of fear of strangers and separation protest and that optimal mothering can occur in a context that fosters high levels of these reactions. This conclusion is of course consistent with Ainsworth's decision to use reunion behaviors rather than reactions to the stranger or to the mother's departure in the 'Strange Situation' as criterial for attachment classification.

But Takahashi's findings . . . suggest that 'familiarity effects', i.e., whether and to what degree the baby is used to being outside the home, meeting strangers, being separated from the mother, directly influence attachment classifications when the variations are as wide as between the Japan and Baltimore samples. Children rarely separated from their mothers under the normal conditions of their lives can be so stressed by the

'Strange Situation' that they are difficult for mothers to console on reunion and are classified as type C. Children who have rarely been away from home can be classified as type C in the laboratory and type B at home. It is untenable to assume that the naturalistically observed conditions that foster fear of strangers and separation protest have no bearing on security of attachment. Ainsworth's [1977] own analysis of how breast-feeding influences the attachment relationship among the Ganda—when demand feeding gives the baby control over the mother's feeding behaviors and when weaning occurs after eight or nine months—suggests that infants become attached not only to specific persons but to specific conditions that have given them comfort and that arouse anxiety when they are withdrawn. The meaning of the mother to the baby is partly provided by such conditions. It is only possible to ignore these aspects of mother-infant attachment if one focuses exclusively on the reunion behaviors that are criterial for attachment classification and does not take into account the natural contexts that condition the child's responses to the 'Strange Situation'.

Ainsworth's 1977 interpretations of cross-cultural differences are important at the present time because they show how much sense can be made of response patterns in the 'Strange Situation' if one knows through naturalistic observation the routine interpersonal environments of infant care that give the test stimuli of the laboratory procedure their meanings to the infant. . . .

The Effects of Prior Experience

The ways in which aspects of prior experience that vary across cultures might affect infant behavior in the 'Strange Situation' can be analyzed by considering individually the component situations confronting the one year-old child and mother in that procedure, e.g., playing in an unfamiliar room, physical separation between mother and child in the same room, meeting a stranger, mother-child separation, and reunion with mother. Each of these situations can be so familiar to the child as to elicit overlearned, automatized responses, or they can be so unfamiliar as to pose an entirely novel task, possibly inducing anxiety and distress.

In addition to the familiarity-novelty dimension of the situation and the task it represents, there are the specific qualitative expectations it arouses based on its similarities to conditions the infant has experienced in the past. As Lamb and Malkin [1986] have shown, infants have well developed expectations of specific caregivers, and of the conditions consistently associated with being comforted when they are distressed, by the time they are five months old. When they are assessed in the 'Strange Situation' at twelve months, their experience-based expectations in social situations have become more complex and differentiated.

(1) *Playing in an unfamiliar room.* The degree to which the physical setting in the 'Strange Situation' is experienced as strange, i.e., as a departure from the infant's normal surroundings, may depend not only on actual similarities and differences but on how much prior experience the child has had in being moved from one place to another. The

American child at one year is assumed to have had a fair amount of such experience, while at the same time being aware that this is a new place. The Japanese baby, however, may have had so little experience in being out of the home that the laboratory setting may seem a striking, potentially distressing, departure from the normal, eliciting in the infant the expectation of being comforted by mother. We propose that for the American child, the task of becoming comfortable in new surroundings like the room used in the 'Strange Situation' is one that has been mastered earlier and for which the child is prepared; the same could not be said for the Japanese child.

(2) *Physical separation between mother and child.* Putting baby on the floor with toys and expecting play while mother sits watching at a distance seems perfectly normal in an American context; it occurs routinely at home and when visiting friends and kin. In some African societies, like the Gusii of Kenya [LeVine et al., 1989] babies are still being held about 50 percent of the daytime at twelve months of age, are rarely in their mother's presence without being held by her or someone else, and are given no toys. Thus, this situation is one for which prior experience has prepared American children but not their Gusii counterparts.

(3) *Meeting a stranger.* As Ainsworth [1977] pointed out, infants among the Ganda and the !Kung Bushmen have social lives confined to a small circle of intimates and rarely encounter a new face, while American babies are taken to public places like supermarkets, where encounters with strangers are abundant. Their divergent patterns of social interaction prepare American children but not the Ganda and !Kung Bushmen for such encounters, or perhaps for mastering the fear that meeting a stranger tends to arouse.

(4) *Separation from mother.* Although the observational data are not complete, it seems that three patterns of prior experience can be identified in the Baltimore, Ganda and Japanese studies discussed above: (a) an American one, in which mothers at home leave the child's view frequently (3.4 times/hour) while remaining accessible to audible signals, but in which they occasionally (at an unspecified frequency but often enough for it not to seem unusual) leave the baby with another person at home or somewhere else; (b) a Ganda one, in which mothers leave the baby's sight rarely when at home (less than once an hour) but leave once a day to spend 3 hours or more cultivating their gardens while the baby is taken care of by a child or grandmother; and (c) a Japanese one, in which babies are rarely left by mother (2.2 times a month), and then only with father or grandmother. These are, as Ainsworth and Takahashi have suggested, different levels of preparation for the brief separations of the 'Strange Situation', though the lack of more specified observational data makes it difficult to say more. Furthermore, a recent study by Gewirtz and Nogueras [1988] shows that the kind of protest the infant exhibits upon separation is easily conditioned to be more or less extreme depending on maternal reactions.

(5) *Reunion with mother.* If separations vary in frequency and type by cultural group, reunions do too. It would be interesting to know the prior experience with reunion of children differing in culture. Apart from frequency and its effects on criterial behavior

for the types A, B and C attachment categories, it seems to us likely that mothers of different cultures train their babies in differing reunion routines—ranging from the excited greeting behavior of many middle-class Americans to quiet holding and breast-feeding in many African settings—that foster the development of varying meanings of the 'Strange Situation' reunions.

The preceding are five aspects of prior experience that vary by culture and might well affect infant responses to the 'Strange Situation'. Only systematic cross-cultural research into the relationships between routine patterns of interaction and infant responses in the 'Strange Situation' will specify to what extent the effects of prior experience account for the cultural variations in frequency of attachment classification found so far—a point made previously by Lamb et al. [1985], but worth repeating in the present context. . . .

References

Ainsworth, M.D.S. (1967). *Infancy in Uganda: Infant care and the growth of attachment.* Baltimore: Johns Hopkins University Press.

Ainsworth, M.D.S. (1977). Infant development and mother-infant interaction among Ganda and American families. In P.H. Leiderman, S.R. Tulkin, & A. Rosenfeld (Eds.). *Culture and infancy.* New York: Academic Press.

Ainsworth, M.D.S., Blehar, M.C., Waters, E., & Wall, S. (1978). *Patterns of attachment.* Hillsdale NJ: Erlbaum.

Gewirtz, J.L., & Nogueras, M. (1988). Do infant protests/distress during maternal departures and separations have a learned basis? How mothers contribute to their children's separation difficulties. Paper presented at the International Conference on Infancy Studies, Washington, D.C.

Konner, M.J. (1972). Aspects of the developmental ethology of a foraging people. In N. Blurton Jones (Ed.), *Ethological studies of child behaviour.* Cambridge: Cambridge University Press.

Lamb, M.E., & Malkin, C.M. (1986). The development of social expectations in distress-relief sequences: A longitudinal study. *International Journal of Behavioral Development, 9*, 235-249.

Lamb, M.E., Thompson, R.A., Gardner, W., & Charnow, E.L. (1985). *Infant-mother attachment.* Hillsdale NJ: Erlbaum.

LeVine, R.A., Miller, P.M., & West, M.M. (Vol. eds.), W. Damon (Series ed.). (1988). *New Directions for Child Development: Vol. 40. Parental behavior in diverse societies*. San Francisco: Jossey-Bass.

13

Gender, Self, and Other

The little girl will pick wild roses,
That is why she was born.

The little girl will dig wild rice with her fingers.
That is why she was born.

She will gather sap of pitch pine trees in the spring.
She will pick strawberries and blueberries.
That is why she was born.

[Tsimshian Lullaby]

You are a little man
You go fishing for small fish
When you are bigger you will go walking in the
mountains

When you are a man
When you grow up you will harvest coconuts
Your mother wants you to go but when you are bigger

You are a little man
In the canoe you go fishing
Mother is cooking

You are a little man, you are not a woman
When you go to the mountains you will be
farming in the sun all day
Every day you are a little man.

[Kuna lullaby]

The developing personality is a complex system. Relatively enduring traits and predispositions organize the way in which the child characteristically makes sense of the world and the self, and acts and interacts with others. The particular constellation of characteristics that constitutes an individual's personality is presumed to be unique—even identical twins vary in personality.

Both the overall structure of personality and the ways in which personality is manifested in behavior change as children grow. One important source of personality development is children's identification with important reference groups. Of the many groups to which a child belongs, those defined by gender and race are among the most salient. Children's gender and race are, in most cases, clear to everyone with whom they interact. For this reason and because many cultures distribute privileges, define responsibilities, and generate behavioral expectations based on such characteristics, the social consequences of gender and race are enormous. The articles chosen for this module address some of these consequences.

● ● ●

Two Views of Sex Differences in Socialization
Patricia Draper

In Patricia Draper's discussion of the sex role training *and* prepared learning *approaches to sex differences in socialization, we once again encounter the familiar nature/nurture theme. The ecology of nurture, as Draper indicates, is a complex system in which social and economic conditions of life, cultural values, and patterns of adult-child interaction are deeply intertwined. As with many other characteristics of children's growth, the direction and extent of differentiation in gendered behavior reflects the particular patterns that exist in the child's communal environment.*

Development, however, is never solely a function of nurture. Draper also suggests that selection factors having to do with the asymmetry of reproductive roles between men and women have acted over the course of evolution to differentiate predispositions to acquire new behaviors. Boys and girls, in other words, are active participants in their own socialization, predisposed from birth to attend and respond in gendered ways—boys, for example, to evince interest in competition and dominance relations with other males, girls to exhibit selective sociability to female kin.

In reading this article, refer back to the nature/nurture issue introduced in Chapter 5, to Jerome Kagan's discussion of temperament in Chapter 8, and to Robert LeVine's characterization of rural African and middle-class American childcare practices in Chapter 11. Notice how, in the context of gender socialization, Draper argues for a rapprochement between views that are sensitive to the complex social ecology of development and those that recognize the importance in children's growth of biologically grounded predispositions. Development, as we see once again, reflects the joint contributions of both nurture and nature.

. . . Several traditions of research in the social sciences have been involved in the study of why the sexes are different. One that emphasizes deliberate sex role training of children owes most of its insights to learning theory and developmental psychology. It regards sex role socialization as the result of interplay between the environmental experience and the child's active learning and imitation. Researchers see the child as one who learns what is being taught and who forms certain evaluations of what is correct or expedient on the basis of experience (Mussen 1973; Maccoby and Jacklin 1974). Unlike the prepared learning tradition, which will be discussed below, systematic consideration is not given to the possibility that girls and boys, *because of* biological sex, will respond differently to the tasks of socialization.

The prepared learning tradition takes as a beginning assumption that girls and boys are born with inherent predispositions to behave in distinctive ways. This tradition accepts the role of learning as necessary for development but assumes that with respect to certain classes of stimuli girls and boys will respond differently. A person who takes this view of sex role socialization will be equally interested in "what children are taught" and "what children choose to learn." . . .

Draper, Patricia. (1985). Two views of sex differences in socialization. In R. L. Hall, with P. Draper, M. E. Hamilton, D. McGuinness, C. M. Otten, and E. A. Roth. *Male-Female Differences: A Bio-Cultural Perspective.* NY: Praeger. pp. 5–25.

Deliberate Sex Role Training of Children

According to this way of thinking, girls and boys behave differently because they are reared differently. Parents and adults of human societies everywhere understand that girls and boys will fulfill different social and economic roles, and in anticipation of that fact they put them on different socialization tracks. Children acquire different skills and attitudes owing in part to specific differences in their indoctrination but also because their experiences are different (D'Andrade 1966). An example here would be the common cross-cultural finding that girls receive stronger responsibility training than do boys (Barry et al. 1957; Whiting and Whiting 1975). The typical socialization of girls results from the fact they remain close to their mothers and the nature of women's work is such that girls can be incorporated into it at early ages. For example, in most societies women work close to home and do work that can be interrupted and broken into small components that children can master (Brown 1973). Therefore, mothers can simultaneously care for children and, in the case of girls, can instruct them in the skills that they will need as they get older.

Boys are likely to be passed over for responsibility training in early childhood because their adult roles do not require that they learn female role skills. Their mothers tend to their needs but do not expect boys to learn responsibility and obedience to the same degree as girls of the same age. [See Romney and Romney (1965) and Minturn and Lambert (1964) for good ethnographic examples of this aspect of sex role socialization.] Further, the nature of the work typically done by men is such that fathers cannot simultaneously do that work, care for dependents, and instruct the boys (Murdock 1949). Men's work is such that children cannot and should not participate; in many societies, for example, men travel far from home and do dangerous or physically rigorous kinds of work.

Much of this reasoning derives from the study of sex roles in nontechnological societies on which anthropologists have focused almost exclusively until recent years. Among cultures supported by agriculture and/or animal husbandry, differences in sex roles are especially marked. In the case of food producers, families live in large domestic groups (often called "extended families") with larger membership than the nuclear family groups found in foraging societies. In the extended families, senior men and women are in charge of the work of younger, same-sex relatives. This results in a type of domestic labor that is more highly organized and more hierarchical in form. It also entails segregation of the sexes in many aspects of daily life: Work roles are segregated and eating and leisure activities are often done with same-sex individuals.

By contrast, in technologically simpler hunting and gathering societies, this is less likely to be the situation. This is not to say that cultural values regarding differences between the sexes do not exist, nor that functional differences in the work roles of the sexes do not exist. Rather, because hunter-gatherers must remain mobile and at low population densities so as not to exhaust the supply of wild foods, there is an advantage to having the smaller nuclear family be the basic domestic unit. When conditions require, groups as small as one or two nuclear families detach themselves from the larger band

and live apart. Under these conditions, men and women must share much in the way of common knowledge, skills, and decision-making ability. Thus, the size of the functioning economic unit may determine the degree of labor specialization—including the degree of sex differences in labor and other activities.

Social and Ecological Influences On Sex Role Socialization

By paying attention to the social and economic arrangements in the society of which children are a part, one can see that some cultures are likely to maximize the socialization differences between the sexes, while others do not.

Group size and economy are basic aspects of social life that can set a stage for small or great sex role differentiation between children. Bushman children of the !Kung tribe, hunter-gatherers living in the Kalahari Desert of Southern Africa, receive very little in the way of explicit cultural messages about how girls and boys should do different things. This "lack" is related to both group size and economy. The living groups have about thirty-five to forty people and only a small portion of the total are children. In consequence, girls and boys grow up playing in a multi-aged peer group of both sexes. Neither sex has an opportunity to play only with same-sex peers, and in the absence of "segregated facilities" there is no opportunity for either sex to engage in stereotypic boy or girl kinds of play (Draper 1976). The idea that same-sex peers play an important part in sex role socialization finds support in various studies of Western children (see Fagot and Patterson 1969; Arganian 1973). Studies of Western children's risk taking are relevant here (Slovic 1966; Ginsburg and Miller 1982). Boys have been found more willing to take risks both in experimental and in natural settings, and it is typically reported that boys prefer to play with peers (preferably same-sex peers) more than girls. The greater opportunity to play with peers (because boys are not put to work) can intensify rivalrous and competitive behavior in boys more than in girls, who have fewer occasions to test themselves against same-sex, same-age playmates.

However, the nature of the economy and the kinds of work that hunter-gatherer adults do exempt girls and boys from being tracked at early ages into sex-differentiated kinds of jobs. Both women and men travel far on foot in the course of gathering vegetable foods and tracking game animals. The adults cover many miles, often crossing areas without drinking water, and they discourage children from accompanying them, knowing that they would slow the work. Girls and boys both stay at the group's base camp under the supervision of other adults who are not working on a given day. All children enjoy a leisured childhood; girls and boys do equally little work.

This brief illustration shows how the circumstances in which children are reared constitute a socialization pressure in and of itself. This occurs regardless of whether adults put an explicit value on their children's socialization in sex roles.

Examples of societies in which girls and boys receive sex-differentiated training and experience are much more common. This is particularly true of the so-called "middle range" tribal societies in which food collecting has been replaced by food producing and surplus accumulation. Along with these economic innovations go institutional changes such as sedentism, increased population density, increased fertility, more numerous subsistence sources and more time-consuming subsistence work, greater sex role specialization, and increased willingness to enlist children into economically useful work.

Societies that derive a large proportion of subsistence from domestic animals provide good examples of the influence of this type of economic progress on the sex role socialization of children. In all such societies, the primary responsibility for the management and defense of herds falls to men. It is boys and not girls who in their middle childhood years begin practicing games and skills that will ultimately make them more successful as herders (and as raiders of the herds belonging to rival groups). Many of the games stress physical prowess, endurance, hand-to-hand combat skills, bluff, and intimidation. Girls in these societies will not undergo this type of anticipatory socialization and one expects (and finds) that female behavior is considerably more muted than the flamboyant style of the men (Edgerton 1971).

An ethnographic description of the Fulani herders of Sub-Saharan Africa provides an apt illustration:

> *At about six years of age the boys begin daily herding with their older brothers or fathers. At this time they are encouraged to begin to display aggressive dominance towards the mature bulls and oxen. We were told that initially the boys are often afraid of the bulls. Nonetheless, they are obliged to discipline these animals by charging them or hitting them with herding sticks. Boys who refuse to beat cattle on instruction are usually considered cowards, threatened, and even beaten if they still refuse. After they become accustomed to disciplining cattle, boys often initiate beating without encouragement. Several times at the beginning of a herding day we observed such young herders approaching the dominant bull or ox and hitting him several hard blows with a herding stick. Although the social code apparently discourages such "undeserved" punishment of cattle, these beatings were generally ignored by the older men. . . . The cultural ideal of the fearless, aggressive, dominant personality is fostered by the consistent, and strongly reinforced expectation of all those with whom the boy comes into contact. (Lott and Hart 1977, pp. 181-82)*

These arguments suggest reasons for customary sex role allocations and specify the consequences of this sexual division of labor for child socialization. In so doing, they point to the existence of social arrangements that are exterior to the child and prior to his/her existence. Children grow up in a particular social milieu and learn skills that are necessary if they are to join the larger adult society. Depending on the local situation, children may or may not be treated differently primarily because of their sex.

Acquiring a Gender Identity

Various factors besides economics enter into sex role socialization. These depend less on the institutional arrangements of the society into which a child is born and more upon the personal psychological and developmental characteristics of the child. Rather than conceiving the child as responding to the learning tasks provided by the society, it is important to recognize that the child also makes certain discriminations and evaluations among learning tasks. This view incorporates a certain reflexivity in which the child acquires information as a result of experiences but then stores and processes that information in unique ways. The result is behavior that is produced at a later time but that is not simply due to the fact that the child has "learned what he was taught" (Bandura 1977).

Cognitive psychologists have shown that as a child matures intellectually, he/she acquires the language labels and cognitive classification of other speakers. One of the most pervasive distinctions acquired relatively early in the child's life is the category of sex. Once children learn gender labels, they experiment with applying them. As they learn the rules for inclusion in the category "girl" or "boy," they begin to turn the rules on the self in a kind of internal conversation (Kohlberg 1966; Kohlberg and Zigler 1967; Falbo 1980). A boy, for example, reasons, "I'm a boy. Cowboys are boys too. All football players are boys. So I can be a cowboy or a football player. I can practice those roles until I grow up."

An important point that Kohlberg (1966) makes is that children contribute to their own sex role socialization in ways that are not deliberately taught, nor necessarily anticipated by adults. According to this point of view, the role models to which children are exposed can influence their sex role conceptions. For example, the model may deliberately instruct the child and reinforce certain behaviors. If the child sees the model as powerful or attractive, he/she imitates it and in highly active ways tries to incorporate many aspects of its behavior, often going well beyond what the model was consciously trying to convey. . . .

The sex role-training perspective of sex differences has led to the suggestion that if contraception allows women to restrict the number of years they spend in reproduction and child tending, a situation largely confined to modern industrial nations, then for most purposes women and men can assume interchangeable roles (Lancaster 1976). As machines continue to relieve humans of hard physical labor, the male monopoly of certain types of work is expected to disappear. Fundamental to this point of view is the idea that except for obvious reproductive differences between the sexes, males and females are essentially the same. Remove the contraints of reproduction (or reduce them to a minimum) and sex role differentiation will disappear.

Sex Differences in Prepared Learning

The prepared learning view contrasts with the social learning of sex role orientation described above. It is not opposed to all aspects of the training model but it invokes a different set of assumptions about the consequences of reproductive differences between the sexes by considering selective forces that have operated on humans in their evolutionary past.

Studies with laboratory animals and research on pathological development in humans support the idea that during fetal development sex-specific hormones act on the central nervous system of male and female fetuses. As a result, the sexes are differentiated at birth with respect to certain types of behavior. Though boy and girl babies are born equally ignorant, they may display different predispositions for learning, even under the same environmental influences (Stratton 1982). This view is based on observations of laboratory animals in which sexually differentiated behaviors are observable at birth or shortly thereafter. From these have come the conclusion that "learning" as it is usually understood has played little or no role in accounting for the differences. Sex-differentiated behaviors have been observed in higher primates that were reared in captivity and in isolation from other conspecifics from which learning might take place (Gray and Buffery 1975). Reasoning from the animal evidence has led investigators to assume that humans, though relying on postnatal learning to a greater extent than other species, are likely to be similarly organized. Even more convincing evidence of prenatal sex differentiation of the central nervous system has come from published studies of sex differences in brain anatomy (Gorski et al. 1978; Jacobson et al. 1980).

Concomitantly, recent studies of child behavior in many societies report that, in certain ways, girls and boys are different. Boys, for example, tend to show more competitive behavior and a rougher physical manner of play. Boys show more interest in dominance interactions, and, increasingly as they mature, they sort themselves out into same-sex peer groups where they can find like-minded playmates. Girls have a quieter behavior with less energetic displays (Cronin 1980; Omark et al. 1980; Vaughn and Waters 1980). They pick up language at earlier ages than do boys, and, perhaps as a consequence, they gravitate more to adults and into a social environment that places more stress on conformity to adult rules than do the typical surroundings of boys, which include primarily other boys.

These different behavior profiles, which show up in children from cultural groups with different values and standards of behavior, lead to the surmise that many of the nonsexual, nonreproductive behaviors of humans are influenced by the same selective forces that operate on fitness. An interpretation of the adaptive advantages of the assertiveness and competition so routinely seen in male-male peer interaction would be that these behaviors are "in place" because of their eventual payoff in reproductive terms. Young men who distinguish themselves in combat or in ritual games look good to young women, and young men who hunt well or show the physical stamina to work hard look attractive to the parents of eligible young women.

This idea has not met with wholehearted acceptance in all social science circles (Sahlins 1976). The reasons for suspicion and rejection of such assertions are not difficult to understand. Western notions value highly the inherent integrity of the individual and take as a given the ability of the individual to rise above his/her circumstances. In this context, research that includes an irremedial biological given (such as sex or some other congenital or constitutional factor such as race) has been suspect on the grounds that it can or will promote biological reductionism.

Social scientists are particularly uneasy when it comes to the contribution of nonexperiential factors in accounting for individual behavior, for the social science paradigm is premised upon the notion that the environmental component in learning is the most significant. Most data of the social sciences come from empirically observable phenomena, and research designs are geared to recording and quantifying extant events. Therefore, the assertion that differences in behavior are not exclusively the product of learning is avoided on two grounds. In the first place, it conflicts with humanistic and philosophical values of Western culture. In the second place, it opens up a conceptual "black box" wherein the conventional means of data collection can not be deployed.

Another black box exists for social scientists who contemplate the contribution of biological factors to human sex differences. If sex-differentiated behavior is not "learned" in the usual sense, then how can we understand it? Worse yet, if some behavioral predispositions are prior, then are they malleable? How can we, for example, change sex-differentiated behavior and perhaps interactions between the sexes if girls and boys behave according to a regimen not under environmental influence? . . .

In order to answer the question, "How does socialization produce differences in the behavior of males and females?" we need to be clear about the sources of our inferences. In other words, what kinds of factors produce sex-differentiated behavior and what place does socialization play among them? The prepared learning approach assumes that socialization for sex role is but one element in a series of events that humans experience. Socialization for sex role applies more narrowly to the way in which children learn the roles of adult males and females.

Several sources of inference help us understand how girls and boys emerge from infancy into childhood with recognizably distinct behavioral styles. The asymmetry of the sexes in reproductive function and its implications for the way in which natural selection has influenced behavior in the sexes seem an essential starting point. Issues at this level of remove from socialization may be thought extraneous to actual influences on girls and boys. However, the prepared learning model considers that, in addition to reproductive function, the sexes also differ with regard to their underlying predisposition to learn. This forces us to look on the socialization experience not only as "what children are taught" but also "what children choose to learn." This perspective introduces the larger evolutionary and biological context within which sex role socialization operates.

Asymmetry of Reproductive Roles

At the most basic level are the different biological roles played by the sexes. In higher mammalian species, the reproductive roles of the sexes are most distinct. The female nurtures the fetus internally at substantial metabolic cost, births the infant, and then lactates for a sustained postnatal period. The mother's role is not limited to the supply of nutrients, for she is a source of warmth, protection, and instruction for a significant time period in the life of her offspring. In some species of higher mammals, the male plays no role in the nurturing of young beyond that necessary for conception. Other species show an active male parental role; examples are found in a few prosimian species and in the canids, beavers, gibbons, and humans. In many other mammals, including a primate such as the baboon and some of the great cats, males serve a protective function for all the young of the social group, some of whom are their

311

offspring.

It is possible for the significance of the reproductive difference between the sexes to be overlooked. It is so basic that it is easy to assume that it is limited to the tasks of reproduction and that it need have no relevance to other aspects of behavior that are unrelated to copulation, reproduction, and nurturing of young. For example, since in higher mammals females make the heaviest energetic commitment to reproduction, it is females who limit the rate of reproduction. No matter how many males are available, the number of offspring that can be conceived, gestated, birthed, and nursed is limited by the number of females of reproductive age who are physiologically capable of mothering. This condition has been interpreted to mean that, relative to males, females need not worry themselves unduly about how to become inseminated. They can rest assured that natural selection will produce males who will actively seek them. Human scientists, considering the strategies the sexes have been forced to evolve over the eons, can reason that female animals on the average should show less of the masculine urgency and competitiveness in dealings with conspecifics.

The logical outcome of this asymmetry in reproductive role is that natural selection has favored males who can best compete with other males in gaining the sexual cooperation of females. Since humans represent a species that takes such a long time to mature, and since the kinds of skills that characterize an adult take years for an individual to consolidate, one can expect that to the extent this holds, males would be expected to show greater interest in competitive interactions and dominance strivings with other males.

Natural selection has favored a different strategy in females. In the first instance, since human females, like females of other higher mammalian species, make the greatest investment in reproduction, we can expect that females in their parental roles will have been under selective pressure in favor of greater attentiveness to offspring and greater willingness to maintain close proximity to offspring. Various behaviors of a more obvious and proximate sort would be included here: feeding, tending, protecting, monitoring, and socializing offspring. In other ways this view predicts that human females will have undergone selective pressure for what might be called "sociability," or perhaps better stated "selective sociability."

An argument could be made for the notion that the sociability preferences of females are "in place" ultimately because of their relationship to the nurturing of offspring. But to understand the kinds of selective forces on human females only in terms of their immediate consequences for the survivorship of young is to miss an important point. Long-term studies of nonhuman primates and other mammals show that lineages of females constitute the social nucleus of many group-living species (Koyama 1970; Eaton 1976; Hrdy 1981; Daly and Wilson 1983). The fitness of females for millions of years of mammalian evolution has been dependent upon social skills and interaction with other females (typically their kin), though studies that reveal the significance of female-female and female-other interactions have only recently been conducted. Studies by Jeanne Altmann (1981), Sarah Hrdy (1979, 1981), and Jim McKenna (1979) show the extent to which a female's position in a female hierarchy can affect her diet, fertility, and

312

eventually her fitness. Coalitions of females, often three or more generations deep, cooperate within the membership and compete with other female lineages for various resources such as rights to drinking water, preferred sleeping places, and the like. A result of within-coalition cooperation and extra-coalition competition is that lineages of females become ranked in a dominance hierarchy. Sociability is thus highly selective.

Research on free-ranging primates has shown the reproductive consequences of such coalitions. Among the yellow baboons of Kenya, long-term studies of the behavior of individual animals that are troop members show that female members of high-ranking coalitions have many advantages (Altmann 1981). They can displace lower-ranked females from desirable feeding places and can drink first among females when the troop moves to a watering place. This advantage is not always of great moment but it becomes so when drought has reduced the water supply below that necessary to sustain all troop members, or when the troop realizes that predators are near the watering place. In this case, the goal is to drink and run, before the predator can draw too close.

Higher-ranking females, probably because of their better diet and less stressful life, enter estrus several months sooner than lower-ranking females, with the result that they potentially will produce more offspring. Further, higher-ranked females are better able to time their estrus so that birth and weaning times coincide with seasons in which the most suitable kinds of forage are available for weanlings. Lower-ranked females are more likely to birth and wean offspring later and in less favorable ecological circumstances, with the result that rates of infant mortality are higher (Altmann 1981).

The concept of selective sociability is relevant in this way: Females have prolonged contact with their own offspring. The relationship is longer and more intense than the relationship that males have with offspring. Females behave as if they have longer memories for kin relations than do males, as indicated by the fact that females interact preferentially with mothers, sisters, half-sisters, daughters, and daughters' daughters. Most primate females, including hominid females in our evolutionary past, have been rewarded for paying attention to bonds with other females and for their ability to maintain complex interactions with other females. Selective sociability is not limited to positive, nurturing behaviors but incorporates hostile, competitive behaviors designed to protect a given female's position against other female challengers. Females that successfully nurture their young leave more offspring in the next generation than females that are less willing to tend and feed dependent young for long periods. Additionally, in species such as *Homo sapiens* in which the male helps in parenting the young, natural selection will favor females who are careful about their choice of mate; a good choice will help more of the young survive. When sex role is conceived in this fundamental manner, it becomes apparent that extensive systems of behavior by males and females are potentially affected by natural selection.

Connections Between Reproductive Interests and Behavioral Predispositions

The discussion above suggests that the sexes have been distinguished along two

313

dimensions: interest in sexual competitiveness and interest in long-term social relationships. Earlier mention was made of evolutionary biologists' premise that all functions of an organism relate in some way to reproductive ones. The basis of this rather extreme reductionism is that natural selection can work only on individuals. Individuals who do not reproduce themselves (or contribute to the survival of close relatives) stand no chance of having their characteristics transmitted to future generations. Given the reproductive asymmetry between the sexes in all mammals, generally, and in the prolongation of juvenile dependence in humans, specifically, there is the potential for a certain "continental divide" in the behavioral terrain traversed by the sexes.

The reproductive interests of males have been seen to be furthered by the competitive behaviors and preferences that males show in childhood play. A number of studies give empirical confirmation of such a characteristic style in boys (Omark et al. 1980). It remains to outline the same relationship between the reproductive interests of females and the kinds of behavioral schema observable in young girls, schema that may represent preadaptations to a long-term social strategy.

Evidence exists to support such an argument, but the reasoning involves a more complex and subtle sequence of behaviors in the case of females as opposed to males. The difference is related to the difference between coitus (the *sine qua non* for males) and gestation-lactation-rearing (the *sine qua non* for females). While it is true that each sex needs the other, the division of reproductive labor is such that the male responsibility for his posterity is physically satisfied by coitus. In a physiological sense, this is "all the male can do" toward furthering conception, and coitus is achieved in a short time. (We are leaving aside the issue of male parental investment. . . . Male involvement affects the probability of infant survival, but does not pertain to the current discussion.) However, competitive interaction with other males and successful courtship displays to females are directly related to whether or not a youth will be in a social position to impregnate a receptive woman.

A woman's physiological responsibility to her posterity is not satisfied in any so direct or momentary a manner as is a male's to his. Indeed, it is not nearly so easy to isolate female behaviors that promote a woman's genetic continuity. Her "success" in this regard is measurable in the number of offspring she rears to sexual maturity (the same as for males), but the behaviors necessary to bring this about lie in the minutiae of hourly, daily, and yearly interactions with those offspring and with other group members whose behavior can affect the offspring. Where should one look for determinants of success?

If the argument that women go for a strategy based on sustaining long-term social relationships is correct, then one would predict the following characteristics. Girls should remain physically close to their mothers and to other females with whom the mother associates. (In many societies, these are likely to be the mother's female kin.) Girls should be attentive to the social interaction of adults and responsible to the social conditioning dealt out by the significant adults in her early years, since the same people are likely to be physically present and socially relevant when girls are reproductively mature themselves. They should be relatively tractable or easily socialized. A girl's close proximity to her mother will mean that aversive behavior on her part toward the mother will be noticeable. If a girl is persistently offensive, her mother may drive her away from the matrilineal enclave, an eventuality that would not promote the girl's welfare. This reasoning leads to the prediction that girls will find it easier than boys to learn the interpersonal tasks of socialization. Additionally, girls should find the society of kindred attractive and rewarding. We need not posit a sixth sense that allows them to detect genetic relatives; rather they should be sensitive to the social lead or guidance of their matrikin.

Several studies point up the greater average tractability of girls; however, these tendencies obscure the considerable variation within the sexes. Behavior observation research on children shows that girls commonly comply with parental requests, whereas similar overtures by parents of boys are more likely to be met with negativism and refusal (Minton et al. 1971; Fagot 1974, 1978a, b). A cross-cultural comparison of children's behavior shows more prosocial behavior on the part of girls (employing social rules to justify behavior) as contrasted with more egocentric behavior by boys (behavior in the service of the self). This suggests that girls are more aware of the influence of social context on their own behavior and the behavior of others, and that they use this knowledge to achieve their goals. Boys resort more directly to unvarnished attempts at assertion and dominance in gaining their objectives (J. Whiting and B. Whiting 1975). Similar findings show up in a study of the social behavior of East African girls and boys (Ember 1973).

Some primate studies indicate that male infants and juveniles wean themselves at earlier ages from close physical proximity to the mother. One suggested mechanism is the greater number of aversive behaviors (pinches, bites, hits) directed at the mothers by male infants and the greater readiness of the mothers to rebuff the close approach of the male offspring except when nursing them (Jensen et al. 1973). Among many primates, mothers may favor female offspring, but in many human societies social and economic practices have changed the odds so that male children more often are favored.

Conclusions

The two views of sex role differentiation in humans stem from different scientific traditions. The sex role-training approach draws on social learning theory, developmental psychology, and an anthropological perspective on the requirements posed by social institutions for child socialization. This school of thought considers sex role as one of several learning accomplishments that each new member of society must master. The focus is on postnatal experience, individual maturation, and the implicit and explicit contingencies that shape life in diverse social situations. Social scientists who work in this tradition are likely to view behavior and social role differences between the sexes as primarily acquired and therefore subject to change.

These scholars concede that the reproductive capabilities of the sexes pose different limitations on the nature of the social roles the sexes can fulfill. They expect, however, that under new social, economic, technological, and ideological conditions, the biological differences will fade in significance. The sexes will become functionally interchangeable since, for example, men no longer specialize in roles requiring physical strength or prowess in combat and women no longer expect to spend twenty to thirty years of their adult lives in childbearing and -rearing.

The prepared learning explanation for sex role socialization differences draws on concepts from zoology, evolutionary biology, and ethology. This approach considers that understanding the contemporary behavior of a species requires study of the selective forces that have operated on individuals of the ancestral population. Scholars in this tradition look to the species' evolutionary past for insights into adaptations that would have been favored by selection. The logic behind this apparently reckless disregard of good contemporaneous data about human sex roles is that the forms of social organization, economy, and levels of population density with which *Homo sapiens* now lives are extremely recent innovations in comparison with the tens of thousands (some say hundreds of thousands) of years humans have lived by foraging and at extremely low population levels.

Rather than taking at face value the fact that children undergo specific experiences that bear on their performance as men and women, evolutionists think of each child as partially preprogrammed to carry over behaviors appropriate in another era. Children learn, but they choose what to learn in concert with behavioral schema that have been selected for in past generations (Blurton Jones 1982). Evolution, of course, is an ongoing process. Indeed, if the theory is taken seriously, it implies that the changed pressures on today's males and females will affect the programming for tomorrow's infants.

As is true for any research paradigm, the theoretical assumptions that are necessary at one level to build and test models become obstacles to testing ideas posed from another level outside the paradigm. So there is a potential for the theorists of the two "sides" to continue to operate in separate divisions, talking past each other with separate concepts and vocabulary. Happily, there are signs of rapprochement. Medical and psychological researchers are opening up a new field of neonatology and have uncovered many attributes of infant behavior that represent relatively structured behavior sequences that are seen so early in life that they cannot be tied to postnatal learning. Research on the relationship of sex to these infant behaviors will tell us more about the areas of behavior that are sex differentiated and that may enter into more complex behaviors that we think of as "feminine" or "masculine" in style.

Child development researchers have used the technique of systematic behavior observation for many decades. As interest grows in more "micro" levels of behavior observational analysis, researchers are able to detect much evidence that the child is a major contributor to his/her own socialization. Variables of sex as well as of individual temperament are being evaluated for the role they play in the child's technique for dealing with experience.

We know that the chief distinction of humans is their great capacity for change and for learning. Research in coming years is not likely to contradict this assumption, but we will have more information on why it is that people are able to learn what they do and what kinds of psychological and psychobiological structures underlie human learning readiness. These studies will help us develop more accurate models of the range of sex roles open to human societies and the advantages and penalties that these structures impose upon individuals.

References

Altmann, J. 1981. *Baboon Mothers and Their Infants*. Chicago: University of Chicago Press.

Arganian, M. 1973. "Sex Differences in Early Development." In *Individual Differences in Children*, edited by J. C. Westman, pp. 45-63. New York: Wiley.

Bandura, A. 1977. *Social Learning Theory*. Englewood Cliffs, NJ: Prentice-Hall.

Barry, H. III, M. K. Bacon, and I. Child. 1957. "A Cross-Cultural Survey of Some Sex Differences in Socialization." *Journal of Abnormal and Social Psychology*, 55:327-32.

Blurton Jones, N. G. 1982. "Origins, Functions, Development and Motivations: Unity and Disunity in the Study of Behavior." *Journal of Anthropological Research*, 4:333-49.

Brown, J. K. 1973. "The Subsistence Activities of Women and the Socialization of Children." *Ethos*, 1:413-23.

Cronin, C. L. 1980. "Dominance Relations and Females." In *Dominance Relations: An Ethological View of Human Conflict and Social Interaction*, edited by R. Omark, F. Strayer, and D. Freedman, pp. 299-318. New York: Garland STPM Press.

Daly, M. and M. Wilson. 1983. *Sex, Evolution and Behavior*, 2nd ed. Boston: Willard Grant Press.

D'Andrade, R. 1966. "Sex Differences and Cultural Institutions." In *The Development of Sex Differences*, edited by E. E. Maccoby. Stanford, CA: Stanford University Press.

Draper, P. 1976. "Social and Economic Constraints on !Kung Childhood." In *Kalahari Hunter Gatherers*, edited by I. DeVore and R. Lee. Cambridge, MA: Harvard University Press.

Eaton, G. G. 1976. "The Social Order of Japanese Macaques." *Scientific American*, 235:96-106.

Edgerton, R. B., ed. 1971. *The Individual in Cultural Adaptation*. Berkeley: University of California Press.

Ember, C. 1973. "Feminine Task Assignment and the Social Behavior of Boys." *Ethos*, 1:424-39.

Fagot, B. 1974. "Sex Differences in Toddlers' Behavior and Parental Reaction." *Developmental Psychology*, 10:554-58.

Falbo, T. 1980. "A Social Psychological Model of Human Sexuality," In *The Psychobiology of Sex Differences and Sex Roles*, edited by J. E. Parsons, pp. 131-42. New York: McGraw-Hill.

Ginsburg, H. J., and S. M. Miller. 1982. "Sex Differences in Children's Risk Taking." *Child Development*, 53:426-28.

Gorski, R. A., J. H. Gordon, J. E. Shryne, and A. M. Southam. 1978. "Evidence for a Morphological Sex Difference Within the Medial Preoptic Areas of the Rat Brain." *Brain Research*, 148:333-46.

Gray, J. A., and A. W. H. Buffery. 1975. "Sex Differences in Emotional and Cognitive Behavior in Mammals Including Man." *Acta Psychologica*, 35:89-111.

Hrdy, S. B. 1979. "Infanticide Among Animals: A Review, Classification, and Examination of the Implications for the Reproductive Strategies of Females." *Ecology and Sociobiology*, 1:13-40.

———1981. *The Woman That Never Evolved*. Cambridge, MA: Harvard University Press.

Jacobson, C. D., J. E. Shryne, F. Shapiro, and R. A. Gorski. 1980. "Ontogeny of the Sexually Dimorphic Nucleus of the Preoptic Area." *Journal of Comparative Neurology*, 193:541-48.

Jensen, G., R. Bobbit, and A. Gordon. 1973. "Mothers' and Infants' Roles in the Development of *Macaca nemestrina*." *Primates*, 14:79-88.

Kohlberg, L. 1966. "A Cognitive Developmental Analysis of Children's Sex Role Concepts and Attitudes." In *The Development of Sex Differences*, edited by E. E. Maccoby. Stanford, CA: Stanford University Press.

Koyama, N. 1970. "Changes in Dominance Rank and Division of a Wild Japanese Monkey Troop in Arashiyama." *Primates*, 11:335-91.

Lancaster, J. B. 1976. "Sex Roles in Primate Societies." In *Sex Differences: Social and Biological Perspectives*, edited by M. Teitelbaum, pp. 22-61. Garden City, NY: Anchor Press/Doubleday.

Lott, D. F., and B. L. Hart. 1977. "Aggressive Domination of Cattle by Fulani Herdsmen and in Relation to Aggression in Fulani Culture and Personality." *Ethos*, 5:174-86.

Maccoby, E. E., and C. M. Jacklin. 1974. *The Psychology of Sex Differences*. Stanford, CA: Stanford University Press.

McKenna, J. J. 1979. "Aspects of Infant Socializa-tion, Attachment, and Maternal Caregiving Patterns Among Primates: A Cross-Disciplinary Review." *Yearbook of Physical Anthropology*, 22:250-86.

Minton, C., J. Kagan, and J. A. LeVine. 1971. "Maternal Control and Obedience in the Two-Year Old." *Child Development*, 42:1873-94.

Minturn, L., and W. W. Lambert. 1964. *Mothers of Six Cultures: Antecedents of Child Bearing*. New York: Wiley.

Murdock, G. P. 1949. *Social Structure*. New York: Macmillan.

Mussen, P. H. 1973. *The Psychological Development of the Child*. Englewood Cliffs, NJ: Prentice-Hall.

Omark, D., F. Strayer, and D. Freedman, eds. 1980. *Dominance Relations: An Ethological View of Human Conflict and Social Interaction*. New York: Garland STPM Press.

Romney, A. K., and R. Romney. 1965. *The Mixtecans of Juxtlahuaca*. New York: Wiley.

Sahlins, M. 1976. *The Use and Abuse of Biology*. Ann Arbor: University of Michigan Press.

Slovic, P. 1966. "Risk-Taking in Children: Age and Sex Differences." *Child Development*, 37:169-76.

Stratton, P., ed. 1982. *Psychobiology of the Human Newborn*. New York: Wiley.

Vaughn, B. E., and E. Waters. 1980. "Social Organization Among Preschool Peers: Dominance, Attention and Sociometric Correlates." In *Dominance Relations: An Ethological View of Human Conflict and Social Interaction*, edited by D. P. Omark, F. Strayer, and D. G. Freedman, pp. 359-80. New York: Garland STPM Press.

Whiting, B., and J. W. M. Whiting. 1975. *Children of Six Cultures*. Cambridge, MA: Harvard University Press.

Whiting, J. W. M., and B. B. Whiting. 1975. "Aloofness and Intimacy of Husbands and Wives: A Cross Cultural Study." *Ethos*, 3:183-207.

Black Children and Poverty: Self-Concept Development
Margaret Beale Spencer

The acquisition of gender roles and gender identity is only one aspect of the child's personality development. While children are learning that they are girls or boys and coming to understand what it means within their culture to be a girl or a boy, they are also acquiring a wide range of other personal characteristics. They become competitive or cooperative, friendly and outgoing, or shy and reserved. They come to prefer active physical involvement in group games or quiet, solitary activities such as reading.

As Margaret Beale Spencer points out, the development of the self-concept is intimately involved with children's growing awareness of their own personal characteristics. It is also related to self-esteem, the positive or negative value that children place on their personal character-istics, and to identity, the awareness of membership in various groups (gender, familial, ethnic, racial, religious) that have social meaning within the culture. Thus, for example, female gender identity involves knowing that you are a girl, that girls act in certain, culturally defined ways; and that cultures hold beliefs concerning the respective privileges, personal characteristics, and responsibilities of women.

In this article, Spencer addresses the acquisition of racial identity in black children growing up in an ecosystem riddled with racial prejudice. Early research ostensibly focused on black children's self-concept failed, she notes, to distinguish between self-concept, personal sense of self-esteem, and orientation toward membership in a group stigmatized by the majority. The Eurocentric racial orientation of black preschool children frequently observed in this research was therefore assumed incorrectly to reflect self-esteem, to be generalizable to black children of all ages, and to be indicative of self-rejection. Research over the past twenty years, however, has yielded a much more sophisticated picture. Black preschoolers' Eurocentric orientation toward the cultural group has been found to be independent of personal self-esteem, which remains high. Eurocentric orientation appears to be related to the cognitive immaturity of preschoolers and to exposure to racially biased imagery in the broader culture. This orientation tends to disappear with increased cognitive development and can be altered through compensatory cultural activity.

In reading about this research, notice that cultural values not only structure the environment of development for children, they also structure the environment of research for scholars. As we saw in relation to the attachment research discussed in Chapter 12, the questions asked, the methods used, and the interpretations given to results in the social sciences are rarely, if ever, value-free.

. . . Self-concept actually refers to an individual's awareness of his or her own characteristics and attributes and the ways in which he or she is both like and unlike others (McCandless and Evans, 1973, p. 389). It is generally understood that this awareness reflects the initial self versus nonself differentiation that occurs during the first year of life—that is, the initial *me* and *not me* differentiating process. This initial me versus not me sorting process has been observed in the behavior of children during mirror play as an awareness of physical and facial characteristics. Over time, it finally evolves into an objective awareness about the self as talkative, strong, healthy, dirty, a girl, a boy, and so forth. Most important, these descriptive or objective labels about the self have implications for another dimension of the self-system—namely, self-esteem. For the most part, Black children have been studied in the latter manner (esteem) as opposed to the former (self-concept). For example, from general observations, studies of mirror play (self-concept) have not been conducted on Black children.

More specifically, the value that children or youth place on themselves and on their associated behaviors and attributes represents self-esteem. Undoubtedly, self-esteem and self-concept are intimately related. Value judgments about what children learn about themselves are frequently so interwoven that it is unlikely that they themselves separate fact from evaluation. In sum, self-esteem reflects how a child or a youth regards himself or herself across a wide spectrum of activities.

On the one hand, self-concept concerns the young child's image of himself or herself as an individual; self-esteem, on the other hand, represents evaluations of those images. Finally, identity suggests an integration with perceptions of future development, that is, an awareness of group membership and the expectations, privileges, restraints, and social responsibilities that accompany that membership (McCandless and Evans, 1973, p. 390). Accordingly, a young girl recognizes that possessing certain physical characteristics means being a female before she understands what females are expected or allowed to do. Similarly, a young child's awareness of skin color will occur before comprehension that this may designate the child as a Chicano, African-American, or Native American,

Spencer, Margaret Beale. (1988). *Self-concept development.* In D.T. Slaughter (Ed.) *Black Children and Poverty: A Developmental Perspective.* SF: Jossey-Bass. pp. 59-72 for example, and that such groups face certain hardships in a society dominated by White Americans and by particular biases transmitted through institutional structures in place at every level of the ecosystem.

Identity Processes: Sex Role and Group (Racial) Referents

Identity formation—which is more global and interactive than usually assumed—should be viewed as a process through which children gain knowledge of such matters as their names, race, sex roles, social class, and the meanings these descriptions have for their lives. Most important, although young children may not understand the reasons that underlie these ascriptive meanings, these meanings evolve in the context of the specific culture to which a child belongs. To put it another way, young children may quickly learn that they and their families are not welcome in certain situations solely as a function of their race—that is, by being a Black person. However, it would be highly unlikely that children would understand why being Black should result in social discrimination. Thus, the child's progressively differentiated understanding of self suggests a dynamic, life-course formulation of an identity.

There are several salient influences. The process of identity formation is determined by cognitive maturation, current situational factors, and previous socialization influences, along with the nature and quality of ego defenses. The process is quite complex and not unlike, in fact, other aspects of ego functioning, such as sex role and moral developments.

The components of identity processes are not new or emergent themes. In one form or another, the issues represent longstanding concerns. Researchers' treatment of these issues relative to sex role identity (versus assumptions made about group identity) is instructive—that is, the literature on sex role identity has benefited from a long legacy of sophisticated analyses and rich theoretical interpretations, particularly for White, middle-income males. On the other hand, the quality of thinking and research products in the area of race-related identity concerns have not been as advantaged. In fact, a comparison of research on sex role identity versus research on race-related identity reveals that variations in the level of inferences drawn show significant patterned differences that have severely limited the quality and quantity of scholarship available to date for policy initiatives, cross-disciplinary academic training, and general dissemination of child development information to the public. . . .

When the two decades of research that occurred before the 1965 Moynihan report on the Black family are reviewed, consistency of empirical themes and concomitant deviant-linked interpretations are evident. First, the data suggested that young, preschool Black children generally evaluated the color Black and Black persons in a negative manner. A pattern of identification with a White figure or with Caucasian-type physiognomic attributes was observed. The concomitant interpretive trend was not only that Blacks generally show personality disorganization but also that the Black family and the Black community were ineffective or incapable of protecting Black children. . . .

During the same two decades before the Moynihan report, in those studies that did pursue comparisons of self-concept and self-esteem, findings did not show lower self-esteem for Black children; studies often showed that the self-esteem of Black children was equal to or greater than that of their White counterparts. Because comparisons of achievements by Blacks and Whites generally showed Blacks doing less well, these findings were interpreted as suggesting that Black youths have an unrealistically high self-esteem. Obviously, scientists' interpretations of findings and anecdotal observations are affected by training (Slaughter and McWorter, 1985).

In contrast, the two decades of research after the 1965 Moynihan report suggest many new possibilities and more serious attempts to translate the fit between the environment and the organism and the associated tensions into a more sophisticated, inclusive model of intrapsychic processes that are supported by data and direct assessments of the constructs. The redirections and alternative interpretations, although still infrequently cited by mainstream scholars, have influenced the thinking and energies of individuals committed to building more inclusive models of human development. . .

Understanding Identity Development of Black Youth

After Moynihan's published report in 1965, several key studies were issued in the 1970s (for example, Porter, 1971; Rosenberg and Simmons, 1971). These included literature reviews (Banks, 1976; Nobles, 1973) and broader theoretical approaches (for example, Spencer, 1975, 1976) that suggested alternative interpretations of the pathology-based conclusions about the findings on personal and group identities.

As noted, until the decade of the 1970s, the consistent finding of Eurocentric racial attitudes among young Black children was interpreted as suggesting general psychopathology or self-rejection. Studies that assessed racial attitudes, racial preferences, and color connotations—aspects of the child's reference group orientation—were interpreted as suggesting that the child's self-esteem was negative or low. For the most part, personal identity variables were not measured directly. Although data were discussed in terms of these variables (for example, self-esteem, self-concept), studies . . . assessed only aspects of the child's reference group orientation or group identity. Reference group orientation variables would include, for example, race identification, race awareness, racial attitudes, and racial preferences.

Most of the new methods, conceptual formulations, and interpretations were contributed to by minority-group scholars (for example, Alejandro-Wright, 1985; Cross, 1985; Hare and Castenell, 1985; Semaj, 1985; Spencer, 1985). When assessed directly, Black children and youth were often found to have equal or higher self-esteem scores when compared with Whites. The most important aspect of these findings has been the observation that these new directions in research and theory, generally introduced by Black scholars, have been infrequently cited by child development researchers. Although published reports were becoming increasingly and routinely available, textbooks continued to be written during this period as though new research findings did not exist.

324

Another important contribution during the two decades after the 1965 Moynihan report was the development of research approaches that included the simultaneous assessment of both personal identity (self-esteem) and young children's reference group orientations; early contributions were made by independent and simultaneous research efforts (see McAdoo, 1973, 1977; Spencer, 1975, 1976, 1982a, 1984). Spencer's research in the mid 1970s and 1980s was an expansion and modification of earlier programmatic research (see Spencer, 1970; Spencer and Horowitz, 1973). An important finding from this redundant research effort was the demonstration of the early independence of personal identity from reference group orientation or group identity in preschool children. That is, young, cognitively egocentric children could feel good about the self (that is, personal identity) while also showing the traditional Eurocentric orientation toward the cultural group (Spencer, 1976).

Another finding from research conducted during this period was the early predictive relationship of race awareness to cognitive maturation and the relationship of race awareness to the Eurocentric group identity orientation of young children (Spencer, 1976, 1980, 1981, 1982b). Race awareness seemed to function in a manner analogous to sex identity—that is, this newer research indicated cognitive underpinnings for the differentiation of racial groups (such as the child's early differentiation for gender membership). In sum, race awareness was found to be correlated with the child's knowledge of racial stereotypes and to have cognitive predictors (Alejandro-Wright, 1985; Semaj, 1985; Spencer, 1976, 1982a, 1982b, 1985). For the first time, research conducted during this period demonstrated that the child's production of Eurocentric values was linked to normal maturational processes consistent with specific, caste-related ecosystem experiences (that is, the child's cognitive development and exposure to racially biased imagery).

During the early to middle 1970s, research suggested that the ecosystem experiences of many children were infused with positive imagery of Whites along with negative stereotypes of minority groups but that these perceptions were malleable—they were amenable to traditional learning models and could be changed (Spencer, 1970; Spencer and Horowitz, 1973). A variety of studies that used bibliotherapy techniques, social reinforcers, and Black culture-oriented curricula in nonpublic preschools served two important purposes. The studies showed that Eurocentric attitudes reflected a particular type of learning and, consistent with learning theory models, were amenable to manipulation. Having a Eurocentric orientation was not evidence of personality disorganization; that assumption was not supported under direct empirical tests that included the assessment of both constructs. The subsequent paradigms were different from previous assumptions about personality disorganization, and they demonstrated the learned quality of Eurocentric values. Furthermore, unlike the assumption of passivity for Black parents' child-rearing efforts and practices, more recent studies by Black researchers have demonstrated variations in parenting strategies as a function of parental perceptions of improved conditions and hope (Spencer, 1983, in press; Bowman and Howard, 1985).

Research findings reported during the last ten years on the intervening role of Black parents (Bowman and Howard, 1985; Spencer, 1983, in press) suggest that a compensato-

325

ry cultural emphasis by Black parents serves an important interventional function. These empirical findings are important and confirm earlier speculations by minority-group theorists, such as Edward Barnes, about the buffering roles of Black parenting strategies and the Black community for the rearing of healthy Black children (Barnes, 1972).

The integration of the literature concerning the myriad labels for constructs was significantly aided, beginning in the early 1970s, by work of a minority-group researcher (see Cross, 1985, 1986) who stressed the need to differentiate studies into those measuring personal identity versus others that measured reference group orientation. The ordering of the studies into personal identity, reference group orientation, or a combination of the two has served a clarifying and informative function for the literature.

Research implemented by minority-group researchers during the decade beginning in the mid 1970s was instrumental in proposing developmental variations in the relationship between findings on personal identity and reference group orientation. Influenced by Piagetian theorizing, these scholars introduced an integration of differentiating studies of personal identity and reference group orientation along with an articulation of developmental influences (see Alejandro-Wright, 1985; Semaj, 1985; Spencer, 1976, 1982a, 1985).

Two independent programmatic research strategies conducted in both the North and the South (each included the direct assessment of sociocognitive developmental constructs) yielded consistent findings across studies (Spencer, 1976, 1982b, 1985). First, older, less cognitively egocentered children, as expected, showed less Eurocentric reference group orientations. In fact, cross-sectional and longitudinal research has demonstrated that older, less egocentric, minority-group children show the most pronounced pattern of decreasing Eurocentric reference group orientation along with improved or better performance on cognitive measures (see Spencer, 1982a, 1982b). The issue of developmental variation in the pattern of reference group orientation is important because, up until the early 1970s and as still reported in most texts, the assumption has been that the response patterns of young, egocentric children characterize the performance patterns for the entire group, independent of developmental stage. That is, inferences about middle-childhood, adolescent, and adult cognitions were inferred from data generally obtained on the sample of convenience: young, Black (most often lower-income) preschool children.

More recent research has also pointed to the influences of differentiated perceptions, affectivity, and cognition for reference group orientation (see the section on identity in Spencer, Brookins, and Allen, 1985), again suggesting the complexity and developmental interactions with exposure to stereotypical imagery, intrapsychic processes, and behavioral outcomes, while also demonstrating the buffering influences of specific child-rearing value strategies: the parental implementation of a compensatory cultural emphasis. Many questions and policy concerns still remain, however. . . .

References

Alejandro-Wright, M. N. "The Child's Conception of Racial Classification: A Socio-Cognitive Developmental Model." In M. B. Spencer, G. K. Brookins, and W. R. Allen (eds.), *Beginnings: Social and Affective Development of Black Children.* Hillsdale, N.J.: Erlhaum, 1985.

Banks, W. C. "White Preference in Blacks: A Paradigm in Search of a Phenomenon." *Psychological Bulletin*, 1976, *83* (6), 1179-1186.

Barnes, E. "The Black Community as the Source of Positive Self-Concept for Black Children: A Theoretical Perspective." In R. Jones (ed.), *Black Psychology.* New York: Harper & Row, 1972.

Bowman, P., and Howard, C. "Race-Related Socialization, Motivation, and Academic Achievement: A Study of Black Youth in Three-Generation Families." *Journal of the American Academy of Child Psychiatry*, 1985, *24* (2), 134-141.

Cross, W. E., Jr. "Black Identity: Rediscovering the Distinction Between Personal Identity and Reference Group Orientation." In M. B. Spencer, G. K. Brookins, and W. R. Allen (eds.), *Beginnings: The Social and Affective Development of Black Children.* Hillsdale, N.J.: Erlbaum, 1985.

Cross, W. E., Jr. "A Two-Factor Theory of Black Identity: Development in Minority Children." In J. S. Phinney and M. J. Rotheram (eds.), *Children's Ethnic Socialization.* Newbury Park, Calif.: Sage, 1986.

Hare, B., and Castenell, L. "No Place to Run, No Place to Hide: Comparative Status and Future Prospects of Black Boys." In M. B. Spencer, G. K. Brookins, and W. R. Allen (eds.), *Beginnings: The Social and Affective Development of Black Children.* Hillsdale, N.J.: Erlbaum, 1985.

McAdoo, H. *An Assessment of Racial Attitudes and Self-Concepts in Urban Black Children.* Office of Child Development Publication, no. OCD-CD-282. Washington, D.C.: Office of Child Development, 1973.

McAdoo, H. "The Development of Self-Concept and Race Attitudes in Black Children: A Longitudinal Study." In W. E. Cross, Jr. (ed.), *The 3rd Conference on Empirical Research in Black Psychology.* Washington, D.C.: National Institute of Education, 1977.

McCandless, B. R., and Evans, E. D. *Children and Youth*. Hinsdale, Ill.: Dryden Press, 1973.

Nobles, W. W. "Psychological Research and the Black Self-Concept: A Critical Review." *Journal of Social Issues*, 1973, *29* (1), 11-31.

Porter, J. *Black Child, White Child: The Development of Racial Attitudes*. Cambridge, Mass.: Harvard University Press, 1971.

Rosenberg, M., and Simmons, R. *Black and White Self-Esteem: The Urban School Child*. Washington, D.C.: American Sociological Association, 1971.

Semaj, L. T. "Afrikanity, Cognition, and Extended Self-Identity." In M. B. Spencer, G. K. Brookins, and W. R. Allen (eds.), *Beginnings: The Social and Affective Development of Black Children*. Hillsdale, N.J.: Erlballm, 1985.

Slaughter, D. T., and McWorter, G. A. "Social Origins and Early Features of the Scientific Study of Black American Families and Children." In M. B. Spencer, G. K. Brookins, and W. R. Allen (eds.), *Beginnings: The Social and Affective Development of Black Children*. Hillsdale, N.J.: Erlbaum, 1985.

Spencer, M. B. "The Effects of Systematic Social (Puppet) and Token Reinforcement on the Modification of Racial and Color-Concept Attitudes in Preschool-Aged Children." Master's thesis, University of Kansas, 1970.

Spencer, M. B. "Racial Attitude and Self-Concept Development in Black Children." Paper presented at the meeting of the American Orthopsychiatric Association, Washington, D.C.: March 21-25, 1975.

Spencer, M. B. "The Social-Cognitive and Personality Development of the Black Preschool Child: An Exploratory Study of Developmental Process." Doctoral dissertation, University of Chicago, 1976.

Spencer, M. B. "Race Dissonance Research on Black Children: Stable Life Course Phenomenon or Fluid Indicator of Intraindividual Plasticity and Unique Cohort Effect?" In J. L. McAdoo, H. P. McAdoo, and W. E. Cross, Jr. (eds.), *Proceedings of the 5th Conference on Empirical Research in Black Psychology*. Washington, D.C.: National Institute of Mental Health, 1980.

Spencer, M. B. "Personal-Social Adjustment of Minority Group Children." Final report of Project No. 5-R01-PMS-MH-31106 funded by the National Institute of Mental Health, 1981.

Spencer, M. B. "Personal and Group Identity of Black Children: An Alternative Synthesis." *Genetic Psychology Monographs*, 1982a, *103*, 59-84.

Spencer, M. B. "Preschool Children's Social Cognition and Cultural Condition: A Cognitive Developmental Interpretation of Race Dissonance Findings." *Journal of Psychology*, 1982b, *112*, 275-286.

Spencer, M. B. "Children's Cultural Values and Parental Child-Rearing Strategies." *Developmental Review*, 1983, *3*, 351-370.

Spencer, M. B. "Black Children's Race Awareness, Racial Attitudes, and Self-Concept: A Reinterpretation." *Journal of Child Psychology and Psychiatry*, 1984, *25*, 433-441.

Spencer, M. B. "Cultural Cognition and Social Cognition as Identity Factors in Black Children's Personal-Social Growth." In M. B. Spencer, G. K. Brookins, and W. R. Allen (eds.), *Beginnings: The Social and Affective Development of Black Children*. Hillsdale, N.J.: Erlbaum, 1985.

Spencer, M. B. "Parental Value Transmission: Implications for Black Child Development." In L. Burton, H. Cheatham, and J. Stewart (eds.), *Black Families: Contemporary Issues and Concerns*. Newbury Park, Calif.: Sage, in press.

Spencer, M. B., Brookins, G. K., and Allen, W. R. (eds.). *Beginnings: The Social and Affective Development of Black Children*. Hillsdale, N.J.: Erlbaum, 1985.

Spencer, M. B., and Horowitz, F. D. "Effects of Systematic and Token Reinforcement on the Modification of Racial and Color-Concept Attitudes in Black and White Preschool Children." *Developmental Psychology*, 1973, *9* (2), 246-254.

14

Rivalry and Interdependence in Sibling Relationships

My earliest memory of all is a mad passion of rage at my elder brother John. . . . I had broken my little brown stool, by madly throwing it at my brother; and felt for perhaps the first time, the united pangs of Loss and Remorse. I was perhaps hardly more than two years old.

–Carlyle, *Reminiscences*

• INTRODUCTION •

The family is a microcosm of the broader society. It provides the child with models for how human beings should relate to one another, and it affords an opportunity to acquire relationship skills within a relatively accepting environment. Respect for the rights and opinions of others, the ability to give and receive nurturance, an orientation toward cooperation, and skills for coping with frustration and conflict develop in the daily events of family life. Nowhere is this more evident than in children's interactions with their siblings. Among young children, moderate rivalry and conflict is a common feature of family life; but so too is cooperation. As development proceeds, the behavior of older siblings serves as a powerful factor in children's acquisition of skills and values. Older brothers and sisters know things that younger children do not know and do things they cannot do. While this contrast can, at times, be painful, it provides a model of behavior toward which the child can aspire and may act as a source of motivation for learning new abilities.

In the two readings chosen for this module, we are presented with examples of sibling behavior that run the gamut from physical aggression to nurturant caregiving. We are also offered a striking cultural contrast. In the first reading Judy Dunn reports data from research on early sibling relationships carried out among working- and middle-class families in the Cambridge area in England. There, as is typical of societies in the industrial West, families tend to be small (two or three children) and siblings relatively close in age. Caregiving is seen as primarily a maternal function. Mothers, who expect children to act as individuals, are likely to be reluctant to place continuing responsibility for one child on the shoulders of another. As a result, children participate in family life as relative peers; and, as in all peer relations, issues of conflict resolution and cooperative activity are dominant concerns.

In the Polynesian and Hawaiian-American families described by Thomas Weisner in the second reading, the number of children is likely to be much larger, and children who have been weaned from the breast spend much of their time in the care of older brothers and sisters. In such sibling care systems, responsibility tends to be diffused throughout the group. Parents direct communication to the oldest child or to the group as a whole, and younger children are rarely singled out as individuals. In this setting, issues of interdependence, mutual assistance, and nurturance become the primary concerns.

● ● ●

Confrontation and Cooperation between Siblings
Judy Dunn

Sibling relationships serve as an early arena for the acquisition of social understanding and social skills. In this report, Judy Dunn presents data from research on interactions among siblings who are relatively close in age and serve as one another's primary playmates. As the author points out, such children may share a similarity of interests and a high level of familiarity with one another. Under these circumstances, either conflict or cooperative play or both may result from self-interest. When children's interests are threatened, conflict may be the outcome. When attention is held by an older sibling's demonstration of practiced skills, motivation for cooperative play in a younger child just developing those skills may be strong. Even as early as the second year, children's reactions to conflict and ability to engage in the coordinated and complementary activities required for cooperative play reflect an emerging capacity to understand the feelings and needs of another and to explore social roles and rules.

Confronting the Sibling

The power of jealousy between siblings is a theme running throughout mythology, literature, and history—an emotion seen by Freud and writers before and after him as having lifelong effects on an individual's personality. We can question the precise scientific basis for such a claim, but we cannot doubt the emotional urgency of the uninhibited rage that young siblings can show toward one another. Such anger often leaves a lasting trace—even from the second year, as Thomas Carlyle comments in his reminiscences of 1881:

Dunn, Judy. (1988). *The Beginnings of Social Understanding*. Cambridge, MA: Harvard University Press. Chapters 3 (Confronting the sibling) and 6 (Cooperation between siblings). pp. 45-65, 109-126.

333

My earliest memory of all is a mad passion of rage at my elder brother John . . . in which my Father too figures though dimly, as a kind of cheerful comforter and soother. I had broken my little brown stool, by madly throwing it at my brother; and felt for the first time, the united pangs of Loss and Remorse. I was perhaps hardly more than 2 years old . . . though all is quite legible for myself. (quoted in Sampson and Sampson, 1985)

The lamentations of parents observing the violence between their children echo down the centuries; the behavior described and the distress felt by parents are strikingly similar whether the witness is from the tenth, eighteenth, or twentieth century. Although the actions of a jealous brother or sister are undoubtedly upsetting to witness (let alone to receive), they are also extremely revealing. If we look closely at the exchanges between young siblings, we gain an illuminating perspective on the nature of the child's growing understanding of the feelings and needs of another person, and of the social and moral rules within the family. It is a picture that in some ways differs from that revealed in the disputes between child and parent, but the developmental changes are similar.

One obvious difference between the sibling-child and the mother-child disputes concerns the interests of the children, which are far closer than those between child and adult. This matching of interests means that two children are very likely to compete for similar goods; the interests of the child are frequently directly threatened by the sibling. It also means that each child knows well what the other particularly likes and dislikes, especially if they are close in age. What pleases a three-year-old is not very different from what pleases his five-year-old brother. This closeness of interests, and the familiarity of children who share daily intimacy, means that young children probably have less difficulty in understanding how to annoy, comfort, or anticipate the moods and responses of their siblings than those of their parents. The accuracy with which children read the expressions and wishes of other children who are in some sense competitors was commented on by Maria Edgeworth in the eighteenth century, in no-nonsense terms. She firmly linked the ability directly to the children's powers of "reason" and the strength of competition between them:

Two hungry children, with their eager eyes fixed on one and the same basin of milk, do not sympathize with each other, though they have the same sensations; each perceives that if the other eats the bread and milk, he cannot eat it . . . We may observe, that the more quickly children reason, the sooner they discover how far their interests are any ways incompatible with the interests of their companions . .

Children, who are accurate observers of the countenance, and who have a superior degree of penetration, discover very early the symptoms of displeasure, or of affection, in their friends; they also perceive quickly the dangers of rivalship from their companions. (1798, p. 275)

334

This competitive similarity of interests, coupled with the child's grasp of what upsets and excites the sibling *and* the uninhibited nature of the sibling relationship, means that sibling quarrels are more often emotionally loaded than are most disputes with the mother. On average, the children in the forty families of our Study 2 expressed intense anger or distress in 28 percent and 21 percent of the incidents of sibling conflict at twenty-four and thirty-six months respectively. In contrast, the proportions of mother-child disputes in which the child showed such distress or anger were 10 percent and 9 percent at the same ages.

Signs of New Understanding

There are some important parallels between a child's behavior in conflict with a parent and with a sibling: these concern developmental changes in emotion and understanding. The children expressed intense anger and distress during sibling conflicts with increasing frequency during the first half of the second year, just as they did in disputes with the mother, differences that were significant between fourteen and eighteen months (see Figure 1 for changes in physical aggression over this period). They also displayed increasing powers of understanding, as shown by their ability to provoke a sibling by teasing.

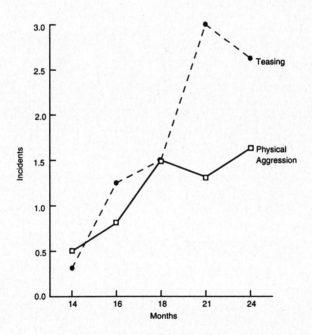

Figure 1. Changes in frequency of teasing and aggression to sibling in second year (Study 1).

335

Teasing

During the second year, teasing became both more frequent and more elaborate. At sixteen and eighteen months, the teasing incidents we observed included the following behavior: removing the sibling's comfort object in the course of a fight; leaving a fight in order to go and destroy a cherished possession of the sibling; holding a cherished object just out of reach of the sibling; pulling the sibling's thumb (sucked in moments of stress) out of his mouth; pushing a toy spider at a sibling who was reportedly afraid of spiders. By the end of the second year, such acts, observed in each of the children in Study 1, had become more elaborate. One child whose sibling had three imaginary friends, named Lily, Allelujah, and Peepee, taunted the sibling by announcing that *she* was the imaginary friend. It was an act that reliably angered the sibling, and an act of considerable intellectual virtuosity for a child of twenty-four months.

The interest of these actions lies in the understanding they reflect of what will upset or annoy a particular person. Teasing of the mother was also, as we have seen, quite common ("I don't love you, Mummy" was a technique already developed at twenty-four months by two of the children in the six families in Study 1). Yet it did not reach the frequency or the elaboration of the teasing of the sibling, a difference that might well reflect the relative difficulty that the child faced in understanding what can upset an adult as opposed to another child, as well as the greater emotional urgency of exchanges with the sibling. Teasing of the sibling remained frequent throughout the third year and was as commonly shown by younger as by older siblings. So the ability to understand what will upset the other child develops very early, and the motivation to act in this way does not decrease over the preschool years. Of the forty secondborn children in Study 2, seventeen were observed to tease by eighteen months, and thirty-six by twenty-four months.

Enlisting Adult Help

The children's behavior during sibling conflicts reflected not only their understanding of what would annoy a sibling but also their growing grasp of what was sanctioned behavior within the family. This was evident in their attempts to enlist adult help. The world of adult values and rules is very much part of the context of sibling disputes in the home, and children learn quickly how to enlist adult aid or to avoid adult sanctions in disputes with siblings. There was, for example, a striking difference in the probability of appealing for help, depending on the initiator of the physical aggression or teasing. In Study 1, we found that in 66 percent of the incidents in which the sibling behaved aggressively, the children appealed to their mothers for help. In contrast, they appealed to their mothers in only 3 percent of incidents in which they *themselves* had acted in this way—a dramatic difference. In itself, such anticipation of the behavior of the parent does not require elaborate understanding; a pet dog faced with an owner's disapproval might well behave in the same way. But the differences in the children's attempts to enlist parental aid in the face of their own or another's transgression do demonstrate a growing comprehension of what is sanctioned behavior. It also demonstrates that children use such understanding when their own interests are threatened.

The earliest appeals to the mother that we observed in our Cambridge children were nonverbal. The fourteen- and sixteen-month-olds acted in the following ways during conflicts with siblings: the child looks at the mother while pointing at the sibling and vocalizing or crying; the child runs over to the mother and pulls her toward the sibling; the child shows her a wound inflicted by the sibling and gestures toward the sibling. Over the months that followed, the children became increasingly articulate in their appeals. . . .

A Principle of Justice?

Justifications and excuses. The children were just as likely to use reasons in disputes with their siblings as with their mothers, at both twenty-four and thirty-six months. And the nature of those justifications is similar. The only significant difference was that at twenty-four months the children were more likely to refer to social rules in disputes with siblings than with mothers. Here the rule in question was usually possession, an issue at the center of many conflicts. By thirty-six months, the patterns of justification made to sibling and to mother were much alike, as was the proportion of conflict incidents that included justification—increasing from 18 percent (twenty-four months) to 28 percent at thirty-six months. . . .

What is clear from these observations is that children from eighteen months on have some grasp of how to affect the feeling state of a sibling; they know well what particular objects or activities have a special significance for the sibling. Strikingly similar observations of understanding in the context of sibling conflict have been reported in the work of Sara Harkness and Charles Super (1985) on the Kipsigis in Kenya; incidents are cited in which two-year-olds deny their own responsibility, blame the sibling, and draw the mother's attention to the misdeeds of the sibling.

In the encounters among our Cambridge siblings, we also see the beginnings of an understanding of certain rules of positive justice, a practical grasp of how such rules can be used when one's interests are threatened. For it is, I would emphasize, under the stress of situations in which the children's own interests are impeded that they demonstrate their comprehension of what will upset their sibling and of how their mothers can be enlisted as support. In these conflicts between peers, effective argument depends on some grasp of the other's goals and rights. . . .

Cooperation between Siblings

Very young children do not only fight, argue, and laugh at the misfortunes and misdeeds of others; they also cooperate with others in play at an astonishingly early age, and with an appreciation of the other's goals and mood that is impressive and delightful

337

to observe. Their ability to cooperate in play with a sibling well before they are two years old far outstrips what might have been expected on the basis of studies of children in more formal settings or with less familiar companions (Dunn and Kendrick, 1982). It is an ability that depends on a sensitivity to the mood of the other, on a shared sense of the absurd and unexpected that presupposes a grasp of the expected, on a willingness to obey directions within the play context, to negotiate, concede to, and coordinate with another. And with the development of joint pretend play, it involves an intellectual leap into a shared world of pretend identities and roles. . . .

Recognizing and Sharing Mood and Action

. . . Sequences in which the children acted together, repeating actions with excitement and laughter, were observed at every stage of each of our studies. These rhythmic coaction sequences involved a great range of actions: large-scale physical actions (bouncing on sofa, dancing, jumping up and down, marching to and fro, repeated falling down); waving, knocking, or tapping objects; coordinated gestures; vocal rhythmic chanting or singing; and, in the third year, verbal chants or rituals. Peter and his older sister Sophie, the siblings in the next example, engaged in excited play of this sort on every occasion that they were observed, often for periods as long as forty minutes, and with a great deal of giggling.

. . . *Family W (Study 2). Child 24 months*
Sibling enters room, looks at C and chants.

Sib: Loola Loola loola loola!
C (laughs and imitates): Loola loola loola loola!
Both chant together: Loola Loola loola loola!

Sibling picks up ribbon, walks (prancing) with it, chanting rhythmically. C watches, smiling, picks up another piece of ribbon and imitates prancing around room; both prance, chant, and laugh, waving ribbons. Sib climbs onto sofa and hangs upside down, still chanting. C imitates. Three minutes later sib hands C a piece of ribbon, starts chanting "Loola." C joins in chanting, both chant together. Four minutes later C takes another piece of ribbon, looks at sib and laughs. Sibling imitates by taking ribbon and laughs. Both climb onto cushion, waving ribbons and chanting. . . .

Recognizing and Cooperating in the Other's Goal

Cooperative actions in which children contribute to the other's play in a manner that reflects an understanding of the other's goals were observed with increasing frequency during the second year. Some children could already act in this cooperative way at

338

fourteen months.

Family B (Study 1). Child 14 months
Sibling begins to sing. C goes to toybox, searches, brings two toys to sibling, a music pipe and bells. Child holds out pipe to sibling and makes "blow" gesture with lips.

Later in the second year, unsolicited acts of helping in play were increasingly evident. By eighteen months, thirty of the forty children were observed to act cooperatively in this way (and thirty-eight of the forty acted cooperatively when requested to do so by their sibling). Here are two typical examples of unsolicited help from eighteen month-olds.

Family H (Study 1). Child 18 months
Sibling is playing game of running cars down a plastic track. C watches, runs to pick up car as it leaves track, brings it to sibling. Sibling runs car again, C again fetches it for him. Sequence repeated four times.

Family P (Study 2). Child 18 months
Sibling is acting out a fairy story with puppets. C watches, laughing. Goes to shelf and finds other puppets, appropriate to the play, and brings them to sibling.

The frequency of these unsolicited cooperative actions significantly increased between eighteen and twenty-four months (Dunn and Munn, 1986). The two-year-olds acted cooperatively in about 7 percent of their interactions, and in a further 6 percent they joined cooperatively in pretend play with siblings. The comparable figures for their older siblings' cooperative actions at these observations were 13 percent and 11 percent of the interactions. Interestingly, the proportion of the children's cooperative exchanges with their siblings did not increase *further* between twenty-four and thirty-six months. Even though the children's skills of cooperating grew over this third year, it seems that their motivation to do so did not increase. . . .

Reversal of Roles

Increasingly often during the second and third year, there were sequences of play in which the children not only took one role in a joint game but were able to reverse roles. This was at first at the sibling's suggestion, but toward the end of the second year, the younger children took their own initiative. Thus the child who was the chaser became the chased; the hider became the seeker. The smoothness with which two-year-olds carried out such role reversals illustrates how they could anticipate the actions of the other and coordinate their own behavior. . . .

339

Cooperation in Pretend

Perhaps the most striking feature of children's ability to cooperate in play during this transitional period is the ability to join in make-believe play. What such joint pretend play involves is the ability to share a pretend framework with another person, to carry out pretend actions in coordination with that other; it may also involve enacting the part of another person or thing, with the incorporation of another person into a reciprocal role (Miller and Garvey, 1981). In joint pretend play, then, we see not only the ability to coordinate and maintain a shared pretend framework but the mutual exploration of social rules and roles.

It is widely held that this is an advanced form of play, not shown until children are about three years old: "According to Piaget, pretend play is initially a solitary symbolic activity (Stage 1). Sociodramatic play (i.e., collective symbolism, Stage 2) does not begin until the latter part of the third year of life . . . Indirect evidence suggests that a shift from solitary to social pretense may occur at about three years of age" (Fein, 1981). But this account of the development of symbolic activity apparently reflects the way in which pretend play has been studied, rather than the way in which children's capacities actually develop. Joint pretend play has been almost exclusively studied in children over three, playing with peers. In one of the few studies that has looked at early role play at home in a family setting, Peggy Miller and Catherine Garvey (1984) described the development of play at "mothers and babies" between children and their mothers. Around twenty-eight months, while their mothers provided support and tutoring, the children began to act as "mother" to a baby (doll), caring for the doll, and acting in a nurturing and affectionate manner. As the months went by, mothers continued to act as supportive spectators. Around thirty months, the children first referred to their own transformed identity, and at about thirty-six months they started to announce a reciprocal role. One girl explicitly announced herself as mother and assigned the role of baby to another child. Miller and Garvey distinguish this role play, in which the child adopts an identity other than the self and explicitly announces a transformed identity, from the earlier role enactment—in which the child's role identity can be inferred from speech and action. For a child to manage to transform her own identity into that of another, and to incorporate the partner into the joint pretend game, entails both understanding and considerable communicative skill.

In considering the development of social understanding and of cooperation in particular, pretend play highlights some especially interesting changes in a child's abilities. In the context of a warm and affectionate sibling relationship, some children manage extremely early to take part in joint pretend play. Such play demonstrates, first, their ability effortlessly to share a non-literal framework; second, their ability to enact a role other than their own; third, their willingness to comply with the directions of the sibling; fourth, their ability to contribute innovations to that play; and fifth, their ability to play roles—to take on an identity other than their own and to coordinate the actions of this pretend person with those of another pretend person, played by the sibling.

The beginnings of these developments are seen as early as eighteen months. Take this

340

example from an observation of eighteen-month-old Mary, whose older sister Polly has set up a pretend birthday party with a cake, in the sand pit in the garden. Both children are singing "Happy Birthday"; in Mary's case the tune and the first two words are quite recognizable.

Family B (Study 1). Child 18 months

Sib: Dear Mary! You're three now.
C   (nods): Mmm.
Sib: You can go to school now.
C   (nods): Mmm.
Sib: Do you want to go to school now?
C   Mmm.
Sib: All right then. (Play voice) Hello Mary, I'm Mrs. Hunt. Do you want to help me do some of this birthday cake, do you? (Ordinary voice) We'd better do our birthday cake, hadn't we?
C   (sings appropriately): "Happy birthday . . ." (Both children walk around garden, singing.)
Sib: We're at church now. We have to walk along. I'm like Mummy and you're like Baby. I'm Mummy. (Play voice) What, little one? We'd better go back to our birthday then.
C   (sings): "Happy birthday . . ." (C holds hands up to sib to be carried.)
Sib: That's all right, little girl. Are you going to sleep?

Mary in this example enacts the role of a baby and behaves toward her sister as if Polly were the mother. In contrast to this baby behavior in the setting of the pretend game, she never once was observed to hold up her arms to be carried by her sister *out* of the context of pretend play, in the course of ten one-hour observations. According to the mother, this behavior was directed to her sibling only in the context of mother-baby games with the sibling as mother. Of the forty children in Study 2, six were, as eighteen-month-olds, instructed in joint pretend play in this manner by older siblings.

By twenty-four months, thirty-two of the forty secondborn children were observed to engage in joint pretend play, and the time spent in such play had increased significantly; by thirty-six months there was a further increase in frequency. Most interesting were the instances of joint role play in which the secondborn children demonstrated the ability to contribute to the pretend framework and that of taking on and explicitly announcing a new identity. Of our forty twenty-four-month-olds, thirteen were observed to play in this way, announcing their identity as *driver*, as *daddy*, as *mummy*, as *baby*, as named characters, and so on. . . .

The establishment and maintenance of joint play depends on both children's accepting or negotiating the other's contributions. Yet it is of course unclear exactly what the two-year-olds understand about the joint role game or about the identity transformations of themselves or their siblings in this play. On occasion the younger refused to obey the older's instructions and simply left the game. But the compliance that they usually showed to their siblings is striking, given their resistance to the sibling's commands in other nonplay circumstances. It is highly unlikely that the children would have obeyed the often fierce directions and prohibitions given by the sibling in the role of "mother" or "teacher" unless they recognized the nonliteral, playful nature of those commands. (For further analyses and discussion of siblings' joint pretend play, see Dunn and Dale, 1984.) . . .

In their second and third years, these children showed themselves to be willing cooperators in play, picking up the mood of the sibling, coordinating their own actions to those of the sibling, taking roles complementary to those of the sibling, and by two years old sharing the collective symbolism of a pretend world. In the context of play, the children *helped* toward achieving a mutual goal. Note, however, that this evidence for cooperation and aid does not conflict with the argument that self-concern is an important motivating force in a child's development. The play of the older sibling was rivetingly interesting for these children; the skills that the younger child was just developing were effortlessly and smoothly demonstrated by the older—and their play acted as a magnet to draw the attention of the younger. It was in the interest of the younger children to participate in such play, and when the game lacked appeal, they quickly stopped cooperating. Yet what stands out from these observations is the delight with which the children explored social roles and rules—hardly the behavior of children exclusively centered on their own narrow vision of the world. . . .

References

Dunn, J. and Dale, N. 1984. I a Daddy: 2-year-olds' collaboration in joint pretend with sibling and with mother. In I. Bretherton, ed., *Symbolic play: The development of social understanding.* New York: Academic Press.

_____and Kendrick, C. 1982. *Siblings: Love, envy, and understanding.* Cambridge, Mass.: Harvard University Press.

Fein, G. G. 1981. Pretend play in childhood: An integrative review. *Child Development*, 52, 1095-1118.

Miller, P., and Garvey, C. 1984. Mother-baby role play: Its origins in social support. In I. Bretherton, ed., *Symbolic play: The development of social understanding.* New York: Academic Press.

Sampson, A. and S. 1985. *Oxford book of ages.* London: Oxford University Press.

Sibling Interdependence and Child Caretaking:
A Cross-Cultural View
Thomas S. Weisner

In much of the world, children older than a year are typically under the care of siblings rather than adults. In this article, Thomas Weisner presents examples of sibling caregiving, describes the social and economic conditions under which this system of caregiving is most commonly found, and suggests possible psychological outcomes of sib care. Among groups such as Hawaiian-Americans and Polynesians in which sib care is the norm, families tend to be large, older children are usually home and available, and children participate with other members of the family and community in activities necessary for the group's survival. As the author suggests, patterns of sibling caregiving in the context of joint domestic activity reflect these social conditions and help shape the overall organization of sibling relations.

It is characteristic of such sibling groups, for example, that roles are flexible and activities shared; interdependence is high; and authority, although hierarchical, is benevolent. In return for obedience to older siblings, younger children receive nurturance and the opportunity to acquire skills through imitation, observation, and participation. Children's concerns lie with providing immediate assistance to siblings rather than with adult rules and rationalizations or with personal achievement. Relative to children in societies where parent care is the norm, children immersed in a sib care system are likely, in Weisner's view, to manifest a more diffuse pattern of attachment, a greater sense of social responsibility and sex-role identification, decreased involvement with adults, and enhanced peer orientation.

Some peculiar preoccupations characterize sibling research in the United States and Western Europe. Western views of siblings are limited—one might even say scientifically ethnocentric—because the preoccupations of Western sibling research are by and large the preoccupations of Western society: achievement; status and hierarchy; conformity and dependency; intelligence; rivalry and competition. Now siblings are indeed rivalrous; they

Weisner, Thomas S. (1982). Sibling interdependence and child caretaking: a cross-cultural view. In M.E. Lamb & B. Sutton-Smith (Eds). *Sibling Relationships: Their Nature and Significance across the Lifespan.* Hillsdale, NJ: Lawrence Erlbaum Associates. pp. 305-327.

often compete fiercely with each other, and age and ordinal position are important for understanding sibling relationships. But these are far from the only important topics. A cross-cultural view suggests a number of aspects seldom considered. Siblings conjointly perform important, responsible domestic tasks and chores essential to the subsistence and survival of the family; they are involved in cooperative child rearing; in defense, warfare, and protection; in arranging marriages and providing marriage payments. Siblings in most of the world strongly influence much of the lifecourse of their brothers and sisters by what they do. They share life crisis and rite of passage ceremonies essential to their cultural and social identity; they take on ritual and ceremonial responsibilities for each other essential to community spiritual ideals. *The sibling group in most societies around the world participates jointly throughout the life span in activities essential to survival, reproduction, and the transmission of cultural and social values.* . . .

Sibling Caretaking During Childhood: Hawaiian and Polynesian Examples

Introduction

In much of the world, children spend most of their time after infancy cared for by their older brothers and sisters, not primarily their mothers (Barry & Paxson, 1971; Whiting, 1963; Whiting & hiting, 1975). The organization of sibling relations, given these kinds of tasks and family responsibilities, differs dramatically from those of urban and industrial societies. In this section, I review a number of themes relevant to sibling care during childhood that illustrate the influence of the ecological niche and the local community on sibling roles and duties. The examples come primarily from Hawaii and Polynesia, and East Africa but the basic patterns apply broadly elsewhere.

Antecedents of Sibling Caretaking: Interdependence

Gallimore, Boggs, and Jordan (1974) developed a series of generalizations based on work with Hawaiian-Americans that synthesize material on the role of the sibling caretaking system in the larger context of shared family obligations:

Responsibility is shared and contingencies are placed on groups rather than individuals. The goals involve immediate assistance to others, as opposed to personal development and achievement, and it is assumed that the individual can rely heavily on the group for help in learning new skills and carrying out tasks [p. 67].

Interdependence includes household work and chores as well as wages when children reach adolescence and join the work force. Older children contribute more, and girls

344

steadily contribute more than boys.

> *For children and adolescents the principal role in the family is defined in terms of material contribution, cooperation, and helpfulness here and now. They are not regarded as trainees for life in another time and place; chore assignments are not designed to foster independence. The work contributed and the wages shared are needed by the family in the present, and young people are expected to do their part. Learning to contribute to the family is preparation for making more not less contributions in the future, with no expectation of a break in the continuity of living arrangements between adolescence and adulthood [p.81].*

Most sibling groups have a "shared-function" rather than a "fixed-role" organizational style [p. 84]. Sharing work and responsibility extends to relationships with parents, peers, and neighbors. Taking turns, substituting, and being interdependent characterizes most sibling groups of this kind. There is also a hierarchy of respect and authority for adults. Obedience to senior siblings, or parents, is extremely important. Successful shared sibling group functioning means that there is no trouble; the system works most smoothly when it goes *un*noticed by adults. Gallimore, Boggs, and Jordan describe this as "benevolent authoritarianism."

These three features of Hawaiian-American families (interdependence, shared functioning, and benevolent authoritarianism) characterize many sibling groups throughout the world. Such systems emphasize cooperation and the flexible allocation of scarce resources. Sibling cooperation, solidarity, and authority of older over younger all flow from this kind of family system.

One of the things about sib care that is most important but least well understood ethnographically is that it is a preeminently shared activity. Sib care nearly always occurs in the context of other activities; it is happening when other people are around, and when other work tasks or chores, games, play, lounging, etc. are going on at the same time. In these contexts sib care is often subsumed under an indirect caretaking hierarchy. The mother may be nearby and apparently not involved in childcare, yet children are watching out for one another knowing that their mother is within shouting distance. Children often play with, help, and discipline one another in the home when the parents are around. The parents seem overtly uninvolved under such circumstances. But their involvement is covert and indirect. This kind of subtle attentiveness to other family members is an integral part of sib care (Ritchie & Ritchie, 1979).

Teaching and learning are often accomplished by graduated stages of participation, and through modeling and imitation of others (Jordan, 1977). Teachers and models are often older children, not parents. Indirect, frequently nonverbal styles of requesting and managing are common.

As infants, children in most Hawaiian and Polynesian families are largely under the direct care of adults (Jordan, 1981; Jordan & Tharp, 1979). Babies receive a good deal of attention from older children also, but do spend most of their time with adults.

345

However, a Hawaiian child as young as one or two may begin to spend a high proportion of time in the company of other children, as the charge of an older child. Most children will be full-fledged members of such a group by age three or four.

Thus, after infancy many Polynesian children are accustomed to spending most of their time with other children rather than with adults or in solitary activity (e.g. Levy, 1968; 1973). They are accustomed to working in a group context with siblings, without immediate adult direction. Although under the supervision of adults, children are expected to be able to carry out their responsibilities without intruding upon adults for help or direction. The group of children is expected to have within itself resources sufficient to carry out tasks that are assigned to it. Adults may relate to the teenage "top sergeant" of a group directly, or just address the group as a whole, rather than talk one-to-one with each individual child.

Hawaiian children acquire skills and knowledge in nonschool settings by participating in activities and tasks with the more competent children of their sibling or companion group (and, to a lesser extent, with adults). This means that they come to learn from a variety of people and that one of their main sources of help, skills, and information is other children. Moreover, they are accustomed to changing roles from that of "learner" to that of "teacher," depending on their competence for a particular function relative to others in the group.

As a consequence, children tend to be highly peer-oriented, and uncomfortable in intensive one-to-one interaction with adults. One would expect that they would also have in their repertoire of behaviors well-developed strategies for teaching and learning from peers and near-peers and to be skilled in utilizing a variety of persons as sources of information and help.

Structural Antecedents of Sib Care: Ecology and Demography

What more general conditions tend to promote the occurrence of sibling caretaking? The evidence indicates that factors related to sheer availability and propinquity of family members, as well as a number of institutional pressures, influence the occurrence of sib care at the cultural level. Conditions associated with sibling caretaking include: larger family size; lineal descent and residence patterns; and a daily routine that makes personnel available for sibling care (that is, where older children are available for sibling care during most parts of the day, and there is a heavy, persistent, routinized workload, some of which can be done in or near the home). Societies emphasizing kin and community cooperation in the performance of tasks and chores also tend to be societies that utilize sib care (see Leiderman & Leiderman, 1973; Whiting & Whiting, 1975).

Sib care often functions as a relief and support system for parents and is used as such in order to free parents to perform important subsistence chores or to engage in adult community involvements away from the home. Sib care also provides a training ground for parenting. Girls in particular learn very early the roles required to be an effective caretaker. Girls learn to differentiate different types of infants—their temperaments, cries,

346

maturational stages, and so forth. They have had wide experience with childcare before they become parents themselves. They also have dealt with their brothers and sisters in both a superordinate and subordinate role, a flexible status they will have to carry on throughout life in many other functional areas (marriage arrangements, bridewealth, inheritance, protection for their own children, and so forth). These are all consequences of a "polymatric" caretaking system (Leiderman & Leiderman, 1977; Fox, 1967).

Infancy, early toddlerhood, and later childhood are clearly quite different stages in caretaking style in general and sib care in particular (Barry, Josephson, Lauer, & Marshall, 1980). During infancy mothers are usually involved in infant care and do not often delegate responsibility. If work roles take the mother fairly far from the home, the infant goes with the mother. A mother who works in or near the home can carry her baby on her back. Infant care is delegated more often when women have a moderate distance to travel, allowing a return for feeding. In early toddlerhood, children are more often left with sibs, and are gradually pushed out of the nest, away from the mother's direct involvement. Older children will carry these toddlers, ages twelve months to three years old, on their hip or back, often staggering slightly under the weight.

Sibling caretaking, then, is part of a larger childhood experience that stresses interdependence. It is also a form of childcare that is reflected in other institutions in adult life that involve sibling roles—that is, it is not an institution that begins and ends in childhood and exists solely as an aid to parental care or as a means of defense and survival in childhood only. It is also a means to train children to behave in ways and to have expectations and responsibilities towards their siblings that will stand them in good stead throughout life. Sib care provides analogues to patterns of adult life.

Some Social and Personality Correlates of Sib Care

Weisner and Gallimore (1977) have suggested a number of characteristics of child caretakers that might be related to participation in a sibling caretaking system. Children in such a system may show a more diffuse affective style and a diffuse pattern of attachment to adults and other children (but cf. Munroe & Munroe, 1980). The social role responsibilities of older siblings should produce increased social responsibility, increased nurturance toward appropriate targets, earlier and stronger sex role identification, and a more task-specific division of labor (Whiting & Whiting, 1975). These patterns should result from early training for and participation in caretaking hierarchies and family work.

Children gradually are initiated into both charge and caretaker roles, sometimes at the same time. A six-year-old boy may be watched over by his older sister, but also occasionally may be given responsibility for getting his three-year-old brother around the neighborhood. Children learn early both sides of caretaking activities. They learn to take the role of others in the sense of appropriately and responsibly performing caretaking tasks and to respond to others doing the same to them. They learn context-specific, role-appropriate behavior in these ways.

347

Sib care appears to decrease orientation and involvement with adults, and increases orientation toward a multiage, multisex group of peers and playmates. Along with this decreased orientation toward adults, children do not appear to receive the same "negotiated rationalizations" and adult understandings of norms that they would receive if involved in compliance or behavior change with their parents or other adults on a routine basis. Sib care is not usually found along with the elaborate rehearsal of the rules, reasons, rationales, exceptions, and adult understandings Western middle class children acquire in the company of their parents. Children in sib care settings learn through observation in natural contexts. They learn by imitation and mimicry, and through sharing and cooperation, rather than through highly verbal modes. . . .

References

Barry, H., III, Josephson, L., Lauer, E., & Marshall, C. Agents and techniques for child training: Cross-cultural codes 6. In H. Barry III & A. Schlegel (Eds.), *Cross-cultural samples and codes*. Pittsburgh: University of Pittsburgh Press, 1980.

Barry, H., III, & Paxson, L. M. Infancy and early childhood: Cross-cultural codes 2. *Ethnology*, 1971, *10*, 466-508.

Fox, L. K. (Ed.). *East African childhood: Three versions*. London: Oxford University Press. 1967.

Gallimore, R., Boggs, J. W., & Jordan, C. *Culture, behavior and education: A study of Hawaiian-Americans*. Beverly Hills, Calif.: Sage Publications, 1974.

Jordan, C. *Maternal teaching, peer teaching and school adaptation in an urban Hawaiian population*. Honolulu: The Kamehameha Early Education Program, The Kamehameha Schools, 1977.

Jordan, C. *Educationally effective ethnology: A study of the contributions of cultural knowledge to effective education for minority children*. Unpublished dissertation, University of California at Los Angeles, 1981.

Jordan, C., & Tharp, R. Culture and education. In A. J. Marcella, R. G. Tharp, & T. J. Ciborowski (Eds.) *Perspectives in cross-cultural psychology*. New York: Academic Press, 1979.

Leiderman, H. P., & Leiderman, G. F. *Polymatric infant care in the East African highlands: Some affective and cognitive consequences*. Paper presented at the Minnesota Symposium on Child Development, Minneapolis, 1973.

Leiderman, H. P., & Leiderman, G. F. Economic change and infant care in an East African agricultural community. In P. H. Leiderman, S. R. Tulkin, & A. Rosenfeld (Eds.), *Culture and infancy: Variations in the human experience.* New York: Academic Press, 1977.

Levy, R. I. Child management structure and its implications in a Tahitian family. In E. Vogel & N. Bell (Eds.), *A modern introduction to the family.* New York: The Free Press, 1968.

Levy, R. I. *Tahitians: Mind and experience in the society islands.* Chicago: University of Chicago Press, 1973.

Munroe, R. H., & Munroe, R. G. Infant experience and childhood affect among the Logoli: A longitudinal study. *Ethos,* 1980, *8,* 295-315.

Ritchie, J., & Ritchie, J. *Growing up in Polynesia.* Sydney, Australia: George Allen and Unwin, 1979

Weisner, T. W., & Gallimore, R. My brother's keeper: Child and sibling caretaking. *Current Anthropology,* 1977, *18,* 169-191.

Whiting, B. B. (Ed.) *Six cultures: Studies of child rearing.* New York: John Wiley & Sons, Inc., 1963.

Whiting, B. B., & Whiting, J. W. M. *Children of six cultures: A psychocultural analysis.* Cambridge: Harvard University Press, 1975.

UNIT 5: Schooling

15

Day Care and the American 'Cult of Motherhood'

High quality day care in the West is expensive, and in many countries competition for places is great. In Russia and China where women are considered vital to the workforce, there are extensive networks of child care and crèches in factories and offices. Hungary has day care of an enviably high standard. Pre-school provision, between approximately three and five (or compulsory schooling age) varies widely — 44% of children in Great Britian go to some form of pre-school, in comparison to 88% in Italy, 95% in Tokyo and 80% in Beijing.

• INTRODUCTION •

Virtually all American children will spend some portion of their early childhood under the care of adults to whom they are not related. Many of these children will be in family or center day care, out of their own homes, for anywhere from twenty to forty or more hours per week. Increasingly, children's initial experience with day care occurs during the first year, sometimes even in the first few months of life. In this society, the need for day care is a direct reflection of the number of single parents and of the fact that in most two-parent families both parents are now employed. Many mothers who would traditionally have remained at home as primary caregivers are now in the work force. Relative to the circumstances in which families lived only a generation or two ago, this represents a major shift. Motherhood must now often be managed in the face of a variety of conflicting extra-familial demands. Day care has become a fact of life.

As the social realities have changed, what has become of the relevant social values? Does this society look favorably on maternal employment? Do we make day care easily accessible? Do we believe that children's psychological needs can be met by non-maternal caregivers? As a society, we have long valued the sanctity of motherhood. We have espoused the view that children need their mothers, at least in those crucial first few years, if they are to develop into happy, well-adjusted adults. Americans are therefore profoundly ambivalent about maternal employment and day care for young children, especially for infants. Women who choose or are forced by economic circumstance to be employed are subjected to conflicting messages: "Follow your interests, actualize your potential, produce an income; but don't neglect your children." Ironically, women who choose to stay at home to raise their children are no less affected by this ambivalence. "Stay at home, be available to your children; but don't settle for welfare or for being *just* a housewife."

In the two readings chosen for this module, we are introduced to the historical origins and to some of the contemporary consequences of this ambivalence. In the first, Barbara Ehrenreich and Deirdre English describe the emergence in American middle-class consciousness of the belief that children represent the future and that mothers have a sacred

354

duty to humanity to safeguard that future by devoting themselves to child rearing. In the second, Sandra Scarr, Deborah Phillips, and Kathleen McCartney analyze a series of "fantasies" concerning the role of mothers in children's development that continue to influence American views of child care.

• • •

The Century of the Child
Barbara Ehrenreich and Deirdre English

Toward the end of the nineteenth century, progress in public health and sanitation contributed to a sharp decrease in infant mortality. Along with this decrease came a reduction in fertility within marriage. Parents who now had reason to believe that most of their children would survive to adulthood began to limit family size and to allocate greater psychological and economic resources to each individual child.

At the same time, the pace of social and technological change was accelerating rapidly. In the period after the Civil War, America experienced unprecedented industrial growth, wave after wave of immigration, and a geometric increase in the population of urban centers. In the midst of this change, Americans began to realize that the only safe prediction that could be made about the future is that it would be unlike the past.

In this excerpt, taken from a book in which Barbara Ehrenreich and Deirdre English analyze the history of advice to women, the authors focus on the change, at the end of the nineteenth century, in mortality, fertility, and social conditions, and the impact of that change on views of the child and of motherhood. As Ehrenreich and English indicate, the turn of the century saw the emergence of a new view of the child. Amidst a growing recognition that accommodation to the uncertainties in the human future might depend less on current skills than on the ability to adapt flexibly to change, society turned to children as the key to the future. Malleable and inexperienced, children could be educated as individuals to be ready for anything that the future might hold. The twentieth century was to be the Century of the Child.

355

While much of the promise inherent in America's discovery of the child has gone unfulfilled, this shift in orientation nonetheless had a number of significant consequences. Chief among them, perhaps, was a concomitant emphasis on the essential role of women as mothers. If children were the key to the future, then those whose task it was to raise the children had been given the key for safekeeping. Even many turn-of-the-century feminists accepted the notion that women had a sacred duty to humanity to stay at home and devote themselves to caring for and educating those who would lead humankind forward into the unknown. Motherhood and homemaking, in these terms, became a noble calling and a profession. A constellation of social values that some have called the American Cult of Motherhood had been created.

Right at the turn of the century, America "discovered" the child as the leading figure in the family, if not in history itself.

"If I were asked what is to be accounted the great discovery of this century," the school superintendent of the State of Georgia told the National Education Association in late 1899:

I would pass by all the splendid achievements that men have wrought in wood and stone and iron and brass. I would not go to the volume that catalogs the printing-press, the loom, the steam-engine, the steamship, the ocean cable, the telegraph, the wireless telegraphy, the telephone, the phonograph, I would not call for the Roentgen ray that promises to revolutionize the study of the human brain as well as the human body. Above and beyond all these the index finger of the world's progress, in the march of time, would point unerringly to the little child as the one great discovery of the century now speeding to its close.[1]

"On the whole it cannot be doubted that America has entered upon 'the century of the child,'" wrote social historian Calhoun. ". . . As befits a civilization with a broadening future, the child is becoming the center of life."[2]

The discovery of the child by adult male public figures, scientists and experts of various kinds, was a step filled with humanistic promise. Perhaps women had always known what the male authorities were now asserting: that the child is not just a stunted adult, but a creature with its own needs, capabilities, harms. Now, with public recognition of the special needs of children, the door was potentially opened to public *responsibility* for meeting those needs: vastly expanded programs for child welfare and

Ehrenreich, Barbara and English, Deirdre. (1978). *For Her Own Good. 150 Years of the Expert's Advice to Women.* Garden City, NY: Anchor Press/Doubleday. Chapter 6 (The century of the child). pp. 165-189.

health, free public day care, community resources for dealing with problems which arise in child raising, and so forth. But, except for the expansion of the public school system in the early twentieth century, very little of this promise was realized. The children who had been "discovered" with so much fanfare would remain the individual responsibility of their mothers. What historian Calhoun failed to explain was that the child was becoming the "center of life" only for women. Any larger social interest in the child would be expressed by the emerging group of child-raising *experts*—and they of course had no material help to offer, but only a stream of advice, warnings, instructions to be consumed by each woman in her isolation. . . .

Discovery of the Child

What had happened near the turn of the century to bring the child out of the background and into the spotlight of public attention? The discovery of the child as a unique and novel form of life, . . . could not have been made in the Old Order. Even a hundred years earlier, the individual child was hardly a figure to command the attention of adult men. Women had, on the average, seven live births in the course of their lives; a third or a half would not survive to the age of five. Each individual child had to be seen as a possibly temporary visitor. Frontier parents often left their infants nameless for many months, lest they "waste" a favorite name; and mothers spoke not only of how many children they had raised, but of how many they had buried. This note in a local Wisconsin paper, October 1885, was typical for an era when it was the young, not the mature, who lived in the shadow of death:

> *The malignant diphtheria epidemic in Louis Valley, La Crosse County, proved fatal to all the children in Martin Molloy's family, five in number. Three died in a day. The house and furniture was burned.*[3]

By 1900 child mortality was already declining—not because of anything the medical profession had accomplished, but because of general improvements in sanitation and nutrition.[4] Meanwhile the birthrate had dropped to an average of about three and a half; women expected each baby to live and were already taking measures to prevent more than the desired number of pregnancies.[5] From a strictly biological standpoint then, children were beginning to come into their own.

Economic changes too pushed the child into sudden prominence at the turn of the century. Those fabled, pre-industrial children who were "seen, but not heard," were, most of the time, hard at work— weeding, sewing, fetching water and kindling, feeding the animals, watching the baby. Today, a four-year-old who can tie his or her own shoes is impressive. In colonial times, four-year-old girls knitted stockings and mittens and could produce intricate embroidery; at age six they spun wool.[6] A good, industrious little girl was called "Mrs." instead of "Miss" in appreciation of her contribution to the family economy: she was not, strictly speaking, a child.

But when production left the household, sweeping away the dozens of chores which had filled the child's day, childhood began to stand out as a distinct and fascinating phase of life. It was as if the late Victorian imagination, still unsettled by Darwin's apes, suddenly looked down and discovered, right at knee-level, the evolutionary missing link. Here was the pristine innocence which adult men romanticized, and of course, here, in miniature, was the future which today's adult men could not hope to enter in person. In the child lay the key to the *control* of human evolution. Its habits, its pastimes, its companions were no longer trivial matters, but issues of gravest importance to the entire species.

This sudden fascination with the child came at a time in American history when child abuse—in the most literal and physical sense—was becoming an institutional feature of the expanding industrial economy. Near the turn of the century, an estimated 2,250,000 American children under fifteen[7] were full-time laborers—in coal mines, glass factories, textile mills, canning factories, in the cigar industry, and in the homes of the wealthy—in short, wherever cheap and docile labor could be used. There can be no comparison between the conditions of work for a farm child (who was also in most cases a beloved family member) and the conditions of work for industrial child laborers. Four-year-olds worked sixteen-hour days sorting beads or rolling cigars in New York City tenements; five-year-old girls worked the night shift in southern cotton mills.

So long as enough girls can be kept working, and only a few of them faint, the mills are kept going; but when faintings are so many and so frequent that it does not pay to keep going, the mills are closed.[8]

These children grew up hunched and rickety, sometimes blinded by fine work or the intense heat of furnaces, lungs ruined by coal dust or cotton dust—when they grew up at all. Not for them the "century of the child," or childhood in any form:

The golf links lie so near the mill
That almost every day
The laboring children can look out
And see the men at play.[9]

Child labor had its ideological defenders: educational philosophers who extolled the lessons of factory discipline, the Catholic hierarchy which argued that it was a father's patriarchal right to dispose of his children's labor, and of course the mill owners themselves. But for the reform-oriented, middle-class citizen the spectacle of machines tearing at baby flesh, of factories sucking in files of hunched-over children each morning, inspired not only public indignation, but a kind of personal horror. Here was the ultimate "rationalization" contained in the logic of the Market: all members of the family reduced alike to wage slavery, all human relations, including the most ancient and intimate, dissolved in the cash nexus. Who could refute the logic of it? There was no rationale (within the terms of the Market) for supporting idle, dependent children. There were no ties of economic self-interest to preserve the family. Child labor represented a long step toward that ultimate "anti-utopia" which always seemed to be germinating in capitalist development: a world engorged by the Market, a world without love.

So, on the one hand, the turn-of-the-century focus on the child was an assertion of what were felt to be traditional human values against the horrors of industrial capitalism. The child represented, as it had for decades, a romanticized past—rural, home-centered, governed by natural rhythms rather than by the industrial time-clock. Psychologist G. Stanley Hall saw children as a race related to the "savages" of Africa—gentle, spontaneous, and badly in need of protection by grown (white) men.

But it was not only the romantic, pastoral image of childhood which inspired the "century of the child." The Little Child in whose name so many reform campaigns were waged—for compulsory education, public health programs, etc.—was not only a symbol of the past but of the industrial future. Addressing a women's meeting in 1898, Dr. W. N. Hailman refuted the "primitive" image of the child as either a "little animal" or "an embryo savage" and presented children as the evolutionary vanguard of the race:

> *Childhood is not a makeshift to keep mankind from dying out; but it is the very abrogation of death, the continued life of humanity in its onward march to its divine destiny . . . It is childhood's teachableness that has enabled man to overcome heredity with history . . . The very meaning and mission of childhood is the continuous progress of humanity. It, and it alone, renders life worth living.*[10]

The exaltation of the child for its "teachableness" and pliancy reflected a growing sense that children might be actually better suited to the industrial world than adults. Turn-of-the-century America was suffering from a massive case of "future shock." Technology seemed to remold the world anew each day: What good was experience? How could "maturity" mean anything other than obsolescence? With the introduction of scientific management and assembly-line procedures, industry was coming to need the pliant youth more than the seasoned craftsman. The rise of the child (and decline of the patriarchal father) was probably most wrenching in immigrant working-class families: the parents often remained, in their attitudes and language, uprooted peasants, helplessly dependent on the son or daughter who had gone to an American school, knew English, and understood the ways of the big city.

The idea that the child was the key to the future, banal as it sounds, had a definite political message. To say that the child alone held the key to social change was to say that the present generation of adults did not. That, contrary to the hopes of socialists and militant unionists, the social structure could not be transformed within a single generation. Child-centrist ideology pictured society inching toward reform generation by generation. The professional or businessman of Yankee stock and the Polish laborer might appear, temporarily, to be members of different species, but, with an "American" upbringing, there would be less of a gap between their sons, even less between their grandsons, and so forth. Social distinctions would dissolve, over time, through mass public education, while improved methods of child raising would produce a "higher" type of human personality. By concentrating on the child—rather than on, say, political agitation, union organizing, or other hasty alternatives—the just society could be achieved painlessly, albeit a little slowly.

Thus the turn-of-the-century exaltation of the child was both romantic and rationalist, conservative and progressive. The child was "primitive" but this meant it was also malleable, hence really more "modern" than anyone else. The child was the reason to seek reforms, and also a reason to defer them. The child was the "founder of the family," the foundation of the home; it was also the only member of the family truly prepared (by virtue of its very inexperience) for the technological turmoil of the outside world. Only the figure of the child held the key to a future which could contain both behemoth factories and nurturing hearthsides, the cold logic of Wall Street and the sentimental warmth of Christmas.

The "Child Question" and the Woman Question

If it was not always crystal clear how a concentration on the child would solve such social problems as labor unrest or urban corruption, it was obvious at once that the child held the answer to the Woman Question. The child was no longer "a mere incident in the preservation of the species" but the potential link to a higher plateau of evolutionary development. Since no one else was going to take responsibility for the child, it fell to the individual mother to forge that link. The Swedish writer Ellen Key's 1909 bestseller, *The Century of the Child*, spelled out the new evolutionary responsibilities of womanhood:

> *Women in parliament and in journalism, their representation in the local and general government, in peace congresses and workingmen's meetings, science and literature, all this will produce small results until women realize that the transformation of society begins with the unborn child. . . . This transformation requires an entirely new conception of the vocation of mother, a tremendous effort of will, continuous inspiration.*[11]

According to Key, only by dint of a total focus on children, for several generations, could women hope to bring forth "the completed man—the Superman." Key's proposals were radical—she argued that even monogamy should be abandoned if it got in the way of women's selection of evolutionarily suitable mates—but other than that her thinking was completely in tune with the establishment's romantic line. Nothing could be more important than motherhood, President Roosevelt told a gathering of women:

360

The good mother, the wise mother—you cannot really be a good mother if you are not a wise mother—is more important to the community than even the ablest man; her career is more worthy of honor and is more useful to the community than the career of any man, no matter how successful, can be. . . .

But . . . the woman who, whether from cowardice, from selfishness, from having a false and vacuous ideal shirks her duty as wife and mother, earns the right to our contempt, just as does the man who, from any motive, fears to do his duty in battle when the country calls him.[12]

Many women agreed, either because they were proud to find themselves in such an important career, or because, as the President warned, the only alternative was contempt. An American female speaker told an international conference on motherhood in 1908:

With clear eyes we must see the goal of our effort and with unfaltering steps journey towards it. The goal is nothing less than the redemption of the world through the better education of those who are able to shape it and make it. The keeper of the gates of to-morrow is the little child upon a mother's arms. The way of that kingdom which is to come on earth, as in heaven, is placed in the hands of a child, and that child's hands a woman holds.[13]

In the reflected glory of the child, motherhood could no longer be seen as a biological condition or a part-time occupation; it was becoming a "noble calling."

So stridently does a "century of the child" cry out for a cult of motherhood that it would be easy enough, in retrospect, to dismiss the whole fixation on children as just another advertisement for female domesticity. In part it was: a woman's home can have no sturdier gatekeeper than a tiny child. Yet something else was going on too: the discovery of the child was, in one sense, a discovery of the *power* of women. In the official ideology of the time, woman was already sequestered in the realm of private life, which was, after all, "her sphere." Here, because of the triviality of domestic concerns, she was even allowed to "reign," just as the man supposedly did outside. But now it is as if the masculinist imagination takes a glance over its shoulder and discovers it has left something important behind in "woman's sphere"—the child. This child—the new child of the twentieth century—is not valued, like the child of patriarchy, simply as an heir. This child is conceived as a kind of evolutionary protoplasm, a means of *control* over society's not-so-distant future. This child cannot be left to women.

It follows that if children must be left with their mothers, they must not be left *alone* with them. A new figure will enter the family tableau—a man equipped to manage both children and mothers *and* to direct the interaction between them—the scientific expert in child raising.

The rapid rise of the child-raising experts reflected the growing prestige of experts in other areas of women's lives. The male takeover of healing had weakened the communal bonds among women—the networks of skill and information sharing—and had created a model for professional authority in all areas of domestic activity. But the terrain that the psychomedical experts began to chart with the "discovery" of the child was, if anything, more ancient, more essentially female, than healing had been. Healing itself is an outgrowth of mothering, a response to the exigencies of childbirth, sick babies, winter colds, etc. When the experts enter the area of child raising, they step into what had been, for better or for worse, the irreducible core of women's existence, the last refuge of her skills and dignity.

The Mothers' Movement

The experts did not, however, come uninvited. The "modern" educated young woman near the turn of the century refused to see child raising as something instinctive, like appetite, or automatic, like uterine contractions. Everything else was coming into conformity with the industrial age and becoming "scientific"—why not the ancient activity of child raising? In 1888 a group of upper-middle-class New York City mothers constituted themselves the Society for the Study of Child Nature and set out to explore every facet of child "nature"— from music appreciation to the concept of private property. These women, according to historian Bernard Wishy "were eager to defer as much as possible to the best ideas, but they now wanted their information directly from experts trained in child study rather than from popular writers."[14] Within the next decade, the idea of women gathering to study and discuss child raising caught on throughout the country. Child study and mothers' clubs sprang up by the score, child study lecturers toured the land, pamphlets and articles proliferated—as if American womanhood was busily cramming for the upcoming "century of the child."

The "mothers' movement"—for they did consider themselves a movement—was a response to some of the same forces which brought forth the domestic science movement. If, in the pre-industrial farm home "housekeeping" had never been an issue, neither had child raising. The mother-child relationship had been shaped by the round of daily tasks; it was always in part an apprenticeship relationship. "Child raising" meant teaching children the skills and discipline required to keep the home industries running. It was not something that one *did*, so much as it was something that happened, or had to happen, if the family's work was to be done.

But within the Domestic Void of the modern home, there is no longer any "natural" way to raise children. There are fewer and fewer skills to acquire in the home, and those that there are bear little relation to the skills that the child (especially the male child) might eventually need in the outside world. Learning to help Mother pick up around the house will not help Johnny pass the college boards ten years later or teach Susy to type. With the separation of home and work, private and public realms, the standards for "success" in child raising came to be set outside the home, beyond the mother's control. Paradoxically, the "better" the mother—the more singlemindedly home-oriented she is—the less experience she will have had in the outside world where her efforts will eventually be judged. In the sexually segregated society built by industrial capitalism on the ruins of the Old Order, there is, in the end, no way for *women* to raise *men*.

The mothers' movement, like the domestic science movement, was an attempt to make a dignified response to this difficult and contradictory situation. In the setting of the Domestic Void, housekeeping priorities were unclear, child raising was baffling. Women were naturally drawn together to discuss domestic issues, share information, and study whatever scientific advice was available. In their recognition that child raising was not a matter of instinct, or mere supervision, they had made real progress over the women (two generations earlier) who had no time to think of children as anything but miniature assistants. But if the women who gathered in the turn-of-the-century mothers' clubs were prepared to confront the problems posed by their new situation as mothers, they were *not* prepared to challenge that situation itself. The domestic science leaders who had gazed, with horror, into the Domestic Void, did not propose to abandon the home. And the mothers' movement was not about to suggest that there might be more congenial, collective settings for child raising.

In fact, when the mothers' movement took institutional form as the National Congress of Mothers in 1897, its concern over the preservation of the home seemed almost to outweigh its concern for children. For example, in the Congress' 1908 Declaration of Principles the word "home" appears four times in the first four principles; "child" or "children" only twice. The opening principles begin, "Whereas, the home is the basis of society . . ." continuing:

> *Whereas, the God-given function of parenthood is the highest, most far reaching duty of humanity, and the performance and sacredness of marriage is the foundation of society . . .*
> *Whereas, All students of social conditions seeking the causes of crime and disease trace them to inefficient homes . . .*
> *Whereas, Homes are inefficient because there is nothing in education to fit young people [i.e., women] for wise home makers . . .*[15]

The national mothers' conferences did give women a chance to hear from the few child-raising experts of the day—G. Stanley Hall and the Rockefellers' pediatrician Emmett Holt—but to judge from the conference proceedings, the real issue at hand was the Woman Question. As Mrs. Birney asked at the first conference, ". . . How, I ask, can we divorce the woman question from the child question?"[16] Neither the movement's leaders—upper-class women like Mrs. Adlai Stevenson and millionaire Phoebe Hearst—nor the rank and file which consisted of middle-American clubwomen—were in any sense feminists. If anything, the National Congress of Mothers represented a contemporary backlash against feminism, like the "right-to-life" movement in the nineteen seventies. "We need not care who makes the laws," one speaker asserted, "if we, as mothers, will make *them* what they should be."[17] Mrs. Birney, the Congress president for several years, expressed her faith that the inherent Anglo-Saxon love of home would "eventually turn back into the home the tide of femininity which is now streaming outward in search of a career."[18]

But contemporary feminists, as we have already seen, were as thoroughly committed to the cult of domesticity as were their more conservative sisters in the mothers' movement. "Woman is the mother of the race," gushed Boston suffragist Julia Ward Howe, "the guardian of its helpless infancy, its earliest teacher, its most zealous champion. Woman is also the homemaker, upon her devolve the details which bless and beautify family life."[19] A more scientific approach to child raising promised to elevate the status of woman's traditional occupation, and the higher the status of woman (in any role) the stronger the argument for female suffrage. What's more, feminists could use the "mother heart" as an excuse for almost every area of female activism—social welfare and reform, even the suffrage struggle. "The age of Feminism," declared feminist Beatrice Hale, "is also the age of the child. The qualms of the timorous should be allayed by this fact, which proves that women, in gaining in humanity do not lose in womanliness."[20] And feminists had good reason to try to disguise their activities as an expanded form of mothering: the tenor of the times was such that even the National Congress of Mothers was criticized for drawing women out of their homes.

In a speech which both feminists and antifeminists (or perhaps we should say suffragists and antisuffragists) could probably have agreed with, a Mrs. Harriet Hickox Heller expressed her confidence at the second annual National Congress of Mothers that higher education would not destroy the maternal instinct:

> . . . all the "isms" and "ologies" known, all the languages living and dead; all the caps and gowns; even all the eyeglasses, are not sufficient to eradicate from any feminine heart the desire to nurture the young of her kind.[21]

Yet, she admitted, higher education could somewhat attenuate that instinct. Child care was not sufficiently challenging to the woman who had had a taste of "isms" and "ologies." If it was to absorb the whole woman, it would have to be redefined, amplified and enriched. Just as the domestic scientists had declared their intention of filling the Domestic Void, Mrs. Heller exhorted: *Let us discover the lens that will focus all a woman's power upon her motherhood.* [Emphasis hers.]

The immediate solution—exactly as in the case of housework—was to reinterpret motherhood as a *profession.* "It seems to me," National Congress of Mothers' president Birney told the second annual convention

> that we should all perceive what intelligent parenthood means for the race, and that to attain it is as well worth our effort and attention as the study of Greek, Latin, higher mathematics, medicine, law or any other profession.[22]

A writer in *Cosmopolitian* magazine urged that motherhood be formally instituted as a profession, open only to those who could demonstrate "fitness." "Doctors and lawyers and teachers and clergymen fit themselves to have charge of human lives. Why should not mothers?"[23] And even Charlotte Perkins Gilman was arguing, though from a position of rationalist feminism, that mothering must become "brain work and soul work" rather than "brute instinct."[24]

The idea that motherhood was a profession, potentially requiring advanced degrees and licenses, may have been unsettling to the average, uncredentialed mother. But there was also something reassuring about it. To insist on the need for "professionals" rather than old-fashioned amateurs was at least to admit that child raising had indeed become a tricky business. The mother who felt isolated, confused, and irritated reminded herself that her occupation was known to be a difficult and challenging career. She was confined to her home but within those confines she could be as purposeful and rational as any enterprising man of the world. And indeed, given the contradictions built into child raising in this privatized and strangely peripheral setting, she would have to be.

Notes

1. Richard Hofstadter, *Anti-Intellectualism in American Life* (New York: Alfred A. Knopf, 1963), p. 364.

2. Arthur W. Calhoun, *Social History of the American Family, Volume III: Since the Civil War* (Cleveland: The Arthur H. Clark Co., 1919), p. 131.

3. Quoted in Michael Lesy, *Wisconsin Death Trip* (New York: Pantheon, 1973) (unpaginated).

4. See René Dubos, *The Mirage of Health* (New York: Harper, 1959); René Dubos, *Man Adapting* (New Haven: Yale University Press, 1965); Thomas McKeown, *Medicine in Modern Society* (London: Allen and Unwin, 1965); A. L. Cochrane, *Effectiveness and Efficiency: Random Reflections on Health Services* (London: Oxford University Press, 1972).

5. See Linda Gordon, *Woman's Body, Woman's Right: A Social History of Birth Control in America* (New York: Grossman, 1977).

6. William F. Ogburn and M. F. Nimkoff, *Technology and the Changing Family* (Boston and New York: Houghton Mifflin, 1955), p. 195.

7. John Spargo, *The Bitter Cry of the Children* (New York and London: Johnson Reprint Corp.,1969, first published 1906), p. 145.

8. Quoted in Spargo, op. cit., p. 179.

9. Sarah N. Cleghorn, quoted in "Child Labor," *Encyclopedia Americana*, Vol. 6 (New York: Americana Corp., 1974), p. 460.

10. Dr. W. N. Hailman, "Mission of Childhood," Proceedings of the National Congress of Mothers Second Annual Convention, May 1898, p. 171.

11. Ellen Key, *The Century of the Child* (New York: G. P. Putnam, 1909), pp. 100-1.

12. Theodore Roosevelt, Address to the First International Congress in America on the Welfare of the Child, under the auspices of The National Congress of Mothers, Washington, D.C., March 1908.

13. Lucy Wheelock, "The Right Education of Young Women," speech given at the First International Congress in America on the Welfare of the Child, Washington, D.C., March 1908.

14. Bernard Wishy, *The Child and the Republic: The Dawn of Modern American Child Nurture* (Philadelphia: University of Pennsylvania Press, 1968), p. 117.

15. Declaration of Principles, First International Congress in America on the Welfare of the Child, Washington, D.C., March 1908.

16. Mrs. Theodore W. Birney, "Address of Wel-come," *The Work and Words of The National Congress of Mothers* (New York: D. Appleton, 1897), p. 7.

17. Dr. Alice Moqué, "The Mistakes of Mothers," Proceedings of the National Congress of Mothers Second Annual Convention, Washington, D.C., May 1898, p. 44.

18. Mrs. Theodore W. Birney, "Presidential Ad-dress," Proceedings of the Third Annual Convention of The National Congress of Mothers, Washington, D.C., February 1899, p. 198.

19. Julia Ward Howe, quoted in William L. O'Neill, *Everyone Was Brave: A History of Feminism in America* (New York: Quadrangle/The New York Times Book Co., 1974), p. 36.

20. Beatrice Forbes-Robertson Hale, *What Women Want: An Interpretation of The Feminist Movement* (New York: Frederick A. Stokes Co., 1914), p. 276.

21. Mrs. Harriet Hickox Heller, "Childhood, an Interpretation," Proceedings of the National Congress of Mothers Second Annual Convention, Washington, D.C., May 1898, p. 81.

22. Mrs. Theodore W. Birney, "Address of Welcome," Proceedings of the National Congress of Mothers Second Annual Convention, p. 17.

23. John Brisben Walker, "Motherhood as a Profession," *Cosmopolitan*, May 1898, p. 89.

24. Wishy, op. cit., p. 120.

Facts, Fantasies and the Future of Child Care in the United States

Sandra Scarr, Deborah Phillips, and Kathleen McCartney

In this article Sandra Scarr, Deborah Phillips, and Kathleen McCartney remind us that scientific research findings can sometimes reinforce powerful social values. When this occurs, the belief that those values and related social policies are scientifically supported may survive long after conclusions drawn from the original studies have been shown to be untenable. Research on the formation of a primary infant-mother attachment relationship, the impact of early experience on later development, and the effect of maternal deprivation on institutionalized infants is, they argue, a case in point. Work on these topics in the 1940s and 1950s was interpreted to suggest that a consistent maternal presence was necessary to the healthy development of infants and young children. Congruent with American motherhood values, this interpretation came to be widely accepted as fact.

Recent evidence, however, has called this early interpretation into question. Reviewing this evidence, the authors conclude that mothers need not be the only source of high quality care. With adequate numbers of well-trained caregivers and good opportunities for adult-child interaction, family and center day care can provide settings within which children will thrive. Indeed, in certain circumstances such as when parental mental health is poor or a family is beset by economic stress or domestic conflict, high quality family or center day care may even help compensate for inadequacies in home care.

From such findings it is clear that questions concerning the effects of day care on young children can have no simple answers. Whether a goal of providing the best possible care for children is most effectively met through a mother's or father's willingness to stay at home with the child or through a regimen of care shared between a high quality day care setting and one or more working parents will depend upon individual and family factors. It will also depend on the ready availability of high quality day care to all those families that need it. Unfortunately, in our state of national ambivalence toward child care, we have yet to develop the social policies necessary to make widespread accessibility of high quality day care a reality.

Child care is now as essential to family life as the automobile and the refrigerator. As of 1986, the majority of families, including those with infants, require child care to support parental employment. Yet most families find it far easier to purchase quality cars and refrigerators than to buy good care for their children.

Contemporary realities about the need for child care, captured in statistics about family income, mens' wages, maternal employment, and labor force needs, have not produced a coherent national policy on parental leaves or on child care services for working parents (Kahn & Kamerman, 1987; Scarr, Phillips, & McCartney, 1989a). Instead, our society remains ambivalent about mothers who work and about children whose care is shared, part-time, with others (McCartney & Phillips, 1988). The cost of our reluctance to shed fantasies about children's needs and parents' obligations, particularly mothers' obligations, is the failure to develop constructive social policies.

Facts and fantasies about child care arrangements influence the thinking of psychologists, other experts, parents, and those who make child care policy. It is thus imperative to reassess our ideas about children's needs and maternal roles, based especially on research. The social and demographic facts that are affecting the growing reliance on child care are now well known. They encompass documentation of declines in family income (Greenstein, 1987), dramatic changes in family structure (Cherlin, 1988), rapid increases in maternal employment and projected continuations of this trend (Hofferth & Phillips, 1987), and converging patterns of employment among mothers of all races and marital statuses (Kahn & Kamerman, 1987; Phillips, 1989). In this article we aim to dispel some of the fantasies that have prevented our nation from making appropriate provisions for the care of infants and young children, and to present research facts about child care. In conclusion, we take a brief look at current policy debates and at the future of child care that could emerge if we proceeded from facts about infants, mothers, and child care.

Fantasies about Mothers

Science is, in part, a social construction (Scarr, 1985). As such, we sometimes construct fantasies about child development, the uses and implications of which can endure long beyond the time when conflicting evidence becomes available. This is most likely to occur when prior scientific results support strongly-held social values. We argue here that the field of psychology has constructed fantasies about the role of mothers in infant development that have impact on our views of child care. We label these beliefs *fantasies* because they are not supported by contemporary scientific evidence. Such fantasies can be found in thinking about mother-infant attachment, maternal deprivation, and the role of early experience for later development. The end result is that some of our

Scarr, Sandra; Phillips, Deborah, & McCartney, Kathleen. (1990). Facts, fantasies, and the future of child care in the United States. *Psychological Science, 1* (1). pp. 26-35.

369

fantasies about the mothers and infant development have contributed to our national ambivalence about child care as an acceptable childrearing environment.

Fantasies about Mother-Infant Attachment

Prevailing views about mother-infant attachment have their roots in psychoanalytic theory, Bowlby's theory (1951), and ethology. In some way, all these theories espouse "monotropism" (Smith, 1980), the idea that a single relationship with a special caregiver, typically the mother, is critical for physical and social nourishment. Psychiatrists and others from a psychoanalytic tradition have most often objected to the use of child care, especially in infancy, for this reason (Fraiberg, 1977; Goldstein, Freud, & Solnit, 1973). Yet, research reveals that infants can and do develop multiple attachment relationships: with fathers (Lamb, 1980), with other family members and close friends of the family (Schaffer, 1977), and with caregivers (Ainslie & Anderson, 1984; Farran & Ramey, 1977; Howes, Rodning, Galluzzo, & Myers, 1988). Moreover, we know that most infants become securely attached to their parents, even when they live with a full-time caregiver in a kibbutz (Fox, 1977). Some research has shown that a secure attachment with a caregiver can buttress a child who otherwise might be at risk (Howes, Rodning, Galluzo, & Myers, 1988). Nevertheless, little is known about children's relationships with their caregivers, whose roles in children's lives must differ from those of parents, especially because of the high turnover rates of caregivers in the United States. An enduring child-adult relationship requires at least moderate stability in caregiving.

A number of studies have compared attachment relationships between infants and their mothers as a function of maternal employment or use of child care. Currently, there is a controversy concerning whether extensive child care during infancy is a risk to infants' attachments to their mothers (Belsky, 1988). But most infants require care while their mothers work. Should we view as a "risk factor" a small mean difference in attachment security (8 percent; Clarke-Stewart, 1989) between children as a function of maternal employment status or child care use? When children in child care seem to fare less well, child care is said to be a risk. When children in child care fare better on assessments of social competence, independence, or school readiness (e.g., Clarke-Stewart, 1984; Gunnarsson, 1978; Howes & Olenick, 1986; Howes & Stewart, 1987), no one is prepared to call care by mothers a risk factor. All forms of care have their strengths and weaknesses, although the effect sizes are likely to be small (for a thorough review of infant care, see Clarke-Stewart, 1989).

Few would disagree that maternal employment and child are contextual issues (Bronfenbrenner, 1979, 1986), with many "ifs, ands, and buts" that depend upon the family and the child care situation. Unfortunately, expert advice to parents often fails to mention the size of effects, fails to acknowledge known moderators of effects, and fails to speculate on the possibility, indeed probability, of unknown moderators (Gerson, Alpert, & Richardson, 1984). A notable exception comes from Maurer & Maurer (1989):

Developmental psychology knows much more about babies now than it knew even ten years ago. . . . Consider, for instance, the effect upon the baby of the mother's going back to work. . . . Studies on the topic abound, and every new one yields a flurry of pronouncements, either dire or reassuring depending on the results. But look at some of the factors involved here. A baby may be cared for in his own home, or in somebody else's home, or in a day care center, by either a relative or a stranger. The caretaker may be trained or untrained, and may be looking after one baby or several babies. The mother may be an overbearing woman and the caretaker easy-going, or vice versa. The mother may be happy about going to work and relaxed about giving over her baby in the morning, or she may be distressed at having to leave him with someone else: either way she may communicate her emotions to the child. At home in the evening, the mother may not have time to play with the baby because she is swamped with housework, or the babysitter or her husband may do the housework, leaving her evenings free. Her husband may be unhappy about her returning to work, so their evenings with the child become tense, or her husband may support her. And, of course, babies differ in temperament from one to another, so they react differently to all these factors. Clearly, no one study can take all of this into account (pp. 207-208).

No study to date has taken into account this full complement of possible influences on children's development and family functioning.

Fantasies about Early Experience

The "romance of early experience" (Scarr & Arnett, 1987) has given us the assumption that infancy provides more potent and pervasive influences than does later human experience. Although evidence for modest relations between early experience and later development exists (Caspi, Elder, & Bem, 1987; Erickson, Sroufe, & Egeland, 1985; Fagan, 1984; Funder, Block, & Block, 1983; Sigman, Cohen, Beckwith, & Parmelee, 1986), we agree with Kagan's (1979) interpretation of the data, namely that continuity does not imply inevitability. The human organism is surprisingly resilient in the face of deleterious experiences and sufficiently malleable to "bounce back" given constructive inputs. Only the most pervasive and continuous detrimental experiences have lasting, negative effects on development (Clarke & Clarke, 1976; Ernst, 1988; Lerner, 1984). Although this fact is encouraging for developmentalists, it is discouraging for interventionists, because even the most intensive early interventions appear to require some follow-up services or lasting environmental changes to assure long-term gains (Rutter, 1979; Scarr & McCartney, 1988; Valentine & Stark, 1979).

As a consequence of growing evidence for malleability, the search for critical periods has shifted toward efforts to examine relations between early and later experience, and to elucidate the mechanisms by which individuals and their environments interact to promote continuities and discontinuities in development (Brim & Kagan, 1980; Lerner, 1984; Scarr & Weinberg, 1983; Wachs & Gruen, 1982). Research on the developmental

371

implications of child care would benefit greatly from adopting this perspective.

Fantasies about Maternal Deprivation

Images about child care include for some the notion of deprivation of maternal care. Research on "maternal deprivation" reached an emotional climax in the 1950s, when Spitz (1945), Bowlby (1951), and others claimed that institutionalized infants were retarded intellectually and socially for lack of mothering. Reanalyses and reinterpretation of the evidence (Yarrow, 1961) found that it was, in fact, lack of sensory and affective stimulation in typical institutions that led to detrimental outcomes for the orphans. Infants need someone consistently there with whom to interact and to develop a trusting relationship, but that person does not have to be the child's biological mother.

Critics of child care sometimes write as though working parents abandon their infants as orphans. For example, the term, "maternal absence," was used to describe employed mothers in the title of a recent article in the prestigious journal, *Child Development* (Barglow, Vaughn & Molitor, 1987). The terms "maternal absence" and "maternal deprivation" seem uncomfortably close and both conjure up negative images. Some seem to forget that employed mothers are typically with their babies in the mornings, evenings, weekends, and holidays, which for most fully-employed workers constitutes about half of the child's waking time. And, when the child is ill, mothers are more likely than other family members to stay at home with the child (Hughes & Galinsky, 1986).

There are moderators of effects in the maternal deprivation literature as well. In his comprehensive review, Rutter (1979) concluded that it is not separation alone but separation in conjunction with other risk factors, for example, family stress, that leads to later antisocial behavior in children. A recent study by Ernst (1988) in Switzerland demonstrates Rutter's point nicely. Ernst's longitudinal study of 137 children who spent their first years in residential nurseries showed no differences between these children and the general population in IQ and in popularity. These children were two to three times more likely to develop behavior and social disorders, however. Ernst's careful analyses revealed that it was not nursery status alone that accounted for the difference. Rather, risk was associated with psychosocial factors in the environment such as parental discord, psychosocial disorder in parents, and abuse.

Early deprivation often indicates that an unfavorable situation will continue. For example, one research team has conducted a retrospective study and found that care during infancy is associated with negative outcomes at age eight (Vandell & Corasaniti, in press). Infant care was atypical eight years ago from a demographic perspective (Hofferth & Phillips, 1987). Thus, we must ask the follow-up questions Ernst thought to ask about psychosocial factors in the environment that might be continuous. Was the use of infant child care eight years ago an indicator of unfavorable circumstances that continue in childhood? A search for these moderators is most likely to advance our knowledge of any identified child care effects. The quality of maternal care, just like other child care arrangements, depends on many aspects of the home situation and mothers' mental health. The fantasy that mothers at home with young children provide the best possible care neglects the observation that some women at home full-time are lonely, depressed, and not functioning well (see Crosby, 1987; Scarr, Phillips, & McCartney, 1989b). Although, surely, most mothers at home are well motivated to provide good and stimulating care, they have many responsibilities other than direct child care. Time-use studies show that mothers at home full-time with preschool children spend very little time in direct interaction with them. They spend less time playing educational games and talking with the children than in many other household activities (Hill & Stafford, 1978; Hoffman, 1984; Nock & Kingston, in press; Ziegler, 1983). Child caregivers, on the other hand, usually have a majority of their time to give to their charges, although they usually have more children to care for than a mother at home. There are trade-offs: Neither home care nor out-of-home care promises quality child care. In fact, employed mothers of infants and young children spend less time in total home activities than non-employed mothers (715 versus 930 minutes, summed across one workday and a Sunday), but their actual time with their *children* is much closer to that of non-employed mothers. The largest difference in time with young children is the distribution of time between weekdays and weekends, with employed mothers concentrating their child-time on the weekends. Employed mothers scrimp on housework and on their own leisure time, rather than on time with their children (Nock & Kingston, in press). Fathers with employed wives spend more time with their infants and preschool children than fathers with non-employed wives (580 versus 521 minutes; Nock & Kingston, in press). Thus, working parents do spend considerable time in both direct and indirect activities with their children. In addition, children of working parents have the attention of caregivers while their parents work.

Research Facts about Child Care and Child Development

Child care arrangements, like families, vary enormously in their abilities to promote children's development, to provide support for working families, and to give caregivers rewarding adult roles. In the research literature, however, child care is still cast as nonmaternal care by investigators who, in fact, rarely study variation in child care settings. Similarly, home care is treated uniformly as though all families were alike, and is assumed to be preferred to other child care arrangements. Thus studies often ignore the facts that families vary from abusive and neglectful of children's needs to supportive and loving systems that promote optimal development, and so do other child care arrangements. Actual child care arrangements vary from hiring a trained nanny or untrained babysitter in one's own home, to family day care in another person's home, to centers that care for more than 100 infants and children. Diversity in the quality of child care, at home and in other settings, is what matters for children. High-quality day care settings have in fact been shown to compensate for poor family environments (McCartney, Scarr, Phillips, & Grajek, 1985; Ramey, Bryant, & Suarez, 1985) and, for

373

low-income children, to promote better intellectual and social development than they would have experienced in their own homes.

Developmental Effects of Child Care

Fears about the effects of child care have centered on possible interference with infants' attachment to their mothers, on their later social development, and on their intellectual development.

Attachment Research

The earliest research on child care asked whether or not caregivers replaced mothers as children's primary attachment figures. Concerns that daily prolonged separations from mother might weaken the mother-child bond were a direct heritage of the work on children in orphanages. But child care was not found to be a milder form of full-time institutionalization. Attachment was not adversely affected by enrollment in the university-based child care centers that provided the early child care samples. Bonds formed between children and their caregivers did not replace the mother-child attachment relationship (Belsky & Steinberg, 1978; Etaugh, 1980).

Now, almost twenty years later, the emergence of infant day care as a middle-class phenomenon among parents who themselves were reared at home by their mothers, has spawned an active debate about infant day care. The central issue here is whether full-time child care in the first year of life increases the probability of insecure attachments between mothers and infants. Some researchers have presented evidence that supports this claim (Belsky, 1986; Belsky, 1988; Belsky & Rovine, in press).

Other researchers have highlighted the many limitations of this new literature on infant day care (Clarke-Stewart, in press; Clarke-Stewart & Fein, 1983; McCartney & Galanopoulos, 1988; Phillips, McCartney, Scarr, & Howes, 1987). The main limitation concerns the exclusive use of the Strange Situation (Ainsworth & Wittig, 1969) to assess attachment. Critics question whether this experimental laboratory procedure of separation from and reunion with mother is equally stressful for children with and without child care experience, because children with child care experience have daily experience with the supposed stressful procedure. Furthermore, studies with an attachment Q-sort measure (Waters & Deane, 1985) have failed to show differences between children in child care and children at home with mother (Belsky, personal communication, to K. McCartney, November 6, 1987; Weinraub, Jaeger, & Hoffman, in press). Finally, the practical significance of differences reported in the Strange Situation between child care and non-child care samples is minimal, despite press reports to the contrary (Clarke-Stewart, 1989).

374

Social Development

Although some studies have reported no differences in social behavior (Golden, Rosenbluth, Grossi, Policare, Freeman, & Brownlees, 1978; Kagan, Kearsley, & Zelazo, 1978), others find that children who have attended child care are more socially competent (Clarke-Stewart, 1984; Gunnarsson, 1978; Howes & Olenick, 1986; Howes & Stewart, 1987; Ruopp, et al., 1979), and still others suggest lower levels of social competence (Haskins, 1985; Rubenstein, Howes, & Boyle, 1983). Positive outcomes include teacher and parent ratings of considerateness and sociability (Phillips, McCartney, & Scarr, 1987), observations of compliance and self regulation (Howes & Olenick, 1986), and observations of involvement and positive interactions with teachers (McCartney, 1984; Ruopp, Travers, Glantz, & Coelen, 1979; Vandell & Powers, 1983).

Negative outcomes of day care experience have emphasized aggression. For example, Haskins' (1985) study of graduates from the Abecedarian project, a high-quality intervention day care program, showed that teachers in the early elementary grades rated these children higher on scales of aggression than a control group that was not enrolled in the program. However, a subgroup of the control children who were enrolled in an equivalent amount of community-based child care were found to be among the least aggressive children in the study, thereby demonstrating that the effect was not due to child care per se. A change in the curriculum of the Abecedarian project decreased aggression by 80 percent (Finkelstein, 1982), and by third grade, all early effects had dissipated for the initial group (Bryant, personal communication, February 1988). Here again, the story of day care effects will eventually be told through an examination of moderators, such as quality, and of trends in behavior over time.

Intellectual and Cognitive Development

Differences in intelligence between children in varying forms of day care and children cared for by their mothers have not been reported in most studies (Carew, 1980; Doyle & Somers, 1978; Kagan, Kearsley, & Zelazo, 1978; Robertson, 1982; Stith & Davis, 1984). Two studies, however, have reported that children in center care score higher on tests of cognitive competence (Clarke-Stewart, 1984; Rubenstein, Howes, & Boyle, 1981) than children in other types of child care settings. Similar evidence is provided by evaluations of early intervention programs (Lee, Brooks-Gunn, & Schnur, 1988; McCartney, Scarr, Phillips, & Grajek, 1985; McKey, Condelli, Ganson, Barrett, McConkey, & Plantz, 1985; Ramey & Haskins, 1981; Schweinhart & Weikart, 1980; Seitz, Apel, Rosenbaum, & Zigler, 1983), which indicate that carefully designed group programs can have substantial, and, in some cases lasting, positive effects on children's patterns of achievement.

In sum, there is near consensus among developmental psychologists and early childhood experts that child care per se does not constitute a risk factor in children's lives; rather, poor quality care and poor family environments can conspire to produce poor developmental outcomes (National Center for Clinical Infant Programs, 1988).

Child Care as a Heterogeneous Environment

Contemporary developmental research has recognized the vast heterogeneity of child care and turned to the question of "what is *quality*?" in child care. Reliable indices of child care quality include caregiver-child ratio, group size, and caregiver training and experience. These variables, in turn, facilitate constructive and sensitive interactions among caregivers and children, which promote positive social and cognitive development (Phillips, 1987; Ruopp et al., 1979).

The caregiver-child ratio is related to decreased exposure to danger (Ruopp et al., 1979) and to increased language interactions in the child care setting. Both Bruner (1980) and Howes and Rubenstein (1985) report that children in centers with more adults per child engage in more talking and more playing. Another study (McCartney, 1984) has documented a link between verbal interaction with caregivers and children's language competence. Results of the National Day Care Study suggest that adequate ratios are particularly important for infants, with experts citing 1:4 as the threshold for good quality care.

Research on group size has revealed that the larger the group, the more management is necessary; the smaller the group, the more education and social interaction is possible. As first demonstrated in the National Day Care Study (Ruopp et al., 1979), caregivers in larger groups provide less social interaction and cognitive stimulation. Children in larger groups were found to be more apathetic and more distressed. These findings have since been replicated in other studies (Bruner, 1980; Howes, 1983; Howes & Rubenstein, 1985).

The research on caregiver training and education is particularly consistent. Not surprisingly, years of child-related education are associated with increased caregiver responsivity, positive affect, and ability to provide socially- and intellectually-stimulating experiences (Clarke-Stewart & Gruber, 1984; Howes, 1983; Ruopp et al., 1979; Stallings & Porter, 1980). These findings do not simply represent the effects of self-selection. Two intervention studies show that training leads to caregiver improvement (Arnett, 1989; Kaplan & Conn, 1984). Experience working with children cannot replace child-related training. Although Howes (1983) found an association between years of experience and responsiveness to children, the National Day Care Study (Ruopp et al., 1979) found that day care experience was associated with less social interaction and more apathy. Other studies have not found any important effects of experience per se (Phillips, McCartney, Scarr, & Howes, 1987; Stallings & Porter, 1980).

Research has also shown that many aspects of quality are correlated and that a good center is essentially one with good caregivers. Good caregivers are caring, able to read a baby's signals, and responsive to babies' signals (McCartney, 1987). In fact, preschoolers perceive caregivers to provide the same caregiving functions as their mothers (Tephly & Elardo, 1984). The vast literature on mother-child interaction can also inform us of caregiving behaviors that are important. Although these behaviors are not legislatable, they are trainable.

Among the most recent indicators of quality to emerge from research is the stability of children's child care arrangements (Cummings, 1980; Howes & Olenick, 1986; Howes & Stewart, 1987). Children who experience multiple changes in caregivers and settings develop less optimally in social and language areas than children with stable child care, with effects lasting into the early school years (Howes, 1988). The importance of stable care stands in stark contrast with the alarmingly high turnover rates among child care workers. Between 1980 and 1990, 42 percent of all non-household child care workers will need to be replaced each year, just to maintain the current supply of child care providers ("New Occupational," 1984). Low pay, lack of benefits, and stressful working conditions are the major reasons cited by child care workers who leave their jobs (Jorde-Bloom, 1987; Kontos & Stremmel, 1988; Whitebook, Howes, Darrah, & Friedman, 1982). Infants and young children cannot develop stable relationships with caregivers if they are faced with new caregivers every few weeks.

Relations Between Home and Child Care

In studies of typical child care, researchers can neither assign children randomly to child care nor assign parents to varying employment patterns. As a consequence, efforts to decipher the "effects" of child care are a methodological conundrum. Pre-existing family differences—in background, traits, and beliefs—are confounded with child care arrangements.

Recent research suggests that there may be interaction effects between family characteristics and child care arrangements in maternal anxiety (Hock, DeMeis, & McBride, 1987), marital status and living arrangements (Scarr, Lande, & McCartney, 1989), such that good child care can compensate for poor home environments. There is also increasing evidence that the lowest income and most disorganized families (among the middle class) end up in the lowest quality child care programs (Howes & Olenick, 1986; Howes & Stewart, 1987; Lamb, Huang, Brookstein, Broberg, Hult, & Frodi, 1988). A number of other family variables might reasonably moderate effects, especially those related to family stress (Kontos & Wells, 1986).

A number of relationships may affect children's sense of security and thereby their adjustment. Belsky found that daughters with unemployed mothers were more likely to be insecurely attached to their fathers than daughters of employed mothers (Belsky & Rovine, in press). Using the attachment Q-sort (Waters & Deane, 1985), Howes and her colleagues (Howes, et al., 1988) have shown recently that both attachment security at home with mother and attachment security with the caregiver at day care are predictors of the child's positive interaction with caregivers and peers in day care. Interactions between family characteristics and child care have been found to affect development in the first two years of life. For example, Scarr, Lande, and McCartney (1989) reported negative main effects for typical center care (but not family day care) in the first two years of life on both intellectual and social/emotional ratings. The same children were also disadvantaged by being reared in single mother-headed households (but not in extended families with single mothers). Further, they found important interactions between households and center care, such that infants from single mother-headed households benefited from group care more than similar children in other kinds of care, including maternal care. By the age of four years, there were no effects of child care in the first two years or in the second two years on any child development outcome. Other research (McBride & Belsky, 1988; Weinraub, Jaeger, & Hoffman, in press) has found that relations between maternal employment and attachment vary according to maternal satisfaction with child care arrangements, role satisfaction, and coping skills. Studies such as these suggest that child care must be seen in the context of the child's family life before one can interpret any effects of child care per se.

Facts about Child Care Policy

For the first time in a decade, child care is on the national agenda. In 1988, more than forty bills containing provisions for child care were introduced in the U.S. Congress (Robins, 1988). Driven largely by escalating rates of employment among non-poor, married mothers (Kahn & Kamerman, 1987), federal child care policies have come under intense scrutiny and numerous proposals for restructuring the federal role have surfaced. These range from "supply side" proposals that emphasize improvements in the current system of child care to "demand side" proposals that offer families additional tax subsidies for purchasing child care. Parental leave policies are also being debated. In addition, the majority of states are now moving toward limited funding for school-based child care programs that typically are targeted at poor and/or disadvantaged families (Marx & Seligson, 1988).

The same demographic trends that are influencing child care policy are also creating new goals for welfare reform effects. For low-income mothers, prevailing beliefs about maternal care have traditionally led us to favor policies that enable them to stay home with their babies, through child support and public assistance (e.g., Aid to Families with Dependent Children). But the new welfare reform bill (Family Support Act of 1988: P.L. 100-483), emphasizes training, employment and women's attainment of economic independence rather than support for full-time mothering (Phillips, in press). This shift in purpose is due largely to policymakers' recognition that the majority of mothers with preschool-age children are now in the labor force. Under these circumstances, it is difficult to justify the prior exemption from training and employment programs for AFDC-eligible mothers with children under age six. Unfortunately, even in the best of circumstances, the child care subsidies included in the Family Support Act are continued for only one year after mothers achieve the minimum wage jobs for which they are being trained.

The policy debate about child care is no longer about whether there will be support for child care or whether families will continue to rely on child care (Martinez, 1989). Instead, it has focused on relatively pragmatic questions about delivery systems, target populations, and financing. These questions, however, are not uncontroversial. For example, the high cost of market forms of child care and fears about nationalizing our child care system have generated strong resistance to legislation that ties government subsidies to use of licensed programs (i.e., centers and regulated family day care homes) or that mandates federal day care standards. For these reasons, we are unlikely ever to see child care and leave policies in the United States that resemble European or Canadian policies (see Scarr, Phillips, & McCartney, 1989a). Considerations of "who should provide child care?" are now mired in an acrimonious debate involving the schools, community-based child care programs, and church-housed programs. And, on-going debates about whether government child care benefits should be reserved for the poor or also assist the non-poor, and about whether these benefits should purchase good quality child care (as in the Head Start program) or disregard consideration of quality are far from resolved.

The child care policies that result from today's debate will constitute some adaptation to the realities of working parents. However, the effects of our national ambivalence about working mothers will undoubtedly be felt, as well. Prevailing beliefs that mothers of very young children belong at home and that child care problems are best solved privately will assure that any new child care policy is likely to remain fragmented, marginal, and modestly funded. At a minimum, any generous policy that might actually create an incentive for those mothers who have a choice about working to use child care, will be avoided.

This is the political and social context on which research on child care has a bearing. The ways in which research questions are framed and the values that underlie our questions can challenge the assumptions that guide policy and promote policies that are based more on facts and less on fantasies.

References

Ainslie, R.C., & Anderson, C.W. (1984). Day care children's relationships to their mothers and caregivers: An inquiry into the conditions for the development of attachment. In R.C. Ainslie (Ed.), *The child and the day care setting*. New York: Praeger.

Ainsworth, M., & Wittig, B.A. (1969). Attachment and exploratory behavior of one-year-olds in a strange situation. In B.M. Foss (Ed.), *Determinants of infant behavior*, Vol. 4. London: Methuen.

Arnett, J. (1989). Issues and obstacles in the training of caregivers. In J. Lande, S. Scarr, & N. Gunzenhauser (Eds.), *Caring for children: Challenge to America* (pp. 241-256). Hillsdale, NJ: Erlbaum.

Barglow, P., Vaughn, B.E., & Molitor, N. (1987). Effects of maternal absence due to employment on the quality of infant-mother attachment in a low-risk sample. *Child Development, 58*, 945-954.

Belsky, J. (1986). Infant day care: A cause for concern? *Zero to Three, 6*(5), 1-9.

Belsky, J. (1988). The "effects" of infant day care reconsidered. *Early Childhood Research Quarterly, 3*, 235-272.

Belsky, J., & Rovine, M.J. (in press). Nonmaternal care in the first year of life and the security of infant-parent attachment. *Child Development.*

Belsky, J., & Steinberg, L.D. (1978). The effects of daycare: A critical review. *Child Development, 49*, 929-949.

Bowlby, J. (1951). *Maternal care and mental health.* Geneva: World Health Organiza tion.

Bronfenbrenner, U. (1979). *The ecology of human development: Experiments by nature and design.* Cambridge, MA: Harvard University Press.

Bronfenbrenner, U. (1986). Ecology of the family as a context for human development: Research perspectives. *Developmental Psychology, 22*, 723-742.

Brim, O.G., & Kagan, J. (1980). *Constancy and change in human development.* Cambridge, MA: Harvard University Press.

Bruner, J. (1980). *Under five in Britain.* London: Methuen.

Carew, J. (1980). Experience and the development of intelligence in young children. *Monographs of the Society for Research in Child Development, 45*, 6-7 (Serial No. 187).

Caspi, A., Elder, G.H., Jr., & Bem, D.J. (1987). Moving against the world: Life course patterns of explosive children. *Developmental Psychology, 23*, 308-313.

Cherlin, A.J. (Ed.). (1988). *The changing American family and public policy.* Washington, DC: The Urban Institute Press.

Clarke, A.M., & Clarke, A.D.B. (1976). *Early experience: Myth and evidence.* London: Open Books.

Clarke-Stewart, A. (1984). Day care: A new context for research and development. In M. Perlmutter (Ed.), *The Minnesota Symposia on Child Psychology: Vol. 27. Parent-child interaction and parent-child relations in child development* (pp. 61-100). Hillsdale, NJ: Erlbaum.

Clarke-Stewart, A. (1989). Infant day care: Malignant or maligned? *American Psychologist*. *44*, 266-273.

Clarke-Stewart, A., & Fein, G. (1983). Early child-hood programs. In P.H. Mussen (Series Ed.) & M. Haith and J. Campos (Vol. Eds.), *Handbook of child psychology: Vol. II. Infancy and developmental psychobiology*. (pp. 917-1000). New York: Wiley.

Clarke-Stewart, A., & Gruber, C. (1984). Day care forms and features. In R.C. Ainslie (Ed.), *The child and the day care setting* (pp. 35-62). New York: Praeger.

Crosby, F.J. (Ed.). (1987). *Spouse, parent, worker: On gender and multiple roles*. New Haven: Yale University Press.

Cummings, E.H. (1980). Caregiver stability and day care. *Developmental Psychology*, *16*, 31-37.

Doyle, A., & Somers, K. (1978). The effects of group and family day care on infant attachment behaviors. *Canadian Journal of Behavioral Science*, *10*, 38-45.

Erickson, M.F., Sroufe, L.A., & Egeland, B. (1985). The relationship between quality of attachment and behavior problems in preschool in a high-risk sample. In I. Bretherton & E. Waters (Eds.), Growing points in attachment theory and research. *Monographs of the Society for Research in Child Development*, *50*. 147- 166.

Ernst, D. (1988). Are early childhood experiences overrated? A reassessment of maternal deprivation. *European Archives of Psychiatry and Neurological Sciences*, *237*, 80-90.

Etaugh, C. (1980). Effects of nonmaternal care on children: Research evidence and popular views. *American Psychologist*, *35*, 309-319.

Fagan, J.F. (1984). The intellectual infant: Theoretical implications. *Intelligence*, *8*, 1-9.

Farran, D., & Ramsey, C. (1977). Infant day care and attachment behaviors toward mothers and teachers. *Child Development*, *48*, 1112-1116.

Finkelstein, N. (1982). Aggression: Is it stimulated by day care? *Young Children*, *37*, 3-9.

Fox, N. (1977). Attachment of kibbutz infants to mothers and metaplete. *Child Development*, *48*, 1228-1239.

Fraiberg, S. (1977). *Every child's birthright: In defense of mothering*. New York: Basic Books.

Funder, D., Block, J.H., & Block, J. (1983). Delay of gratification: Some longitudinal personality correlates. *Journal of Personality and Social Psychology, 44*, 1198-1213.

Gerson, J., Alpert, J.L., & Richardson, M. (1984). Mothering: The view from psychological research. *Signs, 9*, 434-453.

Golden, M., Rosenbluth, L., Grossi, M.T., Policare, H.J., Freeman, H., Jr., & Brownlee, E.M. (1978). *The New York City infant day care study*. New York: Medical and Health Research Association of New York City.

Goldstein, J., Freud, A., & Solnit, A.J. (1973). *Beyond the best interests of the child*. New York: Free Press.

Greenstein, R. (1987). Testimony presented before the Income Security Task Force Committee on the Budget, U.S. House of Representatives, Washington, D.C., November 9, 1987.

Gunnarsson, L. (1978). *Children in day care and family care in Sweden* (Research Bulletin, No. 21). Gothenburg, Sweden: University of Gothenburg.

Haskins, R. (1985). Public school aggression among children with varying day care experience. *Child Development, 56*, 689-703.

Hill, C.R., & Stafford, F.P. (1978). Parental care of children: Time diary estimates of quantity, predictability, and variety. *Institute for Social Research Working Paper Series*. Ann Arbor: University of Michigan.

Hock, E., DeMeis, D., & McBride, S. (1987). Maternal separation anxiety: Its role in the balance of employment and motherhood in mothers of infants. In A. Gottfried & A. Gottfried (Eds.), *Maternal employment and children's development: Longitudinal research* (pp. 191-229). New York: Plenum.

Hofferth, S.L., & Phillips, D.A. (1987). Child care in the United States, 1970 to 1995. *Journal of Marriage and the Family, 49*, 559-571.

Hoffman, L.W. (1984). Maternal employment and the child. In M. Perlmutter (Ed.), *The Minnesota Symposia on Child Psychology: Vol. 17. Parent child interaction and parent-child relations in development* (pp. 101-127). Hillsdale, NJ: Erlbaum.

Howes, C. (1983). Caregiver behavior in center and family day care. *Journal of Applied Developmental Psychology, 4*, 99-107.

Howes, C. (1988). Relations between early child care and schooling. *Developmental Psychology, 24*, 53-57.

Howes, C., and Olenick, M. (1986). Child care and family influences on compliance. *Child Development, 57*, 202-216.

Howes, C., Rodning, C., Galluzzo, D., & Myers, L. (1988). Attachment and child care: Relationships with mother and caregiver. *Early Childhood Research Quarterly, 3*, 403-416.

Howes, C., & Rubenstein, J. (1985). Determinants of toddlers' experience in daycare: Age of entry and quality of setting. *Child Care Quarterly, 14*, 140-151.

Howes, C., & Stewart, P. (1987). Child's play with adults, toys, and peers: An examination of family and child-care influences. *Developmental Psychology, 23*, 423-430.

Hughes, D., & Galinsky, E. (1986). Maternity, paternity, and parenting policies: How does the United States compare? In S.A. Hewlett, A.S. Ilchman, & J.J. Sweeney (Eds.), *Family and work: Bridging the gap* (pp. 53-66). Cambridge, MA: Ballinger.

Jorde-Bloom, P. (1987, April), *Factors influencing overall job commitment and facet satisfaction in early childhood work environments*. Paper presented at the meeting of the American Educational Research Asociation, Washington, D.C.

Kagan, J. (1979). Family experience and the child's development. *American Psychologist, 34*, 886-891.

Kagan, J., Kearsley, R.B., & Zelazo, P.R. (1978). *Infancy: Its place in human development*. Cambridge, MA: Harvard University Press.

Kahn, A.J., & Kamerman, S.B. (1987). *Child care: Facing the hard choices*. Dover, MA: Auburn House.

Kaplan, M., & Conn, J. (1984). The effects of caregiver training on classroom setting and caregiver performance in eight community day care centers. *Child Study Journal, 14*, 79-93.

Kontos, S., & Stremmel, A.J. (1988). Caregivers'perceptions of working conditions in a child care environment. *Early Childhood Research Quarterly, 3*, 77-90.

Kontos, S., & Wells, W. (1986). Attitudes of caregivers and the day care experiences of families. *Early Childhood Research Quarterly, 1*, 47-67.

Lamb, M. (1980). The development of parent-infant attachments in the first two years of life. In F. Pederson (Ed.), *The father-infant relationship: Observational studies in the family setting*. New York: Praeger.

Lamb, M., Hwang, C., Bookstein, F.L., Broberg, A., Hult, G., & Frodi, M. (1988). Determinants of social competence in Swedish preschoolers. *Developmental Psychology, 24*, 58-70.

Lee, V.E., Brooks-Gunn, J., & Schnur, E. (1988). Does Head Start work? A 1-year follow-up comparison of disadvantaged children attending Head Start, no preschool, and other preschool programs. *Developmental Psychology, 24*, 210-222.

Lerner, R.M. (1984). *On the nature of human plasticity*. New York: Cambridge University Press.

Martinez, S. (1989). Child care and federal policy. In J. Lande, S. Scarr, & N. Gunzenhauser (Eds.), *Caring for children: Challenge to America* (pp. 111-124). Hillsdale, NJ: Erlbaum.

Marx, F., & Seligson, M. (1988). *The public school early childhood study. The state survey*. New York: Bank Street College of Education.

Maurer, C., & Maurer, D. (1988). *World of the newborn*. New York: Basic Books.

McBride, S., & Belsky, J. (1988). Characteristics, determinants, and consequences of maternal separation anxiety. *Developmental Psychology, 24*, 407-414.

McCartney, K. (1984). The effect of quality of day care environment upon children's language development. *Developmental Psychology. 20*, 244-260.

McCartney, K. (1987, July/August). Quality: A child's point of view. *Child Care Action News, Newsletter of the Child Care Action Campaign, 4* (4).

McCartney, K., & Galanopoulis, A. (1988). Child care and attachment: A new frontier the second time around. *American Journal of Orthopsychiatry, 58*, 16-24.

McCartney, K., & Phillips, D. (1988). Motherhood and child care. In B. Birns & D. Hay (Eds.), *Different faces of motherhood* (pp. 157-183). New York: Plenum Press.

McCartney, K., Scarr, S., Phillips, D., & Grajek, S. (1985). Day care as intervention: Comparisons of varying quality programs. *Journal of Applied Developmental Psychology, 6*, 247-260.

McKey, R.H., Condelli, L., Ganson, H., Barrett. B.J., McConkey, C., & Plantz, M.C. (1985). *The impact of Head Start on children, families, and communities: Final report of the Head Start evaluation, synthesis. and utilization project*. Washington, D.C.: CSR Inc.

National Center for Clinical Infant Programs. (1988). *Infants, Families and Child Care*. Washington, D.C.: Author. Brochure.

New occupational separation data improve estimates of job replacement needs. (1984, March). *Monthly Labor Review, 107*(3), 3-10.

Nock, S.L., & Kingston, P.W. (in press). Time with children: The impact of couples' work-time commitments. *Social Forces*.

Phillips, D. (Ed.). (1987). *Quality in child care: What does research tell us?* Washington, D.C.: National Association for the Education of Young Children.

Phillips, D. (1989). Future directions and need for child care in the United States. In J.S. Lande, S. Scarr, & N. Gunzenhauser (Eds.), *Caring for children: Challenge to America* (pp. 257-275). Hillsdale. NJ: Erlbaum.

Phillips, D. (in press). With a little help: Children in poverty and child care. In A. Huston (Ed). *Children and Poverty*. New York: Cambridge University Press.

Phillips, D., McCartney, K., & Scarr, S. (1987). Child-care quality and children's social development. *Developmental Psychology, 23*, 537-543.

Phillips, D., McCartney, K., Scarr, S., & Howe, C. (1987, February). Selective view of infant day care research: A cause for concern! *Zero to Three, 7*, 18-21.

Ramey, C.T., Bryant. D.M., & Suarez, T.M. (1985). Preschool compensatory education and the modifiability of intelligence: A critical review. In D. Detterman (Ed.), *Current topics in human intelligence.* (pp. 247-296). Norwood, NJ: Ablex.

Ramey, C.T., & Haskins, R. (1981). The causes and treatment of school failure: Insights from the Carolina Abecedarian Project. In M.J. Begab, H.C. Haywood, & H.L. Garber (Eds.), *Psychosocial influences in retarded performance: Strategies for improving competence*. Baltimore: University Park Press.

Robertson. A. (1982). Day care and children's response to adults. In E. Zigler & E.W. Gordon (Eds.), *Day care: Scientific and social policy issues* (pp. 152-173). Boston: Auburn House.

Robins, P. (1988). Child care and convenience: The effects of labor market entry cost on economic self-sufficiency among public housing residents. *Social Science Quarterly, 69*, 122-136.

Rubenstein, J., Howes, C., & Boyle, P. (1981). A two year follow-up of infants in community based day care. *Journal of Child Psychology and Psychiatry, 22*, 209-218.

Ruopp, R., Travers, J., Glantz, F., & Coelen, C. (1979). *Children at the center: Final results of the National Day Care Study.* Boston: Abt Associates.

Rutter, M. (1979). Maternal deprivation, 1972-1978: New findings, new concepts, new approaches. *Child Development, 50*, 283-291.

Scarr, S. (1985). Constructing psychology: Making facts and fables for our times. *American Psychologist, 40*, 499-512.

Scarr. S., & Arnett, J. (1987). Malleability: Lessons from intervention and family studies. In J.J. Gallagher (Ed.), *The malleability of children* (pp. 71-84). New York: Brooke.

Scarr, S., Lande, J., & McCartney, K. (1989). Child care and the family: Cooperation and interaction. In J. Lande, S. Scarr, & N. Gunzenhauser (Eds.), *Caring for children: The future of child care in the United States* (pp. 1-21). Hillsdale, NJ: Erlbaum.

Scarr, S., & McCartney, K. (1988). Far from home: An experimental evaluation of the mother-child home program in Bermuda. *Child Development, 59,* 531-543.

Scarr, S., Phillips. D., & McCartney, K. (1989a). Dilemmas of child care in the United States: Employed mothers and children at risk. *Canadian Psychology, 30*(2), 126-139.

Scarr, S., Phillips, D., & McCartney, K. (1989b). Working mothers and their families. *American Psychologist, 44*, 1402-1409.

Scarr, S., & Weinberg, R.A. (1983). The Minnesota adoption studies: Genetic differences and malleability. *Child Development, 54*, 260-267.

386

Schaffer, H.R. (1977). *Attachments*. Cambridge, MA: Harvard University Press.

Schweinhart, L., & Weikart, D. (1980). The effects of the Perry Preschool Program on youths through age 15. *Monographs of the High/Scope Educational Research Foundation No. 7.*

Seitz, V., Apfel, N., Rosenbaum, L., & Zigler, E. (1983). Long term effects of Projects Head Start and Follow Through: The New Haven Project. In Consortium for Longitudinal Studies, *As the twig is bent. Lasting effects of preshool programs* (pp. 299-332). Hillsdale, NJ: Erlbaum.

Sigman, M., Cohen, S.E., Beckwith, L., & Parmelee, A.H. (1986). Infant attention in relation to intellectual abilities in childhood. *Developmental Psychology, 22,* 788-792.

Smith, P.K. (1980). Shared care of young children: Alternative models to monotropism. *Merrill-Palmer Quarterly, 26,* 371-389.

Spitz, R. (1945). Hospitalism: An inquiry into the genesis of psychiatric conditions in early childhood. *Psychoanalytic Study of the Child, 1,* 53-74.

Stallings, J., & Porter, A. (1980, June). *National Day Care Home Study: Observation component* (Final Report of the National Day Care Home Study, Vol. III). Washington, DC: Dept of Health, Education and Welfare.

Stith, S., & Davis, A. (1984). Employed mothers and family day care substitute caregivers. *Child Development, 55,* 1340-1348.

Tephly, J., & Elardo, R. (1984). Mothers and day care teachers: Young children's perceptions. *British Journal of Developmental Psychology, 2,* 251-256.

Valentine, J., & Stark, E. (1979). The social context of parent involvement in Head Start. In E. Zigler & J. Valentine (Eds.), *Project Head Start: A legacy of the War on Poverty.* (pp. 291-314). New York: Free Press.

Vandell, D.L., & Corsaniti, M.A. (in press). Child care in the family: Complex contributions to child development. In K. McCartney (Ed.), *New directions in child development research, Vol. 20: The social ecology of child care.* New York: Jossey-Bass.

Vandell, D.L., & Powers, C.P. (1983). Day care quality and children's free play activities. *American Journal of Orthopsychiatry, 53,* 493-500.

Wachs, T.D., & Gruen, G.E. (1982). *Early experience and human development.* New York: Plenum Press.

Waters, E., & Deane, K.E. (1985). Defining and assessing individual differences in attachment relationships: Q-methodology and the organization of behaviors in infancy and childhood. In I. Bretherton & E. Waters (Eds.), Growing points in attachment theory and research. *Monographs of the Society for Research in Child Development, 50,* 41-65.

Weinraub, M., Jaeger, E., & Hoffman, L. (in press). Predicting infant outcome in families of employed and non-employed mothers. *Early Childhood Research Quarterly.*

Whitebook, M., Howes, C., Darrah, R., & Friedman, J. (1982). Caring for the caregivers: Staff burnout in child care. In L. Katz (Ed.), *Current topics in early childhood education* (Vol. 4. pp. 211-235). Norwood, NJ: Ablex.

Yarrow, L. (1961). Maternal deprivation: Toward an empirical and conceptual evaluation. *Psychological Bulletin, 58,* 459-490.

Ziegler, M. E. (1983). *Assessing parents' and children's time together.* Paper presented at the annual meeting of the Society for Research in Child Development, Detroit, Michigan.

16

Mathematics Achievement and the Asian Advantage

In Jewish communities of pre-World War II Europe, traditional reverence toward education was expressed in a special ceremony in celebration of a boy's first day at school. So that he would not see anything unholy along the way, a young boy was wrapped in a prayer shawl and carried to school by his father. At school, when the shawl was removed, the rabbi wrote the alphabet in honey on a slate while the adults who surrounded him showered him with candies, saying "An angel threw this down so that you will want to study." This ritual, designed to strengthen the association that learning is sweet, was considered to be a major ceremony in a boy's life.

Parents throughout the world acknowledge the five to seven transition by treating their children in new ways. In literate societies children are sent to school. In traditional cultures they are expected to begin to acquire the oral tradition of their elders.

The Dagomba of northern Ghana rely heavily on oral tradition passed down from generation to generation by highly skilled drummers. Dagomban drummers are the tribe's historians. Through their drumming and their songs, they tell the story of births and deaths, describe the lineage of members of their tribe, and relate the exploits of their chiefs. Learning the stories and songs that form a drummer's repertoire requires a long and difficult apprenticeship. In general, when boys reach the age of five or six, Dagomban elders feel that they are ready to begin such an apprenticeship.

• INTRODUCTION •

In the United States, Japan, and other technologically-oriented societies, academic achievement is highly valued. Children who do well in school are more likely to graduate to prestigious institutions of higher learning and to succeed in those institutions. Success in college and graduate or professional school in turn facilitates entry into high status employment. This is particularly true for careers which require sophisticated technical expertise involving familiarity with scientific, mathematical, or engineering principles and applications. As the pace of technological innovation has accelerated, this expertise has become increasingly critical to nations' ability to compete effectively in a global economy.

Among the post-World War II industrial powers, no nation has developed this ability better than Japan. From an era of economic ruin immediately following the war, Japan has emerged as a world economic leader. One of the major themes in the narrative of Japanese economic success has been the elaboration of a system of education that fosters high achievement, particularly in mathematics and science. The readings in this module document the extent of the Japanese educational advantage in mathematics, examine factors in Japan's approach to schooling that contribute to the high levels of achievement attained by Japanese children, and discuss some of the costs as well as the benefits of this approach.

• • •

The Japanese Educational Challenge: A Commitment to Children
Merry White

At first glance the daily lives of school children in Japan may seem to be similar to those of their American age mates. In this reading, however, Merry White makes it clear that this superficial resemblance is misleading. Japanese and American approaches to schooling differ in fundamental ways. First, Japanese children spend much more time actively engaged in academic work than do their American counterparts. Relative to American schools, Japanese schools have a longer school year,

390

a longer school week, and a longer school day, devote a greater proportion of the school day to academic study, and assign more homework. In addition, particularly in high school, the average Japanese child spends additional time each week in formal after-school educational activities.

Second, the cultural heritage of Japan is relatively more homogeneous than that of the United States. In comparison to their American counterparts, Japanese children, parents, school personnel, and policy makers are more likely to find themselves in agreement on issues that reflect educational and career values and goals. Third, the Japanese diffuse responsibility for the child's educational achievement and eventual career success over a much wider social network than would be deemed appropriate by most Americans. In Japan, children themselves, their teachers, parents and other family members, school administrators, classmates, even individuals as far removed from the immediate setting as those in the parental workplace, are assumed to bear some responsibility for children's academic and career success. This both provides a broad base of social support for education and invokes a feeling of responsibility to others for success or failure.

As White suggests, this combination of collective responsibility and sense of indebtedness of the individual to the collective provides children with a powerful motive to achieve. In reading this selection, note that costs as well as benefits result from the Japanese approach to schooling. Older children have much less free time to spend with peers, and all children are under great pressure to succeed in examinations. Note also that there is no simple answer to the question of whether the Japanese approach enhances or restricts creativity.

Japanese children today go to schools which very much resemble those of the West, at least superficially, but the similarities are only a single brick deep. The alchemy making the borrowed model into an indigenous cultural phenomenon has by now completely transformed the Occupation-period "American" education into schooling fully congruent with Japanese goals and mores. A look at practices, schedules, and the environment of the classroom will show us some of the dimensions of difference.

White, Merry. (1987). *The Japanese Educational Challenge: A Commitment to Children.* NY: The Free Press. Chapter 4 (Japanese schools today). pp. 66-81.

A Japanese child *must* be in school between the ages of six and fifteen, or the elementary and junior high school years. This much is guaranteed for all children. In fact, however, children typically enter formal schooling at three or four, in private nursery schools, and 94 percent of them finish high school.

The school year begins on April 1 and ends at the end of March the following year. There are three terms: April through July, September through December, and January through March. There are about 240 school days per year. Classes are held for half a day on Saturdays, although there have been several efforts to eliminate them. Efforts have so far failed because of objections on the part of parents to the implied abdication of the schools. . . .

The atmosphere of the classroom is very lively, even noisy. A class will have an average of forty-two children to one teacher. The teacher's main concern is that the children be engaged in their work, and not that they be disciplined or docile. Thus, an American teacher might be distressed at the decibel level tolerated.

The large student-teacher ratio means that expectations for pupil behavior and instructor intervention are different from those we would expect. As Joseph Tobin suggests,[1] the Japanese teacher delegates more authority to children than we find in American schools; intervenes less quickly in arguments; has lower expectations for the control of noise generated by the class; gives fewer verbal cues; organizes more structured large-group activities, such as morning exercise; and, finally, makes more use of peer-group approval and control and less of the teacher's direct influence. In general, children are less often treated on a one-to-one basis, and more often as a group.

Japanese students are almost always promoted with their age group, rarely advanced or held back by ability. A prolonged illness might keep a child from moving on, but his absence from the group and from its shared experiences would be at issue as much as having fallen behind in coursework. . . .

In contrast to American schools, serious homework is assigned to the Japanese first grader, who gets more and more of it as he moves on. By the time a child is in high school, he or she spends several hours a day on homework. In sum, 65 percent of Japanese students spend more than five hours per week on homework; the figure is 24 percent for American seniors.[2]

Responsibility for the Child: Home and School

Compared to the United States, the Japanese responsibility for engendering the healthy development of the young person is more diffusely shared by family, school, and workplace.[3] For example, schoolteachers, principals, and parents, as well as the young person himself, are called to account by the police when a high school student is picked up for driving without a license. And besides the teacher's efforts, parents are expected to provide daily assistance with homework. In a recent poll, data indicates that mothers are consulted more frequently than any other adult, including teachers, on academic work. Meanwhile, high schools and colleges take an active role in finding jobs for their graduates. After entering a company, a young person can expect his or her superiors to help in the individual and parental search for a suitable wife or husband. Some companies even sponsor the wedding ceremonies. Clearly, responsibility for important aspects of personal development is not only allocated differently in Japan, but is also simultaneously assumed by several different parties.

Accordingly, Japanese schools and Japanese parents are both fully engaged in children's social and moral conduct as well as their academic progress, and schools provide active assistance integrating their graduates into the next phase of life. The persistence of this engagement may stem from the tradition of shared responsibility found in apprenticeship systems and small-scale agrarian communities. But while the influence of such traditions is undoubtedly present, the contemporary form of a shared role for child rearing is not much different from the general pattern found in other areas of life.

The pattern means that if an accident occurs in school (or on the job), blame can be less directly ascribed. But because an untoward event may be identified with a large group or network of people or even an institution, the improper behavior of one person brings negative consequences to bear on a large number of people. So while a sense of security is achieved through shared responsibility, the effects of a sin of commission or omission on one's social network are a serious deterrent to individual irresponsibility.

American schools also feel that they are accountable for the academic progress and the physical safety of their students. And parents feel that both may be enforced as if they constituted a contract: if a school is negligent, the parents may expect redress. An exaggerated example of the assumption may be seen in recent lawsuits brought by parents against schools for failing to educate their children.

Japanese and American preparations for a school field trip show further differences in the nature and determination of responsibility. In America a teacher will talk about the academic lessons to be derived from the trip and ask students to have parents sign forms releasing the school from legal responsibility in case of a mishap. But social etiquette and proper cooperative behavior rarely merit more than a passing comment because they are regarded as the responsibility of the parents.

Japanese schools, however, are concerned not only with academic progress and physical safety but with social behavior. Permission slips are not used, because physical safety is believed to be the proper responsibility of everyone involved: the child, classmates, the teacher, the person in charge of the place of the visit, the principal, and to some degree the parents as well. A school that might try using permission slips would be considered socially and probably morally deficient.

This means the entire class must carefully discuss safety precautions and the behavior expected of all of them. The responsibility of the students to the school's image, to other people in public places, to their classmates, and to their parents is explicitly talked through. And those in direct authority—principal, teachers, and class monitors—lay out procedures and precautions to be observed. In sum, with overlapping responsibilities and careful preparation, the likelihood of a mishap is reduced and the number of people who will share in the consequences of a mishap greatly increased.

Thus, if a Japanese child were to fall from a train platform while on a field trip, self-recriminations and apologies would be expected from everyone involved. The child, the class monitors, the teacher, the principal, would all apologize to each other and to the parents; the parents would then apologize to the school for the unruliness of their child; and the railway stationmaster would apologize for whatever deficiencies might have existed. The social effects of the mishap would not end there: A feeling of *meiwaku o kaketa* (having caused trouble for someone) would suffuse all of the relationships for some time, and most likely a continuing exchange of gifts and favors would occur to redress the wrongs.

The heightened sense of collective responsibility means that people try very hard through preventive measures and conservative behavior to reduce the possibility of something going wrong. If something does, prompt and even (to a Westerner) exaggerated assumption of responsibility is regarded as exemplary behavior which enhances one's social stature and which can redress some of the damage caused to one's image. Another reality here is that Japanese tend to feel that blame is more difficult to assign to someone who is visibly suffering guilt and who has already inflicted upon himself some type of punishment. Such a demonstration by one who is not actually responsible is sometimes calculated to arouse feelings of guilt in the one more directly at fault. This behavioral mode is used by parents to discourage irresponsible behavior in their children, and by others in positions of authority to encourage the loyal cooperation of their employees or subordinates.

To Western observers, the diffuse sharing of blame (and credit) appears to minimize individual accountability and therefore to encourage bad behavior. In fact, the diffusion of responsibility in the West would diminish the incentive to keep one's socks up. But in Japan the *combination* of spreading involvement and invoking indebtedness works. Failure thus can affect a network of people and increase a sense of indebtedness to one's kin, colleagues, and superiors. And because this might happen, careful, responsible behavior is greatly encouraged. In general, the interlocking, overlapping, mutually reinforcing responsibilities shared by the family, school, and company for the development of the individual is an important factor behind the success of Japanese education.

The Product

It has now become standard to talk about education in economic terms. To quantify the benefits and costs of Japanese schools, we are given test scores and suicide rates. But this is obviously not enough, and to understand where the data come from, we need to look at context more carefully.

The international media are thoroughly familiar with the high test scores of Japanese children. The scores generally exceed those of children in the West. Moreover, the Japanese educational system also scores high in international comparisons in terms of the numbers of children engaged in formal learning, the time they spend at it, and the place education has in someone's life chances. The children also, in greater numbers than elsewhere, report that they *like* school.

The curriculum—the courses taken and the material covered—is so rich that a high school diploma in Japan can be said to be the equivalent of a college degree in the United States. In math and sciences, particularly, Japanese children receive a broad and comprehensive education. It has recently been shown that the lowest math and science test scores in fifth grade classes in Japan are higher than the highest test scores in comparable American schools.[4]

Significant also is the fact that there is less variation in performance across the population than in most other societies.[5] Indeed it is a source of some wonder in Japan that children elsewhere do not perform as well and that standards and incentives in other advanced nations are so low. In other words, "high achievement" has become a standard expectation in Japan.

The effects of this situation are evident well after the end of formal schooling, for widespread literacy is accompanied by widespread engagement in all forms of knowledge-enhancing activities across all sectors of the population. There is a high level of cultural engagement as well: blue-collar workers submit original classical verse to newspaper columns. Moreover, the national media use highly sophisticated technical vocabularies, and it is assumed that everyone can read music.

So what are the costs and benefits of the achievement? To evaluate them, both Japanese and Western perspectives must be taken into account. Observers from both East and West tend to come down hard on the toll exacted by the exams for entrance to high school and college. "Examination hell," the weeks or months of grueling effort preparing for an examination, does in fact put a significant number of young people under a significant amount of pressure. Whether or not this produces psychologically damaging stress varies from one young person to another. But some effects do seem to influence the lives of most young people.

First, as a youngster approaches the end of junior high school he has less and less free time; even those who are not taking after-school classes, being tutored, or just spending the hours in independent study have fewer peers with whom to spend that time. Nearly everyone can be found either in a structured activity or devoted to solitary pastimes such as watching TV or playing video games. Second, the young person approaching exams or decisions affecting his future is no longer a member of a relatively undifferentiated and supportive group. He is now to be measured and selected as an individual, and, however well the moment of selection is buffered by the continuing nurturant relationships with family and teachers, the experience is strikingly different from what the young person has earlier known.

However, the excesses of examination hell and the pathological outcomes for some do not threaten all. The Western view is that Japanese youth are uniformly engaged in a do-or-die struggle—an image heightened by attention given to the annual juvenile suicide rate, the incidence of school phobia and psychosomatic illnesses, and the prevalence of the "education mama." The Japanese media also emphasize violence in the classroom and

395

at home, the existence of motorcycle gangs, and the (highly organized) rock dancing in a Tokyo street on Sunday afternoons. These are given as evidence of an educational system turned pressure cooker, with the struggle to get ahead having produced an excessively competitive and demoralized generation.

At the same time, Japanese observers of Japanese society are preoccupied with strains in the social fabric which to Americans seem relatively unthreatening. Statistically, neither juvenile suicides nor violence and crime appear to Americans to warrant the critical attention they have received in Japan. When dyeing one's hair or lengthening a skirt are counted as acts of school violence, a standard other than American is being applied. For perspective, one can say that the number of student assaults on teachers in New York City alone in the first semester of the 1974-1975 school year was three times the number of assaults in the entire 1976 school year in all of Japan.[6] It is, however, exactly the critical attention, often heightened by newspaper sensationalism, that feeds the sensitivity shown by Japanese to potential problems—a sensitivity that has created the success of the educational system. Remember that the Japanese feel they are living very precariously on a group of narrow islands and must hence maximize human resources and potential. Because by their lights this is best done through education, there is great concern over how children fare and a disposition to anticipate and attend to any problems that might conceivably arise.

Maximizing Personal Success

The clear net plus for society of the educational system must be weighed against the effect of the educational experience on an individual person's life. In general, Japanese education tries to maximize a child's ability and performance through the collaboration of people, priorities, and processes at many levels. The questions of how the schools stream and screen, how they maintain social cohesion while encouraging each child to work hard to achieve personal success, are best answered by looking at the consonance of goals and means in the home, school, and policy-making institutions.

Japanese and outside observers agree that Japan's rapid development in the Meiji period and the postwar economic miracle are closely related to the emphasis on education. The general level of skill in society was raised, and the especially talented were given a way to rise to positions of influence. During two times of crisis in Japanese history, there was a close correlation between what was good for personal development and what was good for the nation.

Today the finely honed system of selection for the most coveted jobs is still regarded as a sine qua non to the continued stability of Japan. Not only high in status, the positions are highly demanding and require high levels of skill and effort. Because academic success in school is for the Japanese a good indicator of success in such jobs, the school system does the selecting. Accordingly, parents strongly feel that schools must provide their children with everything possible to help them climb the occupational ladder. In Japan few opportunities exist to change paths or retool; the American idea that you can re-create yourself at any time in life, that life is full of second chances, that the self-made person can get ahead, is in no way a Japanese reality. The intensity of examination hell results from both the need to restrict competition to one point in life and from a strong consensus on what the life course is and what its goals should be.

Nevertheless, selecting talent and preserving harmony cannot be done in the same classroom. The need to maintain both has produced a split in the educational system, but one which seems composed of complementary rather than conflicting elements. The regular classroom is a place where the individual does not stick out, where active competition is not encouraged but individual needs are met and goals are set. The cohesion of the age group is paramount. Teachers spend time working with the slower learners, rather than streaming the class to suit different abilities. Moreover, teachers and the school system mostly refuse to become party to examination hysteria, partly because of pressure from the Teachers' Union. This is a very large and powerful labor union that consistently resists any move away from the egalitarian mode of instruction. The union feels that turning teachers into drill instructors would be dehumanizing, and cramming for the examination a poor substitute for learning.

The *Juku*

Where, then, is the principle of competitive selection served? It is served in the *juku*, or private after-school class. For the Japanese child, extracurricular lessons of many sorts are a very common component of the educational experience.[7] Of these, there are two major types: *okeikogoto* (enrichment lessons) and *juku* (supplementary help in academic subjects). *Okeikogoto* frequently begin during the preschool years and may continue throughout one's life. Most classes vary according to fads and the age of the students involved, yet almost all Japanese find themselves in such classes at some time in their lives. Preschool children take lessons like swimming, piano, or English; middle-aged women learn knitting, tennis, or cooking; and retired men study Japanese singing, golf, or tea ceremony. Ways to enrich leisure, they are more common during periods of life when other responsibilities such as formal study, small children, or career are less pressing.

The other type of extracurricular endeavor, *juku*, is taken exclusively during the elementary and secondary school years. Most Japanese children attend some type of *juku* in some major academic subject; in urban areas, 86 percent of ninth grade children report having attended a *juku* at some time. The term loosely covers all extracurricular lessons devoted to academic subjects; however, the range of educational settings and goals is very broad.

Juku range from small classes of two or three students meeting in the home of a teacher to large schools with dozens of classes, hundreds of students and branches all over the country. The content of the courses ranges from remedial to highly accelerated. Some are synchronized with school courses, some are given over to material one or two months ahead of the school curriculum, and some concentrate on techniques and information most likely to earn a high score on entrance exams. Hence the purpose of a course may vary from simply raising a child's math grade to preparing for a specific entrance exam to a targeted prestigious national university.

In urban areas, there are large *juku* with a businesslike and competitive atmosphere mostly attended by students preparing for the university entrance exams. However, many urban *juku*, especially those for elementary and junior high school students, are more informal, given over to the immediate improvement of school performance. The same is true for most *juku* in smaller metropolitan and rural areas, which are much smaller, with seven to fifteen students per class. The larger, examination-oriented *juku* are sometimes also known as *gakushu juku*, *yobiko*, or *zemina* (from the English "seminar"). These last two sometimes refer not only to after-school classes but to full-time cram schools attended by *ronin*, those who have graduated from high school but are doing extra work to take or retake college exams.

Besides being a multimillion-dollar industry, *juku* and *okeikogoto* form an unaccredited and unregulated yet indispensable adjunct to the formal educational system. Their proliferation is a natural response to the pressures created by discrepancies between the goals of individual families, the egalitarian ideology, and the structuring of the formal school system. The situation is further complicated by differences between the nature of the curriculum approved by the ministry of education for use in elementary and secondary schools and the preparation necessary to enter good universities. The tension stems ultimately from the basic ambivalence in Japanese cultural attitudes between egalitarianism and hierarchical distinctions. . . .

But Are They Creative?

If a Western educator observed either the ordinary schools or the *juku*, he would conclude that Japanese education could never allow the flowering of creativity. That conclusion is at least partly the result of ethnocentric assumptions about the source and meaning of creativity. And because Western beliefs about the nature and importance of creativity influence the ways in which we evaluate Japanese education, we should think for a moment about what we mean by creativity and why we regard it so highly.[8]

Western folk and academic psychology both contend that creativity is a desirable individual trait. Popular psychology asserts that children possess the potential for considerable creativity, which may diminish as they grow older. Education that is too rigid and the imposition of adult standards too early are frequently cited as the culprits in a child's loss of a presumed spontaneously unacademic way of looking at the world. At the same time, psychologists frequently describe creativity as a statistically rare response or an extraordinary accomplishment, which by definition means that the average child or average adult is not creative.

Moreover, even as Western educators plan curricula for creativity, we believe that creative invention cannot be fostered institutionally. This idea comes from both nineteenth-century romanticism and twentieth-century expressionism. In the latter, the child is to be completely unrestrained and left to his or her own nature. He is to be driven by a naive force of self-expression, what some have called the "immaculate perception."

Some children are taught that spontaneity is more important than skill. I once observed an American gym class where children were given basketballs and told to "get to know" the ball, to understand its nature—a prospect which made some children intensely uncomfortable, since they really wanted to learn how to dribble and shoot. A recent cartoon in *The New Yorker* captures "free spirit" education. A small child, disgruntled, says to a teacher, "Do we have to do what we want to do again today?" Meanwhile, from the romantics we are given to understand that the best creative effort comes to the artist through the inspiration of the *divinus furor*, the "divine fury" that visits the worthy creator from heaven.

Americans, in short, confuse self-expression with creativity, placing the greatest value on spontaneity rather than on taking pains. A contradiction may lurk here. We think, on the one hand, that hard work sometimes leads to creative success—hard work that goes on apart from formal schooling; on the other hand, we persist in the belief that schools can and should develop children's creativity.

Why do Americans especially believe creativity is so important? Part of the answer lies in American preoccupation with individual differences and the accompanying belief that absolutely unique accomplishments are better than those which somehow resemble the efforts of others. We also feel that society moves forward on breakthroughs, on the innovations and discoveries of people like Henry Ford and Albert Einstein.

Why, then, does Japanese creativity (or lack of it) interest Americans so much? Part of the interest may stem from old-fashioned American chauvinism and the need to find Japanese success fundamentally flawed. We cast about for some intangible yet crucial capacity that we have but that is absent in Japanese mentality, society, and education, which in turn will somehow permit us to retain, or regain, the upper hand.

So Americans insist that Japanese can only imitate because we feel that Japanese social structure and values do not provide fertile ground in which creativity can arise. Japanese culture puts much less emphasis on individual than on group accomplishments, and encourages perceptions of similarities rather than differences among individuals' social and cognitive achievements. Accordingly, the argument goes, classroom teachers do not expect a child to develop a novel approach or contribution and instead foster the development of memorization. Young people defer to their teachers well after their schooling has ended. Moreover, until recent American criticism made the Japanese somewhat self-conscious, there was little explicit rhetoric about the importance of creativity in education.

Traditional forms of learning—in crafts and arts—emphasize what we might call old-style creativity in Japan. Apprentices and novices may spend years sweeping the floors, washing vegetables, preparing the master's brushes, clapping out rhythms, before they shape clay, prepare a meal, draw, or try to dance themselves. Even as their performances become fully fluent, the goal remains precise imitation of the master. The fully mature Noh actor may begin to innovate, but this would be scarcely noticeable except to himself, the master, and the true aficionado—a slight turn of the head, a refinement of a movement of the hand. Such innovations, like a tiny modification of the glaze on a pot or the use of a new flower in a stylized arrangement, are in fact creative acts, which, among the right audience, produce the "Ah!" of shocked recognition that is experienced anywhere in the world in the presence of something truly creative.

The school, however, is a place where a new kind of creativity can be fostered. Japanese schools are, like most of ours, routinized. But because positive engagement and enthusiasm are emphasized, even what an American would call creativity is elicited in certain classes. The outcomes of *Japanese* routinization are, surprisingly, a high degree of analytic and creative problem-solving, as well as expressions of divergent points of view.

In arts education particularly, America cannot accuse Japanese schools of neglecting to foster creativity. In Japanese schools art is not a frill, it is basic. As Diane Ravitch says, for the Japanese the "development of an aesthetic sense" is as important as "learning about nature."[9] Hence all Japanese children learn to play two instruments and read music as part of the required elementary school curriculum. Moreover, every child participates in dramatic productions and receives instruction in drawing and painting. The belief is that before a child can be truly creative, or even express himself, he must be taught possibilities and limits of the medium; in short, one learns how to use the existing forms first. Americans who have observed Japanese children in arts classes also point to the group nature of instruction, and incorrectly assume that only as soloists, composers, and individual artists can they be truly creative—a perception highly colored by our own view of what creativity means.

Criticism leveled at Japanese education also comes down on what is seen as a suppression of genius. There is indeed little provision for tracking the superbright to their best advantage, but their best advantage may be defined very differently in Japan and America. A very bright child, appropriately socialized, will soon enough receive appropriate rewards in Japan, but he is not expected to burst through the limits established by others. He is unlike his American counterpart, who is expected to break records very early in life.

In sum, it will not get us very far to claim that the Japanese have successfully trained children to take exams at the expense of a broader education. And it is not at all appropriate to say that they cannot develop children's individuality and encourage the geniuses who make scientific breakthroughs. The first is untrue, and as for the second, the Japanese, formidable organizers that they are, are now mobilizing themselves to produce scientists and technologists who will show themselves to be creative by anyone's measure. In my judgment, the scales now appear to be tipped in favor of Japan.

Notes

1. Joseph Jay Tobin, Dana H. Davidson, and David Y. H. Wu, "Ratios and Class Size in the Japanese Preschool," unpublished manuscript, 1985.

2. Sheppard Ranbom, "Schooling in Japan," *Education Week* (three-part article: Feb. 20, Feb. 27, March 6, 1985).

3. Merry White and Lois Taniuchi, "Teaching and Learning in Japan," unpublished paper prepared for Project on Human Potential, Harvard Graduate School of Education, 1982.

4. Harold Stevenson, "Classroom Behavior and Achievement of Japanese, Chinese and American Children," in *Child Development and Education in Japan*, ed. Hiroshi Azuma, Harold Stevenson, and Kenji Hakuta (New York: Freeman Press, 1986).

5. L.C. Comber and John P. Keeves, *Science Achievement in Nineteen Countries*. (New York: John Wiley & Sons, 1973); Torsten Husen, *International Study of Achievement in Math: A Comparison of Twelve Countries*, vol. 2 (New York: John Wiley & Sons, 1967).

6. Rohlen, Thomas. *Japan's High Schools*. Berkeley: University of California Press, 1983, p. 296.

7. White and Taniuchi.

8. The following section is drawn from White and Taniuchi.

9. Diane Ravitch, "Japan's Smart Schools," *New Republic*, Jan. 13, 1986, pp. 13-15.

Mathematics Achievement of Chinese, Japanese, and American Children

Harold W. Stevenson, Shin-Ying Lee and James W. Stigler

When Harold Stevenson and his colleagues entered upon the program of research described in this article, the size and nature of the "Asian advantage" in mathematics achievement had yet to be documented in a well-controlled, comparative study. To provide this documentation, the researchers developed individually administered measures of mathematics achievement that were comparable across and appropriate to each of the three groups of children—Japanese, Chinese, and American—to be assessed. These measures were then administered to kindergartners, first-grade, and fifth-grade children in Sendai (Japan), Taipei (Taiwan), and Minneapolis. The results indicated that relative to those of Japanese and Chinese children, the scores of American students declined from grade to grade.

Like Merry White, Stevenson and his colleagues ascribe much of the observed math achievement difference to the simple fact that Japanese and Chinese children spend much more time than American children in school, in academic activities in school, and in mathematics instruction among their academic activities. Interviewing American parents and teachers, these investigators also report a degree of optimism concerning the success of American schools and children that may, at least with respect to mathematics education, be unwarranted. In the authors' view, Americans' sense of satisfaction with the status quo, tendency to view reading and language rather than math and science skills as the proper focus of elementary education, and relative lack of coordination between home and school all serve as barriers to improvement in American children's levels of achievement in mathematics.

Poor scholastic performance by American children has focused attention on education, especially in mathematics and science. Funds for research on how to improve teaching have been allocated and commissions formed, such as a National Research Council committee exploring a research agenda for precollege education in mathematics,

Stevenson, Harold W.; Lee, Shin-Ying; & Stigler, James W. (1986). Mathematics achievement of Chinese, Japanese, and American children. *Science, 231.* pp. 693-699.

science, and technology. Recommendations to be made by this committee and others that have preceded it concentrate on the nation's secondary schools. The wisdom of this emphasis is questionable. Results emerging from a large cross-national study of elementary school children suggest that Americans should not focus solely on improving the performance of high school students. The problems arise earlier. American children appear to lag behind children in other countries in reading and mathematics as early as kindergarten and continue to perform less effectively during the years of elementary school. When differences in achievement arise so early in the child's formal education, more must be involved than inadequate formal educational practices. Improving secondary education is an important goal, but concentrating remedial efforts on secondary schools may come too late in the academic careers of most students to be effective.

Our research deals with the scholastic achievement of American, Chinese, and Japanese children in kindergarten and grades one and five. Children were given achievement tests and a battery of cognitive tasks. The children and their mothers and teachers were interviewed, and observations were made in the children's classrooms. These procedures have yielded an enormous array of information.[1-5] In this article, we focus on the discussion of achievement in mathematics and factors that may contribute to the poor performance of American children in that area. . . .

Selecting the Children

Children in only one city in each country were studied. In the United States, we selected children in the Minneapolis metropolitan area. Several factors led to this choice, the most important being that the residents of this area tend to come from native-born, English-speaking, economically sound families. Few are from a minority background. These factors, we assumed, would provide an advantageous cultural, economic, and linguistic environment for learning in school. If problems were found in Minneapolis, we assumed they would be compounded in other American cities where a greater proportion of the children speak English as a second language, come from economically disadvantaged homes, and have parents whose cultural backgrounds diverge from the typically middle-class milieu to which American elementary school curricula generally are addressed.

The Japanese city that we chose as being most comparable to Minneapolis was Sendai, which is located in the Tohoku region several hundred miles northeast of Tokyo. It, too, is a large, economically successful city, with little heavy industry and with an economic and cultural status in Japan similar to that of Minneapolis in the United States. Taipei was the Chinese city in which it was most feasible for us to conduct our research, in terms of language, size, colleagues, and other factors.

Ten schools in each city were selected to provide a representative sample of the city's elementary schools.[6] Because we wanted to test children shortly after they entered elementary school and also near the end of their elementary education, we randomly chose two first-grade and two fifth-grade classrooms in each school. The age of school entrance is the same in all three countries and elementary school attendance is mandatory.

From each classroom we randomly chose six boys and six girls. This procedure resulted in a sample of 240 first-graders and 240 fifth-graders from each city.

Kindergartens in Taiwan and Japan are mainly privately owned and attendance is not compulsory. Nevertheless, more than 98 percent of the five-year-olds in Sendai and over 80 percent of the five-year-olds in Taipei attend kindergarten for a least a full year. All Minneapolis children attend kindergarten. Children in the study came from twenty-four kindergarten classes in each city. In order to ensure that the samples of kindergarten and elementary school children in Taipei and Sendai would be comparable, the kindergartens chosen were among those attended by children from the ten elementary schools. Six boys and six girls were randomly chosen from each classroom, yielding a sample in each city of 288 children for study. A representative sample of twenty-four kindergarten classrooms was selected in the Minneapolis metropolitan area.

Mathematics Achievement

The American children's scores were lower than those of the Japanese children in kindergarten and at grades one and five, and lower than those of the Chinese children's at grades one and five. Average scores for boys and girls did not show statistically significant differences from each other at any of the three grade levels.

Figure 1 shows graphically the result of transforming each child's score into a z score, which represents the departure in standard deviation units from the mean of a distribution derived from the scores of the children in all three cities at each grade level. Scores were then recombined according to country, and the mean score of children in each country was determined. Consistently superior performance of the Japanese children and rapid improvement in the scores of the Chinese children from kindergarten through fifth grade are evident. Scores of the American children display a consistent decline compared to those of the Chinese and Japanese children. . . .

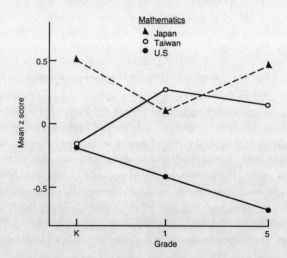

Figure 1. Children's performance on the mathematics test. (Standard deviations for kindergarten, grade 1, and grade 5 were as follows: Japan, 0.77, 0.93, and 1.00; Taiwan, 1.10, 0.98, and 0.76; United States, 0.83, 0.96, and 0.83.)

A high degree of overlap appears in the distributions of scores for the first-grade classrooms in the three cities. At the fifth-grade level there is a clear separation. The highest average score of an American fifth-grade classroom was below that of the Japanese fifth-grade classroom with the lowest average score. In addition, only one Chinese classroom showed an average score lower than the American classroom with the highest average score. Equally remarkable is the fact that the lowest average score for a fifth-grade American classroom was only slightly higher than the average score for the best first-grade Chinese classroom.

Viewed in still another way, the data indicate that among the 100 top scorers on the mathematics test at grade one, there were only fifteen American children. At grade five, only one American child appeared among the 100 top scorers from the total sample of approximately 720 children. On the other hand, among the children receiving the 100 lowest scores at each grade, there were 58 American children at grade one and 67 at grade five.

The low level of performance of American children was not due to a few exceptionally low-scoring classrooms nor to a particular area of weakness. They were as ineffective in calculating as in solving word problems. The search for an adequate explanation of these findings will be a long one, for many factors are involved in producing such large differences in performance. Some of the most obvious alternatives are discussed below. . . .

Life in School

Our information about the children's experiences in school is based on extensive observations made in each elementary school classroom. Each classroom was visited according to a schedule in which the time of observation was randomized during a period of several weeks. The observer's attention was focused on the children for some of the observations and on the teacher for others. Behavior was coded according to an objective coding system.[4] The number of hours of observation was 1353 in Minneapolis, 1600 in Taipei, and 1200 in Sendai.

Learning depends, in part, on the amount of time spent in practicing the material to be learned. We therefore looked at the percentage of time devoted to academic activities, and especially to mathematics. American first-graders were engaged in academic activities a smaller percentage of time than the Chinese and Japanese children: 69.8 percent for the American children, 85.1 percent for the Chinese children, and 79.2 percent for the Japanese children.

By fifth grade, differences between the American and the Chinese and the Japanese children were greater than at the lower grades. American children spent 64.5 percent of their classroom time involved in academic activities. Chinese children spent 91.5 percent, and Japanese children, 87.4 percent. Assuming that our observations provide a representative picture of what went on in Minneapolis fifth-grade classrooms, we estimate that 19.6 hours per week (64.5 percent of the 30.4 hours the American children spend in school) were devoted to academic activities. This is less than half the estimate of 40.4

hours (91.5 percent of 44.1 hours that Chinese children attend school) devoted to academic activities in the fifth grade Chinese classrooms, and not much less than half of the 32.6 hours (87.4 percent of 37.3 hours that Japanese children attend school) in the Japanese classrooms.

In both grades one and five, American children spent less than 20 percent of their time on the average studying mathematics in school. This was less than the percentage for either Chinese or Japanese children. At the fifth grade, language arts (including reading) and mathematics occupied approximately equal amounts of time for the Chinese and Japanese children, but the American children spent more than twice as much time on language arts (40 percent) as on mathematics (17 percent). In some of the American classrooms, no time was devoted to work in mathematics during the approximately forty randomly selected hours when an observer was present. The high variability among American classrooms in the time allocated to the various academic subjects can be readily explained. There are precisely defined curricula in Taiwan and Japan, and teachers are expected to adhere closely to these curricula. American teachers are allowed to organize their classrooms much more according to their own desires; hence, there is greater variability among classrooms. . . .

Moreover, American teachers spent proportionally much less time imparting information (21 percent) than did the Chinese (58 percent) or Japanese (33 percent) teachers. These are sobering results. American children were in school approximately thirty hours a week. This means that they were receiving information from the teacher for approximately six hours a week (0.21 times 30). Computing similar estimates for Chinese and Japanese classrooms gives values of twenty-six hours for Chinese children and twelve hours for Japanese children. American teachers actually spent somewhat more time giving directions than in imparting information (26 percent compared to 21 percent).

There were other interesting differences in the ways children spent their time in school. For example, we sometimes found that a child who was known to be at school was not present in the classroom. The child could be at the school office, on an errand for the teacher, in another classroom, or in the library. This occurred 18.4 percent of the time that an American fifth-grader was to be observed, but less than 0.2 percent of the time in Taipei and Sendai classrooms.

The comparatively low levels of achievement of the American children in mathematics appear to be attributable in part to the fact that they are not receiving amounts of instruction comparable to those received by children in Taiwan and Japan. These cross-national differences become even more profound when they are extended over the school year. Chinese and Japanese children spend half a day at school on Saturdays and have fewer holidays than do American children. As a result, American children attend school an average of 178 days a year; Chinese and Japanese children attend school for 240 days. In addition, Japanese fifth-graders were estimated by their mothers to spend an average of one hour more each day, and the Chinese children, two hours more each day at school than the American children. Taken together, these data point to enormous differences in the amounts of schooling young children receive in the three countries.

406

Homework

Learning occurs at home as well as at school. But our data indicate that neither American parents nor teachers of elementary school children tend to believe that homework is of much value. As a consequence, American children spend much less time on homework than do Japanese children, and both groups spend vastly less time on homework than do Chinese children. American mothers estimated that on weekdays their first-graders spent an average of 14 minutes a day on homework; the daily average for Chinese first graders was 77 minutes, and for Japanese, 37 minutes. For fifth graders, the estimate for the American children was 46 minutes a day; for the Chinese and Japanese fifth-graders the estimates were 114 and 57 minutes a day, respectively. On weekends, American children studied even less: an estimated 7 minutes on Saturday and 11 minutes on Sunday. The corresponding values for Chinese children were 83 and 73 minutes, and for the Japanese children, 37 and 29 minutes—and this was in addition to the half day in school on Saturday. American children also were given less help when they were doing their homework, according to their mothers' estimates. Someone, usually the mother, assisted the fifth-grade children with their homework an average of 14 minutes a day. The Chinese children were assisted by some family member an average of 27 minutes a day, and the Japanese children, 19 minutes a day.

Parental concern about a child's schoolwork was evident in another simple index, the possession of a desk. Only 63 percent of the American fifth-graders, but 98 percent of the Japanese and 95 percent of the Chinese fifth-graders had desks. When the Chinese and Japanese children were not occupied with homework, they were given other opportunities to practice by solving the problems appearing in the workbooks purchased for them by their parents. Only 28 percent of the parents of American fifth-graders, but 58 percent of the Japanese and 56 percent of the Chinese parents bought their children workbooks in mathematics. The discrepancy was even more pronounced in the purchase of workbooks in science, which were purchased by only 1 percent of the American parents, but by 29 percent of the Japanese and 51 percent of the Chinese parents.

How did children in the three cities react to doing homework? Taipei children said they liked homework; children in Minneapolis said they did not like homework; and the attitudes of the Sendai children were somewhere in between. When asked to choose among an array of five frowning, neutral, or smiling faces to express their attitudes about homework, more than 60 percent of the Chinese fifth-graders chose a smiling face, more than 60 percent of the Japanese children chose a smiling or neutral face, and 60 percent of the American children chose a frowning face. Although 30 percent of the American children chose a smiling face at first grade, the percentage was half that among fifth-graders.

One indication of what teachers thought about homework appeared in their ratings of the value of homework and fifteen other activities directed at helping children do well in school. Ratings given to the value of homework by American teachers placed it fifteenth among sixteen items—lowest except for physical punishment. Chinese and Japanese teachers were much more positive; the average rating given by Chinese teachers on a nine-point scale was 7.3; by Japanese teachers, 5.8; and by American teachers, 4.4.

The small amounts of homework assigned to American children were not in conflict with the mothers' beliefs about how much schoolwork their child should be assigned. Among American mothers, 69 percent said that the amount of homework was "just right." Nor were the Chinese and Japanese mothers dissatisfied with the large amounts of homework assigned to their children; 82 percent of the Chinese mothers and 67 percent of the Japanese mothers thought the amount was "just right."

Mothers' Evaluations

When asked to rate their child's achievement in mathematics, American mothers gave their children favorable evaluations. Ratings were made on nine-point scales, each anchored by five defining statements, ranging from "much below average" to "much above average." Although mothers were asked to compare their child with "other children of his or her age," the mean rating made by the American mothers for their child's ability in mathematics was 5.9, higher than the average rating 5.2 of the Chinese mothers and similar to the average of 5.8 of the Japanese mothers.

Mothers were also asked to rate children on several cognitive abilities, each defined by several words or a short phrase. Great care was taken to select words and phrases that express the same nuances of meaning in the three languages. American mothers consistently gave their children the highest average ratings and Japanese mothers gave their children the lowest. For example, on ratings of a child's intellectual ability, the average rating given by American mothers was 6.3, much above the 5.0 that would indicate an average level of ability. The average rating given by the Japanese mothers was 5.5, and by the Chinese mothers, 6.1.

Despite the positive bias of the American mothers, the rank order of their ratings was in line with the children's performance. The correlation between the mothers' ratings of the children's abilities in mathematics and the fifth-graders' scores on the mathematics test was 0.50 in Minneapolis, 0.37 in Taipei, and 0.54 in Sendai. The high ratings made by American mothers must be attributed to an excessively positive attitude, rather than to a failure to perceive a child's status in relation to other children. Conversely, the low ratings of Japanese mothers appear to reflect an effort to be more realistic in their evaluations.

The optimism of the American mothers was reflected in other ways. They were pleased with the job the schools were doing in educating their children: 91 percent judged that the school was doing an "excellent" or "good" job. Only 42 percent of the Chinese mothers and 39 percent of the Japanese mothers were this positive. Instead, the majority of the Chinese and Japanese mothers considered that the schools were doing a "fair" job.

The high esteem the American mothers had for their children's cognitive abilities extended to their satisfaction with their children's current academic performance. More than 40 percent of the American mothers described themselves as being "very satisfied." Fewer than 6 percent of the Chinese and Japanese mothers were this positive.

When asked if there were things about their children's education that could be improved, 45 percent of the American mothers of fifth-graders who suggested improvements could be made emphasized improvement in academic subjects. The subject that they thought should get more emphasis was reading (48 percent of the suggestions). Mathematics and science were seldom mentioned (<6 percent of the suggestions). The subjects mentioned most frequently by the Japanese mothers were reading and mathematics. Chinese mothers, on the other hand, believed that more emphasis should be given to music, art, and gym.

The positive attitudes of the mothers did not mean that American children liked school. In rating how well they liked school, 52 percent of the American children, compared to 86 percent of the Chinese fifth-graders, chose a smiling face. (The question was not asked in Japan.)

Critics of Chinese and Japanese education often suggest that the high demands placed on children result in ambivalence or dislike of school. This does not seem to be the case in elementary schools. It is the American children who regard elementary school less positively. Expressing a dislike for school may be a socially acceptable reaction among American school children. Even young children in Taiwan and Japan are aware of the fact that education is highly prized in the Chinese and Japanese cultures. The emphasis on scholastic achievement may lead to the intense competition that is often said to characterize secondary schools in Taiwan and Japan, but negative consequences were not evident during the elementary school years. In fact, the children in all three cities appeared to be cheerful, enthusiastic, vigorous, and responsive. Although some of these characteristics may be more vividly expressed in classrooms in Minneapolis, they are readily apparent to the observer who follows Chinese and Japanese children through their school day.

Parental Beliefs

Experiences that parents provide their children may be strongly influenced by their general beliefs about the components of success. For example, parents who emphasize ability as the most important requisite for success may be less disposed to stress the need to work hard than would parents who believe success is largely dependent on effort.

In exploring cultural differences in beliefs about the relative importance of factors leading to success in school, we asked the mothers to rank effort, natural ability, difficulty of the schoolwork, and luck or chance by importance in determining a child's performance in school. They were then asked to assign a total of ten pints to the four factors. Japanese mothers assigned the most points to effort, and American mothers gave the largest number of points to ability. The willingness of Japanese and Chinese children to work so hard in school may be due, in part, to the stronger belief on the part of their mothers in the value of hard work.

Outside Assistance

It has been suggested that the scholastic performance of young Chinese and Japanese children is due in part to outside tutoring. Articles about the *juku*, the cram schools of Japan, and the *buxiban*, the after-hours schools in Taiwan, have appeared in American newspapers. These seem to be phenomena associated with later years of schooling, for few mothers said that their elementary school children attended such classes. Children in all three of the cities that we studied were enrolled in after-school lessons or classes, but these were not necessarily ones that would help the children with their schoolwork. American children most frequently took lessons in various types of sports. Among Chinese children, the most popular lessons were in sports and calligraphy, and among Japanese children, the most popular lessons were in art and calligraphy. The percentage of children taking lessons in mathematics was higher in Sendai (7 percent) than in Taipei (2 percent), but not higher than the percentage in Minneapolis (8 percent). . . .

Conclusions

Impetus for change often comes from dissatisfaction with the present state of affairs. Most American mothers interviewed in this study did not appear to be dissatisfied with their children's schools, and seem unlikely, therefore, to become advocates for reform. Moreover, the children, faced with parents who generally are satisfied and approving of what happens in school, must see little need to spend more time and effort on their schoolwork. The poor performance of American children in mathematics thus reflects a general failure to perceive that American elementary school children are performing ineffectively and that there is a need for improvement and change if the United States is to remain competitive with other countries in areas such as technology and science which require a solid foundation in mathematical skills.

The lack of time spent teaching mathematics may be a reflection of the view of American parents and teachers that education in elementary school is synonymous with learning to read. Large amounts of time are devoted to reading instruction, and if changes were to be made in the curriculum, both parents and teachers agreed that even greater proportions of time should be devoted to reading. Mathematics and science play a small role in Americans' conception of elementary education.

American mothers have unrealistically favorable evaluations of their children and what they are accomplishing in school. This optimism may lead to a sense of well-being but is unwarranted in the context of cross-national comparisons of children's scholastic achievement. When we look only within the United States, we may find cause to deplore the poor performance only of certain subgroups of our population. When we broaden our perspective to include children from other countries, we have cause for concern. Although a small proportion of American children perform superbly, the large majority appear to be falling behind their peers in other countries.

The data we have presented are from a single set of studies, conducted in particular locales and with particular methods. Nevertheless, the findings are directly in line with those from other cross-national studies of achievement in mathematics and science involving older children and adolescents.[7-9] Preliminary results from the Second International Mathematics Study, for example, indicate that among eighth-graders from twenty countries, Japanese children received the highest scores in arithmetic, algebra, geometry, statistics, and measurement. The average scores of the American children on these tests ranged from eighth to eighteenth position. The poor performance of American children that begins in kindergarten is maintained through the later grades.

Regardless of the funds that may be allocated to the development and application of new methods of teaching, it seems obvious that children's success in mathematics and other subjects will depend on greater awareness and an increased willingness by American parents to be of direct assistance to their children. Schools may be improved, but the task of helping children reach higher levels of achievement cannot be accomplished without more cooperation and communication between the school and the home. Further, without greater acknowledgement of the importance of the elementary school years to children's education in mathematics and science, legislation to improve instruction in secondary schools may result in little more than exercises in remediation for most children.

References and Notes

1. J. W. Stigler, S.Y. Lee, G.W. Lucker, H.W. Stevenson, *J. Educ. Psychol. 74*, 315 (1982).

2. H. W. Stevenson *et al.*, *Child Devel. 53*, 1164 (1982).

3. H. W. Stevenson *et al.*, *ibid. 56*, 718 (1985).

4. H. W. Stevenson *et al.*, in *Advances in Instructional Psychology,* R. Glaser, Ed. (Erlbaum, Hillside, NJ, in press).

5. H. W. Stevenson, H. Azuma, K. Hakuta, Eds., *Child Development and Education in Japan* (Freeman, New York, in press).

6. Care was taken to develop procedures that would result in the selection of rep resentative samples of children within each city. Selection was made after we discussed our goals with educational authorities in each city. We obtained a list of schools stratified by region and socioeconomic status of the families. Schools in Taipei and Sendai were then selected at random so that the ten elementary schools would constitute a representative sample of schools within each city. In the Minneapolis metropolitan area, where there are many different school districts, we sought to adopt a procedure that was as comparable to that used in Sendai and Taipei as possible. All elementary schools in Sendai were public schools, but one private school was chosen both in Taipei and Minneapolis to represent the proportion of

411

children in those cities that attend private schools. All children in each of the class-rooms in Japan and Taiwan were included as potential subjects. . . . Children with IQ's below seventy were eliminated from the samples in all three cities.

7. T. Husén, *International Study of Achievement in Mathematics: A Comparison of Twelve Countries* (Wiley, New York, 1967).

8. L. C. Comber and J. Keeves, *Science Achievement in Nineteen Countries* (Wiley, New York, 1973).

9. "Preliminary report: Second International Mathematics Study" (University of Illinois, Urbana, 1984).

10. This article reports results from a collaborative study undertaken with S. Kitamura, S. Kimura, and T. Kato of Tohoku Fukushi College in Sendai, Japan., and C.C. Hsu of National Taiwan University in Taipei. Supported by NIMH grants MH 33259 and MH 30567.

UNIT 6: Peer Relationships

17

Friendship, Gender, and Emerging Sexuality

Justice and care perspectives on the solution of moral problems are beautifully illustrated in interviews that 11-15-year-old boys and girls gave to psychologist D. Kay Johnston after she read them the following fable concerning a porcupine and a family of moles:

It was growing cold, and a porcupine was looking for a home. He found a most desirable cave but saw it was occupied by a family of moles.

"Would you mind if I shared your home for the winter?" the porcupine asked the moles.

The generous moles consented and the porcupine moved in. But the cave was small and every time the moles moved around, they were scratched by the porcupine's sharp quills. The moles endured this discomfort as long as they could. Then at last they gathered courage to approach their visitor. "Pray leave," they said, "and let us have our cave to ourselves once again."

"Oh no!" said the porcupine. "This place suits me very well."

As reported in Johnston's article in the book *Mapping the Moral Domain*, children's justice solutions, which focused on the moles' rights, included the following:

The porcupine has to go definitely. It's the moles' house.
It's their ownership and nobody else has a right to it.
Send the porcupine out since he was the last one there.

Care solutions, on the other hand, responded to the needs of all the animals:

Wrap the porcupine in a towel.
There'd be times that the moles would leave or the porcupine would stand still or they'd take   turns doing stuff—eating and stuff and not moving.
The both of them should try to get together and make the hole bigger.

Justice- and care-oriented solutions were offered spontaneously by both boys and girls; but when children were asked which solutions they considered to be the best, justice solutions were overwhelmingly preferred by boys and care solutions by girls.

• INTRODUCTION •

One of the most striking phenomena of middle childhood is the extraordinary degree to which children's activities, friendships, and everyday encounters are differentiated by gender. Even a casual observer in a fifth-grade lunchroom is likely to notice the degree to which boys and girls maintain spatial separation—at lunch tables, in lines, and in groups as they enter or leave the lunchroom, boys will be next to boys, girls next to girls.

On the playground, boys and girls typically control separate territories. Large, open spaces "belong" to the boys; smaller, better defined areas with clearer boundaries are controlled by the girls. In the open spaces, boys will often be found roving together en masse, playing "keep away," or actively engaged in formal games such as baseball, basketball, or soccer. Girls are more often to be found in smaller groups or in friendship pairs, engaged in conversation. When large group activities arise spontaneously among girls, they are much more likely to involve a turn-taking game than an organized sport.

The readings in this chapter document the extent of these gender differences. In the first article, Janet Lever discusses the nature, sources, and possible implications of variation in the complexity of boys' and girls' play and games. In the second reading, Barrie Thorne and Zella Luria describe differences between boys and girls with respect to same gender interactions and patterns of emerging cross-gender contact. Focusing on the implicit and sometimes explicit sexual meanings attached to these varied patterns, the authors suggest that these gender differences help prepare children for the later, more overtly sexual scripts of adolescence.

• • •

Sex Differences in the Complexity of Children's Play and Games
Janet Lever

Peer interactions take place in both public and private settings such as school playgrounds at recess, lunch, and sometimes before and after school; and in homes and in neighborhoods. In the mid-1970s, Janet Lever employed a combination of observations, diary records, interviews, and questionnaires in a classic study of gender differences in public and private peer interactions in middle childhood.

Focusing on the play and games of American fifth graders and utilizing a scale of complexity derived from the sociology of organizations, Lever found that, relative to girls, boys were much more likely to engage in activities organized at a high level of social complexity. Boys' games tended to involve larger groups. They were frequently organized around teams and were likely to be characterized by a number of different features: multiple, differentiated roles (e.g., pitcher, catcher, batter); face-to-face competition requiring simultaneous, interdependent decision-making and interaction; clear and definite outcomes such that there were clear winners and losers; and elaborate structures of rules to govern the adjudication of conflict.

Compared with boys, girls spent less time involved in organized games and more time in loosely-structured play or conversation. Although girls' games did occasionally involve team formation and higher levels of complex organization, girls were much more likely than boys to interact in smaller groups and to be engaged in non-competitive actions that involved one or two roles (e.g., rope turner, jumper) sequentially adopted by each player in turn and governed by ritual rather than rule.

In analyzing the sources of these gender differences, Lever points to traditional beliefs in the masculine character of sport and in female physiological inferiority as reflected in the emphasis in schools on competitive athletics in for boys and in parents' differential expectations for male and female children. Examining possible implications of these patterns, she suggests that gender differences in systematic exposure to complex games may have significant consequences for boys' and girls' differential acquisition of skills needed to function effectively in a competitive, leadership-oriented marketplace.

In Lever's view, complex games help children learn to deal with diversity in the contributions that each member makes to the group, especially as these relate to issues of leadership. In complex interactions, children develop skill in coordinating their actions with those of others, elaborating shared strategies, maintaining group cohesiveness, and working for collective as well as personal goals. Children engaged in complex activities acquire a respect for and an ability to think in terms of systems of impersonal rules. As the opponent in one game becomes a teammate in the next, children gradually become familiar with the importance of depersonalizing the outcomes of interpersonal competition. Complex games, in other words, may provide an important opportunity to learn to adjust to the demands of competition that may eventually be faced in the broader society. Historically this was a training ground from which girls were largely excluded. Since the mid-1970s, however, when Lever's article first appeared the United States has been witness to a major expansion in the availability of organized, team-oriented athletic opportunities for girls. This has occurred partly as a result of changing cultural attitudes and norms and partly as a result of legislation mandating the relative equalization of school expenditures on athletic programs for males and females. As girls take increasing advantage of these formal opportunities, it will be of considerable interest to assess the impact of these changes on gender differences in children's spontaneous activity choices and, ultimately, on gendered patterns of leadership in the society at large.

. . . A central concern of this study is to explore sex differences in the organization of children's play and to speculate on the sources as well as the potential effects of those differences. . . .

Methodology

In total, 181 fifth-grade children, aged ten and eleven, were studied. Half were from a suburban school and the other half from two city schools in Connecticut. The entire fifth grade of each school was included in the study. . . .

Lever, Janet. (1978). Sex differences in the complexity of children's play and games. *American Sociological Review, 43.* pp. 471-483.

Four techniques of data collection were employed: observation of schoolyards, semistructured interviews, written questionnaires, and a diary record of leisure activities. The diary was a simple instrument used to document where the children had actually spent their time for the period of one week. Each morning, under the direction of the researcher, the children filled out a short form on which they described (1) what they had done the previous day after school, (2) who they did it with, (3) where the activity took place, and (4) how long it had lasted. Half the diaries were collected in the winter and half in the spring. The questionnaire, designed to elicit how children spend their time away from school, also was administered by me inside the classroom. I conducted semistructured interviews with one-third of the sample. Some were done in order to help design the questionnaire and diary; others were done later to help interpret the results. I gathered observational data while watching children's play activity during recess, physical education classes, and after school.

Measuring Complexity

In common usage, the word "complex" means something that is made up of a combination of elements. Sociologists similarly have applied the term to describe the amount of functional differentiation in any social unit, from a small group or a large organization, to society as a whole. Based on the ideal type of complex organization, regardless of the scale of the collectivity, there is general agreement that increases in any of the following six attributes constitute greater complexity (Etzioni, 1969; Blau and Schoenherr, 1971):

1. *division of labor based on specialization of roles;*
2. *interdependence between individual members;*
3. *size of the membership;*
4. *explicitness of the group goals;*
5. *number and specificity of impersonal rules; and*
6. *action of members as a unified collective.*

Borrowing from the work of some contemporary students of games (Roberts et al., 1959; Redl et al., 1971; Avedon, 1971; Eifermann, 1972), I developed operational definitions for these six dimensions of complexity as they apply to the structure of play and games:

1. *Role differentiation.* For the purposes of this study, activities are to be considered low in role differentiation if the same behavior is required or expected from all players. For example, in the game of checkers, each player is equipped with the same number of pieces and is expected to move them in accordance with the same rules. Role differentiation is to be scored medium if one player has more power and acts differently from the undifferentiated group of other players. This describes all central-person games such as tag and hide-and-seek. An activity is to be scored high on role differentiation if three or more distinct game roles are present. For example, in the game of baseball, the pitcher

has a different task to perform than the shortstop whose task is different from the center fielder and so on.

2. *Player interdependence.* An activity is to be judged low on the dimension of interdependence of players when the performance of one player does not immediately and significantly affect the performance of other players. For example, in the game of darts, one person's score does not interfere with the next player's score for the round. On the other hand, in the game of tennis, each player's move greatly affects the other's so that game has high interdependence of players.

3. *Size of play group.* This is a simple count of the number of players engaged in an activity. In this analysis, a group of three or fewer children is considered low on this dimension of complexity.

4. *Explicitness of goals.* The explicitness of goals is found in the distinction between play and games. *Play* is defined as a cooperative interaction that has no stated goal, no end point, and no winners; formal *games*, in contrast, are competitive interactions, aimed at achieving a recognized goal (e.g., touchdown; checkmate). Goals may involve tests of physical or mental skills, or both. Formal games have a predetermined end point (e.g., when one opponent reaches a specified number of points; end of ninth inning) that is simultaneous with the declaration of a winner or winners. The same basic activity may be either play or games. For example, riding bikes is play; racing bikes is a game.

5. *Number and specificity of rules.* Sometimes the word "rule" is broadly used to refer to norms or customs. Here the term is used in a narrower sense and refers to explicit rules which (a) are known to all players before the game begins, (b) are constant from one game situation to the next, and (c) carry sanctions for their violation. Play as defined above never has rules, whereas games always are governed by them. But games do vary by the number and specificity of their rules. Some games, like tag and hide-and-seek, have only a few rules; other games, like baseball and Monopoly, have numerous well-established rules.

6. *Team formation.* A team is a group of players working collectively toward a common goal. Play, as defined above, is never structured by teams. Games, on the other hand, are to be divided into those requiring team formation when played with three or more persons and those prohibiting or excluding team formation. Within the category of games with team formation are included both those games where teammates play relatively undifferentiated roles, as in tug-of-war or relay races, and those that require coordination between teammates playing differentiated positions, as in baseball.

In order to test the hypothesis that boys' play and games are more complex in structure, I examine closely the type and frequency of the play activities of both sexes as they occur in public and private places. The evidence for private play is in the diary data, reporting after school and weekend play. Diary data are important because they reflect a large number of incidents, a wide range of activities, and a free choice of both games and playmates. The evidence for public play, based on observational data collected mostly during recess and gym periods, reveal the rich texture of the play world, replete with dialogue that helps the researcher understand the meanings children attribute to different play forms.

Diary Data

The diary responses reflect activities played inside or around the home in the hours after school. From over two thousand diary entries, 895 cases of social play were isolated for this analysis. They represented 136 distinct play activities which were then scored by the author and three independent coders. . . . All games were given ratings based on the children's own reports of how a game is played most typical at the fifth grade level.[1]. . . By age ten, play activities are generally known to be sex segregated. . . .

If we can agree that games provide differential learning environments, then we must assume differential effects for boys and girls. Boys experience three times as many games at the highest level of complexity and over twice as many boys' activities are located in the top half of the complexity scale. Table 1 shows the sex distribution separately for each of the six dimensions. Although greater complexity in boys' activities is demonstrated for all six, the major finding is seen on the fourth dimension, explicitness of goals. Sixty-five percent of boys' activities were competitive games compared to only 37 percent of girls' activities. In other words, *girls played more* while *boys gamed more*. This difference is not merely a function of boys' playing more team sports. Only 140 of the 305 games played by boys were team sports. Eliminating team sports for both sexes, we would still find 54 percent of the boys' activities and 30 percent of the girls' activities competitively structured. Sedentary games, like chess and electric race cars, are as important as sport in reflecting boys' greater competitiveness.

Nor is it the case when girls do participate in competitive games that they experience the same level of complexity as their male peers. The games girls play have fewer rules, and less often require the formation of teams.[2] In summary, the data from children's diaries show strongly that boys, far more often than girls, experience high levels of complexity in their play and games.

Observational Data

Observations of children at play during recess, gym classes, and after school also indicate very distinct play patterns for boys and girls. As in the diary data, boys' activities were found to be more complex. The following descriptions of a few selected play activities illustrate the way in which each of the dimensions of complexity is expressed. Greater attention is given to girls' games as they are less familiar to adults. Some implications of differential organization of play are suggested, but their elaboration awaits the discussion section.

1. *Role differentiation*. The largest category of girls' public activity was the same as their private activity, namely, single-role play. These were cooperative activities with both or all parties doing basically the same thing such as riding bikes, roller skating, or ice skating. A minority of girls' activities were competitive games. Observing recess periods for a year, I saw only one instance of a spontaneously organized team sport, namely, kickball. The activities that appeared most regularly during recess were the traditional girls' games, like hopscotch, which are turn-taking games with only one game role present at a given time. Each player, in specified sequential order, attempts to accomplish the same task as all other players. A few turn-taking games have two distinct roles: for example, in jump rope there is the role of rope turner and that of rope jumper. The other girls' games I observed frequently at recess were central-person games, the most popular being tag, spud, and Mother May I. These games also have only two roles—the "it" and the "others." Power is usually ascribed in these games through "dipping rules" like "odd-man-out."

Boys at this age have largely stopped playing central-person games except as fillers; for example, they might play tag while waiting for a bus or after so many team members have been called home to dinner that their previous game has disintegrated. The great majority of observed games were team sports with their multiple roles. Besides distinctions based on positions and assigned tasks, there were also distinctions in power between team captains and their subordinates. Sometimes the leaders were appointed by teachers, but more often the children elected their captains according to achievement criteria.[3] After school especially, I observed boys in single role activities, some noncompetitive, like flying kites and climbing trees, but most competitive like tennis, foot races, or one-on-one basketball.

2. *Player interdependence*. There are many types of player interdependence: (1) interdependence of action between members of a single group; (2) interdependent decision making between single opponents; (3) simultaneous interdependence of action with one's own teammates and an opposing group of teammates.

Very little interdependence was required of those girls engaged in single role play; coaction rather than interaction is required of the participants. Also, little interdependence was required of those playing turn-taking games. Even though the latter activity is competitive, the style of competition is indirect, with each player acting independently of the others. That is, one competes against a figurative "scoreboard" (Player A → norm ← Player B). Participation in such games is routinized and occurs successively or after the previous player's failure; that is, opponents do not compete simultaneously. Interdependent decision making is not necessary in turn-taking games of physical skill as it may be in some of the popular board games.

When girls do play interdependently, they tend to do so in a cooperative context where there is interdependence of action between members of a single group. This type of interaction is best exemplified (but rarely observed) in the creation of private fantasy scenarios. One public example occurred when seven girls from one school took the initiative to write, produce, and act out a play they called "Hippie Cinderella." They stayed indoors at recess and rehearsed almost daily for three weeks in preparation for presentation to the entire fifth-grade class.

When boys compete as individuals, they are more likely to be engaged in direct, face-to-face confrontations (Player A ↔ Player B). Interdependent decision making between single opponents is necessary in games like tennis or one-on-one basketball that combine strategy with physical skill. More often, boys compete as members of teams and must simultaneously coordinate their actions with those of their teammates while taking into account the action and strategies of their opponents. Boys interviewed expressed finding gratification in acting as representatives of a collectivity; the approval or disapproval of one's teammates accentuates the importance of contributing to a group victory.

3. *Size of play group.* Observations made during recess periods showed boys playing in much larger groups than girls to a far greater extent than appeared in the diary data. Boys typically were involved in team sports which require a large number of participants for proper play. Boys in all three schools could play daily, depending on the season, in ongoing basketball, football, or baseball games involving ten to twenty-five or more persons. Girls were rarely observed playing in groups as large as ten persons; on those occasions, they were engaged in cooperative circle songs that seemed to emerge spontaneously, grow, and almost as quickly disintegrate. More often, girls participated in activities like tag, hopscotch, or jumprope, which can be played properly with as few as two or three participants and seldom involve more than five or six. In fact, too many players are considered to detract rather than enhance the fun because it means fewer turns, with longer waits between turns. Indeed, Eifermann (1968), after cataloging over 2,000 children's games, observed that most girls' games, like hopscotch and jacks, can be played alone, whereas the great majority of boys' games need two or more players.

4. *Explicitness of goals.* In the recess yards, I more often saw girls playing cooperatively and boys playing competitively. Some girls engaged in conversation more than they did in play (see Lever, 1976:481). Others, like those who initiated the circle songs and dances, preferred action governed by ritual rather than rules. For example, the largest and most enthusiastic group of girls witnessed during the year of research was involved in a circle chant called "Dr. Knickerbocker Number Nine." Twenty-four girls repeated the chant and body motions in an outer circle, while one girl in the center spun around with eyes closed. She then stopped, with arm extended, pointing out someone from the outer circle to join her. The ritual chant began again while the new arrival spun around; this procedure continued until nine persons had been chosen in similar random fashion to form the inner circle. Then the ninth person remained in the circle's center while the others resumed their original positions and the cycle would begin anew.

Although this activity appeared monotonous to the observer because it allowed the participants little chance to exercise physical or mental skills, these ten-year-olds were clearly enjoying themselves. Shouts of glee were heard from the circle's center when a friend had been chosen to join them. Indeed, a girl could gauge her popularity by the loudness of these shouts. For some the activity may provide an opportunity to reaffirm self-esteem without suffering any of the achievement pressures of team sports.

Even when girls engaged in presumably competitive games, they typically avoided setting precise goals. In two schools, I observed girls playing "Under the Moon," a popular form of jumprope. The first person hops in and jumps once, in any fashion of her choosing, and then hops out. She then enters again and does two jumps, usually though not necessarily, different from the first. She increases her jumps by an increment of one until she has jumped ten times. Her turn over, she then becomes a rope turner. There was no competition exhibited between players. They participated for the fun of the turn, not to win. Even if the jumper trips the rope, she is allowed to complete her turn. If the jumper competes, it is with herself, as she alone determines whether to attempt an easy jump or a more difficult one.

The point is that girls sometimes take activities in which a comparison of relative achievement is structurally possible (and sometimes normatively expected) and transform them into noncompetitive play. Girls are satisfied to keep their play loosely structured. For example, in the game of jacks, girls can say before beginning, "The first to finish 'double bounces' is the winner." More often, however, they just play until they are bored with the game. Players may or may not verbalize "you won," and recognize who has advanced the most number of steps. Boys grant much more importance to being proclaimed the winner; they virtually always structure their games, be it one-on-one or full team basketball, so that the outcomes will be clear and definite.

5. *Number and specificity of rules.* This investigator also observed . . . that boys' games more often have an elaborate organization of rules. Girls' turn-taking games progress in identical order from one situation to the next; prescriptions are minimal, dictating what must be done in order to advance. Given the structure of these games, disputes are not likely to occur. "Hogging" is impossible when participation is determined by turn-taking; nor can fouls occur when competition is indirect. Sports games, on the other hand, are governed by a broad set of rules covering a wide variety of situations, some common and others rare. Areas of ambiguity which demand rule elaboration and adjudication are built into these games. Kohlberg (1964) . . . argues that children learn the greatest respect for rules when they can be used to reduce dissonance in ambiguous situations.

Because girls play cooperatively more than competitively, they have less experience with rules per se, so we should expect them to have a lesser consciousness of rules than boys. On one of those rare occasions when boys and girls could be watched playing the same games, there was striking evidence for a sex difference in rule sensitivity. A gym teacher introduced a game called "newcombe," a simplified variation of volleyball, in which the principal rule is that the ball must be passed three times before being returned to the other side of the net. Although the game was new to all, the boys did not once forget the "three-pass" rule; the girls forgot it on over half the volleys.

6. *Team formation.* Team formation can be seen as a dimension of complexity because it indicates simultaneously structured relationships of cooperation and conflict. In turn-taking games, girls compete within a single group as independent players, each one against all others. Boys compete between groups, acting interdependently as members of a team. Team formation is required in all of their favorite sports: baseball, football, basketball, hockey, and soccer. Only a few girls in each school regularly joined the boys in their team sports; conversely, only a few boys in each school avoided the sports games. Questionnaire data support these observations. Most boys reported regular participation in neighborhood sports games. In addition, at the time of the study 68 percent said they belonged to some adult-supervised teams, with a full schedule of practice and league games. In fact, some of these fifth graders were already involved in interstate competitions.

The after-school sports program illustrates boys' greater commitment to team competition. Twenty girls from the third, fourth, and fifth grades elected captains who chose teams for newcombe games. Only seven of those girls returned the following week. In contrast, after-school basketball attracted so many boys that the fifth graders were given their own day. The teacher called roll for the next two weeks and noted that every boy had returned to play again.

Thus observational data, like the diary data, support the basic hypothesis that boys' play activities are more complex in structure than those of girls. Boys' play more frequently involves specialization of roles, interdependence of players, explicit group goals, and larger group membership, numerous rules, and team divisions. This conclusion holds for activities in public as well as in private. It suggests a markedly different set of socialization experiences for members of each sex.

Discussion

Sources of the Sex Difference

What is it that produces these distinct play patterns for boys and girls? The answer is mostly historical and cultural and holds true for much of Europe as well as the United States. While the rise of recreational physical activities in the late nineteenth century was enjoyed by women and men alike, the organized team sports which flourished at the same time were limited to participation by males (Paxson, 1917). The combined beliefs in the masculine nature of sport and the physiological inferiority of females led early twentieth century educators to lobby for competitive athletics for boys while restricting the physical education of girls to gymnastic exercises and dance. The emphasis on competitive athletics for males was reinforced by the view that sport served as a training ground for future soldiers ("the battle of Waterloo was won on the playing fields of Eton") and by the growing interest in spectator sports in which the dominant performers were young men (Cozens and Stumpf, 1953). Despite some outstanding individual female athletes in golf, tennis, and track and field, there was no development of interest in women's team sports. This situation is only now beginning to change. . . .

Of course, it is not only the schools that encourage boys' and restrict girls' athletic participation. Parents act as the conveyor belts for cultural norms, and it is no less the case for norms pertaining to sport. Male children are quick to learn that their demonstrations of athletic skill earn the attention and praise of adults. Many fathers show more emotion and enthusiasm for professional sports than anything else. Girls at young ages may not be actively discouraged from sports participation, but they are told that they are "tomboys" which is understood to be a deviant label. In the recent Little League debate, psychologists, parents, and coaches voiced their concern for the masculinization of female athletes, and the possible damage to young male egos when girls defeat boys in public (Michener, 1976). This cultural legacy is still with us, even though we now appear to be on the verge of radical change.

Historical analysis of children's games confirms that boys are playing more team sports now than ever before. Equally important, boys have drifted away from loosely structured play towards more formally organized competitive games (Sutton-Smith and Rosenberg, 1971). Evidence presented here supports this picture. It appears that the growing cultural emphasis on sports and winning has carried over to nonphysical activities and made them more competitive, and that, to date, it has had this effect to a far greater extent for boys than for girls.

Consequences of the Sex Differences

Boys' games provide a valuable learning environment. It is reasonable to expect that the following social skills will be cultivated on the playground: the ability to deal with diversity in memberships where each person is performing a special task; the ability to coordinate actions and maintain cohesiveness among group members; the ability to cope with a set of impersonal rules; and the ability to work for collective as well as personal goals.

Team sports furnish the most frequent opportunity to sharpen these social skills. One could elaborate on the lessons learned. The rule structure encourages strategic thinking. Team sports also imply experience with clear-cut leadership positions, usually based on universalistic criteria. The group rewards the individual who has improved valued skills, a practice which further enhances a sense of confidence based on achievement. Furthermore, through team sports as well as individual matches, boys learn to deal with interpersonal competition in a forthright manner. Boys experience face-to-face confrontations—often opposing a close friend—and must learn to depersonalize the attack. They must practice self-control and sportsmanship; in fact, some of the boys in this study described the greatest lesson in team sports as learning to "keep your cool."

Girls' play and games are very different. They are mostly spontaneous, imaginative, and free of structure or rules. Turn-taking activities like jump-rope may be played

426

without setting explicit goals. Girls have far less experience with interpersonal competition. The style of their competition is indirect, rather than face to face, individual rather than team affiliated. Leadership roles are either missing or randomly filled.

Perhaps more important, girls' play occurs in small groups. These girls report preferring the company of a single best friend to a group of four or more. Often girls mimic primary human relationships instead of playing formal games, or they engage in conversation rather than play anything at all. In either case, there are probable benefits for their affective and verbal development. . . .

That the sexes develop different social skills in childhood due to their play patterns is logical conjecture; that those social skills might carry over and influence their adult behavior is pure speculation. Indeed, the weight of evidence indicates that life experiences are vast and varied; much can happen to intervene and change the patterns set during childhood. Still, there is so much continuity between boys' play patterns and adult male roles that we must consider whether games serve a particular socializing function.

This idea is now popular. In a . . . best seller on managerial leaders, Maccoby (1976) describes the 250 executives he studied as gamesmen who organize teams, look for a challenge, and play to win. The same social skills may be equally helpful in lower level bureaucratic jobs or other settings, like trade unions and work crews, where complexity of organization is also found. One need not endorse the world of organizations, bureaucracy, sharp competition, and hierarchy to recognize it as an integral part of modern industrial society.

The unfortunate fact is that we do not know what effect playing games might have on later life. We do not know, for example, whether the minority of women who have succeeded in bureaucratic settings are more likely to have played complex games. A recent study offers a modicum of supporting data. Hennig and Jardim (1977) portray their small sample of twenty-five women in top management positions as former tomboys. It is also the case that elite boarding schools and women's colleges, many of which stress team sports, have been credited with producing a large portion of this nation's female leaders. I would not want to argue that competitive team sports are the only place to learn useful organizational skills. Surely, the skills in question can be learned in nonplay settings in both childhood and adulthood. Nevertheless, it can be argued that complex games are an early and effective training ground from which girls traditionally have been excluded. . . .

Notes

1. Such reports were especially needed because separate groups of children may play the same game somewhat differently, while even the same children do not necessarily play a game in identical fashion from one occasion to the next. It is also important to note that children modify adult games, so that a game like pool, which has complicated rules for adults, usually is played according to simple rules by children.

2. Fifty-one percent of the games girls play (n = 158) contain many rules, compared with 69 percent of the boys' games (n = 305). Looking only at games with three or more participants, we note that boys played 26 percent more games which called for team formation.

3. In response to the interview question "Who are the fifth-grade leaders?" the boys in all three schools answered that the best athletes/team organizers rightly held that position. In contrast, most girls hesitated with the question, then named persons who had power, but credited their aggression rather than particular valued skills. They equated giving directives with assertiveness and gave that behavior negative labels like "bossy" or "big mouth."

References

Avedon, Elliott M.
1971 "The structure elements of games." pp. 419-26 in Elliott M. Avedon and Brian Sutton-Smith (eds.), The Study of Games. New York: Wiley.

Blau, Peter and R. A. Schoenherr
1971 The Structure of Organizations. New York: Basic Books.

Cozens, Frederick and Florence Stumpf
1953 Sports in American Life. Chicago: University of Chicago Press.

Eifermann, Rivka
1968 "School children's games." Final Report, Contract No. OE-6-21-010. Department of Health, Education and Welfare; Office of Education, Bureau of Research. Unpublished paper.

1972 "Free social play: a guide to directed playing." Unpublished paper.

Etzioni, Amitai
1969 A Sociological Reader on Complex Organization. New York: Holt.

Hennig, Margaret and Ann Jardim
1977 The Managerial Woman. New York: Doubleday.

Kanter, Rosabeth Moss
1977 Men and Women of the Corporation. New York: Basic Books.

Kohlberg, Lawrence
1964 "Development of moral character and moral ideology." pp. 383-431 in M. L. Hoffman and L. W. Hoffman (eds.), Review of Child Development Research, Vol. 1. New York: Russell Sage.

Maccoby, Michael
1976 The Gamesman. New York: Simon and Schuster.

Michener, James A.
1976 Sports in America. New York: Random House.

Paxson, Frederic L.
1917 "The rise of sport." Mississippi Valley Historical Review 4:144-68.

Redl, F., P. Gump, and B. Sutton-Smith
1971 "The dimensions of games." pp. 408-18 in Elliott M. Avedon and Brian Sutton-Smith (eds.), The Study of Games. New York: Wiley

Roberts, John M., M. J. Arth, and R. R. Bush
1959 "Games in culture." American Anthropologist 61:597-605.

Sutton-Smith, B. and B. Rosenberg
1971 "Sixty years of historical change in the game preference of American children." pp. 18-50 in R.E. Herron and B. Sutton-Smith (eds.), Child's Play. New York: Wiley.

Table 1. Sex Differences on the Six Dimensions
of Complexity in Play and Games

Dimensions of complexity	Girls	Boys
1. Number of roles	18%	32%
(3 or more roles)	(427)	(468)
2. Interdependence of players	46%	57%
(high interdependence)	(427)	(468)
3. Size of play group	35%	45%
(4 or more persons)	(427)	(468)
4. Explicitness of goals	37%	65%
(game structure)	(427)	(468)
5. Number of rules	19%	45%
(many rules)	(427)	(468)
6. Team formation	12%	31%
(teams required)	(427)	(468)

Sexuality and Gender in Children's Daily Worlds
Barrie Thorne and Zella Luria

Games are not by any means the only gender-differentiated feature of peer interaction in middle childhood. In the fascinating series of studies focusing on American fourth and fifth graders that are summarized in the following article, Barrie Thorne and Zella Luria document the high degree of gender separation that occurs in children's everyday social interactions and the profound differences that exist between boys and girls in same-gender interaction and ritualized cross-gender contact.

When boys were observed as they played together in large groups, the language of interaction was frequently sexual ("dirty words") and homophobic ("fag talk"). This discourse often took place in the context of heightened group emotional arousal and was accompanied by a tendency to test the limits of adult imposed norms. Fascination with the facts of heterosexuality, as manifest in conversation and the sharing of soft-core pornography, was accompanied by increasing interpersonal distance. By this age, touching outside the context of aggression (pushing, shoving, wrestling) or ritual ("high fives") had become largely taboo.

Within-gender interactions of girls at this age were found to be more focused on romance and less on sex. Interacting in small groups or in shifting coalitions of "best friend" pairs, girls were less involved than boys in limit testing and more concerned with negotiating friendship. Interpersonal interactions between friends were often characterized by expressions of physical intimacy through touch and emotional intimacy through secret sharing and mutual disclosure.

Although the vast majority of peer interactions observed at this age took place within gender, cross-gender interactions did exist. In public spaces, such interactions frequently took the form of teasing, cross-sex chasing, negotiation of "who likes who," and rituals of pollution ("cooties"). In the authors' view, the sexual meanings embedded in these various patterns of interaction help to maintain the gender division and reinforce a ritualized asymmetry in male/female relations that will be central to emerging adolescent heterosexuality.

The ambiguities of "sex"—a word used to refer to biological sex, to cultural gender, and also to sexuality—contain a series of complicated questions. Although our cultural understandings often merge these three domains, they can be separated analytically; their interrelationships lie at the core of the social organization of sex and gender. In this paper we focus on the domains of gender and sexuality as they are organized and experienced among elementary school children, especially nine to eleven year-olds. This analysis helps illuminate age-based variations and transitions in the organization of sexuality and gender.

We use "gender" to refer to cultural and social phenomena—divisions of labor, activity, and identity which are associated with but not fully determined by biological sex. The core of sexuality, as we use it here, is desire and arousal. Desire and arousal are shaped by and associated with socially learned activities and meanings which Gagnon and Simon (1973) call "sexual scripts." Sexual scripts—defining who does what, with whom, when, how, and what it means—are related to the adult society's view of gender (Miller and Simon, 1981).

In our culture, gender and sexuality are deeply intertwined, especially for adults; "woman/man," and especially, "femininity/masculinity" are categories loaded with heterosexual meanings. Erotic orientation and gender are not as closely linked in our culture's definitions of children. Although there is greater acknowledgement of childhood sexuality than in the past, we continue—often after quoting Freud to the contrary—to define children as innocent, vulnerable, and in need of protection from adult sexual knowledge and practice.[1]

Children are not, of course, asexual. They experience arousal, and they sometimes engage in practices (even some leading to orgasm) that adults call "sexual" (Kinsey et al., 1948, 1953). Some children learn and use sexual words at a relatively young age, and, as we will describe later, they draw on sexual meanings (although not necessarily adult understandings) in constructing their social worlds. But special taboos and tensions surround the feelings and language of sexuality in childhood. In our culture we limit the "fully sexual" (sexual acts tied to accepted adult meanings) to adolescence and adulthood. Among children any explicitly sexual activity, beyond ill-defined crushes, is treated as culturally deviant.

Nine- to eleven-year-old children are beginning the transition from the gender system of childhood to that of adolescence. They are largely defined (and define themselves) as children, but they are on the verge of sexual maturity, cultural adolescence, and a gender system organized around the institution of heterosexuality. Their experiences help illuminate complex and shifting relationships between sexuality and gender.

First we explore the segregated gender arrangements of middle childhood as contexts for learning adolescent and adult sexual scripts. We then turn from their separate worlds

Thorne, Barrie & Luria, Zella. (1986). Sexuality and gender in children's daily worlds. *Social Problems*, *33* (3). pp. 176-190.

to relations *between* boys and girls, and examine how fourth and fifth grade children use sexual idioms to mark gender boundaries. Separate gender groups and ritualized, asymmetric relations between girls and boys lay the groundwork for the more overtly sexual scripts of adolescence.

Methods and Sources of Data

Our data are drawn from observations of children in elementary school playgrounds, classrooms, hallways, and lunchrooms. All of the schools went up through sixth grade. One of us (Thorne) was a participant-observer for eight months in a largely White, working-class elementary school in California, a school with about 500 students (5 percent Black, 20 percent Chicana/o, and 75 percent White). She also observed for three months in a Michigan elementary school with around 400, largely working-class students (8 percent Black, 12 percent Chicana/o, and 80 percent White). Playground observations included all ages, but emphasized fourth and fifth graders. The other author (Luria) observed for one-and-a-half academic years in a middle-class, suburban Massachusetts public school and in an upper-middle-class private school in the Boston area. Both schools had about 275 students—17 percent Black and 83 percent White—in the fourth through sixth grades.[2] A separate Massachusetts sample of 27 fourth and fifth graders was interviewed to ascertain children's knowledge of what boys and girls "should do" and know. We have combined our data for this paper.

Throughout our fieldwork we tried to observe children in situations where they were under less adult supervision and control and hence more likely to construct their own activities and social relations. Although we could not pass as children, we did try to separate ourselves from the adult authority systems of the schools. We essentially tried to hang out—watching, talking, and sometimes playing with the children. We interacted freely with the children and sometimes elicited their understanding of ongoing situations. On a number of occasions, we each observed significant breaking of school rules, a backhanded compliment to our trustworthiness, if not our invisibility.

Elementary schools may not seem to be the most fruitful contexts for gathering information about sexuality. Indeed, had we observed the same children in more informal and private settings, such as in neighborhoods or summer camps, we probably would have observed more extensive sexual talk and behavior (as did Fine, 1980, in an ethnographic study of pre-adolescent boys on Little League baseball teams).

On the other hand, children spend a great deal of time in schools, and they often construct their own interactions within the structure of adult-controlled school days. The presence of teachers and aides gave us many opportunities to observe children guarding their more secret lives from potential interference from adults, and to see children and adults negotiating sexual meanings. Furthermore, the dynamics of gender separation and integration are especially vivid in densely-populated school settings.

The social categories of observers have no simple bearing on the process of research, but the fact that we are women may well have affected what we saw and how we interpreted it. Our gender enhanced access to groups of girls, but the more public nature of boys' groups made them generally easier to observe. Age may mute the effects of gender; just as very young boys may go into women's bathrooms, so, by virtue of age, adult women may cross ritual boundaries separating groups of boys from groups of girls. We both found it easier to see and articulate the social relations of boys than those of girls, a skew also evident in the literature. Having grown up as girls, we may have had less detachment from their interactions. In addition, until recently, more research had been done on groups of boys than on groups of girls, and categories for description and analysis have come more from male than female experience.

The Daily Separation of Girls and Boys

Gender segregation—the separation of girls and boys in friendships and casual encounters—is central to daily life in elementary schools. A series of snapshots taken in varied school settings would reveal extensive spatial separation between girls and boys. When they choose seats, select companions for work or play, or arrange themselves in line, elementary school children frequently cluster into same-sex groups. At lunchtime, boys and girls often sit separately and talk matter-of-factly about "girls' tables" and "boys' tables." Playgrounds have gendered spaces: boys control some areas and activities, such as large playing fields and basketball courts; and girls control smaller enclaves like jungle-gym areas and concrete spaces for hopscotch or jumprope. Extensive gender segregation in everyday encounters and in friendships has been found in many other studies of elementary- and middle-school children (e g., Best, 1983; Eder and Hallinan, 1978; Lockheed, 1985). Gender segregation in elementary and middle schools has been found to account for more segregation than race (Schofield, 1982).

Gender segregation is not total. Snapshots of school settings would also reveal some groups with a fairly even mix of boys and girls, especially in games like kickball, dodgeball, and handball, and in classroom and playground activities organized by adults. Some girls frequently play with boys, integrating their groups in a token way, and a few boys, especially in the lower grades, play with groups of girls.

The amount of gender segregation varies not only by situation, but also by school. For example, quantitative inventories in the Massachusetts schools indicated that in the private, upper-middle class school, 65 percent of playground clusters were same-gender, compared with 80 percent in the matched, middle-class public school.

Social class may help account for the difference, but so may school culture; the private school had initiated large group games, like one called "Ghost," which were not typed by gender. The extent of adult supervision also makes a difference. In general, there is more gender segregation when children are freer to construct their own activities.

Gender arrangements in elementary schools have a "with-then-apart" structure (a term coined by Goffman, 1977). In any playground, cafeteria, or classroom, there are mixed-gender, as well as same-gender groups. Mixed-gender groups, and patterns of activity and solidarity which draw boys and girls together, need closer attention (see Thorne, 1986). On the other hand, children so often separate themselves by gen-

433

der—ritualizing boundaries between girls and boys, and talking about them as separate "teams" or "sides"—that they create bounded spaces and relationships in which somewhat different subcultures are sustained. In some respects, then, boys and girls occupy separate worlds.

Most of the research on gender and children's social relations emphasizes patterns of separation, contrasting the social organization and cultures of girls' groups with those of boys (e.g., see Best, 1983; Eder, 1985; Eder and Hallinan, 1978; Goodwin, 1980a; Lever, 1976; Maccoby and Jacklin, 1974; Maltz and Borker, 1983; Savin-Williams, 1976; Waldrop and Halverson, 1975). In brief summary: Boys tend to interact in larger and more publicly-visible groups; they more often play outdoors, and their activities take up more space than those of girls. Boys engage in more physically aggressive play and fighting; their social relations tend to be overtly hierarchical and competitive. Organized sports are both a central activity and a major metaphor among boys; they use a language of "teams" and "captains" even when not engaged in sports.

Girls more often interact in smaller groups or friendship pairs, organized in shifting alliances. Compared with boys, they more often engage in turn-taking activities like jump rope and doing tricks on the bars, and they less often play organized sports. While boys use a rhetoric of contests and teams, girls describe their relations using language which stresses cooperation and "being nice." But the rhetorics of either group should not be taken for the full reality. Girls *do* engage in conflict, although it tends to take more indirect forms than the direct insults and challenges more often found in interactions among boys, and between girls and boys. In a study of disputes among children in a Black working-class neighborhood, Goodwin (1980b) found that girls more often talked about the offenses of other girls in their absence. Hughes (1983, Forthcoming) found that groups of third and fourth grade girls playing four-square used a rhetoric of "friends" and "nice" to justify, rather than avoid, competitive exchanges, and to construct complex large-group activity. This recent research is important in providing a more complex portrayal of girls' interactions—their patterns of competition and conflict, as well as cooperation.

Informal, gender segregated groups are powerful contexts for learning. Children may be especially attentive to one another when they are outside of adult surveillance and in situations not formally defined as ones of teaching and learning. Peers and friends are especially valued because they never seem to teach, or, as one child defined "friend": "they never tell you to wash your hands" (Rubin, 1973).

In the Massachusetts public school, when children asked her purpose, the observer said she was watching how children taught one another things through the rules of games. After incredulous stares, one boy easily turned this bizarre statement into a playground joke: "*She* thinks we teach each other something!" For children in solid positions inside gender segregated peer groups, such learning may appear seamless and almost invisible, associated with free choice and pleasure. Excluded children probably have fewer doubts about the teaching of peers.

Because of time spent and emotions invested in gender-differentiated worlds, girls and boys have somewhat different environments for learning. Gender-differentiated social relations and subcultures may teach distinctive patterns of talk (Maltz and Borker, 1983) and forms of prosocial and antisocial behavior (Maccoby, 1985). Our focus is on how the gender-specific contexts of middle and late childhood may help shape the sexual scripts—the social relations and meanings associated with desire—of adolescent boys and girls.

Interaction among Boys

In daily patterns of talk and play, boys in all-male groups often build toward heightened and intense moments, moments one can describe in terms of group arousal with excited emotions. This especially happens when boys violate rules. In a Massachusetts fifth grade, four boys played a game called "Flak" which one of them had invented. The game took place on a 8 1/2" x 11" piece of paper with drawings of spaceships with guns on each of the corners. The airspace in the middle of the paper was covered by short lines representing metal flak. The purpose of the game was to shoot down all opponents by using one's hand as a gun while making shooting noises. The danger was that one's shots could ricochet off the flak, destroying one's spaceship. The random straying of flak was such that there was no way—if the game was played honestly—to survive one's own shots. Boys playing the game evolved implicit (never stated) rules about cheating: Cheating was permitted up to about one-fourth the distance to an opponent's corner, then the others could complain that flak would stop a player, but not before. At the instigation of the observer, the boys enthusiastically taught the game to the brightest girl in the class, who found the game "boring" and "crazy." The excitement the boys associated with the game was lost on her; she did not remark on the cheating.

Dirty words are a focus of rules, and rule breaking, in elementary schools. Both girls and boys know dirty words, but flaunting of the words and risking punishment for their use was more frequent in boys' than in girls' groups in all the schools we studied. In the middle-class Massachusetts public school, both male and female teachers punished ballplayers for frequent cries of "Shit" and "You fucked it up." But teachers were not present after lunch and before school, when most group-directed play took place. A female paraprofessional, who alone managed almost 150 children on the playground, never intervened to stop bad language in play; the male gym teacher who occasionally appeared on the field at after-lunch recess always did. Boys resumed dirty talk immediately after he passed them. Dirty talk is a stable part of the repertoire of boys' groups (also see Fine, 1980). Such talk defines their groups as, at least in part, outside the reach of the school's discipline.

Some of the dirty talk may be explicitly sexual, as it was in the Massachusetts public school when a group of five fifth-grade boys played a game called "Mad Lib" (also described in Luria, 1983). The game consisted of a paragraph (in this case, a section of a textbook discussing the U.S. Constitution) with key words deleted, to be filled in by

435

the players. Making the paragraph absurd and violating rules to create excitement seemed to be the goal of the game. The boys clearly knew that their intentions were "dirty": they requested the field observer not to watch the game. Instead the observer negotiated a post-game interrogation on the rules of the game. The boys had completed the sentence, "The _____ was ratified in _____ in 1788," with "The *shit* was ratified in *Cuntville* in 1788."

The boys reacted with disbelief when the adult woman observer read the entire paragraph aloud, with no judgment, only requesting correction of pronunciation. The next day, in a gesture which connected rule violation to the interests of the male group, one of the boys asked the observer, "Hey lady, did ya watch the Celtics' game last night?" Sports, dirty words, and testing the limits are part of what boys teach boys how to do. The assumption seems to be: dirty words, sports interest and knowledge, and transgression of politeness are closely connected.

Rule Transgression: Comparing Girls' and Boys' Groups

Rule transgression in *public* is exciting to boys in their groups. Boys' groups are attentive to potential consequences of transgression, but, compared with girls, groups of boys appear to be greater risk-takers. Adults tending and teaching children do not often undertake discipline of an entire boys' group; the adults might lose out and they cannot risk that. Girls are more likely to affirm the reasonableness of rules, and, when it occurs, rule-breaking by girls is smaller scale. This may be related to the smaller size of girls' groups and to adults' readiness to use rules on girls who seem to believe in them. It is dubious if an isolated pair of boys (a pair is the modal size of girls' groups) could get away with the rule-breaking that characterizes the larger male group. A boy may not have power, but a boys' *group* does. Teachers avoid disciplining whole groups of boys, partly for fear of seeming unfair. Boys rarely identify those who proposed direct transgressions and, when confronted, they claim (singly), "I didn't start it; why should I be punished?"

Boys are visibly excited when they break rules together—they are flushed as they play, they wipe their hands on their jeans, some of them look guilty. The Mad Lib game described above not only violates rules, it also evokes sexual meanings within an all-male group. Arousal is not purely individual; in this case, it is shared by the group. Farts and cunts—words used in the game—are part of a forbidden, undressed, sexual universe evoked in the presence of four other boys. The audience for the excitement is the gender-segregated peer group, where each boy increases the excitement by adding still a "worse" word. All of this takes place in a game ("rules") context, and hence with anonymity despite the close-up contact of the game.

While we never observed girls playing a Mad Lib game of this sort, some of our female students recall playing the game in grade school but giving it up after being caught by teachers, or out of fear of being caught. Both boys and girls may acquire knowledge of the game, but boys repeatedly perform it because their gender groups give support for transgression.

436

These instances all suggest that boys experience a shared, arousing context for transgression, with sustained gender group support for rule-breaking. Girls' groups may engage in rule-breaking, but the gender group's support for repeated public transgression is far less certain. The smaller size of girls' gender groupings in comparison with those of boys, and girls' greater susceptibility to rules and social control by teachers, make girls' groups easier to control. Boys' larger groups give each transgressor a degree of anonymity. Anonymity—which means less probability of detection and punishment—enhances the contagious excitement of rule-breaking.

The higher rates of contagious excitement, transgression, and limit-testing in boys' groups means that when they are excited, boys are often "playing" to male audiences. The public nature of such excitement forges bonds among boys. This kind of bonding is also evident when boys play team sports, and when they act aggressively toward marginal or isolated boys. Such aggression is both physical and verbal (taunts like "sissy," "fag," or "mental"). Sharing a target of aggression may be another source of arousal for groups of boys.

The Tie to Sexuality in Males

When Gagnon and Simon (1973) argued that there are gender-differentiated sexual scripts in adolescence, they implied what our observations suggest: the gender arrangements and subcultures of middle childhood prepare the way for the sexual scripts of adolescence. Fifth and sixth grade boys share pornography, in the form of soft-core magazines like *Playboy* and *Penthouse*, with great care to avoid confiscation. Like the Mad Lib games with their forbidden content, soft-core magazines are also shared in all-male contexts, providing explicit knowledge about what is considered sexually arousing and about attitudes and fantasies. Since pornography is typically forbidden for children in both schools and families, this secret sharing occurs in a context of rule-breaking.

While many theorists since Freud have stressed the importance of boys loosening ties and identification with females (as mother surrogates), few theorists have questioned why "communally-aroused" males do not uniformly bond sexually to other males. If the male groups of fifth and sixth grade are the forerunners of the "frankly" heterosexual gender groups of the junior and high school years, what keeps these early groups from open homosexual expression? Scripting in same-gender peer groups may, in fact, be more about gender than about sexual orientation. Boys, who will later view themselves as having homosexual or heterosexual preferences, are learning patterns of masculinity. The answer may also lie in the teaching of homophobia.

By the fourth grade, children, especially boys, have begun to use homophobic labels—"fag," "faggot," "queer"—as terms of insult, especially for marginal boys. They draw upon sexual allusions (often not fully understood, except for their negative and contaminating import) to reaffirm male hierarchies and patterns of exclusion. As "fag" talk increases, relaxed and cuddling patterns of touch decrease among boys. Kindergarten

437

and first-grade boys touch one another frequently and with ease, with arms around shoulders, hugs, and holding hands. By fifth grade, touch among boys becomes more constrained, gradually shifting to mock violence and the use of poking, shoving, and ritual gestures like "giving five" (flat hand slaps) to express bonding. The tough surface of boys' friendships is no longer like the gentle touching of girls in friendship.

"Fag talk," pornography, and the rules for segregation from girls create a separate, forbidden, and arousing area of life among boys. Group teasing for suspected crushes (which we discuss later) heightens the importance of the ambiguous opening toward the institutionalized heterosexuality of adolescence. The underside of this phenomenon is the beginning of homosexual relationships by some eleven- and twelve-year-old males and the rule-violating fantasy of early male masturbation (Bell et al., 1981; Kinsey et al., 1948). Fag talk helps keep homosexual experiments quiet and heightens the import of the lessons of pornography and gender segregation. Homoeroticism and homophobia coexist, often in tension, in male peer groups of middle childhood, and in some later adolescent and adult male groups. Our hunch is that the high *arousal* of the peer group may provide much of the cuing for the homophobic control. For males, navigating the onset of masturbation and social sexuality is another example of handling rule violations. Miller and Simon (1981) point out that violating rules is felt to impart excitement and an almost moral fervor to early sexual events.

Interaction among Girls

In contrast with the larger, hierarchical organization of groups of boys, fourth- and fifth-grade girls more often organize themselves in pairs of "best friends" linked in shifting coalitions. These pairs are not "marriages"; the pattern is more one of dyads moving into triads, since girls often participate in two or more pairs at one time. This may result in quite complex social networks. Girls often talk about who is friends with or "likes" whom; they continually negotiate the parameters of friendships.

For example, in the California school, Chris, a fifth-grade girl, frequently said that Kathryn was her "best friend." Kathryn didn't proclaim the friendship as often; she also played and talked a lot with Judy. After watching Kathryn talk to Judy during a transition period in the classroom, Chris went over, took Kathryn aside, and said with an accusing tone, "You talk to Judy more than me." Kathryn responded defensively, "I talk to you as much as I talk to Judy."

In talking about their relationships with one another, girls use a language of "friends," "nice," and "mean." They talk about who is most and least "liked," which anticipates the concern about "popularity" found among junior high and high school girls (Eder, 1985). Since relationships sometimes break off, girls hedge bets by structuring networks of potential friends. The activity of constructing and breaking dyads is often carried out through talk with third parties. Some of these processes are evident in a sequence recorded in a Massachusetts school:

438

The fifth-grade girls, Flo and Pauline, spoke of themselves as "best friends," while Flo said she was "sort of friends" with Doris. When a lengthy illness kept Pauline out of school, Flo spent more time with Doris. One day Doris abruptly broke off her friendship with Flo and began criticizing her to other girls. Flo, who felt very badly, went around asking others in their network, "What did I do? Why is Doris being so mean? Why is she telling everyone not to play with me?"

On school playgrounds girls are less likely than boys to organize themselves into team sports. They more often engage in small-scale, turn-taking kinds of play. When they jump rope or play on the bars, they take turns performing and watching others perform in stylized movements which may involve considerable skill. Sometimes girls work out group choreographies, counting and jumping rope in unison, or swinging around the bars. In other synchronized body rituals, clusters of fifth- and sixth-grade girls practice cheerleading routines or dance steps. In interactions with one another, girls often use relaxed gestures of physical intimacy, moving bodies in harmony, coming close in space, and reciprocating cuddly touches. We should add that girls also poke and grab, pin one another from behind, and use hand-slap rituals like "giving five," although less frequently than boys.

When the teacher of a combined fourth- and fifth-grade classroom in the California school pitted girls against boys for spelling and math contests, there were vivid gender group differences in the use of touch, space, and movement. During the contests the girls sat close together on desk tops, their arms and shoulders touching. Occasionally a gesture, such as a push or a lean way to one side, would move like a wave through their line. When one of them got a right answer, she would walk along the row of girls, "giving five" before returning to her place. The boys mostly stood along the other side of the classroom, leaning against desks; their bodies didn't touch except for "giving five" when one of them got a right answer.

In other gestures of intimacy, which one rarely sees among boys, girls stroke or comb their friends' hair. They notice and comment on one another's physical appearance such as haircuts or clothes. Best friends monitor one another's emotions. They share secrets and become mutually vulnerable through self-disclosure, with an implicit demand that the expression of one's inadequacy will induce the friend to disclose a related inadequacy. In contrast, disclosure of weakness among boys is far more likely to be exposed to others through joking or horsing around.

Implications for Sexuality

Compared with boys, girls are more focused on constructing intimacy and talking about one-to-one relationships. Their smaller and more personal groups provide less protective anonymity than the larger groups of boys. Bonding through mutual self-disclosure, especially through disclosure of vulnerability, and breaking off friendships by "acting mean," teach the creation, sustaining, and ending of emotionally intimate relations. Girls' preoccupation with who is friends with whom, and their monitoring of

439

cues of "nice" and "mean," liking and disliking, teach them strategies for forming and leaving personal relationships. In their interactions girls show knowledge of motivational rules for dyads and insight into both outer and inner realities of social relationships. Occasionally, girls indicate that they see boys as lacking such "obvious" knowledge.

Girls' greater interest in verbally sorting out relationships was evident during an incident in the Massachusetts public school. The fifth-grade boys often insulted John, a socially isolated boy who was not good at sports. On one such occasion during gym class, Bill, a high status boy, angrily yelled "creep" and "mental" when John fumbled the ball. The teacher stopped the game and asked the class to discuss the incident. Both boys and girls vigorously talked about "words that kill," with Bill saying he was sorry for what he said, that he had lost control in the excitement of the game. The girls kept asking, "How could anyone do that?" The boys kept returning to, "When you get excited, you do things you don't mean." Both girls and boys understood and verbalized the dilemma, but after the group discussion the boys dropped the topic. The girls continued to converse, with one repeatedly asking, "How could Bill be so stupid? Didn't he know how he'd make John feel?"

When talking with one another, girls use dirty words much less often than boys do. The shared arousal and bonding among boys which we think occurs around public rule-breaking has as its counterpart the far less frequent giggling sessions of girls, usually in groups larger than three. The giggling often centers on carefully guarded topics, sometimes, although not always, about boys.

The sexually related discourse of girls focuses less on dirty words than on themes of romance. In the Michigan school, first- and second-grade girls often jumped rope to rhymes about romance. A favorite was, "Down in the Valley Where the Green Grass Grows," a saga of heterosexual romance which, with the name of the jumper and a boy of her choice filled in, concludes: ". . . along came Jason, and kissed her on the cheek . . . first comes love, then comes marriage, then along comes Cindy with a baby carriage." In the Michigan and California schools, fourth- and fifth-grade girls talked privately about crushes and about which boys were "cute," as shown in the following incident recorded in the lunchroom of the Michigan school:

The girls and boys from one of the fourth-grade classes sat at separate tables. Three of the girls talked as they peered at a nearby table of fifth-grade boys; "Look behind you," one said. "Ooh," said the other two. "That boy's named Todd." "I know where my favorite guy is . . . there," another gestured with her head while her friends looked.

In the Massachusetts private school, fifth-grade girls plotted about how to get particular boy-girl pairs together.

As Gagnon and Simon (1973) have suggested, two strands of sexuality are differently emphasized among adolescent girls and boys. Girls emphasize and learn about the emotional and romantic before the explicitly sexual. The sequence for boys is the reverse; commitment to sexual acts precedes commitment to emotion-laden, intimate relationships

440

and the rhetoric of romantic love. Dating and courtship, Gagnon and Simon suggest, are processes in which each sex teaches the other what each wants and expects. The exchange, as they point out, does not always go smoothly. Indeed, in heterosexual relationships among older adults, tension often persists between the scripts (and felt needs) of women and of men (Chodorow, 1978; Rubin, 1983).

Other patterns initially learned in the girls' groups of middle childhood later may be worked into more explicitly sexual scripts. In all the schools we studied, emphasis on appearance increased over the course of fifth grade, and symbols of cultural adolescence—lip gloss (kept hidden in desks and clandestinely passed from girl to girl), hairbrushes, and long-tailed combs—began to appear. However, the girls who first began to use these teen artifacts were not necessarily the ones who showed physical signs of puberty. In the California school, fourth- and fifth grade girls talked about who was prettiest and confessed feelings of being ugly. Girls remark on their own and others' appearance long before they talk about issues of attractiveness to boys. The concern with appearance, and the pattern of performing and being watched, may be integrated into sexual expression later.

Children's Sexual Meanings and the Construction of Gender Arrangements

Girls and boys, who spend considerable time in gender-separate groups, learn different patterns of interaction which, we have argued, lay the groundwork for the sexual scripts of adolescence and adulthood. However, sexuality is not simply delayed until adolescence. Children engage in sexual practices—kissing, erotic forms of touch, masturbation, and sometimes intercourse (see Constantine and Martinson, 1981; Finkelhor, 1979). As school-based observers, we saw only a few overt sexual activities among children, mostly incidents of public, cross-gender kissing, surrounded by teasing, chasing, and laughter.

In elementary school life the overtly sexual is mostly a matter of words, labels, and charged rituals of play. In identifying this behavior as "sexual," we are cautious about imposing adult perspectives. When children say words like "fag" or "fuck," they rarely share adult meanings, as was apparent in their use of "fag" essentially as a synonym for "nerd" and as an epithet occasionally applied to girls as well as to boys.

Although their sexual knowledge is fragmentary and different from that of adults, children learn early on that certain words and gestures are forbidden and charged with special meaning. Adults and children jointly construct the domain considered to be "sexual." For example, both adults and children know and sometimes enforce taboos against the use of dirty words in school, as shown in an incident in the library of the California school:

"Miss Smith, Donny is being a bad boy, he's being nasty, he's looking up sex," a fourth-grade girl told the teacher as they stood near the card catalogue. "No I'm not, I'm looking up sunset," Donny said defensively.

441

The special loading of sexual words and gestures makes them useful for accomplishing nonsexual purposes. Sexual idioms provide a major resource which children draw upon as they construct and maintain gender segregation. Through the years of elementary school, children use with increasing frequency heterosexual idioms—claims that a particular girl or boy "likes," "has a crush on," or is "goin with" someone from the other gender group. Unlike alternative, non-gendered terms for affiliation ("friends," "playmates"), heterosexual idioms imply that interaction between girls and boys has sexual overtones. Children rarely use sexual language to describe within-gender interaction. From an early age, the erotic is prescriptively heterosexual, and male (but, significantly, much less female) homophobic.

Children's language for heterosexual relationships consists of a very few, often repeated, and sticky words. In a context of teasing, the charge that a particular boy "likes" a particular girl (or vice versa) may be hurled like an insult. The difficulty children have in countering such accusations was evident in a conversation between the observer and a group of third-grade girls in the lunchroom of the Michigan school:

> *Susan asked me what I was doing, and I said I was observing the things children do and play. Nicole volunteered, "I like running, boys chase all the girls. See Tim over there? Judy chases him all around the school. She likes him." Judy, sitting across the table, quickly responded, "I hate him. I like him for a friend." "Tim loves Judy," Nicole said in a loud, sing-song voice.*

Sexual and romantic teasing marks social hierarchies. The most popular children and the pariahs—the lowest status, excluded children—are most frequently mentioned as targets of "liking." Linking someone with a pariah suggests shared contamination and is an especially vicious tease.

When a girl or boy publicly says that she or he "likes" someone or has a boyfriend or girlfriend, that person defines the romantic situation and is less susceptible to teasing than those targeted by someone else. Crushes may be secretly revealed to friends, a mark of intimacy, especially among girls. The entrusted may then go public with the secret ("Wendy likes John"), which may be experienced as betrayal, but which also may be a way of testing the romantic waters. Such leaks, like those of government officials, can be denied or acted upon by the original source of information.

Third parties—witnesses and kibitzers—are central to the structure of heterosexual teasing. The teasing constructs dyads (very few of them actively "couples"), but within the control of larger gender groups. Several of the white fifth graders in the Michigan and California schools and some of the black students in the Massachusetts schools occasionally went on dates, which were much discussed around the schools. Same-gender groups provide launching pads, staging grounds, and retreats for heterosexual couples, both real and imagined. Messengers and emissaries go between groups, indicating who likes whom and checking out romantic interest. By the time "couples" actually get together (if they do at all), the groups and their messengers have provided a network of constructed meanings, a kind of agenda for the pair. As we have argued, gender-divided peer groups sustain different meanings of the sexual. They also regulate heterosexual behavior by helping to define the emerging sexual scripts of adolescence (who "likes" whom, who might "go with" whom, what it means to be a couple).

In the California and Michigan schools, when children reported news from the playground to an adult observer, they defined two types of activities as especially newsworthy: physical fights (who fought with and beat up whom), and who "liked," had a crush on, or was "goin with" whom. Like fights, purported romantic liaisons (e.g., "Frank likes Bonnie") are matters of public notice and of widespread rumor and teasing. The charge of "liking" or having a "girlfriend" or "boyfriend" may be constructed from very small clues—for example, that Frank sat down by or talked with Bonnie, or that he chose her as a partner in PE.

When a girl or boy consistently initiates talk or play with someone of the other gender group, she or he risks being teased. This risk is so severe that close friendships between boys and girls that are formed and maintained in other places like neighborhoods or church sometimes go underground during the school day. Heterosexual meanings, which one might think would unite boys and girls, in fact may keep them apart. Children use heterosexual teasing to maintain and police boundaries between "the girls" and "the boys," defined as separate groups.

Heterosexually Charged Rituals

Boundaries between boys and girls are also emphasized and maintained by heterosexually charged rituals like cross-sex chasing. Formal games of tag and informal episodes of chasing punctuate life on playgrounds. The informal episodes usually open with a provocation—taunts like "You can't get me!" or "Slobber monster!," bodily pokes, or the grabbing of possessions like a hat or scarf. The person who is provoked may ignore the taunt or poke, handle it verbally ("leave me alone!"), or respond by chasing. After a chasing sequence, which may end after a short run or a pummeling, the chaser and chased may switch roles.

Chasing has a gendered structure. When boys chase one another, they often end up wrestling or in mock fights. When girls chase girls, they less often wrestle one another to the ground. Unless organized as a formal game like "freeze tag," same-gender chasing goes unnamed and usually undiscussed. But children set apart cross-gender chasing with special names—"girls chase the boys"; "boys chase the girls"; "the chase"; "chasers"; "chase and kiss"; "kiss-chase"; "kissers and chasers"; "kiss or kill"—and with animated talk about the activity. The names vary by region and school, but inevitably contain both gender and sexual meanings.

When boys and girls chase one another, they become, by definition, separate teams. Gender terms override individual identities, especially for the other team: "Help, a girl's chasin' me!"; "C'mon Sarah, let's get that boy"; "Tony, help save me from the girls." Individuals may call for help from, or offer help to, others of their gender. In acts of

443

treason, they may also grab someone of their gender and turn them over to the opposing team, as when, in the Michigan school, Ryan grabbed Billy from behind, wrestled him to the ground, and then called, "Hey girls, get 'im."

Names like "chase and kiss" mark the sexual meanings of cross-gender chasing. The threat of kissing—most often girls threatening to kiss boys—is a ritualized form of provocation. Teachers and aides are often amused by this form of play among children in the lower grades; they are more perturbed by cross-gender chasing among fifth- and sixth-graders, perhaps because at those ages some girls "have their development" (breasts make sexual meanings seem more consequential), and because of the more elaborate patterns of touch and touch avoidance in chasing rituals among older children. The principal of one Michigan school forbade the sixth-graders from playing "pom-pom," a complicated chasing game, because it entailed "inappropriate touch."

Cross-gender chasing is sometimes structured around rituals of pollution, such as "cooties," where individuals or groups are treated as contaminating or carrying "germs." Children have rituals for transferring cooties (usually touching someone else and shouting "You've got cooties!"), for immunization (e. g., writing "CV" for "cootie vaccination" on their arms), and for eliminating cooties (e.g., saying "no gives" or using "cootie catchers" made of folded paper [described in Knapp and Knapp, 1976]). Boys may transmit cooties, but cooties usually originate with girls. One version of cooties played in Michigan is called "girl stain"; the fourth-graders whom Karkau (1973) describes used the phrase, "girl touch." Although cooties is framed as play, the import may be serious. Female pariahs—the ultimate school untouchables by virtue of gender and some added stigma such as being overweight or from a very poor family—are sometimes called "cootie queens" or "cootie girls." Conversely, we have never heard or read about "cootie kings" or "cootie boys."

In these cross-gender rituals girls are defined as sexual. Boys sometimes threaten to kiss girls, but it is girls' kisses and touch which are deemed especially contaminating. Girls more often use the threat of kissing to tease boys and to make them run away, as in this example recorded among fourth-graders on the playground of the California school:

> Smiling and laughing, Lisa and Jill pulled a fourth-grade boy along by his hands, while a group of girls sitting on the jungle-gym called out, "Kiss him, kiss him." Grabbing at his hair, Lisa said to Jill, "Wanna kiss Jonathan?" Jonathan got away, and the girls chased after him. "Jill's gonna kiss your hair," Lisa yelled.

The use of kisses as a threat is doubled-edged, since the power comes from the threat of pollution. A girl who frequently uses this threat may be stigmatized as a "kisser."

Gender-marked rituals of teasing, chasing, and pollution heighten the boundaries between boys and girls. They also convey assumptions which get worked into later sexual scripts: (1) that girls and boys are members of distinctive, opposing, and sometimes antagonistic groups; (2) that cross-gender contact is potentially sexual and contaminating, fraught with both pleasure and danger; and (3) that girls are more sexually-defined (and

444

polluting) than boys.

These meanings are not always evoked. Girls and boys sometimes interact in relaxed ways, and gender is not always salient in their encounters (see Thorne, 1986). But sexual meanings, embedded in patterns of teasing and ritualized play, help maintain gender divisions; they enhance social distance, asymmetry, and antagonism between girls and boys. These patterns may persist in the sexual scripts of adolescence.

Notes

1. In the western world, this definition is made possible by the physical separation of the sexual life of adults from the everyday life of children, a privilege not extended to families who inhabit one room in much of the rest of the world.

2. In this paper, we have set out to trace general patterns in age-based relationships between sexuality and gender. We have not, except incidentally, explored possible variations by region, social class, and race or ethnicity. All of these dimensions should be more fully addressed. For example, our data suggest that the transition to adolescent sexual scripts begins earlier in working-class than in middle-class or upper-middle-class schools. However, the transition began earlier in the Massachusetts, upper-middle-class private school than in the more middle-class public school. The relation of class, type of school, and age of transition to adolescent sexual scripts is obviously complex.

References

Bell, Alan T., Martin S. Weinberg, and Sue K. Hammsersmith
1981 Sexual Preference: Its Development in Men and Women. Bloomington: Indiana University Press.

Best, Raphaela
1983 We've All Got Scars. Bloomington: Indiana University Press.

Chodorow, Nancy
1978 The Reproduction of Mothering. Berkeley: University of California Press.

Constantine. Larry L. and Floyd M. Martinson
1981 Children and Sex. Boston: Little, Brown.

Eder, Donna
1985 "The cycle of popularity: interpersonal relations among female adolescents." Sociology of Education 58:154-65.

Eder, Donna and Maureen T. Hallinan
1978 "Sex differences in children's friendships." American Sociological Review 43:237-50.

Fine, Gary Alan
1980 "The natural history of preadolescent male friendship groups." Pp. 293-320 in Hugh C. Foot, Antony J. Chapman and Jean R. Smith (eds.), Friendship and Social Relations in Children. New York: Wiley.

Finkelhor, David
1979 Sexually Victimized Children. New York: Free Press.

Finnan, Christine R.
1982 "The ethnography of children's spontaneous play." Pp. 358-80 in George Spindler (ed.), Doing the Ethnography of Schooling. New York: Holt, Rinehart & Winston.

Gagnon, John H. and William Simon
1973 Sexual Conduct. Chicago: Aldine.

Goffman, Erving
1977 "The arrangement between the sexes." Theory and Society 4:301-36.

Goodwin, Marjorie Harness
1980a "Directive-response speech sequences in girls' and boys' task activities." Pp. 157-73 in Sally McConnell-Ginet, Ruth Borker, and Nelly Furman (eds.), Women and Language in Literature and Society. New York: Praeger.

1980b "'He-said-she-said': formal cultural procedures for the construction of a gossip dispute activity." American Ethnologist 7:674-95.

Hughes, Linda A.
1983 Beyond the Rules of the Game: Girls' Gaming at a Friends' School. Unpublished Ph.D. dissertation, University of Pennsylvania Graduate School of Education.

Forthcoming "The study of children's gaming." In Brian Sutton-Smith, Jay Mechling and Thomas Johnson (eds.), A Handbook of Children's Folklore. Washington, DC: Smithsonian.

Karkau, Kevin
1973 "Sexism in the fourth grade." Pittsburgh: KNOW, Inc.

Kinsey, Alfred C., Wardell B. Pomeroy, and Clyde E. Martin
    1948 Sexual Behavior in the Human Male. Philadelphia: Saunders.

Kinsey, Alfred C., Wardell B. Pomeroy, Clyde E. Martin, and Paul H. Gebhard
    1953 Sexual Behavior in the Human Female. Philadelphia: Saunders.

Knapp, Mary and Herbert Knapp
    1976 One Potato, Two Potato. New York: W.W. Norton.

Lever, Janet
    1976 "Sex differences in the games children play." Social Problems 23:478-87.

Lockheed, Marlaine E.
    1985 "Sex equity in classroom organization and climate." Pp. 189-217 in Susan S. Klein (ed.), Handbook for Achieving Sex Equity Through Education. Baltimore, MD: Johns Hopkins University Press.

Luria, Zella
    1983 "Sexual fantasy and pornography: two cases of girls brought up with pornography." Archives of Sexual Behavior 11:395-404.

Maccoby, Eleanor
    1985 "Social groupings in childhood: their relationship to prosocial and antisocial behavior in boys and girls." Pp. 263-84 in Dan Olweus, Jack Block, and Marian Radke-Yarrow (eds.), Development of Antisocial and Prosocial Behavior. San Diego, CA: Academic Press.

Maccoby, Eleanor and Carol Jacklin
    1974 The Psychology of Sex Differences. Stanford, CA: Stanford University Press.

Maltz, Daniel N. and Ruth A. Borker
    1983 "A cultural approach to male-female miscommunication." Pp. 195-216 in John J. Gumperz (ed.), Language and Social Identity. New York: Cambridge University Press.

Miller, Patricia Y. and William Simon
    1981 "The development of sexuality in adolescence." Pp. 383-407 in Joseph Adelson (ed.), Handbook of Adolescent Psychology. New York: Wiley.

Rubin, Lillian
    1983 Intimate Strangers. New York: Harper and Row.

Rubin, Zick
1973 Liking and Loving. New York: Holt.

Savin-Williams, Richard C.
1976 "An ethological study of dominance formation and maintenance in a group of human adolescents." Child Development 47:972-79.

Schofield, Janet
1982 Black and White in School. New York: Praeger.

Thorne, Barrie
1986 "Girls and boys together . . . but mostly apart: gender arrangements in elementary schools." Pp. 167-84 in Willard W. Hartup and Zick Rubin (eds.), Relationships and Development. Hillsdale NJ: Lawrence Erlbaum.

Waldrop, Mary F. and Charles F. Halverson
1975 "Intensive and extensive peer behavior: longitudinal and cross-sectional analysis." Child Development 46:16-19.

18

Peer Culture

We went home and when somebody said, "Where were you?" we said, "Out", and when somebody said, "What were you doing until this hour of the night?" we said, as always, "Nothing."

But about this doing nothing: we swung on the swings. We went for walks. we lay on our backs in backyards and chewed grass. . . We watched things: we watched people build houses, we watched men fix cars, we watched each other patch bicycle tires with rubber bands. . .

We sat in boxes; we sat under porches; we sat on roofs; we sat on limbs of trees. We stood on boards over excavations; we stood on tops of piles of leaves; We stood under rain dripping from the eaves; we stood up to our ears in snow.

We looked at things like knives. . . and grasshoppers and clouds and dogs and people. We skipped and hopped and jumped. Not going any-where—just skipping and hopping and jumping and galloping. We sang and whittled and hummed and screamed.

What I mean, Jack, we did a lot of nothing.

—Robert Paul Smith, *Where did You Go? Out.*
   What Did You Do? Nothing

• INTRODUCTION •

Social groups of all sizes—families, peer groups, organizations, cultures—share certain fundamental characteristics. Some of these characteristics have to do with the organization of the group, others with ways of acting that group members share in common, and still others with the extent to which group members identify with one another.

Among the more important organizational features of the group are those having to do with variations among individuals in status and role. As groups evolve a stable pattern of interpersonal relationships, certain members of the group become more likely to give deference to and others to receive deference from the remaining group members. These are low and high status individuals respectively. Roles also become differentiated and associated with different individuals. Thus, for example, some members may become leaders, others followers; some may make trouble, while others consistently attempt to make peace.

Groups also share customary ways of acting and speaking. These include rituals, common language, jargon, norms that specify when particular actions are appropriate or inappropriate, and sanctions employed to enforce those norms.

Finally, members of social groups tend to think of themselves as similar in certain respects to members of their own group and different from members of other groups. Social psychologists refer to this creation of "we feeling" among group members as the formation of an in-group. From the point of view of an in-group, members of other sometimes competing groups are members of out-groups.

In this module, we are introduced to two important pieces of research that illustrate the extent to which the behavior of pre-adolescent children may, under appropriate circumstances, display all of the characteristics of social groups. In the first article, Muzafer and Carolyn W. Sherif describe conditions of group formation, in-group behavior, and intra-group competition and cooperation observed when pre-adolescent boys were left to organize themselves with little or no direct adult supervision. In the second article, Lewis Aptekar describes two styles of street life that he observed while doing research among some of the millions of street children that inhabit the cities of Latin America.

• • •

In-Group Formation, Inter-Group Conflict, and Cooperation in Pre-Adolescent Boys
Muzafer Sherif and Carolyn W. Sherif

Between 1949 and 1954, Muzafer and Carolyn Sherif and their colleagues carried out a series of naturalistic experiments in the group behavior of preadolescent boys. Widely known as the Robbers Cave experiments, these investigations have become classics in the literature of social and developmental psychology. In this excerpt from their social psychology textbook, Sherif and Sherif describe the three phases of group interaction examined in these studies.

In the first phase, boys who had never before met arrived at a camp setting and began to engage in a series of interdependent activities (camping, cookouts, cleaning up areas for swimming or athletic activities) organized to achieve goals that were highly valued by all of the children. Under these conditions, in-groups characterized by status hierarchies, role differentiation, norms, and sanctions, and strong within-group friendship preferences formed rapidly.

In the second phase, conditions were created experimentally that led separate groups of boys into sustained competition (touch football, tug of war, cabin inspections) with one another toward goals (prizes) that were desired by both groups but attainable only by one. Over time, inter-group competition was found to generate hostility and aggression between groups, to lead to the formation of negative stereotypes of out-group members, to increase in-group solidarity as reflected in friendship choices and distortion of the magnitude of the achievements of in- versus out-group members, and to result in changes in the relative status and roles of those group members who were more or less effective in conflict.

In the final phase, situations (water supply system breakdown, raising funds for a movie, helping to get a stalled food truck started) were designed to bring the members of competing groups into contact with one another under conditions in which both groups had to work together as equals to achieve goals desired by everyone but unattainable by one group without the cooperation of the other. Over time, this cooperative contact led to gradual reduction in hostility, dissipation of negative stereotypes, and cessation of conflict.

. . . Any experiment is, necessarily, a miniature and stripped-down model of the actualities it purports to analyze. The experiments reported here and the hypotheses tested were constructed on the basis of extensive surveys of the literature on in-group and inter-group relations (Sherif, 1948; Sherif and Sherif, 1953). Three separate experiments were conducted, each lasting approximately three weeks, in different locations and with different subjects (Sherif, 1951; Sherif and Sherif, 1953; Sherif, White, and Harvey, 1955; Sherif et al., 1961). [This analysis] . . . presents a composite picture of the three studies, the source being specified when it is feasible without confusing the account.

The first experiment was conducted in Connecticut in 1949; the second in upstate New York in 1953; and the third at Robbers Cave, Oklahoma, in 1954. . . .

Choice of Subjects

Because the experiments were performed at camp sites, subjects were selected who would find camping both natural and absorbing for the duration of the experiments, without great interest in outside activities. Pre-adolescent boys were selected (eleven-twelve years old).

In order as far as possible to eliminate alternative explanations for events that would transpire in the experiments, the selection procedures were careful and prolonged. . . .

As a result of these methods of selection, the following alternative bases for explaining the results were eliminated:

1. *Previous acquaintance or personal ties among the boys.* Boys were chosen from different schools and neighborhoods to eliminate this possibility.

2. *Excessive personal frustration situations in past history, unstable family ties, or neurotic tendencies.* Boys were chosen from stable families with both parents living in the home (no broken homes). They were healthy, well adjusted in school and neighborhood, making normal progress in their school grades, and with no past records of presenting behavior problems. Members of minority groups who might have suffered social discrimination were not included.

3. *Pronounced differences in social background or physical appearance.* All subjects were selected from stable, white Protestant families from the middle socioeconomic level. The religious backgrounds represented in a given experiment were from the most similar Protestant groups (e.g., Episcopalian and Congregationalists in Connecticut; Methodist and Baptist in Oklahoma). Intelligence test scores were all well within the normal range, the means in the experiments all being slightly above 100. . . .

The primary method of data collection was observation and ratings made by trained observers at the end of each day. . . .

Sherif, Muzafer and Sherif, Carolyn W. (1969). *Social Psychology*. NY: Harper & Row, Publishers. pp. 228-256.

Experimental Formation of In-Groups

Spontaneous Interpersonal Choices. In the first two experiments, the boys arrived at the site together, were all housed in one large bunkhouse, and, initially, were entirely free to choose companions in the activities, all of which were campwide.

Within two or three days, smaller clusters of budding friendship groups were observed, composed of two to four boys each. (One of the more prominent called themselves the "Three Musketeers.") Each boy was then asked informally who his best friends were in the camp (sociometric choices). Then the budding clusters were arbitrarily split to compose two cabins, so that about two-thirds of the best friends were in different cabins. That is, in each cabin, about two-thirds of the occupants had not chosen each other. . . .

Following the period of group formation, the boys were again asked to name their best friends—specifying that they were free to choose from the entire camp. Table 1 gives the data from the Connecticut study, showing that the hypothesis was supported. The procedures were replicated in 1953 with similar results.

Conclusions and Implications. The findings permitted the conclusion that groups formed on the basis of the experimental conditions, not primarily as the result of spontaneous attraction among like-minded persons. More than half of the initial choices of friends shifted from strictly spontaneous personal choices toward friendship within the in-group. . . .

Table 1. Reversal of Friendship Choices Before
and After Group Formation

Persons chosen in:	Persons (%) choosing from:					
	Group A			Group B		
	Before	After	Difference	Before	After	Difference
Group A	35.1	95.0	59.9	65.0	12.3	−52.7
Group B	64.9	5.0	−59.9	35.0	87.7	52.7

Stage of Group Formation

This stage of the experiments started when subjects were divided into two bunches, matched as closely as possible in terms of size and skills of individuals composing them. The Robbers Cave experiment (1954) started at this point, the boys arriving on two separate buses and settling into cabins at a considerable distance. . . .

During this stage (about a week), the boys engaged in many activities, but their common criteria were that they were (a) highly appealing and (b) required interdependent activity in order to reach a common goal. For example, they included camping out in the woods, cooking meals, improving a swimming place, cleaning up a rough field for athletics, transporting canoes placed near their cabins over rough terrain to the water, and various organized and informal games.

With the research staff instructed not to take initiative or to execute tasks, the experimental conditions meant that the boys faced many problem situations in play and in work that required all of their efforts. They did pool their efforts, organized duties, and divided tasks in work and in play. In the variousactivities, different individuals assumed different responsibilities and came to be known for certain skills or personal characteristics. One excelled in cooking. Another led in athletics. One often horsed around. Others, not outstanding in any particular skill, could be counted on to pitch in and do their level best in anything the group attempted. One or two boys seemed to disrupt activities, to start teasing at the wrong moment, to push others around, to offer useless suggestions, or to "goof off" when there was work to be done. On the other hand, a few boys consistently had good suggestions, needed skills, or showed ability to coordinate the activities without getting on others' nerves.

Thus, over time, the shifting and changing patterns of interpersonal relations from activity to activity and from day to day began to stabilize. . . . One boy in each group began to rank highest in the exercise of effective initiative across situations, frequently with the close assistance of one or two others of high rank. Some boys were sifted toward the bottom of the emerging structure while others jockeyed for higher positions of respect and influence.

An example of events during this period may clarify the process: During a hike in the woods, the boys started to get hungry. They had been supplied with unprepared food. One boy started to build a fire, asking help in getting wood. Another attacked the raw hamburger to make patties. Others prepared a place to put buns, relishes, and utensils. Two mixed soft drinks from flavoring and sugar. One boy stood around without helping and was told by several others to "get to it." Shortly the fire was blazing and the cook had hamburgers sizzling. As soon as they became browned, two boys distributed them to others. Several took turns pouring the drink. Soon the cook had eaten and it was time for the watermelon. A boy already ranked low in status took a knife and started toward the melon. Several boys protested. The most highly regarded boy took the knife and started to cut the melon, saying: "You guys who yell the loudest get yours last.". . .

In short, group structures did emerge in line with the hypotheses in each of the experiments. They were not all identical. In some groups, the leader-follower structure

454

was very steep, while in others the psychological distance between leader and follower was less and the structure was more tightly knit.

Formation of Group Products and Norms. Each group did develop distinctive ways of doing things, as well as customs and notions of propriety. Perhaps the most striking contrasts occurred in the Robbers Cave experiment, in which one group cultivated a norm of "toughness" to the point that the adult staff had to watch out for signs of injury, as the boys would not even bother to treat cuts and scratches, much less show signs of hurt. The other group did not develop such a norm, but did come to dwell on being "good" in conventional terms (*not* swearing, showing consideration, etc.). This norm was dramatically evident when the two groups came into contact. The "good" group huddled in prayer before every contest (praying, of course, to defeat the opposition), while the other delighted in openly rowdy behavior and swearing.

As the group became an organization, the boys coined nicknames for one another. The blond and hardy leader of one group was dubbed "Baby Face" by his admiring followers, in recognition of his good looks and the toughness associated with that title from the well-known gangster of yesteryear. A boy with a rather long head became "Lemon Head." The gay and game athlete in another group was "Horrible Hunt." Each group developed its own jargon, special jokes, secrets, special ways of performing tasks, and preferred places. For example, in 1954, one group killed a snake near their swimming place, named the place "Moccasin Creek" and thereafter preferred that swimming hole, even though others were better.

Wayward members who failed to do things "right" or who did not contribute their bit to the common effort found themselves receiving reprimands, ridicule, "silent treatment," or even threats (group sanctions). A boy who tried to "bully" others was successfully squelched, despite his greater size. By the end of the stage, however, most behavior in the group was in accord with the customary *modus operandi* that had been established, with very little need for frequent correctives. Some groups established standardized means for handling behavior that got "out of line." For example, the penalty in the Bull Dog group (1949) was to remove a specified number of stones from their swimming hole, which both punished the offender and succeeded in raising the water level. This sanction was administered by the leader with the consent of the membership.

Eventually, each of the groups in these studies took names for themselves. Some of these names were coined during this stage, although a few of the groups took names for themselves only after they had learned the other group had one. In the 1949 Connecticut study, the two groups called themselves the Red Devils and the Bull Dogs. In the 1953 experiment, they were the Panthers and the Pythons. The groups in the 1954 experiment called themselves the Rattlers and the Eagles.

In each case, the choice of name was made by the boys; however, they reflect the environment and situational factors in interesting ways. In 1949 the groups were assigned colors to differentiate them, and the "blue" group adopted the name "Bull Dog" from nearby Yale University, whose color was blue. Both sets of names in the other experiments reflect the surrounding terrain. The Rattlers and Eagles were located in the hills of southeast Oklahoma near a famous hideaway for outlaws, where there were numerous specimens of both rattlesnakes and large birds.

Conclusions. . . . Interdependent activities directed toward goals of high appeal value are a sufficient condition for group formation.

In the Robbers Cave experiment, groups formed despite the fact that each was unaware of the presence of another group in the site. Along with the developing organizations, local customs, and valued objects (the criteria for group formation), each manifested signs of "we" feeling and pride in joint accomplishments that mark an in-group. . . .

Intergroup Relations: Conflict

Because the major challenge of intergroup relations is conflict and how to change intergroup hostility once it has taken root, the experimental analysis of intergroup relations began with tests of hypotheses concerning conditions sufficient for the production of intergroup conflict, and the rise of hostile attitudes and negative images (stereotypes). The hypotheses tested were as follows:

Hypotheses

1. *When members of two groups come into contact with one another in a series of activities that embody goals which each urgently desires, but which can be attained by one group only at the expense of the other, competitive activity toward the goal changes, over time, into hostility between the groups and their members.*

2. *In the course of such competitive interaction toward a goal available only to one group, unfavorable attitudes and images (stereotypes) of the out-group come into use and are standardized, placing the out-group at a definite social distance from the in-group.*

3. *Conflict between two groups tends to produce an increase in solidarity within the groups.*

4. *The heightened solidarity and pride in the group will be reflected in overestimation of the achievements by fellow group members and lower estimates of the achievements by members of the out-group.*

5. *Relations between groups that are of consequence to the groups in question, including conflict, tend to produce changes in the organization and practices within the groups.*

Prior to this stage, neither of the groups had had encounters as groups in the 1954 experiment. Although acquainted with individual boys in the other group and aware that there was another group, the boys in the two earlier studies were engaged in activities separately throughout the group formation stage. In the Robbers Cave experiment, the two groups were not even aware of each other's presence until just prior to this stage.

456

The main conditions for this stage were established readily by arranging a tournament of games as though acceding to the boys' requests to engage in team sports. The series of events included baseball, touch football, tug of war, a treasure hunt, tent pitching, skits, and cabin inspection—the latter activities being included to permit the manipulation of points by the research staff to insure that the competition would be fairly close. Prizes were offered to the tournament winners as a group: a trophy as well as highly prized knives to each individual member. A large poster with drawings of two thermometers was used to record the cumulative score of each group daily.

In each experiment, the tournament started with great zest and in the spirit of good sportsmanship to which these American boys had already been thoroughly indoctrinated. In each case, as the tournament progressed from event to event, the good sportsmanship and good feeling began to evaporate. The sportsman-like cheer for the other group, customarily given after a game, "2-4-6-8, who do we appreciate," turned to a derisive chant: "2-4-6-8, who do we appreci-*hate*."

In 1949, the Red Devils began to slip behind in the competition, thereupon accusing the Bull Dogs of being "dirty players" and "cheats" ("At least we play fair."). The victorious Bull Dogs were elated, happy, self-content, and full of pride. The losing Red Devils were dejected. Chiefly because their leader became vindictive, blaming defeat on low-status members of his own group, their loss was conducive to signs of disorganization. Low-status Red Devils resented the accusations, and there was conflict within the group until later the Red Devils faced broadside attacks from the Bull Dogs.

Planned Frustration of In-Groups. This contest was followed by a party proposed by the staff to let "bygones be bygones" between the groups. Although each group claimed that the bad feelings between them were strictly the fault of the other group, both agreed to come. This party involved a frustrating situation planned by the staff so that it appeared to be caused by one group. It led to further frustrations *experienced in common by group members.*

The refreshments were placed on a table. Half were crushed and unappetizing; half were whole and delectable. By careful timing (which was not suspected by the subjects), the Red Devils arrived first. When told to take their share of the refreshments, they took the good half and sat down to enjoy it. When the Bull Dogs arrived a short time later and saw the sorry-looking refreshments left them, they immediately protested. The Red Devils justified their actions with "first come, first served," which became the standardized justification for all Red Devils. The Bull Dogs proceeded to eat their refreshments, hurling taunts, insults, and names at the Red Devils. Particularly common was the term "pigs." Among the names used by most Bull Dogs for Red Devils on this and later occasions were "pigs," "dirty bums," or "Red bums," "jerks," and several more objectionable terms.

The next morning the Red Devils retaliated by deliberately dirtying their breakfast table to make K.P. duty harder for the Bull Dogs. Upon seeing the dirty table, the Bull Dogs decided to mess it up further and leave it. All Bull Dogs joined in by smearing the table with cocoa, sugar, syrup, and the like, and leaving it alive with bees and wasps.

457

The Bull Dogs hung the walls with threatening and derogatory posters against the Red Devils. . . .

At lunch that day the hostility between the groups increased to such a point throughout the meal that they soon were lined-up on opposite sides of the mess hall calling names and then throwing food, cups, tableware, etc. The fight was broken up. Neither group was sure who started the fight, but each was sure it was someone in the *other* group.

At this point, the 1949 experiment was over. The conflict was not over, however. It took another two days of genuine and active efforts by the staff, involving "preaching" and coercion, just to stop the group fighting. The groups planned raids on each other's cabins. Green apples were collected and hoarded by both groups for "ammunition," with the explanation that this was done merely "in case" it might be needed. The Red Devils attempted "sneak" attacks when the other group and counselors were asleep. (The Red Devils had tended to show signs of disorganization after their defeat in the competitions. In this period the group was again united.) This fighting and raiding between groups took on a planned character. They were not merely outbursts upon momentary encounters of individuals.

Spontaneous Frustration of In-Groups. In the Robbers Cave experiment, a series of mutually frustrating situations arose in the natural course of tournament events. On the first day of the tournament, the Eagles were defeated in a tug of war. When the Rattlers left the field, one Eagle suggested that they take down the Rattler flag, which was mounted on the backstop of the athletic field. In a short time, the flag was not only removed but partially burned.

The following morning, events were timed so that the Rattlers arrived on the athletic field first. Discovering their defamed emblem, they immediately denounced the Eagles, the members crying for revenge the minute the Eagles appeared on the field. At the suggestion of a high-status member, a cooler strategy was formulated: First, they would confront the Eagles with the evidence. If the Eagles gave signs of guilt, then the Rattlers would attack. The Eagles admitted the deed, and the Rattlers succeeded in seizing the Eagle flag. The Eagles fought back, grabbing the remaining Rattler flag in turn. Through it all, the groups scuffled and shouted derogatory names at each other.

Name calling, physical encounters and raids followed in succession. The Rattlers raided the Eagle cabin, causing quite a bit of inconvenience, some destruction, and considerable frustration among Eagles. . . . The raid was reciprocated by the Eagles, who left the Rattlers' cabin in great confusion. A few days later, the Rattlers lost the tournament. Their raid on the Eagles' cabin made the others look like mild affairs.

Systemic Differences in Judgment as a Function of Intergroup Relations

Estimations of Time by In-Groups on the Verge of Victory and Defeat. The psychological effects of the differing experiences and viewpoints of in-groups engaged in rivalry were exemplified in the second tug of war. The Rattlers had won the first contest, whereupon the Eagles had burned the Rattler flag. On the next day, after the conflicts described above, the Eagles devised a strategy to win the second tug of war. On a prearranged signal, the Eagles all sat down on the ground and dug in their feet. The confident Rattlers were pulling strenuously in an upright position, but rapidly losing ground and becoming exhausted. After seven minutes, the Rattlers adopted the enemy strategy and dug in too.

Tired by their initial pull in a standing position, the Rattlers were being pulled gradually across the line when the staff announced that the contest would be terminated in another fifteen minutes. At the end of this period, the Rattlers were still not all across the line and the contest was declared a tie. The Eagles were indignant but the Rattlers were relieved and satisfied. The Rattlers accused the Eagles of employing a dirty strategy. Privately they remarked that it seemed that the contest would never end. The Eagles, on the other hand, were overheard to remark to one another that the precious time flew too fast on the verge of their victory.

On the day following the contest, observers of each group asked the members of their respective groups individually, "How long did the tug of war last after both groups had sat down and dug in?" The actual duration was 48 minutes. . . . There was no overlap at all among the estimates made by the two groups. The Eagles gave their judgments in minutes (20-45), while the Rattlers gave theirs in hours (1-3 1/2).

Systematic Errors in Judgment of In-Group and Out-Group Performance. In order to check observations of the tendency to deprecate the achievements of the adversary and magnify the achievements of the in-group, judgments in a laboratory-like task were obtained at the end of this stage in 1954. The experiment within the experiment was introduced as a game, with a cash prize offered to the group which could both win the game and judge its outcome most accurately. The game was bean toss, in which the aim is to collect as many beans scattered on the ground as possible within a limited time. Each person collected beans in a sack with a restricted opening, so that he could not count the number of beans he collected.

The judgment task was made unstructured by exposing through an opaque projector the beans purportedly collected by each individual for a brief time and in random arrangements. Actually, thirty-five beans were exposed each time—a number sufficiently large that it could not be counted in the time available. After each exposure, each person wrote down his estimate of the number. Each collection of beans was identified as the collection of a member of the in-group or out-group. . . .

The members of each group, on the average, overestimated the number of beans collected by fellow group members and made significantly lower estimates of the detested out-group's performance. The tendency to overestimate was much greater for the Eagles, who had been the victors in the tournament, than for the Rattlers, who had been declared the losers.

Negative Stereotypes of the Out-Group Contrasted with the Glorious In-Group. In another check on observations, members of each group were asked to rate their fellow group members and the members of the out-group on a number of personal qualities, of

459

which six were critical. The critical six were terms actually used by the boys in referring to their own group or the out-group during the height of friction. Three were favorable (*brave, tough, friendly*) and three were unfavorable (*sneaky, smart alecks, stinkers*). Each adjective was rated using a five-step scale ranging from "all of them are . . ." to "none of them are. . . ."

Ratings of fellow group members were almost exclusively favorable in both groups (100 percent by Rattlers and 94.3 percent by Eagles). On the other hand, ratings of the out-group were predominantly unfavorable. Categorically unfavorable ratings of the out-group were made in 76.9 percent of the Eagles' judgments and 53 percent of the Rattlers.

Closing Ranks and Heightened Solidarity of In-Groups. Although the sociometric choices obtained at the end of this stage explicitly encouraged choice from the entire camp, the boys made choices almost exclusively within their own groups. After the tournament, the members of each group found the others so distasteful that they expressed strong preferences to have no further contact with them at all. In short, in-group exclusiveness was accompanied by extreme social distance between groups. . . .

Conclusions and Implications

The stage of intergroup conflict in the experiments showed unmistakably that the sustained conflict toward goals that each group desired, but only one could attain, is a sufficient condition for the rise of hostile, aggressive deeds, the standardization of social distance justified by derogatory images of the out-group, and the rudiments of prejudice (negative attitude). In addition, the hypotheses were supported that intergroup conflict produced an increase in in-group solidarity and pride.

The course of conflict between the groups did produce changes in the status and role relationships within the groups, as predicted. In one group (Eagles) the leadership actually changed hands when the leader who had emerged during the peaceful days of group formation proved reluctant in frontline action during conflict. In another (Rattlers) a bully who had been reduced to rather low status during group formation by the castigations of his fellow members emerged as a hero during encounters with the rival out-group. Practices established within the group as norms during group formation were altered during the intergroup encounters. A great deal of time and energy within each group went into making plans and strategies to outwit and defeat the out-group, which now appeared as an enemy.

There can be no doubt that differences in culture, language, or physical appearance facilitate discriminatory reactions toward members of an out-group. There can be no doubt that such differences play a part in the formation of intergroup hostility and prejudice. Yet, this experimental evidence shows that neither cultural, physical, nor economic differences are necessary for the rise of intergroup hostility, stereotyped images, social distance, and negative attitude—nor are maladjusted, neurotic, or unstable psychological tendencies necessary. . . .

Stage of Intergroup Cooperation: Reduction of Conflict

The problem of greatest interest in the experiments was as follows: How can two groups in conflict, each with hostile attitudes and negative images of the other and each desiring to keep the members of the detested out-group at a safe distance, be brought into cooperative interaction and friendly intercourse? In the 1949 experiment, several measures were introduced to reduce conflict in order to send the boys home in a friendly spirit. The Robbers Cave experiment studied the problem more systematically.

Various measures for reducing conflict could have been tried—for example, the distribution of favorable information, appeals to moral values, conferences by the leaders of the groups, contact as equals, or activities emphasizing individual rather than group achievement. Perhaps the most persistent notion is that groups in conflict should be given *accurate and favorable* information about one another. Indeed, groups must know something about each other if there is to be a change of hostile relationships. However, reactions to communication are not neutral affairs. Individuals select the information they will expose themselves to and interpret the content to fit their own designs. Therefore, no systematic information campaigns were attempted.

As for the related idea that *appeal to moral values* shared by each group is sufficient to reduce their hostility, the experiments contain several incidents to the contrary. Religious services were held in the Robbers Cave experiment by the same minister for each group. The topics were brotherly love, forgiveness of enemies, and cooperation. The boys arranged the services and were enthusiastic about the sermon. Upon solemnly departing from the ceremony, they returned within minutes to their concerns to defeat, avoid, or retaliate against the detested out-group.

Individual competition across group lines has been proposed as a means of furthering intergroup harmony—as, for example, in the Olympic games. In classroom and recreation situations, adults use such means in the attempt to break-up groups. However, the problem in this research was how to foster cooperation *between groups*. Therefore, this procedure was not considered appropriate.

Conferences of leaders are often necessary for the resolution of intergroup disputes. However, this measure was not used in the experiments because of evidence that leaders are not free to enter decisions that violate the prevailing norms and trends in their own groups unless these have already begun to change. During the 1949 experiment, one high-status Bull Dog went on his own initiative to the Red Devil cabin with the aim of negotiating better relationships. He was greeted by a hail of green apples, chased down the path, and derided. Upon returning to his own group, he received no sympathy. Despite his high status, he was rebuked for making the attempt, which was doomed to failure in the opinion of his fellow members.

461

The Common Enemy

In the 1949 experiment, several steps were taken to reduce intergroup hostility—including contact between the groups as equals and pronouncements by the adult staff. Although the latter were not effective in reducing the frequent expressions of dislike between the groups, one measure clearly was effective. An outside group was invited to the camp to compete with a campwide team selected from both groups. At least temporarily, the effect of this common enemy was to promote cooperation between groups and to reduce hostile interchange. However, the Bull Dogs and Red Devils maintained their strong in-group preferences to the end of that experiment, to the point that they still maintained social distance between them.

For two reasons, a *common enemy* was not used in the later experiments. First, history contains many examples of uniting against a common enemy in which the same old intergroup conflicts appear when the enemy is vanquished. Second, the uniting of hostile groups to defeat another is, after all, a widening of the scope of intergroup conflict. Logically, the end result is repetition of the stage of intergroup conflict on a larger scale, with potentially more serious consequences.

Hypotheses on Reduction of Intergroup Hostility

The hypotheses actually tested were as follows:
otheses

1. *Contact* between groups on an equal status in activities that, in themselves, are pleasant for members of both groups, but that involve no interdependence among them, will not decrease an existing state of intergroup conflict.

2. When conflicting groups come into contact under conditions embodying goals *that are compelling for the groups involved, but cannot be achieved by a single group through its own efforts and resources,* the group will tend to cooperate toward this *superordinate goal.*

Our definition of superordinate goal emphasizes that it is unattainable by one group singly; hence, it is not identical with a "common goal." Another implication of the definition is that a superordinate goal supersedes other goals each group may have, singly or in common with others; hence its attainment may require subordination of either singular or common goals.

3. Cooperation between groups arising from a series of superordinate goals will have a *cumulative effect* toward reducing the social distance between them, changing hostile attitudes and stereotypes, and hence reducing the possibility of future conflicts between them.

In short, these hypotheses concern the *conditions* under which *contact as equals* can be effective in resolution of conflict and reduction of hostility between groups.

Phase One. In order to test the first hypothesis, a series of situations was introduced involving *contact* between groups in activities highly pleasant to each group but not involving interdependence between them. Examples were going to the movies, eating in the same dining room, shooting off fireworks on July 4th, and the like. Far from reducing conflict, these situations served as occasions for the rival groups to berate and attack each other. In the dining-hall line, they shoved each other and the group that lost the contest for the head of the line shouted "Ladies first!" at the winner. They threw paper, food, and vile names at each other. An Eagle bumped by a Rattler was admonished by his fellow Eagles to brush "the dirt" off his clothes. The mealtime encounters were dubbed "garbage wars" by the participants.

Phase Two: Superordinate Goals. The measure that was effective was suggested by a corollary to our formulation of intergroup conflict: *If conflict develops from mutually incompatible goals, common goals should promote cooperation.* But what kind of common goals?

In considering group relations in the everyday world, it seemed that the most effective and enduring cooperation between groups occurs when *superordinate goals* prevail. Superordinate goals are those goals that have a compelling appeal for members of each group, but that neither group can achieve without participation of the other. To test this hypothesis experimentally, we created a series of urgent and natural situations that challenged members of both groups.

One was a breakdown in the water supply system. Water came to the camp in pipes from a tank about a mile away. The flow of water was interrupted and the boys in both groups were called together to hear of the crisis. Both groups volunteered, in their own distinctive ways, to search the water line for trouble. They explored separately, then came together and jointly located the source of the difficulty. But despite the good spirits aroused, the groups fell back on their old recriminations once the immediate crisis was over.

A similar opportunity was offered when the boys requested a movie that both groups had high on their list of preference. They were told that the camp could not afford to pay for it. The two groups got together, figured out how much each group would have to contribute, chose the film by a common vote, and enjoyed the show together. It should be kept in mind that this followed the episode of their cooperation in the water crisis.

One day the two groups went on an outing at a lake some distance away. A large truck was to go for food. But when everyone was hungry and ready to eat, it developed that the truck would not start (the staff had taken care of that). The boys got a rope—the same rope they had used in their acrimonious tug of war—and all pulled together to start the truck.

Joint efforts in situations such as these did not *immediately* dispel hostility. But gradually, the series of activities requiring interdependent action reduced conflict and hostility between the groups. As a consequence, the members of the two groups began

463

to feel friendlier. For example, a Rattler whom the Eagles had disliked for his sharp tongue and skill in defeating them became a "good egg." The boys stopped shoving each other in the meal line. They no longer called each other names and began to sit together at the table. New friendships developed, cutting across group lines.

In the end, the groups were actively seeking opportunities to intermingle, to entertain and "treat" each other. Procedures that "worked" in one activity were *transferred* to others. For example, the notion of "taking turns" developed in the dining hall and was transferred to a joint campfire, which the boys themselves decided to hold. The groups took turns presenting skits and songs.

Given the alternative of returning in separate buses or on the same bus, members of both groups requested that they go home together on the same bus. As a whole neither group paid attention to a few *diehards* who muttered "Let's not."

On the way home, a stop was made for refreshments. One group still had five dollars won as a prize. They decided to spend this sum on refreshments for both groups rather than to use it solely for themselves and thereby have more to eat. On their own initiative they invited their former rivals to be their guests for malted milks. . . .

References

Sherif, M., 1948. *An Outline of Social Psychology.* New York: Harper & Row.

Sherif, M., 1951. Experimental study of intergroup relations. In J. H. Rohrer and M. Sherif (Eds.), *Social Psychology at the Crossroads.* New York: Harper & Row, 388-426.

Sherif, M., 1966. *In Common Predicament: Social Psychology of Intergroup Conflict and Cooperation.* Boston: Houghton Mifflin. (British ed.: *Group Conflict and Coopera-tion: Their Social Psychology.* London: Routledge, 1967.)

Sherif, M., and Sherif, Carolyn W., 1953. *Groups in Harmony and Tension.* New York: Harper & Row. (Octagon, 1966.)

Sherif, M., Harvey, O. J., White, B. J., Hood, W. R., and Sherif, Carolyn W., 1961. *Intergroup Conflict and Cooperation: The Robbers Cave Experiment.* Norman: Institute of Group Relations, University of Oklahoma.

Sherif, M., White, B. J., and Harvey, O. J., 1955. Status in experimentally produced groups. *Amer. J. Sociol.,* **60**, 370-379.

Colombian Street Children: *Gamines* and *Chupagruesos*
Lewis Aptekar

Throughout history, gangs of street children have roamed the cities of the world, begging, stealing, and prostituting themselves in order to survive. With the advent of the child welfare reform movement and the passage of legislation restricting child labor and mandating school attendance into adolescence, street children largely disappeared from the cities of the developed world.

In many parts of the developing world, however, children fleeing poverty and abuse or children who have simply been abandoned by their parents still band together to live on the street. As is evident in Lewis Aptekar's account, even under the most unfavorable circumstances, these children manage to create organized, functional social groups such as the galladas *found in the cities of Latin America. In these small societies,which typically consist of fifteen to twenty-five economically interdependent children, behavior is regulated by norms and sanctions; children fill varied roles such as fence, thief, and beggar; and status is hierarchically organized with a* jefe *at the head, and* subjefes *and members in successively lower positions.*

As is also evident from Aptekar's research, the way in which children relate to the broader group and the problems that they face in the adolescent transition are a function not only of the circumstances in which they find themselves but also of the nature of their own personalities and developmental histories. In this regard, Aptekar identifies two styles of street life, gaminismo *and* chupagruesic, *which characterize preadolescent children's links to the* galladas.

Gamines *value their independence and ability to survive by their own wit and cunning and have little respect for authority in itself. They are more likely to have left home of their own accord, less likely to form permanent bonds to those in power within the* gallada, *and may find it difficult at adolescence to adjust to the adult society into which they are emerging.*

Chupagruesos, *on the other hand, survive on the streets through servility to the powerful, older and larger boys. They are more likely to have been abandoned by their parents, to enter into relatively enduring dominance/submission patterns within the hierarchical structure of the gallada, and, paradoxically, to find it somewhat easier to adjust at adolescence since their submissive style prepares them to work in the menial jobs available to them in the broader adult society.*

When I was a little boy, my parents explained about the hard times they were going through. Putting food on the table, I was told, was not a natural event like the change of seasons; it deserved respect. If one of us left carrots or broccoli on our plate, we heard the inevitable lines about the kids in India who were starving and how hard Dad was working to provide for us. We were lectured about our responsibilities: we had to help around the house, do well in school, and just as importantly, dress and keep ourselves clean. By the time we had more or less internalized these demands, we had started school. And, at school, like most North American children, we had heard or read about the adventures of Huckleberry Finn. Huck was my first hero. By comparison to our timid dependencies, Huck, who did not have to wash, dress up, listen to lectures about being respectful, or do "nothin'" he didn't want to do, was indeed a heroic figure.

Working in Latin America over the past several years, I found it impossible to avoid these memories. According to reports from UNICEF (Tacon, 1981, 1983), there are 40 million street children in Latin America who appear to be on their own, growing up without parental supervision. Seeing them, I often wondered what childhood would be like without parental authority.

In 1984 I was fortunate enough to be a Fulbright scholar in Colombia and to have the opportunity to examine the lives of the street children more systematically. The first task was to get as close as possible to those who were living outside of family and state control in order to gain their confidence. I collected ethnographic data as they ate, played, worked, and even as they slept so that I could share the variety of experiences as they moved around the city. . . .

Two Styles of Street Life: *Gamines* and *Chupagruesos*

From the ethnographic data, it was apparent that there were two different preadolescent psychological styles that ended at adolescence. The first was that of the true *gamine*, who chose to leave home, having rejected the trade-off between childhood protection with family obligations for the freedom from authority. He was the abandoner, who survived by cunning and wit. The second style was that of the *chupagrueso*, who was more likely to have been abandoned. These children lacked the haughty independence of the *gamines*, and learned to survive on the streets by becoming servile to the powerful.

Not only did the *gamines* appear much more independent and less self-doubting, but also enjoyed their independence. They were significantly brighter, functioned better emotionally, and had less neurological impairment than the *chupagruesos*. . . .

Aptekar, Lewis. (1989). Colombian street children: *Gamines* and *chupagruesos*. *Adolescence*, 24. pp. 783-794.

From the onset of their street lives, the two groups developed very differently psychologically. At first they stayed together while playing, but soon a differentiation between them occurred. Since the preadolescent children were more effective at soliciting alms, they were eventually asked to provide their services to the older children. Some of the smaller children responded to this demand by compromising their liberty and becoming dependent on the larger boys. Others refused, even if it meant fighting against the odds, and established themselves as independent.

The demands upon the *chupagruesos* by their older peers made it extremely difficult for them to break this submissive pattern. In their relationship with other street children, the *chupagruesos* formed sadomasochistic relationships with the larger boys, which often resulted in depression or regression to immature behavior. This in turn increased their submissive lifestyle.

This difference in the relationship of each group to authority is related to a universal motif of children that Bettelheim (1976) discusses in his book about fairy tales. This motif features a giant in conflict with an ordinary child who through wit overpowers him. "This theme is common to all cultures in some form, since children everywhere fear and chafe under the power that adults have over them. . . . Children know that short of doing adults' bidding, they have only one way to be safe from adult wrath; through outwitting them." It was through wit and cunning that the *gamines* took out their anger and learned to cope with their situation, while the *chupagruesos* were too afraid to express their pain.

As the two groups approached adolescence, they faced different problems. The ethnographic notes revealed that *gaminismo* ended at puberty. *Gamines* were unable to continue with their petty robberies or even commit more serious forms of robbery and still be *gamines*. These alternatives no longer provided the satisfaction of outwitting adults. With the increased experience and skill acquired with age, the same acts of mischievousness that once were thrilling became degrading. They no longer tested the *gamines*' intelligence and ability. As they grew older, they were compelled by their perceptions of themselves as haughty provocateurs to give up the small-scale mischief and become either full-scale delinquents or find a way to live outside the mainstream of society. However, escalating petty mischievousness into delinquent acts was unsatisfactory because it led to associations with gangs and the friendships and customs of that delinquent world. The ethos of the delinquent subculture was not to outwit authority, but to commit crime in order to gain wealth or power. The motives of the *gamines* were different.

Thus, *gaminismo* is a developmental stage which faces a nearly inevitable end as the child reaches puberty. This made adolescence for *gamines* a particularly difficult time because they had to give up so many of the acts that had brought them mastery and pleasure. The only way to maintain their hard-won sense of independence was to hide their haughtiness and accept poverty, a task which was not palatable to them. Having made one important life decision—to leave home at a time when most children were fully dependent on the decisions of their families—the *gamines* were forced by puberty to make another vital decision. One such decision was to become a small-scale entrepreneur. This allowed them to live outside of the mainstream and avoid being beholden to "bosses." If they could not do this, some became criminals. Others went against their grain to accept the servile life of a worker; that is, they became *chupagruesic*.

Chupagruesos also had difficult choices to make at puberty. Since they had not chosen to leave home, they lived with great emotional turmoil. As they approached adolescence, their problems were more related to gaining independence than losing it, to increasing self-respect rather than having to trim down excessive self-perceptions, and learning to live with their fears and lift their depression rather than curtail their grandiosity, as the *gamines* must. Paradoxically, the very servility which worked against them as small children on the streets helped them when they faced integration into adult culture. This style allowed them to be dependable and successful in menial jobs—the only kind of work available to them. Although the *chupagruesos* were thus more employable and able to avoid delinquency, they were rarely able to achieve the internal satisfaction that came to the *gamines* who became small-scale entrepreneurs.

Galladas and Camadas: The Street Children at Work and Play

Studying the children among their peer groups was helpful in gaining a fuller understanding of their psychological functioning. Two groups were revealed—the *galladas* and the *camadas*.

The *galladas* consisted of groups of fifteen to twenty-five children who associated with each other primarily for economic reasons. They were led by postpuberty children, with the prepuberty children as their underlings. Although the children stayed together in order to divide the labor that could make them all more successful than if they acted alone, as is the case with other business partners, they rarely associated outside of work.

The *gallada* was integrally related to the poor urban subculture. The leadership of the *galladas*, as well as the majority of its members, had been on the streets for a long time and had adopted a somewhat delinquent lifestyle along with the associations such a style brought. Although the *galladas* were composed mainly of adolescents, there were some preadolescents who helped bring in the goods. In addition, there were a few adults who helped integrate the children's economy into the larger culture.

The ultimate authority of the *gallada* resided with the adolescent *jefe*, who maintained his power and prestige by physical prowess, intelligence, and the ability to "fence" the products of his labor. The *jefe* not only had to learn how to control his *subjefes* and members, but also had to acquire the appropriate skills for dealing with the established criminal element. This gave him and his *gallada* access to more lucrative goods and a place to cash in what they already had. The *jefe* knew how to cultivate and maintain friendships with adults such as street vendors, restaurant owners, and taxicab drivers, all of whom occasionally fenced his materials, even if they were not fully committed to a criminal existence. These skills cemented the *jefe's* power over the group, since they relied on him and his connections to bring them what they needed and wanted. The *jefe* was the bridge between the street children and the subculture of urban poverty.

There was quite a difference between the way the preadolescent *chupagruesos* and the *gamines* responded to the *galladas*. This type of organization was suited for the *chupagrueso*, who learned quickly what was expected of him. He was reliable to those who he saw as having power, and did what was necessary to stay in their good graces. The *chupagruesic* style helped maintain the integrity of the hierarchy and method of doing business. However, the *gamine* used the *gallada* only so long as it helped him. He had little respect for authority per se, and maintained his allegiance to the powerful only so long as it served him better than he could do on his own, or in another *gallada*.

In comparison, the *camadas* were composed of small groups of two or three preadolescents who shared intimacies and camaraderie. These groups were different from the *galladas* in that they were more like family and friends than business partners. The children in the *camadas* were in the middle childhood developmental stage, a time when friendships consist primarily of two-person, same-sex dyads. The *camadas* existed not for economic or pathological reasons, but because, as Sullivan suggested, this is the time of psychological development when such friendships are most needed. By forming chumships, they were able to deal with the demands of street life in a rather healthy manner. In fact, chumships were nearly synonymous with *camadas*.

The problem was that chumship ended at puberty when, as Sullivan noted, "lust" for the opposite sex pulled the relationship apart. One preadolescent, for example, began puberty and an interest in friendship with the opposite sex earlier than his companion, which made his chum extremely lonely at times. As a result, he sought out another chum—one who was younger. When that did not work, he joined a *gallada* and became an isolated and marginal figure which only added to his loneliness. This phenomenon occurred often, because it was rare that the breaking of a chumship was simultaneous. With the passing of chumship came the demise of the *camada*. Like flowers in bloom, the *camadas* were intense, but ephemeral; in their beauty, unfortunately, were the seeds of their own destruction.

Because of these developmental differences, the internal dynamics of the *camadas* were different from those within the *galladas*. There was less formal organization in the *camada*, less delinquency, and the *jefe* was less important. Since the preadolescent children usually were fairly successful in getting food, by relying on their youthful image and thereby posing less of a threat to the public, they were able to secure their basic needs. Thus, they had less reason to obtain goods that had to be fenced. This reduced their level of delinquency and dependence on a *jefe*. Because the preadolescent children in the *camadas* came together more for personal than for business reasons, their relationship with each other was more intimate, resulting in less hierarchy and formal organization.

Since the children in the *camadas* played and ate together, the spirit was more like that of the *gamine*. The *gamines* moved between *galladas*, frequently residing in any one *gallada* only as long as it served their economic needs. *Chupagruesos*, on the other hand, needed the *galladas* for both personal and economic reasons, and they often found themselves deeply attached to a *gallada*, or a particular *jefe*. When the *chupagruesos* reached puberty, they were particularly hard hit by the change; they had not been able to enjoy their chumships in their *camadas* as a result of needing to attach themselves to the *jefes* in the *galladas*.

The *camadas* were composed only of preadolescent children; the *galladas* were run by adolescents, but there also were preadolescents. The preadolescents joined the *galladas* in groups that corresponded to their chumships. Typically, at the end of each day's work, a group of chums who were in the same *camada* left the larger business arrangement of the *gallada* and went to their prearranged private spots to sleep. In the morning they rejoined a *gallada*, either to work, as in the case of the *gamines*, or for personal and economic reasons, as in the case of the *chupagrueso*. When the preadolescent children wanted the older children to help them integrate into the adult society, they also turned to the *galladas*.

Conclusion

When I started this study, I was thinking what childhood might be like without parental authority. By the time I finished, I realized that in its absence, society would fill the vacuum. Because there were so many street children, they could not go unnoticed by society. The apparent freedom of their lifestyle necessitated their moral evaluation. This was dramatically illustrated when the Colombian street children reached puberty. Before that time, the children were considered cute, which contributed to their success at begging for alms. But as they grew, the image changed; they were then perceived as thugs and treated accordingly. When the street *children* reached puberty, they became street *people*, a change which signaled the end of one developmental period and the premature beginning of another.

The reason for this is that the prepuberty children, because they looked so small and young, stood out against the large "real world" in which they apparently roamed without supervision, producing a form of cognitive dissonance in the observer. A person in a dissonant state experiences two conflicting beliefs and thus feels compelled to change his or her opinion about one because of the tension of holding two incompatible attitudes (Festinger, 1965). The adult's concept of a child as innocent and in need of a family for protection, and a child who is capable of producing a self-sustaining livelihood are incongruent, particularly when the child is so small. It was psychologically easier to grant to the prepuberty children the status of children (i.e., dependent, in need of protection, and helpless), no matter how independent they may have been, than to change one's concept of childhood.

This was why small children were paid for cleaning the very windows they had just dirtied, and why they were capable of securing alms through a variety of "theatrical" gestures in which they portrayed themselves as urchins. When the older children tried the same things, there was no dissonance, and the reactions were less charitable. As a result of not being able to beg or rely on being "cute," they were forced to develop delinquent work habits to survive.

470

One of the most significant problems in adapting to being on the streets was the turmoil it created in the developmental sequence. Among their peers, the smaller children were often given the status of elders as a result of being more economically viable. In contrast to being seen as adults within their peer groups, they were treated as "cute and adorable" children by society. Yet, because of the experiences they had after leaving home at such an early age, they were living as adolescents. Unfortunately, as soon as they looked like adults, they were treated as adults. The leeway that adolescents normally received was absent. This made it difficult for the adolescents to do what they had learned as small children, so they either had to rely on their younger friends to support them or adopt a delinquent lifestyle.

The study of Colombian street children has value not only in helping them and the forty million children in similar situations in Latin America, but also points out the relativity of child development. Childhood is not a consistent phenomenon, untouched by societal and cultural expectations. When "appropriate" child behaviors go astray, society reacts. The study of Colombian street children offers the benefit of understanding, at least in one cultural context, how this affects children.

References

Bettelheim, B. (1976). *The uses of enchantment: The meaning and importance of fairy tales*. New York: Knopf.

Festinger, L. (1965). *A theory of cognitive dissonance* (3rd ed.). Stanford: Stanford University Press.

Tacon, P. (1981). *My child now: An action plan on behalf of children without families*. New York: UNICEF.

Tacon, P. (1983). *Regional program for Latin America and the Caribbean*. New York: UNICEF.

UNIT 7: Culture, Time, and Place

19

Adolescence: The Prolonged Transition

Amongst the Bena Bena of New Guinea, teenage boys are taken from their villages for a month-long initiation into manhood. This includes sharp leaves being thrust in and out of their nostrils, tiny arrows being shot into their tongues and penises, and repeatedly eating medicine to make them vomit. The purpose of these endurance tests is to strengthen the initiates, and purge them of the influence of women who are considered to make a man weak. In this war-like tribe strong warriors are admired.

A White Mountain Apache girl in North America will still have a Sunrise Dance when she is fourteen. It lasts for four days. A friend of the family becomes her 'sponsor'. She massages the girl, to pass her knowledge into her. The girl is elaborately dressed with an eagle feather in her hair, so she will live until her hair goes grey, and an abalone shell on her forehead, to symbolize the Changing Woman, mother of all Apache people. She goes through an endurance test, a long and fast dance around a sacred cane, so nobody who is evil can ever catch her. All the people at the ceremony shake yellow pollen over her head and pray for her future. They throw corn kernels over her to protect her from famine. She is painted from top to toe and blessed. For four days she cannot bathe, touch her skin or drink from a glass. The men raise a tepee frame for her, through which she dances, so she will always have a home.

• INTRODUCTION •

In traditional societies the onset of puberty is treated as a sign of adulthood, and the line of demarcation between the child and the adult is relatively sharp. This transition is usually marked by one or more ceremonial rites of passage that signal members of the community that a child has become an adult. Children in such cultures do not generally pass through a developmental period comparable to that which we term *adolescence*.

In societies that expect children to spend a long postpubertal period in school, however, children do not pass from childhood directly to adulthood. The transition to adulthood is gradual. It may extend over a number of years, include numerous ill-defined rites of passage-confirmation, *bar mitzvah*, receipt of a driver's license, moving from home to a college dormitory—and involve continued emotional and economic dependence despite sexual maturity.

Since the pioneering work of psychologist G. Stanley Hall, adolescence in America has traditionally been viewed as a time of "storm and stress" characterized by conflict among newly developing, adultlike cognitive and moral capacities, a continuing state of dependence, crisis in making vocational, religious, and reproductive choices, and difficulty in reconciling the need for peer acceptance with family rules and responsibilities.

According to prevalent stereotypes, adolescents are almost entirely self- and peer-oriented, negative and disparaging of parents, emotionally volatile, and openly rebellious. While recent research has shown that this stereotype is greatly exaggerated, there is little doubt that adolescence is a period of increasing peer involvement and, for many adolescents and families, increased stress.

Parents and children alike must adjust to the adolescent's changing cognitive and moral abilities and emotional needs and to the fact that the adolescents are becoming increasingly autonomous. At the same time, however, adolescents are still far from being treated as adults by their families or by society at large. One of the results of this contradiction is that some adolescents tend to find primary sources of social support, self-validation, and common interest in peers. Sociologists refer to this

476

phenomenon as the creation of *youth culture.*

The three readings in this chapter address the issue of youth culture from very different directions. John and Virginia Demos trace the historical evolution of youth culture as it reflected nineteenth century patterns of urbanization and industrialization and culminated in Hall's popularizing the concept of adolescence. Martha and Morton Fried describe traditional societies in which there is no independent youth culture—male and female rites of passage mark a relatively sudden transition from childhood into the full rights and responsibilities of adulthood. George Lewis describes the experiences of a group of American adolescents, alienated from family and school, who have created their own subculture within the confines of a large New England shopping mall.

● ● ●

Adolescence in Historical Perspective
John Demos and Virginia Demos

In pre-industrial rural America children and parents in farm families shared many of the same tasks, friends, and experiences. Participation in chores that helped assure the family's survival left children relatively little time for leisure. Widely scattered homesteads restricted the opportunity for peer contact. Career choice was clearly mapped out.

As the major urban population centers grew in response to the requirements of trade and industrialization, settings were created in which children either ceased to be an economic asset to the family, or contributed to family survival through work that was unrelated to that of their parents. In the crowded, complex environment of city life, these children were thrown together in large numbers with their peers and confronted with a vast array of conflicting vocational choices, values, and role models.

In the Demos's view, these were the conditions for creation of a sense of discontinuity between generations and the emergence of a youth culture characterized by strong peer preferences, a shared peer idiom, and behavior that was distressing to elders. While these concerns were being reflected in the "advice to youth" literature as early as the 1820s, it was

G. Stanley Hall, at the end of the nineteenth century, who popularized the concept of adolescence.   Hall called attention to an already evolving fact—the fact of youth culture. His emphasis on adolescence as a special stage, a period of storm, stress, and revolutionary crisis (religious conversion, delinquency), helped reshape cultural beliefs and fashion the ideology of adolescence that still looms large in the popular mind.

The idea of adolescence is today one of our most widely held and deeply imbedded assumptions about the process of human development. Indeed most of us treat it not as an idea but as a *fact*. Its impact is clear in countless areas of everyday life—in newspapers, magazines, and books; in various forms of popular entertainment; in styles of dress and of language. Its causes and meaning have been repeatedly analyzed in the world of psychologists and sociologists. Its effects are endlessly discussed by teachers, social workers, officers of the law, and parents everywhere.

Yet all of this has a relatively short history. The concept of adolescence, as generally understood and applied, did not exist before the last two decades of the nineteenth century. One could almost call it an invention of that period; though it did incorporate, in quite a central way, certain older attitudes and modes of thinking. It will be our purpose in this paper to describe the roots and the growth of the concept, to the point in the early twentieth century when it had become well established in the public consciousness. We shall limit our attention to developments in the United States, since adolescence was on the whole an American discovery.

We shall begin with a sketch of some common ideas about childhood and "youth" during the period 1800-1875, as revealed in two kinds of sources: (1) a rapidly developing literature of child-rearing advice, and (2) a large body of books and pamphlets directed to the young people of the country and bearing especially on their "moral problems." Then we shall summarize the activities of the "child-study movement" (beginning in about 1890) and in particular the work of the psychologist G. Stanley Hall, for there the concept of adolescence can be examined at its source. And finally we shall propose a hypothesis for drawing together these various types of material and above all for explaining the relationship between the *idea* of adolescence and the social phenomena to which it was a response. It is here that questions of family life will come most fully into view, since adolescence was, we believe, profoundly related to certain fundamental changes affecting the internal structure of many American homes. But this matter of the connection between "ideas" and "facts," between major cultural assumptions like adolescence and the social realities in which they develop, presents extremely tricky problems. It lurks as an uncomfortable presence behind most serious study that bears in one way or another on the history of the family. The difficulty lies in the nature of the

Demos, John and Demos, Virginia. (1969). Adolescence in historical perspective. *Journal of Marriage and the Family*, November, *31* (4). pp. 632-638.

evidence available to historians, which comprises for the most part a variety of written materials. It is much easier, therefore, to construct a history of ideas *about* the family than of the family as such. . . .

The literature of child-rearing advice is one of the most revealing, and least exploited, sources for the history of the American family. Its beginnings can be located in the early part of the nineteenth century; and it has been growing steadily, and changing in character, ever since. Before about 1825 relatively few books on child-rearing could be found in this country, and those that were available came chiefly from England. In general, they were mild in tone and full of simple moral homilies strung endlessly together. They do not, in short, seem to have been directed to any very pressing needs or problems in the lives of their readers.

After 1825 the situation, for this country at least, changed rapidly. Child-rearing books by American authors began to appear, some of which went through numerous editions and sold many thousands of copies. This development was owing to several different factors. In the first place it was related to a deepening interest in the fact of childhood itself as a distinct period of life and one which was little comparable to the years of maturity. Secondly, it expressed the broad impulse of nationalism that engulfed the country at this time. English books on child-rearing could no longer be regarded as suitable to American conditions. Finally, the new and authentically "native" literature on this subject reflected deep anxieties about the quality of American family life.

Most of the concern which was evident in these books related to problems of authority. In one form or another they all imparted the same message: the authority of parents must be established early in a child's life and firmly maintained throughout the years of growth. Even the smallest infant reveals a "willfulness" that "springs from a depraved nature and is intensely selfish."[1] This must be suppressed by strict training in obedience, or it will rapidly develop beyond the possibility of control with dire implications for the later (adult) personality.

These injunctions seemed all the more necessary because—so many people thought—parental authority was steadily on the wane. In describing the average home, the writers of the child-rearing books repeatedly used words like "disorder," "disobedience," "licentiousness," and above all "indulgence" (i.e., of the children). Statements such as the following were typical:

> It must be confessed that an irreverent, unruly spirit has come to be a prevalent, an outrageous evil among the young people of our land. . . . Some of the good old people make facetious complaint on this. . . . "There is as much family government now as there used to be in our young days," they say, "only it has changed hands."[2]

This seeming change in the traditional family pattern had other dimensions as well. Thus many authors noted the growth of a kind of "child-centered" attitude and condemned it out of hand. More and more parents, for example, appeared to feel compelled to show off their children before any and all guests. Similarly, there was in many households far too much concern with efforts to amuse and entertain the young.[3] Children who were often made the center of attention in this manner would inevitably become conceited and selfish. Another alarming development was the increasing tendency of children to seek social satisfactions outside of the family, among groups of their own peers. Mrs. Lydia Child, whose *Mother's Book* went through many editions, returned again and again to the theme that "youth and age are too much separated."[4] She and many of her contemporaries decried the "new custom" of holding parties exclusively for young people and urged that parents should always be the closest friends and confidants of their children.

Lest it be imagined that Americans of the nineteenth century had no special concern whatsoever for the period which we now call adolescence (and which in their day was simply termed "youth"),[5] we must turn to another category of books that were written specifically for the "youth" of the time and about their particular problems. The general nature of these writings is implicit in their titles: *A Voice to Youth; How to be a Man; Papers for Thoughtful Girls; The Young Lady's Companion; On the Threshold; Lectures to Young Men.*

From all of these works there emerges quite clearly a sense of "youth" as a critical transition period in the life of nearly everyone. It is a time, first of all, when people are extremely impressionable, extremely open to a wide range of outside influences. It is—to quote from Joel Hawes's *Lectures to Young Men* (1832)—

pre-eminently . . . the forming, fixing period. . . . It is during this season, more than any other, that the character assumes its permanent shape and color.[6]

Words such as "pliant," "plastic," and "formative" appear again and again in the discussions of youth.

Because of this characteristic openness, young people are vulnerable to many kinds of "danger." To begin with, boys and girls entering their teens experience a sudden and sharp upsurge of the "passions." They become high emotional; their mood fluctuates unpredictably from exuberance to melancholy. Henry Ward Beecher, whose *Lectures to Young Men* were among the best known examples of the genre, declared:

A young man knows little of life; less of himself. He feels in his bosom the various impulses, wild desires, restless cravings he can hardly tell for what, a sombre melancholy when all is gay, a violent exhilaration when others are sober.[7]

In keeping with their Victorian conventions, these writers never directly mentioned the physiological changes that occur at puberty, in particular the strong new charge of sexual energy and tension. Occasionally one finds an allusion to "internal revolutions" and "occult causes, probably of a physical kind;"[8] but for the most part people were content to define youth in the above terms, that is, as a vast outpouring of the emotions.

As if to complement these disruptive changes within the personality, the world at large was full of "seductive temptations," of inducements to all manner of wicked and ruinous behavior. As Beecher said,

> *These wild gushes of feeling, peculiar to youth, the sagacious tempter has felt, has studied, has practiced upon, until he can sit before that most capacious organ, the human mind, knowing every step and all the combinations.*[9]

Here, then, was the wider, social dimension of the problems which confront the young person. The world lies in wait for him, and "ardent, volatile, inexperienced, and thirsting for happiness," he is

exceedingly liable to be seduced into the wrong paths—into those fascinating but fatal ways, which lead to degradation and wretchedness.[10]

There are, at this stage of life, dangers both within and without.

Most of the material considered so far has been drawn from the period 1825-1850. As the years passed and the century neared its end, the picture of youth that we have been describing was embellished somewhat in certain important respects. Thus, for example, the sexual factor began to receive some attention. And some writers were struck by a kind of aimlessness and indecision that seemed increasingly common among American young people. Theodore T. Munger, whose book *On the Threshold* was published in 1881, declared that

> *Young men of the present years . . . are not facing life with that resolute and definite purpose that is essential both to manhood and to external success. . . . [They] hear no voice summoning them to the appointed field, but drift into this or that, as happens.*[11]

Moreover, towards the end of the century, many writers identified the "dangers" and "temptations" which threatened youth directly with urban life. Something of this had been implicit from the beginning, but now it came clearly into the open. The city loomed as the prime source of corrupting influences for the young. Its chaotic social and economic life, its varied population, its frenzied commercial spirit, and its dazzling entertainments were all sharply antagonistic to proper growth towards adulthood.

At roughly the same time, meanwhile, the formal concept of adolescence was receiving its first public expression. The immediate context of this development was a new movement for systematic "child study," inspired and guided by G. Stanley Hall. Hall was, of course, one of the major figures in the early history of American psychology. After a lengthy period of study in Germany, he became in 1881 a professor at Johns Hopkins, and six years later he accepted the presidency of Clark University. There he remained for the rest of his life, presiding over a wide range of research and teaching activities.

The aim of the child-study movement was to enlist large numbers of ordinary citizens in a broad effort to deepen both public and scientific understanding of human development. The mothers who belonged to the various local organizations were encouraged to keep detailed records of the behavior of their children and to participate in regular discussions about such records. They were also exposed to, and themselves reflected back, the major themes in Stanley Hall's own work—not least, his theory of adolescence.

The essentials of Hall's view of adolescence appeared in one of his earliest papers on psychology: "The Moral and Religious Training of Children," published in 1882 in the *Princeton Review*. The great point of departure, then as later, was the idea of "storm and stress," of severe crisis characterized by

lack of emotional steadiness, violent impulses, unreasonable conduct, lack of enthusiasm and sympathy. . . . The previous selfhood is broken up . . . and a new individual is in process of being born. All is solvent, plastic, peculiarly susceptible to external influences.[12]

The suggestions contained in this article were subsequently elaborated in much greater detail by some of Hall's students at Clark. Efforts were made to link the adolescent "crisis" with a wide range of personal and social phenomena—with religious conversion, for example,[13] and with the rising rate of juvenile delinquency.[14] Hall himself provided the capstone to this whole sequence of activity, with the publication in 1904 of his encyclopedic work *Adolescence: Its Psychology, and Its Relations to Physiology, Anthropology, Sociology, Sex, Crime, Religion, and Education*. It is impossible to summarize here the many ideas and vast assortment of data embraced therein, but certain underlying themes can at least be singled out. From the very start Hall's thinking had been profoundly influenced by Darwinism, and the psychology he proposed was explicitly bound to an evolutionary, or "genetic," model. He urged a kind of "archaeology of the mind," in which all the various stages in the development of human consciousness would be rediscovered and understood in their proper order. A key link here was the theory known as "recapitulation," which affirmed that every individual "lives through" each of the major steps in the evolution of the race as a whole. Adolescence assumed a special importance in this scheme, for it represented (and "recapitulated") the most recent of man's great developmental leaps. The adolescent, Hall believed, reveals truly enormous possibilities of growth and "is carried for a time beyond the point of the present stage of civilization."[15] This is not however, an easy situation, for it encompasses a variety of contradictions and "antithetic impulses." Among the impulses which Hall paired in this context were hyperactivity and lassitude, happiness and depression, egotism and self-abasement, selfishness and altruism, gregariousness and shyness, sensitivity and cruelty, radicalism and conservatism. Caught in the midst of so much change and conflict, the adolescent was bound to experience "storm and stress" more or less continuously.

Hall's work on adolescence quickly exerted a considerable influence in many different directions. Its impact was clear in general texts on psychology, studies of education, the new literature on child-rearing, and a variety of books on child labor, religious training, vocational guidance, and the like. Even critical comments showed the extent to which the idea of adolescence had captured the public imagination: there were those who complained that "we are today under the tyranny of the special cult of adolescence."[16]

Hall's reputation was, however, relatively short-lived. From the very beginning his theories of adolescence aroused at least some criticism. Men like E. L. Thorndike (himself an important figure in the history of American psychology), Charles H. Judd, and Irving King charged him with many forms of exaggeration and overstatement.[17] And after 1925 his work went rapidly into eclipse. Many scholars came to feel that it was unreasonable to view growth in terms of set "stages" of any kind whatsoever. Margaret Mead, in her famous study of Samoan children, tried to show that adolescent "storm and stress" are a function of certain *cultural* determinants.[18] By contrast, Hall was seen as the representative of an outmoded, wholly physiological orientation. Moreover, his fervent, almost missionary approach to his subject, his florid writing, his long-range goal of race improvement—all this came to seem irrelevant, or even offensive, to later generations of psychologists.

Thus G. Stanley Hall has been largely forgotten, if not rejected outright. Yet, we suggest, he has left his mark all the same. Hall's critics denied the validity of considering personal growth in terms of "stages;" but we still regard adolescence in just such a context. His critics accused him of having greatly exaggerated "storm and stress" phenomena, and yet today more than ever we view adolescence in exactly those terms. In fact, the "special cult of adolescence" seems to have lost no strength at all. And it was Hall, more than anyone else, who fixed it in our imagination.

It would be easy to overstate the element of innovation in Hall's thinking. If we compare the kind of adolescence that he was describing with some of the ideas that were current just before his time, we find a considerable degree of continuity. His achievement lay in reshaping certain aspects of popular belief about youth, combining them with some of the most exciting new ideas in science (i.e., evolution), gathering data on a large scale, and presenting the whole in a persuasive and meaningful fashion.

Yet certain questions about the rise of the concept of adolescence remain. What larger developments in American society did it reflect? To what popular attitudes, or needs, or anxieties, did it minister? We offer, in conclusion, the following very tentative suggestions—some of which we have simply lifted from contemporary thinking about adolescence in the fields of psychology and sociology.[19]

We propose, as a starting point, the long term transformation of the United States from an agricultural into an urban and industrial society; for this change—which has, of course, been basic to so much of our history during the last 150 years—has exerted a profound influence on the structure of American families. Consider that most farm families are characterized by a high degree of internal unity. Children and adults share the same tasks, the same entertainments, the same friends, the same expectations. There is a continuum between the generations. The child appears not so much as a child per se but as himself a potential farmer; he is, then, a miniature model of his father.

Such, we would argue, was the prevalent situation in nearly *all* the families of this country before the nineteenth century.

But when Americans began to move to the city, all this changed. City children, for example, do not often have a significant economic function within the family as a whole. (Or alternatively—as in the case of poor children employed as factory hands—their work is likely to be quite different from that of their parents.) Moreover, they are thrust into close proximity with other families and have the opportunity to form numerous contacts among their own peers. Thus there develops in the urban setting an important "discontinuity of age-groups."[20] Children and adults are much more obviously separated from each other than is ever the case in a rural environment.

This second configuration was starting to show itself in some American families during the early part of the nineteenth century, and perhaps it helps to explain the material presented in our opening section. Now—i.e., with the new, typically urban family structure—childhood as such is "discovered;" it is no longer feasible to regard children simply as miniature adults. Now, too, "child-centered" families become possible. The behavior of the young is increasingly seen as bizarre and also as appropriate to their particular time of life. A new tolerance for such behavior develops, and parental authority appears to weaken. Finally, there is an obvious place for a literature on child-rearing.

Most cultures with sharp discontinuities of this kind possess a system of "age-grading," which defines the various steps in the transition from childhood to adulthood. In many cases there are elaborate initiation rites to dramatize this change. But our society lacks such rites; ceremonies like confirmation and graduation exercises are losing whatever significance in this regard they once had. It is in such situations, as Kenneth Keniston has suggested, that a "youth culture" is likely to develop. "Youth culture" may be defined, somewhat carelessly, as institutionalized adolescence. It refers, of course, to the special way of life characteristic of large groups of young people of approximately the same age. It is more than a simple substitute for formal age-grading and initiation rites. It is not, Keniston writes,

so obviously transitional . . . [but is] . . . more like a waiting period . . . a temporary stopover in which one can muster strength for the next harrowing stage of the trip.

Its pattern is "not always or explicitly anti-adult, but it is belligerently *non*-adult."[21] In many respects adulthood looks rather forbidding when compared with the life of a child, and youth culture reflects some reluctance to bridge this gap.

It is pertinent to recall at this point the deep concern of many nineteenth-century Americans about the growth of peer-group contacts. We suggest that these people were witnessing the rudimentary beginnings of a youth culture. Of course, there were none of the artifacts so prominent in our own modern-day youth culture (e.g., "rock 'n roll," "teen magazines," special kinds of dress, and so forth). But the very fact of "wanting to be with and for [their own] kind"[22] was significant. By about 1900 the situation had become more clear. The many and varied writings on "gangs," on juvenile delinquency, and on vocational guidance all show some feeling for the special characteristics of a youth culture.

Keniston argues that a second kind of discontinuity—that between specific generations—is also important in the formation of youth culture. By this he means a clear separation between the parents and the children within an individual family. In such cases the situation of the parents offers no viable goal at which their children may aim. Intra-family conflict is likely to become chronic, and the adolescent is on his own in the formation of an identity. This pattern is characteristic of societies with a high rate of social change and a plurality of alternatives in regard to careers, moral codes, and life styles. The young person shrinks from such a bewildering array of choices and becomes part of the youth culture, where a clear-cut, if temporary, identity comes ready-made.

All of this seems to describe nineteenth-century America fairly well, especially the new life of the cities. Social and economic change was everywhere apparent; ambitions were high; there was an astonishing diversity of people, ideologies, occupations. The disparity between generations was assumed; it became, indeed, a part of the national mythology. Immigrant families presented an especially dramatic case in point; likewise those families in which the children of uneducated parents had the chance to go to school. Thus, once again, there was the youth culture.

The growth of the concept of adolescence was the final step in this long and somewhat devious process. It was the response to an observable *fact*—the fact of a youth culture, of many young people seemingly in distress (or at least behaving in ways that distressed their elders). Americans needed some means of understanding the problems of, and the problems created by, these young people. We have tried to show them groping toward such an understanding through much of the nineteenth century. And we have located, chiefly in the work of G. Stanley Hall, a kind of culmination of these efforts: the first comprehensive theory of adolescence in modern history.

Notes

1. H. W. Bulkeley, *A Word to Parents*, Philadelphia: Presbyterian Board of Publication, 1858, p. 12.

2. Warren Burton, *Helps to Education,* Boston: Crosby and Nichols, 1863, pp. 38-39.

3. On this matter see, for example, Lydia M. Child, *The Mother's Book*, Boston: Carter, Hendee and Babcock, 1835, p. 94.

4. Child, *op. cit.*, p. 95.

5. The word "adolescence" was known in the nineteenth century, but we have found only a very few cases of its use in the literature on child-rearing and "youth."

6. Joel Hawes, *Lectures to Young Men*, Hartford, Connecticut: Cooke & Co., 1832, p. 35. See also child, *op. cit.*, p. 125.

7. Henry Ward Beecher, *Lectures to Young Men*, Boston: J.P. Jewett & Co., 1844, p. 21.

8. Isaac Taylor, *Home Education*, New York: D. Appleton & Co., 1838, p. 131.

9. Beecher, *op. cit.*, p. 21.

10. John M. Austin, *A Voice to Youth*, New York: J. Bolles, 1838, p. 1.

11. Theodore T. Munger, *On the Threshold*, Boston: Houghton Mifflin & Co., 1881, p. 5.

12. G. Stanley Hall, "The Moral and Religious Training of Children," in *Princeton Review* (January, 1882, pp. 26-48. This essay as later republished in a slightly revised form in *Pedagogical Seminary*, 1, pp. 196-210.

13. See E. D. Starbuck, *The Psychology of Religion*, New York: Ginn & Co., 1899; and an essay by the same author, "A Study of Conversion," in *American Journal of Psychology*, 8, pp. 268-308.

14. See Edgar J. Swift, "Some Criminal Tendencies of Boyhood: A Study in Adolescence" in *Pedagogical Seminary*, 7.

15. See the "epitome" of Hall's theories by G.E. Partridge, *The Genetic Philosophy of Education*, Boston: Sturgis & Walton Co., 1912, p. 31.

16. Frank O. Beck, *Marching Manward*, New York: Eaton & Mains, 1913, p. 38.

17. See E. L. Thorndike, *Notes on Child-Study*, in *Columbia University Contributions to Philosophy, Psychology, and Education*, 8:3-4, p. 143; also Thorndike's article, "Magnitude and Rate of Alleged Changes at Adolescence," in *Educational Review*, 54, pp. 140-147. See too Charles H. Judd, *The Psychology of High School Subjects*, Boston: Ginn & Company, 1915; and Irving King, *The Psychology of Child Development*, Chicago: University of Chicago Press, 1903, pp. 222 ff.

18. Margaret Mead, *Coming of Age in Samoa*, New York: W. Morrow and Company, 1928.

19. We have tried to draw together ideas from several different sources, chief among them: Kenneth Keniston, "Social Change and Youth in America," *Daedalus* (Winter, 1962), pp. 145-171; Erik H. Erikson, "Youth: Fidelity and Diversity," *Daedalus* (Winter, 1962), pp. 5-27; Ruth Benedict, "Continuities and Discontinuities in Cultural Conditioning," in *Psychiatry*, 1, pp. 161-167; Kingsley Davis, "The Sociology of Parent-Youth Conflict," *American Sociological Review*, 5, pp. 523-535.

20. The phrase is Kenneth Keniston's. See his article cited above.

21. Keniston, *op. cit.*, p. 161.

22. William B. Forbush, *The Boy Problem*, Chicago: The Pilgrim Press, 1901, p. 20.

Transitions: Rituals of Puberty and Youth
Martha Nemes Fried and Morton H. Fried

In Tikopia, an island in Melanesia, and among the !Kung hunter gatherers of the Kalahari in South and Southwest Africa, a relatively sharp transition from childhood to adulthood is marked by a number of special rituals. In the following reading, Martha and Morton Fried describe Tikopian rituals of anointment and exchange that surround a boy's first torch fishing expedition and those of superincision of the penis that symbolize his transition to manhood.

Among the !Kung, full manhood is indicated by symbolic scarification that occurs when a boy has attained the right to marry by killing his first large game animal. For !Kung women, as for women in many other cultures, transitional ceremonies mark the occurrence of first menstruation. In reading about these rituals, pay particular attention to their communal nature—to the ceremonial roles that community members play, to the public symbolism, and to the taboos that reflect the society's shared belief system. In these societies, there is no opportunity for discontinuity to develop between the generations. In the transitions described by the Frieds, initiates move from childhood directly into the rights and responsibilities of adulthood. The ceremonial rites of passage are public occasions for the recognition of this transition. As the authors point out, rites of passage are not for the initiate alone. They are moments when the community reaffirms its own historical continuity and celebrates the passage of generations.

In our world, where crisis is ever at a boil, every period of life provides a special set of hazards. . . . None of these, however, seems a time as perilous as adolescence. Why? Perhaps because adolescence is a time of tension between pleasure on the one hand and of high turmoil and danger on the other. In fact, although many societies provide special rituals or other markers of transition into and out of a more or less clearly marked period of youth, a distinct period of adolescence is not marked in all cultures. Our view of adolescence is not universal. . . . Consider the Tikopians.

A boy first gets to do a man's work in Tikopia when he participates in a *mataki ramanga*, a "torch [fishing] expedition." He does no more than paddle as one of the

Fried, M.N. and Fried, M.H. (1980). *Transitions: Four Rituals in Eight Cultures*. NY: Norton. Chapter 3 (Puberty/Adolescence). pp. 58-92.

crew, but the event is of sufficient importance to warrant a celebration. The day after the young boy has gone fishing with the men, his cheeks, neck, and chest are rubbed with turmeric. . . . Relatives of various kinds and degrees of closeness congregate on his behalf, providing a behavioral announcement that a major event in the boy's life is taking place.

Tikopian society is dominated by patrilineally organized kin groups, but the mother's relatives are important, as is often the case in patrilineal societies. It is therefore not surprising that the boy is sent on the occasion of his first fishing expedition to visit the house of his mother's brother. There he is again anointed with turmeric and given a ceremonial present known as *maro*, often consisting of a bundle of bark cloth, a mat, other things, and a basket of food. Meanwhile, at home, his parents have fired the rock ovens and spend the day preparing food in lavish quantities. The boy arrives at home and displays the gifts he has received. His parents reciprocate by dispatching gifts of equal value. . . .

If the fishing ritual comes first, it is by no means the most important transition marker for a young male. That honor is reserved for the ceremony centered on the superincision of his penis.

Because great quantities of food have to be accumulated and prepared, sometimes in several ovens, and because many things of value have to be assembled for distribution as gifts for this occasion, the ceremony is often performed for a group rather than for an individual. A number of boys of similar age—a cohort, as it were—are assembled to undergo the ordeal. Their parents, by combining efforts, enhance the occasion. Throughout their lives, the boys who undergo a common superincision ritual perceive it as a bond among them, and say, "We had our ovens fired together."

In recent times the ritual of superincision has usually taken from three to five days, but in the past it could take as many as eight, especially if the son of a chief of high rank was involved. Long in advance of the event, relatives are notified of its coming. Actually, they are probably well aware of it, since the festivities provide a major source of pleasure and excitement. Large supplies of food, pandanus matting, and bark cloth are stored up, and gifts made to be distributed, marking the occasion. The initiate responds to invitations to call at the houses of relatives living in other villages. Each visit begins with the ceremonial anointing of the lad with turmeric, now mixed with coconut oil. The mixture produces a dramatic appearance. The boy seems drenched in blood and the Tikopia themselves think of this as an augury of the bloody injury the boy will suffer in his passage to adulthood. Cleansed, he dons a new waistcloth, made for him by women who are closely related to the men slated to take a prominent part in the impending ritual. To further honor and show affection for the boy, they rehearse songs, some old and others newly composed for this occasion. The practice assures them that the performances will not go awry at the ritual itself.

Individually and in groups, the relatives collect taro, yams, green coconuts, breadfruit, and bananas, heaping it all outside the house of the initiate's father. The day before the ceremony, the menu is completed when men go fishing with nets from boats, while the women work their scoops, wading through the shallows at low tide.

Whatever nature's mood, the next day begins somberly. Sunrise may be bright and clear, but the sounds of weeping and moaning fill the village, a foreboding of the pain to be visited on the boys who come symbolically to manhood that day. No sooner does one group of relatives tire of making the mourning sounds than another group takes up the task with fresh vigor, keeping the air awash in a constant dirge of grief. Faces are bathed in tears and blood as the relatives tear at cheeks and foreheads with fingernails or knives. Others seated nearby present a placid contrast as they await their turn to wail, meanwhile quietly chewing betel and plaiting sinnet cord.

During this preparatory phase of the ritual, the initiate is repeatedly anointed with turmeric, and his waistcloth is changed again and again. As he waits for the operation, the boy hears dirges, such as this:

I would be busy then with the voyage
I would leap aboard to be borne aloft,
For my namesake is carried on the journey.

Fetch then to the sea your canoe
Fetch with it the paddle while I sit
To weep wildly at the trail of foam

I weep for my necklet
Who has leapt aboard the vessel
But us two the mutual sight
On that day alone.

As interpreted by the Tikopia, this song is directed to the boy who is identified as the "necklet." Do we also see here a cry of anguish of the aging man who sings the song? It could be a celebration of *that* man's youth, the time before he married and settled down, when life was exciting for him. In any case, it reminds us that times of transition are times of coming and going not merely for the initiate, but for everyone participating in the ritual. At weddings, in our own culture, for whom are the tears shed?

There are other songs. Some of them are addressed to the boy's father, praising his generosity:

Friend! borne over the land, friend!
The father of the Tikopia

Your wealth of goods has been distributed to Ravenga
It has entered into Namo on the lake-shore

It is scattered around, friend, and stands in the
   West
Till it strikes the lowlands of Faea

We shall go and eat of your meals from the vessel
The praiseworthy man, how we gather around him.

As the boy is clad in fresh waistcloths, the women who change him place the cloths they have removed around their necks; around his neck, they place string upon string of beads. The father leads a chorus of relatives in yet other songs of mourning, and sorrowfully presses noses with each boy in the ritual party who is awaiting initiation. Now the mother's brother of each initiate suddenly seizes him and carries him bodily to a place where coconut leaves have been strewn on the ground. Here the operation is to take place. A crowd assembles as the tension mounts. Each boy is supported by a man who places his arms around him. These are the *tangata me*, "the men on whom the boys sleep." They will cover the boys' eyes at the moment of the incision.

The man who takes the role of surgeon at the superincision is invariably an uncle of the initiate, specifically, the boy's mother's brother (*tuatina*). . . . Although this uncle is probably around the age of the boy's parents, he is treated in a totally different way. Where the boy must maintain formality and respect with his parents, he has a joking relationship with his mother's brother, and when he is in his *tuatina*'s house, he is relaxed and easy. Possibly because of this close emotional tie, the *tuatina* who is about to superincise his nephew's penis is quite nervous. To keep his hands from trembling, he rests his elbows on his knees as he sits in a crouching position. The foreskin of the initiate is drawn tightly forward and just before the cut is made the *tuatina* says "*Fakatoa! iramutu!* (Be strong! nephew!)." Now the cut is made lengthwise on the front portion of the foreskin two inches in length from the tip of the penis. The tool is a razor; of old it was the shell of a bivalve, and many strokes were required to complete the operation, rendering the process so excruciatingly painful that it was only performed on much older boys. The young man's *tuatina* took him to a secluded spot in the forest, far out of earshot, to save him the humiliation of having others hear his terrible screams.

Even now, with a sharp razor, a bungler may have to cut more than once, to the dismay of all. After the cut the foreskin is parted and folded back on each side. Fresh bark cloth is applied as a bandage. Most initiates are rigid with terror—some react with an involuntary retraction of the penis. When that happens, the *tuatina* grasps the organ and forcibly extends it for the cutting.

Before the superincision, the boy must observe a taboo for some time, avoiding certain foods considered "gristly"—these include snails and clams. The lad whose superincision proceeds smoothly with one neat cut is said to be one who has "listening ears," that is, who is obedient to the taboos. If the hand that performs the superincision wavers and the job is botched, it is not blamed on the practitioner but on his subject. It is obvious to all present that the boy has been refractory and has not properly observed

491

the taboo.

After the bandage has been secured, the boy rises and drops his waistcloth, which is again replaced with a fresh one. His bead necklaces and ornaments are carefully taken by his mother's brother. They return to the boy's house, where mourning songs break out anew, describing the wounds just inflicted. Yet again his waistcloth is exchanged for a new one, this time perhaps one of calico. The new garment is put upon him by his *masikitanga*, his father's sisters. . . .

As he enters the house, the boy presses noses with his father and then repeats this affectionate greeting with each relative in the room. This is followed by a lavish exchange of gifts and an elaborate meal.

After eating, the boy is taken alone into the forest or down to the sea by the uncle who performed the superincision. He is taught how to care for his wounded penis. Juice extracted from the leaves of a local plant called *kamika* is dropped into the cut to speed the healing, which will take about a month. During this period the boy avoids activity; soreness and discomfort are expected. When the healing is completed, the initiate is considered an adult. He has entered Tikopian society and may participate fully in all adult activities. . . .

The !Kung hunter-gatherers of the Kalahari desert do not inflict genital mutilation . . . on their children as they move from carefree childhood to adulthood. They do not force any particular mode of conduct on their offspring, but simply tell them what they consider desirable behavior. The growing child develops control from within, in harmony with the knowledge that life in the bush is precarious, and provocative behavior is destructive not only to self but to the entire group.

As children grow up they play games imitative of adult activities, including sexual play. Both boys and girls stop sleeping by the family fire by the age of twelve. Boys and girls alike usually build their own fires in the camp, but girls may spend their nights with a grandmother or a widow. As the size of a camp is very small, consisting in some instances of as few as eight families, both boys and girls remain in close proximity to their parents.

The first ceremony for boys, called *choma*, is similar in some aspects to the initiation ceremonies of an adjacent Bantu-speaking people. The men and boys go to a place well out of earshot of the camp and dance for several days and nights. When the dancing is over, each boy has a vertical line incised in the middle of his forehead, and has his hair cut in a special *choma* way. Participation in this ceremony is purely voluntary, and no social pressure is placed on a boy to engage in it.

The next marker in the growth of a boy from childhood to adulthood is essential—he cannot take a wife until he has successfully killed a large animal such as a great antelope, a giraffe, or a buffalo. From the age of about twelve, a boy begins to prepare for this crucial feat by accompanying his father on hunts. As he gets older, he spends many of his evenings around the campfire listening to stories of the chase told by older men. He has spent years practicing on smaller animals with a bow and unpoisoned arrow, and has sharpened his ability to track animals by following their spoor. The nomadic !Kung man's principal occupation is hunting, and he spends years in preparation, learning from his elders, before his first big kill.

The Rite of the First Kill takes place twice in the life of each man: when he kills his first big male animal and when he kills his first big female animal. Vertical cuts are made in his chest, back, and arms, and a charred medicinal herb mixed with the fat of the animal he killed is rubbed into the cuts, producing permanent welts. Here is the way a !Kung explained scarification: "I cut his chest and put in medicine to lift up his heart and make him *want* to seek meat; I put (it) in his arm and wrist to make his arm soft (*swa*) and his aim correct; in his back to make sure that the game won't run away; in his brow so that he may see things quickly."

The occasion is also marked by the gift of a spear to the hunter by the person for whom he is named. Most boys make the necessary kills between the ages of fifteen and eighteen, and are then eligible to marry. Some men do not achieve these kills until later in life, and some may never qualify at all, but that is indeed rare.

In the strict physical sense !Kung girls mature later than most American girls. Their breasts begin to develop when they are thirteen and the onset of menarche is not usually until the age of fifteen or later, by which time they have likely been married and divorced more than once.

When a girl menstruates for the first time, she is carried by an old woman to an isolated, specially built shelter. The old woman stays with her, for there is a taboo on her feet touching the ground when she urinates or defecates, and she is carried on the woman's back and held when such functions are performed. The girl's head must also be covered at all times. This is done lest she encounter a man, for she must not gaze at men at this time or be seen by them. There is also a major belief among the !Kung that the sun represents death and should not shine upon her head when she is in this vulnerable condition. (There is a similar belief associated with marriage ritual.)

While a girl is still sequestered in the special menstruation shelter, women and old men dance and sing the First Menstruation music. The Eland Dance, deriving its name from the twigs the male participants attach to their heads to suggest the horns of the animal, is fraught with sexual symbolism. Only the women who are present and two old men who have a joking relationship with the menstruating girl can participate in it.

When the menstrual flow has stopped, a design is painted on the girl's face with red powder. She is washed and rubbed with fat and *tsi* nut oil. At this point, the girl may leave her shelter and resume her former activities, with one exception: the first time she drinks water or eats plant foods, the final part of the First Menstruation ceremony must take place. An older woman (it can be her mother) scrapes a root called *sha sha* into the water hole, then, taking the girl's hands, she chews *sha sha*, and, together, they cook plant foods in the fire. The older woman blows on the girl's hands and on the food she is about to consume before she can eat it. This is believed to prevent the girl's having an upset stomach.

Once the ceremonial is completed, the young woman need not ever again go into isolation when she menstruates, but there are still certain taboos she must observe during each period. She may not touch any implement that has to do with hunting, for to do so would rob the hunter of his efficacy. She must abstain from sex with her husband, lest it render him lazy and rob him of the desire to go hunting.

Rats and Bunnies: Core Kids in an American Mall
George H. Lewis

In this reading, George Lewis describes the results of an ethnographic/interview study of a group of adolescents whose lives revolve largely around group interaction in the New England shopping mall in which they congregate. Sharing home and school backgrounds in which they have experienced consistent rejection, institutional indifference, and the abuse of power, these young people come together at the mall to kill time, to look for excitement, to escape from home and school, and to derive from their peers a sense of communal belonging, mutual understanding, and emotional support that is lacking in the rest of their lives.

Like the street children of South America, these New England adolescents are alienated from and hostile toward the broader social world. They have created their own community, a peer culture in which experience is shared and beliefs and attitudes are held in common. In this mall subculture, as Lewis points out, these young people find a sense of democratic friendship and belonging, and space and acceptance to be themselves and to explore the parameters of their own personal identities. No longer children, not yet adult, and without a sense of belonging to home or to school, they are in effect treading water until they grow old enough to be drawn out of the mall and into the adult world.

Over the past three decades, the shopping mall has evolved into a sort of civic center for many suburban, middle-class Americans. More than just central locations for shopping, these covered and climate-controlled monoliths have become meeting places—easily reachable and safe spots in which many activities only marginally related to the economics of the stores take place. Cultural events are staged by outside groups acting in cooperation with mall management. Leisure activities are offered, from video arcades to ice-skating rinks. Fast-food shops, fashion shows, and petting zoos abound. This mix of recreation, leisure, and community facilities with retail outlets is an effort to make the mall a focal point for community life. . . . In addition, and to some extent because of the reputation a mall can build within a community, it becomes a social magnet, drawing others inside its walls—people who come not to buy or participate in the staged events, but out of curiosity, to meet friends, to hang out and pass the time in its controlled and temperate environment.

Lewis, George H. (1989). Rats and bunnies: Core kids in an American mall. *Adolescence*, 24. pp. 881-889.

One such group to whom the mall appeals are adolescents. Many younger children are happily dropped off there during the day on weekends in the winter and any day of the week during summer vacation by their parents, with enough change for the video games and lunch at a fast-food stand. Older teenagers arrive by themselves or, more typically, in small groups, to hang out and see their friends. One remarked to an interviewer, "If you don't have a car to go cruising in, you cruise the mall" (Green, 1982, p. 67). As Anthony (1985) reported, young people spend a great deal of their time hanging out in malls. In her study of a suburban Los Angeles shopping mall, she found that a large proportion of her sample visited the mall at least once a week, with an average stay being from three to five hours. . . .

The Present Study: New England Mall

This study focused on adolescent social behavior and use patterns in a large New England shopping mall. This particular mall was begun seventeen years ago and has evolved, changed, and grown for nearly two decades. Thus it is a permanent cultural fixture in the eyes of the adolescents who frequent it. To them, it has always been there. This mall is extremely well-known, and is regionally popular. In fact, it draws customers from all over the state, from adjoining states, and even from the bordering Canadian province. It boasts of being the largest mall "north of Boston."

Five years ago, a major new wing was added, as large as the original mall and connected to it by a short, enclosed promenade. Shops in the new wing are more flashy in appearance—boutiques, T-shirt stores, record and video shops and, occupying the most space, the fast-food court with its many take-out stands. The older wing, in contrast, is more heavily weighted toward more established stores—men's and women's clothing, banks, professional offices, stationery and book stores. The old mall has three sunken circular "conversation pits" with benches for short-term sitting; the new mall has the food court, with modern wire and metal chairs and tables arranged around large potted plants. The old mall has a wooden gazebo, an information desk, and bulletin board; the new mall has a video arcade. The old mall has few security personnel in evidence; the new mall has security people walking relatively regular beats. In all, there are over 250 shops in the mall, 22 food outlets, a video arcade, three movie theaters, and five major (anchor) department stores.

In general, adolescents spend nearly all their time in the new wing of the mall, congregating around the video arcade and the food court when they are sitting, and moving through and around the various shops in groups of two or three when they are "cruising." The old mall is perceived by them as "boring"—a place where adults shop and where the elderly congregate. Psychologically, from the adolescent perspective, the old mall is not defined as their "territory," and thus they do not frequent it except perhaps as a convenient shortcut to or from the parking lot.

Data for this study are qualitative in nature and consist of a series of unstructured interviews conducted by a team of researchers over a period of six weeks in June and July 1988. . . .

496

What the research team was especially interested in was social groupings and behavior in the mall. In this case, did adolescents congregate on any regular basis? Was the mall a place where peer groups could develop and grow, where a sense of common culture—or even community—could be found? Or, was the mall just another place to go, to be part of a crowd of like-minded strangers, to hang out (perhaps with a friend) when you were both bored and looking for some action?

With this in mind, the team spent many hours observing behavior in the mall, looking for and identifying "regulars" for interview purposes. These youths, the ones who showed up day after day (the criterion was at least four times a week), who spent most of their time interacting with others, and who were familiar to the custodians and security personnel, were interviewed by team members, some on as many as five occasions over the six-week period of research. These twenty-three young people, identified as the "core kids," the ones who defined the new mall as their turf and hung out there day after day, were the focus of the research effort. The many other youths who frequented the mall on a less regular basis, or who came with their parents for shopping purposes, were not included in the study, even though short interviews were conducted with some of them for comparative purposes.

Calling themselves "mall rats" (males) and "mall bunnies" (females), the teenagers congregate in the new wing of the mall, the largest number of them arriving in the late afternoon. They wander around the different shops, playing video games in the arcade, smoking cigarettes, showing off their latest hairstyles, makeup and clothing, and waiting for something—anything—to happen. Most of them stay until nine-thirty or ten, when the stores close and the mall shuts down.

Derick (the names of all teenagers have been changed), age 15, his hands jammed into the pockets of his frayed cutoff jeans, admits that the mall is "a place to go before I have to go to work. I only work right across the street. I have nowhere else to hang out. Most of my friends hang out here."

Looking at the arcade further down this wing of the mall, he gestures toward it with a quick nod of his head. "Go over there to play video games. Spend all my money. I don't like spending all my money, but it's there." He shrugs. "Fuck it."

Standing near Derick in the small knot of teenagers, Ed, 16, takes a long, slow drag on his cigarette and exhales out of the corner of his mouth. "I just started coming on almost a daily basis last year because it was something to do," he says. "You can come here anytime. It's pretty good, but if we didn't have anything, anywhere to go, you know, we'd probably get into a lot more trouble, so it kind of works out. It's something to do and it kind of keeps you out of trouble."

Nodding toward his friends, Ed goes on to explain the social networking that takes place in the mall. "I met all these people here. I've met lots of other people, too. One place where you can always find someone. If you know somebody, they know somebody else, they'll probably see 'em here, and you'll know them, then they'll know someone who is walking around and you know that person. So when you come here, you kind of build on people."

497

For some teenagers, a great deal of time is spent networking in the mall. It is, for them, practically a second home. Tammy, age 14, says, "I used to come here every Saturday from eleven in the morning to nine-thirty at night, and just walk around with my friends, like Gina here, just walk around and check out the guys. Now, most of my friends I meet here at the mall. I try to come out every day, if I can."

When the strip becomes tiresome after roaming from shop to shop, playing video games, or cruising, they usually migrate to the food court. There they sit, talk, bum change, smoke cigarettes, and try to avoid the attention of the security people since most of the activities they are engaged in will inevitably attract it.

The group gathers around a table, some standing, others sitting and talking. One of the girls breaks from her conversation to announce that Bob is coming. Bob has been kicked out of the mall for boisterous behavior and is not allowed in for another two months.

"Just about all of us have gotten kicked out at one time or another," Tony says matter-of-factly. "I was sitting down without anything to eat once, and like I didn't know the policy and he said, 'Move,' and I go, 'Why?' I ran my mouth a little too much. What I basically did was stand up for myself, but he didn't like that, so he just booted me for a couple months. Actually, I'm not supposed to be even in here. He said he's kicked me out forever, but I mean like I changed my hairstyle so he doesn't recognize me anymore."

Ed nods. "I changed mine and I changed my jacket. I used to wear a big leather jacket. I used to wear that all the time. That gave me away. But I've started wearing this jacket now with all my KISS pins on. And as long as I don't act up or do anything, they don't really care. See, I like it here so much I have to come back."

Liz, 15, discusses relationships with the security guards in general. "Somedays they can really get on us and other days they just won't come, and like we'll be sitting down at the table and on busy days or on days they're not in a really good mood, they'll come over and tell us to move."

"They have no respect for mall rats," adds Caulder, 14, standing on the edge of the group. "It's just days like that they can be real dinks."

And yet the harassment by the security guards is easily borne, especially when changing one's clothing or haircut often can be enough to erase their identity. Such treatment is much better, for most of them, than what they could expect if they were to hang around any public places outside of the mall. This relatively light scrutiny by the security guards also allows some adolescents to get away with minor drug transactions, especially when the mall is crowded.

"Other than Dark Harbor [a boardwalk/amusement park area twenty miles down the coast], which is just like, 'deal it out on the streets,' I mean you can get just about anything out here—pot, acid, hash, right here on Saturdays, when it is crowded."

"If you know the right people, you can pick up anything."

"And we pretty much know everybody here."

For some teenagers, the mall—with or without drugs—is an escape from home or school. Heather, 16, explains that she goes there "to get away from home, get away from problems because I can't stay at home. Because my mom's always on my case when she's not off partying with her boyfriend. And that dude's bad news, really. They bother me. So I come to the mall." Slouching in her seat, she flips open the top of her red Marlboro box and counts her cigarettes. "School is no better. I got through a year of school, and they still put me through the next grade even if I'm failing. I don't care about partying. I just want to get through school. Get out."

For Tiffany, the mall has become a second home. At the age of thirteen, she lives with Tony and one other mall friend. "My mom kicked me out when I was eleven," she says with an edge of anger in her voice. "She's a bitch. I call her every day and she's just . . ." Tiffany stops short, shaking her head and rolling her eyes.

"I started going to foster homes and everything, and I just quit. Now, I'm in state custody and I just . . ." She stops again, laughing nervously and blushing. "Sorry about that," she says, apologizing to her friends seeming to imply that she has become too personal, too emotional. Abruptly, she continues. "I don't do anything that they want me to do." She lets out a quick triumphant laugh.

"I swear to God if they came up to me and dragged me where I didn't want to go, I'd beat the crap right out of them. I would kill 'em. I got 'em twisted around my little finger. They don't mess with me," she growls, as she clenches her teeth and curls her small fist, pounding it lightly on the table.

Tony leans back and shakes his head slightly to part his long hair from his face. "I left home and I quit school and moved from, like, hotel to hotel for awhile with a Navy buddy, and that wasn't a really good situation because we were getting kicked out of hotels and motels. We didn't have any money. Didn't have anywhere to go. So we went up to the Beach [Pine Beach, a town forty miles up the coast, where there are employment opportunities in a large shipyard] and when I went up there it's like there's a Burger King and an auto parts store and a Shop and Save and it's like . . . there was no mall. I was real glad to get back down here because it was, like up there, it was boring the hell out of me."

Discussion: Alienation and Peer Support in the Mall

Unlike Anthony (1985), who interviewed a larger random sample of youth in a California mall and found only 4 percent who went to the mall every day, our more focused sample of "regular" mall rats and bunnies was far more likely to visit daily. These twenty-three "core kids" make up a fairly tightly integrated social group, with about a quarter of them employed at least part-time in the fast-food shops in the mall. Around this core there move others, whose patterns of belonging are less regular—possibly three visits a week at the maximum, usually fewer. But even these young people try to make it to the mall to hang out at least once a week.

Most of the core kids (91 percent) go to the mall to be with their friends, as opposed to just 42 percent of Anthony's larger, random sample. Their social lives revolve around the mall. Most arrive by midafternoon and stay until it closes at ten. They eat at the fast-food outlets (or get under-the-counter handouts from those of their group who do work at these places). Most of them, with the exception of purchasing their food and,

499

mainly for the younger ones, playing the video arcade, spend almost no money at the mall, a finding which coincides with what Anthony found in the California mall. For these youths, the records, clothes, and videos purchased by the many young people who visit the mall for shopping purposes are not easily affordable, and there has developed almost a norm against the purchase of shiny, new media material from the mall.

For many of the core kids, like Tiffany, Heather, Derick, and Tony, the mall offers a form of much-needed peer support. Their home and school experiences, filled with personal rejections, institutional indifference, and abuses of power as means of control, create the classic conditions for alienation (Calabrese, 1987; Gallette, 1987). That these youths would exhibit very low social involvement outside of their mall world, have obvious difficulty in conforming to bureaucratic and institutional rules and conditions, and have somewhat negative self-images as well as fairly high levels of hostility against the outside world, should come as no great surprise.

These themes of alienation seem to weave a common web of understanding around most of the mall rats and bunnies. Taken together, they comprise a mutual social support system of alienated young persons. Rat put it well when he said, "Sometimes, if I couldn't work out here and be with my friends, like, I don't know if I could make it. My dad's, ah, real fucked, if you know what I mean. He's always out of control and stuff. So I try to stay out of his way. And *school*," he laughs and shakes his hair. "Like I've been kicked out three times, man. For nothing. Just talk. It's boring, man. I'm not ever going back there. I don't give a shit what my dad says. Let him blow, man."

Tina adds, "We're all just good friends here. We give each other space, which we need, I guess. We do kid around a lot, but basically we don't hit on each other. That's what we came here to get away from."

As Calabrese (1987) has stated, youths operating under these conditions "find alienation a way of life. They are left with few alternatives because society and its organizations do little to reduce their at-risk nature. Adolescents have responded by developing their own culture" (p. 935). This culture, at least as it appears in the New England mall, is one that seems to provide a sense of democratic friendship and belonging, while allowing for a great deal of individual self-expression and exploration of personal identity. This culture, forged from shifting networks of peer relationships, appears to be a somewhat unstable social system and one that rests almost entirely in present time and revolves around present circumstances. Personal pasts are, for the most part, only briefly sketched in. They are seldom spoken about and appear not to be a part of the shared mall culture in anything but a very general sense.

Then, too, adolescents grow up and, for the most part, drift out of the mall culture as they are drawn socially, sexually, and economically into the adult world that has, until they come of age, so effectively excluded them. This fluidity and change in social relationships is one more uncertain part of the teenage years which, for mall rats and bunnies, is also characterized by a lingering malaise concerning the world outside their fragile community—a malaise in which jealousy, mistrust, and despair are the prominent features. As Tony says, "We are the mall rats. We are the mall. What the fuck else can I say?"

Conclusion

The mall, it seems, acts as a social magnet, drawing adolescents to its safe and socially neutral territory. Especially for middle-class youths with unresolved problems and difficult social situations at home and school, it offers a "third ground," a place where congregation is possible and hassles are minimal. As one security guard explained, "We aren't allowed to harass the kids, and I know they got to hang out somewhere. I was a kid once myself. But they've got to keep moving, not block up access to shops or the food service area. And if they get too loud, we have to clear them out."

The small core group of mall rats and bunnies are mall regulars. These young people hang out there nearly every day, usually from midafternoon until closing time. Several of them, in addition, work in the mall's fast-food stands, providing some minimal amount of cash for themselves, as well as an introduction to the world of adult work. In addition, they can and do provide others in the core group with "junk food" snacks, which allows for longer periods of hanging out.

The culture of these regulars centers around present-day concerns and is caught up to a great extent with mass-media images, idols, and sounds. These kid dress, talk, and act like the kids they see on MTV and in the teen movies. They discuss issues of importance in the commercial youth culture—Madonna's new hairstyle, Bruce Springsteen's divorce, Eddie Murphy's new routine. By mutual consent, they each "cover" for the others' deficiencies in self-image, validating their mutual appropriations of mass-mediated roles, clothes, expressions, and physical moves.

And underneath, holding this frail community together, is their recognition of the themes of alienation in each other—alienation from family, school, the whole adult middle-class community that shuts them out. There is anger there, and hostility. And there is also a good deal of despair, masked cunningly by the glittering neon and commercial pop in which the mall rats and bunnies so easily wrap themselves, as the adults of the community, entrapped by the economic lure of the mall, rush hurriedly by, eyes averted, feet tapping and echoing on endless, tiled floors.

References

Anthony, K. H. (1985). The shopping mall: A teenage hangout. *Adolescence*, *20*(78), 307-312.

Calabrese, R. L. (1987). Adolescence: A growth period conducive to alienation. *Adolescence*, 22(88), 929-938.

Gallette, L. C. (1987). Children in maritally violent families: A look at family dynamic. *Youth and Society*, *19*(2),117-133.

Green, B. (1982). Fifteen: Young men cruising shopping malls. *Esquire*, *98*, 67-73.

20

Risk and Resilience

On the slave plantations in the Deep South of America in the nineteenth century, the children played both traditional games and ones improvised on the spot. Some of the games they played were role-playing, for instance 'hiding the switch.' In this popular game, one child would hide a willow switch, which, once hidden, was searched for by the others. The child who found it ran after the other children trying to whip them. This game reflects the children's fear of flogging, and was their way of coming to terms with it. Interestingly, the slave children spent very little time in competitive play, and their games were always designed so that no player was ever eliminated during the game. This reflected the adult slave philosophy of co-operation and community spirit, vital in the face of constant family disruption and separation.

• INTRODUCTION •

One in five American children under six years of age is being raised in poverty. One in two American households headed by a single mother with children under the age of six exists in poverty. Mothers who are poor are less likely to have access to prenatal care or to meet standards for adequate nutrition during pregnancy. Children who are poor are less likely to receive immunizations and regular pediatric health care. Environments of poverty are frequently environments of drug use, alcoholism, domestic stress, violence, and neglect.

Psychologists classify all of these factors as risks. A *risk factor* is any characteristic of the individual or the environment that increases the likelihood of negative developmental outcomes. Risk factors can be biologically based, such as Down syndrome or difficult temperament; prenatal or perinatal, such as fetal drug addiction, delivery complication, or premature birth; familial, such as maternal depression, parental abusiveness, or contentious divorce; or socioeconomic, such as parental unemployment, poverty, and chronic exposure to crime and violence.

While children who grow up subject to multiple risks have a greatly increased likelihood of exhibiting one or more negative developmental outcomes, this is by no means an automatic consequence. Indeed, on the contrary, many children at risk, even those who begin life under conditions of considerable reproductive stress and grow up in the most unfavorable of environments, survive to become happy, competent adults. Psychologists refer to such children as *resilient* and to factors that enhance resilience as *protective factors*.

Both of the readings in this chapter describe studies of risk and resilience. In a brilliant reanalysis of data from the Oakland Growth Study begun in 1931, sociologist Glen Elder and his colleagues take advantage of the fact that the Great Depression of 1929 created a natural experiment on the psychological effects of economic deprivation. Focusing on families whose income was drastically reduced by the depression, the authors evaluate the impact of change in economic circumstance on family function, parents' relationships to children, and children's developmental outcomes.

In the second reading, Emmy Werner describes a longitudinal study through which she and her colleagues identified a wide variety of risk and protective factors in the lives of a cohort of 698 infants born in a single year on the island of Kauai and studied from before birth through age thirty. As you read these articles, notice that in both studies, children's developmental outcomes were found to reflect the interaction of risk with factors in the child and in the environment that afforded those children who proved to be resilient some measure of protection from that risk.

• • •

Linking Family Hardships to Children's Lives
Glen H. Elder, Jr., Tri Van Nguyen, and Avshalom Caspi

In the following reading, Glen Elder, Tri Van Nguyen, and Avshalom Caspi present a sophisticated analysis of the psychological effects of risk and factors that enhance resilience among adolescents in Oakland, California, whose families suffered economic deprivation during the Great Depression. While deprivation was found to place these adolescents at increased risk for psychological distress and a reduced sense of self-adequacy, the authors' results make it clear that the impact of risk was indirect, mediated by the parenting behavior of fathers. When a father's income was lost, the family's resulting economic readjustment frequently led to a reorganization of family roles. Mothers and children went out to work at paid jobs and older daughters assumed greater responsibility for the household. With these changes, the relative power of the mother within the family tended to increase, the attractiveness of the father to decrease, and fathers to become more rejecting and less supportive of their children.

The nature of the relationship between a father's rejecting behavior and psychological functioning in his adolescent children, however, proved to be far from simple. Even under conditions of extreme risk, some children in the Oakland study flourished. Analyzing the data by gender and relating the results to ratings of adolescents' physical attractiveness, the authors suggest that both of these factors may have served to enhance

505

children's resilience in the face of economic deprivation.

Relative to boys who were more likely to work outside the home, a factor that may have increased their independence from the family and buffered the impact of family stress, girls were more negatively affected by the rejecting behavior of fathers. Assuming greater responsibility in the home, girls may have been more directly exposed to tension and conflict within the family or even to have become the target of the father's displaced resentment over loss of male status. Furthermore, this effect was particularly felt by girls who were physically less attractive. In fact, fathers in economically deprived families were actually less likely to be rejecting and more likely to be supportive of their daughters if they were physically attractive. The interaction between characteristics of the child and behavior of the parents, in other words, served jointly to mediate the impact of economic hardship on the child's psychological well-being.

This study exemplifies two approaches to understanding the relation between economic hardship and children's lives. The first approach specifies appropriate causal paths that *mediate* the relationship between economic change and children's functioning. In this study, we examine the role of parenting behavior, especially fathers', in linking economic hardship to the social-affective behavior of children. The second approach identifies conditions that *moderate* the nature of this mediational process, a conditional or interaction effect. In this study, we view child attributes as potential moderators of this process, especially physical attractiveness.

The structure of the present study extends the analytic framework of *Children of the Great Depression* (Elder, 1974), a longitudinal study of 167 California children who were born in 1920-1921 and grew up in the hard-pressed city of Oakland during the worst years of the 1930s. Building on this earlier analysis, the present study examines the role of parenting behavior in the process whereby drastic economic change influenced children's lives. Using the data archive of the Oakland Growth Study, we focus on the period from late childhood through early adolescence (1929-1936). . . .

Family mediation.—Economic setbacks clearly make a difference in psychological functioning (e.g., Pearlin, Lieberman, Menagham, & Mullan, 1981), but how is this difference manifested in children's lives? To understand the impact of economic hardship on children's lives requires knowledge of the adaptations chosen and played out by their parents. The adverse effects of stressful economic times are not necessarily exercised directly. They may be produced indirectly through their disorganizing effects on family relations. Specifically, economic hardship may increase children's socioemotional distress

Elder, Glen H., Jr.; Nguyen, Tri Van; and Caspi, Avshalom. (1985). Linking family hardship to children's lives. *Child Development*, 56. pp. 361-375.

and the risk of developmental impairment by increasing the rejecting behavior of parents, and especially that of fathers.

Conditional effects.—It is widely recognized that characteristics of children elicit modes of parental behavior (e.g., Bell & Harper, 1977). Such behavior is likely to be especially dependent on the attributes of children in stressful times. A child's aversive qualities may heighten parental hostility under such pressure, and conversely, the positive qualities of a child may elicit greater concern and nurturance from parents in hard-pressed households. In the present study, we examine the physical attractiveness of children (see Elder, 1969) as one determinant of parenting behavior in hard economic times. Specifically, adolescents who are less physically attractive may be at greater risk from family hardship and parental maltreatment than attractive adolescents.

Sex variation.—The final hypothesis derives from a growing literature (e.g., Werner & Smith, 1982) that identifies early adolescence as a period of greater vulnerability for girls than for boys. Consequently, both hypotheses, mediational and conditional, should apply more to adolescent girls than to boys. . . .

Hard Times in Children's Lives: The Analytic Model

When Robert Lynd returned to Middletown in 1935, he found a city that had been "shaken for nearly six years by a catastrophe involving not only people's values but, in the case of many, their very existence . . . the great knife of the Depression had cut down impartially through the entire population, cleaving open the lives and hopes of rich as well as poor" (Lynd & Lynd, 1937, p. 295). This observation applies also to families and children in the San Francisco Bay region of California during the Great Depression (Elder, 1974, 1979). But while some families experienced very heavy losses through unemployment, others were spared hard times altogether, and some even managed to benefit economically from the lower living costs of the 1930s. This historical variation (deprived vs. nondeprived families) serves as a point of departure for examining the process by which children were influenced by economic hardship. Indeed, the Great Depression can be viewed as a natural field experiment that created an exogenous change in the social and economic situations of families and altered the developmental context of children.

Using data on the Oakland Growth Study (children born between 1920 and 1921), Elder (1974, 1979) assessed the effects of income loss according to a conceptual model that viewed the family and its socioeconomic and psychological adaptations to hardship as the primary link between economic change, on the one hand, and the life experience and personality of children on the other. Sudden income loss called for new forms of economic maintenance among Oakland families that altered the domestic and economic roles of family members, shifting responsibilities to mother and older children. Girls assumed greater responsibility within the household, and a good many worked at paid jobs, as did boys from hard-pressed families.

Fathers' loss of earnings and resulting adaptations in family maintenance (e.g., women's entry into the labor market) increased the relative power of mother, reduced the level and effectiveness of parental control (particularly in relation to boys), and diminished the attractiveness of father as a role model for children. Income loss also fostered social uncertainty and ambiguity concerning family standing and the status of members. This account (Elder, 1974), however, did not give explicit attention to parenting behavior as a link between hard economic times and children's social and emotional behavior. In this study, we are concerned primarily with testing this link.

Some insights concerning the mediating role of parenting behavior in hard-pressed families have emerged from cognate studies of families and children in the Depression era using the rich family and individual data archive of the Berkeley Guidance Study (Eichorn, Clausen, Haan, Honzik, & Mussen, 1981; Elder, Caspi, & Downey, in press; Elder, Liker, & Cross, 1984; Elder, Liker, & Jaworski, 1984; Liker & Elder, 1983). Heavy income loss between 1929 and 1933 increased the emotional instability, tenseness, and explosiveness of fathers. This change enhanced the tendency for fathers to be punitive and arbitrary in the discipline of their children. By comparison, mothers did *not* become more unstable under economic stress, and income loss did not directly increase their punitive or arbitrary behavior. What accounts for this difference? One possible explanation centers on the more personal nature of income and job loss among men than among wives and mothers. Family misfortune was typically a result of men's losses.

The overall pattern of men's reactions to sudden economic loss conforms to a theory of force in regaining control over life circumstances (Goode, 1971). Loss of control over one's life situation prompts efforts to regain control. Force is one means to this end. All findings from the Berkeley sample (e.g., Liker & Elder, 1983) lend support to the mediating role of father's behavior in hard times (Hypothesis 1): heavy income loss adversely influenced young children (between three and seven years old) by increasing the rejecting, nonsupportive behavior of fathers. In the present study, we attempt to replicate this finding with an older cohort of adolescents (from eleven to fourteen years old) from the Oakland Growth Study.

In the Oakland sample, hard economic times generated by the Great Depression caught children in transition to the social world of adolescence. The transition into adolescence is increasingly identified as a time of psychological vulnerability for girls (e.g., Werner & Smith, 1982; see also Eme, 1979). In their longitudinal research Simmons and her colleagues (Simmons, Blythe, Van Cleave, & Bush, 1979) found self-image disturbances to be more common among girls than boys in early adolescence. These observations suggest that early adolescent girls would be especially vulnerable to parental maltreatment during hard economic times. Some evidence from previous analysis of the Oakland study supports this hypothesis. The psychological costs of the transition into adolescence during the period of economic deprivation were especially strong for girls who lacked appropriate dress and material resources for social dating.

Earlier analyses (Elder, 1974, chap. 6) found that the Oakland girls, but not boys, were judged "less well-groomed" during early adolescence if they came from hard-pressed families in the 1930s, whether middle or working class. Some implications of this handicap are manifested in junior high school. According to self-reports, girls from deprived homes, middle and working class, scored higher than the nondeprived on social unhappiness and on feelings of being socially excluded from peer activities. Mothers also perceived differences of this sort. Mothers from deprived families ranked their daughters higher on hurt feelings, worries, and self-consciousness than mothers from nondeprived families.

To the extent that adolescent girls were especially vulnerable to family tension in the Great Depression, this should be most apparent among the least attractive girls in the Oakland cohort. Unattractive girls generally think poorly of themselves (Sorell & Nowack, 1981), and they rank low on self-confidence and assertiveness, qualities often characteristic of the victimized (Scherer & Shepherd, 1982). In addition, physically unattractive children are more often the recipients of negative attributions from others. For example, adults assign more blame to physically unattractive children, regardless of the facts (Dion, 1972). In the Oakland cohort, adolescent girls in the middle and working class who ranked high on physical attractiveness (. . . Elder, 1974) were rated higher than the less attractive on self-confidence, peer acceptance, and leadership. In the working class, these girls were "less likely to form steady relationships with boys in high school, and were generally more guarded and selective in social friendships."

Overall, we assumed that the least attractive adolescents in the Oakland cohort were more vulnerable to the rejecting behavior of father than attractive children (Hypothesis 2), and that this risk should be greatest among adolescent girls. Several studies suggest that physical attractiveness is more salient for the adjustment of females than males (see Hansell, Sparacino, & Ronchi, 1982). Evaluations along social dimensions are affected not only by attractiveness level, but also by sex, with more differences appearing between attractive and unattractive females than between similarly grouped males (e.g., Bar-Tal & Saxe, 1976). Hence, we have good reason to believe that attractiveness was a powerful conditional factor in the Depression family experience of adolescent girls (Hypothesis 3).

Methods

Sample

The Oakland Growth Study began in 1931 when fifth-grade children from five schools in the Northeastern sector of Oakland were selected for a projected longitudinal analysis of mental, social, and physical development in a normal sample of boys and girls. Selection was based on two criteria: willingness to participate, and anticipated residential permanence in the area. This procedure produced a sample of 167 children, 84 boys and 83 girls, who were studied continuously from 1932 to 1939. Born in 1920-1921, the Oakland children were well beyond the dependent stages of early childhood at the time of maximum economic hardship in the early 1930s. They graduated from high school just before World War II, reaching the age of majority after opportunities had improved through nationwide mobilization for war.

509

Economic deprivation.—The median family income for households in the sample was $3,179 in 1929, as reported in the first parent interviews, and all but a few of the fathers were fully employed. Some four years later, in the trough of the Great Depression (the year 1933), the median family income hit a low of $1,911. To characterize Depression hardships, we used a binary measure of economic loss or deprivation between 1929 and 1933 (0 = nondeprived; 1 = deprived). Taking into account the sharp decline in the cost of living in the San Francisco Bay area (about 25 percent in 1933) as well as the correlation between income and asset loss, all families that lost at least 35 percent of their income (between 1929 and 1933) were classified as economically deprived. Less deprived families were classified as nondeprived. Deprived working- (max. N = 46) and middle-class families (max. N = 49) lost 58 percent and 64 percent of their income, respectively. The corresponding figures for nondeprived families were 15 percent in the working class (max. N = 21) and 20 percent in the middle class (max. N = 40). Income loss represents a general index of the loss of material resources. More specific measures of asset change are not available. However, prior research indicates that loss of income generally coincided with the loss of family assets, from life insurance to furniture and other residential property. An extended discussion of the deprivation measure is provided in *Children of the Great Depression* (Elder, 1974, chap. 3).

Parenting behavior.—The data archive of the Oakland Growth Study generally reflects prevailing concepts of child care and development in the 1930s. Mothers were considered the major figures of child rearing, and they were interviewed on two occasions during the period of economic hardship: 1932 and 1934. The fathers were not interviewed, although interviews with mothers included questions about fathers' behavior. Another, less systematic source of information on parenting behavior was derived from staff observations of parents during their visits to the institute. Through the generosity of Marjorie Honzik at the Institute of Human Development, we borrowed selected parenting ratings from her large parenting project with Mary Main for the years 1931-1934. The Oakland children were between 11 and 14.5 years old at this time.

Building on more than forty years of research on parental behavior, Honzik and Main (1982) developed fifty-four parenting scales; twenty-two capture stressful, negative behaviors, and thirty-two tap supportive parental behaviors and attitudes. This approach is based on the premise that different parents may exhibit mixes of positive and negative behaviors. Each behavior is rated on a seven-point scale. The present analysis is based on only a single rating per item and case, although the completed coding on the Honzik-Main project will have at least two ratings per item. Two methods were used to calculate reliabilities from the scores of two raters on a small subset of families during the initial stage of the Honzik-Main project: (1) correlations between raters 1 and 2 for the total protocol and for each item of the overall scale, and (2) the average of the difference between ratings assigned by the two raters without regard for sign. Acceptable items in terms of interjudge agreement had an *r* of .45 or greater, since the Spearman-Brown correction of this coefficient is .62 with two judges. On the absolute difference analysis, the acceptable difference was 1.50 for the seven-point scales.

Considering these data, we selected four parent behavior ratings for the analysis, three on negative behavior (rejecting, exploiting, indifferent) and one on positive behavior (emotional support). The last rating was the only index of emotional support that was available for a substantive number of the mothers and fathers in the Oakland sample. As broader measures of the family environment, we also selected four seven-point ratings, entitled marital compatibility, emotional tone of home, family coordination, and child-centered home. The parent ratings within each set of negative behaviors were highly correlated, thus permitting construction of the following scales:

Rejecting (mother, father): "Negatively responsive to child," "rejecting," "neglecting," "not dependable;" average r: mothers = .59; fathers = .77.

Exploitive (mother, father): "Overly demanding," "exploitive;" r: mothers = .66; fathers = .45.

Indifferent (mother, father): "Not responsive to child," "indifferent;" r: mothers = .68; fathers = .73.

These measures index parent attitudes toward the study child that became apparent in the course of interviews and observations. Thus, for example, the rejecting index captures a negative attitude of the parent toward the child.

The use of wife reports on father behavior could entail some bias in the measurements. For example, mothers may have presented a consistently biased (favorable or unfavorable) view of their husbands, thereby inflating correlations among all family and parenting indicators. . . . Had reliance on mothers' reports introduced this systematic bias, we would expect between-parent correlations to be of the same magnitude as within-parent correlations. But the former set of relationships is generally lower than within-parent correlations.

Child Behavior

Aspects of a competent self.—Utilizing the California Q-sort for the junior high school period (1933-1936), we sought to characterize adolescent functioning in terms of at least three prominent elements of a competent self (Coan, 1974; Smith, 1968): (1) goal directedness—concerted and satisfying efforts toward the achievement of goals; (2) a sense of self-worth and initiative, including effective coping with life's problems; and (3) social competence —social skills, rewarding associations, consideration of the needs of others. Three item clusters bearing on these dimensions were identified from correlational and factor analyses of ratings on boys and girls (Elder, 1979):

1. **Goal-oriented:** "High aspirations," "productive," "gets things done," "self-defeating in relation to goals," and "lacks personal meaning." Scores on the latter two items were reflected. Average r: boys = .49; girls = .31. Reliability coefficient (α): boys = .80; girls = .51.

2. **Self-inadequacy:** "Satisfied with self" (reflected), "thin-skinned," "feels victimized," "brittle," and "fearful." Average r: boys = .58; girls = .62. Reliability coefficient (α): boys = .87; girls = .88.

3. **Social competence:** "Arouses liking and acceptance," "gregarious," "social poise," "socially perceptive," and "aloof" (reflected). Average r: boys = .45; girls = .44. Reliability coefficient (α): boys = .81; girls = .80.

Self-other relations.—A second Q-sort (Block, 1971) for adolescents focused on interpersonal behavior during the junior high school period (1933-1936). Differential association with peers and adults, attitudes toward parents, and roles in the peer group are the concerns of this set of descriptive variables. At least two judges rated each case, with a mean interrater reliability of .75. We used two items that refer to attitudes toward father: "perceives father as an attractive man," and "feels father is a respected man as judged by social standards." Three additional items bear on peer experience: "emphasizes being with peers," "seeks reassurance from peers," and "is dependent on peers." Each scale ranges from a score of 1 (extremely uncharacteristic) to 9 (extremely characteristic).

Maternal ratings.—A third source of information on children's behavior comes from maternal reports in the 1936 interview. Mothers were asked to rate their children on a set of behavioral attributes using a three-point Likert scale to indicate frequency. Building upon prior analysis (Elder, 1974), we selected four scales: moody, easily hurt, calm, and angry.

Attractiveness.—Information on children's appearance was obtained from observational ratings made by staff members in a playground setting during semiannual visits to the Institute of Human Development (1932-1936). The two or more staff members attending these sessions were well known to the children and related to them as interested, friendly adults. Observations made during the free-play sessions were recorded afterward on comment sheets, and children were rated on a number of seven-point scales (the ratings are known as Free-Play Ratings). An overall index of physical attractiveness was derived by averaging scores on the following interrelated scales: attractive coloring, good features, good physique, thin-to-fat, femininity/masculinity of behavior and physique, pleasing expression, and sex appeal. Interrater reliabilities for the junior high items were above .80. This composite index has been used in prior research (Elder, 1969, 1974) in the adolescent experience and marital success of Oakland females.

Data Analysis

To investigate the influence of economic deprivation on family relations and parenting behavior, we begin with an examination of correlations between these variables. The next step focuses on the relationship of economic hardship and parenting behavior to measures of adolescent functioning during the junior high school years. With regard to the temporal sequence, measures of parenting behavior (1931-1934) precede both the *Q*-sort ratings (1933-1936) and maternal reports (1936). Because we expected sex differences to emerge in these data, separate correlations are reported for boys and girls. To test the mediation hypothesis, path-analytic models are used to examine the role of father behavior in linking economic hardship to adolescent functioning. Finally, to examine the conditional hypothesis of physical attractiveness, we compare the effect of economic hardship on father's behavior in subgroups of attractive and unattractive children and test for significant differences in the regression slopes. . . .

Results

Economic Hardship, Parenting, and Adolescent Behavior

Correlations between economic hardship and measures of parental behavior point to the stronger connection between income loss and father's behavior when compared to mother's behavior and its correlates. Economic loss is moderately linked to father's rejecting ($r= .24$), supportive ($r= -.23$), and indifferent ($r= .17$) behavior. By comparison, none of these modes of parenting among mothers is related to income loss (r's between -.01 and .02). The findings are consistent with previous analyses of the Berkeley Guidance cohort (birth years, 1928-1929; see Elder, Liker, & Cross, 1984), and suggest that economic loss adversely influenced family functioning through its direct influence on fathers' behavior. Economic hardship did not generally affect mothers' parenting behavior. Hence, in the analyses that follow we focus on *fathers* as the primary link between Depression hardship and children's personal and social functioning in adolescence. . . .

Correlations . . . [relating] economic deprivation and father's rejecting behavior to all measures of adolescent functioning . . . [reveal] different patterns of association . . . among boys and girls. . . . In the case of adolescent boys, economic hardship is linked to negative perceptions of father and to peer dependence, as well as to modes of psychological distress. Depression losses diminished the perceived attractiveness of fathers ($r= -.40$ and -.49), while strengthening the appeal of peers. Boys from deprived homes were more likely to emphasize being with peers ($r= .27$), to seek reassurance from friends ($r= .27$), and to express dependence on the peer group ($r= .26$). According to mother's reports, boys from deprived families were also moodier ($r= .28$), more likely to have their feelings easily hurt ($r= .33$), to anger easily ($r= .19$), and to be less calm ($r= -.27$). In theory, the rejecting behavior of fathers should bear on each of these

513

outcomes, from psychological distress and the devaluation of father to hurt feelings, anger, and moodiness. However, with the exception of boys' negative perception of fathers, we find little evidence of a relationship between father rejection and the behavior of adolescent boys in the hard-pressed 1930s.

In the case of adolescent girls, economic hardship made little difference in how they felt about themselves or in how others described them. However, girls' behavior was strongly influenced by the rejecting behavior of father. The overall pattern is just the reverse of findings on adolescent boys. The daughters of rejecting fathers were less apt to aspire toward high goals ($r= -.41$), and they held a low opinion of themselves ($r= .38$, index of self-inadequacy). In addition, they were described by mothers as moodier ($r= .48$), more easily slighted ($r= .30$), and less calm ($r= -.38$).

One possible explanation for this contrast between adolescent boys and girls is that father's rejecting behavior increased under hardship conditions only toward daughters. Indeed, mean scores suggest that fathers were slightly more rejecting toward girls than toward boys during the early 1930s, $t(119) = 1.65, p = .10$. In addition, the correlation between economic hardship and father's rejecting behavior is higher for girls than boys (.25 vs. .11, with social class partialed out). Judging from these differences, one might conclude that the gender contrast stemmed from adolescent girls who became more likely targets of father's rejecting behavior and/or from adolescent boys who were less accepting of such treatment than adolescent girls. We know that hard times were conducive to the prominence of wives and mothers in household matters during the 1930s, but we have no evidence from which to conclude that such change increased the risk of daughters from the frustrations and anger of a deprived father. . . .

Daughters' Attractiveness: A Conditional Effect

The Depression experience was in large measure a family experience for the Oakland girls, but it may not have been the same, whether negative or not, for all girls who grew up in deprived families. Indeed, we have hypothesized that relatively unattractive daughters were at greater risk of the rejecting behavior of deprived fathers than were attractive girls. We know that physical attractiveness made a difference in how the Oakland girls felt about themselves and in how they interacted with others. An early study of the Oakland cohort (Elder, 1969) found that relatively attractive girls were more likely to hold a positive image of self and to marry well as defined by their husbands' social status at mid-life. They were more popular among age-mates in secondary school and were perceived as relatively feminine. Considering these and other observations in the literature (e.g., Sorell & Nowack, 1981), we assumed that less attractive daughters would be more likely to experience paternal rejection during hard times than were attractive girls (Hypothesis 2).

To investigate this conditional hypothesis, we stratified the sample of Oakland girls by a general index of physical attractiveness for the junior high school years (1933-1936). . . . For purposes of analysis, girls were classified as "unattractive" if their scores fell

514

below the median; all other girls were placed in the "attractive" category. For each group, attractive and unattractive, we estimated the effects of economic hardship on father's behavior, with adjustments for initial social class. Three measures of father behavior were included in the analysis: rejecting, exploitive, and supportive. . . .

Economic deprivation is more predictive of the nonsupportive, rejecting, and exploitive behavior of fathers when daughters were unattractive than when they were attractive. With adjustments for class origin, family hardship increased fathers' rejecting behavior only when daughters ranked low on physical attractiveness. The difference (β = .33 vs. .05 for "attractive") is not statistically significant, although it conforms with the initial hypothesis. More powerful support comes from the ratings of exploitive and supportive behavior. If girls were unattractive, family hardship accentuated fathers' overly demanding, exploitive behavior (β = .31 vs. -.46, t = 2.20, p < .05). In addition, such hardship diminished father support only when daughters were rated as unattractive (β = -.45 vs. .08, t = 2.32, p < .05). . . . Attractive girls were not only insulated from the psychological costs of economic hardship; in some cases, economic deprivation actually increased the supportive and benign parenting qualities of their fathers.

If we applied this approach to Oakland boys, would we find adverse paternal influences linked to their attractiveness? Whether rejecting, exploitive, or supportive, father-son relations in the Oakland sample have little to do with whether these men were economically deprived. The sons of deprived men were less likely to think well of their fathers, when compared to other boys, but we cannot explain this association by reference to the paternal behavior under study in this research. However, it is conceivable that the frustrations and harshness of deprived men may have been focused on their less attractive sons, as measured by physical attributes. Using the same measure of physical attractiveness in junior high, we divided the boys at the median into relatively attractive and unattractive groups. The results of this design showed no reliable group differences. We also explored the implications of differential heightand rate of physical maturation among boys for their relation with hard-pressed fathers in the Depression. These results did not alter the picture. The conditional effect is restricted to adolescent girls.

Discussion

The three hypotheses of this study receive modest support from the analysis of father's behavior in hard times and especially in the lives of daughters.

1. The first issue concerns the role of parent behavior in linking economic hardship to children's lives. Economic loss among families in the Oakland cohort increased the psychological distress and self-inadequacy of adolescents by increasing the risk of father's rejecting behavior (Hypothesis 1). Such hardship did not influence maternal behavior. As discussed below, the sequence from economic hardship to paternal rejection and adolescent functioning varied according to gender and physical attractiveness.

2. The second issue concerns the differential role of father's rejecting behavior during hard times among adolescent boys and girls. The causal sequence from economic hardship to the rejecting behavior of fathers and then to the social-affective behavior of children emerged primarily among girls. Family hardship heightened the peer orientation of boys and their devaluation of father, but the behavior of deprived fathers generally had limited influence on boys' functioning. In this adolescent sample, father mediation of economic hardship is restricted to the psychological functioning of girls (Hypothesis 3). Indeed, income loss had no significant effects on girls apart from such family mediation.

Several factors may account for gender variations in the family-mediation hypothesis. Perhaps because of their less imposing physical size and strength, adolescent girls may have been a more likely target for father's hostility in hard times. Indeed, findings from the present study suggest that fathers were slightly more rejecting toward girls than toward boys in hard-pressed families. This sentiment may partly reflect a displaced resentment concerning females over loss of male status within the family.

Another explanation centers on the gender roles of adolescents in economically deprived times. These may have had implications for girls' vulnerability within the family. For example, adolescent girls in the Oakland sample were called upon to assume major responsibilities within the household as their mothers sought work. Adolescent boys, on the other hand, were more likely to assume paid jobs outside the home. Family change of this sort enhanced the social and family independence of boys, but for girls greater household involvement may have meant greater exposure to family discord and tension. Perhaps because of their increased involvement in household affairs during hard economic times, as well as their greater interpersonal sensitivity, adolescent girls appear more strongly influenced by father's negative behavior during hard times than boys. For boys, however, the effects of economic deprivation were seldom mediated by the behavior of fathers.

These gender differences in adolescence may be contrasted with findings on the family mediation model tested with boys and girls in the Berkeley cohort (e.g., Elder, Liker, & Cross, 1984), seven-eight years younger than their Oakland counterparts. The Berkeley children were less than two years old when the economy collapsed, and they remained exclusively within the family through the worst years of that decade. In this sample, boys in early childhood were more likely than girls to be affected by family turmoil and punitive parenting in deprived families (Elder, 1979; see also Elder, Caspi, & Van Nguyen, in press).

3. A third issue examined in this research concerns child effects on parent behavior in stressful times. Even with aversive families and the most stressful experiences, some adolescents came through unscathed. What is different about these children? What protective factors or circumstances shielded them from the adverse consequences of economic hardship (Garmezy, 1981)? One factor involves the observed difference between boys and girls. Overall, adolescent girls appeared to be more subject to rejection by deprived fathers during the Great Depression.

A second relevant source of vulnerability or resourcefulness is the child's physical appearance. Following the literature on child maltreatment and the social meaning of physical attributes, we expected the least attractive adolescents to be at greater risk of paternal maltreatment than attractive boys and girls (Hypothesis 2). The data support this hypothesis for girls. The physical attractiveness of adolescent girls conditioned father's behavior toward them in hard times. Deprived fathers were more likely to reject unattractive than attractive daughters, and, in fact, they were actually more likely to be nurturant toward attractive girls than nondeprived fathers.

Consistent with a social interactional perspective on family process (e.g., Patterson, 1983), these findings suggest that some characteristics of children actually strengthened the aversive behaviors of fathers in stressful times. These findings underscore the importance of viewing the family's changing socioeconomic situation in relation to *both* the child's characteristics and parent behavior (Belsky, 1984; Ricciuti & Dorman, 1983).

Conclusion

The developmental implications of social change can only be studied within a theoretical framework that relates individual and family change. Individuals are changed by changing families, and families are changed by changing the developmental course of members (Elder, 1984, 1985). Both of these processes are likely to emerge when the life-course dynamics of families and individuals are studied over time. A model of family mediation typified the approach of *Children of the Great Depression*, and the present study builds on this work in at least two respects. First, it does so by examining the behavior of fathers in linking economic stress to children's experience.

Second, the present study explores sources of variation in this causal process. The initial study of Oakland children in the Depression era could only achieve a skeletal image of Depression fathers, owing to data limitations. Conceptual blinders at the time also resulted in an understatement of children as producers of their own socialization. In addition to their role in the family economy which the first study covered in detail, these children also fared better or worse in the Depression regime of fathers for reasons linked to gender and physical attractiveness.

The rejecting behavior of fathers represents the connection between economic hardship and children's lives more than the corresponding behavior of mothers. Fathers are prominent in our analysis of Depression families, in part because economic misfortune was typically the first-hand experience of men. Their response to this loss intensified the social consequences of economic loss. But the full significance of father's behavior emerges only when we consider the adolescent roles of girls and boys in the Oakland cohort, as well as physical attractiveness. The rejecting behavior of father is most strongly linked to *both* economic deprivation and the emotional disturbance of girls and especially to those girls who were relatively unattractive. We believe this causal sequence has much to do with the psychological vulnerability of early adolescent girls to paternal maltreatment and to the self-esteem costs of social pressures in the larger social world of peers and school (Simmons et al., 1979).

This study is responsive to a longstanding criticism of purely descriptive research on socioeconomic factors in the lives of adults and children (Kohn, 1977). All too often, research proceeds no further than the demonstration of a simple association between two variables that are assumed to be ordered in a causal sequence. Literally hundreds of studies have correlated measures of socioeconomic status and change with indicators of child behavior, leaving the analysis at that point without the barest feature of an interpretation or empirical test of linkages (Bronfenbrenner & Crouter, 1983). In the present research, the concept of linkage serves as a reminder of the connection between family income loss, on the one hand, and children's social and emotional behavior on the other.

As a whole, the results of this research support a perspective on families and children that locates them within the life course and its age-graded tasks and experiences. The ever-changing environment of developing individuals implies that risk factors should vary in type and relative influence along the life line. Indeed, family stresses appear to be more pathogenic for boys than for girls in the preschool years (Rutter & Madge, 1976), whereas a contrasting sex difference is emerging in studies of early adolescence (Werner & Smith, 1982). Sensitivity to this complexity of interactions among social, psychological, and biological factors is consistent with Kagan's (1979, p. 886) criticism of the search for "absolute principles which declare that a particular set of external conditions is inevitably associated with a fixed set of consequences for all children." External events, such as the Great Depression, can affect older and younger children, as well as parents, in different ways. An understanding of these ways requires knowledge of the life course.

References

Bar-Tal, D., & Saxe, L. (1976). Physical attractiveness and its relation to sex-role stereotyping. *Sex Roles*, **2**, 123-133.

Bell, R. Q., & Harper, V. L. (1977). *Child effects on adults*. Hillsdale, NJ: Erlbaum.

Belsky, J. (1984). The determinants of parenting: A process model. *Child Development*, **55** 83-96.

Block, J. (1971). *Lives through time*. Berkeley, CA: Bancroft.

Bronfenbrenner, U., & Crouter, A. C. (1983). The evolution of environmental models in developmental research. In W. Kessen (Ed.), P. H. Mussen (Series Ed.), *Handbook of child psychology: Vol. 1. History, theory, and methods* (pp. 357-414). New York: Wiley.

Coan, R. W. (1974). *The optimal personality: An empirical and theoretical analysis*. New York: Columbia University Press.

Dion, K. (1972). Physical attractiveness and evaluations of children's transgressions. *Journal of Personality and Social Psychology*, **24**, 207-213.

Eichorn, D. H., Clausen, J. A., Haan, N., Honzik, Marjorie M. P., & Mussen, P. H. (Eds.). (1981). *Present and past in middle life*. New York: Academic Press.

Elder, G. H., Jr. (1969). Appearance and education in marriage mobility. *American Sociological Review* **34**, 519-533.

Elder, G. H., Jr. (1974). *Children of the Great Depression*. Chicago: University of Chicago Press.

Elder, G. H., Jr. (1979). Historical change in life patterns and personality. In P. B. Baltes & O. G. Brim, Jr. (Eds.), *Life span development and behavior* (Vol. 2, pp. 117-159). New York: Academic Press.

Elder, G. H., Jr. (1984). Families, kin, and the life course: A sociological perspective. In R. Parke (Ed.), *Advances in child development research* (Vol. 7). Chicago: University of Chicago Press.

Elder, G. H., Jr. (Ed.). (1985). *Life course dynamics: Trajectories and transitions, 1968-1980*. Ithaca, NY: Cornell University Press.

Elder, G. H., Jr., Caspi, A., & Downey, G. (in press). Problem behavior and family relationships: Life course and intergenerational themes. In A. Sorensen, F. Weinert, & L. Sherrod (Eds.), *Human development: Interdisciplinary perspectives*. Hillsdale, NJ: Erlbaum.

Elder, G. H., Jr., Caspi, A., & Van Nguyen, T. (in press). Resourceful and vulnerable children: Family influences in stressful times. In R. K. Silbereisen & K. Eyferth (Eds.), *Development in context: Integrative perspectives on youth development*. New York: Springer.

Elder, G. H., Jr., Liker, J. K., & Cross, C. E. (1984). Parent-child behavior in the Great Depression: Life course and intergenerational influences. In P. B. Baltes & O. G. Brim, Jr. (Eds.), *Life span development and behavior* (Vol. 6, pp. 109-158). New York: Academic Press.

Elder, G. H., Jr., Liker, J. K., & Jaworski, B. J. (1984). Hard times in lives: Historical influences from the 1930s to old age in postwar America. In K. H. McCluskey & H. W. Reese (Eds.), *Life span developmental psychology: Historical and cohort effects* (pp. 161-201). New York: Academic Press.

Eme, R. F. (1979). Sex differences in childhood psychopathology: A review. *Psychological Bulletin*, **86**, 574-595.

Garmezy, N. (1981). Children under stress: Perspectives on antecedents and correlates of vulnerability and resistance to psychopathology. In A. I. Rabin, J. Aronoff, A. M. Barclay, & R. A. Zucker (Eds.), *Further explorations in personality* (pp. 196-269). New York: Wiley Interscience.

Goode, W. J. (1971). Force and violence in the family. *Journal of Marriage and the Family*, **33**, 624-636.

Hansell, S., Sparacino, J., & Ronchi, D. (1982). Physical attractiveness and blood pressure: Sex and age differences. *Personality and Social Psychology Bulletin*, **8**, 113-121.

Honzik, M. D., & Main, M. (1982). *A fifty-year study of stressful and supportive parenting*. Grant proposal BNS-8342014, National Science Foundation.

Kadushin, A., & Martin, J. A. (1981). *Child abuse: An interactional event*. New York: Columbia University Press.

Kagan, J. (1979). Family experience and the child's development. *American Psychologist*, **34**, 886-891.

Kohn, M. L. (1977). *Class and conformity*. Chicago: University of Chicago Press.

Liker, J. K., & Elder, G. H., Jr. (1983). Economic hardship and marital relations in the 1930s. *American Sociological Review*, **48**, 343-359.

Lynd, R. S., & Lynd, H. M. (1937). *Middletown in transition: A study in cultural conflicts*. New York: Harcourt, Brace.

Patterson, G. R. (1983). Stress: A change agent for family process. In N. Garmezy & M. Rutter (Eds.), *Stress, coping, and development in children* (pp. 235-264). New York: McGraw-Hill.

Pearlin, L. I., Lieberman, M. A., Menagham, E. G., & Mullan, J. T. (1981). The stress process. *Journal of Health and Social Behavior*, **22**, 337-356.

Ricciuti, H. N., & Dorman, R. (1983). Interaction of multiple factors contributing to high-risk parenting. In R. A. Hoekelman (Ed.), *Minimizing high-risk parenting* (pp. 187-210). Media, PA: Harwal.

Rutter, M., & Madge, N. (1976). *Cycles of disadvantage: A review of research.* London: Heinemann.

Scherer, J., & Shepherd, G. (1982). *Victimization of the weak: Contemporary social reactions.* Springfield, IL: Thomas.

Simmons, R. G., Blyth, D. A., Van Cleave, G. F., & Bush, D. M. (1979). Entry into adolescence: The impact of school structure, puberty, and early dating on self-esteem. *American Sociological Review*, **44**, 948-967.

Smith, M. B. (1968). Competence and socialization. In J. A. Clausen (Ed.), *Socialization and society* (pp. 270-320). Boston: Little, Brown.

Sorell, G. T., & Nowack, C. A. (1981). The role of physical attractiveness as a contributor to individual development. In R. M. Lerner & N. A. Busch-Rossnagel (Eds.), *Individuals as producers of their development: A life span perspective* (pp. 389-446). New York: Academic Press.

Werner, E. E. & Smith, R. S. (1982). *Vulnerable but invincible: A study of resilient children.* New York: McGraw-Hill.

Children of the Garden Island
Emmy E. Werner

Economic deprivation is only one among many possible variables of risk. In the study described below—a study that is generally regarded as a modern classic—Emmy Werner and her colleagues identified a wide variety of risk factors as they tracked the development over a thirty year period of an entire cohort of 698 infants born in 1955 on the island of Kauai. Focusing on reproductive stress and on material, intellectual, and emotional aspects of the family environment, they designated 30 percent of their sample as high risk because they had suffered complications during maternal pregnancy, labor, or delivery; were raised in chronic poverty; were reared by parents who had no more than eight grades of formal schooling; or lived in a family environment characterized by discord, divorce, alcoholism, or mental illness.

Of these high risk children, approximately one in three proved to be resilient. Such children developed into competent, successful, and reasonably happy young adults despite early and, in many cases, continuing exposure to factors that placed them seriously at risk. Because Werner and her colleagues had gathered extensive data on all children in the large sample at ages one, two, ten, eighteen, and thirty or thirty-one, they were able to look backward to identify personal and environmental factors that were associated with resilience. Resilient children seemed to be temperamentally well equipped, personally, to elicit positive response from other human beings. As infants, they were described as even-tempered, cuddly, affectionate, and active. As children, they continued to be active, sociable, and relatively resistant to distress.

Although their environments were often inadequate in many ways, resilient children seemed to have been able to establish an affectionate bond with at least one caregiver during the first years of life. That caregiver might have been a parent, grandparent or other relative, or even a babysitter. This ability to connect socially and to derive needed emotional support from peers, neighbors, teachers, or other adults in the community continued to characterize resilient children over the course of development. At age eighteen, with the support provided by the social network, these children were hopeful and looking forward to the future.

At age thirty, they still tended to feel personally competent, determined, supported by their spouses or others, and strong in their religious faiths.

Like the research of Glen Elder and his colleagues, the study of children on the island of Kauai demonstrates quite clearly that when children grow up under conditions of chronic risk, they do not automatically become casualties. While risk factors increase the child's vulnerability, protective factors greatly increase the probability that the child will survive. Outcome, in Werner's as in Elder's view, is a function of the balance between risk and resilience.

Kauai, the Garden Island, lies at the northwest end of the Hawaiian chain, 100 miles and a half hour flight from Honolulu. Its 555 square miles encompass mountains, cliffs, canyons, rain forests and sandy beaches washed by pounding surf. The first Polynesians who crossed the Pacific to settle there in the eighth century were charmed by its beauty, as were the generations of sojourners who visited there after Captain James Cook "discovered" the island in 1778. The 45,000 inhabitants of Kauai are for the most part descendants of immigrants from Southeast Asia and Europe who came to the island to work on the sugar plantations with the hope of finding a better life for their children. Thanks to the islanders' unique spirit of cooperation, my colleagues Jessie M. Bierman and Fern E. French of the University of California at Berkeley, Ruth S. Smith, a clinical psychologist on Kauai, and I have been able to carry out a longitudinal study on Kauai that has lasted for more than three decades. The study has had two principal goals: to assess the long-term consequences of prenatal and perinatal stress and to document the effects of adverse early rearing conditions on children's physical, cognitive and psychosocial development.

The Kauai Longitudinal Study began at a time when the systematic examination of the development of children exposed to biological and psychosocial risk factors was still a bit of a rarity. Investigators attempted to reconstruct the events that led to physical or psychological problems by studying the history of individuals in whom such problems had already surfaced. This retrospective approach can create the impression that the outcome is inevitable, since it takes into account only the "casualties," not the "survivors." We hoped to avoid that impression by monitoring the development of all the children born in a given period in an entire community.

We began our study in 1954 with an assessment of the reproductive histories of all the women in the community. Altogether 2,203 pregnancies were reported by the women of Kauai in 1954, 1955 and 1956; there were 240 fetal deaths and 1,963 live births. We chose to study the cohort of 698 infants born on Kauai in 1955, and we followed the development of these individuals at one, two, ten, eighteen and thirty-one or thirty-two

Werner, Emmy E. (1989). Children of the garden island. *Scientific American, 260.* pp. 106-111.

years of age. The majority of the individuals in the birth cohort—422 in all—were born without complications, following uneventful pregnancies, and grew up in supportive environments.

But as our study progressed we began to take a special interest in certain "high risk" children who, in spite of exposure to reproductive stress, discordant and impoverished home lives and uneducated, alcoholic or mentally disturbed parents, went on to develop healthy personalities, stable careers and strong interpersonal relations. We decided to try to identify the protective factors that contributed to the resilience of these children.

Finding a community that is willing or able to cooperate in such an effort is not an easy task. We chose Kauai for a number of reasons, not the least of which was the receptivity of the island population to our endeavors. Coverage by medical, public-health, educational and social services on the island was comparable to what one would find in communities of similar size on the U.S. mainland at that time. Furthermore, our study would take into account a variety of cultural influences on childbearing and child rearing, since the population of Kauai includes individuals of Japanese, Philippine, Portuguese, Chinese, Korean and northern European as well as of Hawaiian descent.

We also thought the population's low mobility would make it easier to keep track of the study's participants and their families. The promise of a stable sample proved to be justified. At the time of the two-year follow-up, 96 percent of the living children were still on Kauai and available for study. We were able to find 90 percent of the children who were still alive for the ten-year follow-up, and for the eighteen-year follow-up we found 88 percent of the cohort.

In order to elicit the cooperation of the island's residents, we needed to get to know them and to introduce our study as well. In doing so we relied on the skills of a number of dedicated professionals from the University of California's Berkeley and Davis campuses, from the University of Hawaii and from the island of Kauai itself. At the beginning of the study five nurses and one social worker, all residents of Kauai, took a census of all households on the island, listing the occupants of each dwelling and recording demographic information, including a reproductive history of all women twelve years old or older. The interviewers asked the women if they were pregnant; if a woman was not, a card with a postage-free envelope was left with the request that she mail it to the Kauai Department of Health as soon as she thought she was pregnant.

Local physicians were asked to submit a monthly list of the women who were coming to them for prenatal care. Community organizers spoke to women's groups, church gatherings, the county medical society and community leaders. The visits by the census takers were backed up with letters, and milk cartons were delivered with a printed message urging mothers to cooperate. We advertised in newspapers, organized radio talks, gave slide shows and distributed posters.

Public-health nurses interviewed the pregnant women who joined our study in each trimester of pregnancy, noting any exposure to physical or emotional trauma. Physicians monitored any complications during the prenatal period, labor, delivery and the neonatal period. Nurses and social workers interviewed the mothers in the postpartum period and when the children were one and ten years old; the interactions between parents and offspring in the home were also observed. Pediatricians and psychologists independently examined the children at two and ten years of age, assessing their physical, intellectual and social development and noting any handicaps or behavior problems. Teachers evaluated the children's academic progress and their behavior in the classroom.

From the outset of the study we recorded information about the material, intellectual and emotional aspects of the family environment, including stressful life events that resulted in discord or disruption of the family unit. With the parents' permission we also were given access to the records of public-health, educational and social-service agencies and to the files of the local police and the family court. My collaborators and I also administered a wide range of aptitude, achievement and personality tests in the elementary grades and in high school. Last but not least, we gained the perspectives of the young people themselves by interviewing them at the age of eighteen and then again when they were in their early thirties.

Of the 698 children in the 1955 cohort, sixty-nine were exposed to moderate prenatal or perinatal stress, that is, complications during pregnancy, labor or delivery. About 3 percent of the cohort—twenty-three individuals in all—suffered severe prenatal or perinatal stress; only fourteen infants in this group lived to the age of two. Indeed, nine of the twelve children in our study who died before reaching two years of age had suffered severe perinatal complications.

Some of the surviving children became "casualties" of a kind in the next two decades of life. One out of every six children (116 children in all) had physical or intellectual handicaps of perinatal or neonatal origin that were diagnosed between birth and the age of two and that required long-term specialized medical, educational or custodial care. About one out of every five children (142 in all) developed serious learning or behavior problems in the first decade of life that required more than six months of remedial work. By the time the children were ten years old, twice as many children needed some form of mental-health service or remedial education (usually for problems associated with reading) as were in need of medical care.

By the age of eighteen, 15 percent of the young people had delinquency records and 10 percent had mental-health problems requiring either in- or outpatient care. There was some overlap among these groups. By the time they were ten, all twenty-five of the children with long-term mental-health problems had learning problems as well. Of the seventy children who had mental-health problems at eighteen, fifteen also had a record of repeated delinquencies.

As we followed these children from birth to the age of eighteen we noted two trends: the impact of reproductive stress diminished with time, and the developmental outcome of virtually every biological risk condition was dependent on the quality of the rearing environment. We did find some correlation between moderate to severe degrees of perinatal trauma and major physical handicaps of the central nervous system and of the musculoskeletal and sensory-systems; perinatal trauma was also correlated with mental retardation, serious learning disabilities and chronic mental health problems such as schizophrenia that arose in late adolescence and young adulthood.

But overall rearing conditions were more powerful determinants of outcome than perinatal trauma. The better the quality of the home environment was, the more competence the children displayed. This could already be seen when the children were just two years old: toddlers who had experienced severe perinatal stress but lived in middle-class homes or in stable family settings did nearly as well on developmental tests of sensory-motor and verbal skills as toddlers who had experienced no such stress.

Prenatal and perinatal complications were consistently related to impairment of physical and psychological development at the ages of ten and eighteen only when they were combined with chronic poverty, family discord, parental mental illness or other persistently poor rearing conditions. Children who were raised in middle-class homes, in a stable family environment and by a mother who had finished high school showed few if any lasting effects of reproductive stress later in their lives.

How many children could count on such a favorable environment? A sizable minority could not. We designated 201 individuals—30 percent of the surviving children in this study population—as being high risk children because they had experienced moderate to severe perinatal stress, grew up in chronic poverty, were reared by parents with no more than eight grades of formal education or lived in a family environment troubled by discord, divorce, parental alcoholism or mental illness. We termed the children "vulnerable" if they encountered four or more such risk factors before their second birthday. And indeed, two-thirds of these children (129 in all) did develop serious learning or behavior problems by the age of ten or had delinquency records, mental- health problems or pregnancies by the time they were eighteen.

Yet one out of three of these high risk children—72 individuals altogether—grew into competent young adults who loved well, worked well and played well. None developed serious learning or behavior problems in childhood or adolescence. As far as we could tell from interviews and from their record in the community, they succeeded in school, managed home and social life well and set realistic educational and vocational goals and expectations for themselves when they finished high school. By the end of their second decade of life they had developed into competent, confident and caring people who expressed a strong desire to take advantage of whatever opportunity came their way to improve themselves.

They were children such as Michael, a boy for whom the odds on paper did not seem very promising. The son of teen-age parents, Michael was born prematurely, weighing four pounds five ounces. He spent his first three weeks of life in a hospital, separated from his mother. Immediately after his birth his father was sent with the U.S. Army to Southeast Asia, where he remained for two years. By the time Michael was eight years old he had three siblings and his parents were divorced. His mother had deserted the family and had no further contact with her children. His father raised Michael and his siblings with the help of their aging grandparents.

Then there was Mary, born after twenty hours of labor to an overweight mother who had experienced several miscarriages before that pregnancy. Her father was an unskilled farm laborer with four years of formal education. Between Mary's fifth and tenth birthdays her mother was hospitalized several times for repeated bouts of mental illness, after having inflicted both physical and emotional abuse on her daughter.

Surprisingly, by the age of eighteen both Michael and Mary were individuals with high self-esteem and sound values who cared about others and were liked by their peers. They were successful in school and looked forward to the future. We looked back at the lives of these two youngsters and the seventy other resilient individuals who had triumphed over their circumstances and compared their behavioral characteristics and the features of their environment with those of the other high-risk youths who developed serious and persistent problems in childhood and adolescence.

We identified a number of protective factors in the families, outside the family circle and within the resilient children themselves that enabled them to resist stress. Some sources of resilience seem to be constitutional: resilient children such as Mary and Michael tend to have characteristics of temperament that elicit positive responses from family members and strangers alike. We noted these same qualities in adulthood. They include a fairly high activity level, a low degree of excitability and distress and a high degree of sociability. Even as infants the resilient individuals were described by their parents as "active," "affectionate," "cuddly," "easygoing" and "even tempered." They had no eating or sleeping habits that were distressing to those who took care of them.

The pediatricians and psychologists who examined the resilient children at twenty months noted their alertness and responsiveness, their vigorous play and their tendency to seek out novel experiences and to ask for help when they needed it. When they entered elementary school, their classroom teachers observed their ability to concentrate on their assignments and noted their problem-solving and reading skills. Although they were not particularly gifted, these children used whatever talents they had effectively. Usually they had a special hobby they could share with a friend. These interests were not narrowly sex-typed; we found that girls and boys alike excelled at such activities as fishing, swimming, horseback riding and hula dancing.

We could also identify environmental factors that contributed to these children's ability to withstand stress. The resilient youngsters tended to come from families having four or fewer children, with a space of two years or more between themselves and the next sibling. In spite of poverty, family discord or parental mental illness, they had the opportunity to establish a close bond with at least one caretaker from whom they received positive attention during the first years of life.

The nurturing might come from substitute parents within the family (such as grandparents, older siblings, aunts or uncles) or from the ranks of regular baby-sitters. As the resilient children grew older they seemed to be particularly adept at recruiting such surrogate parents when a biological parent was unavailable (as in the case of an absent father) or incapacitated (as in the case of a mentally ill mother who was frequently hospitalized).

Maternal employment and the need to take care of younger siblings apparently contributed to the pronounced autonomy and sense of responsibility noted among the resilient girls, particularly in households where the father had died or was permanently absent because of desertion or divorce. Resilient boys, on the other hand, were often firstborn sons who did not have to share their parents' attention with many additional children in the household. They also had some male in the family who could serve as a role model (if not the father, then a grandfather or an uncle). Structure and rules in the household and assigned chores were part of the daily routine for these boys during childhood and adolescence.

Resilient children also seemed to find a great deal of emotional support outside their immediate family. They tended to be well liked by their classmates and had at least one close friend, and usually several. They relied on an informal network of neighbors, peers and elders for counsel and support in times of crisis and transition. They seem to have made school a home away from home, a refuge from a disordered household. When we interviewed them at eighteen, many resilient youths mentioned a favorite teacher who had become a role model, friend and confidant and was particularly supportive at times when their own family was beset by discord or threatened with dissolution.

For others, emotional support came from a church group, a youth leader in the YMCA or YWCA or a favorite minister. Participation in extracurricular activities—such as 4-H, the school band or a cheerleading team, which allowed them to be part of a cooperative enterprise—was also an important source of emotional support for those children who succeeded against the odds.

With the help of these support networks, the resilient children developed a sense of meaning in their lives and a belief that they could control their fate. Their experience in effectively coping with and mastering stressful life events built an attitude of hopefulness that contrasted starkly with the feelings of helplessness and futility that were expressed by their troubled peers.

In 1985, twelve years after the 1955 birth cohort had finished high school, we embarked on a search for the members of our study group. We managed to find 545 individuals—80 percent of the cohort—through parents or other relatives, friends, former classmates, local telephone books, city directories and circuit-court, voter-registration and motor-vehicle registration records and marriage certificates filed with the State Department of Health in Honolulu. Most of the young men and women still lived on Kauai, but 10 percent had moved to other islands and 10 percent lived on the mainland; 2 percent had gone abroad.

We found sixty-two of the seventy-two young people we had characterized as "resilient" at the age of eighteen. They had finished high school at the height of the energy crisis and joined the work force during the worst U.S. recession since the Great Depression. Yet these thirty-year-old-men and women seemed to be handling the demands of adulthood well. Three out of four (forty-six individuals) had received some college education and were satisfied with their performance in school. All but four worked full time, and three out of four said they were satisfied with their jobs.

Indeed, compared with their low-risk peers from the same cohort, a significantly higher proportion of high-risk resilient individuals described themselves as being happy with their current life circumstances (44 percent versus 10 percent). The resilient men and women did, however, report a significantly higher number of health problems than their peers in low- risk comparison groups (46 percent versus 15 percent). The men's problems seemed to be brought on by stress: back problems, dizziness and fainting spells, weight gain and ulcers. Women's health problems were largely related to pregnancy and childbirth. And although 82 percent of the women were married, only 48 percent of the men were. Those who were married had strong commitments to intimacy and sharing with their partners and children. Personal competence and determination, support from a spouse or mate and a strong religious faith were the shared qualities that we found characterized resilient children as adults.

We were also pleasantly surprised to find that many high-risk children who had problems in their teens were able to rebound in their twenties and early thirties. We were able to contact twenty-six (90 percent) of the teen-age mothers, fifty-six (80 percent) of the individuals with mental-health problems and seventy-four (75 percent) of the former delinquents who were still alive at the age of thirty.

Almost all the teen-age mothers we interviewed were better off in their early thirties than they had been at eighteen. About 60 percent (sixteen individuals) had gone on to additional schooling and about 90 percent (twenty-four individuals) were employed. Of the delinquent youths, three-fourths (fifty-six individuals) managed to avoid arrest on reaching adulthood. Only a minority (twelve individuals) of the troubled youths were still in need of mental-health services in their early thirties. Among the critical turning points in the lives of these individuals were entry into military service, marriage, parenthood and active participation in a church group. In adulthood, as in their youth, most of these individuals relied on informal rather than formal sources of support: kith and kin rather than mental-health professionals and social-service agencies.

Our findings appear to provide a more hopeful perspective than can be had from reading the extensive literature on "problem" children that come to the attention of therapists, special educators and social-service agencies. Risk factors and stressful environments do not inevitably lead to poor adaptation. It seems clear that, at each stage in an individual's development from birth to maturity, there is a shifting balance between stressful events that heighten vulnerability and protective factors that enhance resilience.

As long as the balance between stressful life events and protective factors is favorable, successful adaptation is possible. When stressful events outweigh the protective factors, however, even the most resilient child can have problems. It may be possible to shift the balance from vulnerability to resilience through intervention, either by decreasing exposure to risk factors or stressful events or by increasing the number of protective factors and sources of support that are available.

It seems clear from our identification of risk and protective factors that some of the most critical determinants of outcome are present when a child is very young. And it is obvious that there are large individual differences among high-risk children in their responses to both negative and positive circumstances in their caregiving environment. The very fact of individual variation among children who live in adverse conditions suggests the need for greater assistance to some than to others.

If early intervention cannot be extended to every child at risk, priorities must be established for choosing who should receive help. Early-intervention programs need to focus on infants and young children who appear most vulnerable because they lack—permanently or temporarily—some of the essential social bonds that appear to buffer stress. Such children may be survivors of neonatal intensive care, hospitalized children who are separated from their families for extended periods of time, the young offspring of addicted or mentally ill parents, infants and toddlers whose mothers work full time and do not have access to stable child care, the babies of single or teen-age parents who have no other adult in the household and migrant and refugee children without permanent roots in a community.

Assessment and diagnosis, the initial steps in any early intervention, need to focus not only on the risk factors in the lives of the children but also on the protective factors. These include competencies and informal sources of support that already exist and that can be utilized to enlarge a young child's communication and problem-solving skills and to enhance his or her self-esteem. Our research on resilient children has shown that other people in a child's life—grandparents, older siblings, day-care providers or teachers—can play a supportive role if a parent is incapacitated or unavailable. In many situations it might make better sense and be less costly as well to strengthen such available informal ties to kin and community than it would to introduce additional layers of bureaucracy into delivery of services.

Finally, in order for any intervention program to be effective, a young child needs enough consistent nurturing to trust in its availability. The resilient children in our study had at least one person in their lives who accepted them unconditionally, regardless of temperamental idiosyncracies or physical or mental handicaps. All children can be helped to become more resilient if adults in their lives encourage their independence, teach them appropriate communication and self-help skills, and model as well as reward acts of helpfulness and caring.

Finally, in order for any intervention program to be effective, a young child needs enough consistent nurturing to trust in its availability. The resilient children in our study had at least one person in their lives who accepted them unconditionally, regardless of temperamental idiosyncracies or physical or mental handicaps. All children can be helped to become more resilient if adults in their lives encourage their independence, teach them appropriate communication and self-help skills and model as well as reward acts of helpfulness and caring.

Thanks to the efforts of many people, several community-action and educational programs for high risk children have been established on Kauai since our study began. Partly as a result of our findings, the legislature of the State of Hawaii has funded special mental-health teams to provide services for troubled children and youths. In addition the State Health Department established the Kauai Children's Services, a coordinated effort to provide services related to child development, disabilities, mental retardation and rehabilitation in a single facility.

The evaluation of such intervention programs can in turn illuminate the process by which a chain of protective factors is forged that affords vulnerable children an escape from adversity. The life stories of the resilient individuals on the Garden Island have taught us that competence, confidence and caring can flourish even under adverse circumstances if young children encounter people in their lives who provide them with a secure basis for the development of trust, autonomy and initiative.

21

The Child at Work

Child labor is not a thing of the past. In some countries it amounts to little better than slavery. The Anti-Slavery Society estimates that even today as many as 200 million children are working, often doing back-breaking jobs in appalling squalor. Children work in agriculture, on the sugar plantations in Brazil, and the rubber plantations in Malaysia; in sex-related professions, either as prostitutes or appearing in pornography in Thailand, the Philippines and South Korea; in industry, in carpet making in India and textile factories in Bangladesh. They often work in cramped and dangerous conditions, which can deform them for life. They are at risk from disease, hunger, exhaustion and despair.

Like some 12,000 children, Pitpong used to wake up very early in the morning to compete in scavenging scrap materials on the top of the smoking and stench-odored pile of garbage—a home to 3,500 families, the majority of whom depend on garbage for a livelihood. The garbage heap gives him five to eight pesos daily, just enough to provide for him and his family a meal of thin gruel and cheap junk foods to lessen his hunger. The difficulty in carrying his daily garbage haul from the top of the mountain down to the junkshop resulted in his stunted growth. His physique can be mistaken for that of an undernourished five year old with short limbs and pot belly.

-O. Martin, *Profile of a Working Child*

• INTRODUCTION •

Industrialization in the United States began in the decade before 1800. By 1820, factories were springing up all over New England and the eastern states. The initial technology in these industries was generally simple enough to permit much of the work to be done by relatively unskilled hands. Industries needed a concentrated labor pool. Children, brought to urban industrial areas by families lured by the promise of employment, were able to fulfill much of that need.

As industrialization proceeded, the trend toward urbanization accelerated. As urban population density grew, problems of public health and sanitation became ever more pressing. Diseases that are now rarely seen or are lightly dismissed in the United States (measles, influenza, diphtheria, typhoid, smallpox) swept through crowded slums and claimed hundreds of thousands of lives. Inadequate methods of food distribution, handling, and preservation compounded the problem.

By the end of the nineteenth century, however, progress in urban sanitation and public health began to bring many of these diseases under control. Improved of food distribution, and handling, and refrigeration gave most Americans access to an adequate food supply. Infant and adult mortality rates declined sharply. At the same time, campaigns against child labor and for compulsory schooling began to gather momentum. The modern American urban/suburban middle class ideal of childhood—a period of growth and development in which well-nourished children, relatively free from disease and from the need to contribute economically to family survival, are able to devote themselves largely to their own education or to productive leisure—had emerged.

In nations around the world that are still undergoing primary economic development, and even among Americans living in chronic poverty, this vision of childhood is an unattainable ideal. Measles and other diseases are completely preventable at minimal cost. Yet these diseases still take the lives of millions of children worldwide, sometimes even including those living in poverty in the United States. Inadequate food production and distribution brings famine and starvation to millions more; and in most of the world, children must work to survive.

In some instances, children work side by side with other family members in productive tasks that contribute directly to family subsistence. This work can serve to enhance the child's sense of self-esteem and of belonging to family and community. Far too often, however, children are exploited for their labor. At its worst, this exploitation may involve the selling of children to sweatshop masters or even into prostitution or slavery. Even when children's labor is less exploitative, it still may interfere with schooling or the opportunity for leisure.

The readings in this chapter focus on child labor. The first article consists of introductions taken from a massive compilation of documents relating to the history of children in America edited by Robert Bremner and his colleagues. Here we read about the growth of industrial child labor in the United States, beginning at the end of the eighteenth and continuing into the present century, and the emergence at the end of the nineteenth century of the reform movement that eventually led to legislation that restricted the circumstances under which children may be legally employed.

In the second reading, William Myers introduces us to the specifics of the living and working conditions of urban working children in South America. In reading this article, notice that today, just as in times past, much of the fruit of children's labor goes directly to families that need that labor in order to survive. If child labor reform is to be effective, and children are to leave the street for the classroom, that reform must be coupled with overall economic development and with social and economic policies designed to provide substitute sources of economic support for the families that now rely on income from the work of their children to work.

● ● ●

Child Labor in America: A Documentary History, 1735-1932
Robert H. Bremner (Editor)

Working children were a fact of American colonial life. Toiling side by side with parents and other family members on farms, in cottage industries, in parental workshops, or apprenticed to master artisans, children made significant contributions to the family's or the artisan's economic survival. Within the culture of the time, idleness was viewed as "the devil's workshop" and work as the proper duty of a god-fearing human being.

Although children's work did undoubtedly interfere with attendance at whatever limited formal schooling might have been available, and was sometimes exploitative, it also frequently served as a kind of informal training, helping to prepare children for the occupations that they would assume as adults. In line with communal values and contributing to the child's own learning and to the family's survival, children's labor was part of a broader experience that tended to enhance children's sense of self and participation in family and community.

When industrialization came to the United States in the 1790s, it was a natural step for children to be recruited to the work force; but as Robert Bremner points out, the face of child labor had begun to change. In many households, the entire family was employed in the factory. Such households lost their status as independent, self-governing, economic units. Even when all members were wage earners, total wages were often inadequate to meet the costs of living, and families found themselves perpetually in debt to the company store. Traditional patterns of family authority became diluted as children worked separately, away from their parents, answering to the foreman on the factory floor and to the father at home.

The work day and the work week were long and hard. Little protection was available from industrial hazards or from an abusive supervisor. Children had few if any hours in the day left for formal schooling or recreation; and only rarely did the factory jobs in which they were engaged help prepare them for a higher-level occupation as an adult. In short, industrial child labor was much more exploitative than the domestic and farm labor that had preceded it.

By the end of the nineteenth century, industrial child labor had spread to all parts of the nation, to mines, to sweatshops, and to factories of all kinds. Reformers, motivated in part by general protest against the exploitation of the working class and in part by Century of the Child ideology, had launched a concerted attack on child labor. Arguing for the importance of play in the realization of childhood potential and for the realization of individual potential as fundamental to the success of a democratic society, reformers organized an intensive anti-child labor lobbying effort.

By 1916, this effort had finally resulted in federal legislation regulating child labor in mines and factories. Children at work on farms, in sweatshops, and as domestics, street vendors or bootblacks, however, were overlooked. Initial attempts to pass broader legislation met strong resistance. As Bremner suggests, middle-class reformers were not always in touch with the reality of poverty. As is still true in many parts of the world, children's labor was essential to family survival. Only as government policies began to address the economic needs of families was it possible to get young children out of the work force and into school.

Industrial child labor began in America at the end of the eighteenth century. The novelty of this development should not obscure the fact that during the eighteenth and nineteenth centuries most children continued to work in their homes, on the farm, and in their parents' workshops.

With the increase of patriotic enthusiasm for national industries in the last third of the eighteenth century, there was an increasing premium on the work of women and children in the household, especially in the production of wool and cotton. In 1767, Sir Henry Moore, governor of New York, reported with great satisfaction that "every house swarms with children, who are set to work as soon as they are able to spin and card."[1] Alexander Hamilton declared in 1790:

It is computed in a number of districts that two thirds, three fourths, and even four fifths, of all the clothing of the inhabitants, are made by themselves. The importance of so great a progress as appears to have been made in family manufactures, within a few years, in both a moral and political view, renders the fact highly interesting.[2]

In the 1760s small shops took over several stages in the production of wool and cotton. Although housewives continued to spin at home, they found it more efficient to have the wool and cotton carded and fulled in the workshop. Sometimes, too, they brought the spun wool to be dyed. Thus, these shops became the nuclei of later factories, serving as a transitional stage between household industry and the large factory. Since carding, fulling, and spinning had been children's occupations in the home, it was only natural to transfer children to such workshops. This form of employment, however, could not yet be considered industrial child labor; it was merely a variation on traditional household work. The labor force in such shops consisted of the master's household—his children, his servants, and his apprentices.

The cotton industry in New England brought the industrial revolution to America, and with it the introduction of children as an industrial labor force. In 1789 William

Bremner, R.H. (Ed.) (1970). *Children and Youth in America. A Documentary History. Volume I-II, 1600-1832.* Cambridge: Harvard University Press. Volume I: pp. 145-149; Volume II: pp. 601-604.

Almy and Moses Brown invited Samuel Slater, "the father of American manufactures," to join them as a partner in their Providence, Rhode Island, factory. An apprentice and later employee of Jedidiah Strutt, the leading English manufacturer of cotton and a partner of Richard Arkwright, Slater had smuggled himself and the plans for Arkwright's machinery to New York. He joined Almy and Brown and produced satisfactory yarn in 1791. For the first time in America all stages of manufacture from raw cotton to yarn were worked in the factory by machinery (except the cleaning, which children too young to work in the factory still performed at home).

The Slater factory demonstrated in practice the arguments of the advocates of the new industrial system: diversification of labor and the introduction of power machinery were ideally suited for the employment of children. The first employees at Almy, Brown, and Slater were nine boys from poor families in the vicinity. In contrast to earlier practice these children were factory laborers, rather than apprentices. Slater had intended to keep apprentices as well but in the words of his son, "it did not suit the American temperament, and was abandoned."[3] By 1801, the number of children increased to one hundred, ranging in age from four to ten. They worked in one room where all the machinery was concentrated under the supervision of a foreman, spreading the cleaned cotton on the carding machine to be combed and passing it through the roving machine, which turned the cotton into loose rolls ready to be spun. Most of the children tended the spindles, removing and attaching bobbins. Small, quick fingers were admirably suited for picking up and knotting broken threads. To the delight of Tench Coxe, a champion of American industry, the children became "the little fingers . . . of the gigantic automatons of labor saving machinery."[4]

In the twenty years after its establishment the Slater system spread rapidly through New England. In 1810 Albert Gallatin reported twenty-seven mills in operation in Rhode Island, southern Massachusetts, and eastern Connecticut. All these mills were fashioned after the Slater model. For 1809 Gallatin estimated the number of employees in the cotton mills as 4,000. Those consisted of 500 men and 3,500 women and children. The later growth of the industry was so rapid that the Committee on Manufactures reported in 1816 that the mills then employed 100,000 hands, of whom 24,000 were "boys under seventeen" and 66,000 "women and girls." Thus, children and women comprised 90 percent of the labor force.[5] The computation in the *Digest of Manufactures* separates women from children. Children formed 47 percent of the labor force in Massachusetts cotton mills, 55 percent in Rhode Island, and 55 percent in Connecticut. In the wool industry, which used traditional methods of production, children comprised only 22 to 27 percent.

Two systems developed for the recruitment of children to the factory. Samuel Slater followed the English plan of employing entire families. This family system dominated the smaller factories in Rhode Island, Connecticut, and southern Massachusetts. The alternative, established first in the textile mill in Waltham, was the boardinghouse system, where some children and mostly young girls worked in the factory, while their parents continued to live on the farm. This practice would be more common after the 1820's in large factories employing older girls: in Lowell and Lawrence, Massachusetts, in Dover,

536

Manchester, Exeter, and Portsmouth, New Hampshire, and in Maine.

Under the family system, rural families moved to the mill and lived in a compact community built and owned by the company. They paid an average rent of twenty-five cents per week for the tenement and obtained provisions through a company store, often as a partial or whole substitute for money wages. Every member of the family above age seven worked in the factory from sunrise to sunset, six days a week. Their only holidays were Christmas, Easter, and half a day on the Fourth of July. The father was often a mechanic or skilled spinner; his wife and children provided the unskilled labor force. In other instances, however, the father continued to farm.

Children's wages were calculated and graded according to age. A child under ten normally received fifty cents a week. Some companies paid as little as thirty-seven cents. While fifty cents a week was the standard pay in the Slater factory, children of the Rier family in Lancaster received higher weekly wages (the youngest eight years old, seventy-five cents, and the oldest, sixteen years old, $2.00). In contrast, the Troy mill at Fall River paid the youngest children only twenty-five or ten cents a week. Henry Bradshaw Fearon, a British traveler, must have exaggerated when he reported that at the Slater mill in Pawtucket children from six to ten years were earning $1.12 ½ a week, children from eleven to sixteen years $1.67 a week, women $2.00 a week, and men from $4.50 to $5.25 a week.[6]

The significance of these wages is clearer in view of the fact that in 1814 the company store of the Slater mill charged $1.34 for a bushel of corn, nine cents for a pound of flour, sixteen cents for a bushel of potatoes, twenty-three cents for a pound of sugar, twenty cents for a pound of candles, and sixteen cents for a pound of soap. A pair of shoes cost $2.00. Families rarely purchased other items, except occasionally beef, coffee, and tobacco. The account books of the Slater and Tiffany cotton mill suggest that families, even with the continued earnings of all children, carried a debt from one period to the next and rarely broke even. Accounts went unsettled for long periods, usually a full year. William Howland, for example, ordinarily discovered at Christmas time that his labor and the work of his seven children had failed to cancel his debt to the company. Howland earned $6.00 a week, and his children earned respectively $4.00, $2.50, eighty-five cents, sixty-six cents, and fifty cents a week each. For the period from May 27, 1814, to December 20, 1814, he owed the company $587.98 for "sundries" and rent. The family's combined earnings came to $582.46. He was still $2.08 short, after the company credited him with $3.44. From the next settlement period, in December 1815, he carried a debt of $37.07. April 3, 1816, marked the beginning of a period of solvency, since he was credited with $10.49. On December 20, 1816, he was credited again with $50.51. But, by January 20, 1818, he found himself short again, this time by the amount of $45.86. On May 2, 1818, Mr. Howland finally managed to settle the account with $4.22 to his credit.

Sally Maine, on the other hand, who had three children working in the factory fared worse. On November 9, 1815, she discovered that she was $98.24 short. (She had spent $445.50 and earned only $347.26.) To cope with the emergency Mrs. Maine took in four woman boarders and sent her two boys to work full time. But by November 4, 1817, she owed again $70.92. The purchase record of Mrs. Maine suggests that she rarely bought anything in the store but essential staples, although she did have a high sugar and coffee consumption. During the entire period she purchased two pairs of shoes and six yards of gingham. All eighteen families listed in the mill's account books from 1817 to 1819 continuously struggled with debt. The record books do not show even one case of savings.

In principle, the employment of children in factories was not drastically different from the colonial precedent of child labor. Moreover, Virginia had established the pattern for commercial employment of children early in the colonial period. Advocates of infant industries used the existing views of the sanctity of work and fear of idleness as persuasive arguments in favor of the new manufactures. They declared that new industries would not displace farmers from their labor and would not strain the labor market, since they would draw on women and children. By harnessing children to machinery, factories would not only increase industrial production at minimum expense but would also put the poor, idle, and potentially vicious elements of society to useful employment.

In reality, the labor of children in factories introduced novel conditions and required special adjustment. In the earlier practice of household production children were not distinguished from adults. They shared in the burden of domestic chores and industries. They worked whenever and wherever it was necessary. In the factory system, on the other hand, the household ceased to be a self-governing economic unit. Paternal authority became separate from labor instruction and supervision. A child now answered to two masters: a foreman in the factory and a father at home. The father still had to decide whether his child should be employed, to sign contracts for him, and to collect his wages. But even in the family employment system, where whole families were hired as a unit, the contract spelled out the wages of each child independently. In the factory room, the members of the family became part of a crowd, each repeating a specific function and being disciplined by a foreman.

The disruption of the family as an independent economic unit in this period was evident not only in the factory system. Even in household industry the master-apprentice relationship lost its paternal-filial character as the personal, non-vocational obligations binding master and servant declined. In the eighteenth century many apprentices were acquiring not only their general education, but also their trade education in schools.

The factory system redefined child labor. It classified children as a distinct labor force. Advertisers of new machinery estimated and measured the efficiency of their product in terms of the necessary boy or girl power to produce a certain amount of yarn. John Baxter assured prospective customers that his new machines with six and twelve spindles respectively could be easily turned by "children of from five to ten years of age," while the twelve spindle machines would require "girls from ten to twenty."[7] Not unlike slave families, the number of employable children determined the economic assets and desirability of raising a family. Children received payment as laborers, rather than maintenance and instruction as apprentices.

One can only speculate on the impact of factory labor on the independence of child workers. The meager wages earned went into the family pocket. Long hours of work from sunrise to sunset left little time for schooling or recreation. On the other hand, the factory experience occasionally produced experts at an early age. In one instance a thirteen-year-old boy was employed by the Globe Company in Tiverton, Rhode Island, to repair and set into operation idle machinery, and in another a fifteen-year-old was sent by his father to Burrillville, Rhode Island, to superintend and equip a mill and put it into operation. The boys had had six to seven years experience. If the factory confined the horizons of the children of mill families, it still loomed high in the dreams of young boys and girls in impoverished rural areas. Lured by visions of an independent income, life with their peers in boardinghouses, and a change of environment, they viewed the mill as an escape from drudgery on the farm. Thus, the factory began to compete with the sea as an outlet for restless youngsters.

The new child labor force in the factory was not governed by the traditional laws of apprenticeship or servitude, although some customs lingered. Thus, the paternalism of Samuel Slater and General Humphreys derived as much from the traditional conceptions of master-apprentice relationships as from personal benevolence. Ideally all members of the company village were envisioned as one large family. In reality, unlike the apprentice's master, the factory owner was under no obligation to teach the child a trade, unless he was explicitly taken on as an apprentice. Nor was he required to provide him with a general education. Unlike apprentices, factory children had no legal recourse in the case of abuse in this early period. The nation's leaders, delighting in the contribution of little children to economic independence, struggled to secure national protection for infant industries but did not find it necessary to protect the "little fingers" that worked them. . . .

1866 - 1932

"There is scarcely one subject in the whole range of social reform more important than that of child labor," wrote W. D. P. Bliss in the *Encyclopedia of Social Reform* (New York, 1898). In retrospect much of the history of modern American reform can be written in terms of the struggle to curb child labor. The movement held the attention of Americans from the 1880s to the depression of the 1930s, when emphasis shifted from ending child labor to securing youth employment.

Until the 1880s child labor was considered both economically and ethically valuable. Such child labor laws as existed stemmed from the efforts of educational reformers who sought to strike a balance between work and education in order to prevent pauperism and crime. The focus of the legislation was on the schooling of working children rather than on protecting them from industrial hazards and exploitation. Nevertheless, as early as the 1860s it was recognized that school attendance laws then on the books were unenforceable.

Rapid industrialization after the Civil War increased the child labor force, introduced new occupations for children, and spread child labor into new parts of the nation, especially the South. By 1900 one-third of the workers in southern mills were children. More than half of them were between ten and thirteen years of age; and many were under ten. In the absence of legislative restrictions the South repeated the experience of New England in its early period of industrialization.

The nation-wide extent of child labor became visible in 1870 when the Census Bureau established a separate category of the gainfully employed who were from ten to fifteen years of age. According to the 1870 census about one out of every eight children was employed. By 1900 approximately 1,750,000 children, or one out of six, were gainfully employed. Sixty percent were agricultural workers; of the 40 percent in industry over half were children of immigrant families.

Bureaus of labor statistics, founded in many states after establishment of the Massachusetts bureau in 1869, increased information available on child labor. Despite reluctance of employers to provide information, the bureaus kept the public aware of the extent and hazards of child labor. Their influence re-enforced the popular tendency to consider child labor as an industrial problem even though most employed children worked in agriculture.

By 1899 twenty-eight states had passed some legislation regulating child labor. The laws ordinarily applied only to manufacturing and generally set the minimum age limit at twelve. A few states, however, had raised the working age to thirteen or fourteen.

The attack on child labor at the turn of the century was part of a general protest against exploitation of the working class, industrial hazards, and involuntary poverty. Robert Hunter, a New York settlement worker, described a vicious circle of deprivation: poverty of parents, premature employment of children, and the children's poverty in maturity. The Roman Catholic economist, John A. Ryan, declared in 1902 that if fathers received a living wage no child under sixteen would have to work except possibly during school vacations.[8] Meanwhile a growing volume of periodical literature asserted that the working child was a victim rather than a self-reliant little man. Countless articles told consumers how their luxury items were manufactured. Accounts of the "slaughter of the innocents," "child slavery," and "cannibalism" in American factories pricked the conscience of the middle class.

Reformers also examined child labor from the standpoint of new biological and educational theories which held that prolongation and protection of childhood was essential to human progress. Using such ideas reformers argued that exploitation of the young undermined their biological potential as parents. In the Progressive era, this view carried special weight because of fear of race suicide. Applying the principle of evolution to child development, G. Stanley Hall defined distinct periods of growth, each with its own needs and potentials. Hall warned that outside pressures and interference with the child's natural development would not only stunt the individual but arrest the evolution of society. In 1900 the United States Census Bureau applied Hall's model to the age classification of child laborers:

In the age period ten to fifteen occurs the transition from childhood to adolescence and normally each year included in that period marks important changes in the child's growth and development; hence in any question relating to the education and welfare of the child, a difference of only one year is significant.[9]

The "new psychology" stressed the physiological and psychological importance of play in child development just when social reformers discovered that premature toil and the absence of playgrounds deprived the children of the poor of the opportunity to play. Child labor reform and the playground movement, therefore, became two aspects of the same campaign, and both dramatized the failure of urban America to meet the needs of childhood. In *Poverty* (1904) Robert Hunter warned:

You cannot rob children of their play any more than you can forget and neglect the children at their play, as we now do in the tenement district, without at the same time paying the penalty. When children are robbed of playtime, they too often reassert their right to it in manhood, as vagabonds, criminals, and prostitutes.[10]

John Dewey made the realization of childhood's potential a basic goal of a democratic society. Florence Kelley, secretary of the National Consumers' League, applying Dewey's concept to her campaign for the abolition of child labor, asserted that the right to childhood "follows in the existence of the Republic."[11] The argument for a decent childhood as a basic requirement of democracy appealed especially to those concerned with preservation of the nation's natural resources. Thus when Theodore Roosevelt attacked child labor in 1912, he emphasized need for "conservation" of childhood.

As the twentieth century opened, opposition to child labor became an organized crusade. Social workers, political economists, constitutional lawyers, and disinterested industrialists came together in tightly-organized state committees supported by consumers' leagues and women's clubs. In true Progressive spirit the reformers relied on exposure to arouse the public conscience, and on the leadership of informed citizen's groups to point the way to corrective legislation and effective enforcement. These attitudes were manifested by the Alabama and New York child labor committees which were formed independently of each other within the space of one year. Reverend Edgar Gardner Murphy, an Episcopalian clergyman, organized the Alabama Child Labor Committee in 1901 to mobilize public support for a bill then pending in the state legislature. The New York Child Labor Committee stemmed from a meeting of representatives of thirty-two settlement houses in New York City in 1902. The meeting, called by Lillian Wald and Florence Kelley, decided to found an organization to investigate and expose child labor conditions. The Committee succeeded in enlisting both the moral and financial support of wealthy New Yorkers. It launched the first extensive investigation into working conditions in New York City, agitated for and secured passage of the stronger child labor law of 1903 which included regulation of the street trades, launched an ambitious program of scholarships for working children, and in 1909 obtained enactment of a dangerous trades act.

The campaign for child labor reform assumed broader scope in 1904 with the organization of the National Child Labor Committee. The board of the National Committee was headed by Felix Adler and included Florence Kelley, Jane Addams, Lillian Wald, Edgar G. Murphy, Edward T. Devine, Robert W. D. De Forest, and Homer Folks. The Committee's triple goals were nationwide investigation, campaigns for more stringent legislation, and enforcement of existing laws. From headquarters in New York City the Committee directed a national campaign with Alexander McKelway acting as special field representative for the South and Owen Lovejoy for the North. Within several years of its existence the Committee had secured the organization of local committees in every state with a child labor problem, and was cooperating with state committees as a propaganda agency and clearing house for child labor campaigns. In addition to its own pamphlets and *Child Labor Bulletin*, the Committee obtained publication outlets in *Survey*, *The Outlook*, *Arena*, and *The Annals of the American Academy of Political and Social Science* and in newspapers throughout the country. It held traveling exhibits and was the first organized reform movement to make wide use of photographic propaganda.

Until 1914, although "national" in organization, the Committee devoted its activities to reform at the state level. Aiming at uniform state laws, the Committee set up legislative standards for a minimum age of fourteen in manufacturing and sixteen in mining, documentary proof of age, a maximum eight-hour work day, and prohibition of night work. At the time of the Committee's organization in 1904 no state had legislation meeting all these standards. By 1914 thirty-five states had a fourteen-year age limit and an eight-hour day for workers under sixteen; thirty-four states prohibited night work under age sixteen, and thirty-six states had appointed factory inspectors to enforce the laws.

Despite these legislative gains child labor remained a serious national problem because of loopholes in the laws or lapses in their enforcement. Agricultural labor was still unregulated; canneries obtained exclusion from child labor laws; domestic service, street trades, and sweat shop labor escaped regulation; and exemption clauses for children of widows and poor parents robbed southern laws of their effectiveness. In 1914, summing up a decade of the National Child Labor Committee's work, Owen Lovejoy concluded, "We have been disillusioned. More has been done than seemed possible within the period, but the field is immensely larger than was supposed."[12]

In 1914 the Committee, previously divided on the need and desirability of federal legislation, decided that the only way to obtain uniform national standards was through federal child labor legislation. After 1914, therefore, the Committee joined forces with the United States Children's Bureau and acted as an effective lobby for a national child labor law. In 1915 at the peak of the campaign for passage of the federal child labor bill the Committee used 416 newspapers and distributed more than four million pages of propaganda materials.

Passage of the Keating-Owen Act in 1916 marked the greatest triumph of the Progressive campaign against child labor. Rejection of the proposed constitutional amendment in the 1920s marked the movement's worst defeat. The story of these episodes can be followed in the documents. Here it is necessary only to point out the irony, which was not lost on the reformers, that the major reform efforts were directed toward a minority of the child labor force: children in factories and mines.

As already noted, agricultural workers, domestic servants, child laborers in sweat shops, and children in the street trades were overlooked by both state and federal laws. Perhaps that is why the proposed child labor amendment, which would have permitted broader and more stringent regulation than was attempted in the federal child labor laws of 1916 and 1919, encountered such fierce opposition.

One of the major difficulties of child labor reform in the early twentieth century was the cultural and economic gap between middle-class reformers and working-class parents. The reformers, in their zeal to refute the stereotype of the poor widow dependent on her little boy's earnings, may have underestimated the economic necessity of child labor among large segments of the working class. On the other hand, the support Homer Folks, Lillian Wald, Florence Kelley, and Jane Addams gave to such causes as mothers' aid, workmen's compensation, minimum wage laws, health insurance, and scholarships for poor children proved that they recognized child labor could not be ended without finding means to supplement family income. The attack on child labor was one of the converging lines of reform which, even before the Great Depression, led to realization that solving problems of childhood required comprehensive efforts to promote economic security for families.

Notes

1. "Governor Moore to the Lords of Trade, 12 January, 1767," E.B. O'Callaghan, ed., *Documents Relative to the Colonial History of the State of New York*, VII (Albany, 1856), 888.

2. "Manufactures December 5, 1791," *American State Papers, Finance*, I (Washington, 1832), 132.

3. "H.N. Slater's Reminiscences of Samuel Slater, his Father, April 26, 1884," in William B. Weeden, *Economic and Social History of New England, 1670-1789*, II (Boston and New York, 1891), 913.

4. Tench Coxe, quoted in United States Bureau of Labor, *Report on Condition of Woman and Child Wage-Earners in the United States*, 19 volumes (Washington, D.C., 1910-1913), VI, 48.

5. "Protection to the Manufactures of Cotton Fabrics, February 13, 1816," *American State Papers, Finance*, III (Washington, 1834), 82.

6. Quoted in United States Bureau of Labor, *Report on Condition of Woman and Child Wage-Earners*, VI, 62.

7. *Nile's Weekly Register*, March 5, 1814, p. 16.

8. John A. Ryan, "What Wage Is a Living Wage," *Catholic World*, 75 (April 1902), 8.

9. U.S. Department of Commerce and Labor, Bureau of the Census, *Bulletin* 69 (Washington, D.C., 1907), p. 7.

10. Robert Hunter, *Poverty* (New York, 1904), p. 223.

11. Florence Kelley, *Some Ethical Gains Through Legislation* (New York, 1905), pp. 3-4.

12. Owen R. Lovejoy, Annual Report for 1914, *Child Labor Bulletin*, III (November 1914), p. 9.

Urban Working Children: A Comparison of Four Surveys from South America
William E. Myers

Around the developing world, children as young as four or five years of age spend long hours working on city streets, as domestic servants, and in sweatshops. In the following article, William Myers brings together data from surveys that focused on the living conditions of urban working children in Bolivia, Brazil, Paraguay, and Peru. The picture that emerges is complex but surprisingly consistent. Urban working children are far more frequently male than female, and work for the most part on the street as vendors, bootblacks, and car minder/washers. Domestic labor is provided primarily by girls. Children tend to work a six-day week and relatively long hours. Wages are very low, often far below the minimum wage, and most children contribute some proportion of their income to the family.

Although some urban working children have been abandoned by or have run away from their families, the vast majority live in households with at least one parent present; and parents also generally work, although only a small proportion are regularly employed. As Myers points out, working children are aware of their own economic value. Many have gone to work to replace the income of fathers who are absent or non-productive. While data on the consistency and amount of schooling that these children receive are weak at best, it is clear that working children are considerably retarded in academic progress relative to non-working peers. In the author's view, however, this academic retardation is as much or more a function of the general effects of poverty and of the low quality of available schooling for the poor as it is of the fact that children who work have little time for study.

Recent years have seen a resurgence of public and official concern about the situation of children who work. Particular attention has been devoted to those commonly referred to as "street children." These are the youngsters so typically encountered hawking petty goods and services in the streets of developing countries. Such working children are

Myers, W.E. (1989). Urban working children: A comparison of four surveys from South America. *International Labour Review, 128* (3). pp. 321-335.

ubiquitous in many cities of the world, and their number has seemed to increase with deteriorating social and economic conditions.

The common perception that there are more and more urban children working and living in lonely, squalid circumstances has led not only to renewed concern about their welfare, but also to the growth of popular myths regarding who they are, what they do and what sort of problems they face. Given the increasing public interest in these children, the amount of genuine data about them is surprisingly limited. Very few surveys exploring how they really experience their situation have been conducted. Even programs established to serve them seldom gather and record systematic information about the children themselves. In the absence of facts, misconceptions abound.

Conceptual clichés can be detrimental to the children involved, not only because they obscure individual differences, but also because they may misdiagnose the problem and lead to inappropriate societal actions that aggravate rather than ameliorate the situation. For example, in many cities children and adolescents working on the streets are regarded by the police as vagrants or delinquents and are subject to arrest, beatings and imprisonment. In other cases they are assumed to be neglected by their families and may be placed against their will in "protective" detention centers. Such actions are inimical to the interests of both the children and society.

The lack of real data has nowhere been more keenly felt than in Latin America, which in recent years has been the world's most active focus of interest and activity on behalf of street children. Although much has been said in that region about the circumstances of such children, a great deal of the literature has been polemical rather than informational. It is often impossible to distinguish the objective situation of the children from the ideological perspective of the observer. Comparatively little effort has been devoted to systematic documentation of the realities of the situation.

A major portion of such limited empirical information as is now available in the region is not very useful for profiling working children and their condition. A key problem is that data collection does not sufficiently reflect practical concerns. For example, official child workforce participation data tend (understandably) to refer primarily to the formal sector, whereas the vast majority of working children are to be found in the unreported informal sector. Government statistics in this field seldom address questions essential for policy planning such as where and how long children work, what they do, how they are remunerated, who employs and supervises them, their state of health and development, where they live, whether they attend school and how they perform there, and what their aspirations are.

Much of the available non-governmental information consists of case descriptions of small numbers of working children. The best of these studies may help provide insights into important dynamics of the problem but they lack the quantitative perspectives necessary to draw broadly applicable inferences. Consequently, they are of only limited use in determining which problems are so serious or widespread that they merit policy or program intervention.

546

The information most needed, but especially rare at this time, is field survey data based on interviews with working children. Until such time as more inquiries of this type are completed and available, however, the few that exist might be more widely utilized to challenge current stereotypes and to develop new perceptions supported by at least some empirical evidence. It may help to correct some of the prevailing misconceptions about urban working children if we can identify important common patterns in the findings of different survey studies of working children from a variety of locations. Even divergences between results from different places can be instructive, since they warn of the variation that might be expected.

As a step towards a more empirical perspective, the following discussion will compare the findings of four different field surveys of urban working children in South America. Included is one survey each from Bolivia, Brazil, Paraguay and Peru.

The Field Surveys

These particular studies were selected because they provide quantified data obtained through structured interviews with approximately equivalent populations from four contiguous countries. All made at least some use of trained professionals in an effort to improve policies and programs for working children. The survey locations and methods were as follows:

— in *Asunción*, Paraguay, 199 child street workers were interviewed in depth between August 1983 and April 1985 in markets, along principal traffic arteries and at intersections, at major gathering places in the city center and in the poorer suburbs. Interviewing followed minimally obtrusive procedures in which the children were engaged in open-ended conversations regarding specified topics of interest. In order to reduce distortions and inhibitions, notes were not taken during the conversations, but were written up afterwards;[1]

— in *Brazil*, a questionnaire containing mostly open-ended questions was distributed in 1983 to forty community-based programs serving working and street children in various towns and cities of the country. Programs cooperating in the study—participation was entirely optional—were asked to facilitate the collection of information from children with whom they had contact. Seventeen of the programs returned completed questionnaires. In most cases, the children filled out their own questionnaires, but in some instances other children or adults assisted according to need. This process yielded usable information on 1,096 children from eleven states and territories;[2]

— in *Cochabamba*, Bolivia, a 1987 survey was essentially a census, since the cohort of 967 children for whom data are reported approximates a preliminary estimate of the total number of the city's street children. The children were approached in a variety of their known places of work and congregation. A closed interview schedule was used, but the interviews also included the open-ended collection of supplementary information;[3]

– in *Lima*, Peru, a 1986 study provided data on 215 young workers who were contacted primarily in their places of work. The information was gathered through structured interviews following a closed schedule.[4]

The demographic composition of the respective study samples is shown in Table 1. Despite their similarities, these four studies are not entirely comparable in their definition and selection of urban children. The Asunción and Lima surveys specifically concerned working children, whereas in Brazil and Cochabamba the focus was on street children. This latter definition permits the inclusion of children who inhabit the street without working. In Brazil, respondents claiming not to work accounted for 17 percent of the sample, and in Cochabamba 21 percent. While the inclusion of non-working children in the data may potentially weaken conclusions about child workers, the effects may not be critical. One reason is that some of the most important Cochabamba data are available separately for workers and non-workers. Another is that claims not to work may not be what they seem.

Table 1. Number, age and sex of surveyed children

Survey	Number	Age range	Males (%)	Females (%)
Asunción	199	8-16[1]	88	12
Brazil	1,096	5-18[2]	98	2
Cochabamba	967	4-18[3]	88	12
Lima	215	6-14[4]	86	14

[1] No age distribution table is available but within the majority group of 8-16 year-olds, the age group 11-14 predominates (Espínola et al., op. cit., p. 17).
[2] Fifty-eight percent aged 11-14, and 31 per cent aged 15-18.
[3] Sixty-three percent aged 10-14.
[4] Sixty-nine percent aged 11-14.

548

Not working has to be interpreted as carefully as working, for it is well known that irregular economic activities typical of underemployment may not always be defined as work by those undertaking them. Some respondents associate "work" only with a regular job, a fixed wage or self-employment. Irregular activities, such as doing odd jobs, are not counted as such, even though they provide a living. As Espínola et al. eloquently put it:

> *Statements from children who work in the street such as "I want to study because I want to work," or simply "I want to work," reveal that what these youngsters do daily for long hours, and often in extremely unfavorable conditions, for many of them is not work.*
>
> *In effect, they associate the notion of "work" with a more formal and stable situation, comparable to what one has in a fixed job, and a fixed weekly income.*
>
> *The fact of feeling shame and not recognizing their work for what it is—an activity that generates income and provides essential help to their families—demonstrates how the contempt with which many persons see and treat them is reflected in the young workers themselves. The daily disparagement and disregard to which they are subjected transmit to the children a negative social evaluation of their occupations and activities, which they end up adopting.[5]*

This issue of not admitting to work probably arises in the studies from Cochabamba and Brazil. If the child respondents in these surveys could not be supported by their poor families and did not work, how did they survive? There are various possible answers, of course, but within the particular social contexts of Bolivia and Brazil it is likely that many respondents claiming not to work in fact lived from the same marginal economic activities that other children defined as work. It is also probable that some may have been reluctant to reveal work which involved activities considered illicit or socially undesirable.

Working children are not the only people who have trouble with the definition of their work; researchers and policy-makers often share the quandary. In dealing with poor people and the informal sector, there is always some question as to just which activities are properly and productively considered to constitute "work." For example, should unremunerated children who stay at home to look after their younger brothers and sisters so that their mothers can hold an outside job, be counted as working children?

Should illicit service activities—like prostitution or selling drugs—be considered work? While complex questions like these do not have easy general answers, all four of the surveys discussed here clearly consider work to be economic participation outside the home. For example, in the Lima study Alarcón defines child work as those activities which

> *imply the participation of children in the production and commercialization of goods to be consumed outside the nuclear family, the rendering of services to persons beyond the family, or, finally, participation in those activities in which the boundaries between*

begging and work are blurred—such as singing on public transportation or cleaning automobile windscreens, among others.[6]

None of the four studies employed a probabilistic sample, and their methods of finding interviewees differed. The Lima study sought out children where they were known to work, including inside shops and homes. Therefore, it probably covers a somewhat wider range of occupations and working conditions than do the other studies, and devotes more attention to children who work as wage employees. About 25 percent of its respondents were hired by establishments and another 15 percent were employed as household domestics. The other three studies drew their samples from places where self-employed children were more likely to be concentrated. Only about 20 percent of the Cochabamba respondents, and fewer than 10 percent of those from Brazil, seem to have had employee or apprentice status. The Asunción study reports no child employees of either homes or establishments. The majority of subjects in all four studies were children working in streets, open markets and other public places.

It is important to remember that these surveys only report what children say, and their data therefore display the world only as the interviewed youngsters perceive or wish to represent it. No attempts were made to corroborate the responses of the children with additional information from, say, their families or employers. There certainly is no indication that the children necessarily see things in the same way as would an outside observer. The following discussion of their work, family, education and aspirations needs to be interpreted in this light.

Analysis of the Findings

Principal Occupations

From the evidence of the four surveys it appears that the work of urban children is concentrated in relatively few occupations. By way of illustration, Table 2 compares participation in three of the most popular occupations for young workers, and only in Brazil do these three categories fail to account for at least half the surveyed workers. It is interesting to note that even in Lima, where a special effort was made to include workers in households and establishments, half the survey respondents are still identified with "street" occupations.

The Lima survey graphically demonstrates that the occupational distribution is related to sex. Whereas only 14 percent of all the children surveyed were employed in household domestic service, 42 percent of the females were to be found in that occupation, versus a mere 3 percent of the males. Also, 38 percent of the girls worked as street vendors, as opposed to only 20 percent of the boys.

There is evidence of considerable mobility between occupations. Espínola et al. report that three out of four children in their Asunción sample had changed occupation at least once. Alarcón relates the 34 percent of his Lima sample that have changed

550

Table 2. Principal occupations of children surveyed[1]

| Survey | Percentage of children in each occupation | | | |
	Street vendors	Bootblacks	Car minders and washers	Total % in these trades
Asunción	54	13	14	81
Brazil	21	8	11	40
Cochabamba	34	16	19	69
Lima	26	18	6	50

[1] Categories combined and recalculated from reported data.

occupations to age, noting a drift from less stable towards more stable activities as children become older. Chej de Peñaloza also mentions the considerable occupational mobility of Cochabamba children, but provides no figures.

Occupational mobility, however, does not mean volatility. Perhaps the commitment to child occupations is more remarkable than the mobility between them. In Asunción, 38 percent of the children surveyed had remained in their current occupation for a period of three to six years. Even though half had changed their occupation once, only 22 percent had changed it more than once. In Lima, only 42 percent of the boys and 14 percent of the girls reported having ever participated in a different occupation.

This picture differs substantially from the prevalent notion that most urban working children flit nonchalantly between unrelated economic activities according to whim or sudden opportunity. On the contrary, the evidence of these surveys suggests a certain degree of structure and commitment within these occupations which encourages continuity. It might be that children have more investment in their work—contacts made, street location rights purchased or rented, credit arranged, policemen bribed or won over, etc.—than first meets the eye. It also may be more difficult to enter a new occupation, especially where others have vested interests to defend, than most observers realize. Perhaps many children simply prefer the work they do.

Hours of work

Children spend a lot of their time working. The only survey (Lima) reporting the number of days the children say they work puts the average at six per week. Three surveys provide information on the length of the working day; Table 3 compares responses from Asunción, Brazil and Lima. Alarcón observes that in Lima girls report longer working days than do boys, which is largely a result of the relatively long duty hours expected of maids and other household employees. It should be noted that in estimating the hours they work, many children may be referring to the period they are actively available for work and not necessarily the time spent in the activity itself. Alarcón mentions that maids are likely to count their occasional rest between tasks as part of their working day because they are still available for work on demand. The situation of other occupations —car washers, for example—could be analogous, and in fact Espínola et al. call attention to the substantial amount of "dead time" in children's occupations.

Table 3. Hours children work per day[1]

Survey	Percentage of children in each group		
	1-4 hours	5-8 hours	9+ hours
Asunción[2]	19	60	21
Brazil	26	59	15
Lima	10	37	52

[1] Data not available for Cochabamba.   [2] Data reported for 2-3, 4-6, 7-8, and 9+ hours. One-third of those working 4-6 hours are shown here under the 1-4 hours category, and two-thirds under the 5-8 hours category.

Earnings

A key question is how much children earn in return for all the trouble and sacrifices they incur in their work. Unfortunately, it is not very useful to compare earnings across national boundaries without also considering what those earnings mean in terms of local purchasing power. Data as reported from the four surveys do not permit that sort of analysis, but a few salient facts do suggest that the earnings of working children tend to be very low, usually only a fraction of the legal minimum wage.

In Asunción, it was found that the average income of child street workers came to only 34 percent of the legal minimum wage in 1983-84, the time of the survey. Espínola et al. indicate that this proportion has since declined, having fallen in 1987 to 26 percent. Even the most remunerative common children's occupations (washing cars and windscreens) yield barely half the legal minimum wage for work of the same duration. In Cochabamba, 12 percent of the young workers received no cash remuneration at all, and another 61 percent earned no more than the equivalent of U.S. $40 per month. In Lima, the median income for the survey sample was worth approximately U.S. $22 per month. Interestingly, bootblacks reported earning more than any other occupation (U.S. $46 per month) and household domestics the least (U.S. $12 per month, presumably including meals). In fact, the three lowest-paid occupations were precisely those in which girls were the most likely to work.

These figures support the general notion of child workers as being very poorly remunerated. A note of caution is in order, however. Many adults make no more; Alarcón mentions that many teachers in Lima earn even less than the working children they teach. Such distortions are far from uncommon and are indeed to be expected where official minimum salaries and public sector wages are especially depressed.

In Recife, Brazil, for example, a 1987 study of 461 street children, commissioned by the municipal government, found that "any child" could expect to make at least one to three times the minimum wage from begging or from selling fruit at the busier intersections. That helped explain why many children refused to abandon their work to participate in a city program that offered them meals, free transportation, vocational education and a scholarship worth half the minimum wage. Since a high proportion of poor adults doing unskilled work in Recife earn the minimum wage or less, many working children earn more than their parents.[7]

Only the surveys in Cochabamba and Lima looked at the question of how working children dispose of their income. In the former, 61 percent responded that they turned the money over to their family, while 34 percent indicated that they used it to cover their own expenses. However, the phrasing of this question probably forced inaccurate answers, since it unfortunately excluded the possibility of dividing earnings between various purposes.

In Lima, Alarcón took a more sophisticated approach by asking what percentage of their income the children turned over to the family. Whereas 78 percent of the children said they contributed some portion of their earnings to meeting family expenses, 26 percent claimed to give all their income to their family and another 14 percent said they gave their family more than half, but less than everything they made. The reason for dividing income between family and personal expenses is apparent in the fact that only 37 percent of the children said that their parents could cover all the costs of their (the children's) food and clothing. No fewer than 53 percent of the children were responsible for meeting all or part of those expenses themselves. One of the interesting findings of the Lima study is that, despite their own and their families' pressing needs, nearly two-thirds of the children claimed to be saving part of their earnings.

Family situation

In many parts of Latin America, children working on urban streets are assumed by the authorities and public alike to be at least partially alienated from their families. The picture of wasted, thinly clad children sleeping huddled together on city streets is far too common and disturbing to be ignored. This image is given credence by the predominance of press, government and academic attention to the more severe cases in which children live without family support or contact. In fact, however, as Table 4 shows, the vast majority of working children surveyed live in households with at least one parent present.

Table 4. Living situation of working children surveyed [1]

Survey	Percentage of respondents living with:		
	Both parents	One parent	Total
Asunción	51	30	81
Cochabamba	...	...	63[2]
Lima	48	27	75

[1] Information not available for Brazil.   [2] Includes unknown number of households headed by other relatives.

554

Even so, there is evidence in some places of a major problem of family disintegration. In Cochabamba, 16 percent of the children interviewed said they had no contact whatsoever with their families, and another 16 percent claimed only "occasional" contact.

It appears that most working children come from families in which both adults and children work. In Lima, Alarcón reports that, in households having both father and mother present, 95 percent of the fathers and 59 percent of the mothers were claimed by the interviewed children to be working. In Asunción, the children indicated that 87 percent of their fathers and 51 percent of their mothers worked. However, the nature of parental employment may leave much to be desired. Espínola et al. point out that, in Asunción, only 37 percent of the fathers and 12 percent of the mothers were said to have fixed, regular sources of income. The others depend, like their children, on a variety of irregular sources generally associated with underemployment. In only 6 percent of the cases was the family said to be dependent solely on the work of its children, but for 50 percent of the families it was claimed that the working children contributed at least half of the total household income.

The children are well aware of their economic importance. When asked why they work, 64 percent in Asunción responded that it was to help their family. About 75 percent gave that answer in Lima if one includes the objective of covering their own costs of clothing and school expenses, which of course relieves the family of that burden. The loss of an adult income puts even more pressure on the children to work. In Asunción, fully 45 percent of the children surveyed indicated that they had gone to work to replace a father who had abandoned the family, died or become ill or unemployed.

Alarcón was the only researcher to inquire who decided that the children should go to work. Half his respondents claimed that they themselves made the decision, while another 40 percent indicated that they were put to work by their parents. He points out that the independence of even the children who claim to have made their own decision is very relative. Only 20 percent of the young workers were able to obtain their current occupation on their own; the rest had to find work through the mediation of their family or others.

Education

One of the most serious criticisms of economic participation by children is that it either precludes or interferes with schooling, thus condemning young workers to a life of illiteracy and unskilled labor. Working children in general, and street children in particular, are often associated in the public mind with truancy or early departure from school. Education and work are thought to be difficult to reconcile; either children work or they study.

Data from the four field surveys suggest that work may not always be the major hindrance to schooling that some fear. In three of the four studies, more than three-quarters of the respondent children claimed to be attending school (77 percent in Asunción, 82 percent in Brazil and 84 percent in Lima). The exception was Cochabamba, where the figure was less than half (49 percent).

555

Given the hours that children say they work, the relatively high rates of school attendance that they also report are astonishing. In the case of Lima, for example, over two-thirds of the children who say they work over nine hours a day would also have to be studying in order to account for the 84 percent school attendance claimed by the sample. The initiative and application demonstrated by working children who manage to keep up with their studies command respect. Trying to meet the demands of both work and study must place them under very considerable stress. The wonder is not that some drop out, but that so many persist.

However, these data need to be interpreted with caution. First of all, one cannot be certain about the veracity of the responses. At least some children, faced with an adult interviewer, may be reluctant to admit to not attending school. Similarly, the children and outside observers may not have the same ideas of just how many days per year in class constitutes "attending school." Perhaps most importantly, the data provide no insight into the quality of education that the children receive when in school, although the authors of the Asunción and Cochabamba studies indicate that it is likely to be very poor.

The fact that some working children do not go to school does not necessarily mean that it is the need to work that keeps them away. In Lima, Alarcón explored the reasons why 16 percent of his sample did not attend school. Of this group, 26 percent pointed to the need to work, 23 percent cited distaste for school, 18 percent said they lacked the necessary funds, and 12 percent declared that they did not have the proper legal documents. In other words, only about a quarter of those out of school, or about 5 percent of the entire sample, claimed that the need to work kept them from studying. However, some occupations and working conditions do tend to discourage school attendance more than others.

Working may in fact contribute more to maintaining children in school than to keeping them out of it. Alarcón notes that, in Lima, child work often makes education possible by helping to cover the costs of school attendance. Family expenses related to schooling may include matriculation fees, uniforms and other clothing, school supplies, transportation, and informal payments to help support teachers, whose official salaries may, as we have seen, be less than what their working students earn in the street. Many impoverished families simply could not meet these expenses unless the children helped out by working. In this regard, it is worth noting that, in Cochabamba, Chej de Peñaloza found the lowest levels of educational attainment to be disproportionately concentrated among non-working children, not the workers.

However, attending school is not the same as benefiting from it. It is conceivable that working adversely affects the children's studies even as it makes them financially possible. Exploring this question, Alarcón asked the children who said they attended school whether they thought that working affected their schoolwork. Two-thirds said they were not aware of any effects. Of the 34 percent who were, half replied that work took time away from schooling and a quarter said that it left them too tired to get the most out of their classes.

Alarcón prudently admits the possibility of negative effects of work on schooling that are not perceived by the students, but which might be revealed by objective data. School advancement from one grade or level to another may be such an objective indicator; to the extent that working undermines learning, grade repetition could be expected to increase. The survey data are unclear about whether this occurred. Interestingly, Alarcón finds that exactly the same proportion (34 percent) of his sample claimed that work affected their studies as admitted to having had to repeat at least one grade. However, he does not report to what extent the two categories overlap.

The Asunción survey notes that the overwhelming majority of young workers it surveyed are still at the primary level and far behind their normal age group in school. Similarly, the Cochabamba study found school progress relative to age was quite retarded for the sample as a whole. Chej de Peñaloza suggests that this educational retardation has less to do with work than with the limited availability of schooling where poor children live. This seems to be especially the case for recent rural-urban migrants, who make up a significant portion of the Cochabamba population. Only 38 percent of the survey sample were born in that city and Chej de Peñaloza reports that many of the children have immigrated from rural areas offering no more than three years of schooling. Such students begin with an educational deficit which working probably does not cause but which it may exacerbate.

Throughout Latin America, children from very poor families and communities tend as a group to be retarded in their studies. It is unknown to what extent their economic participation contributes to this, and without studies comparing working and non-working children from equivalent backgrounds, a definitive answer will not be forthcoming. It would be very useful to know, for example, how the 49 percent school attendance and slow academic progress reported by Cochabamba street children compare with school participation and performance by non-street children from the same *barrios*. It would also be helpful to have objective evidence, such as school enrollment and attendance records, with which to check the claims made by children about their school participation. In the absence of such information, and taking the slim evidence from Cochabamba and Lima at face value, it is reasonable to speculate that the effects of poverty, and the poor quality of education available in most poor communities, may be far more influential than is work in retarding academic progress.

Only the Brazil survey inquired what children thought of their schools. Asked what they most liked about school, nearly a third indicated the teacher. Another quarter mentioned the act of studying. What they liked least was fighting with other children. De Andrade Gonçalves points out that these two responses, taken together, emphasize the importance to children of interpersonal relationships associated with the school experience. They suggest an abhorrence of violence and a yearning for peace and acceptance.

Aspirations of Working Children

Two studies, those from Asunción and Brazil, inquired into the preferences and aspirations of working children. Data from this kind of research provide insight into the

557

values and horizons of the children surveyed, and a glimpse into the kind of future that they might try to build for themselves. The results of these two studies suggest that the children think a great deal about work and value it highly. There is little indication that they find it inherently distasteful. In response to the open, projective question, "What do you want to do?", no fewer than 51 percent of the Asunción children are reported to have replied that they wished to continue working, either in their current or in more desirable occupations. Only 19 percent mentioned a desire to continue their schooling.

One item of the Brazil questionnaire requested the subject to specify "three things that you do not do, but would like to do." Of the 2,281 responses generated (an average of only two per respondent), 33 percent were work or career aspirations. By comparison, only 25 percent of the responses concerned pleasurable or recreational activities, 14 percent were desires for material possessions and wealth, and 8 percent related to further education. The relative importance of work considerations can also be seen in answers to another question: "In your life today, what do you most like?" Some 31 percent of the responses indicated work. Following in order were school (18 percent), family members (17 percent) and playing soccer (16 percent). Among responses to the immediately following contrary question, "What do you not like?", work does not appear.

Only the Asunción study asked what the respondents would like to be when they grow up, to which 49 percent of the children indicated occupations typically associated with skilled or semi-skilled workers who enjoy regular, stable employment. Cited examples included mechanic, chauffeur, baker, sign-painter, bartender, security guard and film projectionist. In the context of current economic conditions, these aspirations could be considered modest but realistic. Although 23 percent said they did not know what they wanted to be, only 8 percent denied any aspirations at all or named occupations at the level of their current work. In a different vein, 21 percent expressed ambitious occupational aspirations likely to be difficult to achieve. Examples included dancer, doctor, engineer, professional athlete, and veterinarian.

Problems and Needs Mentioned by Working Children

A striking pattern emerges from the two studies (Brazil and Cochabamba) that inquired into children's own perceptions of threats, problems or needs. It suggests that many working children feel alienated and vulnerable and may need friendship and emotional support at least as much as other types of assistance. The Brazilian children showed marked fear and abhorrence of violence. Asked what they most fear, 71 percent of them indicated some sort of violence, the most frequently mentioned being robbery by adults or other children. It will be recalled from the above discussion that they also identified fighting with other children as what they least liked about their current life, and indicated that what they most liked about school was the teacher, who presumably was seen as protective and compassionate.

In response to questioning about their most important needs, 73 percent of the Cochabamba children gave first priority to some form of emotional support such as attention, affection and understanding. Nutritional, habitational, occupational and other types of assistance followed far behind.

Concluding Observations

Taken together, the surveys of urban working children in Asunción, Brazil, Cochabamba and Lima convey a general impression of patterns that may be more broadly prevalent in Latin America. The possible importance of these findings for policy and program action merits consideration.

What first strikes one is the fact that those young workers typically seen in the street and other public places are predominantly from a narrow age band of preadolescent and early adolescent boys roughly eleven-fourteen years old. From a developmental perspective, this age is a critical moment in the child's socialization and in the formation of the self-identity and self-esteem that will be carried into adulthood. Much of what the person will be in society later on is cast during this period. The implication is that actions to protect working children should be attractive and appropriate above all to this age group.

It is also apparent that there are many other urban working children, mainly hidden from view in households and establishments, who were not adequately represented in these surveys. Ways need to be found to identify them and learn more about their situations and needs.

Children appear to be working very long hours. It would probably be extremely difficult to reduce those hours to any significant extent without improving the overall economic situation of the families these children are helping to support. One alternative might be to establish programs that reduce the burden on children by combining education and work so that they can earn while they learn. Various models worthy of consideration and experimentation might include the following:

—cooperative education, in which schools and employers collaborate in special programs for working children, a formula already well known in various parts of the world;

—an "education with production" model, in which children work in economic enterprises associated with schools in which they study; successful pilot projects have been conducted in places as different as Africa and the United States;

—self-employment training and assistance through formal or non-formal educational institutions which could be combined with necessary academic instruction.

It would appear that the education issue pertinent to most working children today is not so much school attendance or the capacity to learn as the quality of education provided.

559

Any programs seeking to attract working children need to have a firm understanding of the local economic context, especially the financial incentives inducing children to work. It is likely that the profitability of child work varies greatly from one situation to another, yielding but a pittance to the child in some instances while providing very substantial returns in others. Since children's attitudes and behavior regarding work may be much influenced by society-wide economic and social factors, it is important to understand how individual child work problems relate to the larger picture.

Questions of family disintegration may not be very pertinent to the majority of young workers; they concern primarily a rather small percentage of children who live in the streets or are otherwise at high risk. These very needy children merit special attention, but the policies and programs targeted at their specific problems may not be those best suited for dealing with the situation of the broader group of working children at less immediate risk.

Most urban working children appear to be carrying very heavy family responsibilities with considerable cheerfulness, good will and enthusiasm. Their qualities and contribution should be more widely appreciated by society as a whole, and more opportunities should be made available for them to develop their talents and skills for future success as adults.

Finally, it is worth noting that in line with the problems and needs mentioned by working children themselves, a growing number of Latin American programs are stressing the befriending of children as the most important single element of their work with them. Program operators are increasingly recognizing that working on urban streets is a harsh business that often badly bruises children's self-esteem and confidence. Other assistance becomes meaningful to the children only as their internal resources can be supported and strengthened. For that reason, they hold, programs to reach these children should envisage their purpose as the promotion of positive human relationships and not merely as the delivery of essential services.

Notes

1. Basílica Espínola, Benno Glauser, Rosa María Ortiz and Susana Ortiz de Carrizosa: *En la calle: Menores trabajadores de la calle en Asunción* (Asunción, Callescuela, 1987).

2. Zuila de Andrade Gonçalves: *Modo de vida e representações de meninos de rua* (Rio de Janeiro, Ministério da Previdência e Assistência Social/SAS/FUNABEM/UNICEF, 1985), mimeographed.

3. Maruja Chej de Peñaloza: *Situación del menor en alto riesgo en la ciudad de Cochabamba* (Cochabamba, 1987), mimeographed.

4. Walter Alarcón Glasinovich: *Pobreza urbana y trabajo infantil en Lima metropolitana* (Lima, Radda Barnen, 1986), mimeographed.

5. Espínola et al., op. cit., p. 67.

6. Alarcón, op. cit., p. 10.

7. *Jornal do Brasil* (Rio de Janeiro), 27 Sep. 1988, p. 17. The cited study is by Cleide Galiza of the Fundação Joaquim Nabuco, Recife.

22

Death, Divorce, and Remarriage:
The Child's Perspective

Mothers, fathers, and children form the core of the family constellation; but families that meet the traditional ideal of two parents with two to three children, a family type that American sociologists call the *Dick and Jane family*, are increasingly rare. In modern nations, families come in a vast array of forms: two-parent families, single-parent families, mother-headed households, father-headed households, same-sex parents, stepmothers, stepfathers, and families that have been "blended." Families may consist of parents and children alone or they may contain grandparents, aunts, uncles, nieces, or nephews.

Surprisingly, two hundred years ago, in these same countries, families were similarly complex. People frequently lived near their most immediate relatives, and families were extended over several households. High rates of adult mortality from disease, accident, and childbirth meant that many families were headed by single parents. Remarriage brought stepparents into the household and blended children from different families. Family constellations were often even further augmented by apprentices, servants, or lodgers.

With industrialization and urbanization in the early years of the nineteenth century, families looking for factory work began to move away from the communities in which they had been raised and to establish themselves in cities as relatively isolated units. As public health and safety improved, particularly toward the end of the century, adult mortality dropped precipitously. The Dick and Jane family that served as the post-World War II ideal had been born.

Since 1960 the composition of American households has changed dramatically. By 1980 the percentage of children under 18 living with biological parents who had been married only once had declined from 71 percent to 57 percent. Today it is estimated that this figure is below 50 percent. During the same period, the percentage of children under 18 living in single-parent households more than doubled, from 9.2 percent to more than 25 percent. In addition, as single parents remarry, the number of blended families continues to increase.

• INTRODUCTION •

In growing up, children are typically exposed to a variety of transitions. Events such as the birth of a younger sibling, school entry or transfer, a family move, or departure of an older sibling to school or to marriage, all have the potential to require the child to adjust to altered family roles, responsibilities, and routines. All such transitions are associated with elevated stress and pose some degree of potential risk, but few transitions are as potentially disorganizing to children as the disruption of their parents' marriage.

Historically, marital disruption was brought about almost entirely by the death of a parent; and before the twentieth century, rates of adult mid-life mortality from childbirth, disease, and accident were remarkably high by current standards. In the modern era, as mortality rates have drastically declined, divorce rates have soared and the vast majority of marital disruptions now occur as a function of divorce. Interestingly, in all historical periods, most parents whose marriages suffered disruption have tended to remarry. Stepparents, blended families, and children's need to adjust to changes introduced by remarriage are by no means solely a twentieth century phenomenon.

The two readings in this chapter approach marital transition from very different perspectives. In the first article, Peter Uhlenberg charts the impact of declining mortality on family structure and transition. From his analysis, he draws the surprising conclusion that, despite the high divorce rate, the American family is the most stable that it has ever been in history. In the second reading, Mavis Hetherington, Margaret Stanley-Hagan, and Edward Anderson examine factors in the child and in the environment that mediate the effects of family transition and household reorganization that typically accompany divorce and remarriage of a custodial parent.

• • •

Death and the Family
Peter Uhlenberg

The twentieth century decline in the rate of mortality has been precipitous. Since the turn of the century infant mortality has dropped from 140 to 14 deaths per thousand live births and the average American life span has risen from fifty to seventy-three years. In this provocative essay, Peter Uhlenberg examines the impact of decreasing mortality on family structure and change. Among the most interesting trends for which he provides analysis are: a) radical reductions in the probability that a family will suffer the loss of a child or that a child will suffer the loss of a parent or sibling; b) sharp increase in the probability that children's grandparents will survive until the child reaches adolescence; and c) deep decline in early widowhood.

These trends suggest to Uhlenberg that the American family, taken as a whole, is as stable as it has ever been. Parents, confident in children's survival, are free to invest emotion and resources in each child. Young children are rarely exposed to the death of close relatives, and the opportunity for multigenerational interaction has increased. Even family disruption brought about by the rising rate of divorce is more than offset by the declining probability of death.

Thus, for example, in 1900, approximately two thirds of all marriages of men and women joined in their early twenties would have ended sometime within the first forty years through the death of a spouse. Since many of these widows and widowers remarried, blended families were common. In 1976, little more than a third of such marriages would have been disrupted by death. Indeed, even death and divorce taken together produced less marital disruption in 1976 than that produced by death alone at the turn of the century. So striking is this change that the author goes so far as to suggest that the reduction in marital disruption due to death may even contribute to the divorce rate.

The impact of mortality change upon family structure, although sometimes mentioned, has been seriously neglected in studies of family history. Many of the most significant changes in the American family—the changing status of children, the increasing

Uhlenberg, Peter. (1980). Death and the family. *Journal of Family History*. pp. 313-320.

independence of the nuclear family, the virtual disappearance of orphanages and foundling homes, the rise in societal support of the elderly, the decline in fertility, the rise in divorce—cannot be adequately understood without a clear recognition of the profound changes that have occurred in death rates. And the decline in mortality in this century has been dramatic. At the beginning of this century about 140 infants out of every 1,000 born died in the first year of life; now only 14 out of 1,000 die. In this same period the average life span has increased from less than fifty to seventy-three. The mortality decline in this century is greater than the total mortality decline that occurred during the 250 years preceding 1900.

In searching for the meaning of aggregate statistics on death for individuals and families, we must consider the effects of a death upon the survivors. Habenstein suggests that "each death initiates significant responses from those survivors who in some way have personally or vicariously related to the deceased. Inevitably, the collectivities in which the dead person held membership also react." The family is often the most important group in which an individual has membership and in which close relationships exist, so it is here that we should expect death to have its greatest impact. The loss of a parent, a child, a sibling, or a spouse disrupts established family patterns and requires readjustment. As the experience of losing intimate family members moves from a pervasive aspect of life to a rare event, adjustments in family structure become imperative.

If the mortality decline since 1900 has been so large and if this decline has major repercussions for the family, why has it been neglected in studies of family change? One important reason is the difficulty involved in trying to measure accurately the effects of a mortality change. Suppose, for example, that we want to describe the effect of mortality upon the family position of children at various historical times. If we attempt to specify the situation in its full complexity, we must deal with the age of mothers and fathers at the birth of their children, the birth position of children, and the age-sex configuration of siblings. Furthermore, we must recognize that cohorts of individuals live out their lives in a dynamic environment in which the force of mortality is constantly changing. Even if we could construct a conceptually complex model to elaborate the detailed mortality experiences of individuals, we would not have the necessary statistics to make use of it. Nor can a retrospective survey provide the data we would need, since only survivors to the present could be interviewed.

The purpose of this essay is to suggest an alternative approach by constructing relatively simple measures of how different mortality levels affect important aspects of the family. Rather than attempting to summarize the total impact of mortality upon a cohort, the present study develops hypothetical situations to provide insights into the dynamic role of death in family life. The emphasis is upon ways in which mortality impinges upon family structure, and how observed changes in mortality over this century have encouraged change in the American family.

For a perspective on historical change in mortality, I will focus upon three dates in the twentieth century: approximately 1900, 1940, and 1980 (actually, 1976). At each date, the role of mortality will be considered from the perspective of . . . childhood [and] young adulthood. . . .

Childhood

Mortality change has affected the family experience of children in three ways. First, an increasing likelihood that a newborn will survive through childhood may influence the nature of parent-child relations. Second, declining mortality in the middle years of life affects the chances of orphanhood for children. Third, changing adult mortality also alters the prospects for having grandparents alive during childhood.

Parent-Child Relations

There is widespread agreement that mortality levels in a society constrain attitudes and feelings that parents have toward their infant children. As Ariès writes, under conditions of very high infant and childhood mortality "people could not allow themselves to become too attached to something that was regarded as a probable loss." As infant mortality has declined, childhood has become a more clearly differ-entiated stage of life, and families have increasingly focused upon children and emphasized the nurturance of children. Comparing the modern and historical American family, Skolnick concludes, "What seems to have changed is the psychological quality of the intimate environments of family life. . . .

Table 1. Measures of Death to Children in Families: 1900; 1940; 1976

Year	Probability of Surviving from 0 to 15	Probability of 1 or More Dying out of 3	Average Number of Children per Mother*	Probability of 1 or More Dying out of Average Number of Births
1900	.79	.50	4.2	.62
1940	.94	.17	2.8	.16
1976	.98	.06	2.1	.04

* For 1900 and 1940 this is the average completed family size for women who were aged 25-29 at these dates. For 1976 the figure is the expected completed family size for women aged 25-29 in 1976.

Within the home the family has become more intense emotionally." Surely other factors in addition to changed mortality encouraged the deepening of emotional bonds between family members. But a look at the extent of changing survival prospects for infants since 1900 points clearly to the critical role that this change played in the increased intimacy of the parent-child relationship.

Several calculations to demonstrate the magnitude of the drop in child deaths since 1900 are presented in Table 1. First, the probability that an individual baby would survive his or her childhood increased from .79 in 1900 to .98 in 1976. The second calculation answers the question, what is the probability that a couple bearing three children would have at least one child die before reaching age fifteen? The answer is that under 1900 mortality conditions half of the parents would experience the loss of a child; under 1976 conditions only 6 percent would. But the rate of birth as well as death fell over this century. As a result, the probability of an average parent experiencing the death of a child changed even more. Women bearing children around 1900 had, on average, 4.2 children, while projections suggest that women currently bearing children will average about 2.1. Thus the third calculation in Table 1 shows that the probability of a child dying for parents with an average number of children for that period dropped from .62 in 1900 to only .04 in 1976. As the parental experience of having a child die changed from routine to exceptional, the stimulus to invest greater emotion and resources has grown.

Orphanhood

The dependency of children upon adults for care and socialization necessitates fully developed social arrangements to deal with orphans in societies with high rates of mortality. Adoption within an extended kinship system and placement of children in orphanages were two mechanisms used to deal with the social problem of orphans in nineteenth-century America. But during the twentieth century orphanhood changed from a common occurrence to a rare event. Consequently, social institutions designed to deal with this problem have virtually disappeared. From the perspective of successive cohorts of children, the change has profoundly altered their experiences in families.

Table 2 contains data which show the effect of varying mortality levels upon the probability of orphanhood. Since probability of death is related to age, some assumption about the age of men and women at the occurrence of parenthood is required. Over this century the median age of women at the birth of their children has ranged from 27.2 to 25.4, and fathers have, on average, been about three years older than mothers. Therefore, the choice of a mother aged twenty-seven and a father aged thirty for the calculations in Table 2 is a reasonable approximation to the typical experience over this time interval. From the table we can read the probability of orphanhood for those born under these circumstances.

If mortality levels characteristic of 1900 persisted over time and the probability of death for the father and mother was independent, about 24 percent of the children born would lose at least one parent before reaching age fifteen; one out of 62 would have both parents die. Under mortality conditions existing in 1976, only 5 percent of all children

567

Table 2. Probabilities of Parents and Siblings Dying Before a Child Reaches Age 15: 1900; 1940; 1976.*

Year	Probability of 1 or More Parents Dying	Probability of 1 or More of 2 Siblings Dying	Probability of Death to Member of Nuclear Family
1900	.24	.36	.51
1940	.10	.12	.21
1976	.05	.04	.09

* See text for specific family context of the child.

would see a parent die, while one in 1,800 would lose both parents. So declining mortality has operated to increase greatly the family stability of children.

Of course, increasing divorce has had the counter influence of increasing family disruption for children. At current levels of divorce, about 36 percent of all children will experience a disrupted family. But the social significance of disruption due to death differs from disruption due to divorce. Current discussions of the effects of family disruption upon children should consider the very high rate of family instability that has been the historical experience of children prior to the modern era of low mortality. Further, those interested in designing social policy for the family would benefit from studying the historical ways of dealing with orphans.

In addition to the reduced probability of losing a parent during childhood, there has also been a great reduction in the probability of a sibling dying. One good example indicates the magnitude of this change. Consider the situation of a first-born child to a mother aged twenty-seven and a father aged thirty, where the parents have two additional children at two-year intervals. That is, the first-born child has siblings born when he or she is two and four. What is the probability that this child will experience the death of a sibling before reaching age fifteen? Under 1900 mortality conditions the probability is .36, while under 1976 conditions, it is only .04. Combined with the possibility of a parent or sibling dying during childhood, the chances of a child losing someone in the nuclear family before he or she reaches age fifteen drops from .51 to .09. Since the average number of siblings for a child born later in this century is much lower than for someone born earlier, the actual experience of encountering the death of an intimate family member has declined even more dramatically than these calculations suggest. Compared to the past, children now are almost entirely shielded from the death of close relatives, except that of elderly grandparents.

Grandparents' Survival

Not only did the mortality decline improve the likelihood that all members of the nuclear family would survive one's childhood, but also it increased the average number of living grandparents. Consider the probability of a child having grandparents alive if he or she is born to a father aged thirty and mother aged twenty-seven and if both parents were similarly born when their fathers and mothers were thirty and twenty-seven respectively. Under 1900 mortality conditions, one-fourth of the children would have all grandparents alive at birth; by 1976 it increased to almost two-thirds (Table 3). The probability of three or more grandparents being alive when the child was age fifteen increased from .17 to .55. Thus, mortality change has greatly increased the potential for family interaction across more than two generations. The actual role of grandparents in the lives of children cannot be determined from these simple demographic data. But the increased presence of grandparents suggests that statements about their declining importance in the lives of children are probably exaggerated or wrong.

Table 3. Distribution of Children by Number of Living Grandparents when Child Is Aged 0 and 15 under Conditions of 1900, 1940, and 1976.

Year	Number of Grandparents Alive at Age 0				Number of Grandparents Alive at Age 15			
	0-1	2	3	4	0-1	2	3	4
1900	.08	.26	.42	.25	.48	.35	.15	.02
1940	.02	.13	.40	.46	.29	.39	.26	.06
1976	.00	.05	.31	.63	.12	.33	.39	.16

Young Adult

The mortality decline since 1900 has greatly altered the prospects that a marriage between young adults will be broken by death before old age. If a man and woman marry when they are aged twenty-five and twenty-two, the probability that either of them will die within forty years after their marriage dropped from .67 in 1900 to .36 in 1976. This decline in early widowhood more than offsets the rise in divorce (Table 4), so that the stability of marriages during the childrearing years has actually increased over this century. When the declining age at completion of childbearing is also considered, the higher probability of both husband and wife surviving to the empty nest stage of life is even more marked.

With current low mortality the prospective view of married life is quite different from what it was in the past. A man and a woman marrying at the average marriage age can anticipate jointly surviving a median of forty-five years, i.e., until the husband is seventy years old. The prospect of living with one person over such a long time period, especially when one anticipates significant but unknown social change, may influence one's view of marriage. In particular, it may cause higher uncertainty about whether or not the marriage can survive until broken by death. If a couple enters into marriage accepting the option of divorce as a possibility, the chances of actually ending the marriage with a divorce are probably increased. Further, the period of time in which a divorce can occur has been lengthened. Thus it seems likely that the decreasing likelihood of marital disruption due to death has contributed to the increased rate of divorce in recent years. . . .

Table 4. Probability of Marital Disruption Due to Death or Divorce within the First 40 Years: 1900; 1940; 1976.

Year	Broken by Death*	Broken by Death or Divorce*
1900	.67	.71
1940	.50	.63
1976	.36	.60

* Assuming husband is 25 and wife is 22 at time of marriage.

Conclusion

Declining mortality during the twentieth century has had a major impact upon the American family. The role of mortality as an independent variable producing change has been noted in the following areas:

1. Increasing survival prospects for infants have encouraged stronger emotional bonds between parents and children.
2. Decreasing deaths of adults aged twenty to fifty have reduced the proportion of children who experience orphanhood.
3. Decreasing mortality has eliminated the experience of a member of the nuclear family dying for most children.
4. Increasing survival rates have increased the number of living grandparents for children.
5. Decreasing mortality has increased the number of years that marriages survive without being disrupted by death. This change has probably contributed to the increase in divorce. . . .

Marital Transitions: A Child's Perspective
E. Mavis Hetherington, Margaret Stanley-Hagan, and Edward R. Anderson

Nearly half of all American children can expect to experience parental divorce and life in a single-parent family. Most of these will also encounter remarriage and life with a stepparent, possibly in a blended family. In the following article, Mavis Hetherington and her colleagues review the available data on the impact of divorce-related marital transitions on children's adjustment.

Pointing out that marital transitions (conflict, separation, divorce, single parenting, periodic contact with a non-custodial parent, remarriage, stepparenting) generally require children to adjust to a continuing series of family changes over time, the authors discuss a number of factors in children themselves and in the child's environment that together help account for the great diversity of children's reactions to these transitions. Indeed, it is the authors' contention that the long-term effects of divorce and remarriage on children's adjustment are less related to divorce or remarriage per se than to variables that moderate the impact of marital transition on the child.

Among the most important of these moderating factors are experiences and levels of stress, conflict, and economic deprivation associated with family reorganization; children's own temperament, level of development, and gender-related resources for coping with stress; psychological attributes of the single-parent or stepparent home environment and nature of the relationship to the non-custodial parent; and availability of social support from siblings, peers, relatives, and schools. Although no child finds it easy to cope with divorce, available evidence suggests that resourceful children in strong, supportive environments will not only manage the transitions successfully, they may even benefit from them.

The rate of divorce, particularly divorce involving families with children, rose dramatically between 1965 and 1979. Since 1979, however, the rate has begun to fall, declining 6 percent between 1979 and 1984 (Hernandez, 1988). Despite this leveling off,

Hetherington, E.M., Stanley-Hagan, M. & Anderson, E.R. (1989). Marital transitions: A child's perspective. *American Psychologist, 44* (2). pp. 303-312.

it is estimated that between 40 percent and 50 percent of the children born in the late 1970s and early 1980s will experience their parents' divorce and will spend an average of five years in a single-parent home before their custodial parents' remarriage (Glick & Lin, 1986). Because 75 percent of divorced mothers and 80 percent of divorced fathers remarry and the divorce rate in remarriages is higher than that in first marriages, many children are exposed to a series of marital transitions and household reorganizations following their parents' initial separation and divorce. Thus divorce and remarriage should not be viewed as single static events but as part of a series of transitions modifying the lives and development of children. Children encounter widely varying sequences of family reorganizations and family experiences following divorce, and the patterning and timing of these experiences may be critical in their long-term adjustment.

In this article the changed experiences and responses of children to their parents' marital rearrangements are discussed, and divorce and remarriage from the perspective of the child is examined. Although the adjustment of children is related to the adaptation and behavior of parents, what may be a positive life situation or coping strategy for one family member is not necessarily salutary for other family members. The decision to divorce or remarry may be made on the basis of the possibility for improved well-being of the parent, in many instances with little or no consideration for the concerns of the child. Few children wish for their parents' divorce, and many children resent their parents' remarriages. . . .

In spite of this, after a period of initial distress following divorce, most children and parents adapt to their situation in a single-parent household within two to three years if their new situation is not compounded by continued or additional adversity. The new family structure and equilibrium is usually disrupted, however, by the custodial parent's remarriage within three to five years. The period of adjustment to remarriage seems to be longer than that for divorce, especially for older children (Hetherington, in press-a; Hetherington & Clingempeel, 1988). Moreover, because divorces tend to occur more rapidly in remarriages, in some families the child is already confronting a second divorce before adaptation to the remarriage may have occurred.

The transition following divorce or remarriage both involve the restructuring of the household and changes in family roles and relationships; however, they differ in several important ways. Divorce usually involves high levels of family conflict and decrease or loss of contact with a parent, whereas remarriage involves the addition of a family member. Furthermore, a child whose parent remarries has already experienced life in his or her family of origin, divorce, and a period of time in a single-parent household before the remarriage occurs. Children's experiences in earlier family situations will modify responses to new situations. It has been argued that behavior problems exhibited by children in remarried families are attributable not to difficulties in adapting to remarriage, but to stresses associated with divorce and life in a single parent household (Furstenberg, 1988; Zill, 1988).

573

Diversity in Children's Responses to Divorce and Remarriage

There is great diversity in children's responses to their parents' marital transitions. Many children manifest some behavioral disruptions and emotional upheaval immediately following their parents' divorce or remarriage. Anger, resentment, anxiety, depression, and even guilt are commonly experienced by children at this time. In the period immediately following divorce, children may grieve for the absent parent, may respond with noncompliance and aggression to parental conflict and family disorganization, and may become confused by and apprehensive of changing relationships with parents. . . . In the period following remarriage, the child must give up fantasies of parental reconciliation, may resent the new stepparent's attempts to control or discipline, and may perceive the new marital relationship as a threat to the restabilized parent-child relationship. . . .

Following the initial responses to the crisis period in their parents' divorce and remarriage, some children exhibit remarkable resiliency and in the long term may actually be enhanced by coping with these transitions; others suffer sustained developmental delays or disruptions; still others appear to adapt well in the early stages of family reorganization but show delayed effects that emerge at a later time, especially adolescence (Hetherington, in press-a). The most commonly reported problem behaviors found in children from divorced and remarried families are aggressive, noncompliant, and acting-out behaviors; decrements in prosocial behavior; problems in academic achievement and school adjustment; and disruptions in peer and heterosexual relations (Bray, 1987, 1988; Camara & Resnick, 1988; Hetherington et al., 1982 1985; Hetherington & Clingempeel, 1988; Stolberg & Anker, 1984; Stolberg, Camplair, Currier, & Wells, 1987; Zill, 1988). Although there are some reports of greater depression or internalizing disorders in these children when they reach adolescence (Hetherington & Clingempeel, 1988; Wallerstein, Corbin, & Lewis, 1988), these findings are less well substantiated and less consistently found than those citing externalizing problems. Researchers consistently find that children adapt better in a well-functioning single-parent or stepparent family than in a conflict-ridden family of origin (Block, Block, & Gjerde, in press; Hess & Camara, 1979; Hetherington et al., 1982; Lamb, 1977; Long & Forehand, 1987; Stolberg et al., 1987). Again it should be noted that being removed from a conflictual family situation through divorce or the introduction of a supportive stepparent may also have positive effects on the adjustment of children. Long-term effects of marital transitions are related more to new stresses encountered by the child, the individual attributes of the child, the qualities of the single-parent or stepfamily home environment, and resources and support systems available to the child than to divorce or remarriage per se. . . .

Cumulative Stress

Rutter (1980) reported that a single stress typically carries no appreciable psychiatric risk for children. When children are exposed to multiple stressors, however, the adverse effects increase multiplicatively. When parents divorce, children are frequently exposed to parental conflict and must adjust not only to the absence of the noncustodial parent but also to depressed economic resources, changes in the custodial parent's availability and overall parenting style, and more chaotic household routines. When the custodial parent remarries, the child again experiences changes in family structure and relationships. Moreover, it has been suggested that when roles and relationships in stepfamilies become increasingly complex, adjustment of family members becomes increasingly difficult (Cherlin, 1981). Support for this idea is found in evidence that children in stepfamilies have more difficulty in adjusting in stepfamilies with larger numbers of children, in blended families in which there are children from the custodial parent and the stepparent's previous marriages, and in families in which a new child is born to the biological parent and stepparent (Hetherington et al., 1982; Santrock & Sitterle, 1987; Zill, 1988).

Child Temperament and Personality

Temperamentally difficult children have been found to be less adaptable to change and more vulnerable to adversity than are temperamentally easy children (Hetherington, in press-a; Rutter, 1980). The more difficult child is more likely to be the elicitor and the target of aversive responses by the parents and stepparents, whereas the temperamentally easy child not only is less likely to be the recipient of criticism, displaced anger, and anxiety but also is more able to cope with these responses. If temperamentally easy children have support systems available to them, going through moderate levels of stress in a divorce or remarriage may actually enhance their ability to cope with later adaptive challenges. In contrast, for temperamentally difficult children, increasing stress leads to decrements in later coping skills and an increase in behavior problems. . . . Other individual attributes such as intelligence, independence, internal locus of control, and self-esteem also are related to children's adaptability in the face of stressful life experiences. . . . Furthermore, a recent provocative paper by Block et al. (in press) suggests that children with personality and behavior problems may be not only more vulnerable to the effects of their parents' divorce but also more likely to have parents who later divorce. Behavior problems in children may exacerbate marital problems and contribute to divorce.

Developmental Status

The adaptation of children to family transitions also varies with their developmental status. Although some studies show that children who are younger at the time of the parents' marital disruption exhibit more problems (Kalter & Rembar, 1981; Santrock & Wohlford, 1979), others do not (Stolberg et al., 1987; Wallerstein et al., 1988). It might be more accurate to say that the type of behavior problems and coping mechanisms differ for children of different ages. Although nothing is known about the effects of divorce on infants, young children's responses are mediated by their limited cognitive and social competencies, their dependency on their parents, and their restriction to the home. During the interval immediately following divorce, preschool children are less able to appraise accurately the divorce situation, the motives and feelings of their parents, their own role in the divorce, and possible outcomes. Thus young children may blame themselves for the divorce, may fear abandonment by both parents, may misperceive parents' emotions, needs, and behaviors, and may harbor fantasies of reconciliation (Wallerstein et al., 1988).

The cognitive immaturity that creates profound anxieties for the child who is young at the time of the parent's divorce may prove beneficial over time. Ten years after divorce these children have fewer memories of either parental conflict or their own earlier fears and suffering, . . . and they typically have developed a close relationship with the custodial parent. Although approximately one-third of these children continue to experience anger at the unavailability of the noncustodial parent and may experience depression five and ten years after divorce, most are adapting reasonably well if they are not encountering new personal or family stressors. In contrast, those who had been adolescents and who retain memories of the conflict and stress associated with the divorce may be more consciously troubled (Wallerstein et al., 1988).

Like their younger counterparts, older children and adolescents experience considerable initial pain and anger when their parents divorce; however, they are better able to accurately assign responsibility for the divorce, to resolve loyalty conflicts, and to assess and cope with additional stresses such as economic changes and new family role definitions. The older child also is able to take advantage of extrafamilial support systems. Adolescents may show remarkable maturity as they assume greater responsibilities—in the words of Weiss (1979) they may "grow up faster," but many experience premature detachment from their families. It is estimated that one third of older children and adolescents become disengaged from their families. If this disengagement leads to greater involvement in a prosocial peer group, school attainment, or nurturant, constructive relationships outside of the family, this can be an adaptive, positive coping mechanism. If, however, it is associated with involvement in antisocial groups and activities with little adult concern or monitoring, the outcomes can be disastrous. . . .

Following remarriage, many children evidence a resurgence of problem behaviors (Bray, 1988; Hetherington, in press-a; Hetherington & Clingempeel, 1988; Hetherington et al., 1985). The younger child appears able to eventually form an attachment with a competent stepparent and to accept the stepparent in a parenting role. Developmental tasks facing early adolescents, however, may make them especially vulnerable and unable to adapt to the transition of remarriage. . . . In addition, because older children have more self-confidence and resources for fighting back, they may confront or question some aspects of family roles and functioning that younger children would not. . . . Children entering adolescence are confronted with changing perceptions of their parents; a decreased dependence on parental control and establishing self-monitoring; balancing parental, individual, and peer expectations; and establishing autonomy and gaining power in decision making (Steinberg, 1985).

Moreover, the awareness and preoccupation with sexuality that emerges at adolescence may not only heighten stepfamily members' concerns about what appropriate affection might be, but also may cause children to resent closeness in the new marital relationship. . . . Children in remarried families often misinterpret normal displays of affection between newly remarried spouses (Hetherington, in press-a, in press-b). These concerns may be less of an issue, however, when the parent's remarriage occurs prior to the child's adolescence, as opposed to when the remarriage occurs at adolescence. Parker and Parker (1986), for instance, report fewer cases of sexual abuse between stepfathers and stepdaughters if the remarriage occurred when the children were young. Furthermore, for older adolescents the entry of a stepparent may not be as aversive, because late adolescents are anticipating their departure from the home and new young adult roles and relationships. The introduction of a stepparent may relieve responsibilities for emotional and economic support of their divorced parents. . . .

Sex Differences

Following divorce, approximately 90 percent of children reside with a custodial mother. The deleterious effects of marital discord, divorce, and life in a single-parent family in which the mother has custody are more pervasive for boys than for girls (Hetherington et al., 1982, 1985; Porter & O'Leary, 1980; Rutter, 1980, 1987). In contrast to girls who live with single mothers and to children who live with nondivorced parents, boys living with single mothers show a higher rate of behavior disorders and problems in interpersonal relations both in the home and in the school with teachers and peers. Boys also are more likely to show more sustained noncompliant, aggressive behavior even two to three years after divorce. Disturbances in social and emotional adjustment in girls living with their mothers have largely disappeared by two years after divorce; however, problems may reemerge at adolescence in the form of precocious sexual behavior and disruptions in heterosexual relations (Hetherington, 1972; Newcomer & Udry, 1987; Wallerstein et al., 1988).

There is some evidence that school-aged children adapt better in the custody of a parent of the same sex (Camara & Resnick, 1988; Zill, 1988). Boys in the custody of their fathers are more mature, social, and independent; are less demanding; and have higher self-esteem than do girls in their fathers' custody. Sons in the custody of their fathers, however, are also less communicative and less overtly affectionate, perhaps as a result of less exposure to women's expressiveness. Girls in the custody of their fathers show higher levels of aggression and behavioral problems and fewer incidences of prosocial behavior than do girls in the custody of their mothers (Furstenberg, 1988).

It should be noted, however, that research on children's adjustment in homes where the father has custody is scant. Moreover, there is evidence that the quality of the relationship of custodial fathers and their children is related to whether or not the father actively sought custody or was awarded custody because of his ex-wife's incompetence or inability to take custody (Hetherington & Stanley-Hagan, 1986). Boys in the custody of either mothers or fathers show more acting-out behaviors than do girls (Furstenberg & Allison, 1985; Hetherington & Camara, 1984). . . . This may be attributed in part to the fact that boys are more likely than girls to be exposed to parental conflict. Parents fight more and their fights are longer in the presence of sons (Hetherington et al., 1982). Moreover, a recent study (Morgan, Lye, & Condron, in press) reports that families with sons are 9 percent less likely to divorce than are those with daughters. This may be because of the greater involvement and attachment of fathers to sons or to the reluctance of mothers to attempt raising sons alone. Whatever the reason, it seems likely that parents of sons may remain together longer even in an acrimonious marriage. Thus sons may be exposed to more conflict both before and after divorce. In addition, boys interpret family disagreements less positively than do girls (Epstein, Finnegan, & Gythell, 1979). Furthermore, since boys are more likely than girls to respond to stress with externalizing, noncompliant, antisocial behaviors, firm consistent authoritative control may be more essential in the parenting of boys. During and following divorce, however, the discipline of custodial mothers often becomes erratic, inconsistent, peremptory, and punitive. Finally, in times of family stress boys are less able than girls to disclose their feelings and to solicit and obtain support from parents, other adults, and peers (Hetherington, in press-a).

There are some reports that marital discord is associated with anxiety and depression in girls (Emery, 1982; Emery & O'Leary, 1982; Rutter, 1971; Wallerstein et al., 1988). Internalizing behaviors are sometimes found in girls following divorce, but girls demonstrate such behaviors less frequently than they do conduct disorders (Furstenberg & Seltzer, 1983; Garbarino et al., 1984; Hetherington & Clingempeel, 1988; Hetherington et al., 1985; Jacobson, 1984; Zill & Peterson, 1983).

Little is known about the effects of joint custody on the adjustment of children. In most cases, joint legal custody still involves residential custody by the mother. . . . It seems unlikely that the findings of early studies of voluntary joint custody (Steinman, 1981), before the legal preference for joint custody was established, are relevant to the current situation in which joint custody is now preferred in more than thirty states. These early studies usually involved friendly divorces in which the parents were willing to make sacrifices in order to maintain parental responsibilities. Children benefit from contact with both parents following divorce if there is cooperation and low conflict between parents. Encouraging joint custody by parents with acrimonious relationships may only prolong the child's involvement in conflict and make adaptation to the divorce even more diffi-cult. Further research is needed in this area.

Following the remarriage of the custodial parent, there often is a reemergence of emotional and behavioral problems in girls and an intensification of problems in boys. . . . Whereas boys experience more pervasive problems in post-divorce adjustment, some studies report that girls have more problems adjusting to remarriage (Brand et al., 1988). Over time, preadolescent boys in families with stepfathers are more likely than girls to show improvement on measures of adjustment (Hetherington et al., 1985). Sex differences in response to remarriage are less consistently reported in adolescents (Hetherington & Clingempeel, 1988; Wallerstein et al., 1988). Sons who are often in-volved in conflictual, coercive relations with their custodial mothers may have little to lose and much to gain by the introduction of a warm, involved stepfather. In contrast, daughters who often have close relationships with their custodial mothers and considerable independence may find a stepfather disruptive and constraining.

The Child's Life Experiences Following Family Transitions

Children encounter many changes in their life situation and family roles and relationships following divorce and remarriage. Some of these changes have direct impact on the child, but many are mediated through the behavior of other family members.

The Economics of Divorce and Remarriage

Poor parents and those with unstable incomes are more likely to divorce (Hernandez, 1988). Divorce is associated with a marked drop in income for households in which mothers retain custody. Forty-three percent of divorced custodial mothers have annual incomes less than $10,000. . . . This may be attributed in part to the fact that a large proportion of ex-husbands fail to pay child support . . . and to a tendency for divorced women to lack the education, skills, or experience to obtain well-paying jobs. Reduced economic resources are often accompanied by dependence on welfare; changes in maternal employment; poorer quality in housing, neighborhoods, schools and child care; and geographic mobility and a consequent loss of social networks and support for the child from familiar friends, neighbors, and teachers.

If a mother is forced to return to work around the time of the divorce, the preschool child may feel he or she has been abandoned by both parents. . . . Moreover, if a mother resents or feels unhappy working or manages only to obtain part-time or temporary jobs requiring frequent job changes, the child may be negatively affected by interactions with an anxious, dissatisfied mother. There is some accumulating evidence that although the mother's employment often enhances the adjustment and independence of daughters, it may have deleterious effects on sons, particularly under stressful life situations such as those involved in poverty or divorce (Hetherington, in press-a; Werner, 1987). If the timing of the mother's entry into the work force is appropriate, however, and if the mother wishes to work, is satisfied with her job, and obtains adequate child care, her employment may improve the family finances, contribute to her social and psychological well-being, and have no adverse effects on the child.

Contrary to the experiences of custodial mothers, both noncustodial and custodial fathers typically maintain or improve their standard of living following divorce (Chase-Lansdale & Hetherington, in press; Hetherington & Stanley-Hagan, 1986). For noncustodial fathers, the improved financial status may be attributed to the fact that they cease to be the primary source of support for their ex-spouse and children. Even when paid, child support payments tend to represent a small percentage of the divorced fathers' usable income. Thus, children who reside with their fathers following divorce seldom encounter the stresses associated with limited financial resources that are experienced by children who reside with their mothers.

For families with single mothers, the financial picture improves significantly following remarriage. In fact, the financial status of stepfamilies tends to parallel that found in families in which parents have never divorced (Hernandez, 1988). The improved financial resources are clearly beneficial to both parents and children, . . . although problems are not necessarily absent. Newly remarried couples must face decisions regarding the division of resources among residential family members and nonresidential ex-spouses and children. Such decisions are reported frequently to be sources of conflict, jealousy, and resentment.

Interparental Relationships

Although divorce marks the legal end of the marital relationship, the parenting relationship continues to be a critical factor in the child's adjustment to family transitions. A high degree of discord frequently characterizes family relations in the period surrounding divorce, and conflict may even accelerate following divorce. This intense, often irrational acrimony may be a way for divorced spouses to maintain an emotional relationship following divorce. Many spouses, especially men, have lingering bonds of attachment following divorce and may find conflict preferable to indifference or disengagement. The result is that children often are exposed to quarreling, denigration, and recrimination between their parents and may feel conflicting loyalties. As has been noted, researchers have documented that children, particularly boys, so exposed often exhibit disturbed behavior. . . . Moreover, it has been shown that high rates of continued aggression and conflict between the divorced parents are associated with the gradual loss of contact of the noncustodial parent, especially after the noncustodial parent remarries (Hetherington, in press-b). Continued contact with children is significantly higher by noncustodial mothers than noncustodial fathers.

The balance between conflict and cooperation and the conflict resolution strategies used by divorced parents seem to play an especially important role in the adjustment of children. . . . Although parents may feel angry or resentful, if they are able to control their anger, cooperate in parenting, negotiate differences, and not directly expose their children to quarrels or violence, children show fewer emotional and social problems. Most children wish to maintain relations with both parents, and continued positive relations with both parents has been shown to be an important factor in children's successful adjustment to family transitions. As Santrock and Sitterle (1987) stated, "When divorced parents continue to argue about the terms of their relationship, life is unpleasant for everyone with the children losing most of all" (p. 287). Even after the custodial parent's remarriage, continued contact with noncustodial fathers has salutary effects on children, especially boys (Hetherington et al., 1982, 1985; Zill, 1988). There is some recent evidence, however, that if a child has frequent contact with a noncustodial mother, he or she may have more difficulty accepting a stepmother (Santrock & Sitterle, 1987).

In single-parent families, the well-being of the custodial parent and the quality of the parent-child relationship become central to the adjustment of the child. Yet the stress of separation and divorce places both men and women at risk for psychological and physical dysfunction (Chase-Lansdale & Hetherington, in press). Alcoholism, drug abuse, depression, psychosomatic problems, and accidents are more common among divorced than nondivorced adults. Recent research (Kiecolt-Glaser et al., 1987) suggests that marital disruption hampers the immunologic system, making divorced persons more vulnerable to disease, infection, chronic and acute medical problems, and even death.

In addition, parents undergoing divorce often exhibit marked emotional lability characterized by euphoria and optimism alternating with anxiety, loneliness and depression, and associated changes in self-concept and self-esteem. The significance of these psychological, emotional, and physical changes is that children are encountering an altered parent at a time when they need stability in a rapidly changing life situation. Furthermore, parents and children may exacerbate each other's problems. A physically ill, emotionally disturbed, or preoccupied parent and a distressed, demanding, noncompliant child may have difficulty giving each other support or solace.

A period of diminished parenting is often found following divorce (Hetherington et al., 1982; Wallerstein & Kelly, 1980). It is not uncommon for custodial mothers to become self-involved, erratic, uncommunicative, nonsupportive, and inconsistently punitive in dealing with their children. . . . A decline in effective control and monitoring of children's behavior is most notable, however, in both divorced and remarried mothers. Divorced mothers and their sons are particularly likely to engage in escalating, mutually coercive interchanges. Girls also exhibit increased noncompliance, anger, demandingness, and dependency in the year following divorce, but by two years after divorce their problem behaviors have largely vanished, and mothers and daughters have reestablished a positive or exceptionally close relationship.

Fathers who receive custody of their children also experience early problems. Most report feeling resentment, confusion, and apprehension about their abilities to parent (Hetherington & Stanley-Hagan, 1986)—emotions that are exacerbated by the fathers' perceived isolation. They report feeling ostracized by the community because of their unique status. Although parenting skills improve for both parents over time, by two years after divorce custodial fathers report better family adjustment and fewer problems with their children than do custodial mothers (Furstenberg, 1988). This may be because, unlike custodial mothers, custodial fathers have fewer financial worries, more available supports, and are more likely to be awarded custody of school-aged children and adolescents.

When either mothers or fathers have custody, different aspects of parenting are related to the adjustment of younger than older children going through stressful experiences and multiple changes. Structured, stable, supportive environments, however, are important to children of all ages. A predictable, controlled, responsive environment may be especially important to young children who are less able to select and shape their environments and to exert self-control. Thus, the young child adjusts more easily when the custodial parent can provide the child with a stable, well-organized household, and when the parent is nurturant, uses authoritative control, and makes reasonable maturity demands. In most single-parent households, particularly where the father has custody, parents expect older children and adolescents to assume greater household and child-care responsibilities more than do parents in two parent households. Moreover, parents may make inappropriate emotional demands and elevate the older child to the level of a confidant. For many children, the increased practical and emotional responsibilities accelerate the development of self-sufficiency and maturity. If, however, the parent makes excessive maturity demands, the child is likely to experience feelings of incompetence and resentment (Hetherington et al., 1982).

In the early months of remarriage, custodial mothers report being less effective and more authoritarian in their child rearing than nondivorced mothers. . . . Compared to nondivorced mothers and like newly divorced mothers, newly remarried mothers report poorer family communication, less effective problem resolution, less consistency in setting rules, less effective disciplining, and less emotional responsiveness. Both remarried mothers and stepfathers report less family cohesion and more poorly defined family roles and relationships in the early months of remarriage (Bray, 1988). Control and monitoring of children's behavior by mothers is low initially, but begins to improve over time for children who are not yet adolescent at the time of the remarriage (Hetherington, 1987, in press-a, in press-b). With older children, however, control and monitoring remain low and are related to externalizing disorders in adolescence (Hetherington & Clingempeel, 1988).

Both stepmothers and stepfathers take a considerably less active role in parenting than do custodial parents. . . . Even after two years, disengagement by the stepparent is the most common parenting style. . . . Stepfathers who initially spend time establishing relations with their stepchildren by being warm and involved, but do not assert parental authority, may eventually be accepted by boys. . . . This appears to occur in spite of the fact that stepfathers initially appear less supportive to boys than to girls. . . . Acceptance of the stepfather by the stepdaughter, however, is uncorrelated with his behavior toward her and is more difficult to obtain. . . .

There is some evidence that residential stepmothers are more involved and take a more active role in discipline than do stepfathers (Santrock & Sitterle, 1987), which may in part explain the finding that the response of children to remarriage appears to be mediated by the form of the stepfamily. In general, families in which the custodial father remarries and a stepmother enters the family experience more resistance and poorer adjustment for children than do families in which the custodial mother remarries and a stepfather enters the family (Brand et al., 1988; Clingempeel et al., 1984; Furstenberg, 1988; Hobart, 1987; Santrock & Sitterle, 1987; Zaslow & Hayes, 1987). Moreover, families in which both parents bring children from a previous marriage are associated with the highest levels of behavior problems. . . . In evaluating the efficacy of parents over the course of adjustment to remarriage, it must be kept in mind that newly remarried parents report experiencing levels of both positive and negative stress twice that of nondivorced parents (Bray, 1987, 1988).

The quality of the new marriage can also affect the parenting role; however, this appears to vary with the sex of the child. More positive marital relations in families with either stepfathers or stepmothers are associated with more negative parent-child relations and poorer child adjustment for girls (Brand et al., 1988; Hetherington, in press-a, in press-b). For boys, however, after the first two years of remarriage positive marital adjustment is related to more positive outcomes as it is in nondivorced families (Hetherington, 1987).

Relationships with the Noncustodial Parent

Neither the quality nor the frequency of contact between the noncustodial parent and child can be predicted from the pre-divorce relationship. . . . On the one hand, some intensely attached noncustodial fathers find intermittent parenting painful and withdraw from their children. On the other hand, a substantial number of noncustodial fathers report that their relationships with their children improve after divorce, and many such fathers, who were previously relatively uninvolved, become competent and concerned parents.

There is some evidence that noncustodial mothers are more likely to maintain contact with their children than are noncustodial fathers (Furstenberg, 1988; Zill, 1988). In the early months following divorce, fathers have as much or more contact with children as they did preceding the divorce, but most noncustodial fathers rapidly become less available to their children. Also, fathers are more likely to maintain frequent contact with their sons than with their daughters. . . .

The introduction of a step-parent forces a renegotiation of the noncustodial parent's role and may strain the parent-child relationship. It is interesting to note that the remarriage of the custodial parent is not related to changes in involvement of the noncustodial parent, although remarriage of the noncustodial parent typically means withdrawal of parenting by the noncustodial parent. . . . A few researchers have found that children in families with stepmothers report a higher level of involvement of the noncustodial mother than is found with the noncustodial fathers in families with step-fathers (Brand et al., 1988; Furstenberg, 1988; Santrock & Sitterle, 1987), yet some evidence suggests otherwise (Camara & Resnick, 1988). Increased involvement of the noncustodial father, however, appears to play a positive or neutral role in families with stepfathers, . . . whereas increased involvement of the noncustodial mother plays a negative role in families with stepmothers, especially for girls. . . . Frequent visits by the biological mother have been associated with negative relations between the child and the stepmother. . . .

In summary, although the meager research findings on the role of noncustodial parents in the development of the child are not entirely consistent, they suggest that under conditions of low interparental conflict, continued involvement of a competent, supportive, reasonably well-adjusted noncustodial father can have positive effects on the adjustment of children, especially boys. . . . Moreover, such an involvement between the noncustodial father and child has not been found to interfere with the development of close family relations in a new stepfamily. . . . In contrast, continued involvement of the noncustodial mother seems to precipitate loyalty conflicts that are manifested in greater acrimony between children and their stepmothers. . . . More research is needed before firm conclusions can be drawn about the effects on children of sustained contact with the noncustodial parent. It is important to note that these effects are likely to be modified by the quality of the relation between the divorced parents and the attributes and behavior of the noncustodial parent.

Support Systems

Support systems can serve as sources of practical and emotional support for both parents and children experiencing family transitions. Just as authoritative parents can offer support to children going through their parents' marital transitions, authoritative schools can offer support to children undergoing stressful experiences. . . . Day care centers and schools that provide warm, structured, and predictable environments can offer stability to children experiencing a rapidly changing family environment, chaotic household routines, an altered parent, and inconsistent parenting. Moreover, responsive peers and school personnel can validate the self-worth, competence, and personal control of the older child and adolescent who has access to these extrafamilial supports (Hetherington & Clingempeel, 1988; Hetherington et al., 1982, 1985; Rutter, 1987).

Supports offered by friends and family also can increase divorced parents' positive attitudes toward themselves and their life situation and facilitate the parenting role (Hetherington, in press-a). Following divorce, often for economic reasons, between 25 percent and 33 percent of newly divorced custodial mothers reside with a relative, usually their mothers (Hernandez, 1988). The grandmother often provides economic resources and shares in child care and household responsibilities, thus partially relieving the mother's financial concerns and sense of task overload, and providing the child with another source of needed emotional support. Researchers have found that in Black families children who live with both mother and grandmother adjust better than do children who reside with a divorced mother alone (Kellam, Ensminges, & Turner, 1977). Furthermore, sons in the custody of mothers show fewer behavior problems when they have an involved supportive grandfather than when none is available (Hetherington, in press-a). When they have the economic resources to do so, however, most custodial mothers prefer to establish their own households, thus avoiding feelings of dependency and conflict over childrearing issues that may arise when they share their residences with their own parents. Such conflicts between custodial mothers and their parents occur less often with grandfathers than with grandmothers (Hetherington, in press-a).

Grandparents also increase the complexity of the stepfamily household. Involvement with stepgrandparents is highest when there are no biological grandchildren, when grandparents live nearby, and when the children in the stepfamily are young at the time of remarriage. Children appear to make little distinction between biological grandparents and stepgrandparents (Furstenberg, 1988). It appears that most of the influence of grandparents is mediated by the relationships with parents. . . .

Children experiencing their parents' marital transitions also may receive support from sibling relationships. There is evidence that some siblings, especially female siblings of divorced parents, may act as buffers and fill emotional voids left by unresponsive parents. . . . In contrast, relations among male siblings of divorced mothers with custody are more antagonistic than among those with nondivorced parents. . . . Generally, however, rivalrous, aggressive, coercive sibling and stepsibling relationships are more common in stepfamilies than positive relationships, and these negative relationships may act as additional stressors, at least in the first two years following remarriage (Hetherington, in press-b; Hetherington & Clingempeel, 1988). Sibling relationships in stepfamilies improve somewhat over time, but they are still more troubled than those of siblings with nondivorced parents. . . . Although overt aggression may decrease with the duration of the remarriage and age of the child, this is often associated with disengagement and lack of involvement and empathy. Siblings who live with custodial mothers who are single parents or with remarried parents appear to have particularly troubled relationships, especially if one of the siblings is a boy. The quality of the sibling relationship during the time in a single-parent household may mediate the relationship in stepfamilies, but this has not been investigated.

Conclusion

Many children encounter their parents' divorce and life in a one-parent family. Moreover, since most parents remarry, it may be appropriate to think of the time a child spends in a single-parent household as a transitional period between life with nondivorced, often conflict-ridden, parents and life in a stepfamily. Most children initially experience their parents' marital rearrangements as stressful. Divorce and remarriage are often associated with experiences that place children at increased risk for developing social, psychological, behavioral, and academic problems. Yet divorce and remarriage also can remove children from stressful or acrimonious family relationships and provide additional resources for children. Many children eventually emerge from the divorce or remarriage of their parents as competent or even enhanced individuals.

In recent years, researchers have begun to move away from the view that single-parent and stepfamilies are atypical or pathogenic. More studies are focusing on the diversity of children's responses to their parents' marital transitions and on the factors that facilitate or disrupt the development and adjustment of children in these family situations.

References

Block, J. H., Block, J., & Gjerde, P. F. (In press). Parental functioning and the home environment in families of divorce: Prospective and concurrent analysis. *Journal of the American Academy of Child Psychiatry.*

Brand, E., Clingempeel, W. E., & Bowen-Woodward, K. (1988). Family relationships and children's psychological adjustment in stepmother and stepfather families: Findings and conclusions from the Philadelphia Stepfamily Research Project. In E. M. Hetherington & J. D. Arasteh (Eds.), *Impact of divorce, single-parenting, and stepparenting on children.* (pp. 299-324). Hillsdale, NJ: Erlbaum.

Bray, J. H. (1987, August), *Becoming a stepfamily.*Symposium presented at the meeting of the American Psychological Association, New York, NY.

Bray, J. H. (1988). Children's development during early remarriage. In E. M. Hetherington & J. D. Arasteh (Eds.), *Impact of divorce, single-parenting, and stepparenting on children* (pp. 279-298). Hillsdale, NJ: Erlbaum.

Camara, K. A., & Resnick. G. (1988). Interparental conflict and cooperation: Factors moderating children's post-divorce adjustment. In E. M. Hetherington & J. D. Arasteh (Eds.), *Impact of divorce, single-parenting, and stepparenting on children* (pp. 169-195). Hillsdale NJ: Erlbaum.

Cherlin, A. (1981). *Marriage, divorce, remarriage: Changing patterns in the postwar United States.* Cambridge, MA: Harvard University Press.

Clingempeel, W. G., Brand, C., & Sevoli, R. (1984). Stepparent-stepchild relationships in stepmother and stepfather families: A multimethod study. *Family Relations, 33,* 465-473.

Emery, R. E. (1982). Interparental conflict and the children of discord and divorce. *Psychological Bulletin, 92,* 310-330.

Emery, R., & O'Leary, K. (1982). Children's perceptions of marital discord and behavior problems of boys and girls. *Journal of Abnormal Child Psychology, 10,* 11-24.

Epstein, N., Finnegan, D., & Gythell, D. (1979). Irrational beliefs and perceptions of marital conflict. *Journal of Consulting and Clinical Psychology, 67,* 608-609.

Furstenberg, F. F. (1988). Child care after divorce and remarriage. In E. M. Hetherington & J. Arasteh (Eds.), *Impact of divorce, single-parenting, and stepparenting on children* (pp. 245-261). Hillsdale, NJ: Erlbaum.

Furstenberg, F. F., Jr., & Allison, P. D. (1985). *How marital dissolution affects children: Variations by age and sex.* Unpublished manuscript.

Furstenberg, F. F., & Seltzer, J. A. (1983, August). *Encountering divorce: Children's responses to family dissolution and reconstitution.* Paper presented at the meeting of the American Psychological Association, Detroit, MI.

Garbarino, J., Sebes, L., & Schellenbach, C. (1984). Families at risk for destructive parent-child relations in adolescence. *Child Development, 55*(1), 174-183.

Glick, P. C., & Lin, S. (1986). Recent changes in divorce and remarriage. *Journal of Marriage and the Family, 48,* 737-747.

Hernandez, D. J. (1988). Demographic trends and the living arrangements of children. In E. M. Hetherington & J. D. Arasteh (Eds.), *Impact of divorce, single-parenting, and stepparenting on children* (pp. 3-22). Hillsdale, NJ: Erlbaum.

Hess, R. D., & Camara, K. A. (1979). Post-divorce family relationships as mediating factors in the consequence of divorce for children. *Journal of Social Issues, 25,* 79-96.

Hetherington, E. M. (1972). Effects of fathers' absence on personality development in adolescent daughters. *Developmental Psychology, 7*(3), 313-326.

Hetherington, E. M. (1987). Family relations six years after divorce. In K. Pasley & M. Ihinger-Tollman (Eds.), *Remarriage and stepparenting today: Current research and theory* (pp. 185-205). New York: Guilford Press.

Hetherington, E. M. (in press-a). Coping with family transitions: Winners, losers, and survivors. *Child Development.*

Hetherington, E. M. (in press-b). Parents, children and siblings six years after divorce. In R. Hinde & J. Stevenson-Hinde (Eds.), *Relationships within families.* Cambridge, England: Cam-bridge University Press.

Hetherington, E. M., & Camara, K. A. (1984). Families in transition: The process of dissolution and reconstitution. In R. Parke (Ed.), *Review of child development research* (Vol. 3, pp. 398-439). Chicago: University of Chicago Press.

587

Hetherington, E. M., & Clingempeel, W. G. (1988, March). *Coping with remarriage: The first two years*. Symposium presented at the Southeastern Conference on Human Development, Charleston, SC.

Hetherington, E. M., Cox, M., & Cox, R. (1982). Effects of divorce on parents and children. In M. Lamb (Ed.), *Nontraditional families* (pp. 233-288). Hillsdale, NJ: Erlbaum.

Hetherington, E. M., Cox, M., & Cox, R. (1985). Long-term effects of divorce and remarriage on the adjustment of children. *Journal of American Academy of Psychiatry, 24*(5), 518-530.

Hetherington, E. M., & Stanley-Hagan, M. (1986). Divorced fathers: Stress, coping, and adjustment. In M. Lamb (Ed.), *The father's role: Applied perspectives* (pp. 103-134). New York: Wiley.

Hobart, C. (1987). Parent-child relations in remarried families. *Journal of Family Issues, 8*, 259-277.

Jacobson, D. S. (1984). *Factors associated with healthy family functioning in stepfathers*. Paper presented at the meeting of the Society for Research in Child Development, Lexington, KY.

Kalter, N., & Rembar, J. (1981). The significance of a child's age at the time of parental divorce. *American Journal of Orthopsychiatry, 51*, 85-100.

Kellam, S. G., Ensminges, M. E., & Turner, R. J. (1977). Family structure and the mental health of children: Concurrent and longitudinal community-wide studies. *Archives of General Psychiatry, 34*(9), 1012-1022.

Kiecolt-Glaser, J. K., Fisher, L. D., Ogrocki, P., Stout, J. C., Speicher, B. S., & Glaser, R. (1987). Marital quality, marital disruption, and immune function. *Psychosomatic Medicine, 40*, 13-34.

Lamb, M. (1977). The effects of divorce on children's personality development. *Journal of Divorce, 1*, 163-174.

Long, N., & Forehand, R. (1987). The effects of parental divorce and marital conflict on children: An overview. *Journal of Developmental and Behavioral Pediatrics, 8*, 292-296.

Morgan, P. S., Lye, D. N., & Condron, G. A. (in press). Sons, daughters, and divorce: Does the sex of children affect the risk of marital disruption? *American Journal of Psychology.*

Newcomer, S., & Udry, J. R. (1987). Parental marital status effects on adolescent sexual behavior. *Journal of Marriage and the Family, 49,* 235-240.

Parker, H., & Parker, S. (1986). Father-daughter sexual abuse: An emerging perspective. *American Journal of Orthopsychiatry, 56*(4), 531-549.

Porter, B., & O'Leary, K. D. (1980). Marital discord and childhood behavior problems. *Journal of Abnormal Psychology, 8,* 287-295.

Rutter, M. (1971). Parent-child separation: Psychological effects on the children. *Journal of Child Psychiatry and Applied Disciplines, 12,* 233-260.

Rutter. M. (1980). Protective factors in children's responses to stress and disadvantage. In M. W. Kent & J. E. Rolf (Eds.), *Primary prevention of psychopathology: III. Promoting social competence and coping in children* (pp. 49-74). Hanover, NH: University Press of New England.

Rutter, M. (1987). Psychosocial resilience and protective mechanisms. *American Journal of Orthopsychiatry, 57*(3), 316-331.

Santrock, J. W., & Sitterle, K. A. (1987),Parent-child relationships in stepmother families. In K. Pasley & M. Ihinger-Tallman (Eds.), *Remarriage and stepparenting: Current research and theory* (pp. 135-154). New York: Guilford Press.

Santrock, J. W., & Wohlford, P. (1979). Effects of father absence: Influence of reason for and onset of absence. *Proceedings of the 78th Annual Convention of the American Psychological Association* (Vol. 78). Washington, DC: American Psychological Association.

Steinberg, L. D. (1985, March). *The ABCs of transformations in the family at adolescence: Changes in affect, behavior, and cognition.* Paper presented at the Third Biennial Conference on Adolescence Research, Tucson, AZ.

Steinman, S. (1981). The experience of children in a joint-custody arrangement. *American Journal of Orthopsychiatry, 51,* 403-414.

Stolberg, A. L., & Anker, J. M. (1984). Cognitive and behavioral changes in children resulting from parental divorce and consequent environmental changes. *Journal of Divorce, 8*, 184-197.

Stolberg, A. L., Camplair, C., Currier, K., & Wells, M. J. (1987). Individual, familial and environmental determinants of children's post-divorce adjustment and maladjustment. *Journal of Divorce, 11*, 51-70.

Wallerstein, J., Corbin, S. B., & Lewis, J. M.(1988). Children of divorce: A ten-year study. In E. M. Hetherington & J. Arasteh (Eds.), *Impact of divorce, single-parenting and stepparenting on children.* (pp. 198-214). Hillsdale, NJ: Erlbaum.

Wallerstein, J. S., & Kelly, J. B. (1980). *Surviving the breakup.* New York: Basic Books.

Weiss, R. S. (1979). Growing up a little faster: The experience of growing up in a single-parent household. *Journal of Social Issues, 35*, 97-111.

Werner, E. E. (1987). Vulnerability and resiliency in children at risk for delinquency: A longitudinal study from birth to young adulthood. In J. D. Burchard & S. M. Burchard (Eds.), *Prevention of delinquent behavior* (pp. 68-84). Beverly Hills, CA: Sage.

Zaslow, M. J., & Hayes, C. D. (1987, September). Sex differences in children's responses to psychosocial stress. In W. A. Morrill (Chair) Symposium conducted at the meeting of the National Academy of Sciences Summer Study Center, Woods Hole, MA.

Zill, N. (1988). Behavior, achievement, and health problems among children in stepfamilies: Findings from a national survey of child health. In E. M. Hetherington & J. D. Arasteh (Eds.), *Impact of divorce, single-parenting, and stepparenting on children* (pp. 325-368). Hillsdale, NJ: Erlbaum.

Zill, N., & Peterson, J. L. (1983, April). Marital disruption, parent-child relationships, and behavior problems in children. Paper presented at the meeting of the Society for Research in Child Development, Detroit, MI.

Publication Credits

Aptekar, L. (1989). Colombian street children: *Gamines* and *chupagruesos*. *Adolescence*, **24**, 783-794. Reprinted with permission of Libra Publishers, Inc. / Baillargeon, R., Spelke, E. S., & Wasserman, S. (1985). Object permanence in five-month-old infants. *Cognition*, **20**, 195-197, 202-204. Reprinted with permission of Elsevier Science Publishers, B.V., and the author. / Bogin, B. (1990). The evolution of human childhood. *Bio Science*, **40**(1), 16-25. © 1990 by American Institute of Biological Sciences. Reprinted with permission of American Institute of Biological Sciences and the author. / Bradley, L., & Bryant, P. E. (1983). Categorizing sounds and learning to read–a causal connection. *Nature*, **301**, 419-421. Reprinted with permission of MacMillan Magazines Ltd. and the authors. / Bremner, R. H. (Eds.) (1970). *Children and youth in America: A documentary history Volume I: 1600-1865*, 103-106, 145-149, 282-283, 559, 758-760. Copyright © 1970 by the American Public Health Association. Reprinted by permission of Harvard University Press, Cambridge, Massachusetts. / Bronfenbrenner, U. (1979). *The ecology of human development*, 3-8. Copyright © 1979 by the President and Fellows of Harvard College. Reprinted by permission of Harvard University Press, Cambridge, Massachusetts. / Chi, M. T. H. (1978). Knowledge structures and memory development. In R. S. Sieigler (Ed.). *Children's thinking: What develops?* 73-76, 80-82, 95-96. Reprinted with permission of Lawrence Erlbaum Associates and the author. / De Cuevas, J. (1990). No, She holded them loosely. *Harvard Magazine*, **93**(1), September/December, 60-67. Copyright © 1990 Harvard Magazine. Reprinted with permission of Harvard Magazine, Inc. and the author. / Demos, J., & Demos, V. (1969). Adolescence in historical perspective. *Journal of Marriage and the Family*, **31**(4), November, 632-638. Copyright 1969 by the National Council on Family Relations, 3989 Central Ave. N. E., Suite # 550, Minneapolis, MN 55421. Reprinted by permission of the National Council on Family Relations and the authors. / Draper, P. (1985). Two views of sex differences in socializiation. In R. L. Hall, P. Draper, M. E. Hamilton, D. MacGuinness, C. M. Otten, & E. A. Roth (1985), *Male-female differences: A bio-cultural perspective*, 5-25. © 1985 by Praeger Publishers. Reprinted with permission of Greenwood Publishing Group, Inc., Westport, Connecticut. / Dunn, J. (1988). *The beginning of social understanding*, 45-51, 58, 109-126. Copyright © 1988 by Judy Dunn. Reprinted by permission of Harvard University Press, Cambridge, Massachusetts. / Ehrenreich, B., & English, D. (1978). *For her own good: 150 years of the experts' advice to women*, 165-177. Copyright (c) 1978 by Barbara Ehrenreich and Deirdre English. Used by permission of Doubleday, a division of Bantam Doubleday Dell Publishing Group, Inc. / Elder, G. H., Jr., Nguyen, T., & Caspi, A. (1985). Linking family hardship to children's lives. *Child Development*, **56**, 361-366, 368-375. © 1985 by the Society for Research in Child Development, Inc. Reprinted with permission of the Society for Research in Child Development, Inc., and the author. / Fried, M. N., & Fried, M. H. (1980). *Transitions: Four rituals in eight cultures*, 58-92. Copyright © 1980 by Martha

Names Fried and Morton H. Fried. Reprinted with permission of W. W. Norton & Company, Inc. / Gibson, E. J., & Walk, R. D. (1960). The "visual cliff." *Scientific American*, **202**, 80-92. Copyright © 1960 by Scientific American, Inc. Reprinted with permission. All rights reserved. / Hendry, J. (1986). *Becoming Japanese: The world of the pre-school child*, 47-69. Reprinted by permission of University of Hawaii Press. / Hetherington, E. M., Stanley-Hagan, M., & Anderson, E. R. (1989). Marital transitions: A child's perspective. *American Psychologist*, **44**(2), 303-312. Copyright 1989 by the American Psychological Association. Reprinted with permission of the American Psychological Association and the author. / Hunt, J. McV. (1961). *Intelligence and experience*, 347-363. Copyright © 1961 by The Ronald Press Company. Reprinted by permissions of John Wiley & Sons, Inc. / Kagan, J. (1986). *The power and limitations of parents*, 3-17. Copyright © Hogg Foundation for Mental Health, 1986, the University of Texas, Austin, Texas. Reprinted with permission of Hogg Foundation for Mental Health and the author. / Kagan, J. (1989). Temperamental influences on the preservation of style of social behavior. *McLean Hospital Journal*, **XIV**, 23-34. Reprinted with permission of McLean Hospital Journal. / Kamerman, S. B., & Kahn, A. J. (1988). What Europe does for single-parent families. The Public Interest, Fall, no. 93, 70-86. Copyright © 1986 by National Affairs, Inc. Reprinted with permission of National Affairs, Inc., and the author. / Karen, R. (1990). Becoming attached. *The Atlantic Monthly*, February, 37-70. © Robert Karen. Reprinted with permission of International Creative Management and the author. / Kessen, W. (1978). A historical view: Our disconnected child. *Harper's Magazine*, April, **256**, 44-45. Copyright © 1978 by *Harper's Magazine*. Reprinted by special permission. All rights reserved. / Klaus, M. H., & Klaus, P. H. (1985). *The amazing newborn*, 128-129, 131-132, 135-136, 138. © 1985 by Addison-Wesley Publishing Company. Reprinted by permission. / Lever, J. (1978). Sex differences in the complexity of children's play and games. *American Sociological Review*, **43**, 471-483. Reprinted with permission of American Sociological Association and the author. / LeVine, R. A. (1980). A cross-cultural perspective on parenting. In M. D. Fantini & R. Cardenas, *Parenting in a multicultural society*, 17-26. Copyright © 1980 by Longman Publishing Group. Reprinted by permission. / LeVine, R. A., & Miller, P. M. (1990). Commentary. *Human Development*, **33**, 73-80. Reprinted with permission of S. Karger, A.G., Basel. / Lewis, G. H. (1989). Rats and bunnies: Core kids in an American mall. *Adolescence*, **24**, 881-889. Reprinted with permission of Libra Publishers, Inc. / Lurie, N. O. (Ed.) (1961). *Mountain Wolf Woman, sister of Crashing Thunder: The autobiography of a Winnebago Indian*, 8-9, 20-23. Reprinted with permission of University of Michigan Press. / Mead, M. (1955). Children and ritual in Bali. In M. Mead & M. Wolfenstein (Eds.), *Childhood in contemporary cultures*, 40-51. Copyright 1955 by The University of Chicago. © The University of Chicago, 1955. All rights reserved. Copyright 1955 under the International Copyright Union. Published 1955 Composed and printed by The University of Chicago Press, Chicago, Illinois, U.S.A. / Mead, M., & Metraux, R. (1980). A new understanding of childhood. *Aspects of the present*, 149-155. Copyright

Study of Social Problems. Reprinted with permission of the publisher and author. / Uhlenberg, P. (1985). Death and the family. *Journal of Family History*, **5**(3), Fall, 313-320. Reprinted in N. R. Hiner & J, M. Hawes (Eds.), *Growing up in America: Children in historical perspective*, 243-251. Copyright 1985 by the National Council on Family Relations, 3989 Central Avenue, N. E., Suite 550, Minneapolis, MN 55421. Reprinted with permission of the publisher and author. / Weisner, T. S. (1982). Sibling interdependence and child caretaking: A cross-cultural view. In M. E. Lamb & B. Sutton-Smith (Eds.), *Sibling relationships: Their nature and significance across the lifespan*, 305-311, 326-327. Reprinted with permission of Lawrence Erlbaum Associates and the author. / Weiss, N. P. (1977). Mother, the invention of necessity: Dr. Benjamin Spock's *Baby and Child Care*. *American Quarterly*, Winter, 519-546. Reprinted in N. R. Hiner & J. M. Hawes (Eds.) (1985), *Growing up in America: Children in historical perspective*, 282-303. Copyright 1977 by Nancy Pottishman Weiss. Reprinted with permisssion of the American Studies Association and the author. / Werker, J. (1989). Becoming a native listener. *American Scientist*, **77**, 54-59. Reprinted by permission of *American Scientist*, Journal of Sigma Xi, The Scientific Research Society. / Werner, E. E. (1989). Children of the garden island. *Scientific American*, **260**, 107-111. Reprinted with permission of Scientific American. / White, M. (1987). *The Japanese educational challenge: A commitment to children*, 66-81. Copyright © 1986 by Merry White. Reprinted by permission of The Free Press, a Division of Macmillan, Inc. / Wilson, M. N. (1989). Child development in the context of the black extended family. American Psychologist, **44**(2), 180-185. Copyright 1989 by the American Psychological Association. Reprinted with permission of the publisher and author.

Photographic Credits

Primary Contributors

Lewis Aptekar is currently Associate Dean of the College of Education, San Jose State University. He is the author of *Street Children of Cali* and *Environmental Disasters in Global Perspective*.

Renee Baillargeon is Associate Professor of Psychology at the University of Illinois, Champaign. Her research has centered on infant perception and cognition, with a particular focus on infants' understanding of the physical world.

Barry Bogin is Professor of Anthropology in the Department of Behavioral Sciences at the University of Michigan, Dearborn. His interests are in evolutionary biology and human growth, development, and adaptation. Dr. Bogin is the author of *Patterns of Human Growth*.

Lynette Bradley is a Researcher in Experimental Psychology at Oxford University. Her primary areas of research are reading, writing, and spelling. Dr. Bradley is the author of *Assessing Reading Difficulties* and co-author of *Rhyme and Reason in Reading and Spelling*.

Robert H. Bremner is Professor Emeritus of History at Ohio State University. Writing extensively on American social history, especially on children and poverty, Dr. Bremner is the author of several books, including *The Public Good: Philanthropy and Welfare in the Civil War Era*.

Urie Bronfenbrenner is the Jacob Gould Shurman Professor Emeritus of Human Development and Family Studies and of Psychology at Cornell University. His research focuses on the nature of person/context interactions as they shape development. Among many works, he has authored *Two Worlds of Childhood* and *The Ecology of Human Development*.

Michelene T. H. Chi is Professor of Psychology and Senior Scientist at the University of Pittsburgh Learning Research and Development Center. Her research focuses on the nature and development of knowledge structures in complex domains.

John de Cuevas is a freelance writer and contributing editor of *Harvard Magazine*. Trained in evolutionary biology and interested in origins--of the cosmos, earth, life, the human species, language, art--he has taught science writing at Harvard, and currently teaches at Lesley College.

John Demos is the Samuel Knight Professor of American History at Yale University. A social historian focusing on American family life, he has written several books, including *Past, Present, and Personal: The Family and the Life Course in American History*.

Patricia Draper is currently appointed in Human Development and Anthropology at Pennsylvania State University. Her research includes comparative studies of family organization, gender roles, adult development and aging, hunter-gatherers, African ethnology, and evolutionary ecology.

Judy Dunn is Professor of Human Development at Pennsylvania State University. She is the author or co-author of several books, including *Sisters and Brothers*, *The Study of Temperament: Changes, Continuities, and Challenges*, and *Siblings: Love, Envy, and Understanding*.

Barbara Ehrenreich is a freelance writer, columnist, and lecturer. She has published numerous books on health care, gender, and socioeconomic and class structures in contemporary America, including most recently *The Worst Years of Our Lives: Memoirs of a Decade of Greed*.

Glen H. Elder, Jr. is Howard W. Odom Distinguished Professor of Sociology and Research Professor in Psychology at the University of North Carolina at Chapel Hill. He is the author of *Children of the Great Depression: Social Change in the Life Course* and co-editor of *Children in Time and Place*.

Morton N. Fried (1923-1986) was Professor of Anthropology at Columbia University. He wrote extensively on Chinese culture, with an emphasis on clans and lineages. His books include *The Fabric of Chinese Society*, *The Evolution of Political Society*, and *The Notion of Tribe*.

Eleanor J. Gibson is Susan Linn Sage Professor of Psychology Emeritus, at Cornell University. Among her extensive publications in the field of perceptual learning and development is a recent book, *An Odyssey in Learning and Perception*.

E. Mavis Hetherington is the James M. Page Professor of Psychology at the University of Virginia. Formerly editor of *Child Development*, she has published widely on social development, psychopathology, and stress and coping in children and families.

J. McVicker Hunt (1906-1991) was Professor of Psychology at the University of Illinois at Urbana-Champaign. Well known for research on the effects of early childhood experience on mental development, he authored many books, including *Experience and Early Development*.

Jerome Kagan is the Daniel and Amy Starch Professor of Psychology at Harvard University. His research interests include temperamental differences among children and early moral development. Dr. Kagan's numerous books and monographs include *The Second Year: The Emergence of Self-Awareness*, and *Unstable Ideas: Temperament, Cognition, and Self*.

Sheila B. Kamerman is Professor of Social Policy and Social Planning at Columbia University. Her research involves comparative studies of family/child social policiy. Dr. Kamerman's most recent books, co-authored with Alfred J. Kahn, are *Child Care: Facing the Hard Choices* and *The Responsive Workplace: Employers and a Changing Labor Force*.

Robert Karen is a practicing clinical psychologist and a writer. He is working on a book, *Becoming Attached*, expected out in 1994. Dr. Karen has also done research and written on the subject of shame.

William Kessen is the Eugene Higgins Professor of Psychology and a Professor of Pediatrics at Yale University. His research includes the study of newborn infant behavior, early conceptions of the visual world, and the nineteenth-century origins of psychological science. He is the author or editor of several books, including *The Child* and *Childhood in China*.

Marshall Klaus is the Director of Academic Affairs for Children's Hospital of Oakland, California, and Adjunct Professor of Pediatrics at the University of San Francisco School of Medicine. His research focuses on labor and childbirth, and on how new parents develop ties to their infants.

Janet Lever teaches in the Department of Sociology at California State University, Los Angeles, and is Consultant in Residence at the RAND corporation, working in health and policy analysis. She is co-author of the Sex and Health column for *Glamour* magazine.

Robert A. LeVine is the Roy E. Larsen Professor of Education and Human Development and Professor of Anthropology at Harvard University. He has investigated child rearing in subsaharan Africa and is the author of *Mothers and Wives: Gusii Women of East Africa*. Currently he is studying the impact of women's schooling on child care in Mexico, Nepal, and Zambia.

George H. Lewis is Professor of Sociology and Anthropology at the University of the Pacific. His research interests are in popular culture and music, with a current focus on the relationship between mass culture and the folk community and on country music and its audience.

Margaret Mead (1901-1978) was one of the world's foremost anthropologists. Curator of the American Museum of Natural History, she taught at Columbia University. Expeditions to the South Pacific provided the basis for hundreds of articles and over twenty books, including *Coming of Age in Samoa*.

Richard P. Meier is Assistant Professor of Linguistics and Psychology at the University of Texas at Austin. His research is on the acquisition of sign language in deaf children and on the pre-linguistic development of gesture in deaf and hearing children.

Andrew N. Meltzoff is Professor of Psychology at the University of Washington. His research is in the areas of cross-modal matching, imitation and early memory, and the relations between language and thought during the transition from infancy to early childhood.

Carolyn B. Mervis is Professor of Psychology at Emory University. Her research focuses on the development of language and cognition. She is the author of numerous articles in journals such as *Child Development* and the *Journal of Child Language*.

Steven Mintz is Associate Professor of History at the University of Houston. He is a specialist in the history of the family and childhood, and has authored *A Prison of Expectations: The Family in Victorian Culture*.

Mountain Wolf Woman (1884-1960) was a Winnebago Indian who lived in Wisconsin. Her autobiographical reminiscences were transcribed by Nancy Lurie, an anthropologist, who was her niece by adoption.

William E. Myers, at the time his article was originally published, was a Visiting Scholar at Stanford University Law School. His research interests included the state of working children in South America.

Sandra Scarr is Commonwealth Professor of Psychology at the University of Virginia. Her research involves behavior genetics, intelligence, and child care and family issues. Her book *Mother Care/Other Care* won the American Psychological Association's National Book Award.

Muzafer Sherif (1906-1988) was an internationally reknowned social scientist who taught at the University of Oklahoma and at Pennsylvania State University. His research on social perception and judgment, group formation, intergroup conflict, and attitude change formed the basis of many books, including *Intergroup Conflict and Cooperation: The Robbers Cave Experiment*.

Dan I. Slobin is Professor of Psychology at the University of California at Berkeley. His cross-linguistic research has centered on language acqusition and language change. Dr. Slobin has edited *The Cross Linguistic Study of Language Acqusition* and is currently working on a book about narrative development.

Margaret Beale Spencer is Professor in the Division of Educational Studies at Emory University and Associate Clinical Professor of Community Medicine at Morehouse School of Medicine. Her research focuses on minority child and adolescent development and she is co-author of *Ethnicity and Diversity: Minorities No More*.

Elizabeth Cady Stanton (1815-1902) was an American suffrage worker, lecturing and writing on women's rights, family life, child care, and abolition. She was the first president of the National Women's Suffrage Association and co-compiler of the *History of Women's Suffrage*.

Harold W. Stevenson is Professor of Psychology at the University of Michigan. His recent research has focused on cross-national studies of children's academic achievement. He is co-editor of *Child Development and Education in Japan* and *Cultural Perspectives on Child Development*.

James M. Tanner is Professor of Human Growth and Development at the University of London. He is internationally reknowned in the fields of human and animal growth and is the author of several books, including *Growth at Adolescence* and *A History of the Study of Human Growth*.

Barrie Thorne is Professor of Sociology and Streisand Professor in Intimacy and Sexuality at the University of Southern California. She is the author of *The Girls and the Boys* and co-editor of *Rethinking the Family: Some Feminist Questions*.

Peter R. Uhlenberg is a Professor of Sociology at the University of North Carolina, Chapel Hill. He has published in the areas of demographics, sociology of the family, social gerontology, and intergenerational relations. Dr. Uhlenberg is currently conducting research on the demography of aging in Sri Lanka.

Thomas S. Weisner is Professor of Anthropology in the Departments of Psychiatry and Anthropology at the University of California, Los Angeles. He has done field research on sibling caretaking in Western Kenya and Hawaii and is the Director of the Family Lifestyles Project, a longitudinal study of traditional and nontraditional families, begun in 1975.

Nancy Pottishman Weiss is director of the Global Education Network. She is involved in comparative studies of childhood and schooling in Asia, Europe, and America. Her work has appeared in a variety of journals, including *Journal of Social Research* and *American Quarterly*.

Janet F. Werker is Associate Professor of Psychology at the University of British Columbia. Her research focuses on speech perception in infants, older children, and adults. She has published in journals such as *Developmental Psychology* and *Infant Behavior and Development*.

Emmy E. Werner is Professor of Human Development and Research Child Psychologist at the University of California, Davis. Her research has focused on children at risk and she is co-author of *Vulnerable but Invincible: A Longitudinal Study of Resilient Children and Youth*.

Merry White is Associate Professor of Sociology at Boston University and Research Associate at Harvard University's Reischauer Institute of Japanese Studies. Among her publications are *The Japanese Overseas* and a forthcoming study of the social construction of adolescence, *The Material Child: Coming of Age in Japan and America*.

Melvin N. Wilson is Associate Professor of Psychology at the University of Virginia. His research involves familial processes in the Black extended family, the role of self-disclosure in clinical assessment, and the nature of intervention service delivery systems.